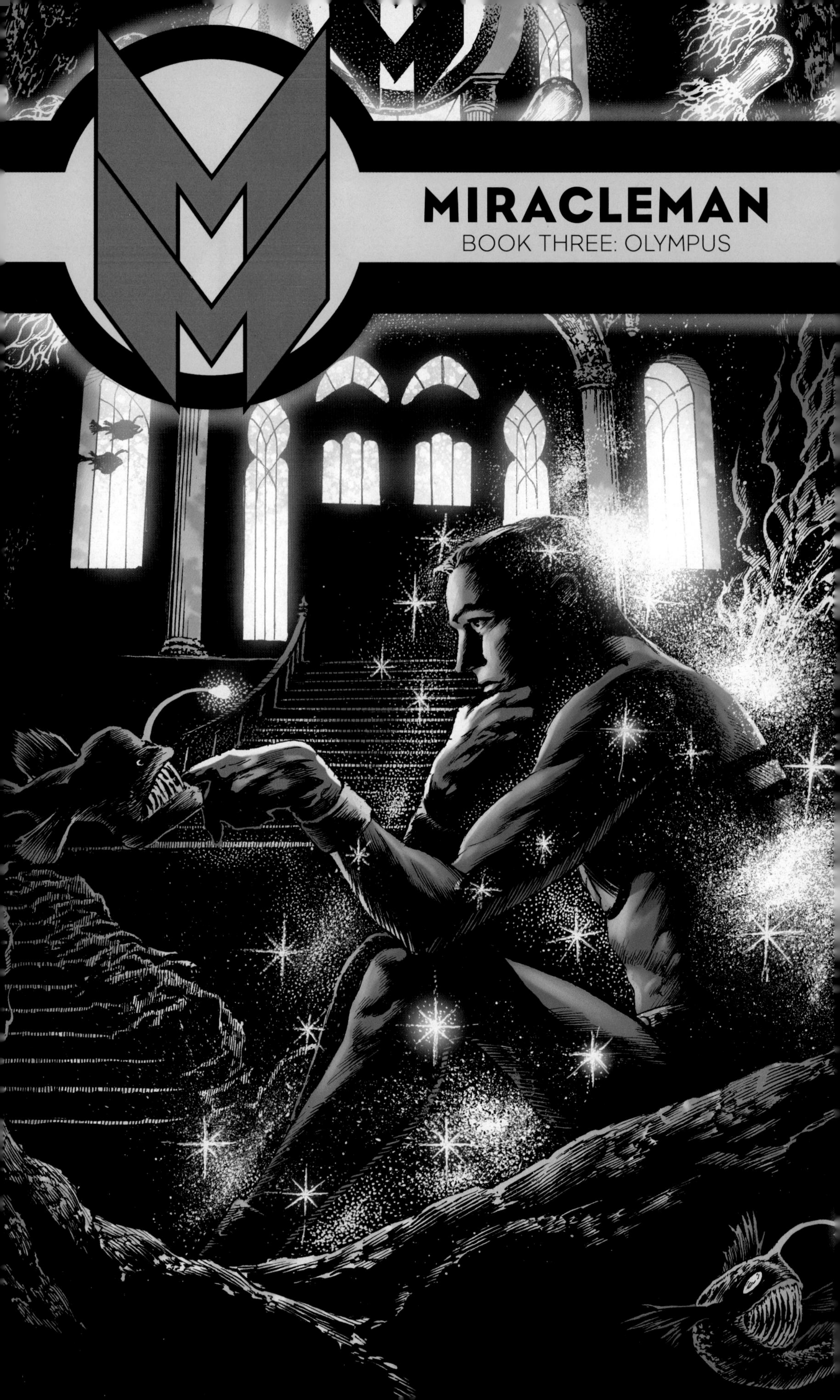
MIRACLEMAN
BOOK THREE: OLYMPUS

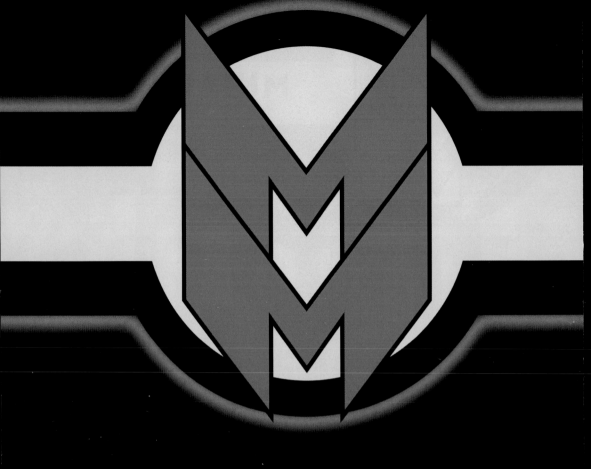

RESTORATION & COLLECTION EDITOR – **CORY SEDLMEIER**

BOOK DESIGN – **JEFF POWELL** · MANAGER, TALENT RELATIONS – **GEORGE BELIARD**

SVP PRINT, SALES & MARKETING – **DAVID GABRIEL** · EDITOR IN CHIEF – **AXEL ALONSO**

CHIEF CREATIVE OFFICER – **JOE QUESADA** · PUBLISHER – **DAN BUCKLEY** · EXECUTIVE PRODUCER – **ALAN FINE**

**SPECIAL THANKS FOR THE CONTRIBUTION OF ORIGINAL ARTWORK –**

JOHN TOTLEBEN, THOMAS YEATES, SAM PARSONS, NEIL GAIMAN, DR. SRIHARI NAIDU, VINCENT ZURZOLO & METROPOLIS COLLECTIBLES, HERITAGEAUCTIONS.COM, JONATHAN BAYLIS, KEITH VERONESE, JAMIE CUFR, STEVE & RICH DONNELLY, GENE KOGAN, KEVIN MASON, ROBERT JAQUIER, JASON GREENFIELD, CHRIS PUCKELWARTZ, OYSTEIN SORENSEN, MICHAEL BROWNING, MICHAEL SWEET, SCOTT DUNBIER, JOSEPH MELCHIOR, DAVID MANDEL, JAMES ROWLAND, AARON BUSHEY, STEVEN LEE, JONATHAN HOMICH, DARREN HINERMAN, JIM PASCOE, JOHN KALISZ, RALPH MATHIEU, MARTIN KELLER, MALCOLM BOURNE, JON B. COOKE, RANDY SCOTT, ZAK MULLIGAN, AARON WEISBROD AND PAUL SHIPLE



---

**MIRACLEMAN BOOK THREE: OLYMPUS.** Contains material originally published in magazine form as MIRACLEMAN #11-16 and ALL-NEW MIRACLEMAN ANNUAL #1. First printing 2015. ISBN# 978-0-7851-5466-2. Published by MARVEL WORLDWIDE, INC., a subsidiary of MARVEL ENTERTAINMENT, LLC. OFFICE OF PUBLICATION: 135 West 50th Street, New York, NY 10020. Copyright © 2015 Marvel Characters, Inc. All rights reserved. All characters featured in this issue and the distinctive names and likenesses thereof, and all related indicia are trademarks of Marvel Characters, Inc. No similarity between any of the names, characters, persons, and/or institutions in this magazine with those of any living or dead person or institution is intended, and any such similarity which may exist is purely coincidental. **Printed in the U.S.A.** ALAN FINE, EVP - Office of the President, Marvel Worldwide, Inc. and EVP & CMO Marvel Characters B.V.; DAN BUCKLEY, Publisher & President - Print, Animation & Digital Divisions; JOE QUESADA, Chief Creative Officer; TOM BREVOORT, SVP of Publishing; DAVID BOGART, SVP of Operations & Procurement, Publishing; C.B. CEBULSKI, SVP of Creator & Content Development; DAVID GABRIEL, SVP Print, Sales & Marketing; JIM O'KEEFE, VP of Operations & Logistics; DAN CARR, Executive Director of Publishing Technology; SUSAN CRESPI, Editorial Operations Manager; ALEX MORALES, Publishing Operations Manager; STAN LEE, Chairman Emeritus. For information regarding advertising in Marvel Comics or on Marvel.com, please contact Niza Disla, Director of Marvel Partnerships, at ndisla@marvel.com. For Marvel subscription inquiries, please call 800-217-9158. **Manufactured**

# MIRACLEMAN

## BOOK THREE: OLYMPUS

STORY
# THE ORIGINAL WRITER

ART
# JOHN TOTLEBEN

WITH THANKS TO **THOMAS YEATES**

COLOR ART
# STEVE OLIFF

LETTERING
**JOE CARAMAGNA**

ART RESTORATION
**MICHAEL KELLEHER & KELLUSTRATION**

MIRACLEMAN CREATED BY **MICK ANGLO**

# MIRACLEMAN
## BOOK THREE: OLYMPUS

## LEGENDS & APOCRYPHA

1987

THE JULY MORNING: BIG, HOT, EMPTY, NOT QUITE BROKEN.

THE TOY CITY: EMERGING STOREY BY STOREY FROM COOL GREY HAZE; BARELY AWAKE BUT DREAMING HARD...

REAMING OF NEW MUSIC, EW THOUGHTS, NEW PAINTINGS, NEW WORLD EVERY DAY.

EVERY DAY.

SOMETIMES, TOY CITIZENS CLAMBER UP HERE ASKING FAVOURS; THIS DISEASE NEEDS CURING, THAT RIVER MOVING. SOMETIMES I SAY YES.

THEY WEAR HELMETS FOR THE THIN AIR; WEAR FEAR IN DAMP CRESCENTS BENEATH THEIR SHIRT ARMS.

FUNNY LITTLE BUBBLE-HEADS.

EVENTUALLY, ONE WILL SUFFER A HEART ATTACK WHILE IMPLORING ME TO SQUARE THE CIRCLE OR GRANT IMMORTALITY...

IMMORTALITY.

FATHER, HOW YOU WOULD HAVE LAUGHED TO SEE THIS.

YOUR FACE IS COLD NOW, TANNED SILVER BY THE SPOTLIGHTS.

THE JULY MORNING: BIG, HOT, EMPTY, SILENT.

CROSSING TO THE LECTERN, CLIMBING ITS STEPS RATHER THAN FLYING, I OPEN A BOOK WITH STEEL PAGES.

I HAVE LEGENDS TO WRITE; TALES OF HOW IT FEELS TO LIVE IN A MYTHOLOGY.

I SIT HERE, IN MY STILL, HIGH PLACE, AND TEST THE KEENNESS OF MY STYLUS AGAINST AN UPRAISED FINGERTIP.

THERE; A NEEDLE OF BLOODY LIGHT, AN AFTERTASTE OF OZONE...

I AM READY TO BEGIN.

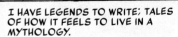

5

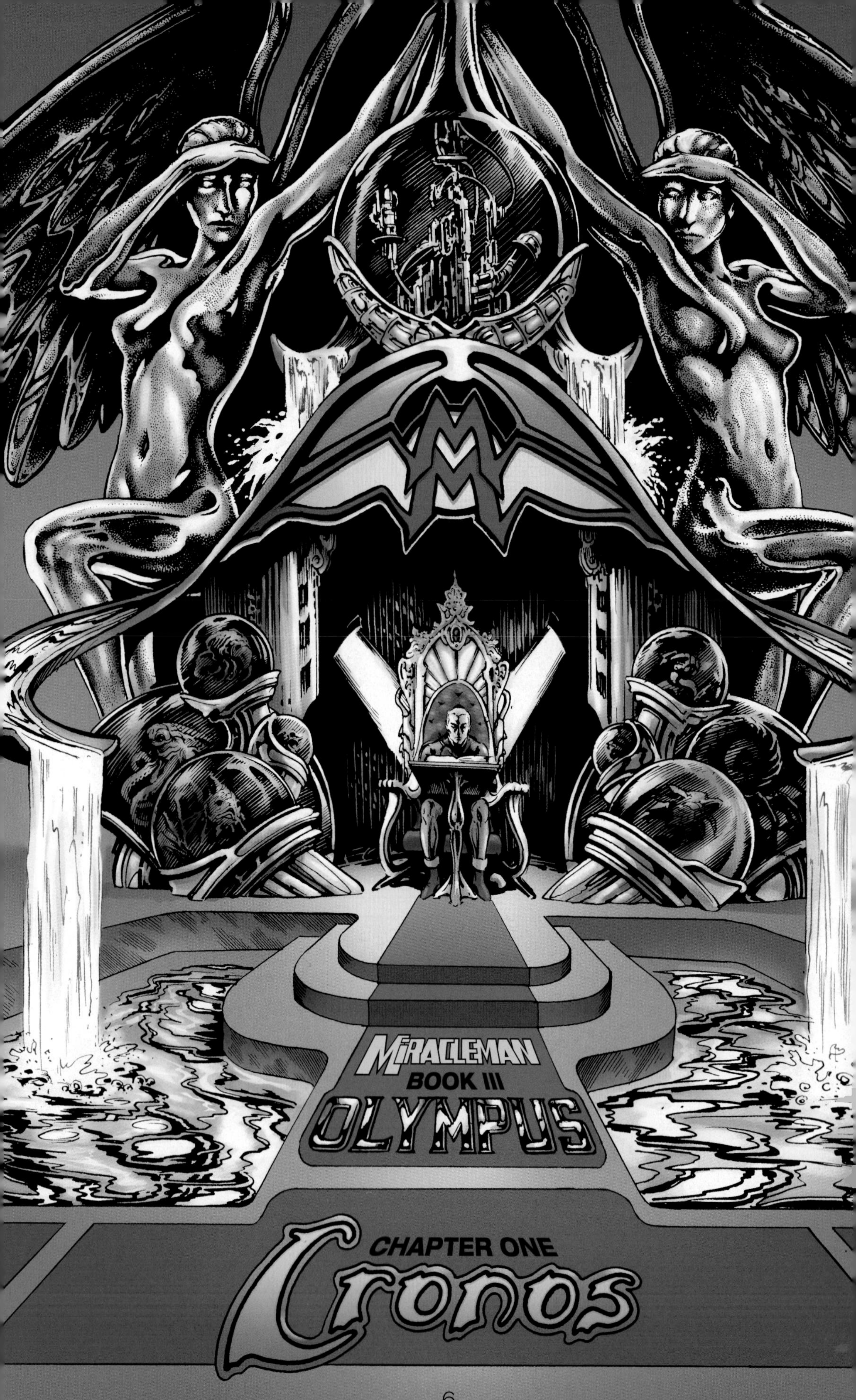
MIRACLEMAN
BOOK III
OLYMPUS
CHAPTER ONE
Cronos

After creation came a time when young gods fought their Titan fathers…

THE **TIME** WAS NOVEMBER 1982; THE **PLACE**, LESS **CERTAIN**. WHERE DID IT **BEGIN**? WITH **ME**? OR **HER**? WITH **HIM**, BATES, THE **ADVERSARY**?

YES.

YES, PERHAPS IT BEGAN WITH **HIM**.

…AND THEY ALL STARTED CALLING ME **NAMES**!

OH, JOHNNY, I'M **SORRY**. YOU **WANTED** TO MIX WITH OTHER CHILDREN, BUT SOME OF THEM ARE, WELL, **DIFFICULT**...

THEY S-SAID 'HERE'S MASTER BATES...'

OH, **DON'T**. DON'T **CRY**.

LOOK, SINCE YOUR **RECOVERY** YOU'VE BEEN DOING SO **WELL**. YOU MUSTN'T LET THESE BULLIES SET YOU **BACK**. STAND **UP** TO THEM.

YOU DON'T **UNDERSTAND**! I **WANTED** TO! I WANTED TO...TO...

YES? IT'S OKAY, JOHNNY. YOU WANTED TO **WHAT**?

"NOTHING. NOTHING IMPORTANT. IT DOESN'T MATTER."

"I'D LIKE TO BE ON MY OWN NOW, PLEASE."

…and in the place of his confinement, the Adversary tested the shackles that bound him, tugging at them. They creaked, but did not break.

7

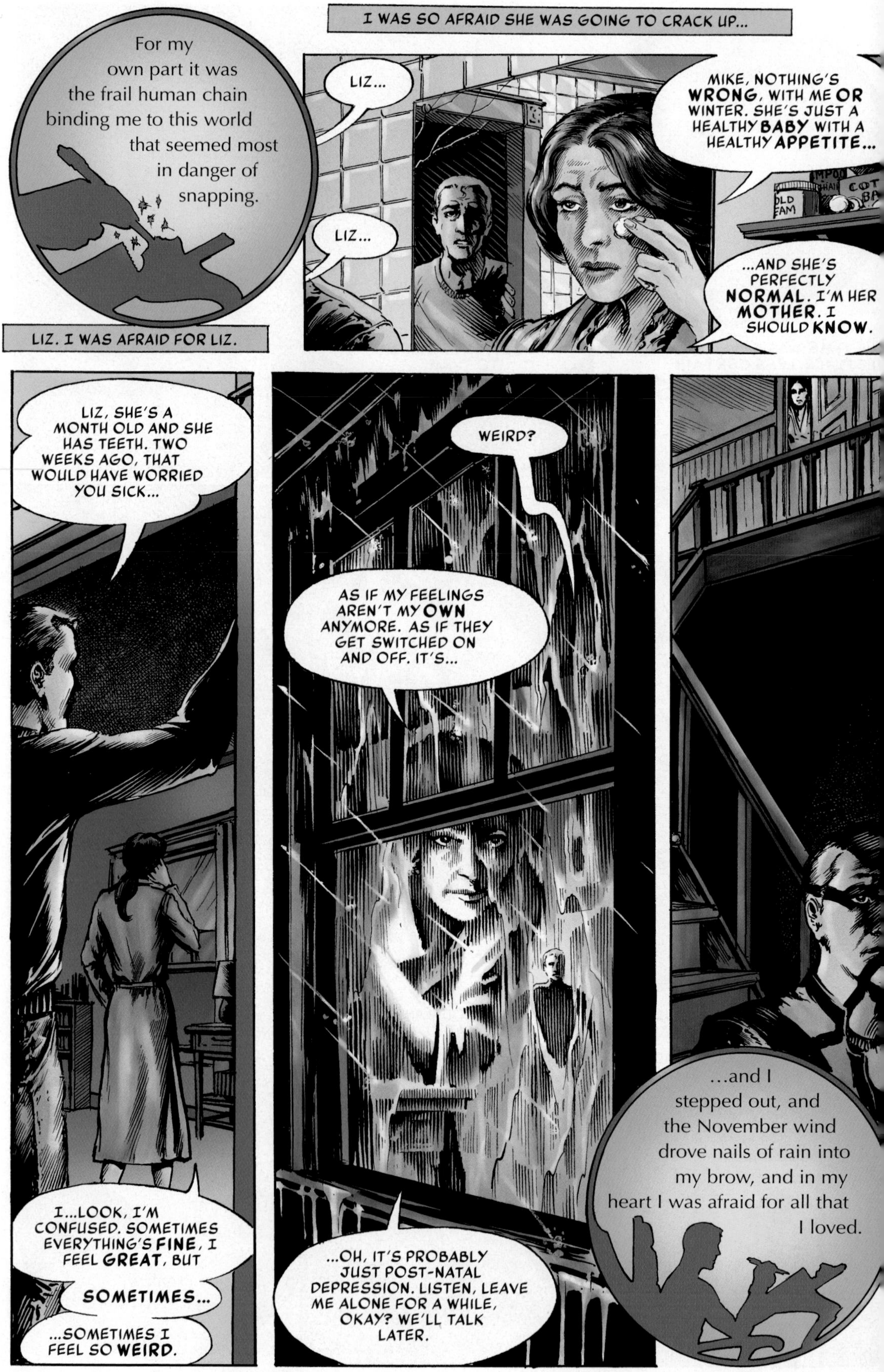

For my own part it was the frail human chain binding me to this world that seemed most in danger of snapping.
LIZ. I WAS AFRAID FOR LIZ.
I WAS SO AFRAID SHE WAS GOING TO CRACK UP...
LIZ...
LIZ...
MIKE, NOTHING'S WRONG, WITH ME OR WINTER. SHE'S JUST A HEALTHY BABY WITH A HEALTHY APPETITE...
...AND SHE'S PERFECTLY NORMAL. I'M HER MOTHER. I SHOULD KNOW.
LIZ, SHE'S A MONTH OLD AND SHE HAS TEETH. TWO WEEKS AGO, THAT WOULD HAVE WORRIED YOU SICK...
I...LOOK, I'M CONFUSED. SOMETIMES EVERYTHING'S FINE, I FEEL GREAT, BUT
SOMETIMES...
...SOMETIMES I FEEL SO WEIRD.
WEIRD?
AS IF MY FEELINGS AREN'T MY OWN ANYMORE. AS IF THEY GET SWITCHED ON AND OFF. IT'S...
...OH, IT'S PROBABLY JUST POST-NATAL DEPRESSION. LISTEN, LEAVE ME ALONE FOR A WHILE, OKAY? WE'LL TALK LATER.
...and I stepped out, and the November wind drove nails of rain into my brow, and in my heart I was afraid for all that I loved.

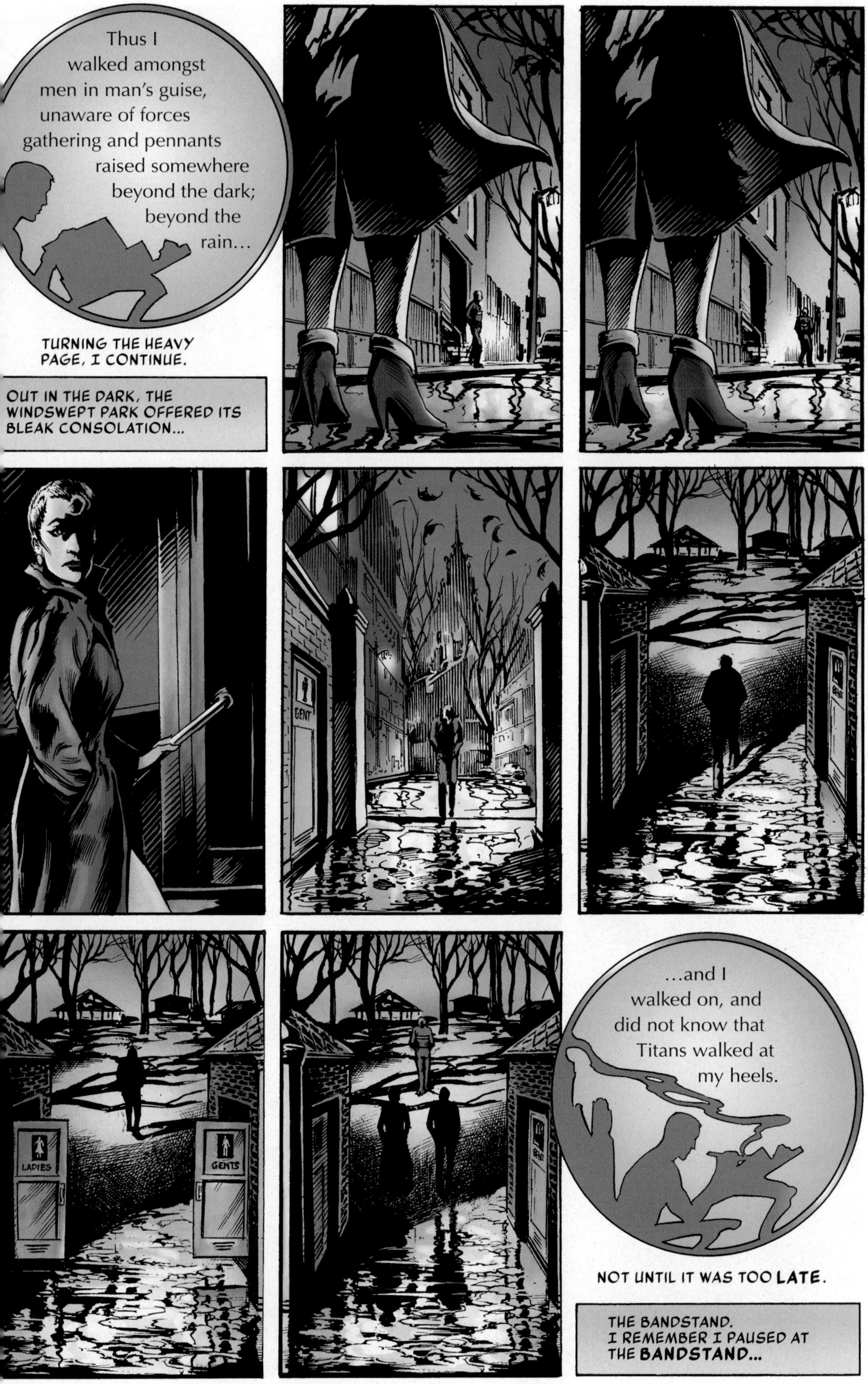
Thus I walked amongst men in man's guise, unaware of forces gathering and pennants raised somewhere beyond the dark; beyond the rain...
TURNING THE HEAVY PAGE, I CONTINUE.
OUT IN THE DARK, THE WINDSWEPT PARK OFFERED ITS BLEAK CONSOLATION...
GENT
LADIES
GENTS
...and I walked on, and did not know that Titans walked at my heels.
NOT UNTIL IT WAS TOO LATE.
THE BANDSTAND. I REMEMBER I PAUSED AT THE BANDSTAND...

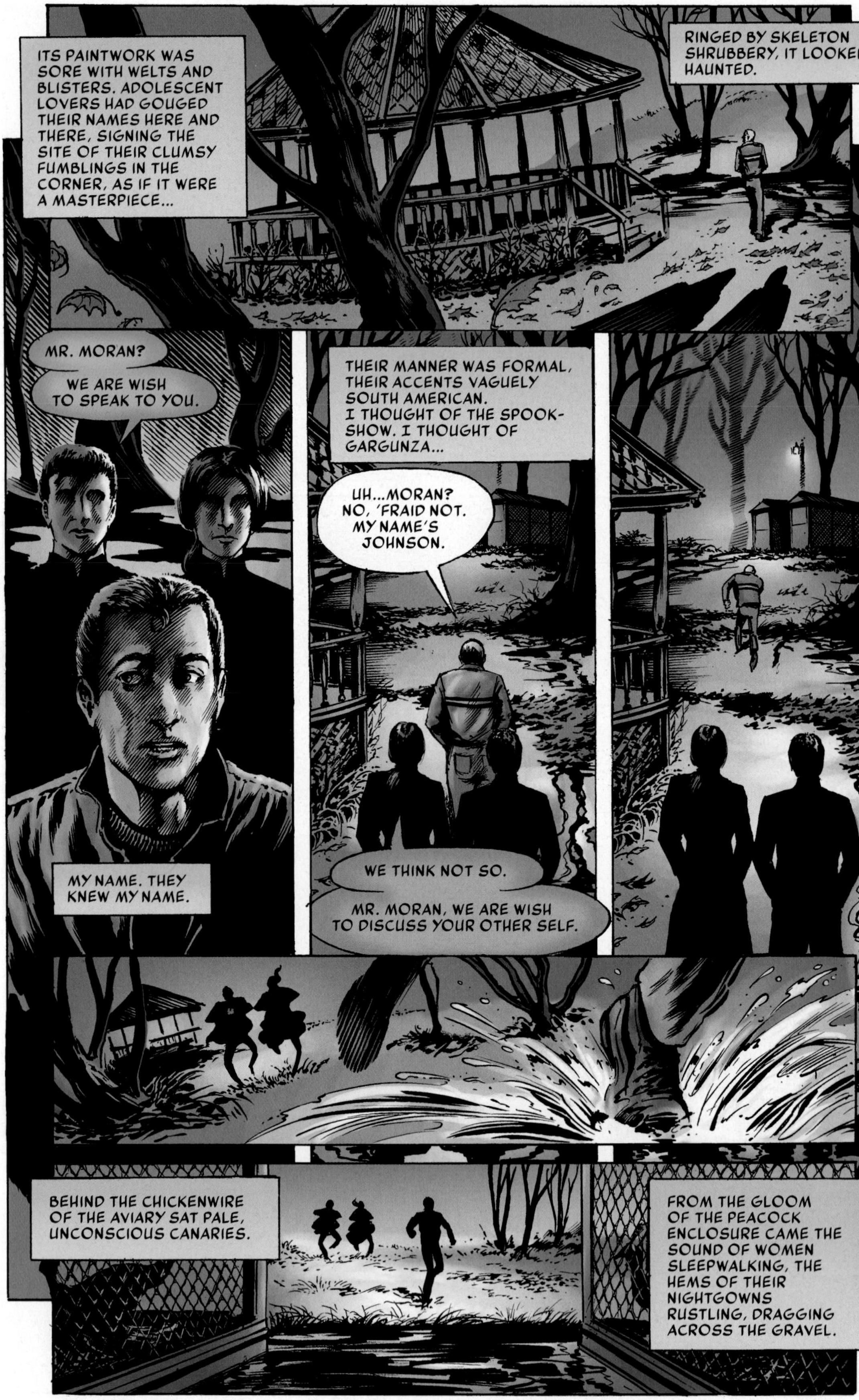
ITS PAINTWORK WAS SORE WITH WELTS AND BLISTERS. ADOLESCENT LOVERS HAD GOUGED THEIR NAMES HERE AND THERE, SIGNING THE SITE OF THEIR CLUMSY FUMBLINGS IN THE CORNER, AS IF IT WERE A MASTERPIECE...
RINGED BY SKELETON SHRUBBERY, IT LOOKED HAUNTED.
MR. MORAN?
WE ARE WISH TO SPEAK TO YOU.
MY NAME. THEY KNEW MY NAME.
THEIR MANNER WAS FORMAL, THEIR ACCENTS VAGUELY SOUTH AMERICAN. I THOUGHT OF THE SPOOK-SHOW. I THOUGHT OF GARGUNZA...
UH...MORAN? NO, 'FRAID NOT. MY NAME'S JOHNSON.
WE THINK NOT SO.
MR. MORAN, WE ARE WISH TO DISCUSS YOUR OTHER SELF.
BEHIND THE CHICKENWIRE OF THE AVIARY SAT PALE, UNCONSCIOUS CANARIES.
FROM THE GLOOM OF THE PEACOCK ENCLOSURE CAME THE SOUND OF WOMEN SLEEPWALKING, THE HEMS OF THEIR NIGHTGOWNS RUSTLING, DRAGGING ACROSS THE GRAVEL.

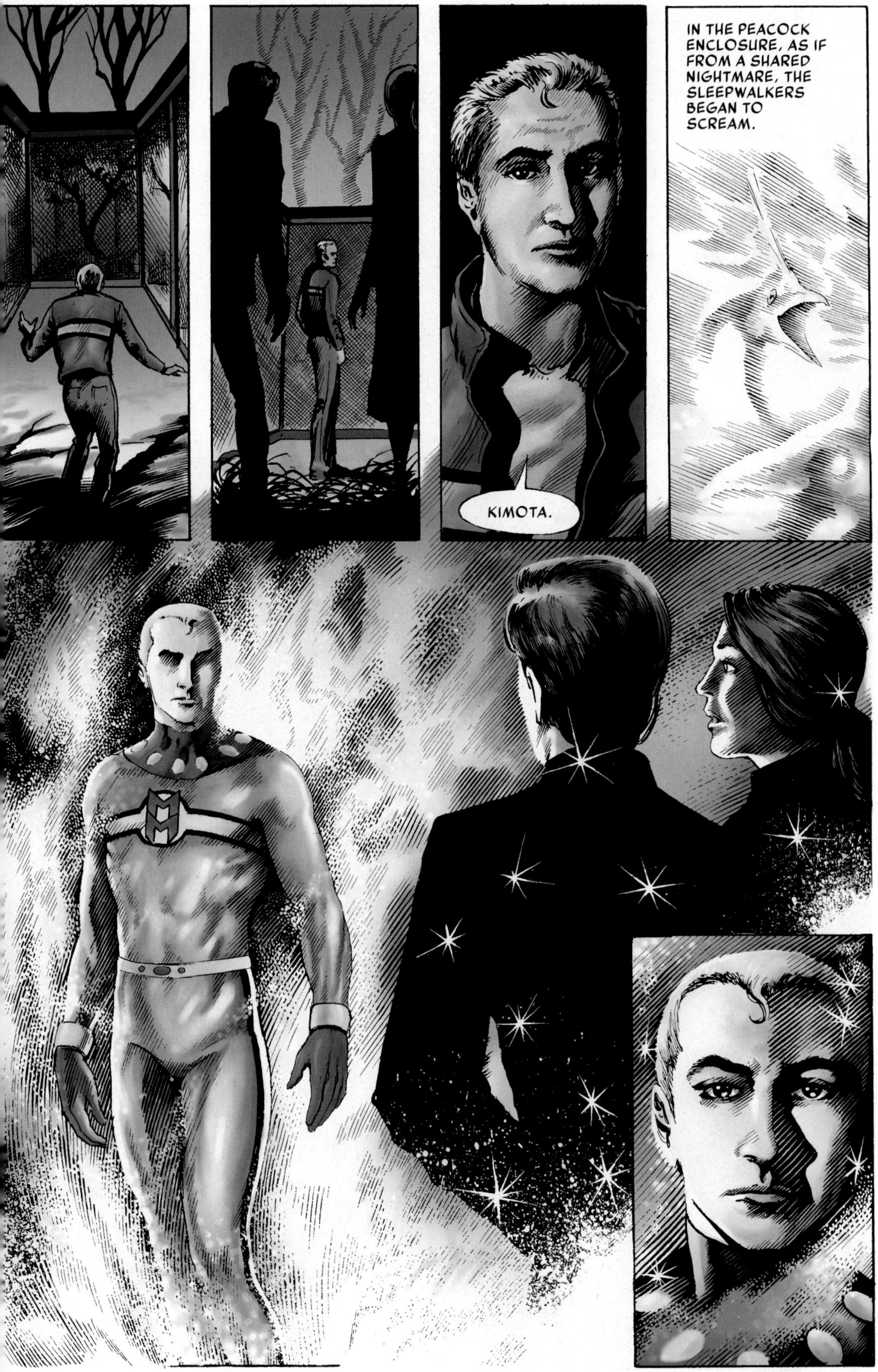
KIMOTA.
IN THE PEACOCK ENCLOSURE, AS IF FROM A SHARED NIGHTMARE, THE SLEEPWALKERS BEGAN TO SCREAM.

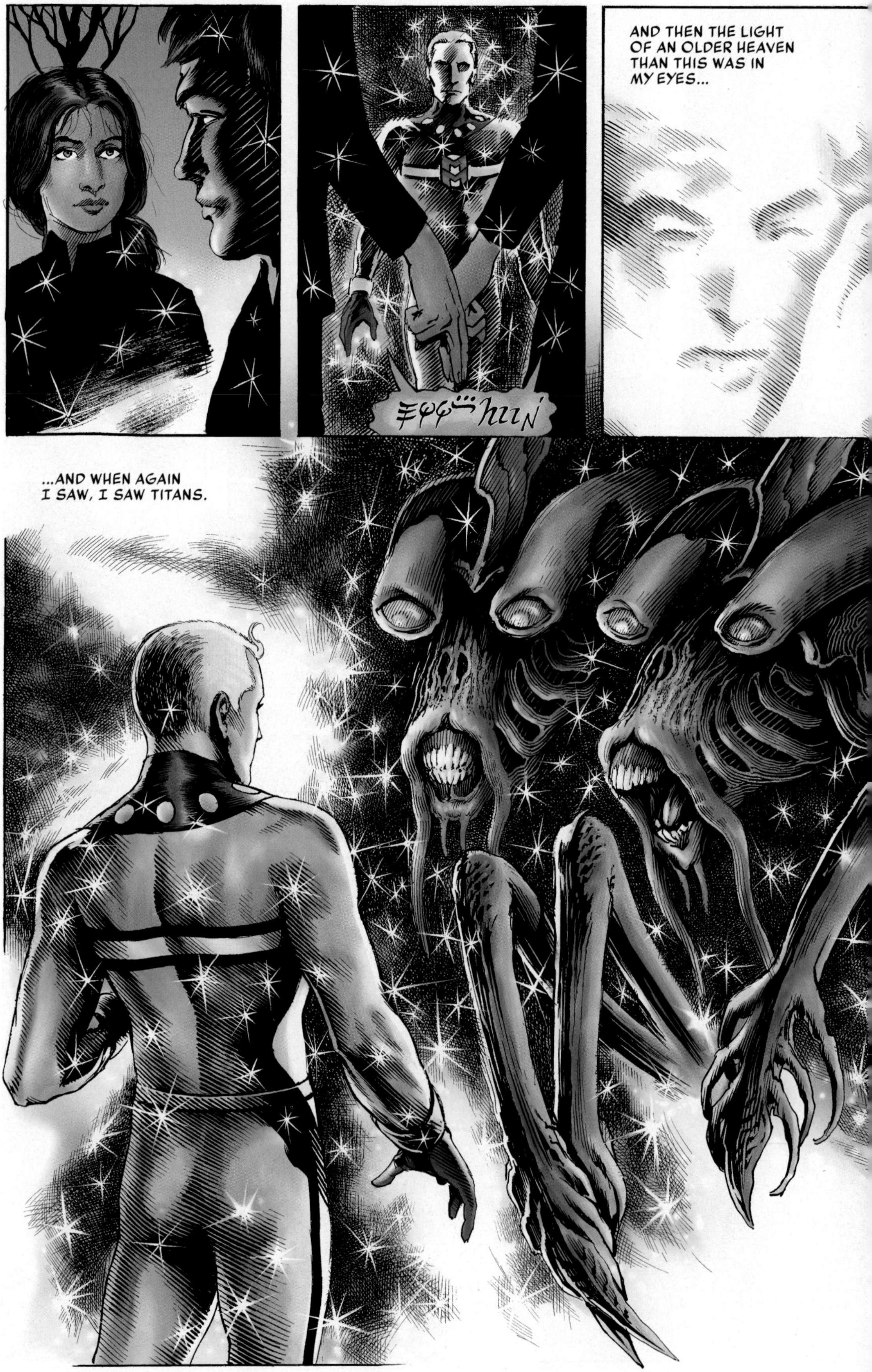
AND THEN THE LIGHT OF AN OLDER HEAVEN THAN THIS WAS IN MY EYES...
...AND WHEN AGAIN I SAW, I SAW TITANS.

I knew them not for Titans then, knew not that Cronos was arrived to confiscate the thunderbolts of a delinquent Zeus.

This was before such concepts were defined, or inked, white hot, upon immortal steel.

THIS WAS BEFORE THE TIME OF NAMES AND NAMING, IN DAYS THAT KNEW A BLOODIER IMPERATIVE, KNEW NO CREED SAVE BALLISTICS, NO FAITH BUT IN THE RITUAL OF TENSE...

...AND SPRING...

...AND THRUST.

LIPS PAINTED WITH BLOOD, I CLUNG TO THE BIRDSHIT-STREAKED CHAINLINK, WHERE CONVICTS HAD MARKED OFF THE DAYS OF THEIR SENTENCE IN CHALK ON PENITENTIARY WALLS.

THE TITANS ADVANCED, MY CONFIDENCE DEPARTING WITH THE BIRDS.

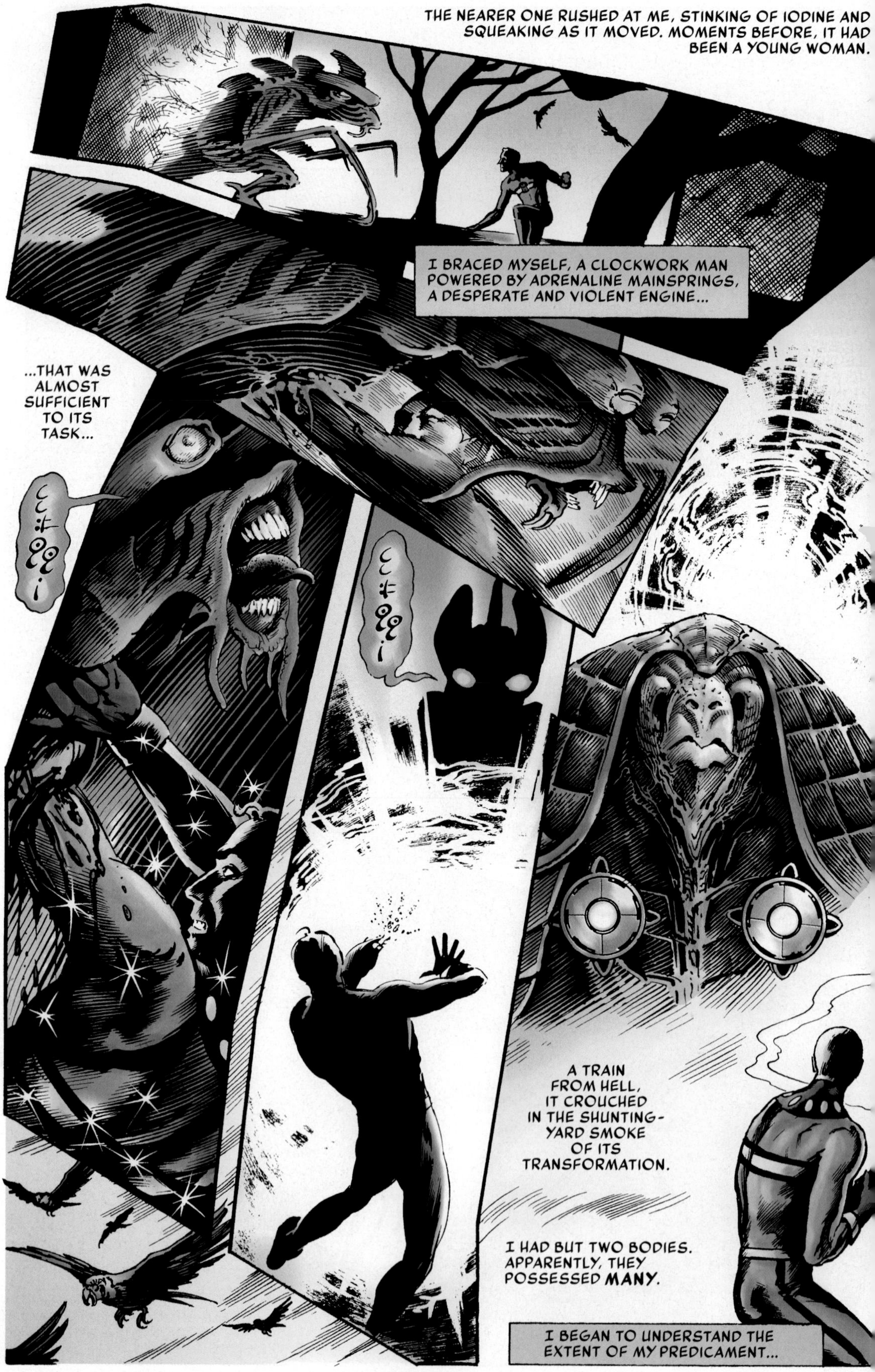
THE NEARER ONE RUSHED AT ME, STINKING OF IODINE AND SQUEAKING AS IT MOVED. MOMENTS BEFORE, IT HAD BEEN A YOUNG WOMAN.
I BRACED MYSELF, A CLOCKWORK MAN POWERED BY ADRENALINE MAINSPRINGS, A DESPERATE AND VIOLENT ENGINE...
...THAT WAS ALMOST SUFFICIENT TO ITS TASK...
A TRAIN FROM HELL, IT CROUCHED IN THE SHUNTING-YARD SMOKE OF ITS TRANSFORMATION.
I HAD BUT TWO BODIES. APPARENTLY, THEY POSSESSED **MANY**.
I BEGAN TO UNDERSTAND THE EXTENT OF MY PREDICAMENT...

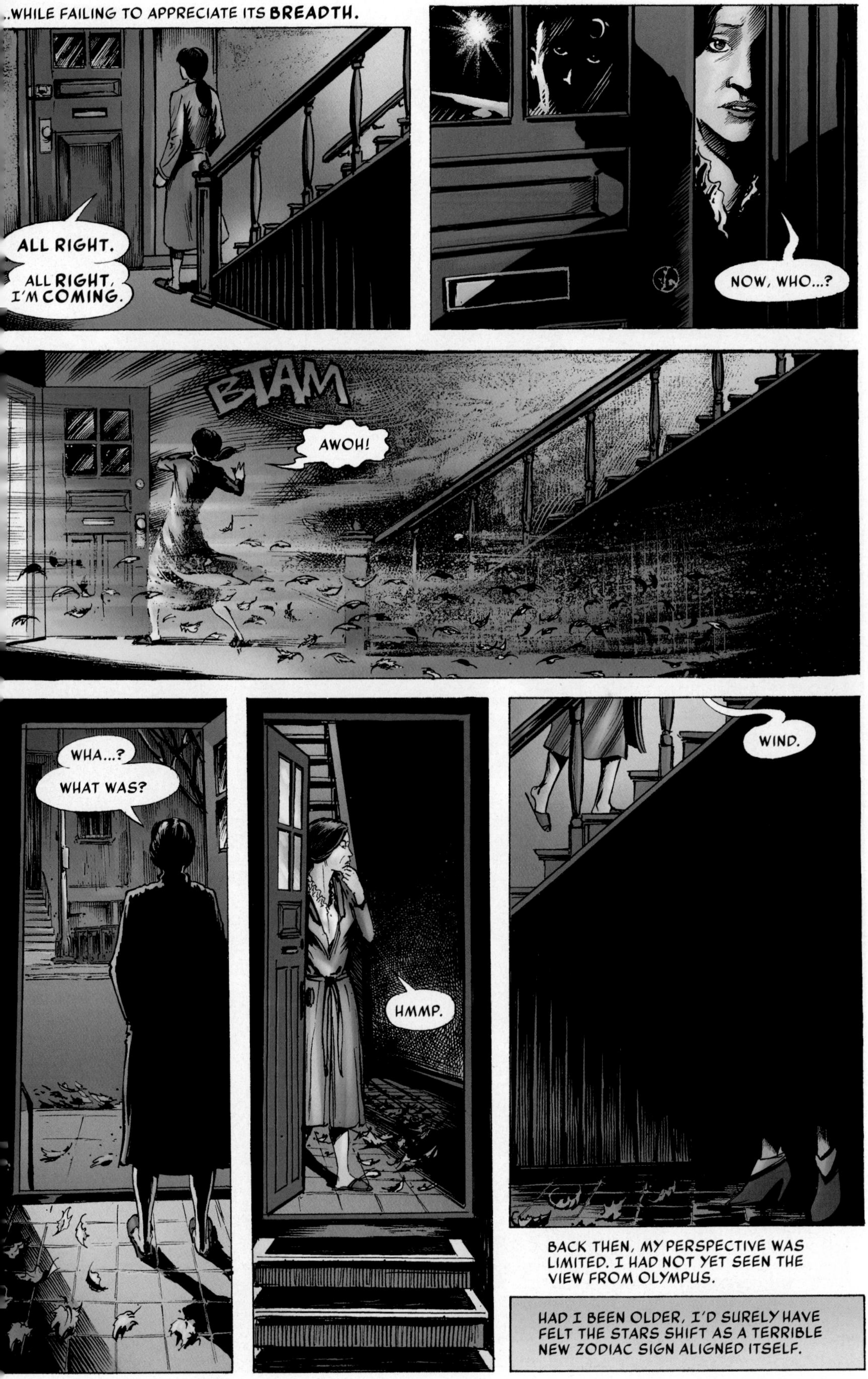

..WHILE FAILING TO APPRECIATE ITS BREADTH.
ALL RIGHT.
ALL RIGHT, I'M COMING.
NOW, WHO...?
BTAM
AWOH!
WHA...?
WHAT WAS?
HMMP.
WIND.
BACK THEN, MY PERSPECTIVE WAS LIMITED. I HAD NOT YET SEEN THE VIEW FROM OLYMPUS.
HAD I BEEN OLDER, I'D SURELY HAVE FELT THE STARS SHIFT AS A TERRIBLE NEW ZODIAC SIGN ALIGNED ITSELF.

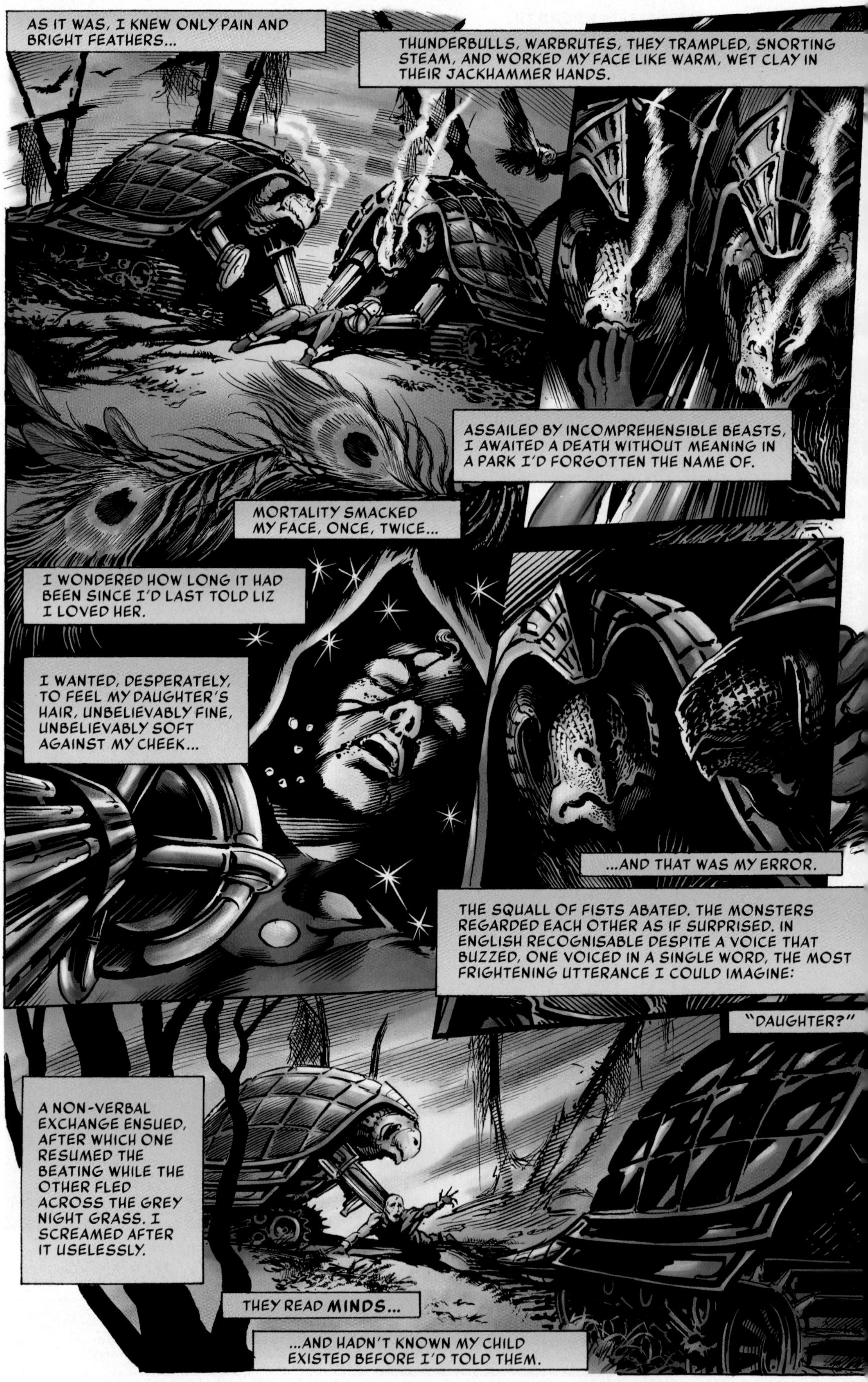
AS IT WAS, I KNEW ONLY PAIN AND BRIGHT FEATHERS...
THUNDERBULLS, WARBRUTES, THEY TRAMPLED, SNORTING STEAM, AND WORKED MY FACE LIKE WARM, WET CLAY IN THEIR JACKHAMMER HANDS.
ASSAILED BY INCOMPREHENSIBLE BEASTS, I AWAITED A DEATH WITHOUT MEANING IN A PARK I'D FORGOTTEN THE NAME OF.
MORTALITY SMACKED MY FACE, ONCE, TWICE...
I WONDERED HOW LONG IT HAD BEEN SINCE I'D LAST TOLD LIZ I LOVED HER.
I WANTED, DESPERATELY, TO FEEL MY DAUGHTER'S HAIR, UNBELIEVABLY FINE, UNBELIEVABLY SOFT AGAINST MY CHEEK...
...AND THAT WAS MY ERROR.
THE SQUALL OF FISTS ABATED. THE MONSTERS REGARDED EACH OTHER AS IF SURPRISED. IN ENGLISH RECOGNISABLE DESPITE A VOICE THAT BUZZED, ONE VOICED IN A SINGLE WORD, THE MOST FRIGHTENING UTTERANCE I COULD IMAGINE:
"DAUGHTER?"
A NON-VERBAL EXCHANGE ENSUED, AFTER WHICH ONE RESUMED THE BEATING WHILE THE OTHER FLED ACROSS THE GREY NIGHT GRASS. I SCREAMED AFTER IT USELESSLY.
THEY READ **MINDS**...
...AND HADN'T KNOWN MY CHILD EXISTED BEFORE I'D TOLD THEM.

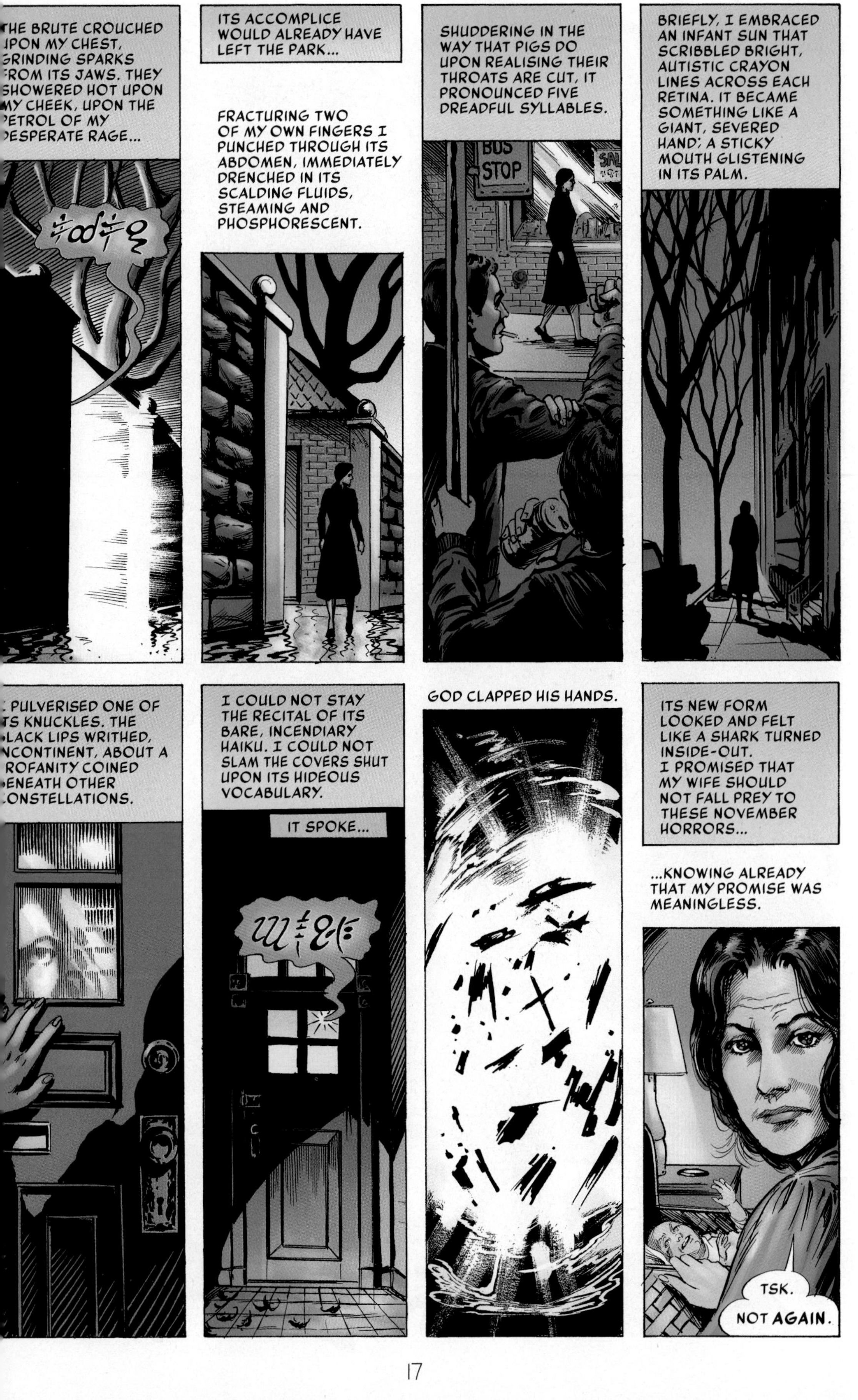
THE BRUTE CROUCHED UPON MY CHEST, GRINDING SPARKS FROM ITS JAWS. THEY SHOWERED HOT UPON MY CHEEK, UPON THE PETROL OF MY DESPERATE RAGE...
ITS ACCOMPLICE WOULD ALREADY HAVE LEFT THE PARK...
FRACTURING TWO OF MY OWN FINGERS I PUNCHED THROUGH ITS ABDOMEN, IMMEDIATELY DRENCHED IN ITS SCALDING FLUIDS, STEAMING AND PHOSPHORESCENT.
SHUDDERING IN THE WAY THAT PIGS DO UPON REALISING THEIR THROATS ARE CUT, IT PRONOUNCED FIVE DREADFUL SYLLABLES.
BUS STOP
BRIEFLY, I EMBRACED AN INFANT SUN THAT SCRIBBLED BRIGHT, AUTISTIC CRAYON LINES ACROSS EACH RETINA. IT BECAME SOMETHING LIKE A GIANT, SEVERED HAND; A STICKY MOUTH GLISTENING IN ITS PALM.
I PULVERISED ONE OF ITS KNUCKLES. THE BLACK LIPS WRITHED, INCONTINENT, ABOUT A PROFANITY COINED BENEATH OTHER CONSTELLATIONS.
I COULD NOT STAY THE RECITAL OF ITS BARE, INCENDIARY HAIKU. I COULD NOT SLAM THE COVERS SHUT UPON ITS HIDEOUS VOCABULARY.
IT SPOKE...
GOD CLAPPED HIS HANDS.
ITS NEW FORM LOOKED AND FELT LIKE A SHARK TURNED INSIDE-OUT. I PROMISED THAT MY WIFE SHOULD NOT FALL PREY TO THESE NOVEMBER HORRORS...
...KNOWING ALREADY THAT MY PROMISE WAS MEANINGLESS.
TSK.
NOT AGAIN.

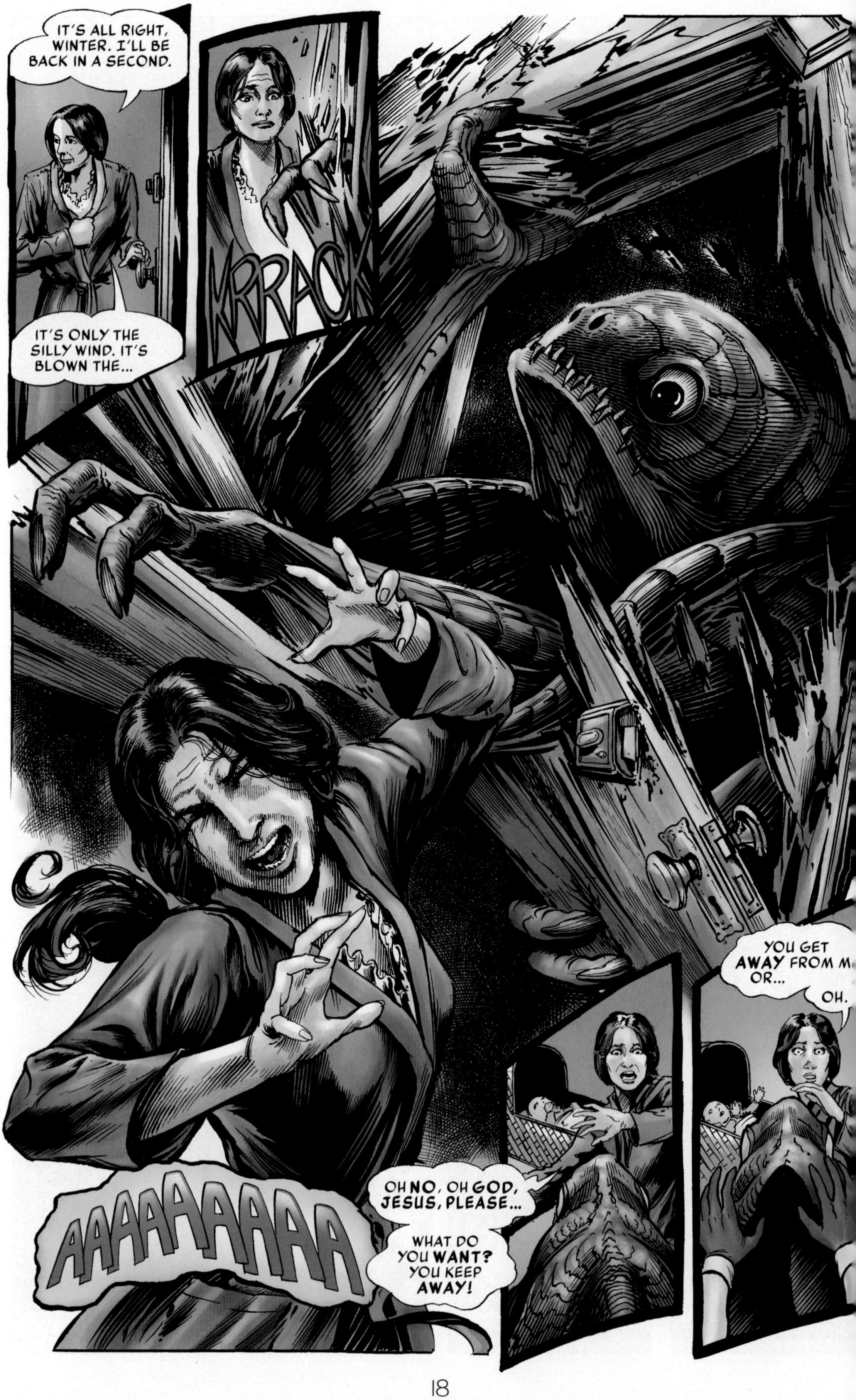
IT'S ALL RIGHT, WINTER. I'LL BE BACK IN A SECOND.
IT'S ONLY THE SILLY WIND. IT'S BLOWN THE...
KRRACK
AAAAAAAAA
OH NO, OH GOD, JESUS, PLEASE...
WHAT DO YOU WANT? YOU KEEP AWAY!
YOU GET AWAY FROM M
OR...
OH.

ASSUMING YOU CAN STILL UNDERSTAND ENGLISH IN THIS BODY, I WANT YOU TO KNOW THAT I'VE JUST CRUSHED YOUR LARYNX.

KLITCH

YOU SEE, THERE ARE **SOME** SITUATIONS YOU JUST **CAN'T** TALK YOUR WAY OUT OF.

TO HAVE SEEN HER THEN, AS LIZ DESCRIBED HER LATER: COLD AND GLITTERING, A STATUE OF CUT GLASS, IMMACULATE SAVE FOR GAUNTLETS DARKENED BY UNEARTHLY BLOOD...

APHRODITE, RISEN FROM THE CHURNING FOAM WHERE FELL THE MANHOOD OF CRONOS.

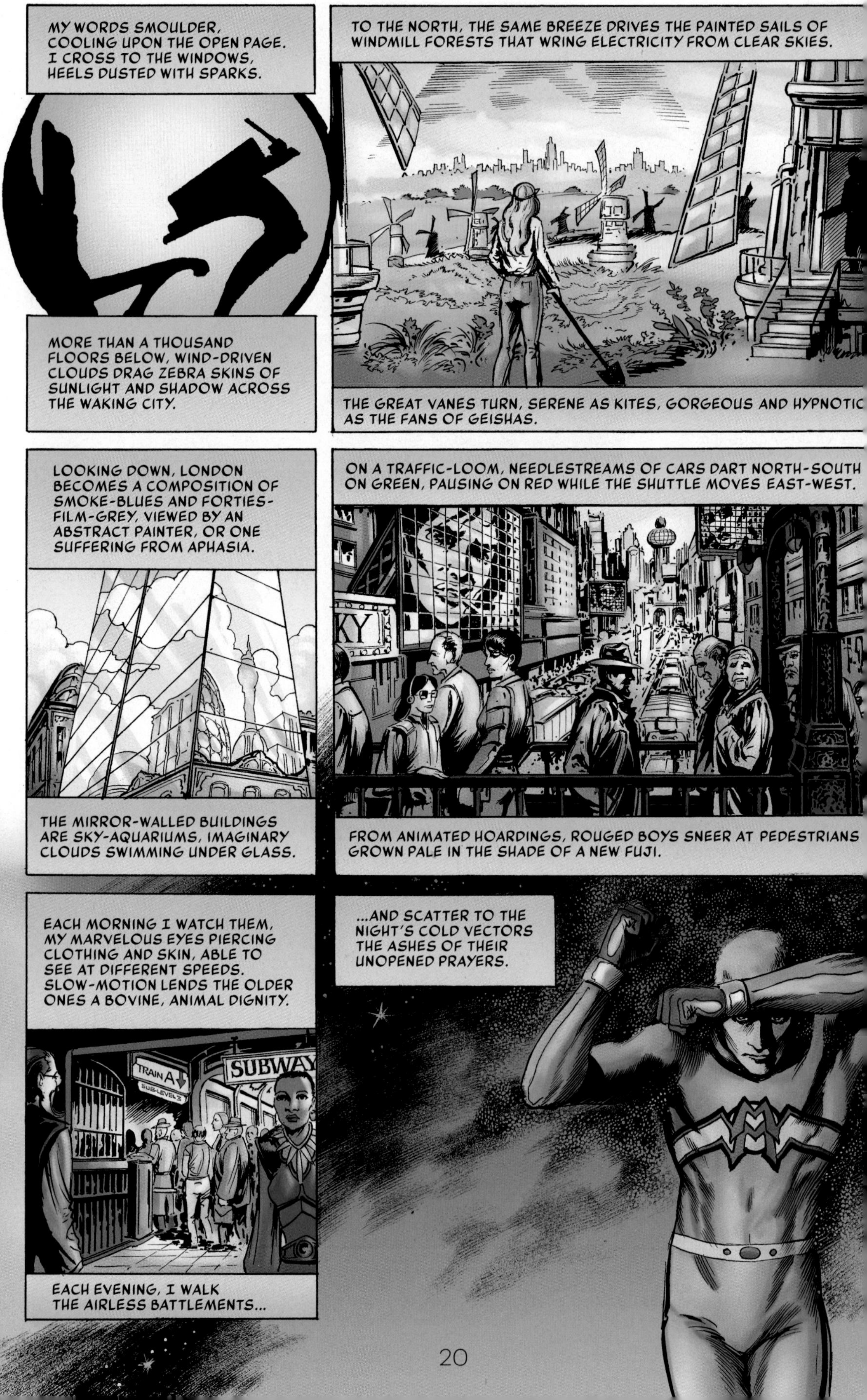
MY WORDS SMOULDER, COOLING UPON THE OPEN PAGE. I CROSS TO THE WINDOWS, HEELS DUSTED WITH SPARKS.
MORE THAN A THOUSAND FLOORS BELOW, WIND-DRIVEN CLOUDS DRAG ZEBRA SKINS OF SUNLIGHT AND SHADOW ACROSS THE WAKING CITY.
TO THE NORTH, THE SAME BREEZE DRIVES THE PAINTED SAILS OF WINDMILL FORESTS THAT WRING ELECTRICITY FROM CLEAR SKIES.
THE GREAT VANES TURN, SERENE AS KITES, GORGEOUS AND HYPNOTIC AS THE FANS OF GEISHAS.
LOOKING DOWN, LONDON BECOMES A COMPOSITION OF SMOKE-BLUES AND FORTIES-FILM-GREY, VIEWED BY AN ABSTRACT PAINTER, OR ONE SUFFERING FROM APHASIA.
THE MIRROR-WALLED BUILDINGS ARE SKY-AQUARIUMS, IMAGINARY CLOUDS SWIMMING UNDER GLASS.
ON A TRAFFIC-LOOM, NEEDLESTREAMS OF CARS DART NORTH-SOUTH ON GREEN, PAUSING ON RED WHILE THE SHUTTLE MOVES EAST-WEST.
KY
FROM ANIMATED HOARDINGS, ROUGED BOYS SNEER AT PEDESTRIANS GROWN PALE IN THE SHADE OF A NEW FUJI.
EACH MORNING I WATCH THEM, MY MARVELOUS EYES PIERCING CLOTHING AND SKIN, ABLE TO SEE AT DIFFERENT SPEEDS. SLOW-MOTION LENDS THE OLDER ONES A BOVINE, ANIMAL DIGNITY.
TRAIN A
SUB-LEVEL 3
SUBWAY
EACH EVENING, I WALK THE AIRLESS BATTLEMENTS...
...AND SCATTER TO THE NIGHT'S COLD VECTORS THE ASHES OF THEIR UNOPENED PRAYERS.

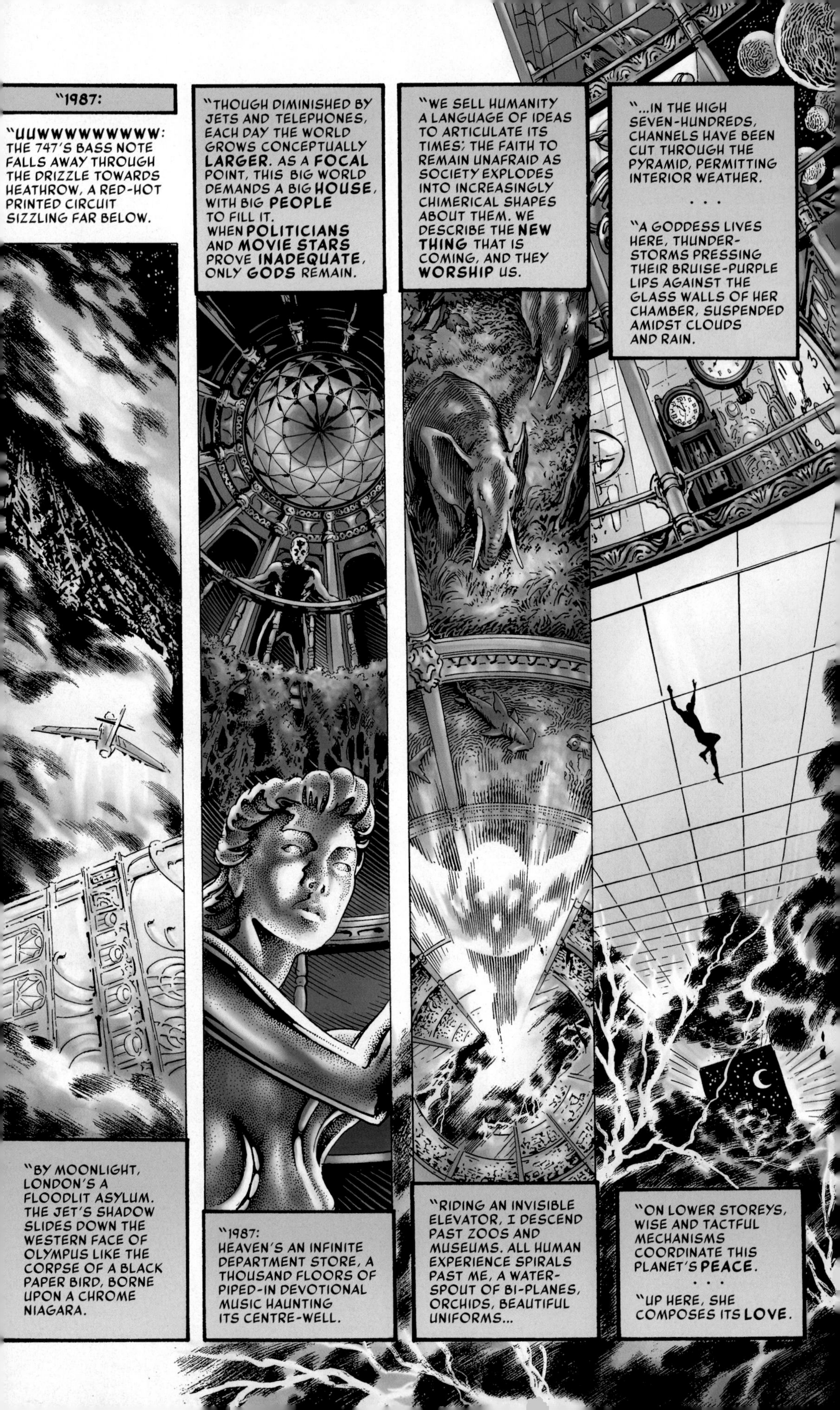
"1987:
"UUWWWWWWWWW: THE 747'S BASS NOTE FALLS AWAY THROUGH THE DRIZZLE TOWARDS HEATHROW, A RED-HOT PRINTED CIRCUIT SIZZLING FAR BELOW.
"BY MOONLIGHT, LONDON'S A FLOODLIT ASYLUM. THE JET'S SHADOW SLIDES DOWN THE WESTERN FACE OF OLYMPUS LIKE THE CORPSE OF A BLACK PAPER BIRD, BORNE UPON A CHROME NIAGARA.
"THOUGH DIMINISHED BY JETS AND TELEPHONES, EACH DAY THE WORLD GROWS CONCEPTUALLY LARGER. AS A FOCAL POINT, THIS BIG WORLD DEMANDS A BIG HOUSE, WITH BIG PEOPLE TO FILL IT. WHEN POLITICIANS AND MOVIE STARS PROVE INADEQUATE, ONLY GODS REMAIN.
"1987: HEAVEN'S AN INFINITE DEPARTMENT STORE, A THOUSAND FLOORS OF PIPED-IN DEVOTIONAL MUSIC HAUNTING ITS CENTRE-WELL.
"WE SELL HUMANITY A LANGUAGE OF IDEAS TO ARTICULATE ITS TIMES; THE FAITH TO REMAIN UNAFRAID AS SOCIETY EXPLODES INTO INCREASINGLY CHIMERICAL SHAPES ABOUT THEM. WE DESCRIBE THE NEW THING THAT IS COMING, AND THEY WORSHIP US.
"RIDING AN INVISIBLE ELEVATOR, I DESCEND PAST ZOOS AND MUSEUMS. ALL HUMAN EXPERIENCE SPIRALS PAST ME, A WATER-SPOUT OF BI-PLANES, ORCHIDS, BEAUTIFUL UNIFORMS...
"...IN THE HIGH SEVEN-HUNDREDS, CHANNELS HAVE BEEN CUT THROUGH THE PYRAMID, PERMITTING INTERIOR WEATHER.
. . .
"A GODDESS LIVES HERE, THUNDER-STORMS PRESSING THEIR BRUISE-PURPLE LIPS AGAINST THE GLASS WALLS OF HER CHAMBER, SUSPENDED AMIDST CLOUDS AND RAIN.
"ON LOWER STOREYS, WISE AND TACTFUL MECHANISMS COORDINATE THIS PLANET'S PEACE.
. . .
"UP HERE, SHE COMPOSES ITS LOVE.

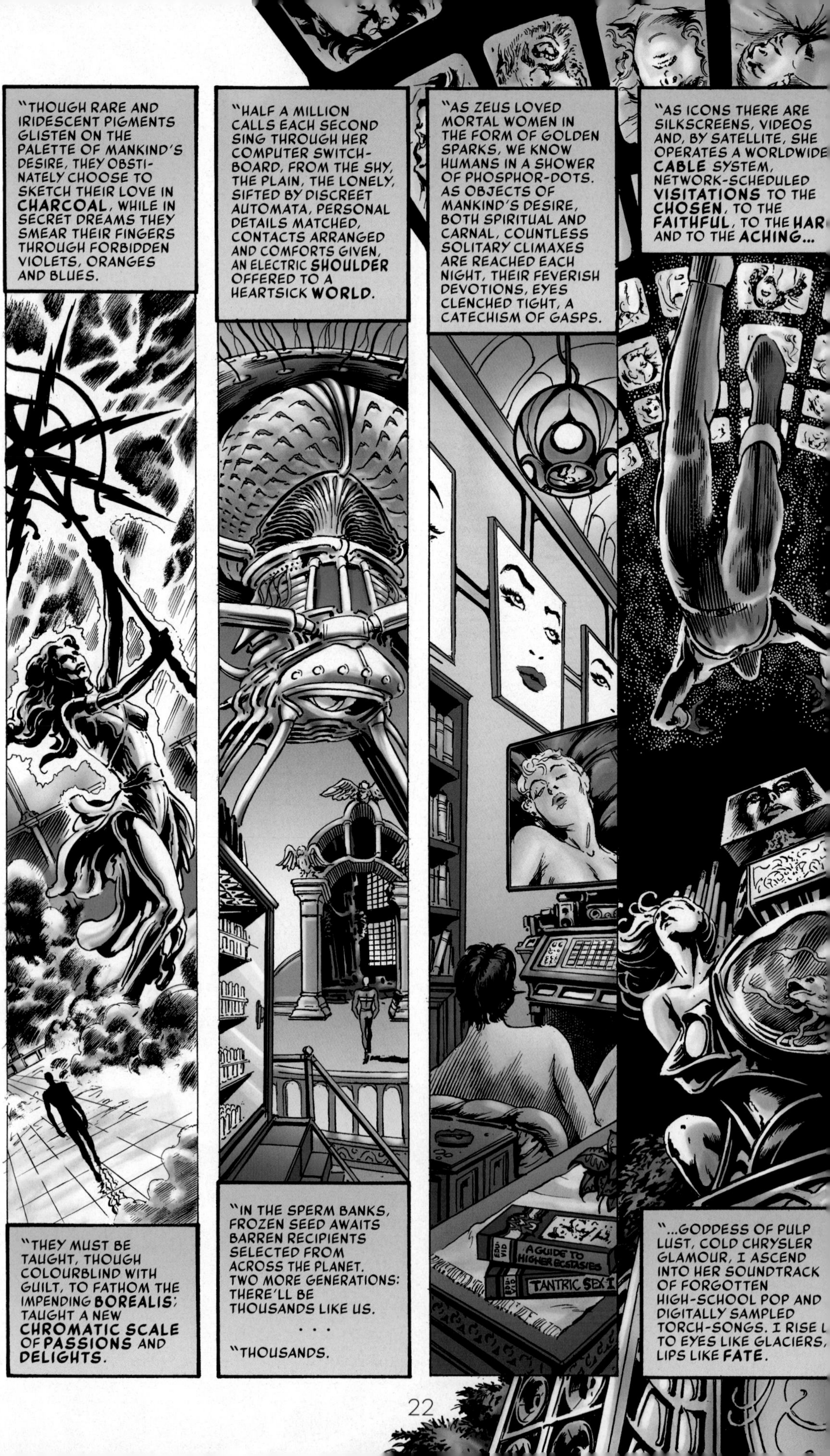
"THOUGH RARE AND IRIDESCENT PIGMENTS GLISTEN ON THE PALETTE OF MANKIND'S DESIRE, THEY OBSTINATELY CHOOSE TO SKETCH THEIR LOVE IN CHARCOAL, WHILE IN SECRET DREAMS THEY SMEAR THEIR FINGERS THROUGH FORBIDDEN VIOLETS, ORANGES AND BLUES.
"THEY MUST BE TAUGHT, THOUGH COLOURBLIND WITH GUILT, TO FATHOM THE IMPENDING BOREALIS; TAUGHT A NEW CHROMATIC SCALE OF PASSIONS AND DELIGHTS.
"HALF A MILLION CALLS EACH SECOND SING THROUGH HER COMPUTER SWITCHBOARD, FROM THE SHY, THE PLAIN, THE LONELY, SIFTED BY DISCREET AUTOMATA, PERSONAL DETAILS MATCHED, CONTACTS ARRANGED AND COMFORTS GIVEN, AN ELECTRIC SHOULDER OFFERED TO A HEARTSICK WORLD.
"IN THE SPERM BANKS, FROZEN SEED AWAITS BARREN RECIPIENTS SELECTED FROM ACROSS THE PLANET. TWO MORE GENERATIONS: THERE'LL BE THOUSANDS LIKE US.
. . .
"THOUSANDS.
"AS ZEUS LOVED MORTAL WOMEN IN THE FORM OF GOLDEN SPARKS, WE KNOW HUMANS IN A SHOWER OF PHOSPHOR-DOTS. AS OBJECTS OF MANKIND'S DESIRE, BOTH SPIRITUAL AND CARNAL, COUNTLESS SOLITARY CLIMAXES ARE REACHED EACH NIGHT, THEIR FEVERISH DEVOTIONS, EYES CLENCHED TIGHT, A CATECHISM OF GASPS.
A GUIDE TO HIGHER ECSTASIES
TANTRIC SEX
"AS ICONS THERE ARE SILKSCREENS, VIDEOS AND, BY SATELLITE, SHE OPERATES A WORLDWIDE CABLE SYSTEM, NETWORK-SCHEDULED VISITATIONS TO THE CHOSEN, TO THE FAITHFUL, TO THE HAR AND TO THE ACHING...
"...GODDESS OF PULP LUST, COLD CHRYSLER GLAMOUR, I ASCEND INTO HER SOUNDTRACK OF FORGOTTEN HIGH-SCHOOL POP AND DIGITALLY SAMPLED TORCH-SONGS. I RISE TO EYES LIKE GLACIERS, LIPS LIKE FATE.

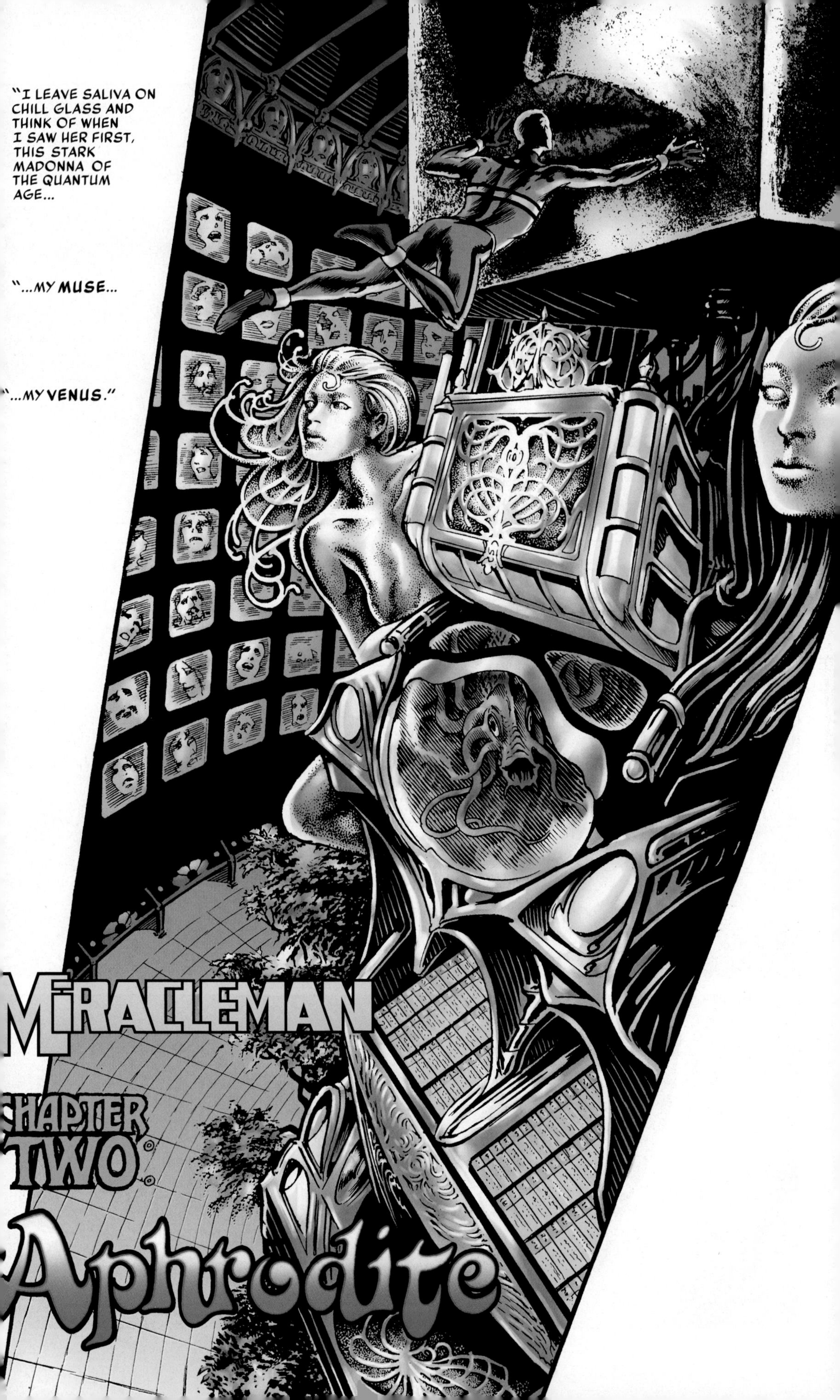
"I LEAVE SALIVA ON CHILL GLASS AND THINK OF WHEN I SAW HER FIRST, THIS STARK MADONNA OF THE QUANTUM AGE...
"...MY MUSE...
"...MY VENUS."
MIRACLEMAN
CHAPTER TWO
Aphrodite

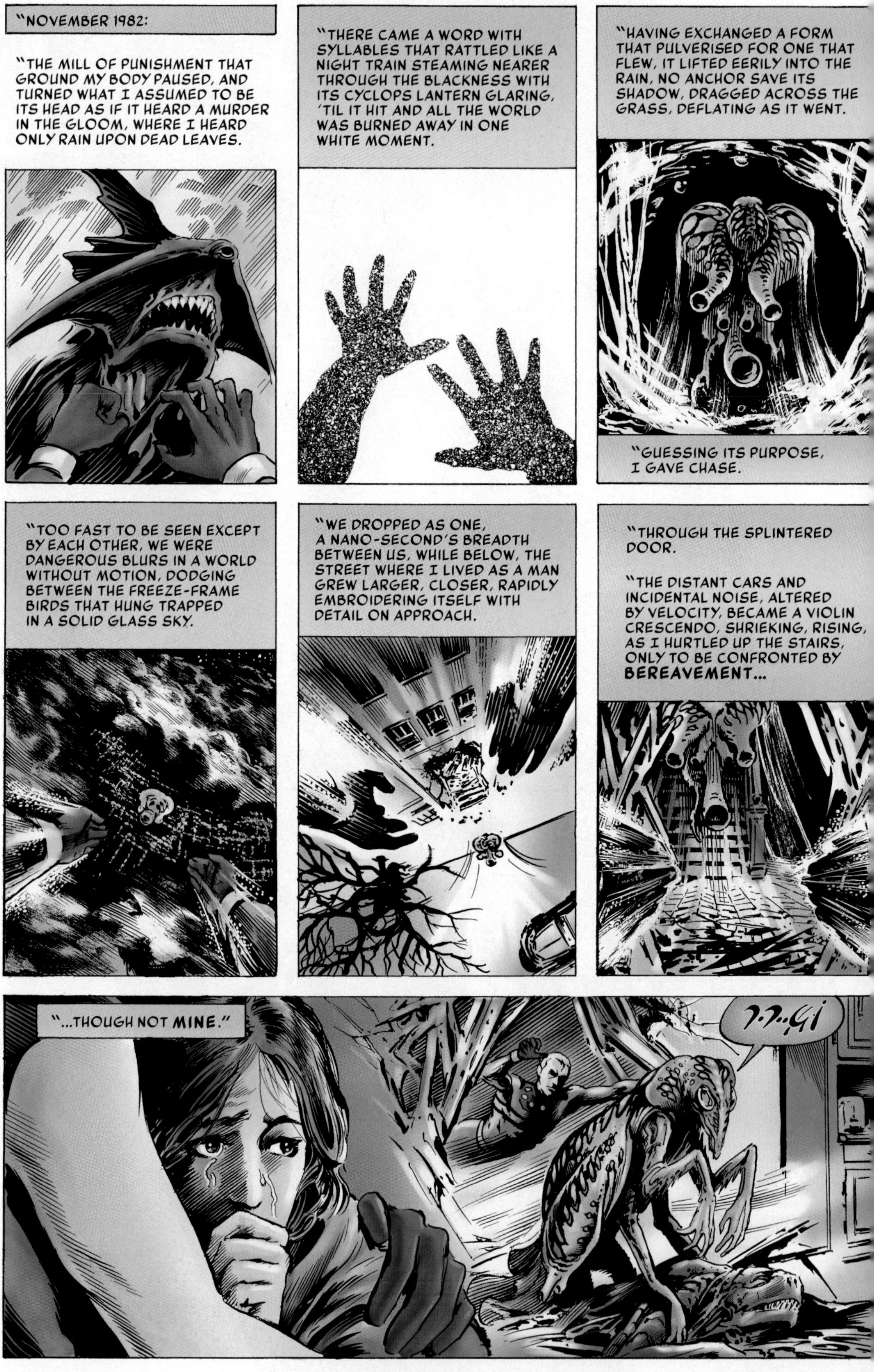
"NOVEMBER 1982:
"THE MILL OF PUNISHMENT THAT GROUND MY BODY PAUSED, AND TURNED WHAT I ASSUMED TO BE ITS HEAD AS IF IT HEARD A MURDER IN THE GLOOM, WHERE I HEARD ONLY RAIN UPON DEAD LEAVES.
"THERE CAME A WORD WITH SYLLABLES THAT RATTLED LIKE A NIGHT TRAIN STEAMING NEARER THROUGH THE BLACKNESS WITH ITS CYCLOPS LANTERN GLARING, 'TIL IT HIT AND ALL THE WORLD WAS BURNED AWAY IN ONE WHITE MOMENT.
"HAVING EXCHANGED A FORM THAT PULVERISED FOR ONE THAT FLEW, IT LIFTED EERILY INTO THE RAIN, NO ANCHOR SAVE ITS SHADOW, DRAGGED ACROSS THE GRASS, DEFLATING AS IT WENT.
"GUESSING ITS PURPOSE, I GAVE CHASE.
"TOO FAST TO BE SEEN EXCEPT BY EACH OTHER, WE WERE DANGEROUS BLURS IN A WORLD WITHOUT MOTION, DODGING BETWEEN THE FREEZE-FRAME BIRDS THAT HUNG TRAPPED IN A SOLID GLASS SKY.
"WE DROPPED AS ONE, A NANO-SECOND'S BREADTH BETWEEN US, WHILE BELOW, THE STREET WHERE I LIVED AS A MAN GREW LARGER, CLOSER, RAPIDLY EMBROIDERING ITSELF WITH DETAIL ON APPROACH.
"THROUGH THE SPLINTERED DOOR.
"THE DISTANT CARS AND INCIDENTAL NOISE, ALTERED BY VELOCITY, BECAME A VIOLIN CRESCENDO, SHRIEKING, RISING, AS I HURTLED UP THE STAIRS, ONLY TO BE CONFRONTED BY BEREAVEMENT...
"...THOUGH NOT MINE."

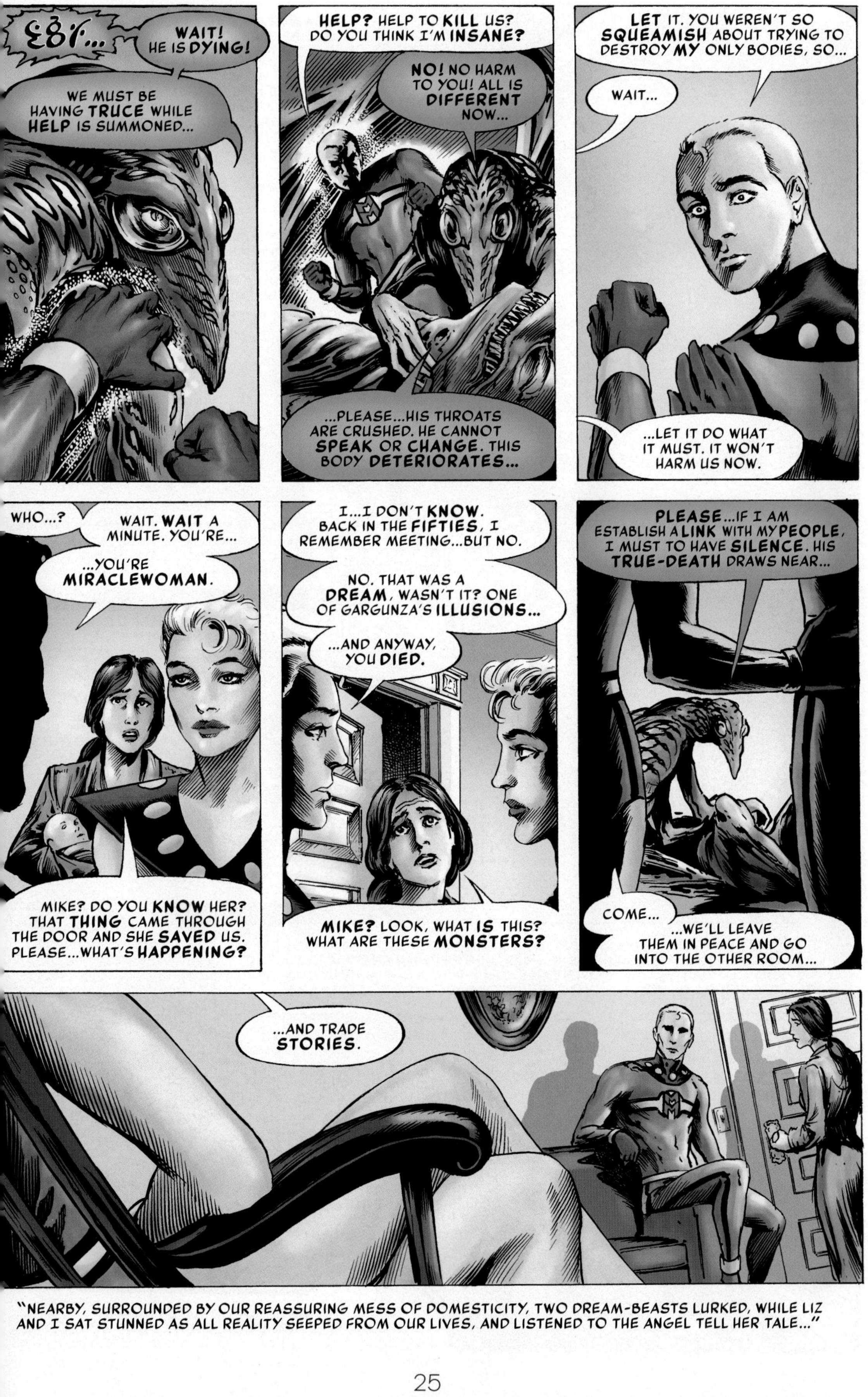
WAIT! HE IS DYING!
WE MUST BE HAVING TRUCE WHILE HELP IS SUMMONED...
HELP? HELP TO KILL US? DO YOU THINK I'M INSANE?
NO! NO HARM TO YOU! ALL IS DIFFERENT NOW...
...PLEASE...HIS THROATS ARE CRUSHED. HE CANNOT SPEAK OR CHANGE. THIS BODY DETERIORATES...
LET IT. YOU WEREN'T SO SQUEAMISH ABOUT TRYING TO DESTROY MY ONLY BODIES, SO...
WAIT...
...LET IT DO WHAT IT MUST. IT WON'T HARM US NOW.
WHO...?
WAIT. WAIT A MINUTE. YOU'RE...
...YOU'RE MIRACLEWOMAN.
MIKE? DO YOU KNOW HER? THAT THING CAME THROUGH THE DOOR AND SHE SAVED US. PLEASE...WHAT'S HAPPENING?
I...I DON'T KNOW. BACK IN THE FIFTIES, I REMEMBER MEETING...BUT NO.
NO. THAT WAS A DREAM, WASN'T IT? ONE OF GARGUNZA'S ILLUSIONS...
...AND ANYWAY, YOU DIED.
MIKE? LOOK, WHAT IS THIS? WHAT ARE THESE MONSTERS?
PLEASE...IF I AM ESTABLISH A LINK WITH MY PEOPLE, I MUST TO HAVE SILENCE. HIS TRUE-DEATH DRAWS NEAR...
COME...
...WE'LL LEAVE THEM IN PEACE AND GO INTO THE OTHER ROOM...
...AND TRADE STORIES.

"NEARBY, SURROUNDED BY OUR REASSURING MESS OF DOMESTICITY, TWO DREAM-BEASTS LURKED, WHILE LIZ AND I SAT STUNNED AS ALL REALITY SEEPED FROM OUR LIVES, AND LISTENED TO THE ANGEL TELL HER TALE..."

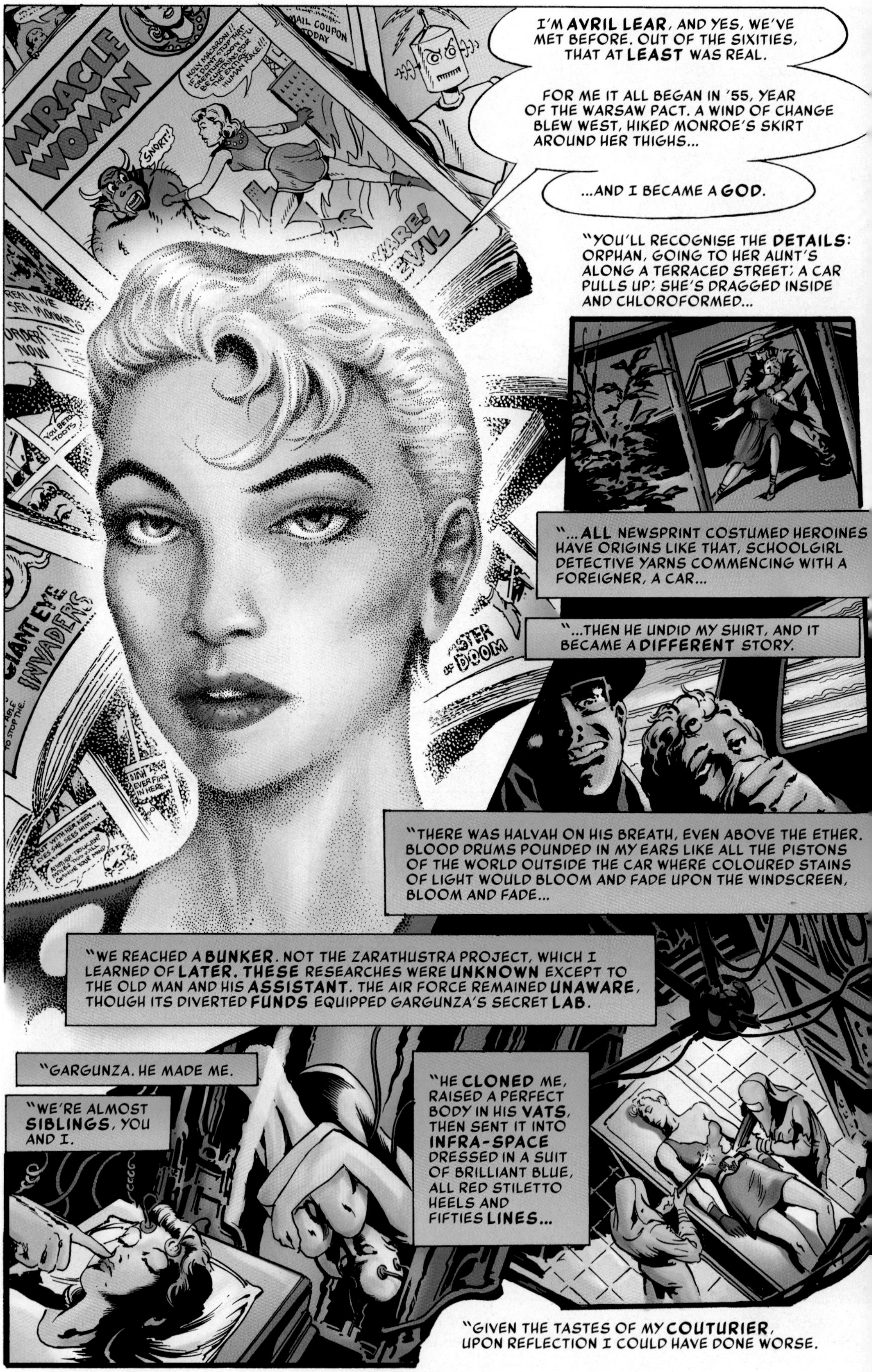
I'M AVRIL LEAR, AND YES, WE'VE MET BEFORE. OUT OF THE SIXTIES, THAT AT LEAST WAS REAL.
FOR ME IT ALL BEGAN IN '55, YEAR OF THE WARSAW PACT. A WIND OF CHANGE BLEW WEST, HIKED MONROE'S SKIRT AROUND HER THIGHS...
...AND I BECAME A GOD.
MIRACLE WOMAN
SNORT!
"YOU'LL RECOGNISE THE DETAILS: ORPHAN, GOING TO HER AUNT'S ALONG A TERRACED STREET; A CAR PULLS UP; SHE'S DRAGGED INSIDE AND CHLOROFORMED...
"...ALL NEWSPRINT COSTUMED HEROINES HAVE ORIGINS LIKE THAT, SCHOOLGIRL DETECTIVE YARNS COMMENCING WITH A FOREIGNER, A CAR...
"...THEN HE UNDID MY SHIRT, AND IT BECAME A DIFFERENT STORY.
GIANT EYE INVADERS
"THERE WAS HALVAH ON HIS BREATH, EVEN ABOVE THE ETHER. BLOOD DRUMS POUNDED IN MY EARS LIKE ALL THE PISTONS OF THE WORLD OUTSIDE THE CAR WHERE COLOURED STAINS OF LIGHT WOULD BLOOM AND FADE UPON THE WINDSCREEN, BLOOM AND FADE...
"WE REACHED A BUNKER. NOT THE ZARATHUSTRA PROJECT, WHICH I LEARNED OF LATER. THESE RESEARCHES WERE UNKNOWN EXCEPT TO THE OLD MAN AND HIS ASSISTANT. THE AIR FORCE REMAINED UNAWARE, THOUGH ITS DIVERTED FUNDS EQUIPPED GARGUNZA'S SECRET LAB.
"GARGUNZA. HE MADE ME.
"WE'RE ALMOST SIBLINGS, YOU AND I.
"HE CLONED ME, RAISED A PERFECT BODY IN HIS VATS, THEN SENT IT INTO INFRA-SPACE DRESSED IN A SUIT OF BRILLIANT BLUE, ALL RED STILETTO HEELS AND FIFTIES LINES...
"GIVEN THE TASTES OF MY COUTURIER, UPON REFLECTION I COULD HAVE DONE WORSE.

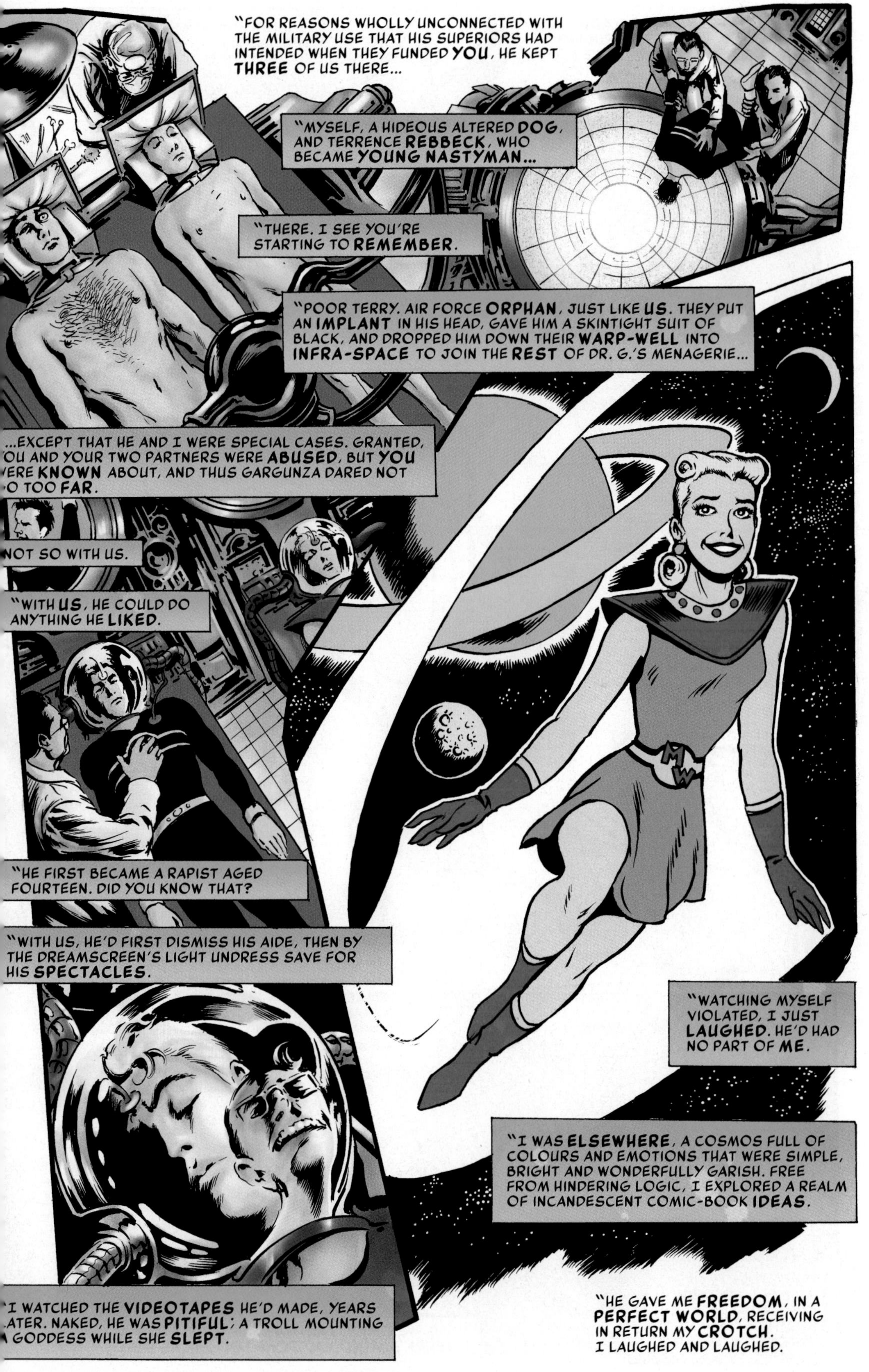
"FOR REASONS WHOLLY UNCONNECTED WITH THE MILITARY USE THAT HIS SUPERIORS HAD INTENDED WHEN THEY FUNDED YOU, HE KEPT THREE OF US THERE...
"MYSELF, A HIDEOUS ALTERED DOG, AND TERRENCE REBBECK, WHO BECAME YOUNG NASTYMAN...
"THERE. I SEE YOU'RE STARTING TO REMEMBER.
"POOR TERRY. AIR FORCE ORPHAN, JUST LIKE US. THEY PUT AN IMPLANT IN HIS HEAD, GAVE HIM A SKINTIGHT SUIT OF BLACK, AND DROPPED HIM DOWN THEIR WARP-WELL INTO INFRA-SPACE TO JOIN THE REST OF DR. G.'S MENAGERIE...
...EXCEPT THAT HE AND I WERE SPECIAL CASES. GRANTED, OU AND YOUR TWO PARTNERS WERE ABUSED, BUT YOU ERE KNOWN ABOUT, AND THUS GARGUNZA DARED NOT O TOO FAR.
NOT SO WITH US.
"WITH US, HE COULD DO ANYTHING HE LIKED.
"HE FIRST BECAME A RAPIST AGED FOURTEEN. DID YOU KNOW THAT?
"WITH US, HE'D FIRST DISMISS HIS AIDE, THEN BY THE DREAMSCREEN'S LIGHT UNDRESS SAVE FOR HIS SPECTACLES.
"WATCHING MYSELF VIOLATED, I JUST LAUGHED. HE'D HAD NO PART OF ME.
"I WAS ELSEWHERE, A COSMOS FULL OF COLOURS AND EMOTIONS THAT WERE SIMPLE, BRIGHT AND WONDERFULLY GARISH. FREE FROM HINDERING LOGIC, I EXPLORED A REALM OF INCANDESCENT COMIC-BOOK IDEAS.
I WATCHED THE VIDEOTAPES HE'D MADE, YEARS ATER. NAKED, HE WAS PITIFUL; A TROLL MOUNTING GODDESS WHILE SHE SLEPT.
"HE GAVE ME FREEDOM, IN A PERFECT WORLD, RECEIVING IN RETURN MY CROTCH. I LAUGHED AND LAUGHED.

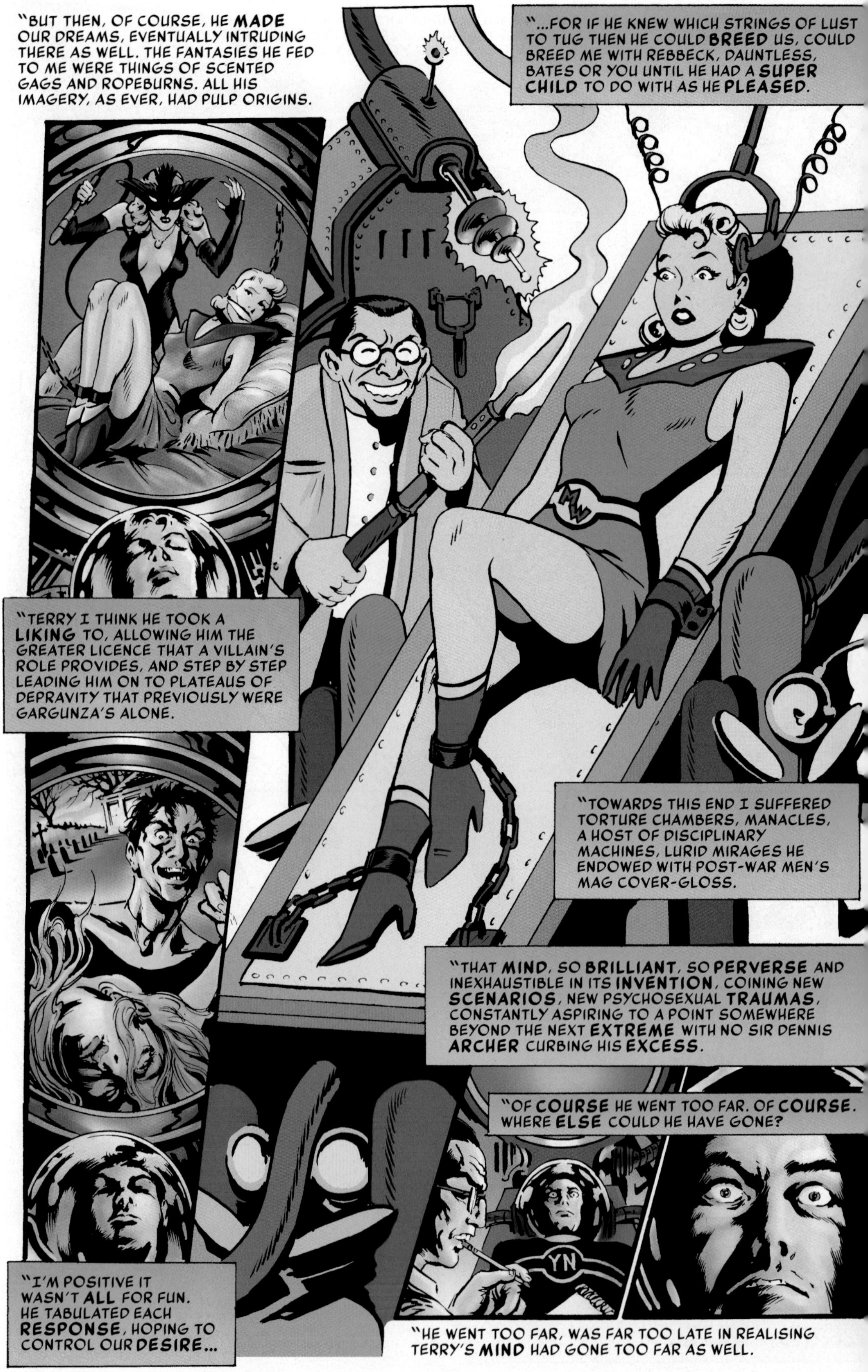
"BUT THEN, OF COURSE, HE MADE OUR DREAMS, EVENTUALLY INTRUDING THERE AS WELL. THE FANTASIES HE FED TO ME WERE THINGS OF SCENTED GAGS AND ROPEBURNS. ALL HIS IMAGERY, AS EVER, HAD PULP ORIGINS.
"...FOR IF HE KNEW WHICH STRINGS OF LUST TO TUG THEN HE COULD BREED US, COULD BREED ME WITH REBBECK, DAUNTLESS, BATES OR YOU UNTIL HE HAD A SUPER CHILD TO DO WITH AS HE PLEASED.
"TERRY I THINK HE TOOK A LIKING TO, ALLOWING HIM THE GREATER LICENCE THAT A VILLAIN'S ROLE PROVIDES, AND STEP BY STEP LEADING HIM ON TO PLATEAUS OF DEPRAVITY THAT PREVIOUSLY WERE GARGUNZA'S ALONE.
"TOWARDS THIS END I SUFFERED TORTURE CHAMBERS, MANACLES, A HOST OF DISCIPLINARY MACHINES, LURID MIRAGES HE ENDOWED WITH POST-WAR MEN'S MAG COVER-GLOSS.
"THAT MIND, SO BRILLIANT, SO PERVERSE AND INEXHAUSTIBLE IN ITS INVENTION, COINING NEW SCENARIOS, NEW PSYCHOSEXUAL TRAUMAS, CONSTANTLY ASPIRING TO A POINT SOMEWHERE BEYOND THE NEXT EXTREME WITH NO SIR DENNIS ARCHER CURBING HIS EXCESS.
"I'M POSITIVE IT WASN'T ALL FOR FUN. HE TABULATED EACH RESPONSE, HOPING TO CONTROL OUR DESIRE...
"OF COURSE HE WENT TOO FAR. OF COURSE. WHERE ELSE COULD HE HAVE GONE?
"HE WENT TOO FAR, WAS FAR TOO LATE IN REALISING TERRY'S MIND HAD GONE TOO FAR AS WELL.

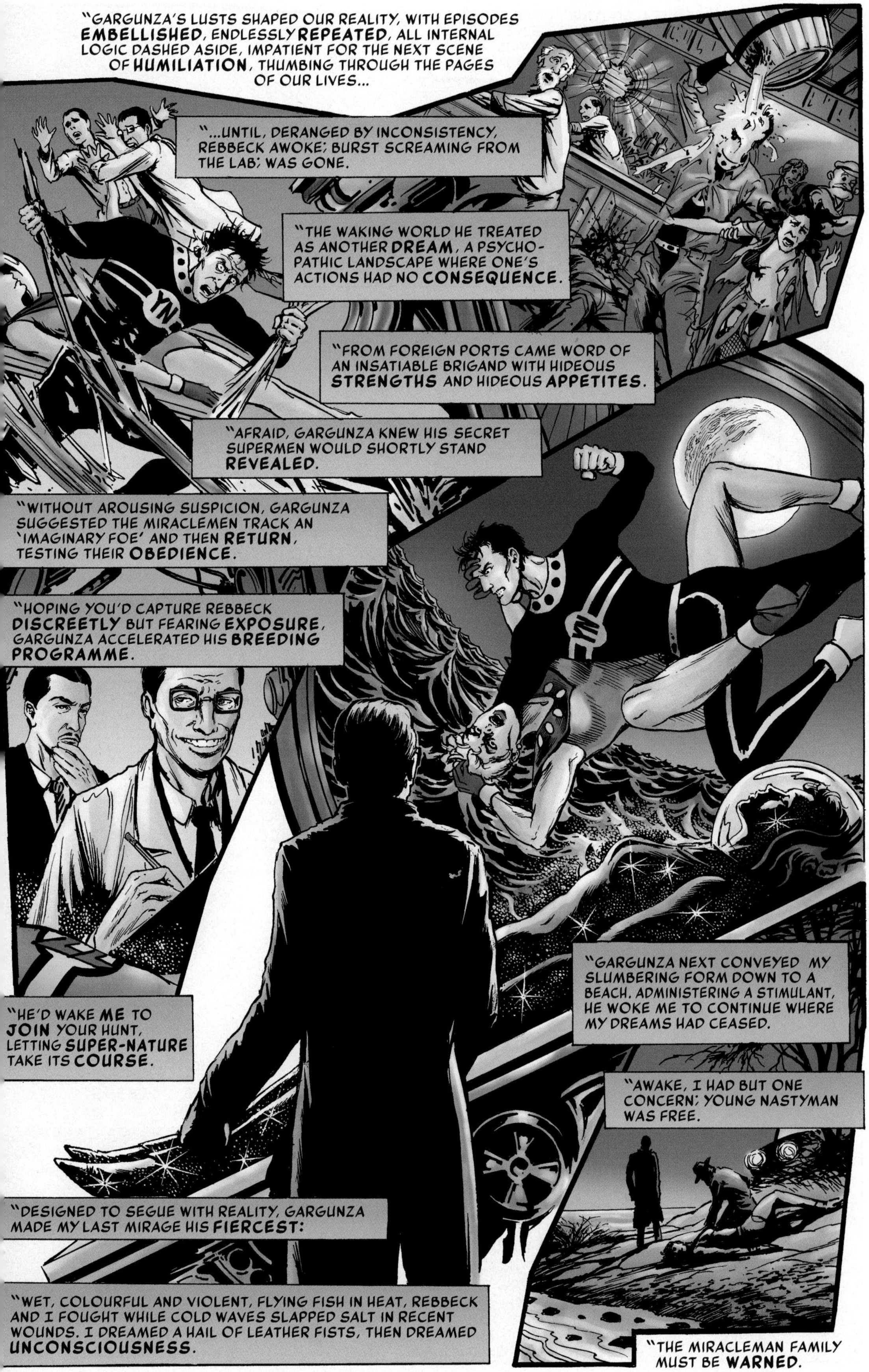
"GARGUNZA'S LUSTS SHAPED OUR REALITY, WITH EPISODES EMBELLISHED, ENDLESSLY REPEATED, ALL INTERNAL LOGIC DASHED ASIDE, IMPATIENT FOR THE NEXT SCENE OF HUMILIATION, THUMBING THROUGH THE PAGES OF OUR LIVES...
"...UNTIL, DERANGED BY INCONSISTENCY, REBBECK AWOKE; BURST SCREAMING FROM THE LAB; WAS GONE.
"THE WAKING WORLD HE TREATED AS ANOTHER DREAM, A PSYCHO-PATHIC LANDSCAPE WHERE ONE'S ACTIONS HAD NO CONSEQUENCE.
"FROM FOREIGN PORTS CAME WORD OF AN INSATIABLE BRIGAND WITH HIDEOUS STRENGTHS AND HIDEOUS APPETITES.
"AFRAID, GARGUNZA KNEW HIS SECRET SUPERMEN WOULD SHORTLY STAND REVEALED.
"WITHOUT AROUSING SUSPICION, GARGUNZA SUGGESTED THE MIRACLEMEN TRACK AN 'IMAGINARY FOE' AND THEN RETURN, TESTING THEIR OBEDIENCE.
"HOPING YOU'D CAPTURE REBBECK DISCREETLY BUT FEARING EXPOSURE, GARGUNZA ACCELERATED HIS BREEDING PROGRAMME.
"HE'D WAKE ME TO JOIN YOUR HUNT, LETTING SUPER-NATURE TAKE ITS COURSE.
"GARGUNZA NEXT CONVEYED MY SLUMBERING FORM DOWN TO A BEACH. ADMINISTERING A STIMULANT, HE WOKE ME TO CONTINUE WHERE MY DREAMS HAD CEASED.
"AWAKE, I HAD BUT ONE CONCERN; YOUNG NASTYMAN WAS FREE.
"DESIGNED TO SEGUE WITH REALITY, GARGUNZA MADE MY LAST MIRAGE HIS FIERCEST:
"WET, COLOURFUL AND VIOLENT, FLYING FISH IN HEAT, REBBECK AND I FOUGHT WHILE COLD WAVES SLAPPED SALT IN RECENT WOUNDS. I DREAMED A HAIL OF LEATHER FISTS, THEN DREAMED UNCONSCIOUSNESS.
"THE MIRACLEMAN FAMILY MUST BE WARNED.

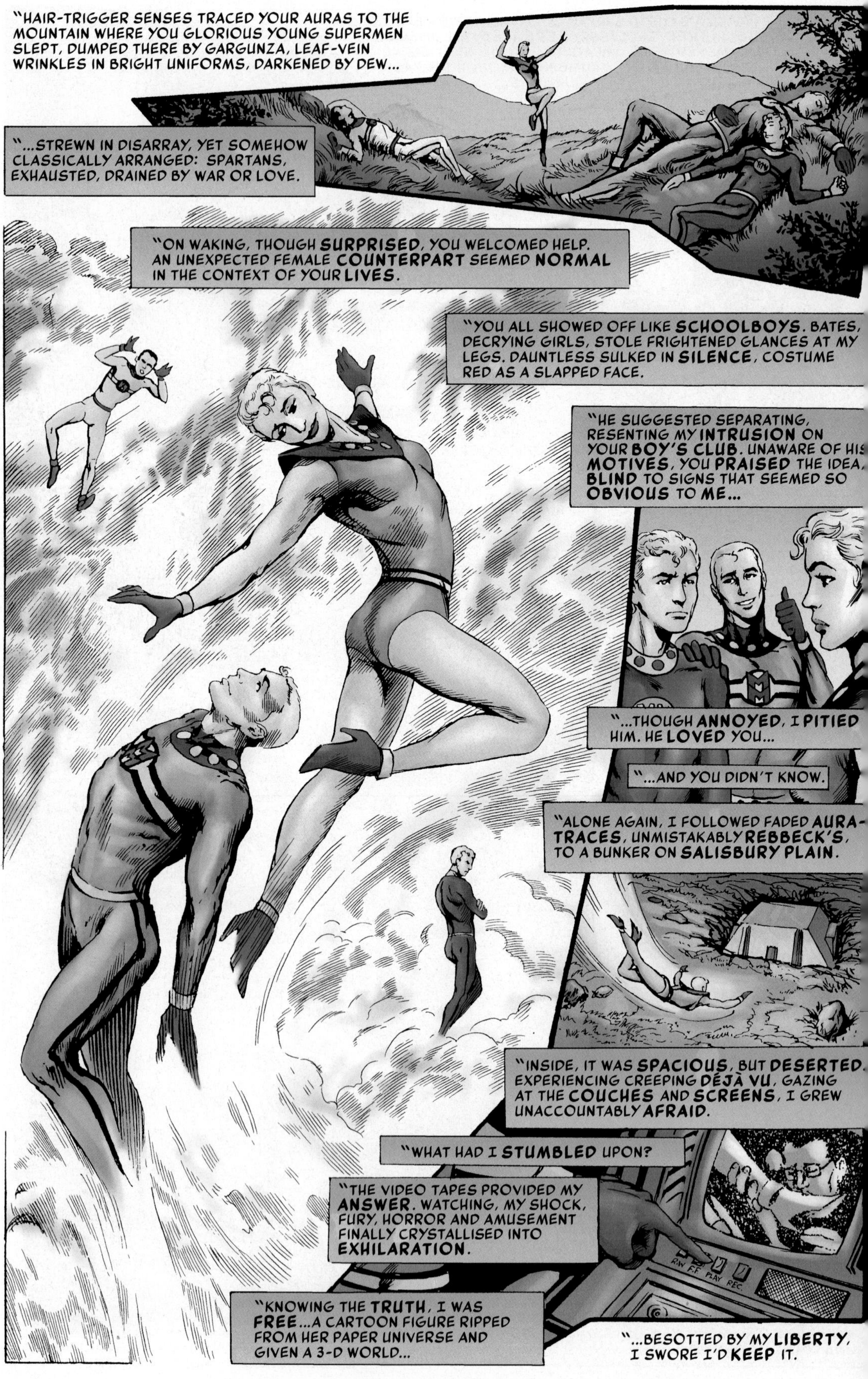

"HAIR-TRIGGER SENSES TRACED YOUR AURAS TO THE MOUNTAIN WHERE YOU GLORIOUS YOUNG SUPERMEN SLEPT, DUMPED THERE BY GARGUNZA, LEAF-VEIN WRINKLES IN BRIGHT UNIFORMS, DARKENED BY DEW...
"...STREWN IN DISARRAY, YET SOMEHOW CLASSICALLY ARRANGED: SPARTANS, EXHAUSTED, DRAINED BY WAR OR LOVE.
"ON WAKING, THOUGH SURPRISED, YOU WELCOMED HELP. AN UNEXPECTED FEMALE COUNTERPART SEEMED NORMAL IN THE CONTEXT OF YOUR LIVES.
"YOU ALL SHOWED OFF LIKE SCHOOLBOYS. BATES, DECRYING GIRLS, STOLE FRIGHTENED GLANCES AT MY LEGS. DAUNTLESS SULKED IN SILENCE, COSTUME RED AS A SLAPPED FACE.
"HE SUGGESTED SEPARATING, RESENTING MY INTRUSION ON YOUR BOY'S CLUB. UNAWARE OF HIS MOTIVES, YOU PRAISED THE IDEA, BLIND TO SIGNS THAT SEEMED SO OBVIOUS TO ME...
"...THOUGH ANNOYED, I PITIED HIM. HE LOVED YOU...
"...AND YOU DIDN'T KNOW.
"ALONE AGAIN, I FOLLOWED FADED AURA-TRACES, UNMISTAKABLY REBBECK'S, TO A BUNKER ON SALISBURY PLAIN.
"INSIDE, IT WAS SPACIOUS, BUT DESERTED. EXPERIENCING CREEPING DÉJÀ VU, GAZING AT THE COUCHES AND SCREENS, I GREW UNACCOUNTABLY AFRAID.
"WHAT HAD I STUMBLED UPON?
"THE VIDEO TAPES PROVIDED MY ANSWER. WATCHING, MY SHOCK, FURY, HORROR AND AMUSEMENT FINALLY CRYSTALLISED INTO EXHILARATION.
R.W. F.F. PLAY REC.
"KNOWING THE TRUTH, I WAS FREE...A CARTOON FIGURE RIPPED FROM HER PAPER UNIVERSE AND GIVEN A 3-D WORLD...
"...BESOTTED BY MY LIBERTY, I SWORE I'D KEEP IT.

"SCANNING ACCELERATED VIDEOS, SKIMMING FILES, I SHOWERED IN PICTURES, WORDS, NEW NUMBERS, 'TIL MY SENSITISED MIND STUNG, UNBEARABLY, EXQUISITELY...

"...GARGUNZA AND CRASHED ALIENS ASIDE, I LEARNED ABOUT MY VALUE, TOO GREAT FOR GARGUNZA TO RELINQUISH WHILE I LIVED...

"...THUS I MUST DIE."

"RESUMED, MY SEARCH LED TO A BLEAK, ICELANDIC BROTHEL, UNSTAFFED SAVE FOR REBBECK'S WOMAN, THREE DAYS DEAD. I DOUBT HE KNEW OR CARED.

"I EXPLAINED EVERYTHING, SUGGESTED FAKING DEATH, TRICKING GARGUNZA, BUT, DERANGED BY THE COLLISION OF GRIM PRESENT AND FICTITIOUS PAST, REBBECK ATTACKED.

"HE WAS SO DISSIPATED BY HIS CRUMBLING REASON AND DECAYING WILL, NOTHING IN HIS TORMENTED EYES EXCEPT A PLEA FOR DEATH.

"ABOVE VOLCANOES GARGLING MOLTEN ROCK, WE FOUGHT. I CAN'T RECALL WHO FIRST PROPELLED OUR FIGHT TOWARDS THEIR SMOULDERING SPARK-INFESTED MOUTHS.

"IN COOLING-TOWER ACOUSTICS, CURSES RANG LIKE ANVILS. LUKE-WARM, LAVA SPLASHED AGAINST MY FLANKS. I SWILLED SOME 'ROUND MY MOUTH, SPAT FIRE.

"POOR TERRY, POWERS FADING, FIRST PERSPIRED, THEN BLISTERED, EYEBROWS SINGEING. TEARS STEAMED BRIEFLY ON MY CHEEKS.

"HE FLICKERED, LIKE A FAULTY T.V. THEN, A FLASH, A TEARING SOUND...

"...AS THE VOLCANO BURST, I HALF-GLIMPSED SOMETHING WITH TOO MANY FACES, BORN UPON THE FIREFLOOD'S SIZZLING BREAST.

"LATER, RETRIEVING THOSE REMAINS, THE SPOOKSHOW MISTOOK THEM FOR YOUNG MIRACLEMAN'S.

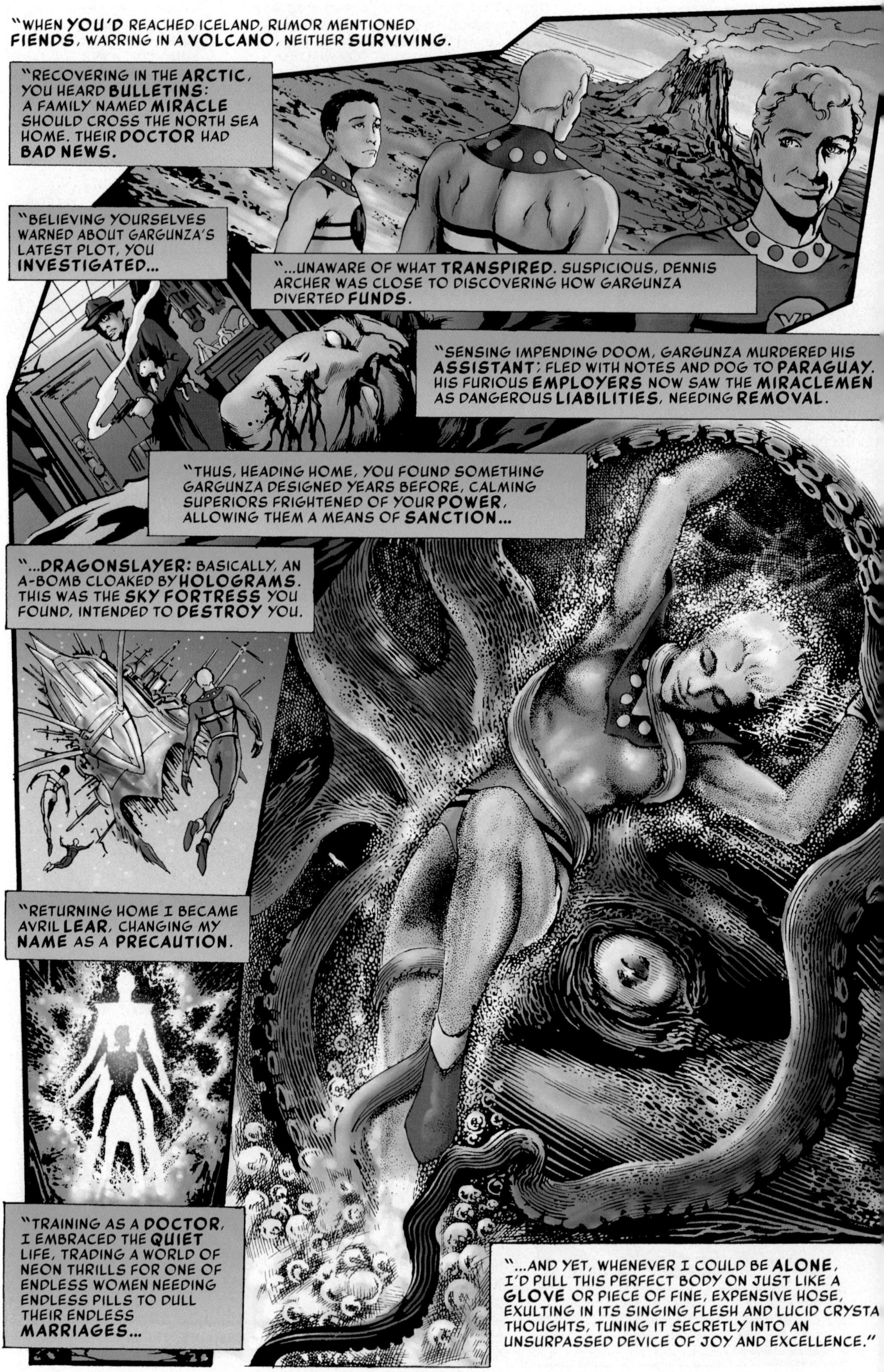

"WHEN YOU'D REACHED ICELAND, RUMOR MENTIONED FIENDS, WARRING IN A VOLCANO, NEITHER SURVIVING.
"RECOVERING IN THE ARCTIC, YOU HEARD BULLETINS: A FAMILY NAMED MIRACLE SHOULD CROSS THE NORTH SEA HOME. THEIR DOCTOR HAD BAD NEWS.
"BELIEVING YOURSELVES WARNED ABOUT GARGUNZA'S LATEST PLOT, YOU INVESTIGATED...
"...UNAWARE OF WHAT TRANSPIRED. SUSPICIOUS, DENNIS ARCHER WAS CLOSE TO DISCOVERING HOW GARGUNZA DIVERTED FUNDS.
"SENSING IMPENDING DOOM, GARGUNZA MURDERED HIS ASSISTANT; FLED WITH NOTES AND DOG TO PARAGUAY. HIS FURIOUS EMPLOYERS NOW SAW THE MIRACLEMEN AS DANGEROUS LIABILITIES, NEEDING REMOVAL.
"THUS, HEADING HOME, YOU FOUND SOMETHING GARGUNZA DESIGNED YEARS BEFORE, CALMING SUPERIORS FRIGHTENED OF YOUR POWER, ALLOWING THEM A MEANS OF SANCTION...
"...DRAGONSLAYER: BASICALLY, AN A-BOMB CLOAKED BY HOLOGRAMS. THIS WAS THE SKY FORTRESS YOU FOUND, INTENDED TO DESTROY YOU.
"RETURNING HOME I BECAME AVRIL LEAR, CHANGING MY NAME AS A PRECAUTION.
"TRAINING AS A DOCTOR, I EMBRACED THE QUIET LIFE, TRADING A WORLD OF NEON THRILLS FOR ONE OF ENDLESS WOMEN NEEDING ENDLESS PILLS TO DULL THEIR ENDLESS MARRIAGES...
"...AND YET, WHENEVER I COULD BE ALONE, I'D PULL THIS PERFECT BODY ON JUST LIKE A GLOVE OR PIECE OF FINE, EXPENSIVE HOSE, EXULTING IN ITS SINGING FLESH AND LUCID CRYSTA THOUGHTS, TUNING IT SECRETLY INTO AN UNSURPASSED DEVICE OF JOY AND EXCELLENCE."

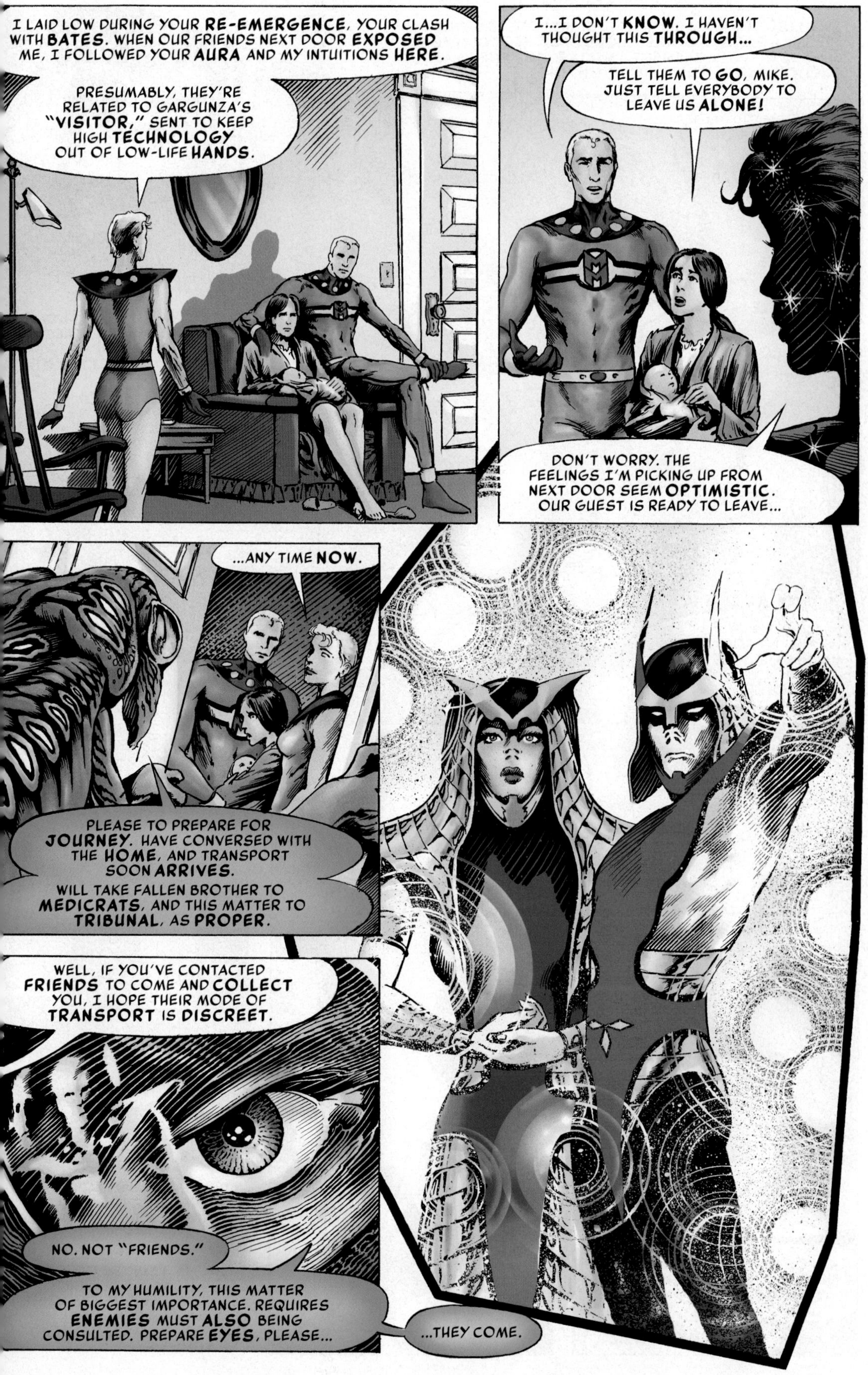

I LAID LOW DURING YOUR RE-EMERGENCE, YOUR CLASH WITH BATES. WHEN OUR FRIENDS NEXT DOOR EXPOSED ME, I FOLLOWED YOUR AURA AND MY INTUITIONS HERE.
PRESUMABLY, THEY'RE RELATED TO GARGUNZA'S "VISITOR," SENT TO KEEP HIGH TECHNOLOGY OUT OF LOW-LIFE HANDS.
I...I DON'T KNOW. I HAVEN'T THOUGHT THIS THROUGH...
TELL THEM TO GO, MIKE. JUST TELL EVERYBODY TO LEAVE US ALONE!
DON'T WORRY. THE FEELINGS I'M PICKING UP FROM NEXT DOOR SEEM OPTIMISTIC. OUR GUEST IS READY TO LEAVE...
...ANY TIME NOW.
PLEASE TO PREPARE FOR JOURNEY. HAVE CONVERSED WITH THE HOME, AND TRANSPORT SOON ARRIVES.
WILL TAKE FALLEN BROTHER TO MEDICRATS, AND THIS MATTER TO TRIBUNAL, AS PROPER.
WELL, IF YOU'VE CONTACTED FRIENDS TO COME AND COLLECT YOU, I HOPE THEIR MODE OF TRANSPORT IS DISCREET.
NO. NOT "FRIENDS."
TO MY HUMILITY, THIS MATTER OF BIGGEST IMPORTANCE. REQUIRES ENEMIES MUST ALSO BEING CONSULTED. PREPARE EYES, PLEASE...
...THEY COME.

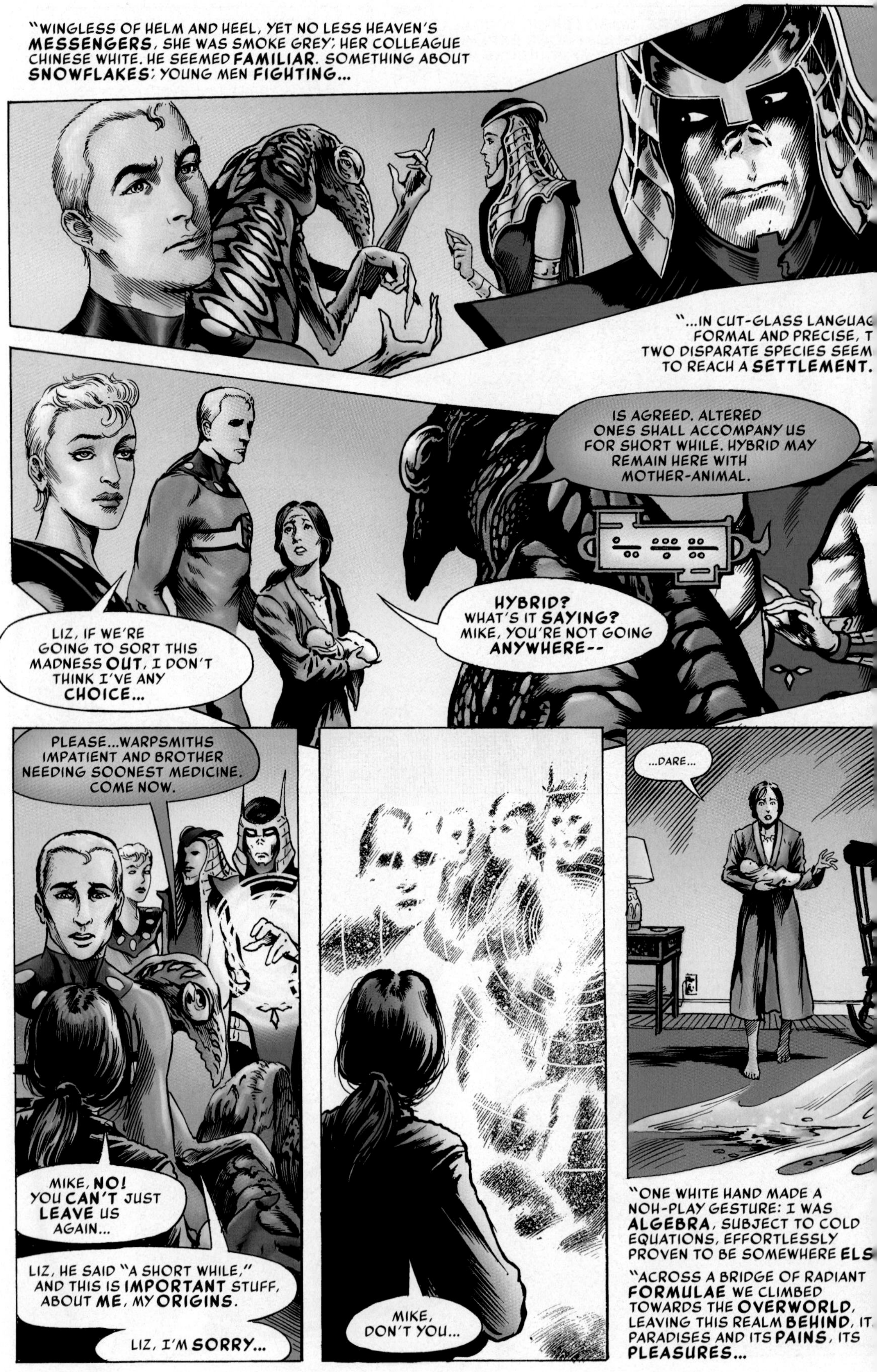

"WINGLESS OF HELM AND HEEL, YET NO LESS HEAVEN'S MESSENGERS, SHE WAS SMOKE GREY; HER COLLEAGUE CHINESE WHITE. HE SEEMED FAMILIAR. SOMETHING ABOUT SNOWFLAKES; YOUNG MEN FIGHTING...
"...IN CUT-GLASS LANGUAG FORMAL AND PRECISE, T TWO DISPARATE SPECIES SEEM TO REACH A SETTLEMENT.
IS AGREED. ALTERED ONES SHALL ACCOMPANY US FOR SHORT WHILE. HYBRID MAY REMAIN HERE WITH MOTHER-ANIMAL.
HYBRID? WHAT'S IT SAYING? MIKE, YOU'RE NOT GOING ANYWHERE--
LIZ, IF WE'RE GOING TO SORT THIS MADNESS OUT, I DON'T THINK I'VE ANY CHOICE...
PLEASE...WARPSMITHS IMPATIENT AND BROTHER NEEDING SOONEST MEDICINE. COME NOW.
MIKE, NO! YOU CAN'T JUST LEAVE US AGAIN...
LIZ, HE SAID "A SHORT WHILE," AND THIS IS IMPORTANT STUFF, ABOUT ME, MY ORIGINS.
LIZ, I'M SORRY...
MIKE, DON'T YOU...
...DARE...
"ONE WHITE HAND MADE A NOH-PLAY GESTURE: I WAS ALGEBRA, SUBJECT TO COLD EQUATIONS, EFFORTLESSLY PROVEN TO BE SOMEWHERE ELS
"ACROSS A BRIDGE OF RADIANT FORMULAE WE CLIMBED TOWARDS THE OVERWORLD, LEAVING THIS REALM BEHIND, IT PARADISES AND ITS PAINS, ITS PLEASURES...

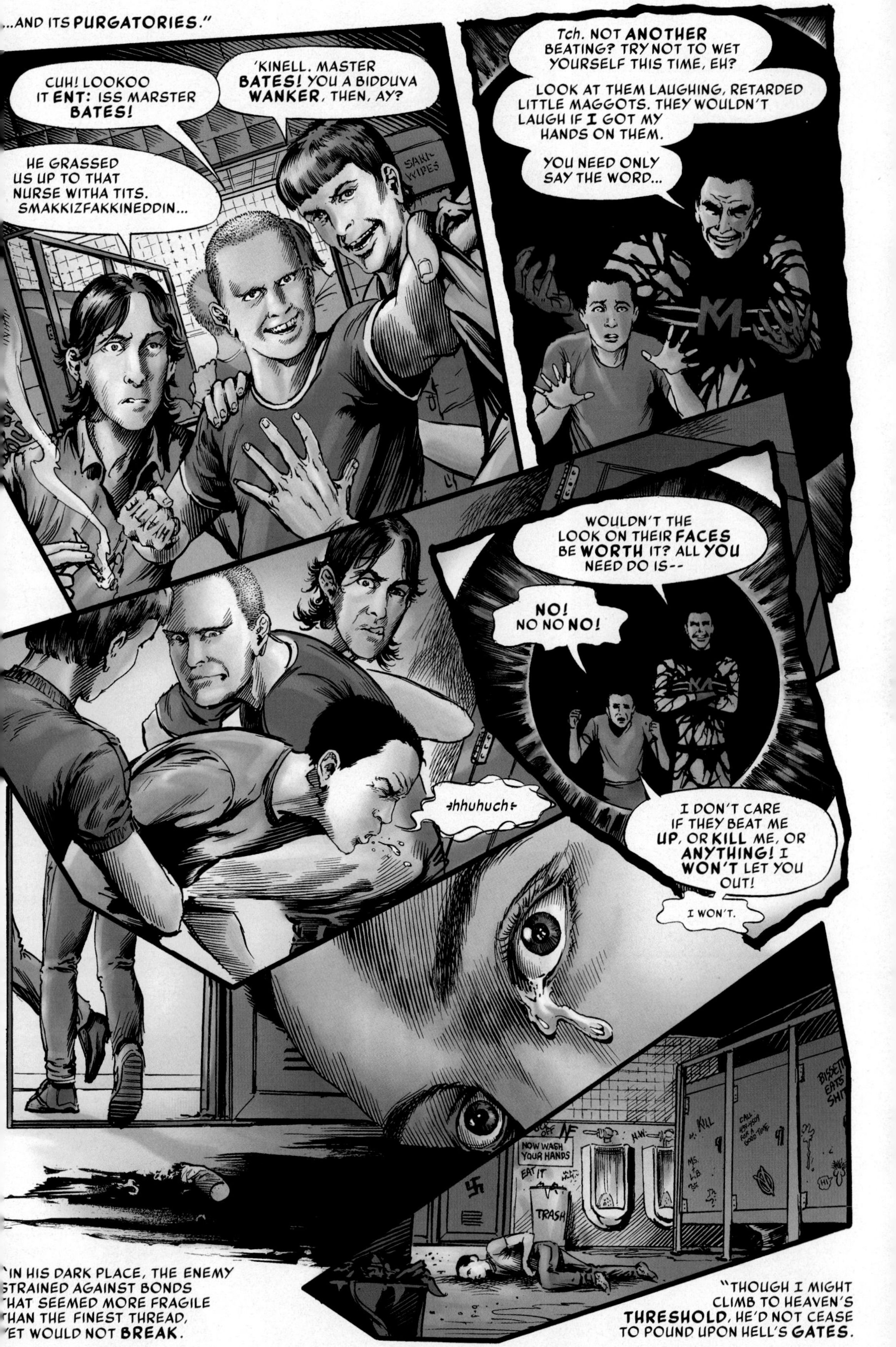
...AND ITS PURGATORIES."
CUH! LOOKOO IT ENT: ISS MARSTER BATES!
'KINELL. MASTER BATES! YOU A BIDDUVA WANKER, THEN, AY?
HE GRASSED US UP TO THAT NURSE WITHA TITS. SMAKKIZFAKKINEDDIN...
SANI-WIPES
Tch. NOT ANOTHER BEATING? TRY NOT TO WET YOURSELF THIS TIME, EH?
LOOK AT THEM LAUGHING, RETARDED LITTLE MAGGOTS. THEY WOULDN'T LAUGH IF I GOT MY HANDS ON THEM.
YOU NEED ONLY SAY THE WORD...
WOULDN'T THE LOOK ON THEIR FACES BE WORTH IT? ALL YOU NEED DO IS--
NO! NO NO NO!
ahhuhuch
I DON'T CARE IF THEY BEAT ME UP, OR KILL ME, OR ANYTHING! I WON'T LET YOU OUT!
I WON'T.
NOW WASH YOUR HANDS
EAT IT
TRASH
KILL
BISSETT EATS SHIT
"IN HIS DARK PLACE, THE ENEMY STRAINED AGAINST BONDS THAT SEEMED MORE FRAGILE THAN THE FINEST THREAD, YET WOULD NOT BREAK.
"THOUGH I MIGHT CLIMB TO HEAVEN'S THRESHOLD, HE'D NOT CEASE TO POUND UPON HELL'S GATES.

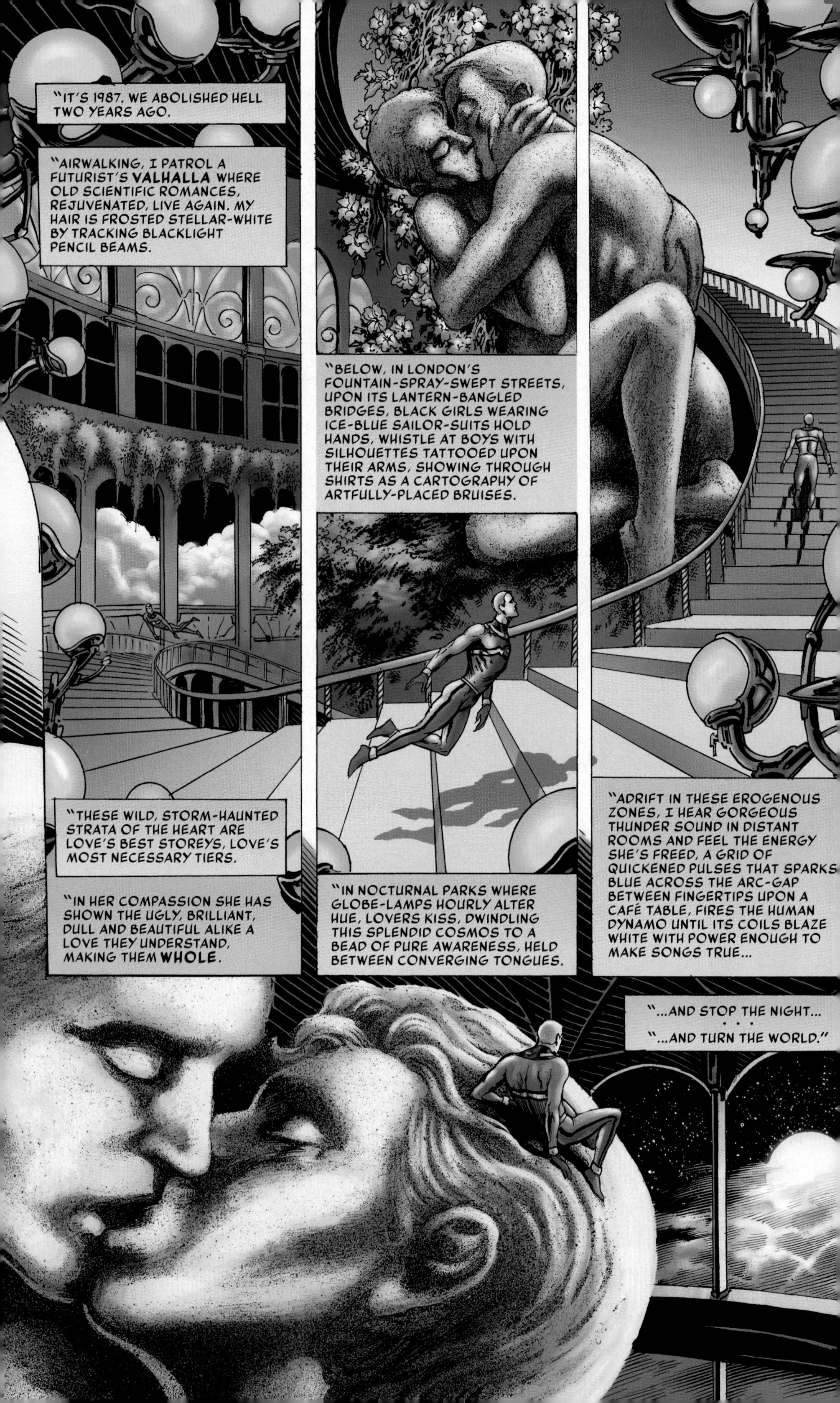
"IT'S 1987. WE ABOLISHED HELL TWO YEARS AGO.
"AIRWALKING, I PATROL A FUTURIST'S **VALHALLA** WHERE OLD SCIENTIFIC ROMANCES, REJUVENATED, LIVE AGAIN. MY HAIR IS FROSTED STELLAR-WHITE BY TRACKING BLACKLIGHT PENCIL BEAMS.
"BELOW, IN LONDON'S FOUNTAIN-SPRAY-SWEPT STREETS, UPON ITS LANTERN-BANGLED BRIDGES, BLACK GIRLS WEARING ICE-BLUE SAILOR-SUITS HOLD HANDS, WHISTLE AT BOYS WITH SILHOUETTES TATTOOED UPON THEIR ARMS, SHOWING THROUGH SHIRTS AS A CARTOGRAPHY OF ARTFULLY-PLACED BRUISES.
"THESE WILD, STORM-HAUNTED STRATA OF THE HEART ARE LOVE'S BEST STOREYS, LOVE'S MOST NECESSARY TIERS.
"IN HER COMPASSION SHE HAS SHOWN THE UGLY, BRILLIANT, DULL AND BEAUTIFUL ALIKE A LOVE THEY UNDERSTAND, MAKING THEM **WHOLE**.
"IN NOCTURNAL PARKS WHERE GLOBE-LAMPS HOURLY ALTER HUE, LOVERS KISS, DWINDLING THIS SPLENDID COSMOS TO A BEAD OF PURE AWARENESS, HELD BETWEEN CONVERGING TONGUES.
"ADRIFT IN THESE EROGENOUS ZONES, I HEAR GORGEOUS THUNDER SOUND IN DISTANT ROOMS AND FEEL THE ENERGY SHE'S FREED, A GRID OF QUICKENED PULSES THAT SPARKS BLUE ACROSS THE ARC-GAP BETWEEN FINGERTIPS UPON A CAFÉ TABLE, FIRES THE HUMAN DYNAMO UNTIL ITS COILS BLAZE WHITE WITH POWER ENOUGH TO MAKE SONGS TRUE...
"...AND STOP THE NIGHT...
"...AND TURN THE WORLD."

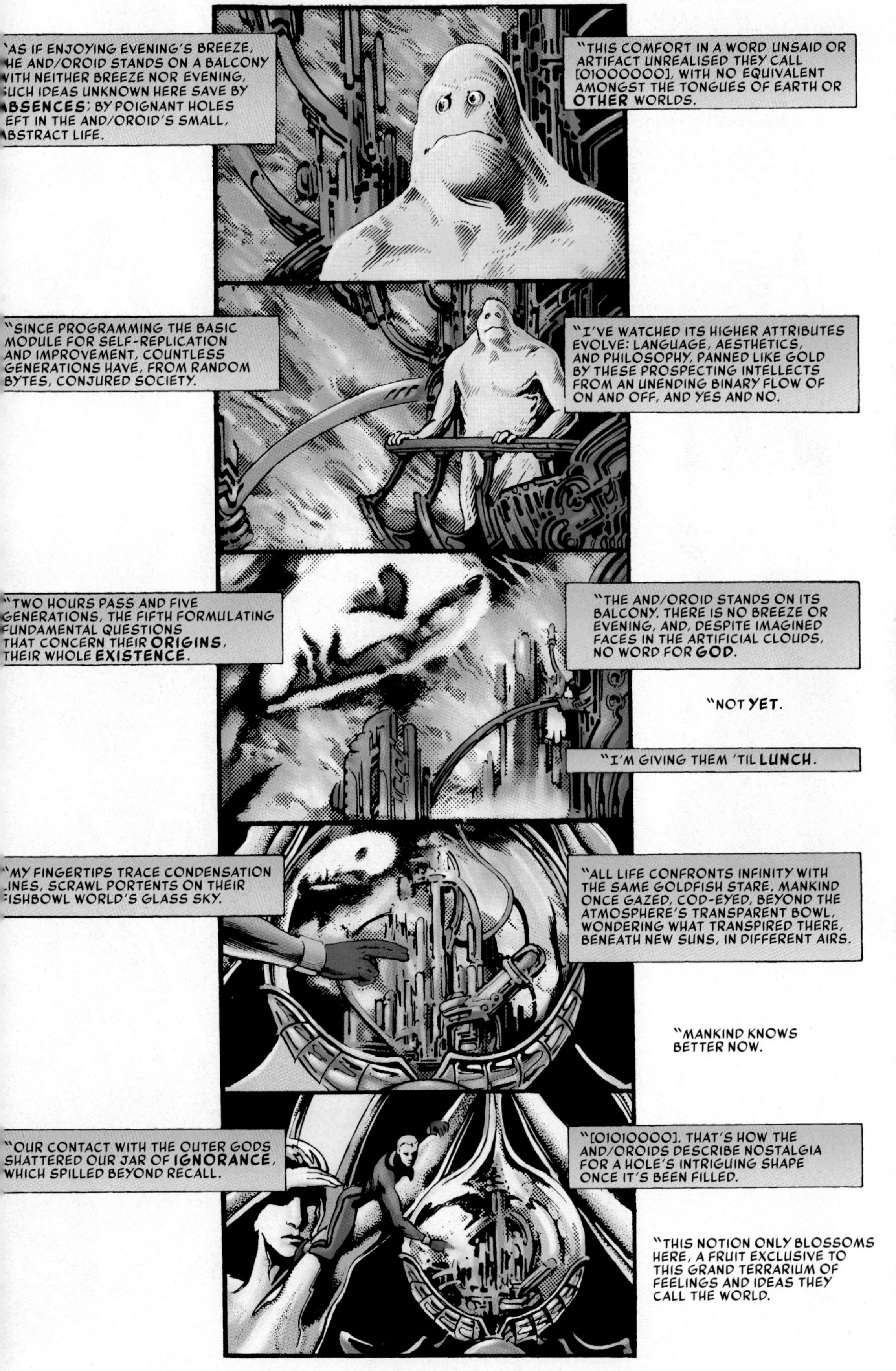
"AS IF ENJOYING EVENING'S BREEZE, THE AND/OROID STANDS ON A BALCONY WITH NEITHER BREEZE NOR EVENING, SUCH IDEAS UNKNOWN HERE SAVE BY ABSENCES; BY POIGNANT HOLES LEFT IN THE AND/OROID'S SMALL, ABSTRACT LIFE.
"THIS COMFORT IN A WORD UNSAID OR ARTIFACT UNREALISED THEY CALL [01000000], WITH NO EQUIVALENT AMONGST THE TONGUES OF EARTH OR OTHER WORLDS.
"SINCE PROGRAMMING THE BASIC MODULE FOR SELF-REPLICATION AND IMPROVEMENT, COUNTLESS GENERATIONS HAVE, FROM RANDOM BYTES, CONJURED SOCIETY.
"I'VE WATCHED ITS HIGHER ATTRIBUTES EVOLVE: LANGUAGE, AESTHETICS, AND PHILOSOPHY, PANNED LIKE GOLD BY THESE PROSPECTING INTELLECTS FROM AN UNENDING BINARY FLOW OF ON AND OFF, AND YES AND NO.
"TWO HOURS PASS AND FIVE GENERATIONS, THE FIFTH FORMULATING FUNDAMENTAL QUESTIONS THAT CONCERN THEIR ORIGINS, THEIR WHOLE EXISTENCE.
"THE AND/OROID STANDS ON ITS BALCONY. THERE IS NO BREEZE OR EVENING, AND, DESPITE IMAGINED FACES IN THE ARTIFICIAL CLOUDS, NO WORD FOR GOD.
"NOT YET.
"I'M GIVING THEM 'TIL LUNCH.
"MY FINGERTIPS TRACE CONDENSATION LINES, SCRAWL PORTENTS ON THEIR FISHBOWL WORLD'S GLASS SKY.
"ALL LIFE CONFRONTS INFINITY WITH THE SAME GOLDFISH STARE. MANKIND ONCE GAZED, COD-EYED, BEYOND THE ATMOSPHERE'S TRANSPARENT BOWL, WONDERING WHAT TRANSPIRED THERE, BENEATH NEW SUNS, IN DIFFERENT AIRS.
"MANKIND KNOWS BETTER NOW.
"OUR CONTACT WITH THE OUTER GODS SHATTERED OUR JAR OF IGNORANCE, WHICH SPILLED BEYOND RECALL.
"[01010000]. THAT'S HOW THE AND/OROIDS DESCRIBE NOSTALGIA FOR A HOLE'S INTRIGUING SHAPE ONCE IT'S BEEN FILLED.
"THIS NOTION ONLY BLOSSOMS HERE, A FRUIT EXCLUSIVE TO THIS GRAND TERRARIUM OF FEELINGS AND IDEAS THEY CALL THE WORLD.

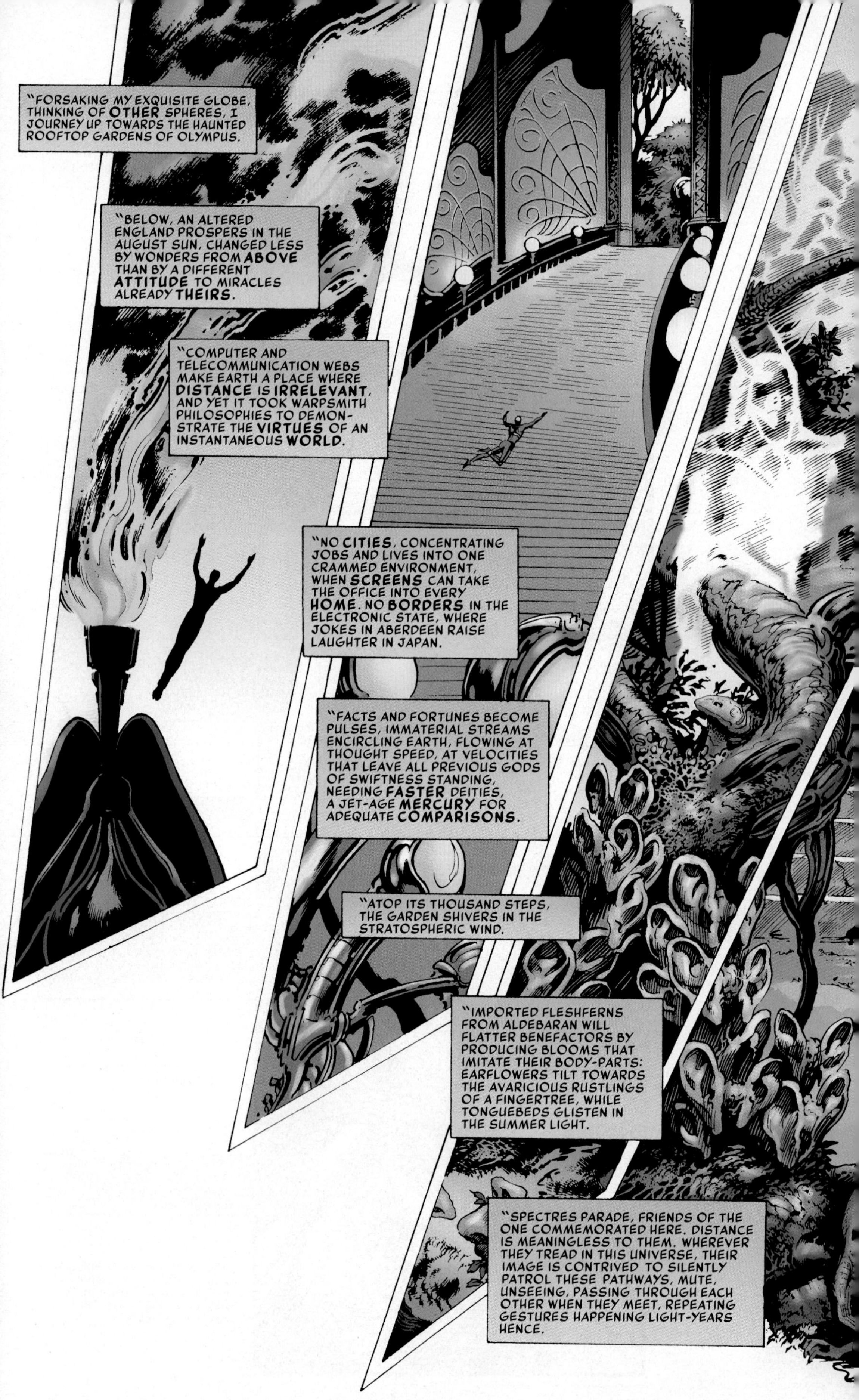
"FORSAKING MY EXQUISITE GLOBE, THINKING OF OTHER SPHERES, I JOURNEY UP TOWARDS THE HAUNTED ROOFTOP GARDENS OF OLYMPUS.
"BELOW, AN ALTERED ENGLAND PROSPERS IN THE AUGUST SUN, CHANGED LESS BY WONDERS FROM ABOVE THAN BY A DIFFERENT ATTITUDE TO MIRACLES ALREADY THEIRS.
"COMPUTER AND TELECOMMUNICATION WEBS MAKE EARTH A PLACE WHERE DISTANCE IS IRRELEVANT, AND YET IT TOOK WARPSMITH PHILOSOPHIES TO DEMON-STRATE THE VIRTUES OF AN INSTANTANEOUS WORLD.
"NO CITIES, CONCENTRATING JOBS AND LIVES INTO ONE CRAMMED ENVIRONMENT, WHEN SCREENS CAN TAKE THE OFFICE INTO EVERY HOME. NO BORDERS IN THE ELECTRONIC STATE, WHERE JOKES IN ABERDEEN RAISE LAUGHTER IN JAPAN.
"FACTS AND FORTUNES BECOME PULSES, IMMATERIAL STREAMS ENCIRCLING EARTH, FLOWING AT THOUGHT SPEED, AT VELOCITIES THAT LEAVE ALL PREVIOUS GODS OF SWIFTNESS STANDING, NEEDING FASTER DEITIES, A JET-AGE MERCURY FOR ADEQUATE COMPARISONS.
"ATOP ITS THOUSAND STEPS, THE GARDEN SHIVERS IN THE STRATOSPHERIC WIND.
"IMPORTED FLESHFERNS FROM ALDEBARAN WILL FLATTER BENEFACTORS BY PRODUCING BLOOMS THAT IMITATE THEIR BODY-PARTS: EARFLOWERS TILT TOWARDS THE AVARICIOUS RUSTLINGS OF A FINGERTREE, WHILE TONGUEBEDS GLISTEN IN THE SUMMER LIGHT.
"SPECTRES PARADE, FRIENDS OF THE ONE COMMEMORATED HERE. DISTANCE IS MEANINGLESS TO THEM. WHEREVER THEY TREAD IN THIS UNIVERSE, THEIR IMAGE IS CONTRIVED TO SILENTLY PATROL THESE PATHWAYS, MUTE, UNSEEING, PASSING THROUGH EACH OTHER WHEN THEY MEET, REPEATING GESTURES HAPPENING LIGHT-YEARS HENCE.

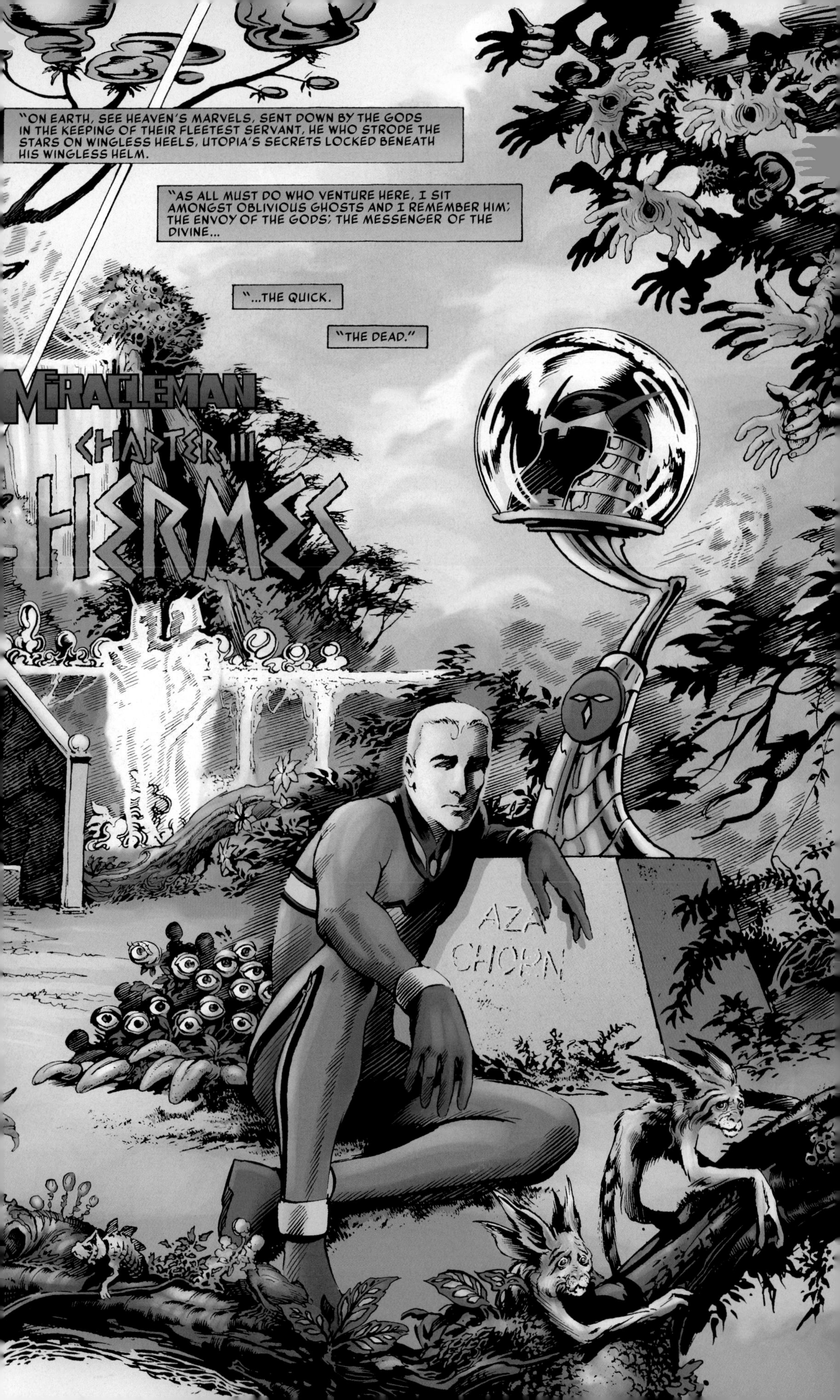

"ON EARTH, SEE HEAVEN'S MARVELS, SENT DOWN BY THE GODS IN THE KEEPING OF THEIR FLEETEST SERVANT, HE WHO STRODE THE STARS ON WINGLESS HEELS, UTOPIA'S SECRETS LOCKED BENEATH HIS WINGLESS HELM.
"AS ALL MUST DO WHO VENTURE HERE, I SIT AMONGST OBLIVIOUS GHOSTS AND I REMEMBER HIM; THE ENVOY OF THE GODS; THE MESSENGER OF THE DIVINE...
"...THE QUICK.
"THE DEAD."
MIRACLEMAN
CHAPTER III
HERMES
AZA CHORN

"ALMOST FIVE YEARS AGO NOW, SINCE THE FIRST TIME THAT WE MET, WHEN FIRST I WAS TRANSPORTED BY HIS POWER. ALL I RECALL IS MY WIFE STUMBLING FORWARD, REACHING OUT..."

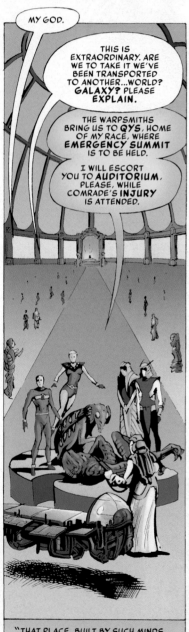

MY GOD.

THIS IS EXTRAORDINARY. ARE WE TO TAKE IT WE'VE BEEN TRANSPORTED TO ANOTHER...WORLD? GALAXY? PLEASE EXPLAIN.

THE WARPSMITHS BRING US TO QYS, HOME OF MY RACE, WHERE EMERGENCY SUMMIT IS TO BE HELD.

I WILL ESCORT YOU TO AUDITORIUM, PLEASE, WHILE COMRADE'S INJURY IS ATTENDED.

"THAT PLACE, BUILT BY SUCH MINDS, THEIR ATTITUDE TO SPACE LAID BARE WITHIN ITS EVERY LINE."

WAIT A MINUTE...WHAT'S OUR CONNECTION WITH THIS "EMERGENCY SUMMIT"?

YOUR WORLD! BABY BORN THERE NOW, YOU SEE? NOT OF ANIMAL STATUS.

CHANGES EVERYTHING. QYS AND WARPSMITHS MUST NEGOTIATE PLACE FOR NEW WORLD IN INTELLIGENT SPACE.

COME, THIS WAY. EVERYTHING WILL TO BECOME CLEAR.

"INTELLIGENT SPACE"?

"THE DISTANT WALLS' ACOUSTICS MADE A TAPELOOP OF EACH SOUND, EACH WORD WORD. THE DISTANT DISTANT WALLS..."

MIRACLEWOMAN, I'M LOST. ARE THESE THE ALIENS THAT CRASHED IN WILTSHIRE, DECADES AGO?

MOST PROBABLY.. AND PLEASE, IT WOULD BE EASIER TO CALL ME AVRIL.

EXCUSE ME? DO WE CORRECTLY ASSUME YOU ORIGINATED THE MULTIPLE-BODY TECHNOLOGY OUR CREATOR UTILISED?

YES. QYS WEAR MANY SKINS. SEE: PORTAL AHEAD, FOR VIEWING WARDROBE IN UNDERSPACE.

"...AND EVERYTHING WAS NEW: NEW SHAPES, A NEW VOCABULARY OF SCENTS..."

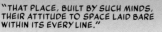

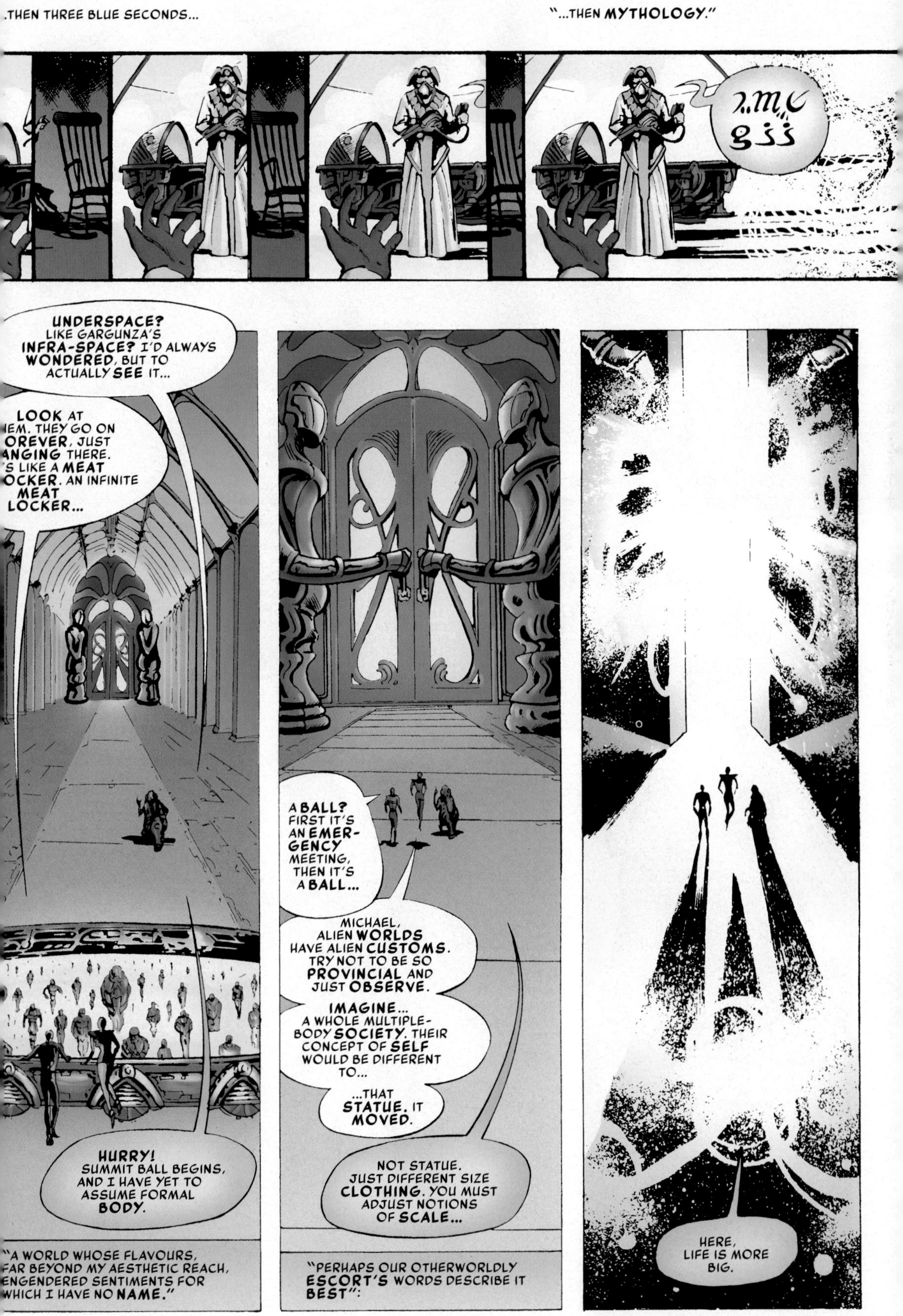

.THEN THREE BLUE SECONDS...
"...THEN MYTHOLOGY."
UNDERSPACE? LIKE GARGUNZA'S INFRA-SPACE? I'D ALWAYS WONDERED, BUT TO ACTUALLY SEE IT...
LOOK AT IEM. THEY GO ON OREVER, JUST ANGING THERE. 'S LIKE A MEAT OCKER. AN INFINITE MEAT LOCKER...
HURRY! SUMMIT BALL BEGINS, AND I HAVE YET TO ASSUME FORMAL BODY.
"A WORLD WHOSE FLAVOURS, FAR BEYOND MY AESTHETIC REACH, ENGENDERED SENTIMENTS FOR WHICH I HAVE NO NAME."
A BALL? FIRST IT'S AN EMERGENCY MEETING, THEN IT'S A BALL...
MICHAEL, ALIEN WORLDS HAVE ALIEN CUSTOMS. TRY NOT TO BE SO PROVINCIAL AND JUST OBSERVE.
IMAGINE... A WHOLE MULTIPLE-BODY SOCIETY. THEIR CONCEPT OF SELF WOULD BE DIFFERENT TO...
...THAT STATUE. IT MOVED.
NOT STATUE. JUST DIFFERENT SIZE CLOTHING. YOU MUST ADJUST NOTIONS OF SCALE...
"PERHAPS OUR OTHERWORLDLY ESCORT'S WORDS DESCRIBE IT BEST":
HERE, LIFE IS MORE BIG.

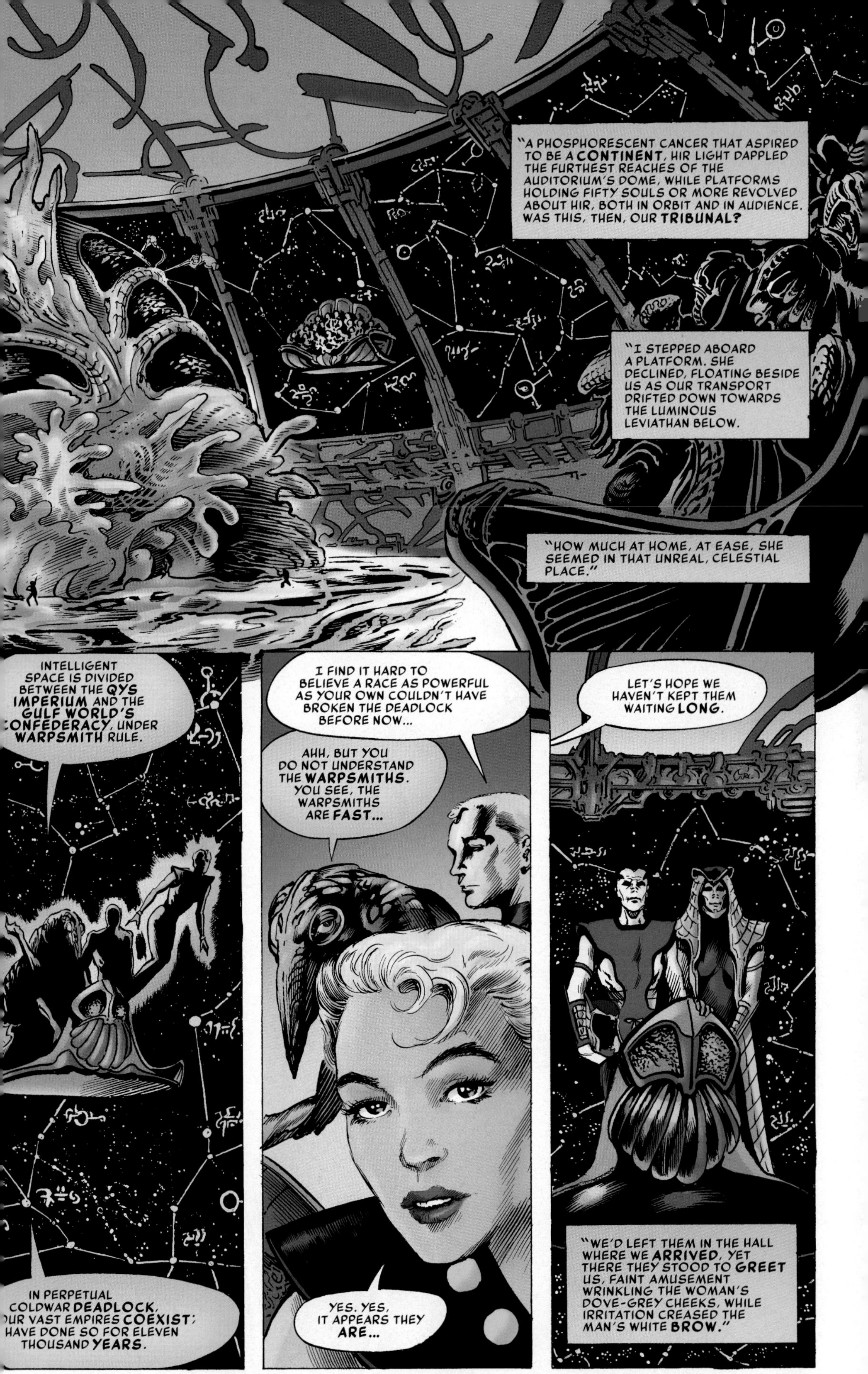
"A PHOSPHORESCENT CANCER THAT ASPIRED TO BE A CONTINENT, HIR LIGHT DAPPLED THE FURTHEST REACHES OF THE AUDITORIUM'S DOME, WHILE PLATFORMS HOLDING FIFTY SOULS OR MORE REVOLVED ABOUT HIR, BOTH IN ORBIT AND IN AUDIENCE. WAS THIS, THEN, OUR TRIBUNAL?
"I STEPPED ABOARD A PLATFORM. SHE DECLINED, FLOATING BESIDE US AS OUR TRANSPORT DRIFTED DOWN TOWARDS THE LUMINOUS LEVIATHAN BELOW.
"HOW MUCH AT HOME, AT EASE, SHE SEEMED IN THAT UNREAL, CELESTIAL PLACE."
INTELLIGENT SPACE IS DIVIDED BETWEEN THE QYS IMPERIUM AND THE GULF WORLD'S CONFEDERACY, UNDER WARPSMITH RULE.
IN PERPETUAL COLDWAR DEADLOCK, OUR VAST EMPIRES COEXIST; HAVE DONE SO FOR ELEVEN THOUSAND YEARS.
I FIND IT HARD TO BELIEVE A RACE AS POWERFUL AS YOUR OWN COULDN'T HAVE BROKEN THE DEADLOCK BEFORE NOW...
AHH, BUT YOU DO NOT UNDERSTAND THE WARPSMITHS. YOU SEE, THE WARPSMITHS ARE FAST...
YES. YES, IT APPEARS THEY ARE...
LET'S HOPE WE HAVEN'T KEPT THEM WAITING LONG.
"WE'D LEFT THEM IN THE HALL WHERE WE ARRIVED, YET THERE THEY STOOD TO GREET US, FAINT AMUSEMENT WRINKLING THE WOMAN'S DOVE-GREY CHEEKS, WHILE IRRITATION CREASED THE MAN'S WHITE BROW."

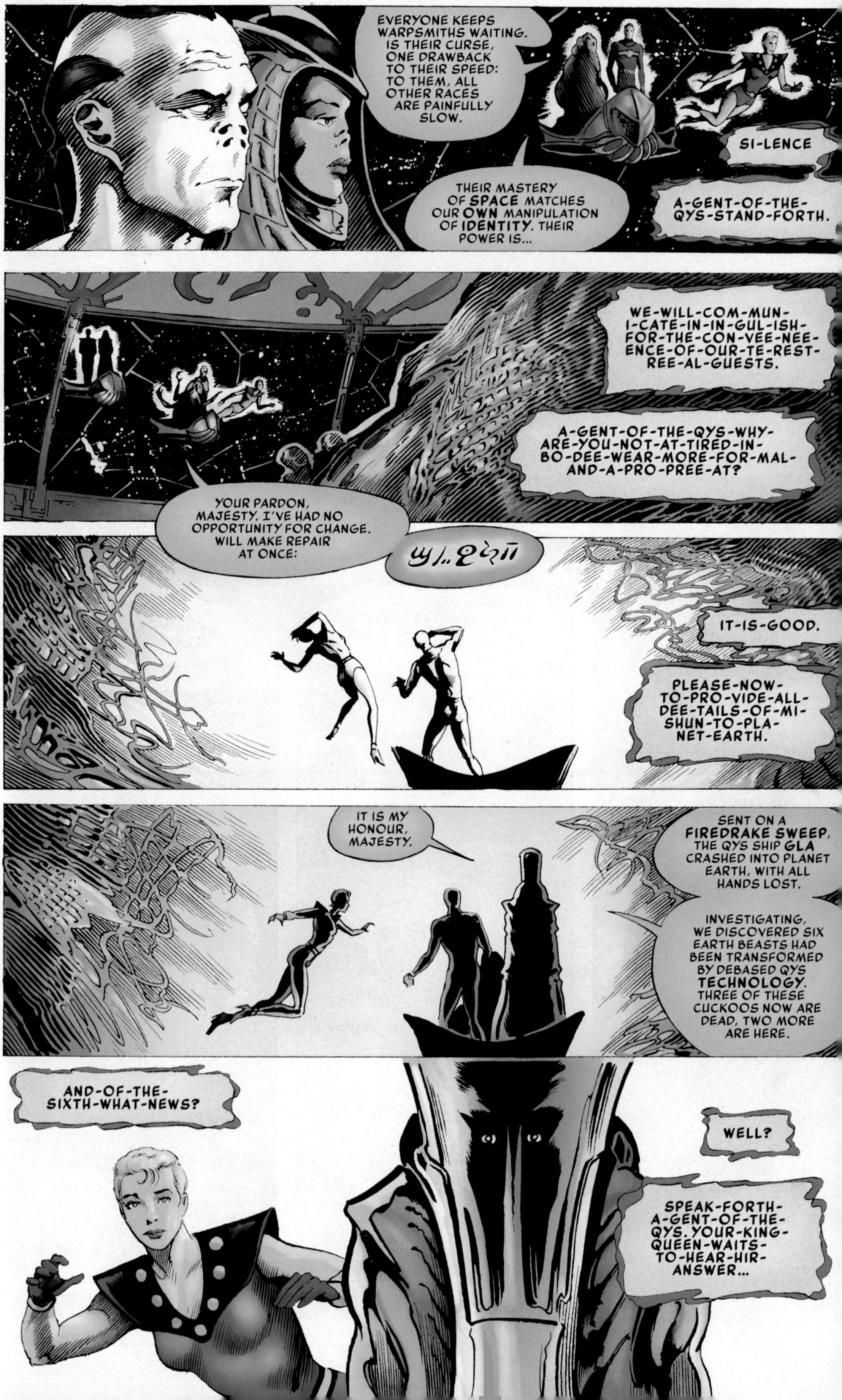
EVERYONE KEEPS WARPSMITHS WAITING. IS THEIR CURSE, ONE DRAWBACK TO THEIR SPEED: TO THEM, ALL OTHER RACES ARE PAINFULLY SLOW.
THEIR MASTERY OF SPACE MATCHES OUR OWN MANIPULATION OF IDENTITY. THEIR POWER IS...
SI-LENCE
A-GENT-OF-THE-QYS-STAND-FORTH.
WE-WILL-COM-MUN-I-CATE-IN-IN-GUL-ISH-FOR-THE-CON-VEE-NEE-ENCE-OF-OUR-TE-REST-REE-AL-GUESTS.
A-GENT-OF-THE-QYS-WHY-ARE-YOU-NOT-AT-TIRED-IN-BO-DEE-WEAR-MORE-FOR-MAL-AND-A-PRO-PREE-AT?
YOUR PARDON, MAJESTY. I'VE HAD NO OPPORTUNITY FOR CHANGE. WILL MAKE REPAIR AT ONCE:
IT-IS-GOOD.
PLEASE-NOW-TO-PRO-VIDE-ALL-DEE-TAILS-OF-MI-SHUN-TO-PLA-NET-EARTH.
IT IS MY HONOUR, MAJESTY.
SENT ON A FIREDRAKE SWEEP, THE QYS SHIP GLA CRASHED INTO PLANET EARTH, WITH ALL HANDS LOST.
INVESTIGATING, WE DISCOVERED SIX EARTH BEASTS HAD BEEN TRANSFORMED BY DEBASED QYS TECHNOLOGY. THREE OF THESE CUCKOOS NOW ARE DEAD, TWO MORE ARE HERE.
AND-OF-THE-SIXTH-WHAT-NEWS?
WELL?
SPEAK-FORTH-A-GENT-OF-THE-QYS. YOUR-KING-QUEEN-WAITS-TO-HEAR-HIR-ANSWER...

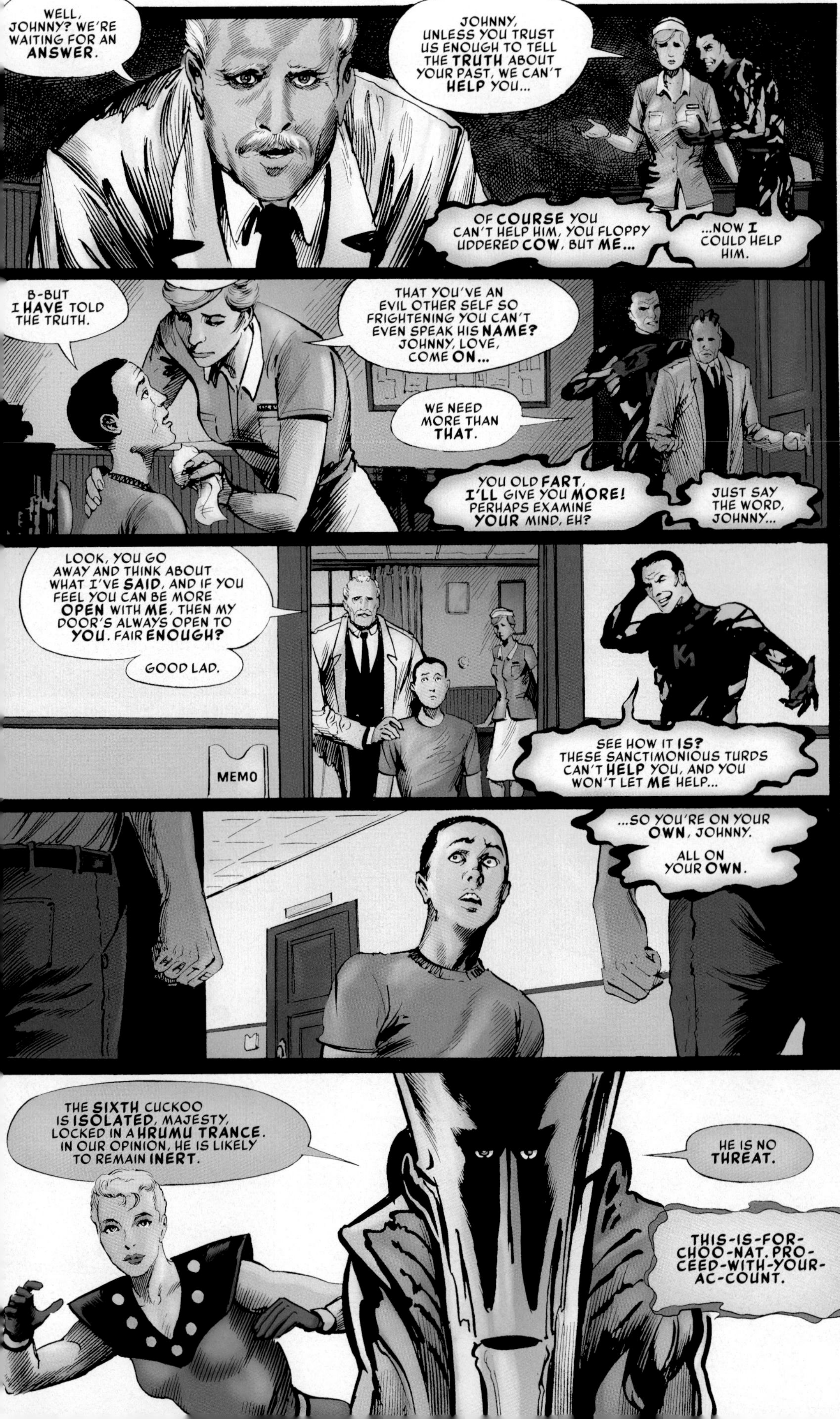

WELL, JOHNNY? WE'RE WAITING FOR AN ANSWER.
JOHNNY, UNLESS YOU TRUST US ENOUGH TO TELL THE TRUTH ABOUT YOUR PAST, WE CAN'T HELP YOU...
OF COURSE YOU CAN'T HELP HIM, YOU FLOPPY UDDERED COW, BUT ME...
...NOW I COULD HELP HIM.
B-BUT I HAVE TOLD THE TRUTH.
THAT YOU'VE AN EVIL OTHER SELF SO FRIGHTENING YOU CAN'T EVEN SPEAK HIS NAME? JOHNNY, LOVE, COME ON...
WE NEED MORE THAN THAT.
YOU OLD FART, I'LL GIVE YOU MORE! PERHAPS EXAMINE YOUR MIND, EH?
JUST SAY THE WORD, JOHNNY...
LOOK, YOU GO AWAY AND THINK ABOUT WHAT I'VE SAID, AND IF YOU FEEL YOU CAN BE MORE OPEN WITH ME, THEN MY DOOR'S ALWAYS OPEN TO YOU. FAIR ENOUGH?
GOOD LAD.
MEMO
SEE HOW IT IS? THESE SANCTIMONIOUS TURDS CAN'T HELP YOU, AND YOU WON'T LET ME HELP...
...SO YOU'RE ON YOUR OWN, JOHNNY.
ALL ON YOUR OWN.
THE SIXTH CUCKOO IS ISOLATED, MAJESTY, LOCKED IN A HRUMU TRANCE. IN OUR OPINION, HE IS LIKELY TO REMAIN INERT.
HE IS NO THREAT.
THIS-IS-FOR-CHOO-NAT. PRO-CEED-WITH-YOUR-AC-COUNT.

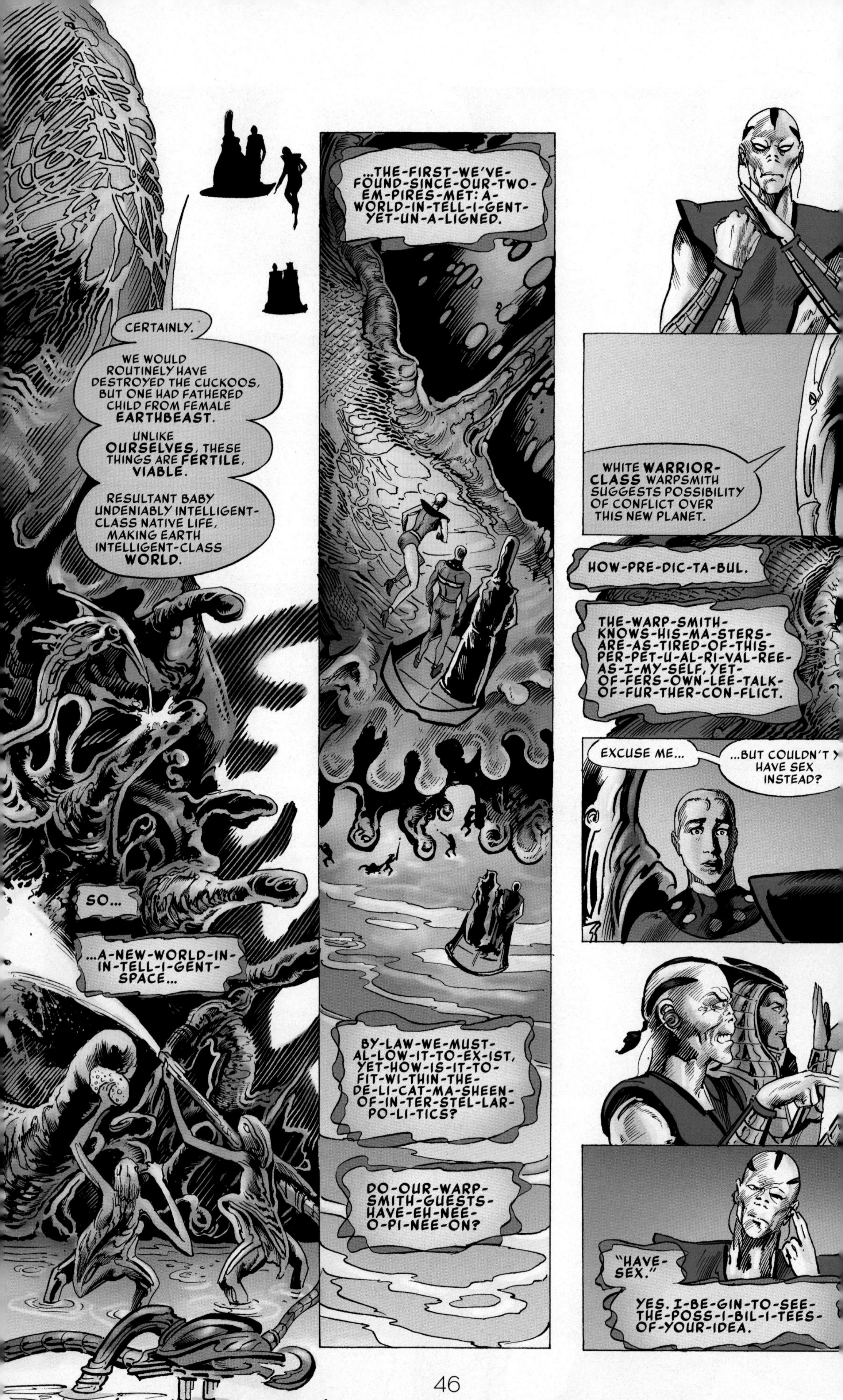
CERTAINLY.
WE WOULD ROUTINELY HAVE DESTROYED THE CUCKOOS, BUT ONE HAD FATHERED CHILD FROM FEMALE EARTHBEAST.
UNLIKE OURSELVES, THESE THINGS ARE FERTILE, VIABLE.
RESULTANT BABY UNDENIABLY INTELLIGENT-CLASS NATIVE LIFE, MAKING EARTH INTELLIGENT-CLASS WORLD.
SO...
...A-NEW-WORLD-IN-IN-TELL-I-GENT-SPACE...
...THE-FIRST-WE'VE-FOUND-SINCE-OUR-TWO-EM-PIRES-MET: A-WORLD-IN-TELL-I-GENT-YET-UN-A-LIGNED.
BY-LAW-WE-MUST-AL-LOW-IT-TO-EX-IST, YET-HOW-IS-IT-TO-FIT-WI-THIN-THE-DE-LI-CAT-MA-SHEEN-OF-IN-TER-STEL-LAR-PO-LI-TICS?
DO-OUR-WARP-SMITH-GUESTS-HAVE-EH-NEE-O-PI-NEE-ON?
WHITE WARRIOR-CLASS WARPSMITH SUGGESTS POSSIBILITY OF CONFLICT OVER THIS NEW PLANET.
HOW-PRE-DIC-TA-BUL.
THE-WARP-SMITH-KNOWS-HIS-MA-STERS-ARE-AS-TIRED-OF-THIS-PER-PET-U-AL-RI-VAL-REE-AS-I-MY-SELF, YET-OF-FERS-OWN-LEE-TALK-OF-FUR-THER-CON-FLICT.
EXCUSE ME...
...BUT COULDN'T HAVE SEX INSTEAD?
"HAVE-SEX."
YES. I-BE-GIN-TO-SEE-THE-POSS-I-BIL-I-TEES-OF-YOUR-IDEA.

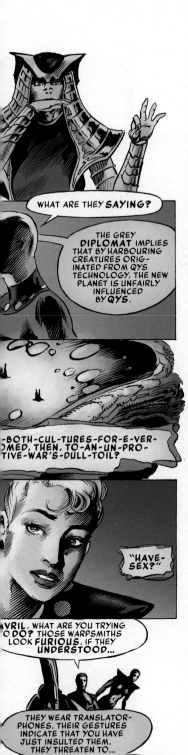

WHAT ARE THEY **SAYING?**

THE GREY **DIPLOMAT** IMPLIES THAT BY **HARBOURING** CREATURES ORIG- INATED FROM QYS TECHNOLOGY, THE NEW PLANET IS UNFAIRLY INFLUENCED BY QYS.

-BOTH-CUL-TURES-FOR-E-VER-
OMED, THEN, TO-AN-UN-PRO-
TIVE-WAR'S-DULL-TOIL?

"HAVE- SEX?"

VRIL, WHAT ARE YOU TRYING O DO? THOSE **WARPSMITHS** LOOK **FURIOUS.** IF THEY UNDERSTOOD...

THEY WEAR **TRANSLATOR- PHONES.** THEIR GESTURES INDICATE THAT YOU HAVE JUST INSULTED THEM. THEY THREATEN TO...

...NO. WAIT...

...THEY APOLOGISE FOR **MISUNDERSTANDING** YOU. THEIR **TRANSLATORS** HAVE JUST RELAYED AN ADDITIONAL LAYER OF POSSIBLE **MEANING** TO THEM. IT SEEMS TO **PACIFY** THEM.

DAMNED IF **I** DO.

IT'S **OBVIOUS.** IF TWO **ORGANISMS** OR TWO **CULTURES** ARE FORCED INTO **CONTACT,** IT CAN BE **THANATIC** AND **DESTRUCTIVE,** OR **EROTIC** AND **CREATIVE.**

YOU-SUH-JEST-OUR-
CUL-TURES-MA-REE,
U-SING-YOUR-NEU-
TRAL-PLA-NET-FOR-
OUR-COURT-SHIP.

AN-IM-PRESS-IVE CON-CEPT.

DE-SPITE-YOUR-
UG-LI-NESS MAY-
I-COM-PLI-MENT-
YOUR-THIN-KING?

ALL-SO, YOUR-
DEE-EN-AY-SPY-
RALS-ARE-VE-
REE-PRI-TEE.

I-MUST-CON-SULT-
MY-AD-VI-SORS.
GO-NOW.

"STILL DAZZLED BY OUR **AUDIENCE,** WE RETURNED THE WAY WE CAME, COMING AT LAST TO FARAWAY **RECEPTION ROOMS.**

"THE **WARPSMITHS** WERE THERE, WAITING FOR US.

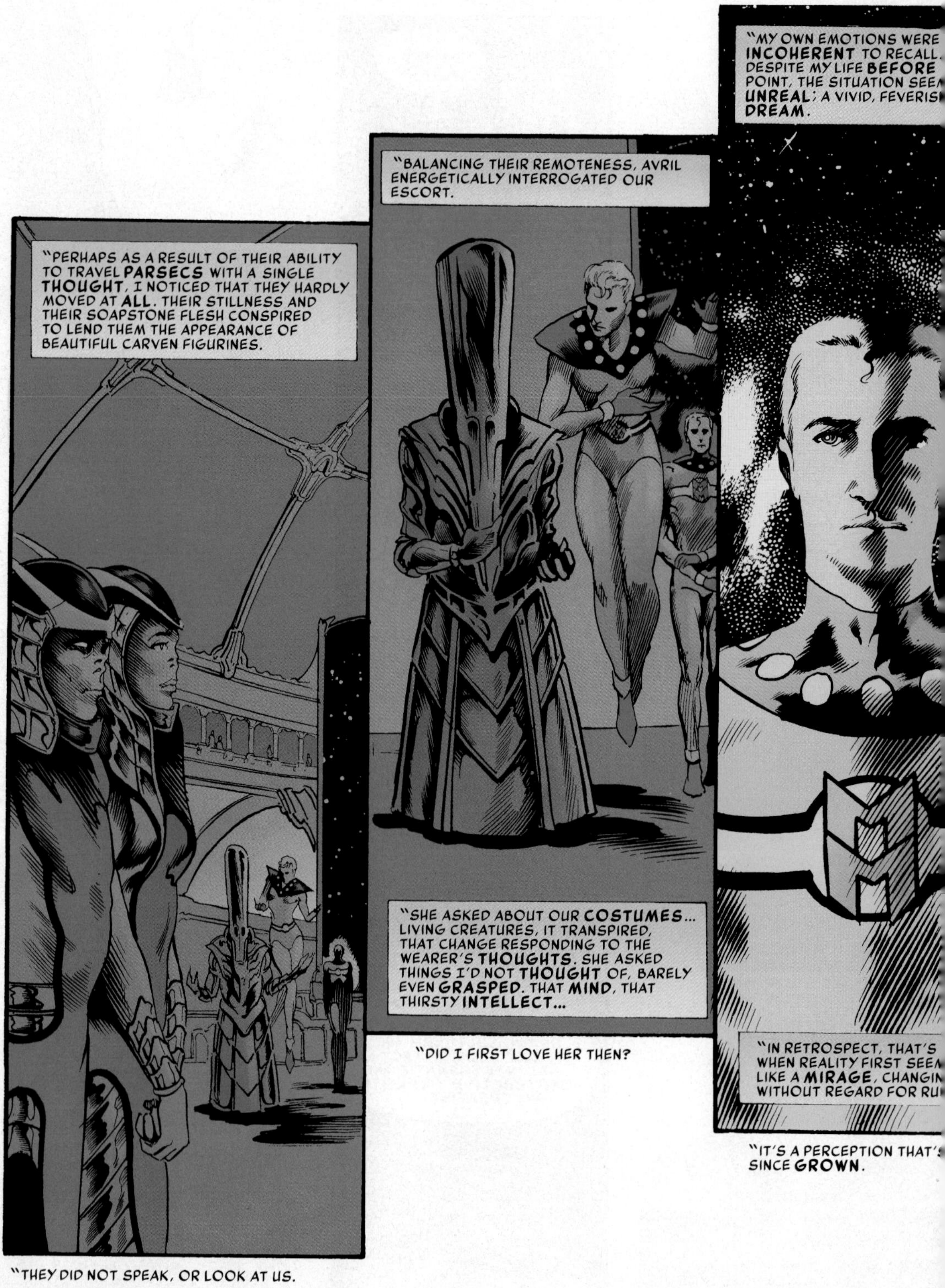
"PERHAPS AS A RESULT OF THEIR ABILITY TO TRAVEL PARSECS WITH A SINGLE THOUGHT, I NOTICED THAT THEY HARDLY MOVED AT ALL. THEIR STILLNESS AND THEIR SOAPSTONE FLESH CONSPIRED TO LEND THEM THE APPEARANCE OF BEAUTIFUL CARVEN FIGURINES.
"THEY DID NOT SPEAK, OR LOOK AT US.
"BALANCING THEIR REMOTENESS, AVRIL ENERGETICALLY INTERROGATED OUR ESCORT.
"SHE ASKED ABOUT OUR COSTUMES... LIVING CREATURES, IT TRANSPIRED, THAT CHANGE RESPONDING TO THE WEARER'S THOUGHTS. SHE ASKED THINGS I'D NOT THOUGHT OF, BARELY EVEN GRASPED. THAT MIND, THAT THIRSTY INTELLECT...
"DID I FIRST LOVE HER THEN?
"MY OWN EMOTIONS WERE INCOHERENT TO RECALL. DESPITE MY LIFE BEFORE POINT, THE SITUATION SEE UNREAL; A VIVID, FEVERIS DREAM.
"IN RETROSPECT, THAT'S WHEN REALITY FIRST SEE LIKE A MIRAGE, CHANGIN WITHOUT REGARD FOR RU
"IT'S A PERCEPTION THAT' SINCE GROWN.

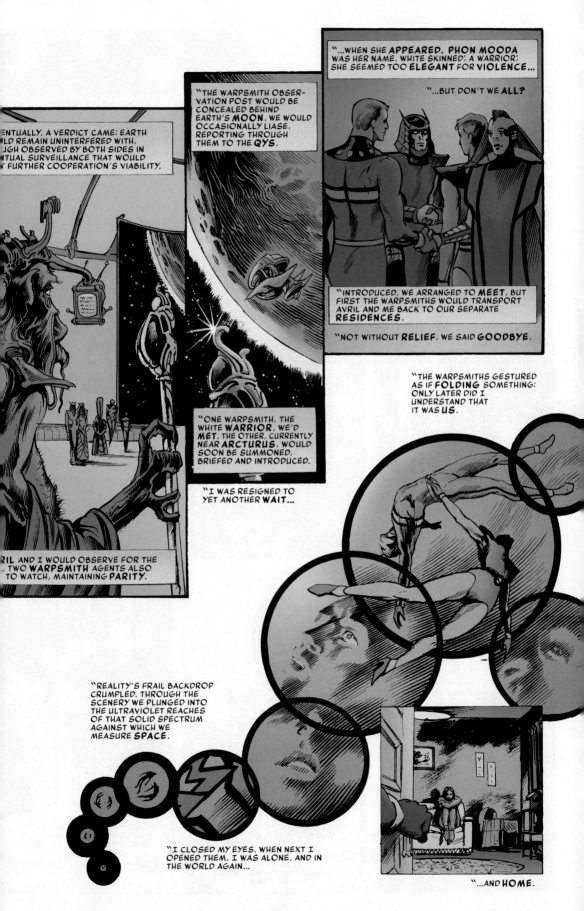

"...WHEN SHE **APPEARED**. PHON MOODA WAS HER NAME. WHITE SKINNED; A WARRIOR; SHE SEEMED TOO **ELEGANT** FOR **VIOLENCE**...

"...BUT DON'T WE **ALL?**

ENTUALLY, A VERDICT CAME: EARTH
[W]LD REMAIN UNINTERFERED WITH,
[THO]UGH OBSERVED BY BOTH SIDES IN
[MU]TUAL SURVEILLANCE THAT WOULD
[TE]T FURTHER COOPERATION'S VIABILITY.

"THE WARPSMITH OBSER-
VATION POST WOULD BE
CONCEALED BEHIND
EARTH'S **MOON**. WE WOULD
OCCASIONALLY LIASE,
REPORTING THROUGH
THEM TO THE **QYS**.

"INTRODUCED, WE ARRANGED TO **MEET**, BUT
FIRST THE WARPSMITHS WOULD TRANSPORT
AVRIL AND ME BACK TO OUR SEPARATE
**RESIDENCES**.

"NOT WITHOUT **RELIEF**, WE SAID **GOODBYE**.

"THE WARPSMITHS GESTURED
AS IF **FOLDING** SOMETHING:
ONLY LATER DID I
UNDERSTAND THAT
IT WAS **US**.

"ONE WARPSMITH, THE
WHITE **WARRIOR**, WE'D
**MET**. THE OTHER, CURRENTLY
NEAR **ARCTURUS**, WOULD
SOON BE SUMMONED,
BRIEFED AND INTRODUCED.

"I WAS RESIGNED TO
YET ANOTHER **WAIT**...

[AV]RIL AND I WOULD OBSERVE FOR THE
[_], TWO **WARPSMITH** AGENTS ALSO
[_] TO WATCH, MAINTAINING **PARITY**.

"REALITY'S FRAIL BACKDROP
CRUMPLED. THROUGH THE
SCENERY WE PLUNGED INTO
THE ULTRAVIOLET REACHES
OF THAT SOLID SPECTRUM
AGAINST WHICH WE
MEASURE **SPACE**.

"I CLOSED MY EYES. WHEN NEXT I
OPENED THEM, I WAS ALONE, AND IN
THE WORLD AGAIN...

"...AND **HOME**.

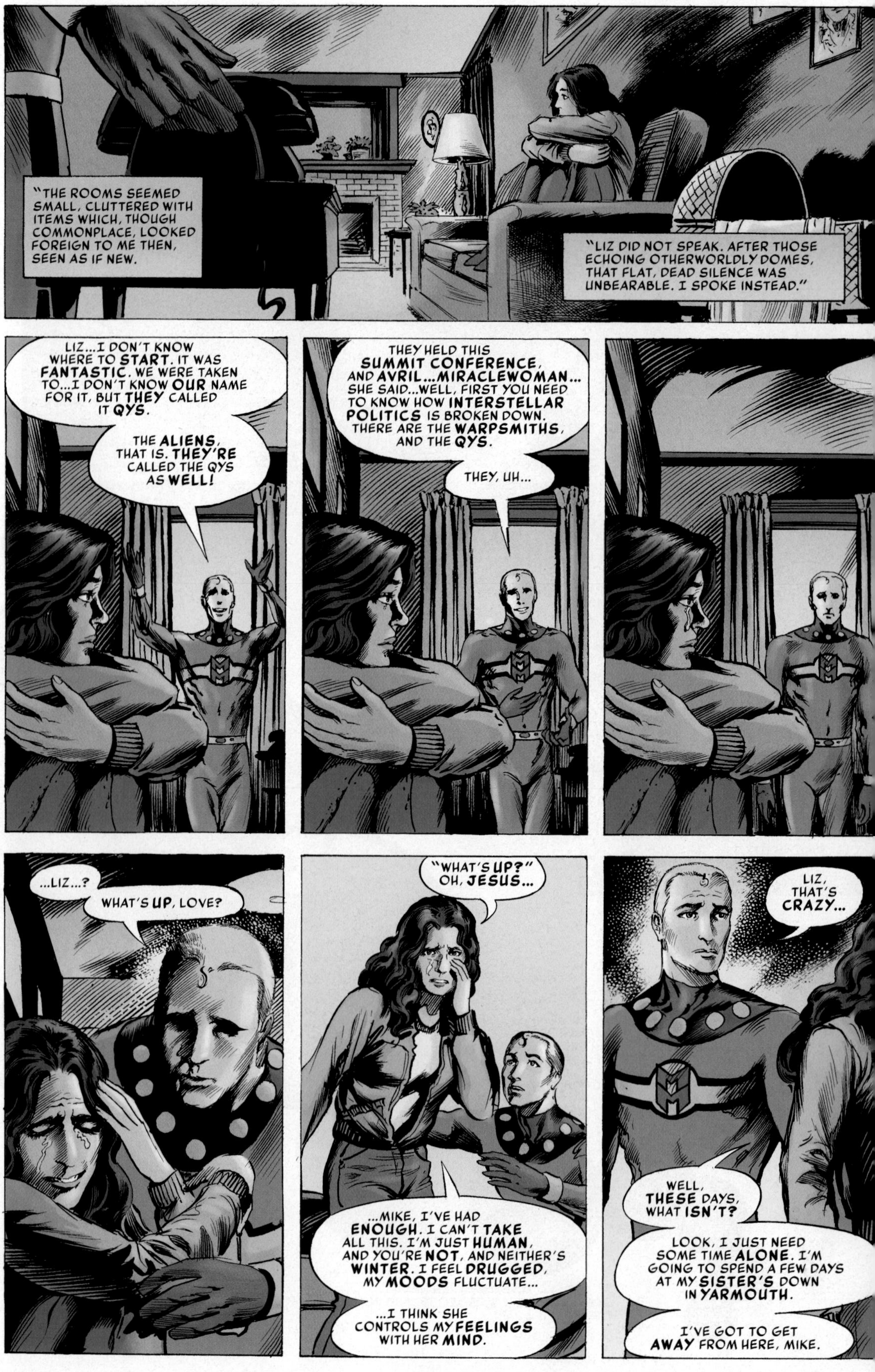
"THE ROOMS SEEMED SMALL, CLUTTERED WITH ITEMS WHICH, THOUGH COMMONPLACE, LOOKED FOREIGN TO ME THEN, SEEN AS IF NEW.
"LIZ DID NOT SPEAK. AFTER THOSE ECHOING OTHERWORLDLY DOMES, THAT FLAT, DEAD SILENCE WAS UNBEARABLE. I SPOKE INSTEAD."
LIZ...I DON'T KNOW WHERE TO START. IT WAS FANTASTIC. WE WERE TAKEN TO...I DON'T KNOW OUR NAME FOR IT, BUT THEY CALLED IT QYS.
THE ALIENS, THAT IS. THEY'RE CALLED THE QYS AS WELL!
THEY HELD THIS SUMMIT CONFERENCE, AND AVRIL...MIRACLEWOMAN... SHE SAID...WELL, FIRST YOU NEED TO KNOW HOW INTERSTELLAR POLITICS IS BROKEN DOWN. THERE ARE THE WARPSMITHS, AND THE QYS.
THEY, UH...
...LIZ...?
WHAT'S UP, LOVE?
"WHAT'S UP?" OH, JESUS...
...MIKE, I'VE HAD ENOUGH. I CAN'T TAKE ALL THIS. I'M JUST HUMAN, AND YOU'RE NOT, AND NEITHER'S WINTER. I FEEL DRUGGED, MY MOODS FLUCTUATE...
...I THINK SHE CONTROLS MY FEELINGS WITH HER MIND.
LIZ, THAT'S CRAZY...
WELL, THESE DAYS, WHAT ISN'T?
LOOK, I JUST NEED SOME TIME ALONE. I'M GOING TO SPEND A FEW DAYS AT MY SISTER'S DOWN IN YARMOUTH.
I'VE GOT TO GET AWAY FROM HERE, MIKE.

LIZ, THIS IS SO **SUDDEN.** CAN'T WE **TALK?**

LATER. LATER WE'LL TALK.

I'VE THOUGHT IT THROUGH, AND I HAVE TO LEAVE **NOW.** I **LOVE** YOU, MIKE. I LOVE **BOTH** OF YOU. I'LL BE BACK SOON.

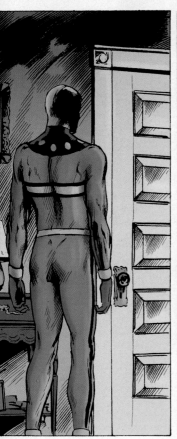

FATHER?

I THINK IT'S TIME WE DISCUSSED **MOTHER,** DON'T YOU?

"FIVE YEARS AGO NOW.

"FIVE SHORT YEARS SINCE FIRST I WALKED ON OTHER WORLDS OR HEARD THE VOICE OF **WINTER.**

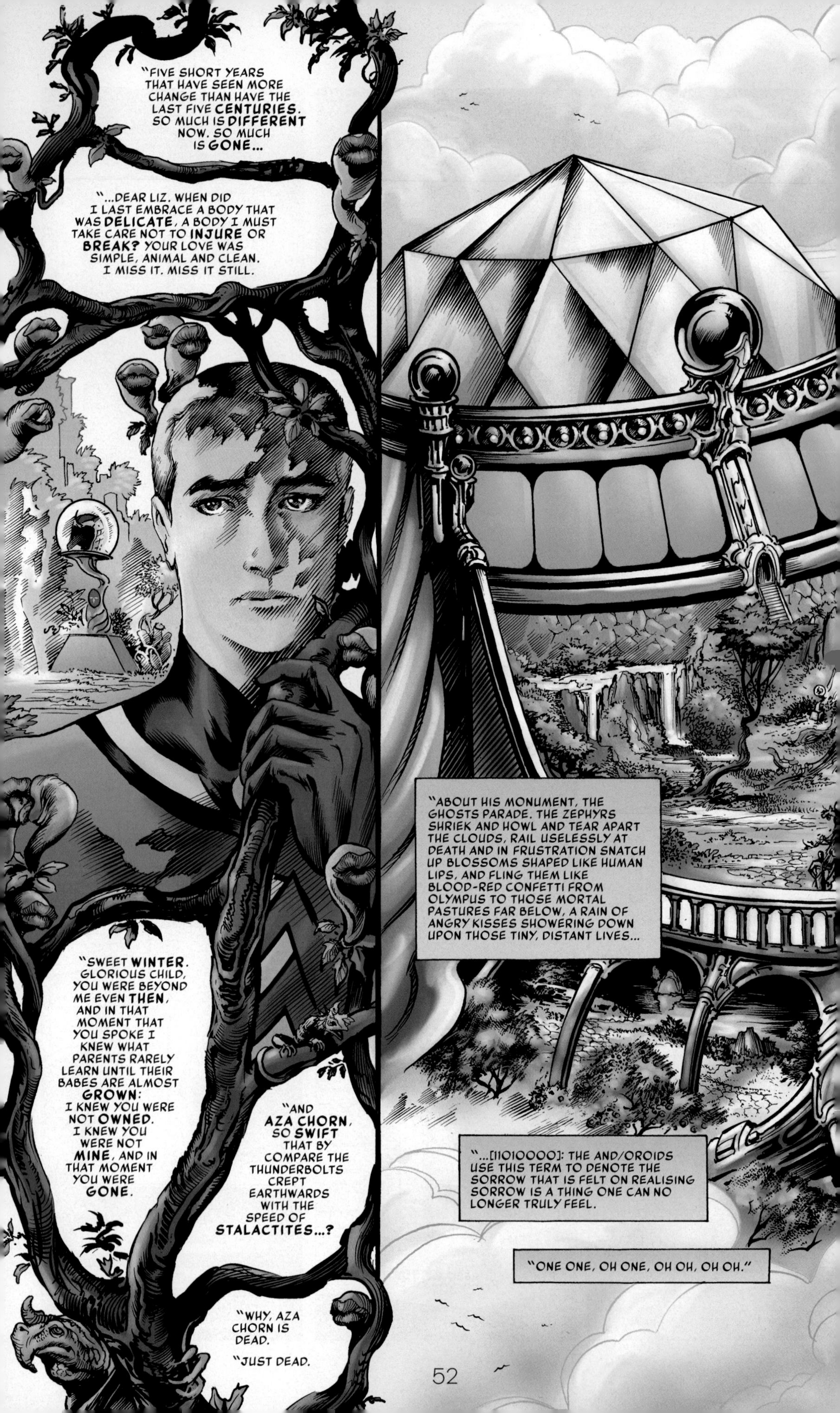
"FIVE SHORT YEARS THAT HAVE SEEN MORE CHANGE THAN HAVE THE LAST FIVE CENTURIES. SO MUCH IS DIFFERENT NOW. SO MUCH IS GONE...
"...DEAR LIZ. WHEN DID I LAST EMBRACE A BODY THAT WAS DELICATE, A BODY I MUST TAKE CARE NOT TO INJURE OR BREAK? YOUR LOVE WAS SIMPLE, ANIMAL AND CLEAN. I MISS IT. MISS IT STILL.
"SWEET WINTER. GLORIOUS CHILD, YOU WERE BEYOND ME EVEN THEN, AND IN THAT MOMENT THAT YOU SPOKE I KNEW WHAT PARENTS RARELY LEARN UNTIL THEIR BABES ARE ALMOST GROWN: I KNEW YOU WERE NOT OWNED. I KNEW YOU WERE NOT MINE, AND IN THAT MOMENT YOU WERE GONE.
"AND AZA CHORN, SO SWIFT THAT BY COMPARE THE THUNDERBOLTS CREPT EARTHWARDS WITH THE SPEED OF STALACTITES...?
"WHY, AZA CHORN IS DEAD.
"JUST DEAD.
"ABOUT HIS MONUMENT, THE GHOSTS PARADE. THE ZEPHYRS SHRIEK AND HOWL AND TEAR APART THE CLOUDS, RAIL USELESSLY AT DEATH AND IN FRUSTRATION SNATCH UP BLOSSOMS SHAPED LIKE HUMAN LIPS, AND FLING THEM LIKE BLOOD-RED CONFETTI FROM OLYMPUS TO THOSE MORTAL PASTURES FAR BELOW, A RAIN OF ANGRY KISSES SHOWERING DOWN UPON THOSE TINY, DISTANT LIVES...
"...[11010000]: THE AND/OROIDS USE THIS TERM TO DENOTE THE SORROW THAT IS FELT ON REALISING SORROW IS A THING ONE CAN NO LONGER TRULY FEEL.
"ONE ONE, OH ONE, OH OH, OH OH."

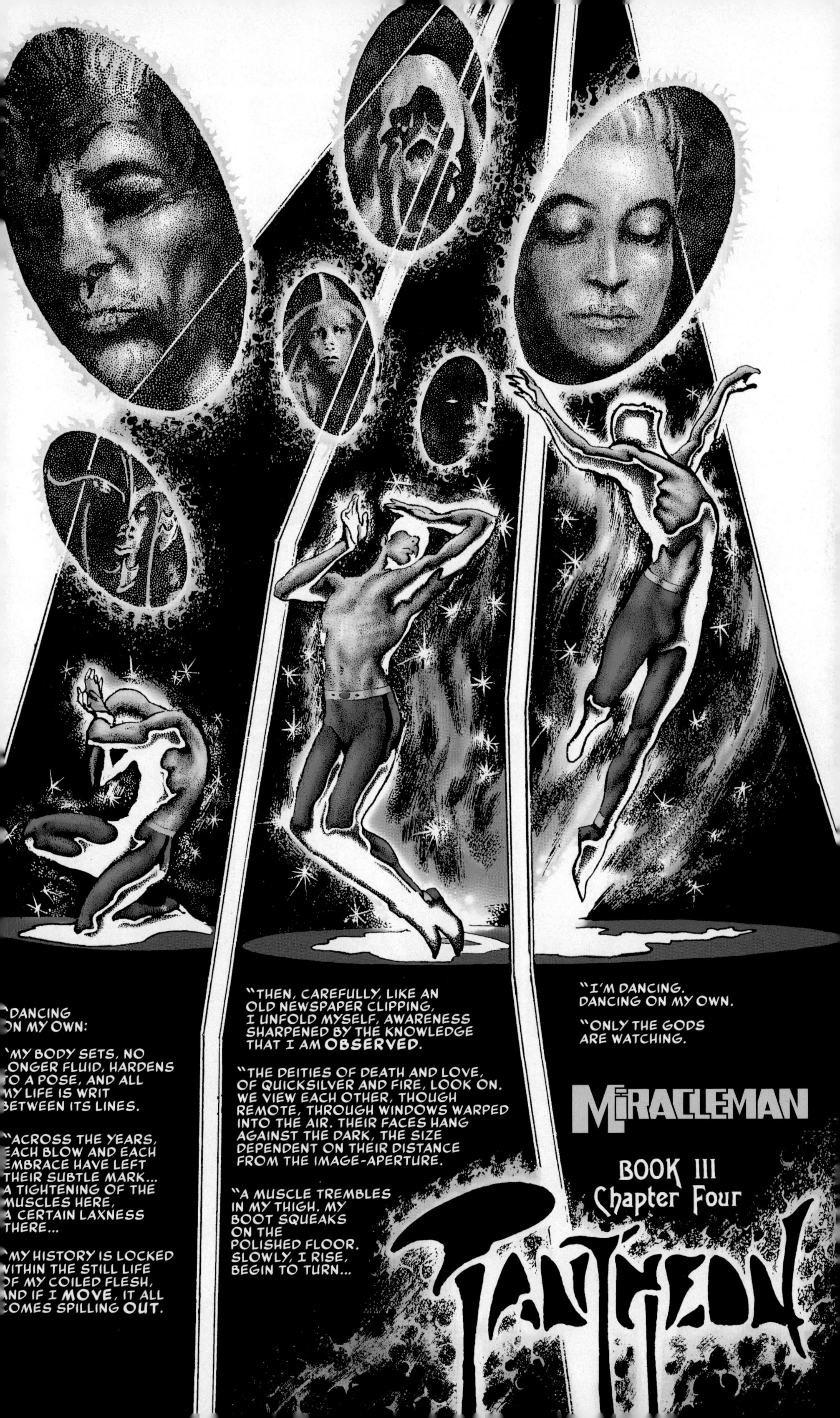
"DANCING
ON MY OWN:
'MY BODY SETS, NO
ONGER FLUID, HARDENS
TO A POSE, AND ALL
MY LIFE IS WRIT
BETWEEN ITS LINES.
"ACROSS THE YEARS,
EACH BLOW AND EACH
EMBRACE HAVE LEFT
THEIR SUBTLE MARK...
A TIGHTENING OF THE
MUSCLES HERE,
A CERTAIN LAXNESS
THERE...
"MY HISTORY IS LOCKED
WITHIN THE STILL LIFE
OF MY COILED FLESH,
AND IF I MOVE, IT ALL
COMES SPILLING OUT.
"THEN, CAREFULLY, LIKE AN OLD NEWSPAPER CLIPPING, I UNFOLD MYSELF, AWARENESS SHARPENED BY THE KNOWLEDGE THAT I AM OBSERVED.
"THE DEITIES OF DEATH AND LOVE, OF QUICKSILVER AND FIRE, LOOK ON. WE VIEW EACH OTHER, THOUGH REMOTE, THROUGH WINDOWS WARPED INTO THE AIR. THEIR FACES HANG AGAINST THE DARK, THE SIZE DEPENDENT ON THEIR DISTANCE FROM THE IMAGE-APERTURE.
"A MUSCLE TREMBLES IN MY THIGH. MY BOOT SQUEAKS ON THE POLISHED FLOOR. SLOWLY, I RISE, BEGIN TO TURN...
"I'M DANCING. DANCING ON MY OWN.
"ONLY THE GODS ARE WATCHING.
MIRACLEMAN
BOOK III
Chapter Four
PANTHEON

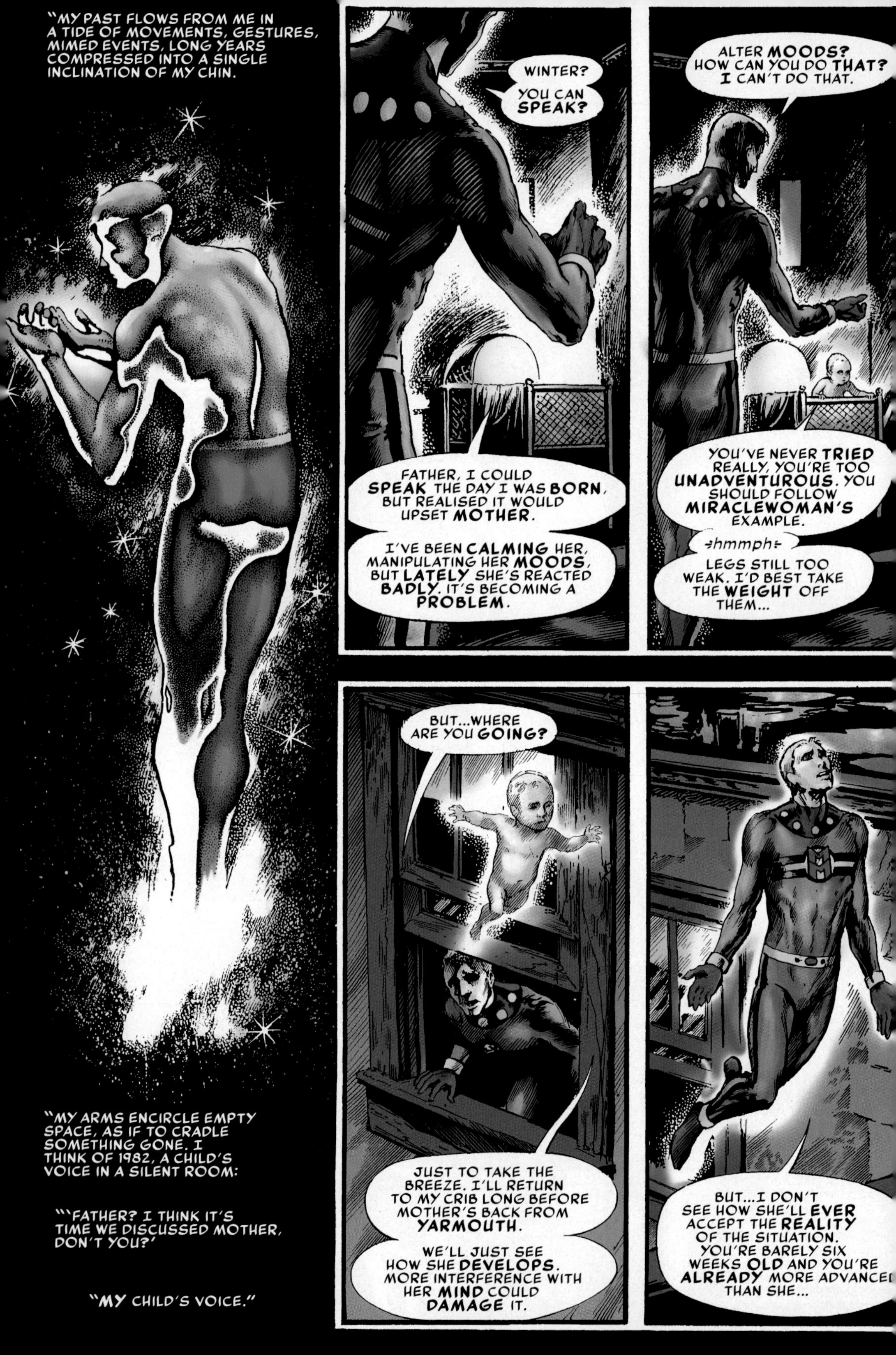
"MY PAST FLOWS FROM ME IN A TIDE OF MOVEMENTS, GESTURES, MIMED EVENTS, LONG YEARS COMPRESSED INTO A SINGLE INCLINATION OF MY CHIN.
"MY ARMS ENCIRCLE EMPTY SPACE, AS IF TO CRADLE SOMETHING GONE. I THINK OF 1982, A CHILD'S VOICE IN A SILENT ROOM:
"'FATHER? I THINK IT'S TIME WE DISCUSSED MOTHER, DON'T YOU?'
"MY CHILD'S VOICE."
WINTER?
YOU CAN SPEAK?
FATHER, I COULD SPEAK THE DAY I WAS BORN, BUT REALISED IT WOULD UPSET MOTHER.
I'VE BEEN CALMING HER, MANIPULATING HER MOODS, BUT LATELY SHE'S REACTED BADLY. IT'S BECOMING A PROBLEM.
ALTER MOODS? HOW CAN YOU DO THAT? I CAN'T DO THAT.
YOU'VE NEVER TRIED REALLY, YOU'RE TOO UNADVENTUROUS. YOU SHOULD FOLLOW MIRACLEWOMAN'S EXAMPLE.
hmmph
LEGS STILL TOO WEAK. I'D BEST TAKE THE WEIGHT OFF THEM...
BUT...WHERE ARE YOU GOING?
JUST TO TAKE THE BREEZE. I'LL RETURN TO MY CRIB LONG BEFORE MOTHER'S BACK FROM YARMOUTH.
WE'LL JUST SEE HOW SHE DEVELOPS. MORE INTERFERENCE WITH HER MIND COULD DAMAGE IT.
BUT...I DON'T SEE HOW SHE'LL EVER ACCEPT THE REALITY OF THE SITUATION. YOU'RE BARELY SIX WEEKS OLD AND YOU'RE ALREADY MORE ADVANCED THAN SHE...

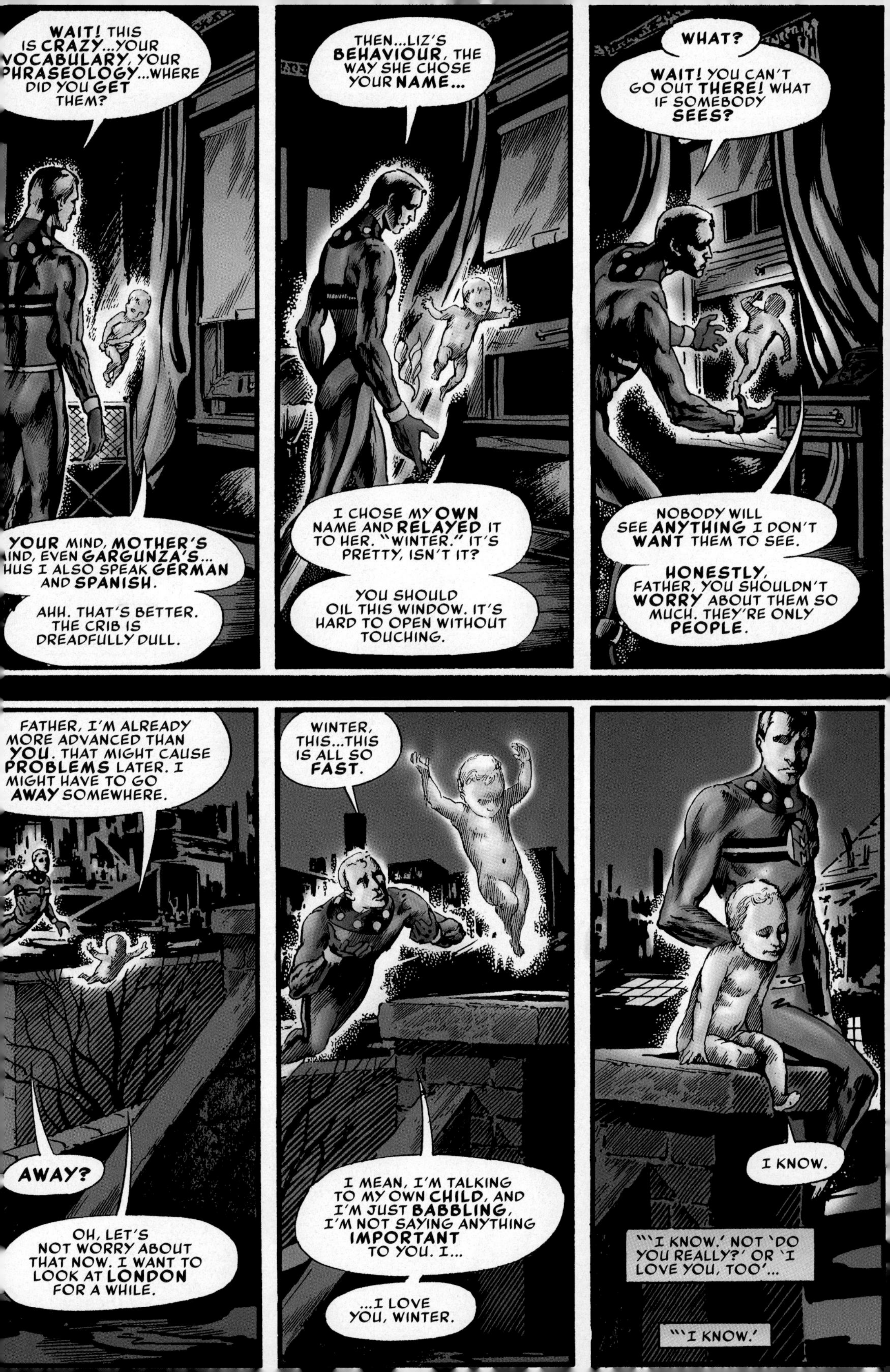
WAIT! THIS IS CRAZY...YOUR VOCABULARY, YOUR PHRASEOLOGY...WHERE DID YOU GET THEM?
YOUR MIND, MOTHER'S MIND, EVEN GARGUNZA'S... THUS I ALSO SPEAK GERMAN AND SPANISH.
AHH. THAT'S BETTER. THE CRIB IS DREADFULLY DULL.
THEN...LIZ'S BEHAVIOUR, THE WAY SHE CHOSE YOUR NAME...
I CHOSE MY OWN NAME AND RELAYED IT TO HER. "WINTER." IT'S PRETTY, ISN'T IT?
YOU SHOULD OIL THIS WINDOW. IT'S HARD TO OPEN WITHOUT TOUCHING.
WHAT?
WAIT! YOU CAN'T GO OUT THERE! WHAT IF SOMEBODY SEES?
NOBODY WILL SEE ANYTHING I DON'T WANT THEM TO SEE.
HONESTLY, FATHER, YOU SHOULDN'T WORRY ABOUT THEM SO MUCH. THEY'RE ONLY PEOPLE.
FATHER, I'M ALREADY MORE ADVANCED THAN YOU. THAT MIGHT CAUSE PROBLEMS LATER. I MIGHT HAVE TO GO AWAY SOMEWHERE.
AWAY?
OH, LET'S NOT WORRY ABOUT THAT NOW. I WANT TO LOOK AT LONDON FOR A WHILE.
WINTER, THIS...THIS IS ALL SO FAST.
I MEAN, I'M TALKING TO MY OWN CHILD, AND I'M JUST BABBLING, I'M NOT SAYING ANYTHING IMPORTANT TO YOU. I...
...I LOVE YOU, WINTER.
I KNOW.
"'I KNOW.' NOT 'DO YOU REALLY?' OR 'I LOVE YOU, TOO'...
"'I KNOW.'

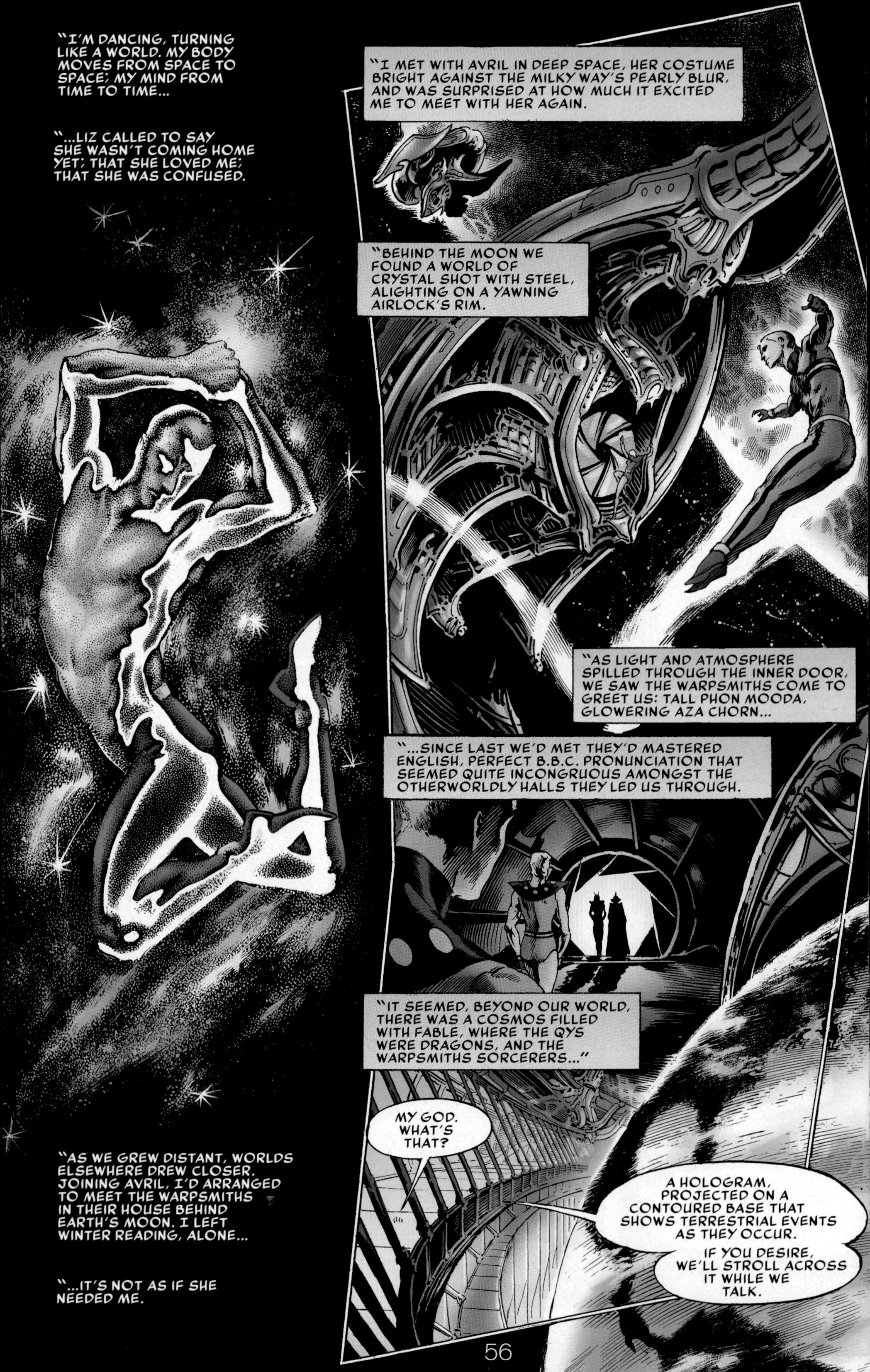
"I'M DANCING, TURNING LIKE A WORLD. MY BODY MOVES FROM SPACE TO SPACE; MY MIND FROM TIME TO TIME...
"...LIZ CALLED TO SAY SHE WASN'T COMING HOME YET; THAT SHE LOVED ME; THAT SHE WAS CONFUSED.
"AS WE GREW DISTANT, WORLDS ELSEWHERE DREW CLOSER. JOINING AVRIL, I'D ARRANGED TO MEET THE WARPSMITHS IN THEIR HOUSE BEHIND EARTH'S MOON. I LEFT WINTER READING, ALONE...
"...IT'S NOT AS IF SHE NEEDED ME.
"I MET WITH AVRIL IN DEEP SPACE, HER COSTUME BRIGHT AGAINST THE MILKY WAY'S PEARLY BLUR, AND WAS SURPRISED AT HOW MUCH IT EXCITED ME TO MEET WITH HER AGAIN.
"BEHIND THE MOON WE FOUND A WORLD OF CRYSTAL SHOT WITH STEEL, ALIGHTING ON A YAWNING AIRLOCK'S RIM.
"AS LIGHT AND ATMOSPHERE SPILLED THROUGH THE INNER DOOR, WE SAW THE WARPSMITHS COME TO GREET US: TALL PHON MOODA, GLOWERING AZA CHORN...
"...SINCE LAST WE'D MET THEY'D MASTERED ENGLISH, PERFECT B.B.C. PRONUNCIATION THAT SEEMED QUITE INCONGRUOUS AMONGST THE OTHERWORLDLY HALLS THEY LED US THROUGH.
"IT SEEMED, BEYOND OUR WORLD, THERE WAS A COSMOS FILLED WITH FABLE, WHERE THE QYS WERE DRAGONS, AND THE WARPSMITHS SORCERERS..."
MY GOD. WHAT'S THAT?
A HOLOGRAM, PROJECTED ON A CONTOURED BASE THAT SHOWS TERRESTRIAL EVENTS AS THEY OCCUR.
IF YOU DESIRE, WE'LL STROLL ACROSS IT WHILE WE TALK.

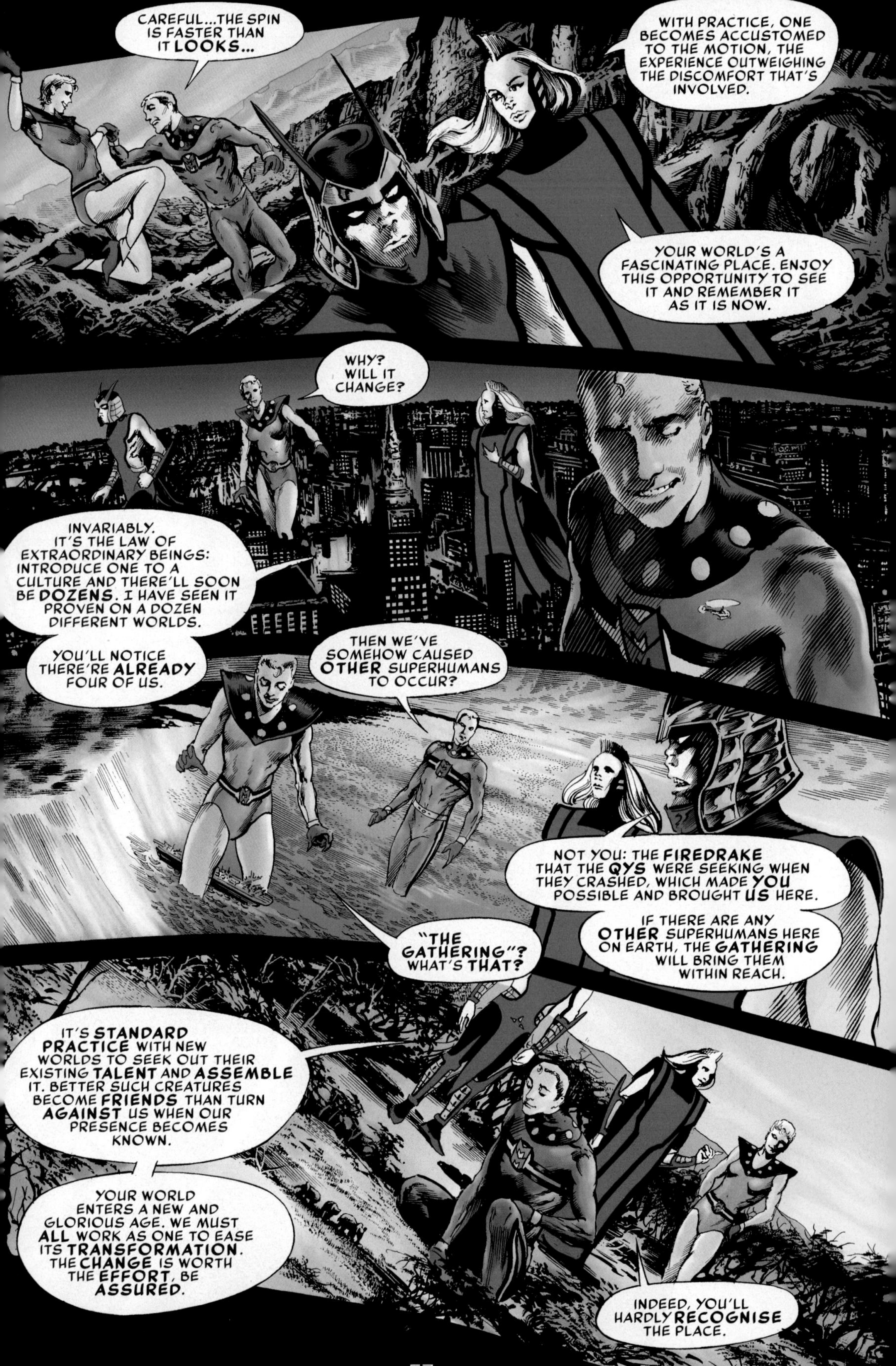

CAREFUL...THE SPIN IS FASTER THAN IT LOOKS...
WITH PRACTICE, ONE BECOMES ACCUSTOMED TO THE MOTION, THE EXPERIENCE OUTWEIGHING THE DISCOMFORT THAT'S INVOLVED.
YOUR WORLD'S A FASCINATING PLACE. ENJOY THIS OPPORTUNITY TO SEE IT AND REMEMBER IT AS IT IS NOW.
WHY? WILL IT CHANGE?
INVARIABLY. IT'S THE LAW OF EXTRAORDINARY BEINGS: INTRODUCE ONE TO A CULTURE AND THERE'LL SOON BE DOZENS. I HAVE SEEN IT PROVEN ON A DOZEN DIFFERENT WORLDS.
YOU'LL NOTICE THERE'RE ALREADY FOUR OF US.
THEN WE'VE SOMEHOW CAUSED OTHER SUPERHUMANS TO OCCUR?
NOT YOU: THE FIREDRAKE THAT THE QYS WERE SEEKING WHEN THEY CRASHED, WHICH MADE YOU POSSIBLE AND BROUGHT US HERE.
IF THERE ARE ANY OTHER SUPERHUMANS HERE ON EARTH, THE GATHERING WILL BRING THEM WITHIN REACH.
"THE GATHERING"? WHAT'S THAT?
IT'S STANDARD PRACTICE WITH NEW WORLDS TO SEEK OUT THEIR EXISTING TALENT AND ASSEMBLE IT. BETTER SUCH CREATURES BECOME FRIENDS THAN TURN AGAINST US WHEN OUR PRESENCE BECOMES KNOWN.
YOUR WORLD ENTERS A NEW AND GLORIOUS AGE. WE MUST ALL WORK AS ONE TO EASE ITS TRANSFORMATION. THE CHANGE IS WORTH THE EFFORT, BE ASSURED.
INDEED, YOU'LL HARDLY RECOGNISE THE PLACE.

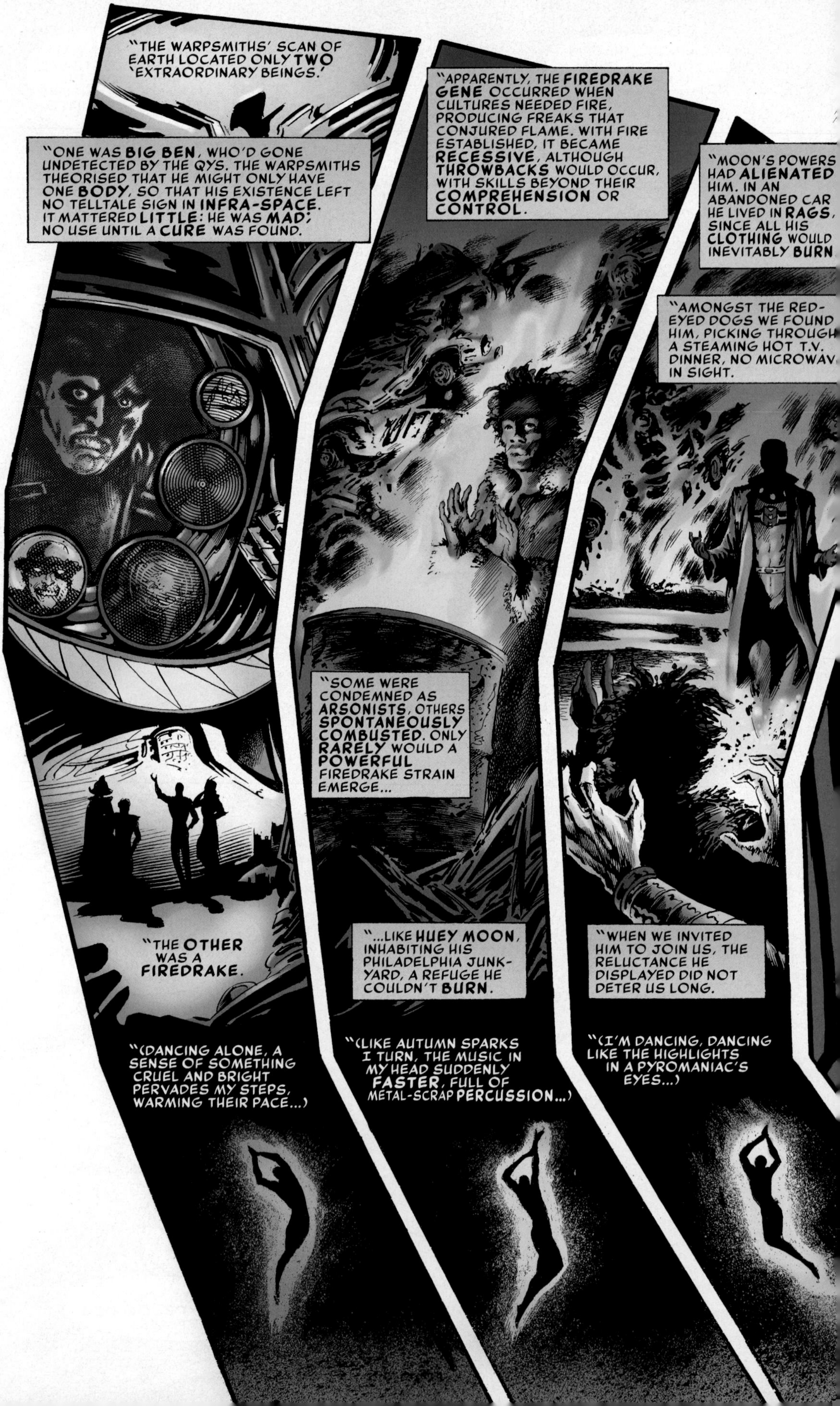
"THE WARPSMITHS' SCAN OF EARTH LOCATED ONLY TWO 'EXTRAORDINARY BEINGS.'
"ONE WAS BIG BEN, WHO'D GONE UNDETECTED BY THE QYS. THE WARPSMITHS THEORISED THAT HE MIGHT ONLY HAVE ONE BODY, SO THAT HIS EXISTENCE LEFT NO TELLTALE SIGN IN INFRA-SPACE. IT MATTERED LITTLE: HE WAS MAD; NO USE UNTIL A CURE WAS FOUND.
"THE OTHER WAS A FIREDRAKE.
"(DANCING ALONE, A SENSE OF SOMETHING CRUEL AND BRIGHT PERVADES MY STEPS, WARMING THEIR PACE...)
"APPARENTLY, THE FIREDRAKE GENE OCCURRED WHEN CULTURES NEEDED FIRE, PRODUCING FREAKS THAT CONJURED FLAME. WITH FIRE ESTABLISHED, IT BECAME RECESSIVE, ALTHOUGH THROWBACKS WOULD OCCUR, WITH SKILLS BEYOND THEIR COMPREHENSION OR CONTROL.
"SOME WERE CONDEMNED AS ARSONISTS, OTHERS SPONTANEOUSLY COMBUSTED. ONLY RARELY WOULD A POWERFUL FIREDRAKE STRAIN EMERGE...
"...LIKE HUEY MOON, INHABITING HIS PHILADELPHIA JUNK-YARD, A REFUGE HE COULDN'T BURN.
"(LIKE AUTUMN SPARKS I TURN, THE MUSIC IN MY HEAD SUDDENLY FASTER, FULL OF METAL-SCRAP PERCUSSION...)
"MOON'S POWERS HAD ALIENATED HIM. IN AN ABANDONED CAR HE LIVED IN RAGS, SINCE ALL HIS CLOTHING WOULD INEVITABLY BURN
"AMONGST THE RED-EYED DOGS WE FOUND HIM, PICKING THROUGH A STEAMING HOT T.V. DINNER, NO MICROWAV IN SIGHT.
"WHEN WE INVITED HIM TO JOIN US, THE RELUCTANCE HE DISPLAYED DID NOT DETER US LONG.
"(I'M DANCING, DANCING LIKE THE HIGHLIGHTS IN A PYROMANIAC'S EYES...)

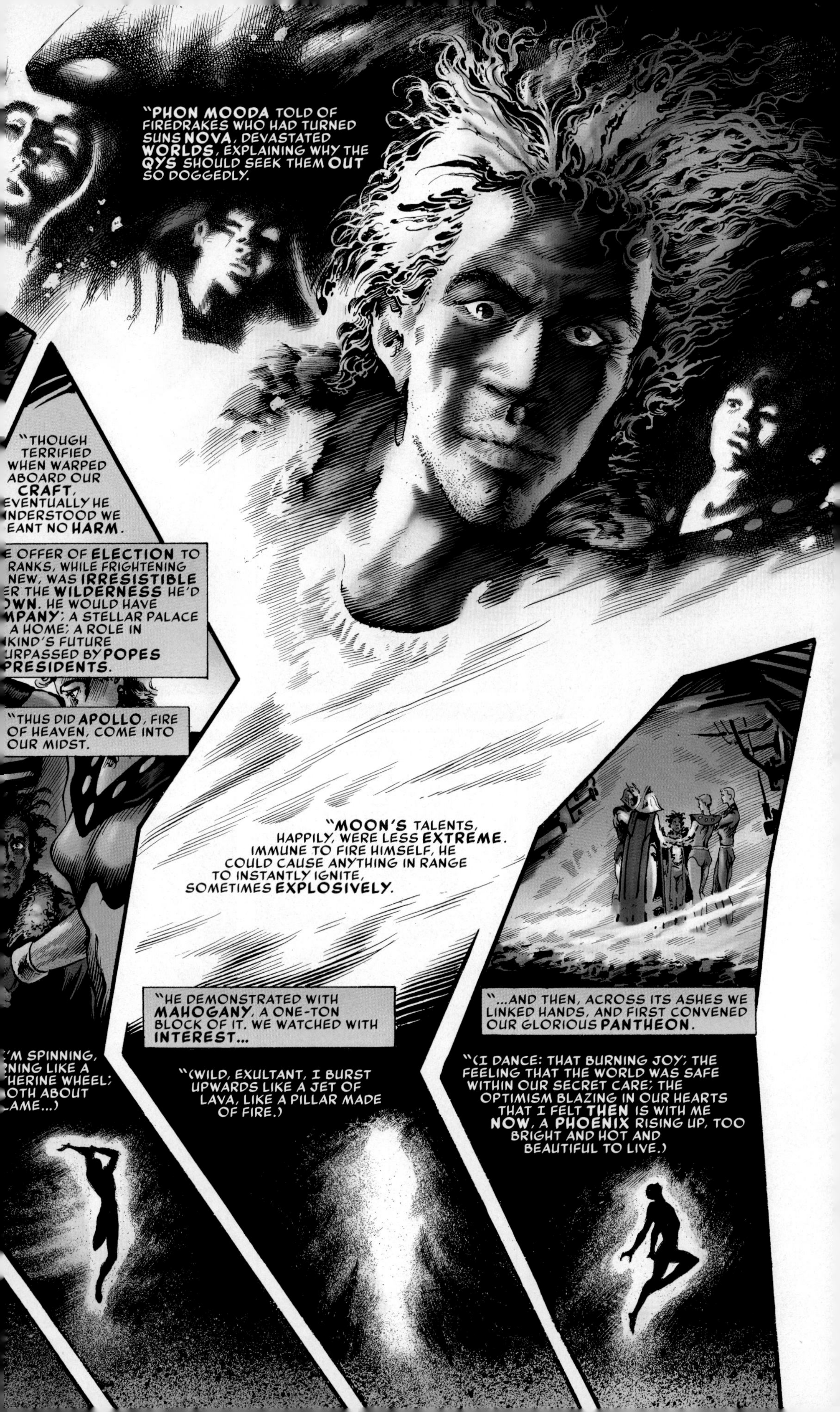
"PHON MOODA TOLD OF FIREDRAKES WHO HAD TURNED SUNS NOVA, DEVASTATED WORLDS, EXPLAINING WHY THE QYS SHOULD SEEK THEM OUT SO DOGGEDLY.
"THOUGH TERRIFIED WHEN WARPED ABOARD OUR CRAFT, EVENTUALLY HE NDERSTOOD WE EANT NO HARM.
E OFFER OF ELECTION TO RANKS, WHILE FRIGHTENING NEW, WAS IRRESISTIBLE ER THE WILDERNESS HE'D OWN. HE WOULD HAVE MPANY; A STELLAR PALACE A HOME; A ROLE IN KIND'S FUTURE URPASSED BY POPES PRESIDENTS.
"THUS DID APOLLO, FIRE OF HEAVEN, COME INTO OUR MIDST.
"MOON'S TALENTS, HAPPILY, WERE LESS EXTREME. IMMUNE TO FIRE HIMSELF, HE COULD CAUSE ANYTHING IN RANGE TO INSTANTLY IGNITE, SOMETIMES EXPLOSIVELY.
"HE DEMONSTRATED WITH MAHOGANY, A ONE-TON BLOCK OF IT. WE WATCHED WITH INTEREST...
"...AND THEN, ACROSS ITS ASHES WE LINKED HANDS, AND FIRST CONVENED OUR GLORIOUS PANTHEON.
'M SPINNING, RNING LIKE A HERINE WHEEL; OTH ABOUT AME...)
"(WILD, EXULTANT, I BURST UPWARDS LIKE A JET OF LAVA, LIKE A PILLAR MADE OF FIRE.)
"(I DANCE: THAT BURNING JOY; THE FEELING THAT THE WORLD WAS SAFE WITHIN OUR SECRET CARE; THE OPTIMISM BLAZING IN OUR HEARTS THAT I FELT THEN IS WITH ME NOW, A PHOENIX RISING UP, TOO BRIGHT AND HOT AND BEAUTIFUL TO LIVE.)

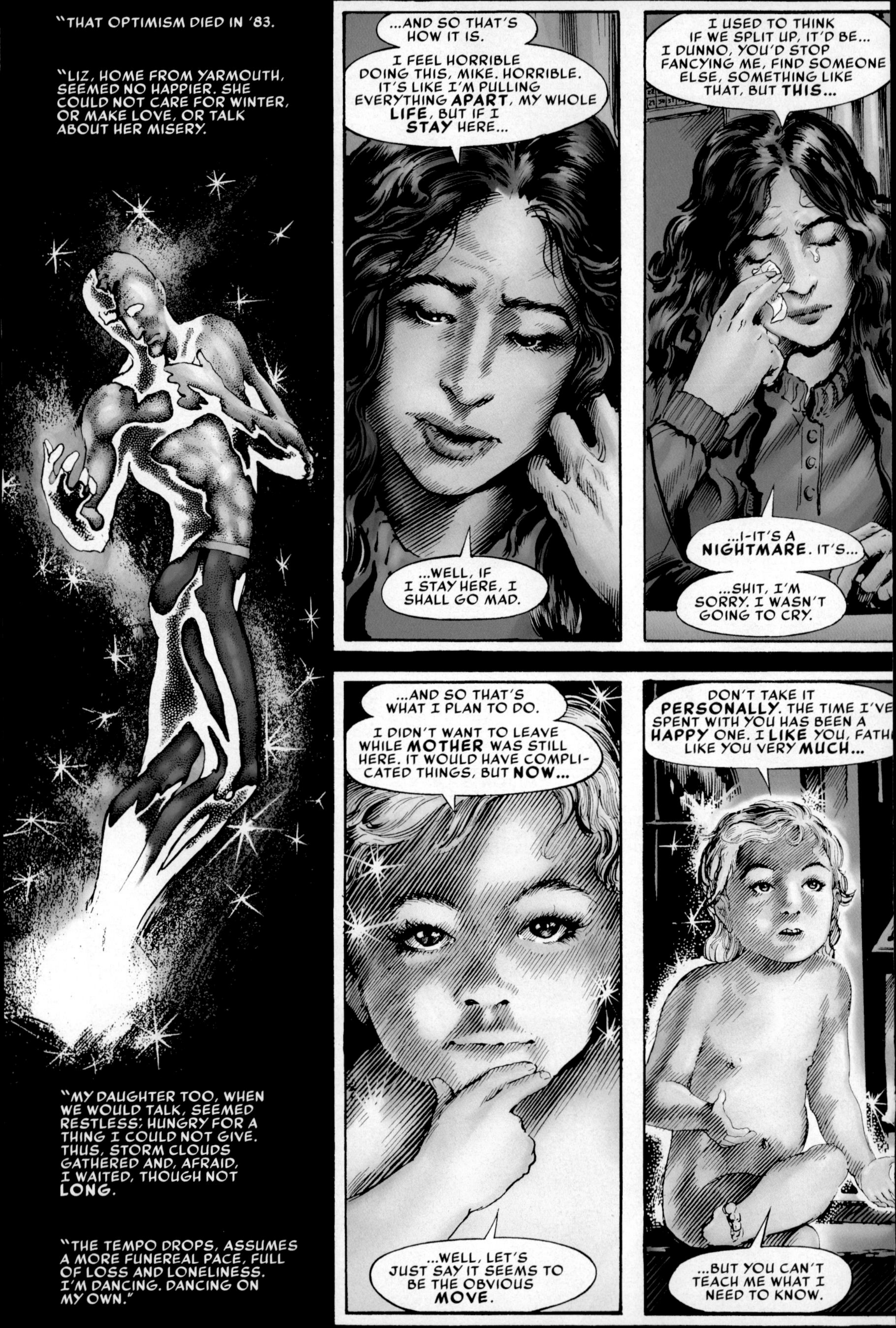
"THAT OPTIMISM DIED IN '83.
"LIZ, HOME FROM YARMOUTH, SEEMED NO HAPPIER. SHE COULD NOT CARE FOR WINTER, OR MAKE LOVE, OR TALK ABOUT HER MISERY.
...AND SO THAT'S HOW IT IS.
I FEEL HORRIBLE DOING THIS, MIKE. HORRIBLE. IT'S LIKE I'M PULLING EVERYTHING **APART**, MY WHOLE **LIFE**, BUT IF I **STAY** HERE...
...WELL, IF I STAY HERE, I SHALL GO MAD.
I USED TO THINK IF WE SPLIT UP, IT'D BE... I DUNNO, YOU'D STOP FANCYING ME, FIND SOMEONE ELSE, SOMETHING LIKE THAT, BUT **THIS**...
...I-IT'S A **NIGHTMARE**. IT'S...
...SHIT, I'M SORRY. I WASN'T GOING TO CRY.
"MY DAUGHTER TOO, WHEN WE WOULD TALK, SEEMED RESTLESS; HUNGRY FOR A THING I COULD NOT GIVE. THUS, STORM CLOUDS GATHERED AND, AFRAID, I WAITED, THOUGH NOT **LONG**.
"THE TEMPO DROPS, ASSUMES A MORE FUNEREAL PACE, FULL OF LOSS AND LONELINESS. I'M DANCING. DANCING ON MY OWN."
...AND SO THAT'S WHAT I PLAN TO DO.
I DIDN'T WANT TO LEAVE WHILE **MOTHER** WAS STILL HERE. IT WOULD HAVE COMPLICATED THINGS, BUT **NOW**...
...WELL, LET'S JUST SAY IT SEEMS TO BE THE OBVIOUS **MOVE**.
DON'T TAKE IT **PERSONALLY**. THE TIME I'VE SPENT WITH YOU HAS BEEN A **HAPPY** ONE. I **LIKE** YOU, FATH LIKE YOU VERY **MUCH**...
...BUT YOU CAN'T TEACH ME WHAT I NEED TO KNOW.

IT'S JUST, I DON'T **BELONG** HERE ANYMORE, WITH YOU AND WINTER. YOU'RE **BEYOND** ME.

EVEN SLEEPING WITH YOU, IT FEELS **WRONG**, LIKE **BEASTIALITY**, LIKE I'M AN **ANIMAL** AND YOU'RE...OH, I DON'T KNOW...A HIGHER **SPECIES**.

LOOK, I... I BETTER GO. MY TRAIN'S AT FOUR. I'LL BE IN TOUCH. I'LL WRITE SOMETIME, AND...

...AND I'M SORRY, MIKE. I'M SORRY FOR US ALL.

THE **QYS**, CONVERSELY, HAVE USED VARIOUS SUPERHUMAN FORMS FOR **CENTURIES**. THEIR INSIGHTS WILL PROVIDE THE EDUCATION I REQUIRE.

IF LIGHTSPEED IS **SURPASSABLE**, I SHOULD BE THERE WITHIN THE **YEAR**. IF **NOT**...WELL, THEN, IT MAY TAKE SLIGHTLY **LONGER**.

SOMEDAY, WHEN I'M **BACK**, I'LL TEACH YOU ALL THE THINGS I'VE **LEARNED**. UNTIL THEN, KEEP YOURSELF IN **HEALTH**...

...AND FATHER, DO NOT LOOK SO **SAD**.

IT'S SUCH A LOVELY UNIVERSE.

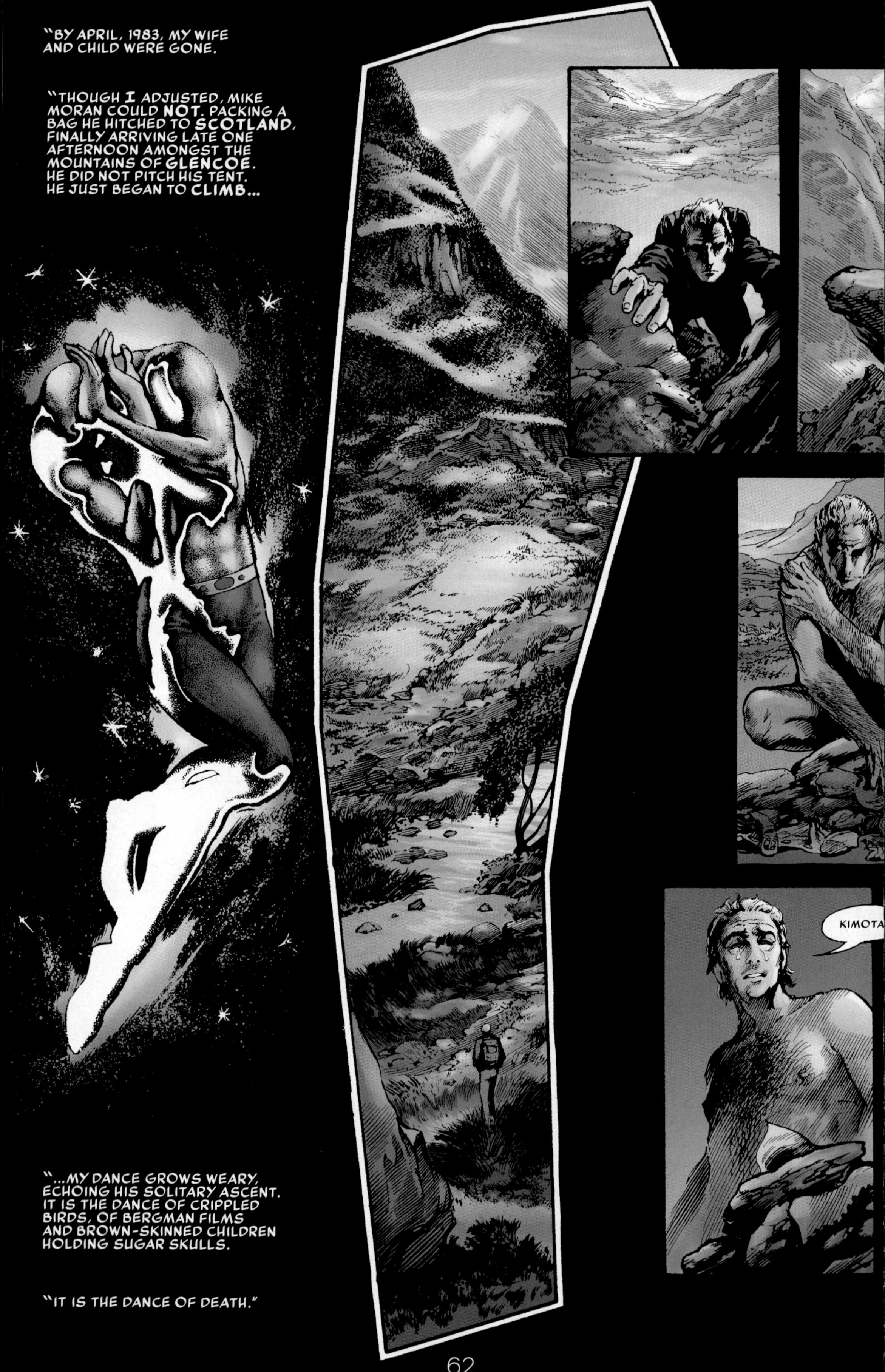
"BY APRIL, 1983, MY WIFE AND CHILD WERE GONE.
"THOUGH I ADJUSTED, MIKE MORAN COULD NOT. PACKING A BAG HE HITCHED TO SCOTLAND, FINALLY ARRIVING LATE ONE AFTERNOON AMONGST THE MOUNTAINS OF GLENCOE. HE DID NOT PITCH HIS TENT. HE JUST BEGAN TO CLIMB...
"...MY DANCE GROWS WEARY, ECHOING HIS SOLITARY ASCENT. IT IS THE DANCE OF CRIPPLED BIRDS, OF BERGMAN FILMS AND BROWN-SKINNED CHILDREN HOLDING SUGAR SKULLS.
"IT IS THE DANCE OF DEATH."
KIMOTA

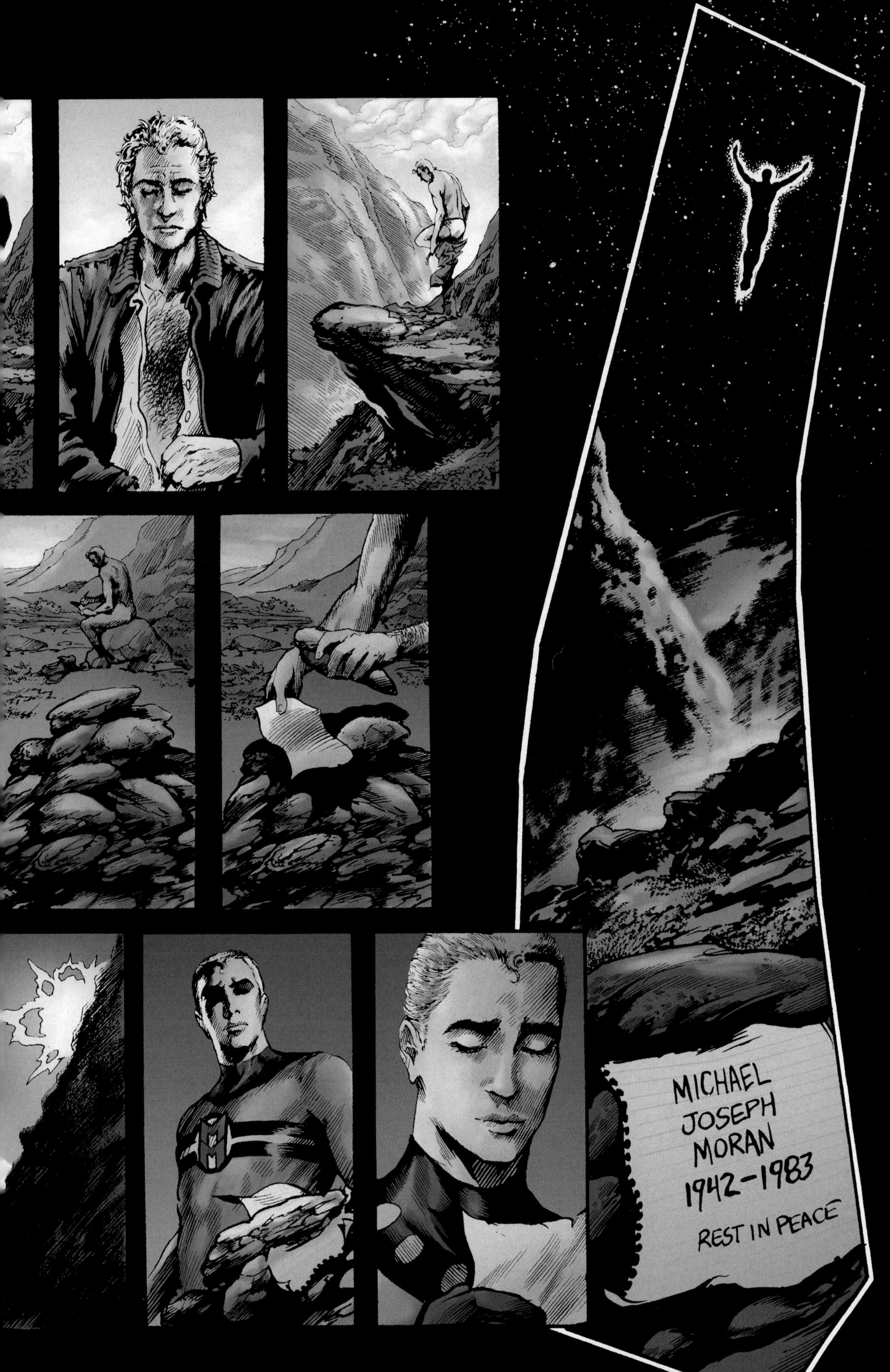
MICHAEL
JOSEPH
MORAN
1942-1983
REST IN PEACE

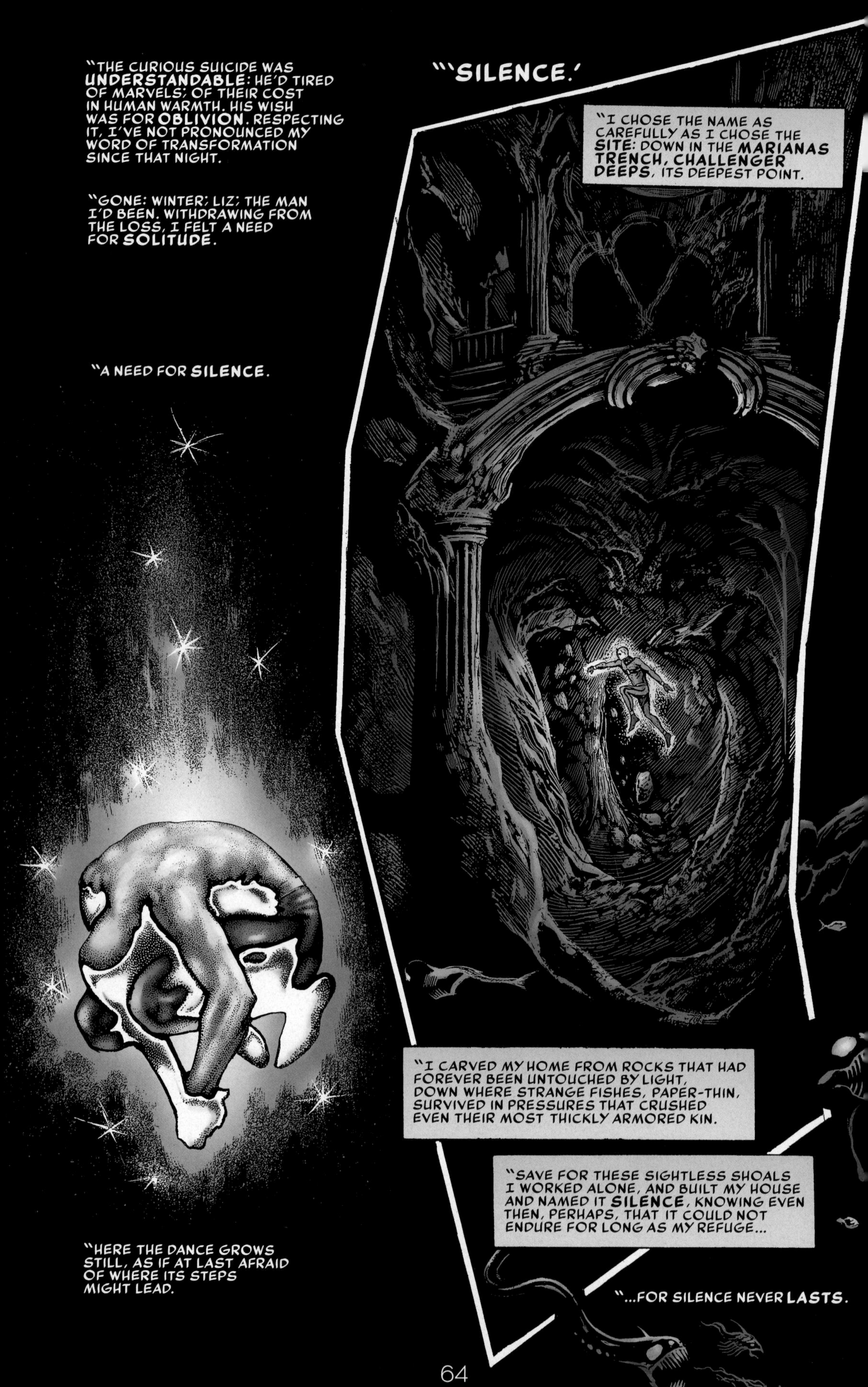
"THE CURIOUS SUICIDE WAS UNDERSTANDABLE: HE'D TIRED OF MARVELS; OF THEIR COST IN HUMAN WARMTH. HIS WISH WAS FOR OBLIVION. RESPECTING IT, I'VE NOT PRONOUNCED MY WORD OF TRANSFORMATION SINCE THAT NIGHT.
"GONE: WINTER; LIZ; THE MAN I'D BEEN. WITHDRAWING FROM THE LOSS, I FELT A NEED FOR SOLITUDE.
"A NEED FOR SILENCE.
"HERE THE DANCE GROWS STILL, AS IF AT LAST AFRAID OF WHERE ITS STEPS MIGHT LEAD.
"'SILENCE.'
"I CHOSE THE NAME AS CAREFULLY AS I CHOSE THE SITE: DOWN IN THE MARIANAS TRENCH, CHALLENGER DEEPS, ITS DEEPEST POINT.
"I CARVED MY HOME FROM ROCKS THAT HAD FOREVER BEEN UNTOUCHED BY LIGHT, DOWN WHERE STRANGE FISHES, PAPER-THIN, SURVIVED IN PRESSURES THAT CRUSHED EVEN THEIR MOST THICKLY ARMORED KIN.
"SAVE FOR THESE SIGHTLESS SHOALS I WORKED ALONE, AND BUILT MY HOUSE AND NAMED IT SILENCE, KNOWING EVEN THEN, PERHAPS, THAT IT COULD NOT ENDURE FOR LONG AS MY REFUGE...
"...FOR SILENCE NEVER LASTS.

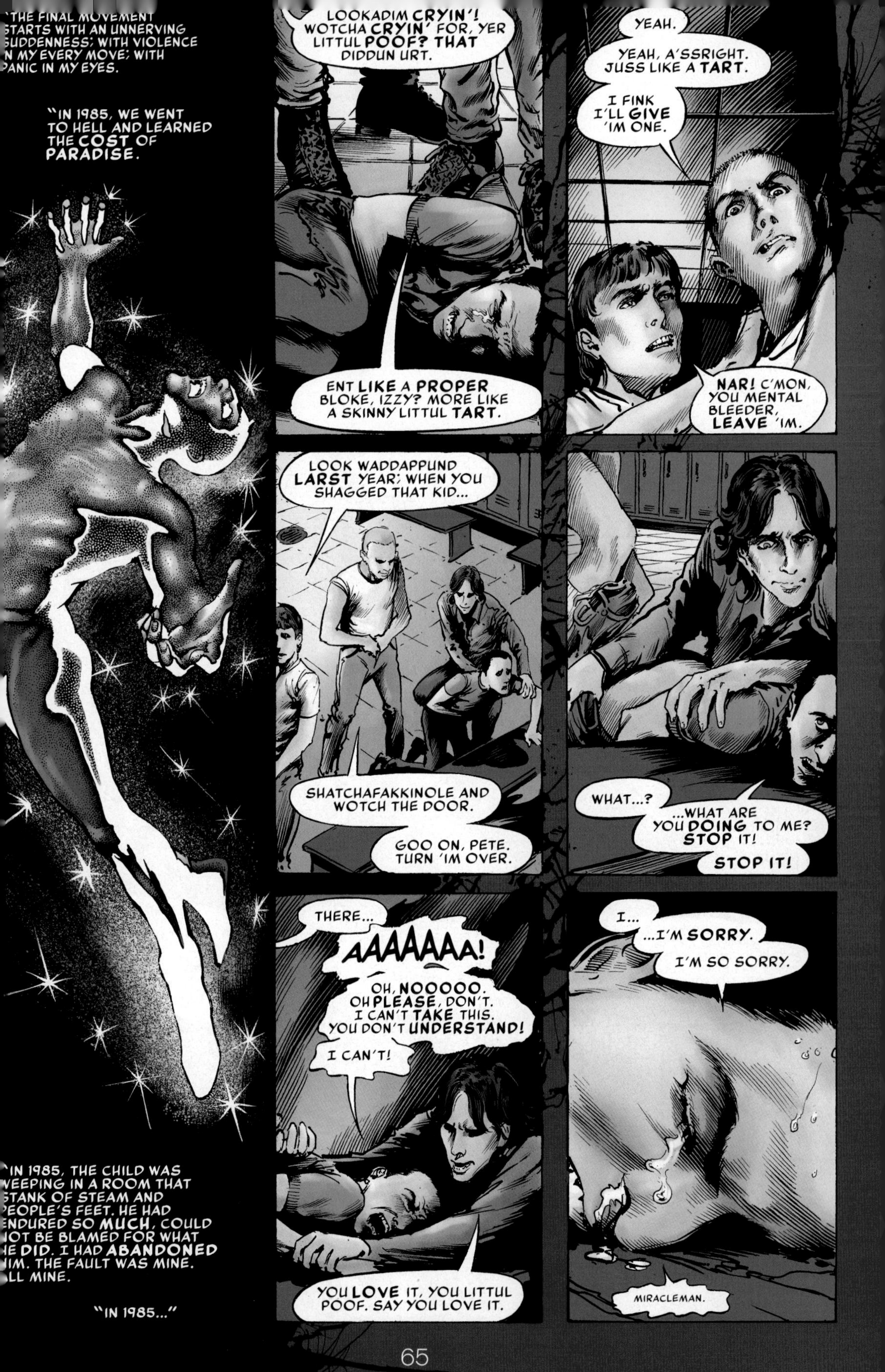
"THE FINAL MOVEMENT
STARTS WITH AN UNNERVING
SUDDENNESS; WITH VIOLENCE
IN MY EVERY MOVE; WITH
PANIC IN MY EYES.
"IN 1985, WE WENT TO HELL AND LEARNED THE COST OF PARADISE.
LOOKADIM CRYIN'! WOTCHA CRYIN' FOR, YER LITTUL POOF? THAT DIDDUN URT.
ENT LIKE A PROPER BLOKE, IZZY? MORE LIKE A SKINNY LITTUL TART.
YEAH.
YEAH, A'SSRIGHT. JUSS LIKE A TART.
I FINK I'LL GIVE 'IM ONE.
NAR! C'MON, YOU MENTAL BLEEDER, LEAVE 'IM.
LOOK WADDAPPUND LARST YEAR; WHEN YOU SHAGGED THAT KID...
SHATCHAFAKKINOLE AND WOTCH THE DOOR.
GOO ON, PETE. TURN 'IM OVER.
WHAT...?
...WHAT ARE YOU DOING TO ME? STOP IT!
STOP IT!
THERE...
AAAAAAA!
OH, NOOOOO. OH PLEASE, DON'T. I CAN'T TAKE THIS. YOU DON'T UNDERSTAND!
I CAN'T!
YOU LOVE IT, YOU LITTUL POOF. SAY YOU LOVE IT.
I...
...I'M SORRY.
I'M SO SORRY.
MIRACLEMAN.
"IN 1985, THE CHILD WAS
WEEPING IN A ROOM THAT
STANK OF STEAM AND
PEOPLE'S FEET. HE HAD
ENDURED SO MUCH, COULD
NOT BE BLAMED FOR WHAT
HE DID. I HAD ABANDONED
HIM. THE FAULT WAS MINE.
ALL MINE.
"IN 1985..."

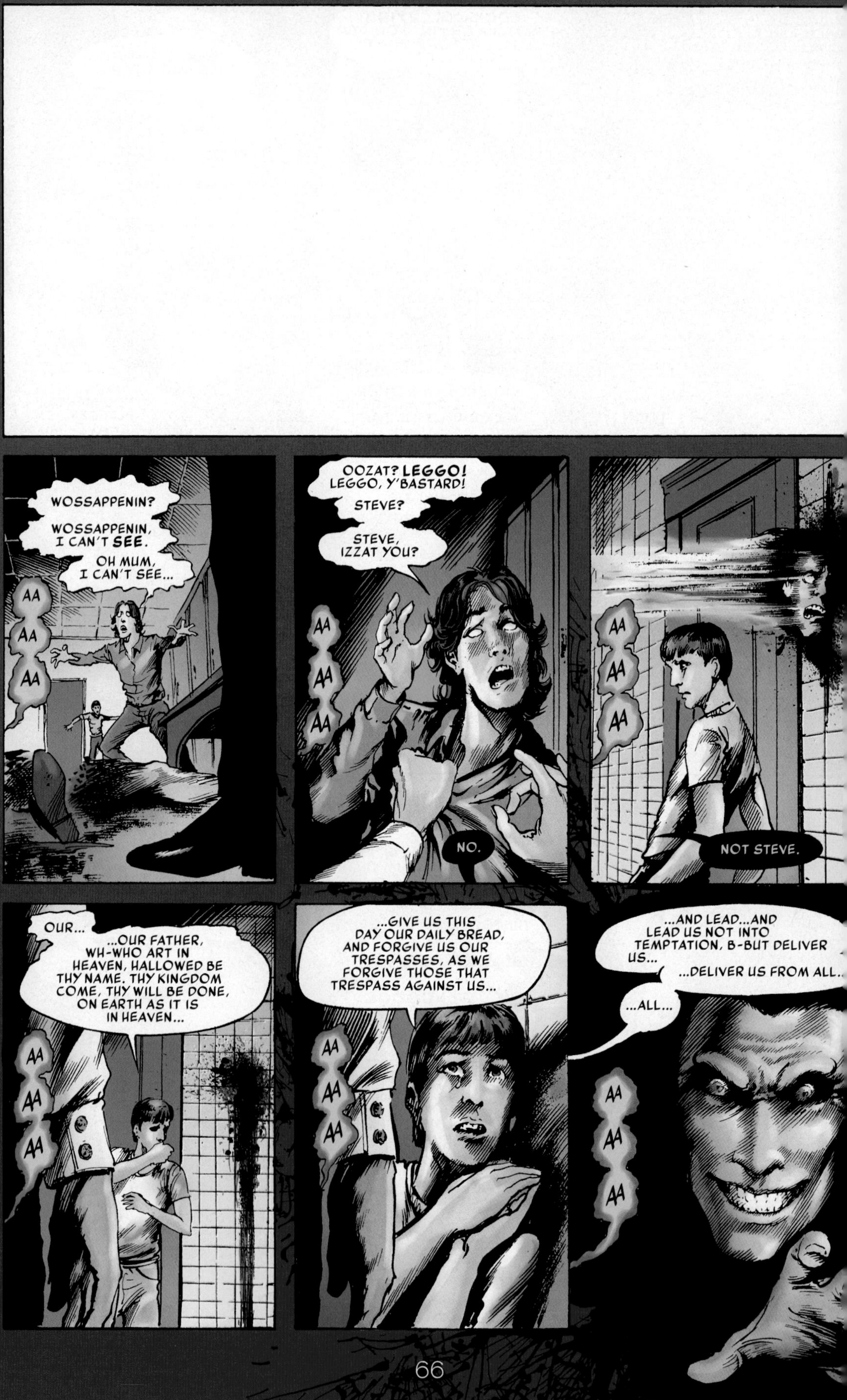
WOSSAPPENIN?
WOSSAPPENIN, I CAN'T SEE.
OH MUM, I CAN'T SEE...
AA AA AA
OOZAT? LEGGO! LEGGO, Y'BASTARD!
STEVE?
STEVE, IZZAT YOU?
AA AA AA
NO.
AA AA AA
NOT STEVE.
OUR...
...OUR FATHER, WH-WHO ART IN HEAVEN, HALLOWED BE THY NAME. THY KINGDOM COME, THY WILL BE DONE, ON EARTH AS IT IS IN HEAVEN...
AA AA AA
...GIVE US THIS DAY OUR DAILY BREAD, AND FORGIVE US OUR TRESPASSES, AS WE FORGIVE THOSE THAT TRESPASS AGAINST US...
AA AA AA
...AND LEAD...AND LEAD US NOT INTO TEMPTATION, B-BUT DELIVER US...
...DELIVER US FROM ALL...
...ALL...
AA AA AA

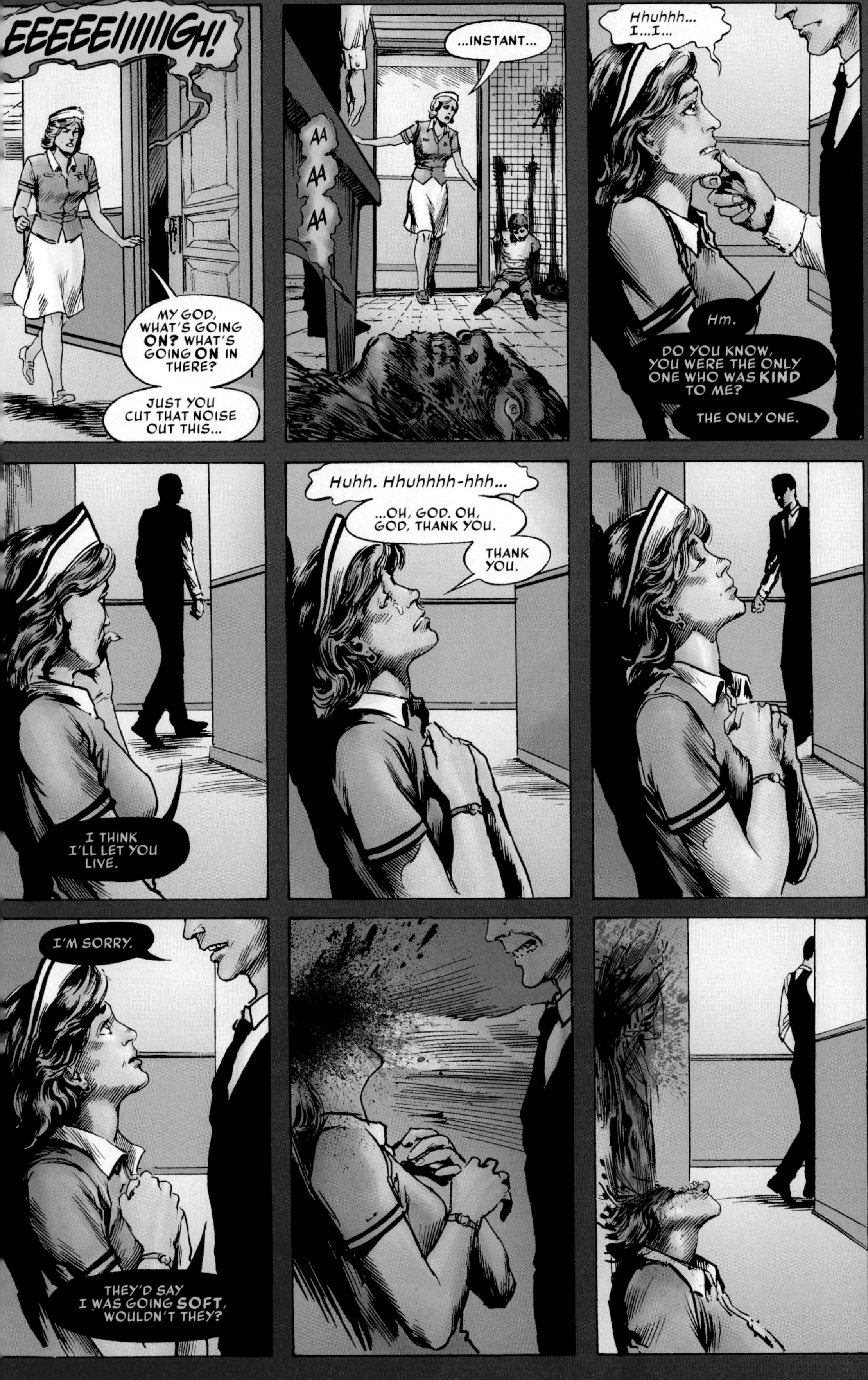
EEEEEIIIIIIGH!
MY GOD, WHAT'S GOING ON? WHAT'S GOING ON IN THERE?
JUST YOU CUT THAT NOISE OUT THIS...
...INSTANT...
AA AA AA
Hhuhhh... I...I...
Hm.
DO YOU KNOW, YOU WERE THE ONLY ONE WHO WAS KIND TO ME?
THE ONLY ONE.
I THINK I'LL LET YOU LIVE.
Huhh. Hhuhhhh-hhh...
...OH, GOD. OH, GOD, THANK YOU.
THANK YOU.
I'M SORRY.
THEY'D SAY I WAS GOING SOFT, WOULDN'T THEY?

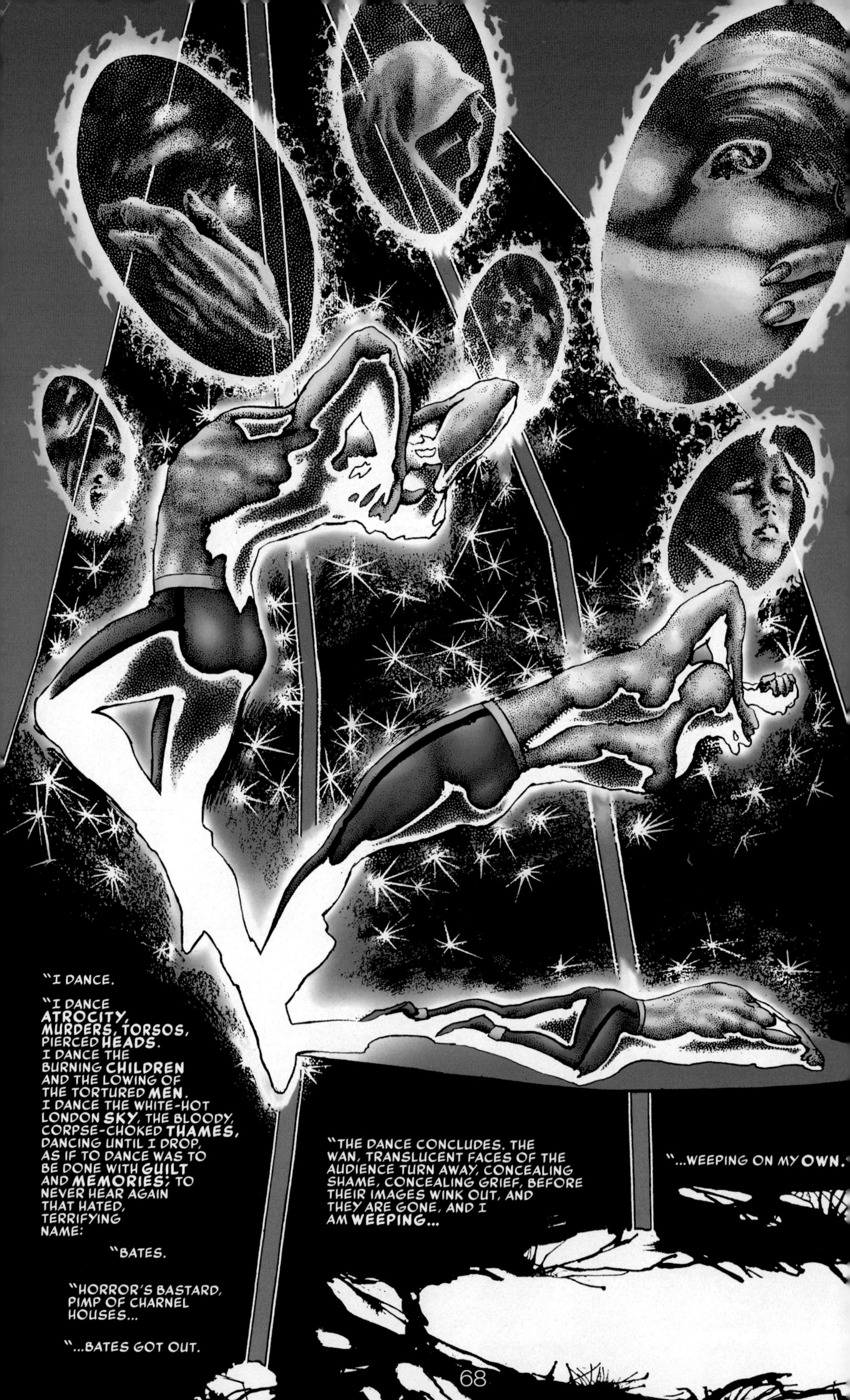
"I DANCE.
"I DANCE ATROCITY, MURDERS, TORSOS, PIERCED HEADS. I DANCE THE BURNING CHILDREN AND THE LOWING OF THE TORTURED MEN. I DANCE THE WHITE-HOT LONDON SKY, THE BLOODY, CORPSE-CHOKED THAMES, DANCING UNTIL I DROP, AS IF TO DANCE WAS TO BE DONE WITH GUILT AND MEMORIES; TO NEVER HEAR AGAIN THAT HATED, TERRIFYING NAME:
"BATES.
"HORROR'S BASTARD, PIMP OF CHARNEL HOUSES...
"...BATES GOT OUT.
"THE DANCE CONCLUDES. THE WAN, TRANSLUCENT FACES OF THE AUDIENCE TURN AWAY, CONCEALING SHAME, CONCEALING GRIEF, BEFORE THEIR IMAGES WINK OUT, AND THEY ARE GONE, AND I AM WEEPING...
"...WEEPING ON MY OWN."

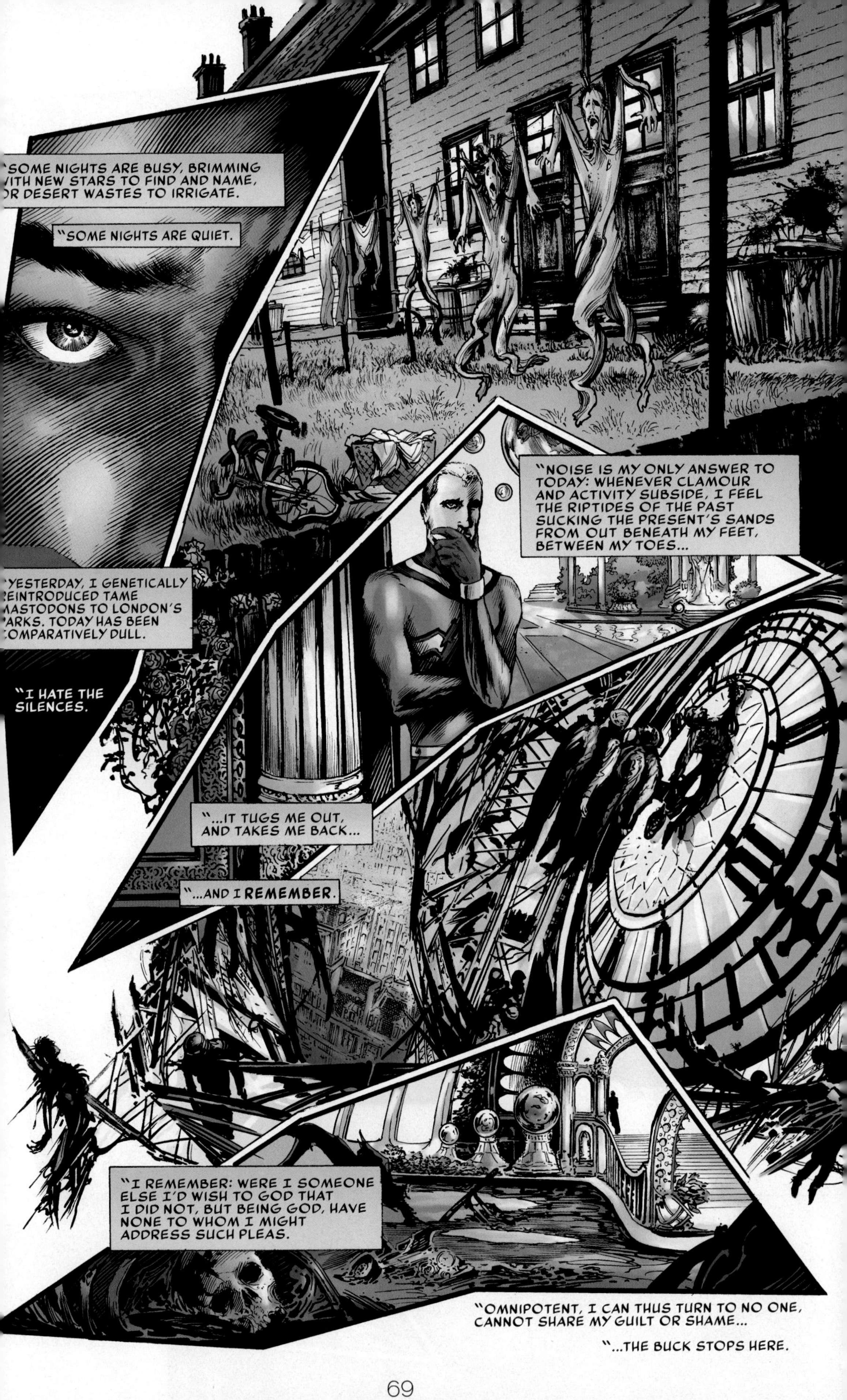
"SOME NIGHTS ARE BUSY, BRIMMING WITH NEW STARS TO FIND AND NAME, OR DESERT WASTES TO IRRIGATE.
"SOME NIGHTS ARE QUIET.
"YESTERDAY, I GENETICALLY REINTRODUCED TAME MASTODONS TO LONDON'S PARKS. TODAY HAS BEEN COMPARATIVELY DULL.
"I HATE THE SILENCES.
"NOISE IS MY ONLY ANSWER TO TODAY: WHENEVER CLAMOUR AND ACTIVITY SUBSIDE, I FEEL THE RIPTIDES OF THE PAST SUCKING THE PRESENT'S SANDS FROM OUT BENEATH MY FEET, BETWEEN MY TOES...
"...IT TUGS ME OUT, AND TAKES ME BACK...
"...AND I REMEMBER.
"I REMEMBER: WERE I SOMEONE ELSE I'D WISH TO GOD THAT I DID NOT, BUT BEING GOD, HAVE NONE TO WHOM I MIGHT ADDRESS SUCH PLEAS.
"OMNIPOTENT, I CAN THUS TURN TO NO ONE, CANNOT SHARE MY GUILT OR SHAME...
"...THE BUCK STOPS HERE.

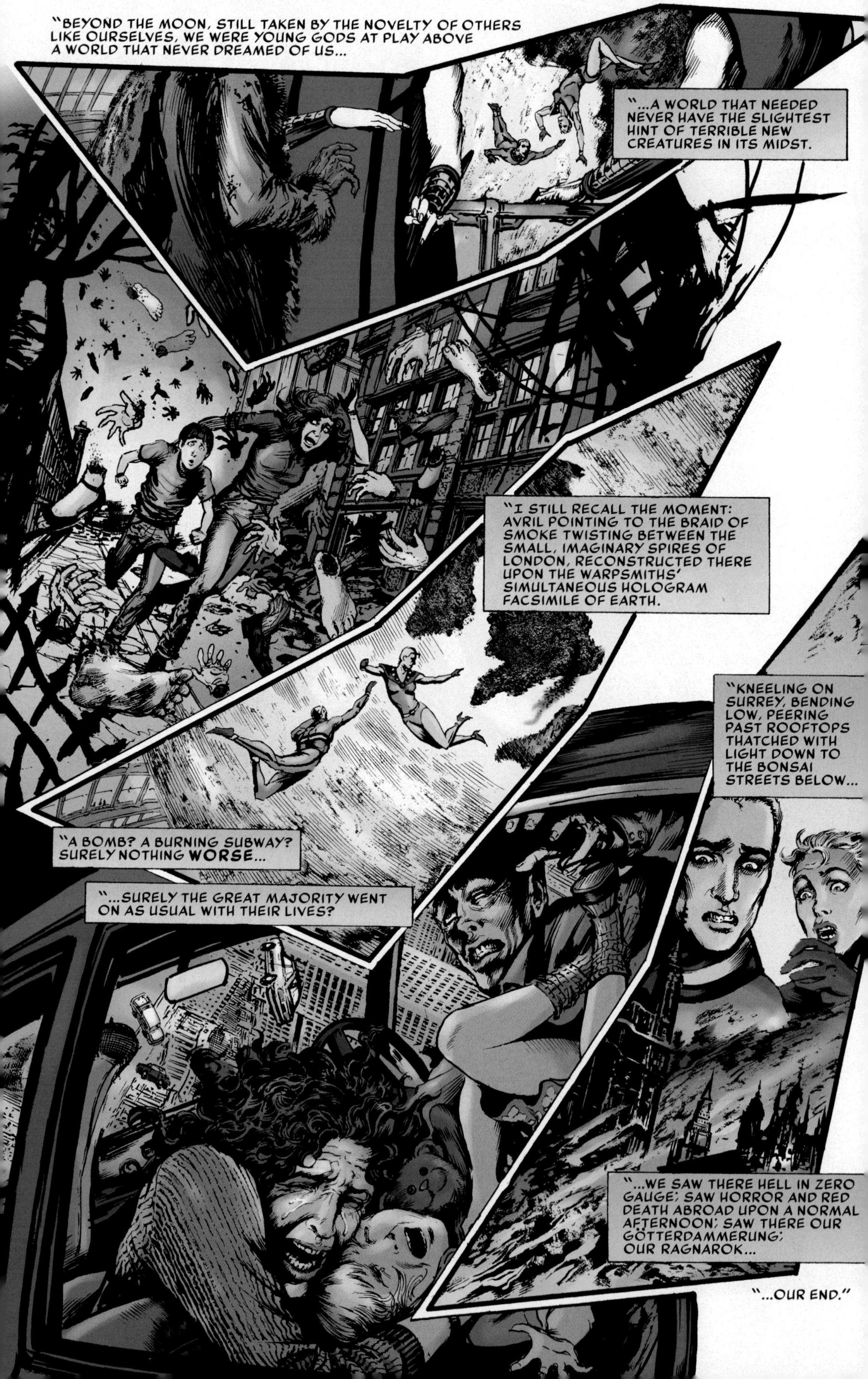
"BEYOND THE MOON, STILL TAKEN BY THE NOVELTY OF OTHERS LIKE OURSELVES, WE WERE YOUNG GODS AT PLAY ABOVE A WORLD THAT NEVER DREAMED OF US...
"...A WORLD THAT NEEDED NEVER HAVE THE SLIGHTEST HINT OF TERRIBLE NEW CREATURES IN ITS MIDST.
"I STILL RECALL THE MOMENT: AVRIL POINTING TO THE BRAID OF SMOKE TWISTING BETWEEN THE SMALL, IMAGINARY SPIRES OF LONDON, RECONSTRUCTED THERE UPON THE WARPSMITHS' SIMULTANEOUS HOLOGRAM FACSIMILE OF EARTH.
"A BOMB? A BURNING SUBWAY? SURELY NOTHING **WORSE**...
"...SURELY THE GREAT MAJORITY WENT ON AS USUAL WITH THEIR LIVES?
"KNEELING ON SURREY, BENDING LOW, PEERING PAST ROOFTOPS THATCHED WITH LIGHT DOWN TO THE BONSAI STREETS BELOW...
"...WE SAW THERE HELL IN ZERO GAUGE; SAW HORROR AND RED DEATH ABROAD UPON A NORMAL AFTERNOON; SAW THERE OUR GÖTTERDAMMERUNG; OUR RAGNAROK...
"...OUR END."

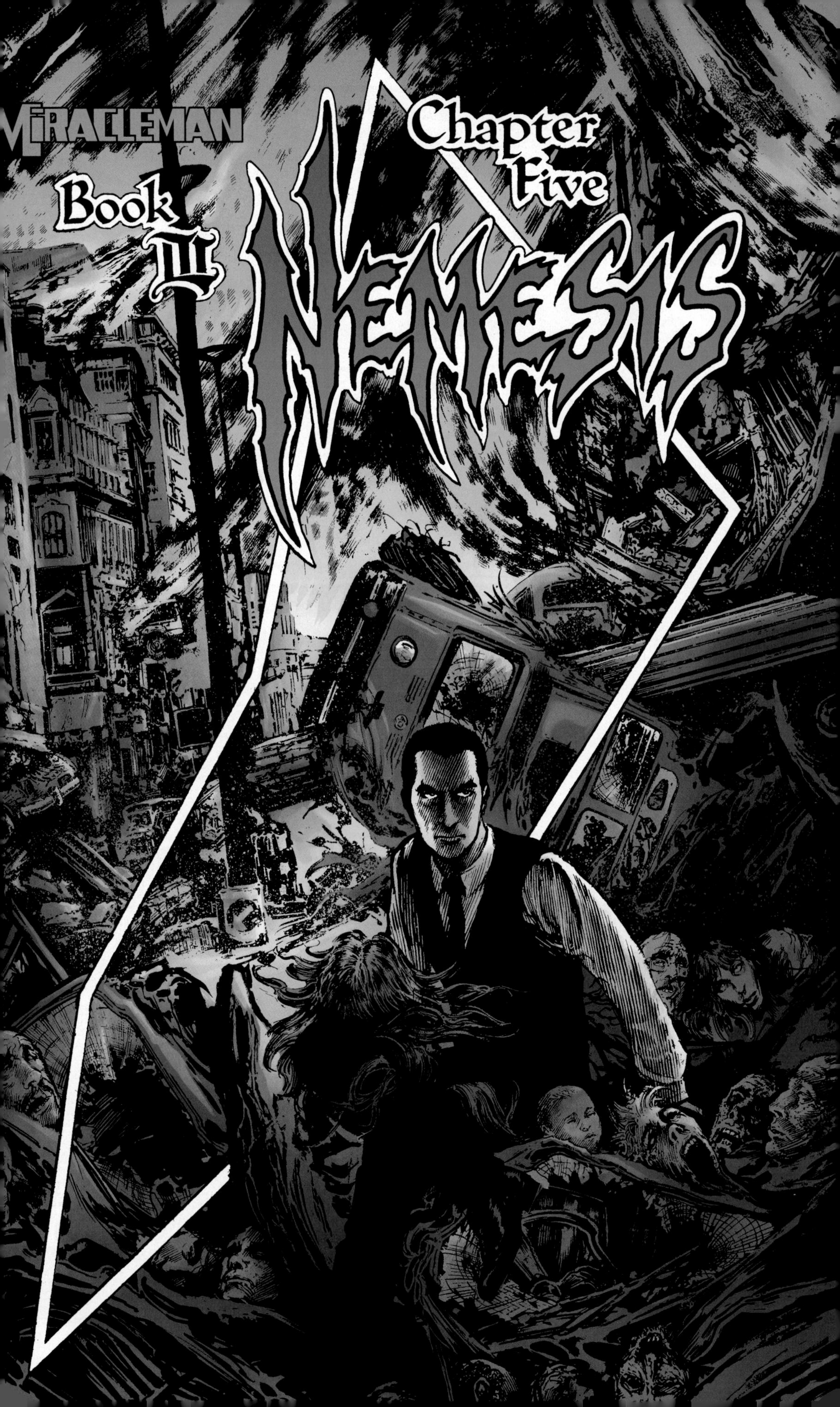

MIRACLEMAN
Book VI
Chapter Five
Nemesis

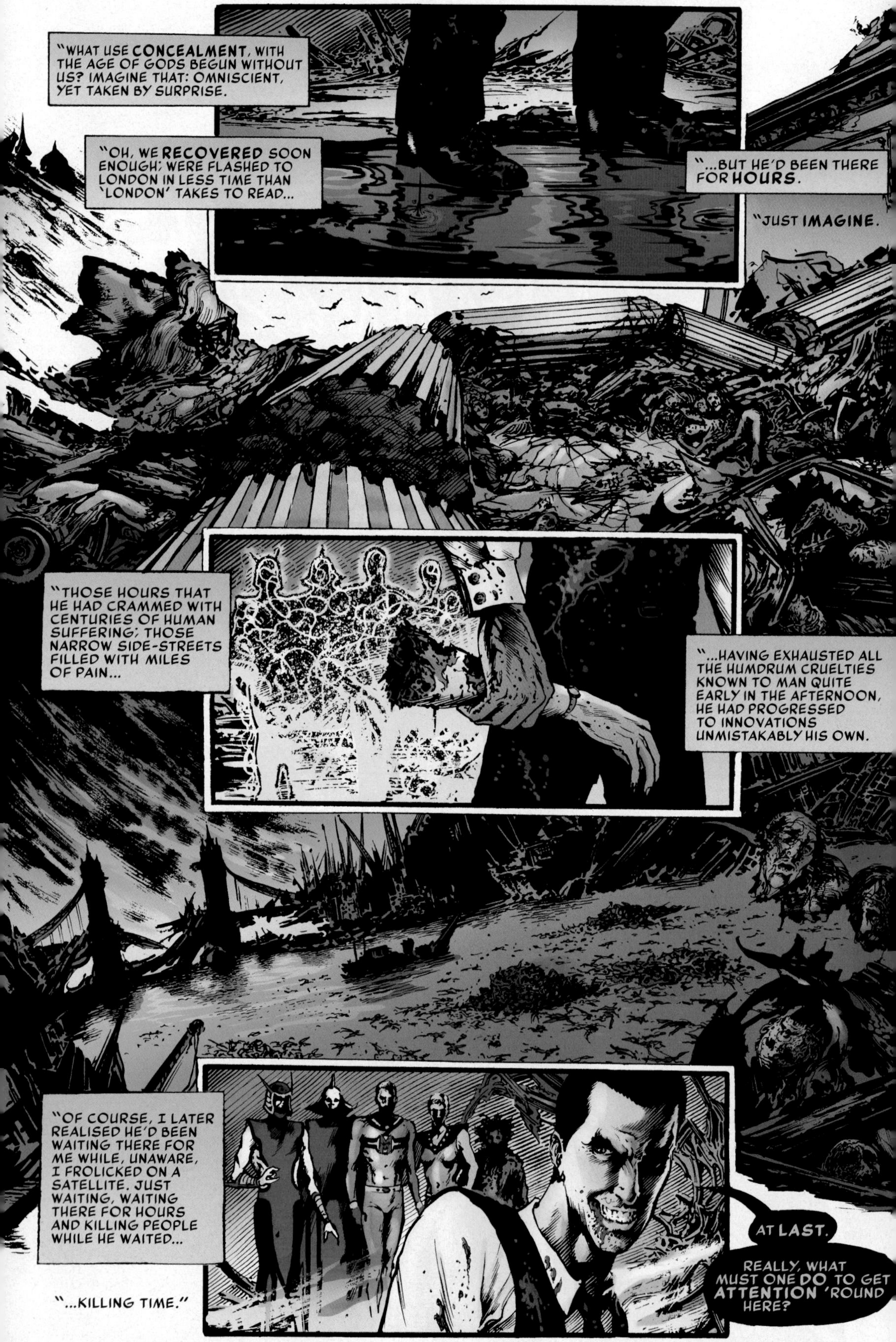
"WHAT USE CONCEALMENT, WITH THE AGE OF GODS BEGUN WITHOUT US? IMAGINE THAT: OMNISCIENT, YET TAKEN BY SURPRISE.
"OH, WE RECOVERED SOON ENOUGH; WERE FLASHED TO LONDON IN LESS TIME THAN 'LONDON' TAKES TO READ...
"...BUT HE'D BEEN THERE FOR HOURS.
"JUST IMAGINE.
"THOSE HOURS THAT HE HAD CRAMMED WITH CENTURIES OF HUMAN SUFFERING; THOSE NARROW SIDE-STREETS FILLED WITH MILES OF PAIN...
"...HAVING EXHAUSTED ALL THE HUMDRUM CRUELTIES KNOWN TO MAN QUITE EARLY IN THE AFTERNOON, HE HAD PROGRESSED TO INNOVATIONS UNMISTAKABLY HIS OWN.
"OF COURSE, I LATER REALISED HE'D BEEN WAITING THERE FOR ME WHILE, UNAWARE, I FROLICKED ON A SATELLITE. JUST WAITING, WAITING THERE FOR HOURS AND KILLING PEOPLE WHILE HE WAITED...
"...KILLING TIME."
AT LAST.
REALLY, WHAT MUST ONE DO TO GET ATTENTION 'ROUND HERE?

"AND THEN WE FOUGHT. GIVEN THE SPEED OF THOUGHT AND MOTION SHARED BY ALL THE COMBATANTS, THAT OPENING SKIRMISH TOOK BUT SECONDS...

"...SECONDS THAT ERASED THE LANDMARKS OF TWO HUNDRED YEARS; THAT BLEW THE PAST AWAY...

"...AND LAUNCHED MYTHOLOGIES THAT SHALL ENDURE UNTIL THE SUN GROWS RED, AND OVERRIPE, AND COLD.

"HE JUST ATTACKED, NOT ASKING WHO THE OTHERS WERE. I WONDERED IF HE'D EVER WOKEN FROM GARGUNZA'S DREAMS. IF HE BELIEVED THOSE SENSELESS FANTASIES WERE TRUE, WHY NOT AS WELL ACCEPT A WARPSMITH, CARING LITTLE WHENCE IT CAME...

"...AND LESS WHAT IT COULD DO?

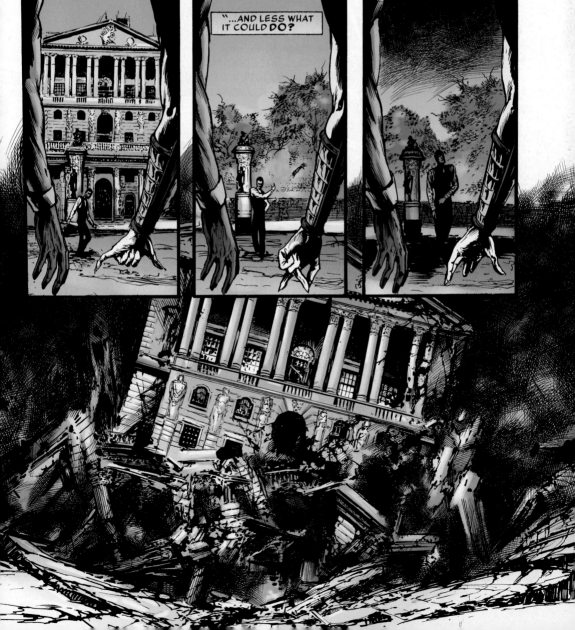

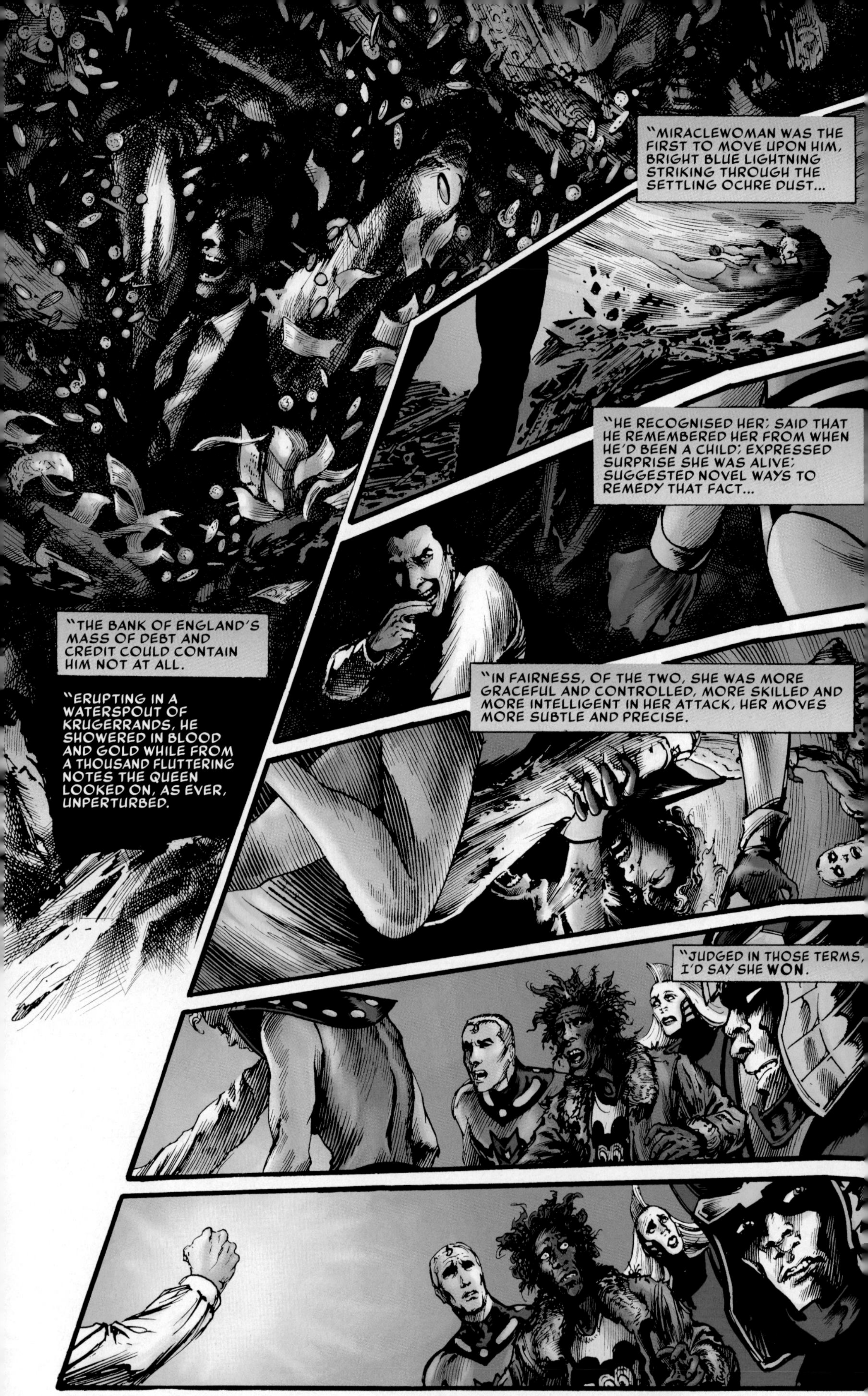
"MIRACLEWOMAN WAS THE FIRST TO MOVE UPON HIM, BRIGHT BLUE LIGHTNING STRIKING THROUGH THE SETTLING OCHRE DUST...
"HE RECOGNISED HER; SAID THAT HE REMEMBERED HER FROM WHEN HE'D BEEN A CHILD; EXPRESSED SURPRISE SHE WAS ALIVE; SUGGESTED NOVEL WAYS TO REMEDY THAT FACT...
"THE BANK OF ENGLAND'S MASS OF DEBT AND CREDIT COULD CONTAIN HIM NOT AT ALL.
"ERUPTING IN A WATERSPOUT OF KRUGERRANDS, HE SHOWERED IN BLOOD AND GOLD WHILE FROM A THOUSAND FLUTTERING NOTES THE QUEEN LOOKED ON, AS EVER, UNPERTURBED.
"IN FAIRNESS, OF THE TWO, SHE WAS MORE GRACEFUL AND CONTROLLED, MORE SKILLED AND MORE INTELLIGENT IN HER ATTACK, HER MOVES MORE SUBTLE AND PRECISE.
"JUDGED IN THOSE TERMS, I'D SAY SHE WON.

"THERE WAS NO PAUSE AND NO RESPITE. [H]E LEAPT FOR AZA CHORN, FAST AS A CHEETAH; [A]S A MAMBA; AS AN INK-BLACK THUNDERBOLT.

"YET WHEN THEY BRAG [A]MONGST THEMSELVES, [T]HE CATS AND SNAKES AND [S]HEETS OF LIGHTNING USE [O]NE ULTIMATE COMPARISON, [A]LBEIT SPARINGLY:

"'FAST AS A WARPSMITH.'

"POOR MARBLE ARCH. IT COULD [A]FFORD NO MORE RESTRAINT [T]HAN COULD THE BANK OF [E]NGLAND. WOULD THAT AZA [C]HORN HAD TELEPORTED [G]ATES ELSEWHERE AND NOT [R]EMOVED SO CHARMING AND [P]REPOSTEROUS A FOLLY [F]ROM OUR SKYLINE...

"...BUT THEN, HE COULD NOT HAVE KNOWN, NOT BEING RAISED AROUND THESE PARTS."

IT DIDN'T HOLD HIM. NOW IT'S UP TO ME...

NO, LET THE **FIREDRAKE** BUY US TIME. I MUST LOCATE A MEANS BY WHICH TO PURCHASE EXTRA **POWER**.

[I]T WILL REQUIRE A TRIP TO **HOD**, [M]Y HOMEWORLD, GALAXIES AWAY.

WHAT? BUT...

THERE. IT IS ARRANGED.

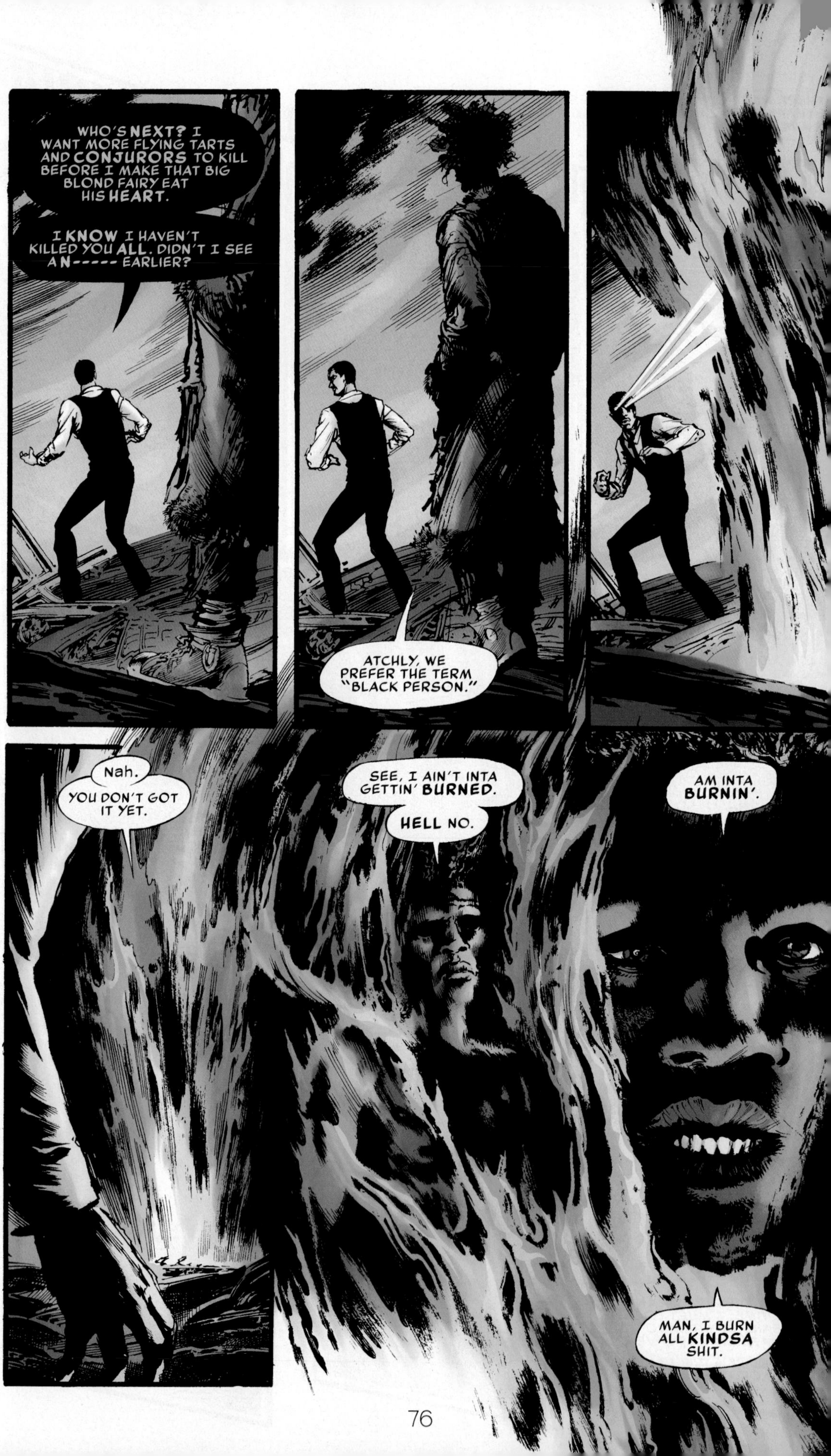
WHO'S NEXT? I WANT MORE FLYING TARTS AND CONJURORS TO KILL BEFORE I MAKE THAT BIG BLOND FAIRY EAT HIS HEART.
I KNOW I HAVEN'T KILLED YOU ALL. DIDN'T I SEE A N----- EARLIER?
ATCHLY, WE PREFER THE TERM "BLACK PERSON."
Nah.
YOU DON'T GOT IT YET.
SEE, I AIN'T INTA GETTIN' BURNED.
HELL NO.
AM INTA BURNIN'.
MAN, I BURN ALL KINDSA SHIT.

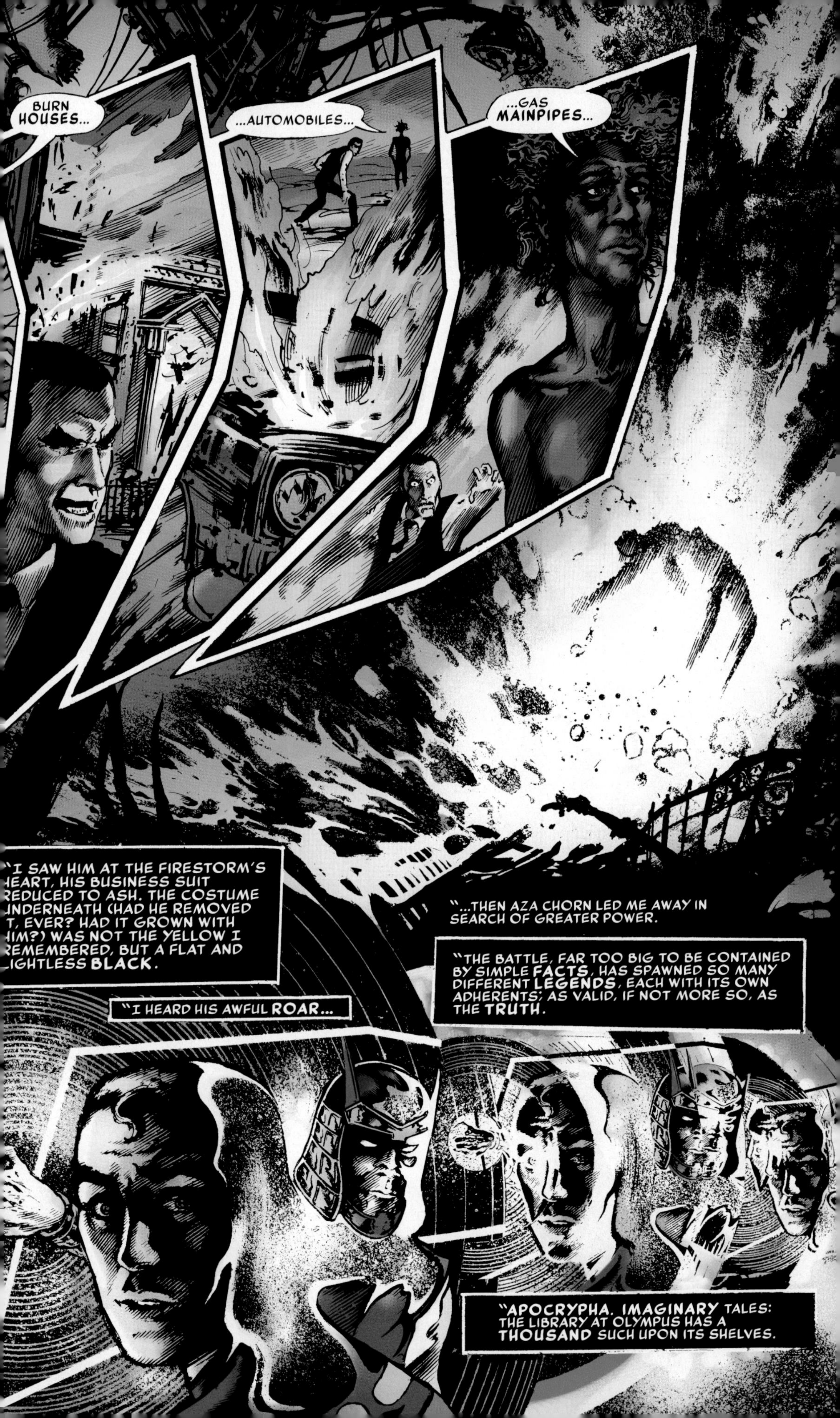

BURN HOUSES...
...AUTOMOBILES...
...GAS MAINPIPES...
"I SAW HIM AT THE FIRESTORM'S HEART, HIS BUSINESS SUIT REDUCED TO ASH. THE COSTUME UNDERNEATH (HAD HE REMOVED IT, EVER? HAD IT GROWN WITH HIM?) WAS NOT THE YELLOW I REMEMBERED, BUT A FLAT AND LIGHTLESS BLACK.
"I HEARD HIS AWFUL ROAR...
"...THEN AZA CHORN LED ME AWAY IN SEARCH OF GREATER POWER.
"THE BATTLE, FAR TOO BIG TO BE CONTAINED BY SIMPLE FACTS, HAS SPAWNED SO MANY DIFFERENT LEGENDS, EACH WITH ITS OWN ADHERENTS; AS VALID, IF NOT MORE SO, AS THE TRUTH.
"APOCRYPHA. IMAGINARY TALES: THE LIBRARY AT OLYMPUS HAS A THOUSAND SUCH UPON ITS SHELVES.

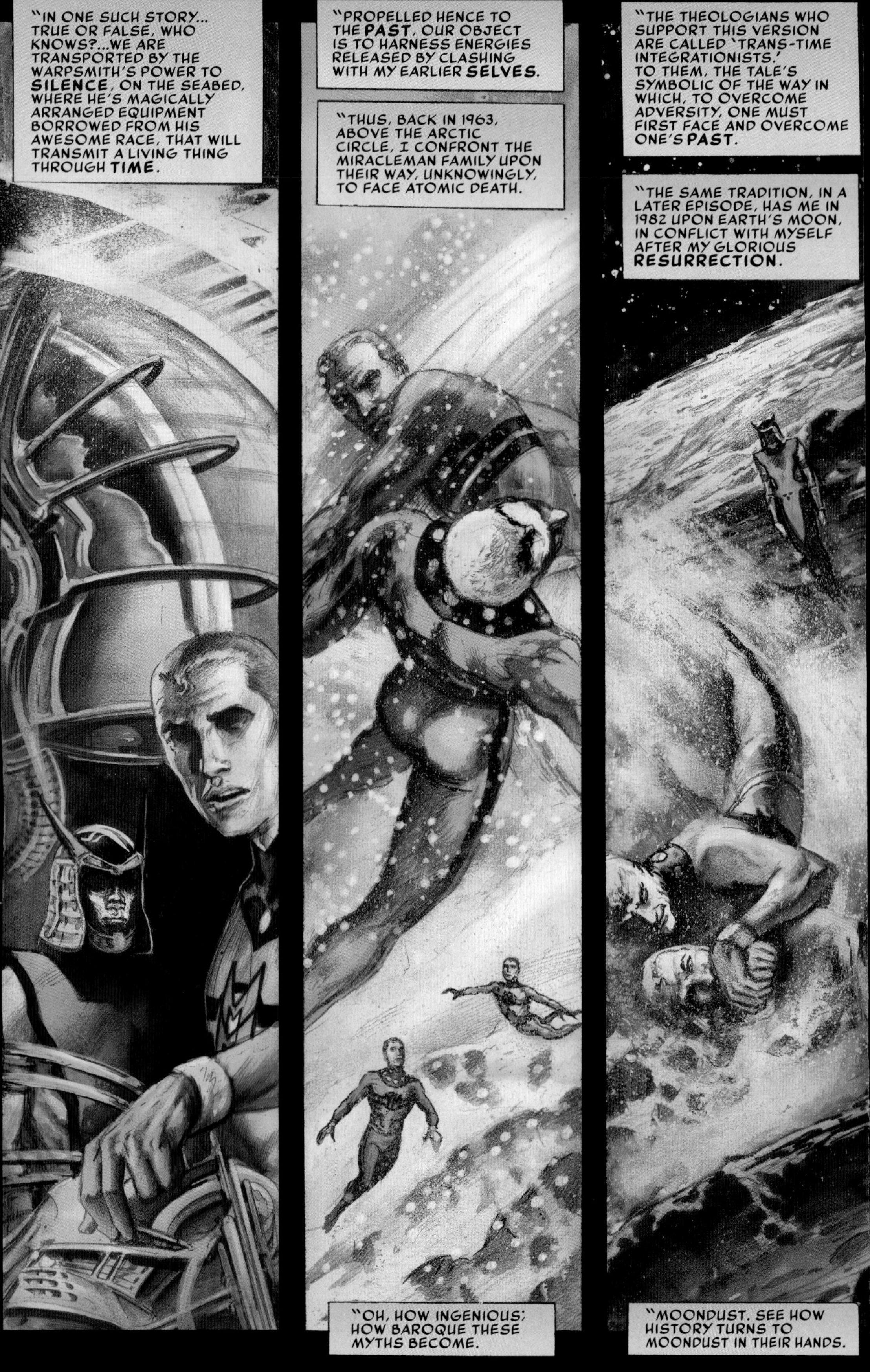
"IN ONE SUCH STORY... TRUE OR FALSE, WHO KNOWS?...WE ARE TRANSPORTED BY THE WARPSMITH'S POWER TO SILENCE, ON THE SEABED, WHERE HE'S MAGICALLY ARRANGED EQUIPMENT BORROWED FROM HIS AWESOME RACE, THAT WILL TRANSMIT A LIVING THING THROUGH TIME.
"PROPELLED HENCE TO THE PAST, OUR OBJECT IS TO HARNESS ENERGIES RELEASED BY CLASHING WITH MY EARLIER SELVES.
"THUS, BACK IN 1963, ABOVE THE ARCTIC CIRCLE, I CONFRONT THE MIRACLEMAN FAMILY UPON THEIR WAY, UNKNOWINGLY, TO FACE ATOMIC DEATH.
"OH, HOW INGENIOUS; HOW BAROQUE THESE MYTHS BECOME.
"THE THEOLOGIANS WHO SUPPORT THIS VERSION ARE CALLED 'TRANS-TIME INTEGRATIONISTS.' TO THEM, THE TALE'S SYMBOLIC OF THE WAY IN WHICH, TO OVERCOME ADVERSITY, ONE MUST FIRST FACE AND OVERCOME ONE'S PAST.
"THE SAME TRADITION, IN A LATER EPISODE, HAS ME IN 1982 UPON EARTH'S MOON, IN CONFLICT WITH MYSELF AFTER MY GLORIOUS RESURRECTION.
"MOONDUST. SEE HOW HISTORY TURNS TO MOONDUST IN THEIR HANDS.

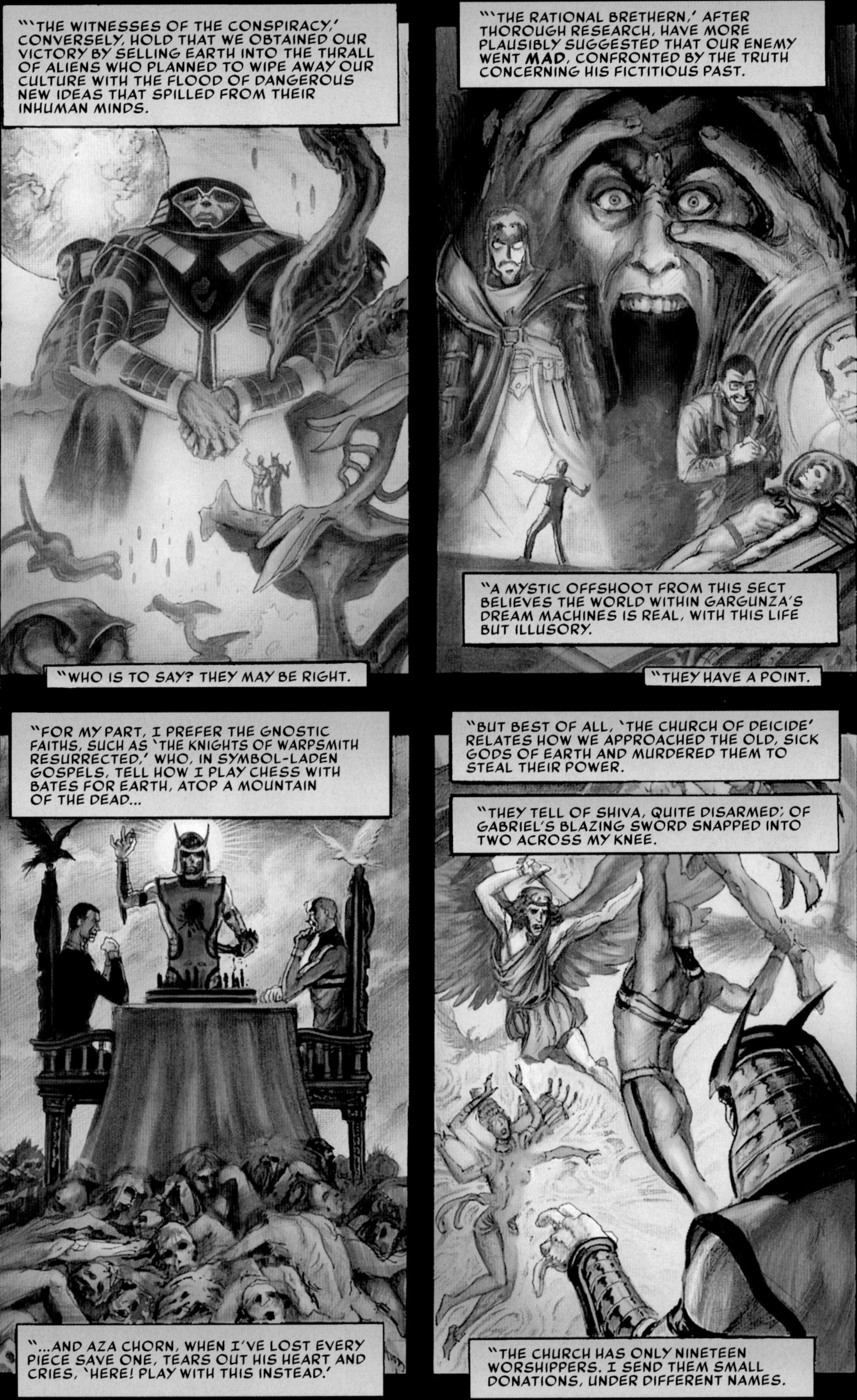
"'THE WITNESSES OF THE CONSPIRACY,' CONVERSELY, HOLD THAT WE OBTAINED OUR VICTORY BY SELLING EARTH INTO THE THRALL OF ALIENS WHO PLANNED TO WIPE AWAY OUR CULTURE WITH THE FLOOD OF DANGEROUS NEW IDEAS THAT SPILLED FROM THEIR INHUMAN MINDS.
"WHO IS TO SAY? THEY MAY BE RIGHT.
"'THE RATIONAL BRETHERN,' AFTER THOROUGH RESEARCH, HAVE MORE PLAUSIBLY SUGGESTED THAT OUR ENEMY WENT MAD, CONFRONTED BY THE TRUTH CONCERNING HIS FICTITIOUS PAST.
"A MYSTIC OFFSHOOT FROM THIS SECT BELIEVES THE WORLD WITHIN GARGUNZA'S DREAM MACHINES IS REAL, WITH THIS LIFE BUT ILLUSORY.
"THEY HAVE A POINT.
"FOR MY PART, I PREFER THE GNOSTIC FAITHS, SUCH AS 'THE KNIGHTS OF WARPSMITH RESURRECTED,' WHO, IN SYMBOL-LADEN GOSPELS, TELL HOW I PLAY CHESS WITH BATES FOR EARTH, ATOP A MOUNTAIN OF THE DEAD...
"...AND AZA CHORN, WHEN I'VE LOST EVERY PIECE SAVE ONE, TEARS OUT HIS HEART AND CRIES, 'HERE! PLAY WITH THIS INSTEAD.'
"BUT BEST OF ALL, 'THE CHURCH OF DEICIDE' RELATES HOW WE APPROACHED THE OLD, SICK GODS OF EARTH AND MURDERED THEM TO STEAL THEIR POWER.
"THEY TELL OF SHIVA, QUITE DISARMED; OF GABRIEL'S BLAZING SWORD SNAPPED INTO TWO ACROSS MY KNEE.
"THE CHURCH HAS ONLY NINETEEN WORSHIPPERS. I SEND THEM SMALL DONATIONS, UNDER DIFFERENT NAMES.

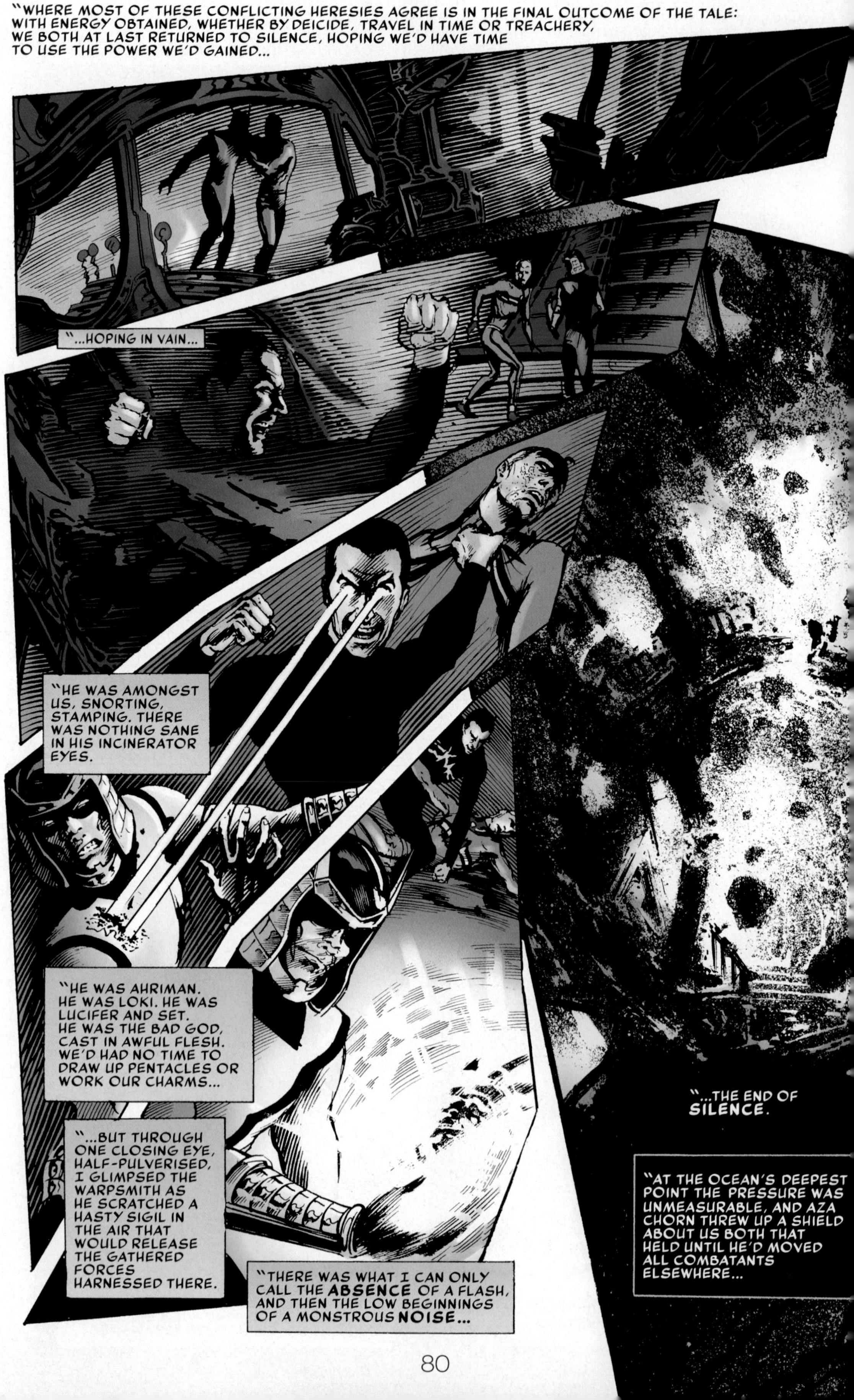
"WHERE MOST OF THESE CONFLICTING HERESIES AGREE IS IN THE FINAL OUTCOME OF THE TALE: WITH ENERGY OBTAINED, WHETHER BY DEICIDE, TRAVEL IN TIME OR TREACHERY, WE BOTH AT LAST RETURNED TO SILENCE, HOPING WE'D HAVE TIME TO USE THE POWER WE'D GAINED...
"...HOPING IN VAIN...
"HE WAS AMONGST US, SNORTING, STAMPING. THERE WAS NOTHING SANE IN HIS INCINERATOR EYES.
"HE WAS AHRIMAN. HE WAS LOKI. HE WAS LUCIFER AND SET. HE WAS THE BAD GOD, CAST IN AWFUL FLESH. WE'D HAD NO TIME TO DRAW UP PENTACLES OR WORK OUR CHARMS...
"...BUT THROUGH ONE CLOSING EYE, HALF-PULVERISED, I GLIMPSED THE WARPSMITH AS HE SCRATCHED A HASTY SIGIL IN THE AIR THAT WOULD RELEASE THE GATHERED FORCES HARNESSED THERE.
"THERE WAS WHAT I CAN ONLY CALL THE ABSENCE OF A FLASH, AND THEN THE LOW BEGINNINGS OF A MONSTROUS NOISE...
"...THE END OF SILENCE.
"AT THE OCEAN'S DEEPEST POINT THE PRESSURE WAS UNMEASURABLE, AND AZA CHORN THREW UP A SHIELD ABOUT US BOTH THAT HELD UNTIL HE'D MOVED ALL COMBATANTS ELSEWHERE...

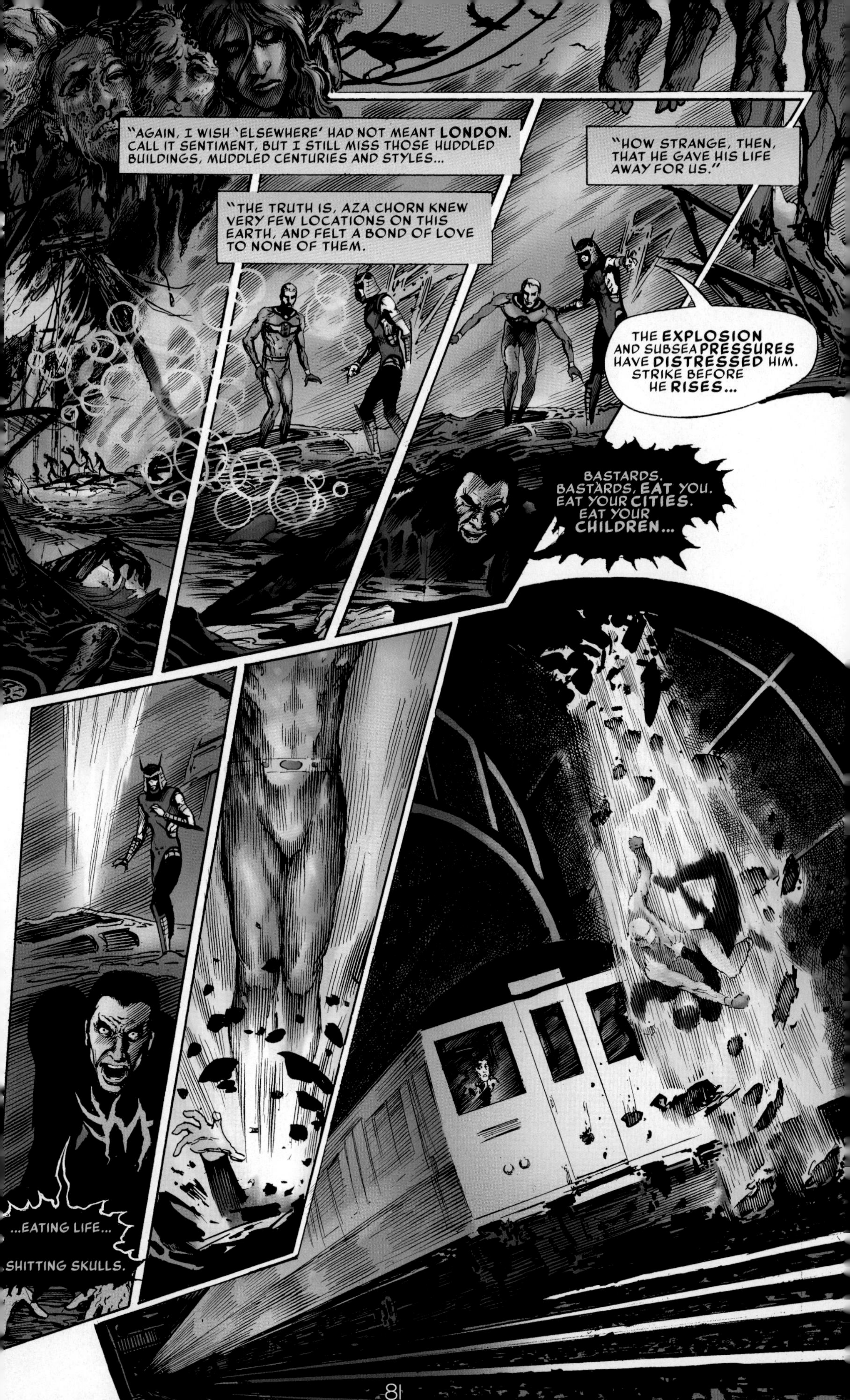
"AGAIN, I WISH 'ELSEWHERE' HAD NOT MEANT LONDON. CALL IT SENTIMENT, BUT I STILL MISS THOSE HUDDLED BUILDINGS, MUDDLED CENTURIES AND STYLES...
"THE TRUTH IS, AZA CHORN KNEW VERY FEW LOCATIONS ON THIS EARTH, AND FELT A BOND OF LOVE TO NONE OF THEM.
"HOW STRANGE, THEN, THAT HE GAVE HIS LIFE AWAY FOR US."
THE EXPLOSION AND SUBSEA PRESSURES HAVE DISTRESSED HIM. STRIKE BEFORE HE RISES...
BASTARDS. BASTARDS, EAT YOU. EAT YOUR CITIES. EAT YOUR CHILDREN...
...EATING LIFE...
SHITTING SKULLS.

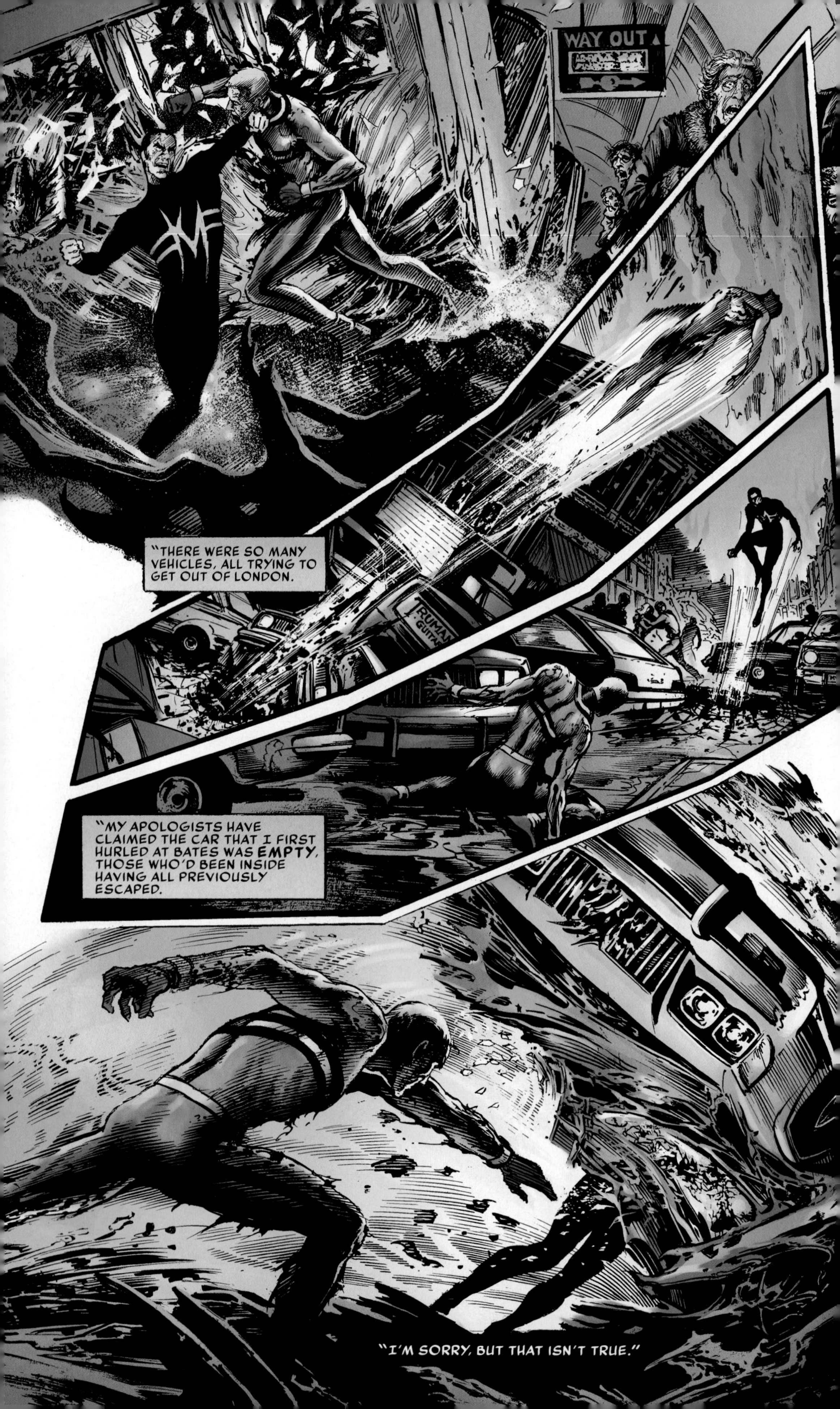
WAY OUT
"THERE WERE SO MANY VEHICLES, ALL TRYING TO GET OUT OF LONDON.
TRUMAN GUITARS
"MY APOLOGISTS HAVE CLAIMED THE CAR THAT I FIRST HURLED AT BATES WAS EMPTY, THOSE WHO'D BEEN INSIDE HAVING ALL PREVIOUSLY ESCAPED.
"I'M SORRY, BUT THAT ISN'T TRUE."

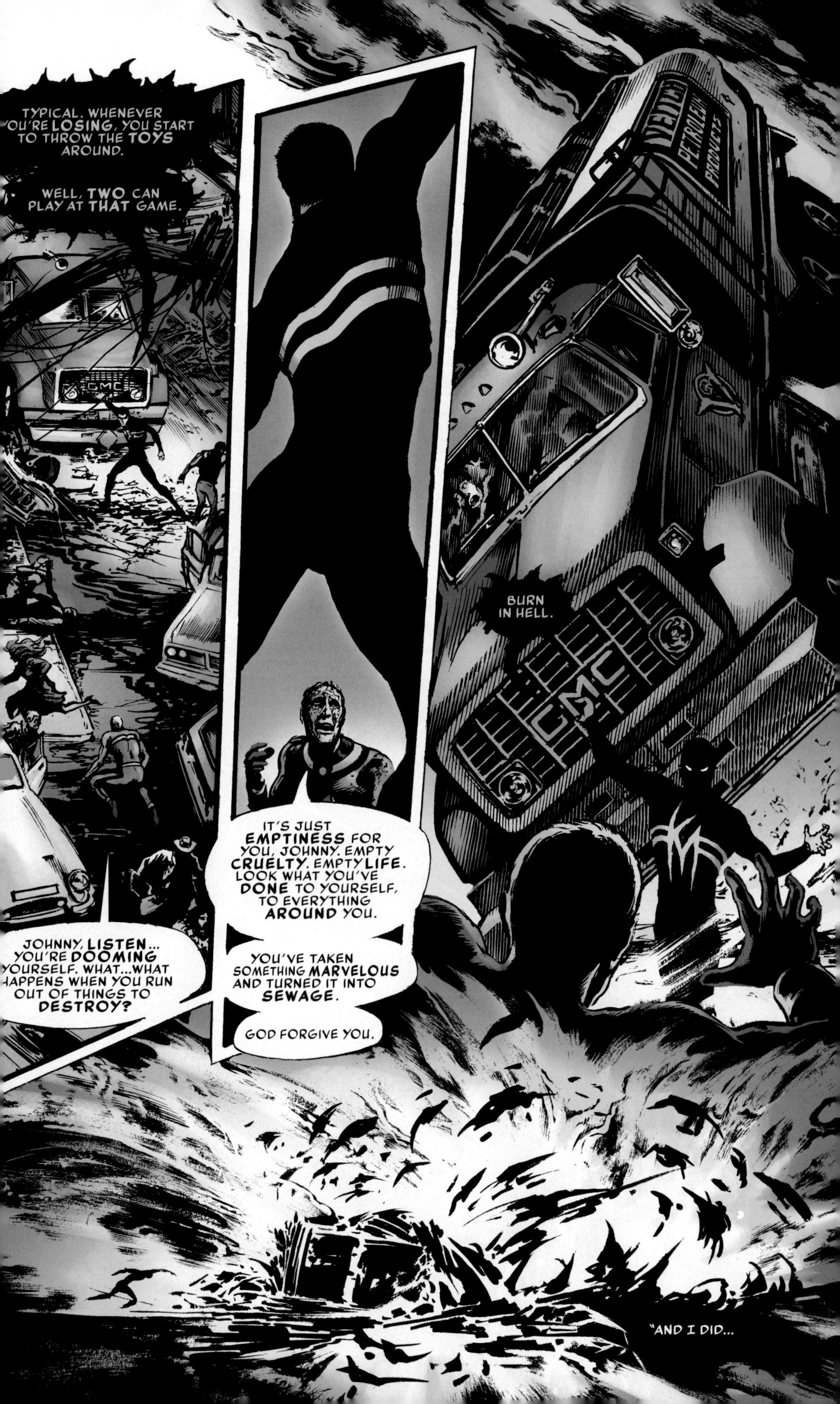
TYPICAL. WHENEVER YOU'RE LOSING, YOU START TO THROW THE TOYS AROUND.
WELL, TWO CAN PLAY AT THAT GAME.
BURN IN HELL.
IT'S JUST EMPTINESS FOR YOU, JOHNNY. EMPTY CRUELTY. EMPTY LIFE. LOOK WHAT YOU'VE DONE TO YOURSELF, TO EVERYTHING AROUND YOU.
JOHNNY, LISTEN... YOU'RE DOOMING YOURSELF. WHAT...WHAT HAPPENS WHEN YOU RUN OUT OF THINGS TO DESTROY?
YOU'VE TAKEN SOMETHING MARVELOUS AND TURNED IT INTO SEWAGE.
GOD FORGIVE YOU.
"AND I DID...

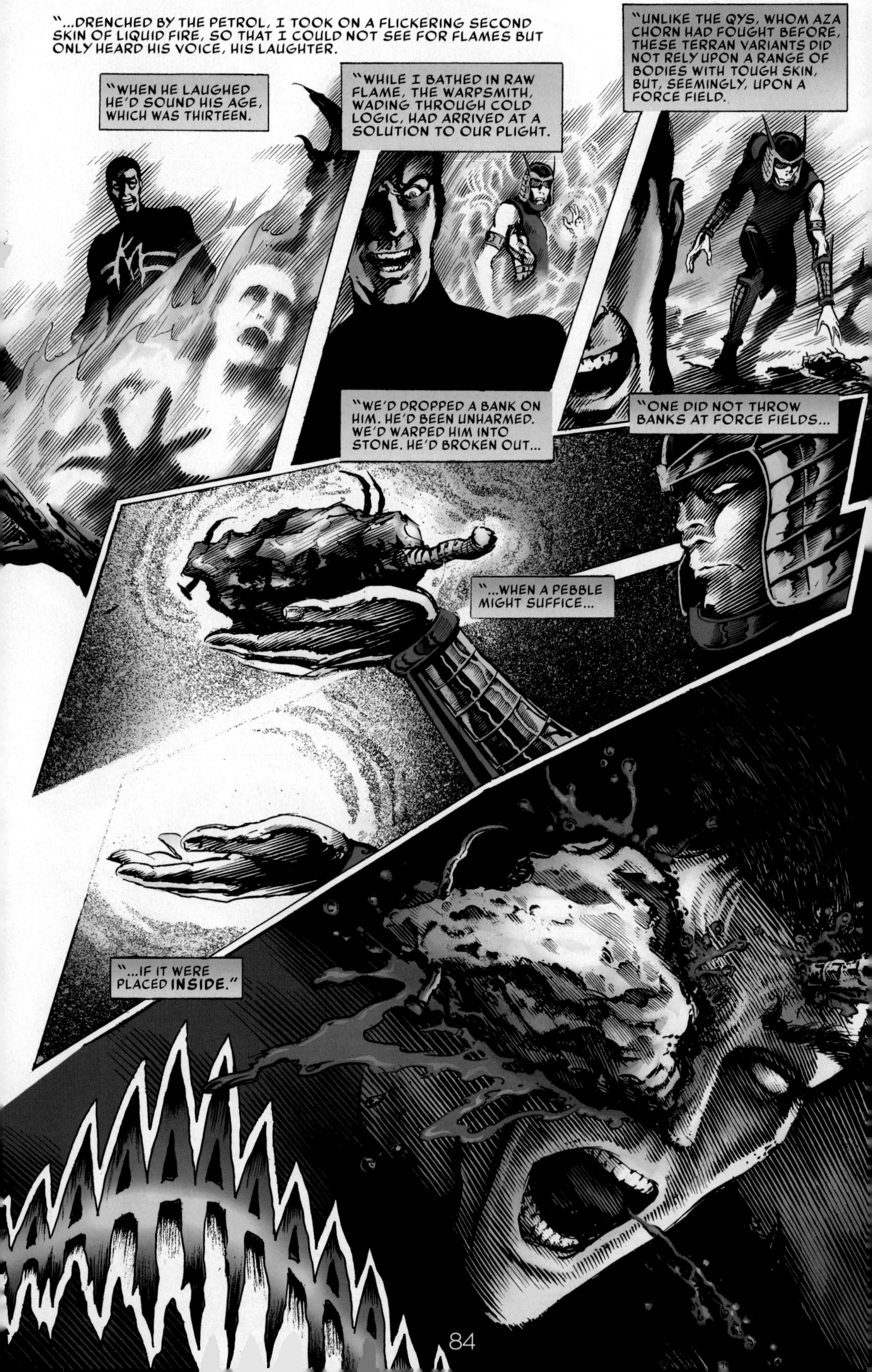
"...DRENCHED BY THE PETROL, I TOOK ON A FLICKERING SECOND SKIN OF LIQUID FIRE, SO THAT I COULD NOT SEE FOR FLAMES BUT ONLY HEARD HIS VOICE, HIS LAUGHTER.
"WHEN HE LAUGHED HE'D SOUND HIS AGE, WHICH WAS THIRTEEN.
"WHILE I BATHED IN RAW FLAME, THE WARPSMITH, WADING THROUGH COLD LOGIC, HAD ARRIVED AT A SOLUTION TO OUR PLIGHT.
"UNLIKE THE QYS, WHOM AZA CHORN HAD FOUGHT BEFORE, THESE TERRAN VARIANTS DID NOT RELY UPON A RANGE OF BODIES WITH TOUGH SKIN, BUT, SEEMINGLY, UPON A FORCE FIELD.
"WE'D DROPPED A BANK ON HIM. HE'D BEEN UNHARMED. WE'D WARPED HIM INTO STONE. HE'D BROKEN OUT...
"ONE DID NOT THROW BANKS AT FORCE FIELDS...
"...WHEN A PEBBLE MIGHT SUFFICE...
"...IF IT WERE PLACED INSIDE."

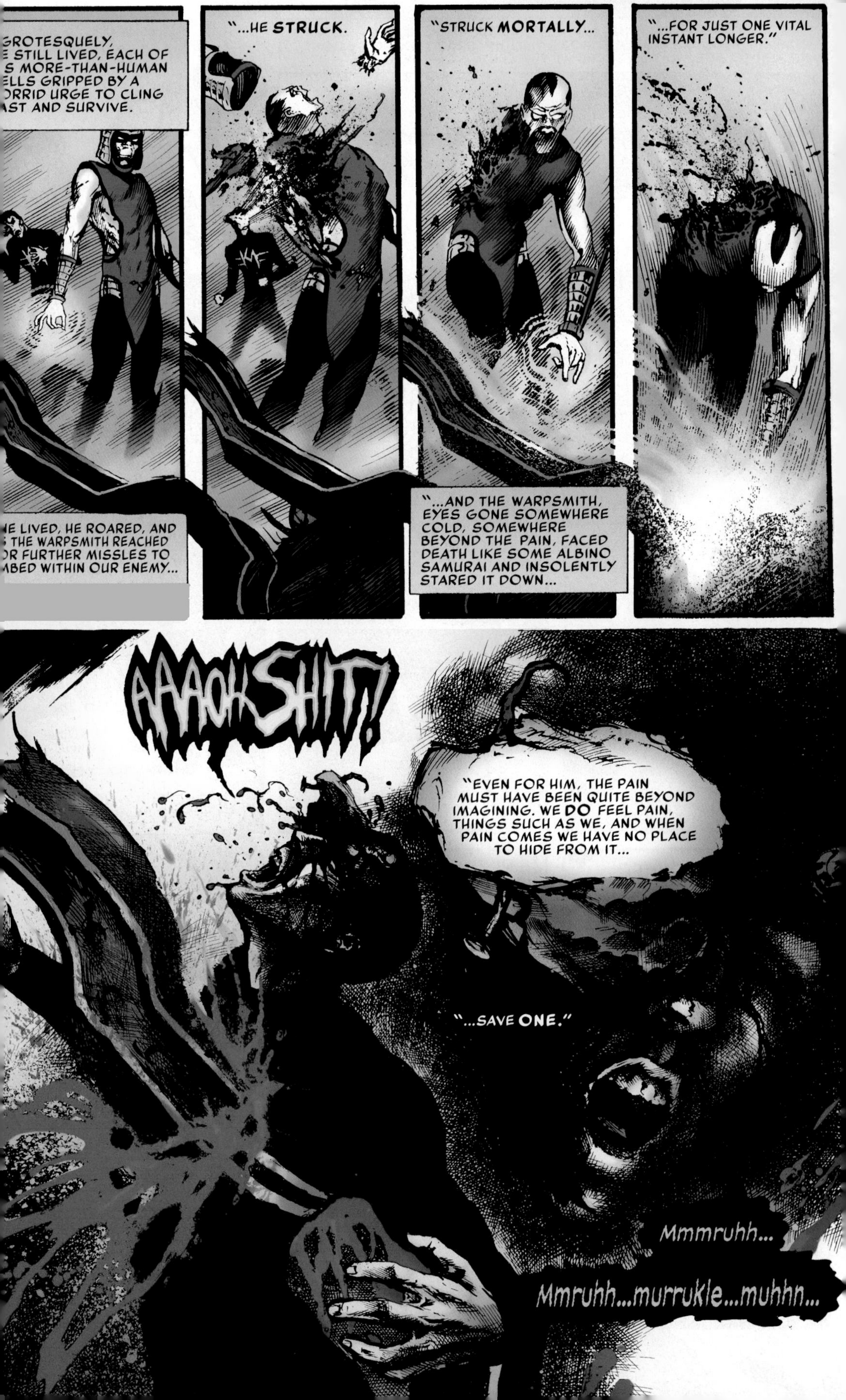
GROTESQUELY,
E STILL LIVED, EACH OF
S MORE-THAN-HUMAN
ELLS GRIPPED BY A
ORRID URGE TO CLING
AST AND SURVIVE.
"...HE STRUCK.
"STRUCK MORTALLY...
"...FOR JUST ONE VITAL INSTANT LONGER."
E LIVED, HE ROARED, AND
S THE WARPSMITH REACHED
OR FURTHER MISSLES TO
MBED WITHIN OUR ENEMY...
"...AND THE WARPSMITH, EYES GONE SOMEWHERE COLD, SOMEWHERE BEYOND THE PAIN, FACED DEATH LIKE SOME ALBINO SAMURAI AND INSOLENTLY STARED IT DOWN...
AAAOH SHIT!
"EVEN FOR HIM, THE PAIN MUST HAVE BEEN QUITE BEYOND IMAGINING. WE DO FEEL PAIN, THINGS SUCH AS WE, AND WHEN PAIN COMES WE HAVE NO PLACE TO HIDE FROM IT...
"...SAVE ONE."
Mmmruhh...
Mmruhh...murrukle...muhhn...

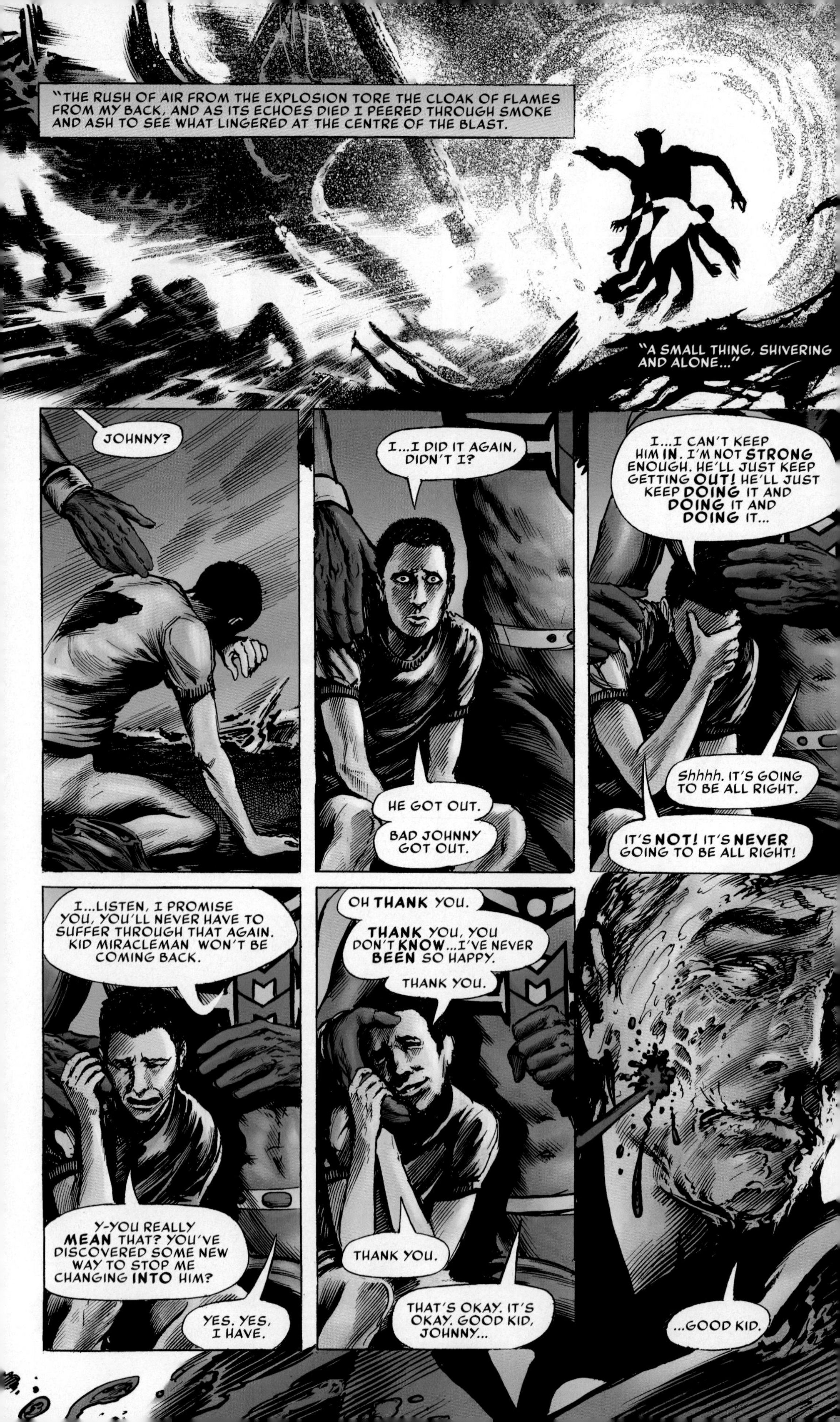
"THE RUSH OF AIR FROM THE EXPLOSION TORE THE CLOAK OF FLAMES FROM MY BACK, AND AS ITS ECHOES DIED I PEERED THROUGH SMOKE AND ASH TO SEE WHAT LINGERED AT THE CENTRE OF THE BLAST.
"A SMALL THING, SHIVERING AND ALONE..."
JOHNNY?
I...I DID IT AGAIN, DIDN'T I?
HE GOT OUT.
BAD JOHNNY GOT OUT.
I...I CAN'T KEEP HIM IN. I'M NOT STRONG ENOUGH. HE'LL JUST KEEP GETTING OUT! HE'LL JUST KEEP DOING IT AND DOING IT AND DOING IT...
Shhhh. IT'S GOING TO BE ALL RIGHT.
IT'S NOT! IT'S NEVER GOING TO BE ALL RIGHT!
I...LISTEN, I PROMISE YOU, YOU'LL NEVER HAVE TO SUFFER THROUGH THAT AGAIN. KID MIRACLEMAN WON'T BE COMING BACK.
Y-YOU REALLY MEAN THAT? YOU'VE DISCOVERED SOME NEW WAY TO STOP ME CHANGING INTO HIM?
YES. YES, I HAVE.
OH THANK YOU.
THANK YOU, YOU DON'T KNOW...I'VE NEVER BEEN SO HAPPY.
THANK YOU.
THANK YOU.
THAT'S OKAY. IT'S OKAY. GOOD KID, JOHNNY...
...GOOD KID.

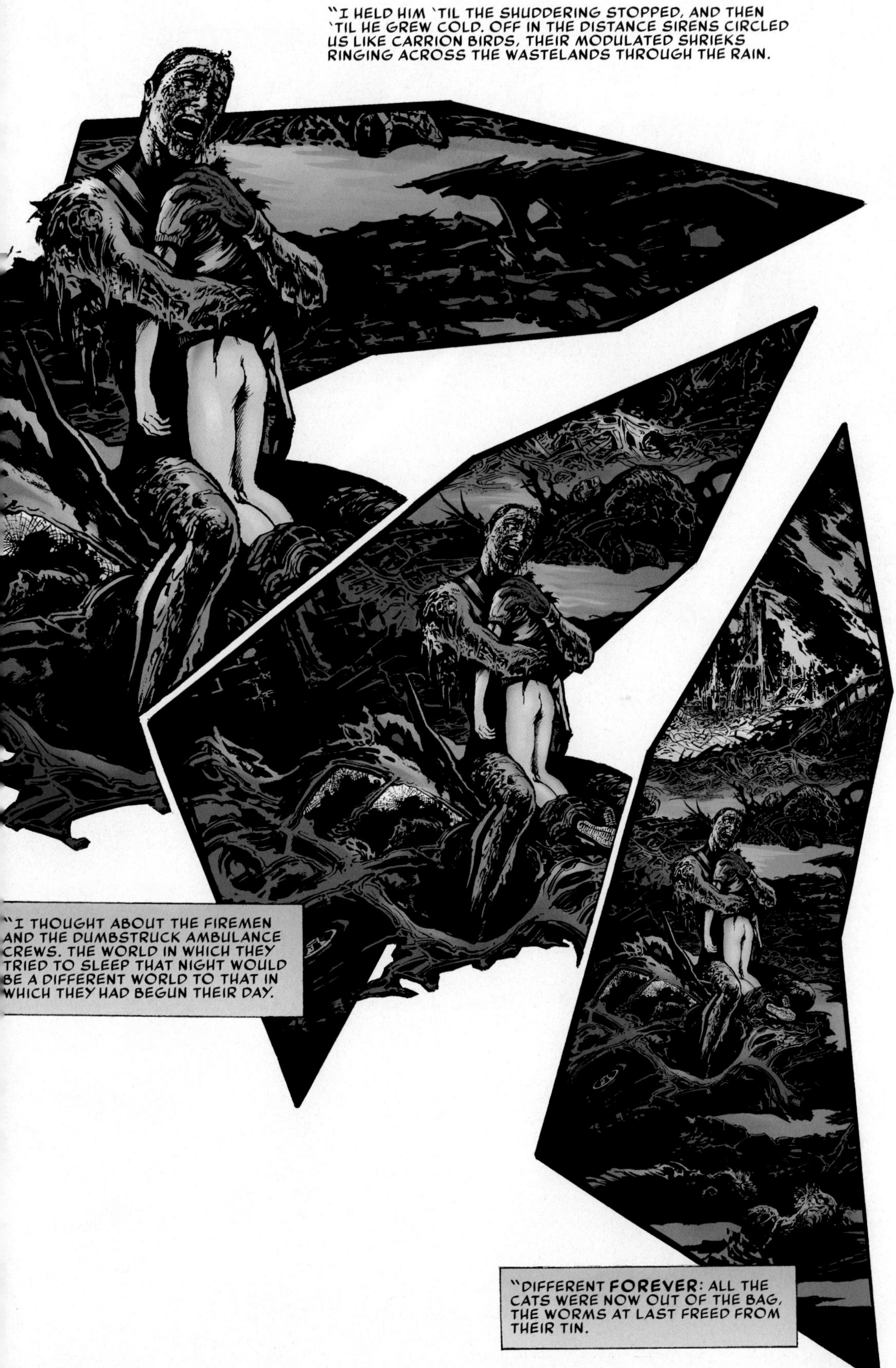
"I HELD HIM `TIL THE SHUDDERING STOPPED, AND THEN `TIL HE GREW COLD. OFF IN THE DISTANCE SIRENS CIRCLED US LIKE CARRION BIRDS, THEIR MODULATED SHRIEKS RINGING ACROSS THE WASTELANDS THROUGH THE RAIN.
"I THOUGHT ABOUT THE FIREMEN AND THE DUMBSTRUCK AMBULANCE CREWS. THE WORLD IN WHICH THEY TRIED TO SLEEP THAT NIGHT WOULD BE A DIFFERENT WORLD TO THAT IN WHICH THEY HAD BEGUN THEIR DAY.
"DIFFERENT FOREVER: ALL THE CATS WERE NOW OUT OF THE BAG, THE WORMS AT LAST FREED FROM THEIR TIN.

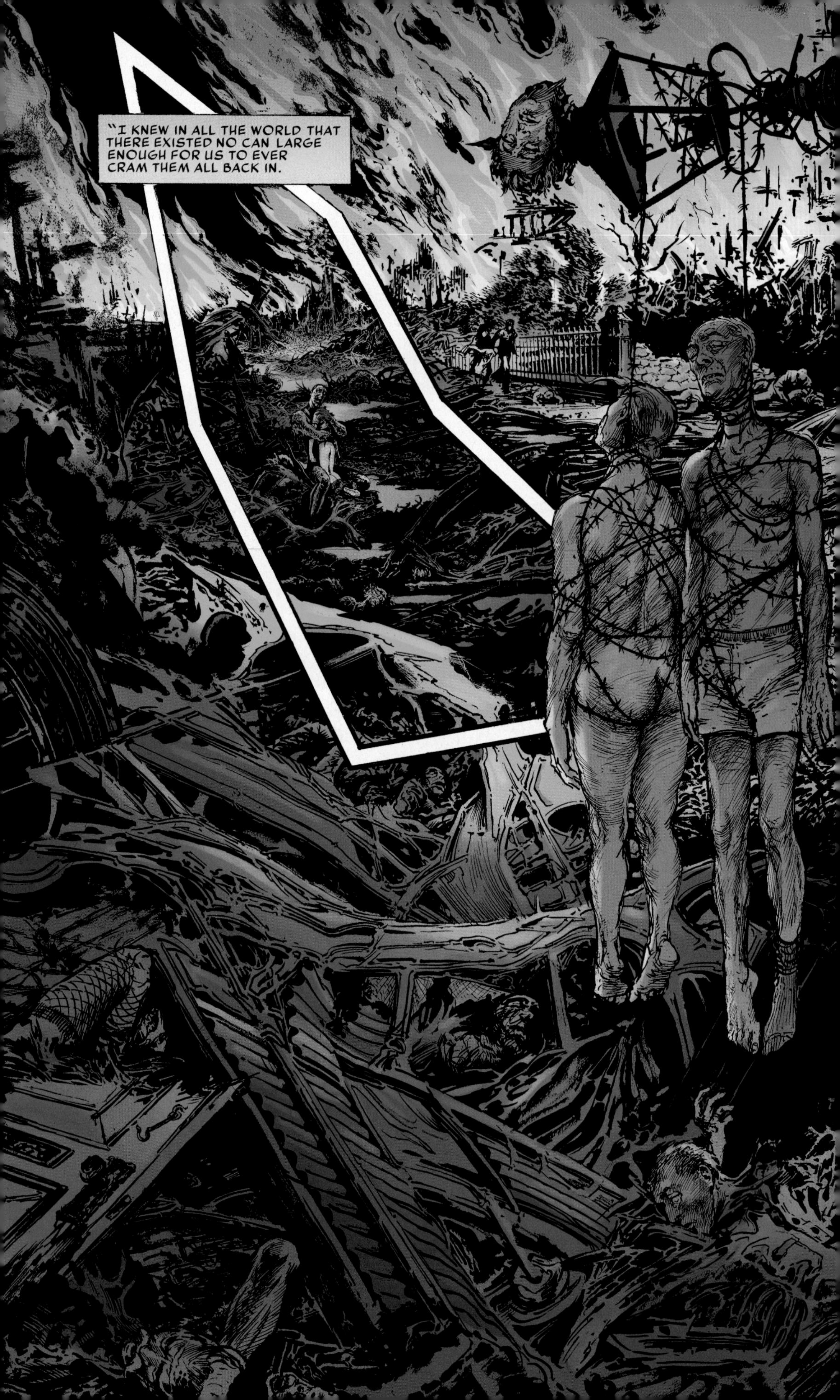
"I KNEW IN ALL THE WORLD THAT THERE EXISTED NO CAN LARGE ENOUGH FOR US TO EVER CRAM THEM ALL BACK IN.

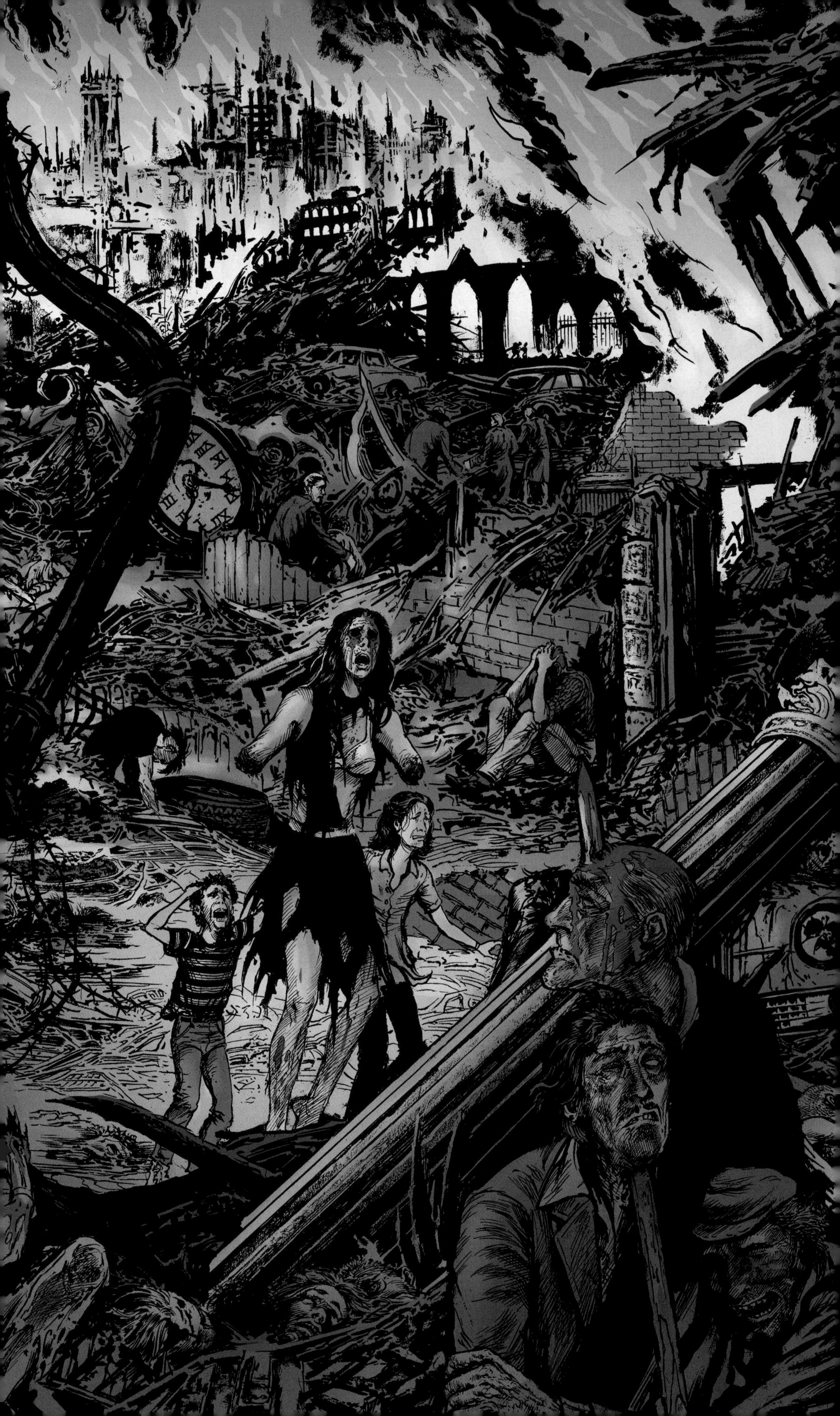

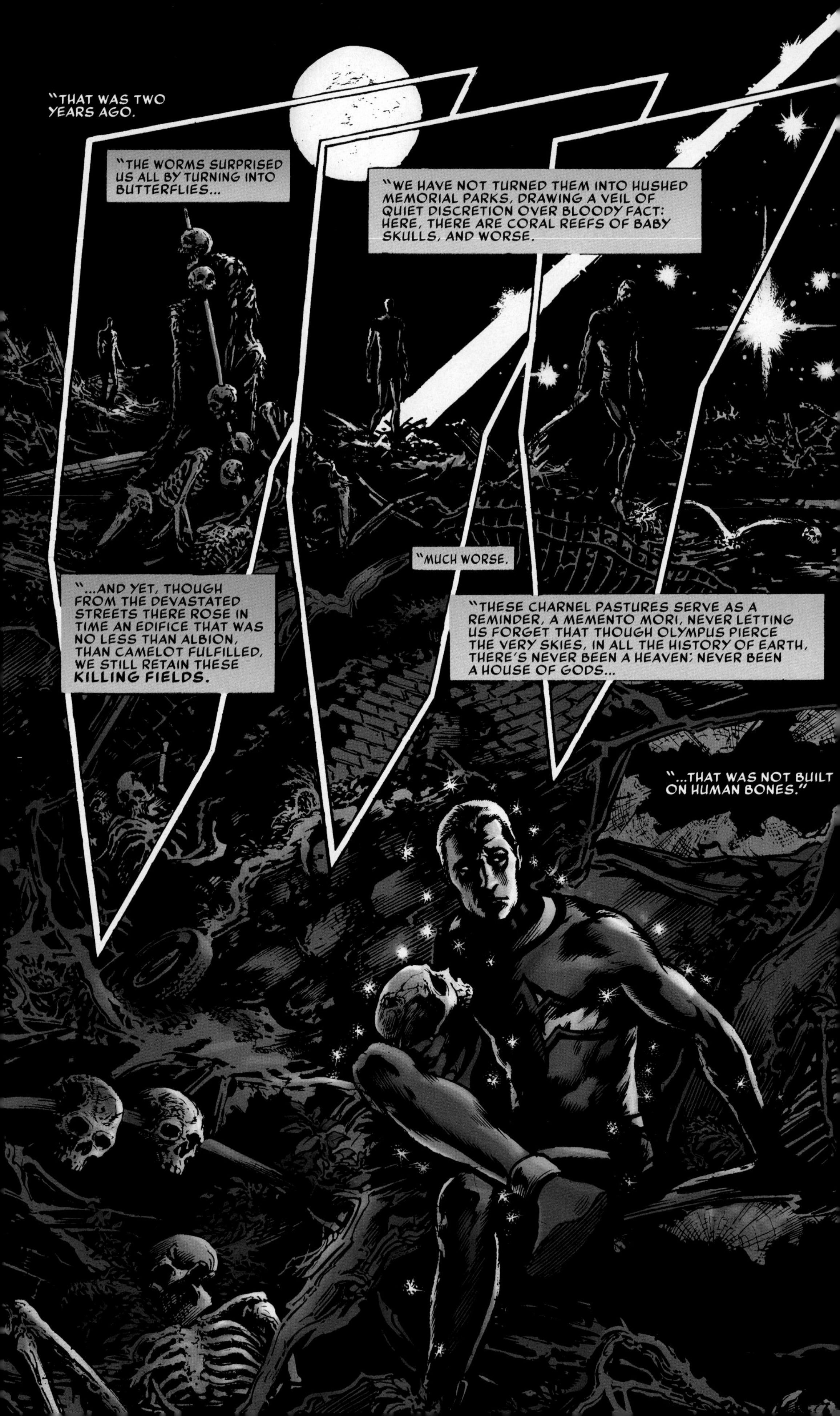
"THAT WAS TWO YEARS AGO.
"THE WORMS SURPRISED US ALL BY TURNING INTO BUTTERFLIES...
"WE HAVE NOT TURNED THEM INTO HUSHED MEMORIAL PARKS, DRAWING A VEIL OF QUIET DISCRETION OVER BLOODY FACT: HERE, THERE ARE CORAL REEFS OF BABY SKULLS, AND WORSE.
"MUCH WORSE.
"...AND YET, THOUGH FROM THE DEVASTATED STREETS THERE ROSE IN TIME AN EDIFICE THAT WAS NO LESS THAN ALBION, THAN CAMELOT FULFILLED, WE STILL RETAIN THESE KILLING FIELDS.
"THESE CHARNEL PASTURES SERVE AS A REMINDER, A MEMENTO MORI, NEVER LETTING US FORGET THAT THOUGH OLYMPUS PIERCE THE VERY SKIES, IN ALL THE HISTORY OF EARTH, THERE'S NEVER BEEN A HEAVEN; NEVER BEEN A HOUSE OF GODS...
"...THAT WAS NOT BUILT ON HUMAN BONES."

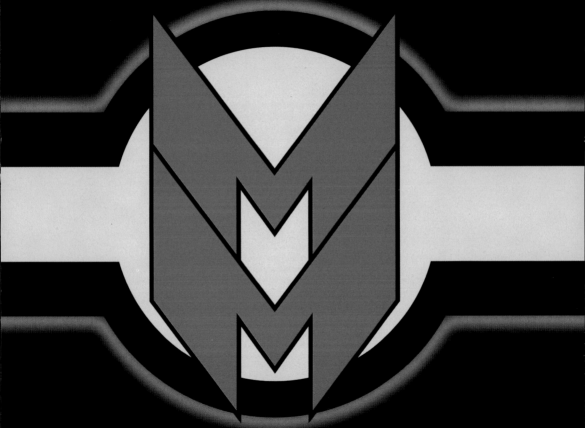

"It's been five years since my rebirth. Though I'd suspected that the people would in some way mark the anniversary, I'd hoped, rather uncharitably, that they would not see fit to sacrifice small goats or children in my name.

"As it transpired, I was quite touched: They made a bonfire on the wasteland that was once Trafalgar Square and on it heaped their comic books, their films and novels filled with horror, science fiction, fantasy, and as it burned they cheered; cheered as the curling, burning pages fluttered up into the night; cheered to be done with times when wonder was a sad and wretched thing made only out of paper, out of celluloid.

"A Telex came from Tokyo this morning. Their geneticists have reared a mouse that levitates; a glowing rabbit that can talk. Oh what a world, with super mice and atom rabbits, yet I dream of *more*.

"I dream suburbias where every child is brave and funny, where a green-skinned scientist cackling at dusk or a journey to the sherbet-wastes of Mars are childhood commonplaces. I dream teenagers, the boys with letter sweatshirts, girls with single brushstroke brows, in endless ice cream parlours, never growing old or running out of flavours; dream them in moon-chilled jalopies when their sitcom day is through...the delicate perfume of sex and leatherette pervades the air, the radios playing new Gene Vincent songs, new episodes of discontinued but beloved shows.

"I dream a world of heroes and exciting clothes, hoods cut away to show the hair or leotards made out of flags. I dream insignia, dream lightning flashes, planets, letters, stars; of bob-cut women wearing red stilettos, ice-blue half-length capes; of men in dominos, transparent blouses, slashing elegance of line in every wrinkle, every crease. I dream names like Doctor Satellite, Lady October, Johnny Analogue. I dream a world where everyone has sidekicks and caves to keep their eerie souvenirs.

"I dream of cities that old futurists would weep with joy to see, of wharfside neighbourhoods where tough kids track down spies, where crumbling tenements contort to teetering and eccentric shapes that seem to spell out words against the night.

"I dream a Piccadilly Circus where magicians dressed in toppers, tails or turbans wave hypnotically and conjure birds made out of steam, or scented fish or flowers that speak in verse for the delighted evening crowds. I dream of an Embankment where tall men with somber cloaks and names like Kismet, Destiny, or Fate will entertain a passerby with stories of her life to come, or chill her blood with supernatural parables, and all the while their hat-brim shadows hide their eyes.

"I dream of rugged, mustard-yellow monsters from the deep, with vulgar and percussive names like Zax and Rul-Rah-Room. I dream a world of dreams fulfilled, a place where ecstasy and not his brother pain has run amok, and even as I dream I know my dreams are almost true, a planet of attained desire and concrete fantasy that spins and glitters, balanced on the diamond capstone of Olympus.

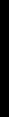

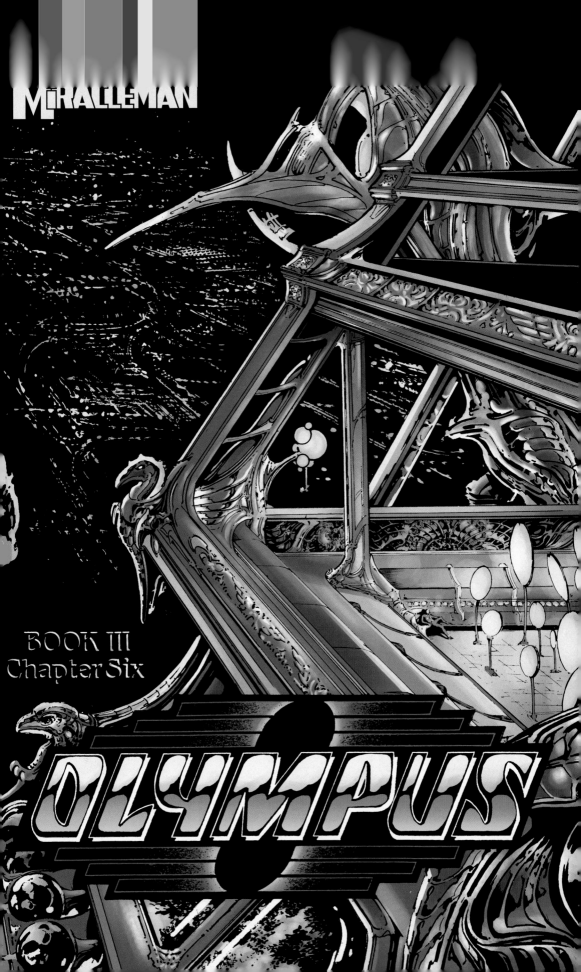

MIRACLEMAN

BOOK III
Chapter Six

OLYMPUS

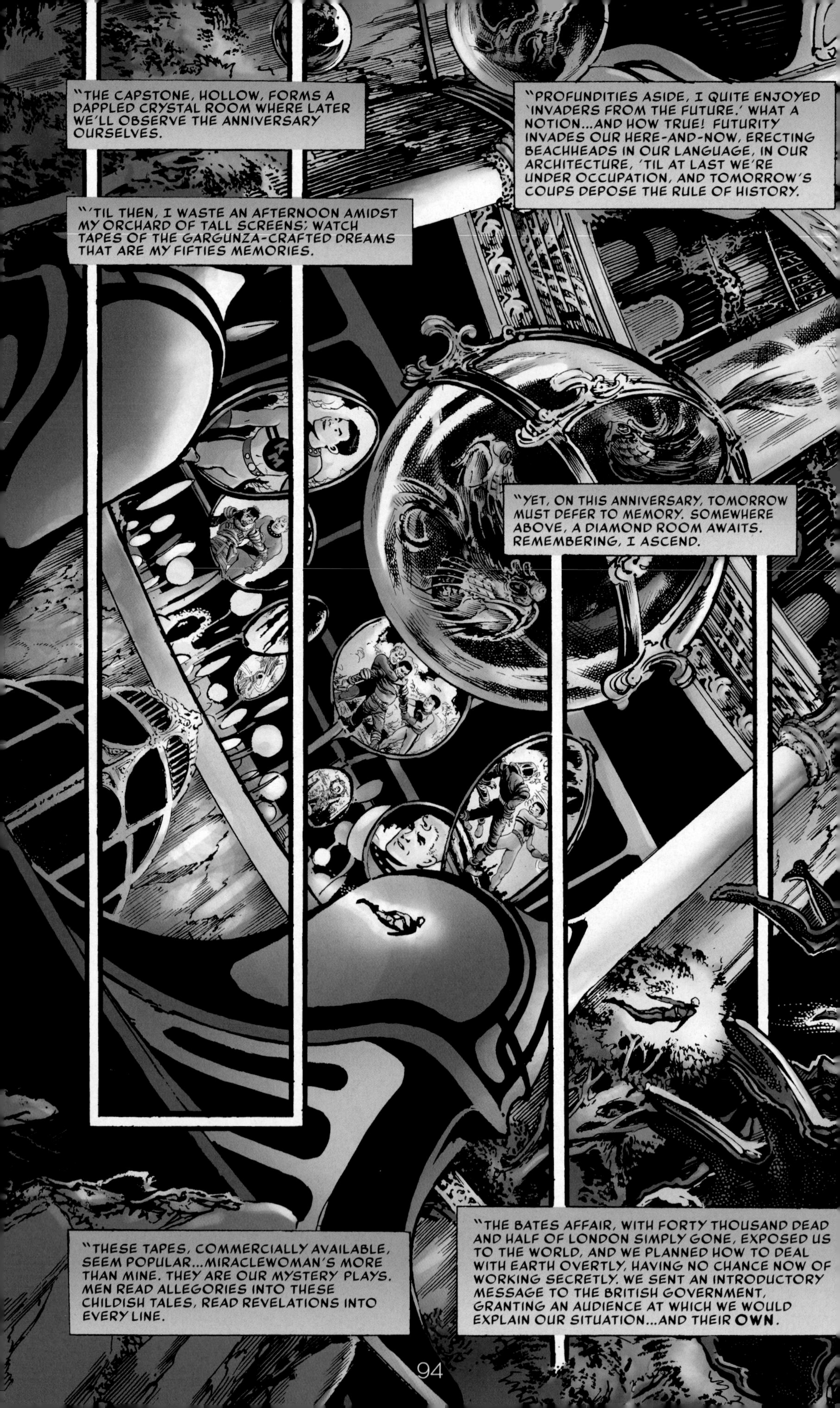
"THE CAPSTONE, HOLLOW, FORMS A DAPPLED CRYSTAL ROOM WHERE LATER WE'LL OBSERVE THE ANNIVERSARY OURSELVES.
"'TIL THEN, I WASTE AN AFTERNOON AMIDST MY ORCHARD OF TALL SCREENS; WATCH TAPES OF THE GARGUNZA-CRAFTED DREAMS THAT ARE MY FIFTIES MEMORIES.
"PROFUNDITIES ASIDE, I QUITE ENJOYED 'INVADERS FROM THE FUTURE.' WHAT A NOTION...AND HOW TRUE! FUTURITY INVADES OUR HERE-AND-NOW, ERECTING BEACHHEADS IN OUR LANGUAGE, IN OUR ARCHITECTURE, 'TIL AT LAST WE'RE UNDER OCCUPATION, AND TOMORROW'S COUPS DEPOSE THE RULE OF HISTORY.
"YET, ON THIS ANNIVERSARY, TOMORROW MUST DEFER TO MEMORY. SOMEWHERE ABOVE, A DIAMOND ROOM AWAITS. REMEMBERING, I ASCEND.
"THESE TAPES, COMMERCIALLY AVAILABLE, SEEM POPULAR...MIRACLEWOMAN'S MORE THAN MINE. THEY ARE OUR MYSTERY PLAYS. MEN READ ALLEGORIES INTO THESE CHILDISH TALES, READ REVELATIONS INTO EVERY LINE.
"THE BATES AFFAIR, WITH FORTY THOUSAND DEAD AND HALF OF LONDON SIMPLY GONE, EXPOSED US TO THE WORLD, AND WE PLANNED HOW TO DEAL WITH EARTH OVERTLY, HAVING NO CHANCE NOW OF WORKING SECRETLY. WE SENT AN INTRODUCTORY MESSAGE TO THE BRITISH GOVERNMENT, GRANTING AN AUDIENCE AT WHICH WE WOULD EXPLAIN OUR SITUATION...AND THEIR **OWN**.

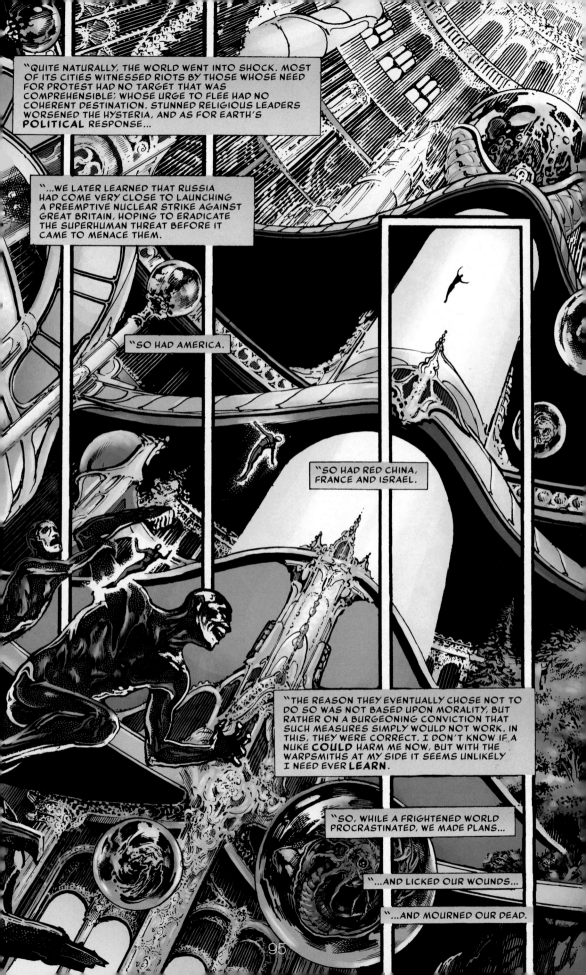

"QUITE NATURALLY, THE WORLD WENT INTO SHOCK. MOST OF ITS CITIES WITNESSED RIOTS BY THOSE WHOSE NEED FOR PROTEST HAD NO TARGET THAT WAS COMPREHENSIBLE; WHOSE URGE TO FLEE HAD NO COHERENT DESTINATION. STUNNED RELIGIOUS LEADERS WORSENED THE HYSTERIA, AND AS FOR EARTH'S **POLITICAL** RESPONSE...

"...WE LATER LEARNED THAT RUSSIA HAD COME VERY CLOSE TO LAUNCHING A PREEMPTIVE NUCLEAR STRIKE AGAINST GREAT BRITAIN, HOPING TO ERADICATE THE SUPERHUMAN THREAT BEFORE IT CAME TO MENACE THEM.

"SO HAD AMERICA.

"SO HAD RED CHINA, FRANCE AND ISRAEL.

"THE REASON THEY EVENTUALLY CHOSE NOT TO DO SO WAS NOT BASED UPON MORALITY, BUT RATHER ON A BURGEONING CONVICTION THAT SUCH MEASURES SIMPLY WOULD NOT WORK. IN THIS, THEY WERE CORRECT. I DON'T KNOW IF A NUKE **COULD** HARM ME NOW, BUT WITH THE WARPSMITHS AT MY SIDE IT SEEMS UNLIKELY I NEED EVER **LEARN.**

"SO, WHILE A FRIGHTENED WORLD PROCRASTINATED, WE MADE PLANS...

"...AND LICKED OUR WOUNDS...

"...AND MOURNED OUR DEAD.

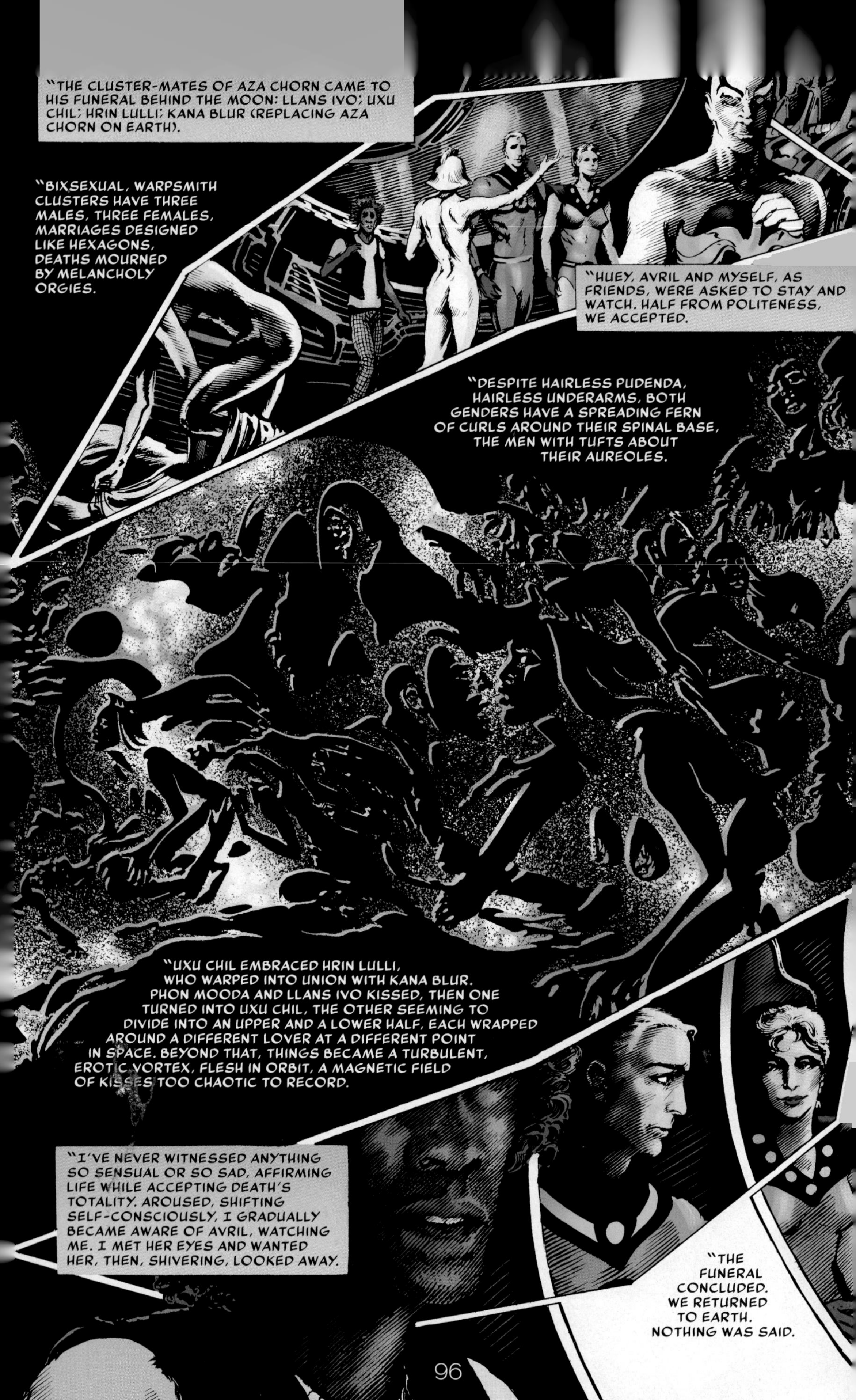
"THE CLUSTER-MATES OF AZA CHORN CAME TO HIS FUNERAL BEHIND THE MOON: LLANS IVO; UXU CHIL; HRIN LULLI; KANA BLUR (REPLACING AZA CHORN ON EARTH).
"BIXSEXUAL, WARPSMITH CLUSTERS HAVE THREE MALES, THREE FEMALES, MARRIAGES DESIGNED LIKE HEXAGONS, DEATHS MOURNED BY MELANCHOLY ORGIES.
"HUEY, AVRIL AND MYSELF, AS FRIENDS, WERE ASKED TO STAY AND WATCH. HALF FROM POLITENESS, WE ACCEPTED.
"DESPITE HAIRLESS PUDENDA, HAIRLESS UNDERARMS, BOTH GENDERS HAVE A SPREADING FERN OF CURLS AROUND THEIR SPINAL BASE, THE MEN WITH TUFTS ABOUT THEIR AUREOLES.
"UXU CHIL EMBRACED HRIN LULLI, WHO WARPED INTO UNION WITH KANA BLUR. PHON MOODA AND LLANS IVO KISSED, THEN ONE TURNED INTO UXU CHIL, THE OTHER SEEMING TO DIVIDE INTO AN UPPER AND A LOWER HALF, EACH WRAPPED AROUND A DIFFERENT LOVER AT A DIFFERENT POINT IN SPACE. BEYOND THAT, THINGS BECAME A TURBULENT, EROTIC VORTEX, FLESH IN ORBIT, A MAGNETIC FIELD OF KISSES TOO CHAOTIC TO RECORD.
"I'VE NEVER WITNESSED ANYTHING SO SENSUAL OR SO SAD, AFFIRMING LIFE WHILE ACCEPTING DEATH'S TOTALITY. AROUSED, SHIFTING SELF-CONSCIOUSLY, I GRADUALLY BECAME AWARE OF AVRIL, WATCHING ME. I MET HER EYES AND WANTED HER, THEN, SHIVERING, LOOKED AWAY.
"THE FUNERAL CONCLUDED. WE RETURNED TO EARTH. NOTHING WAS SAID.

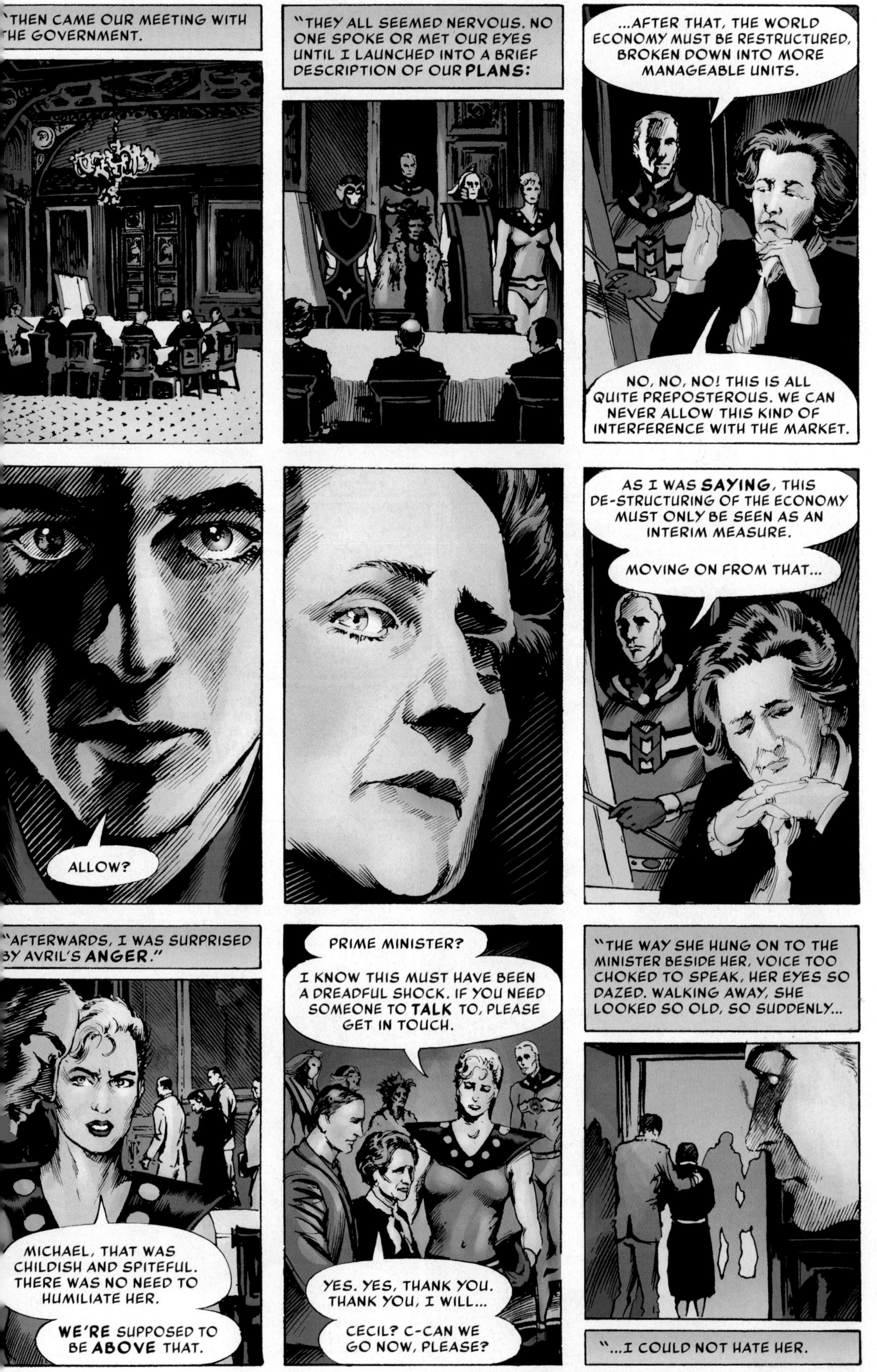
"THEN CAME OUR MEETING WITH THE GOVERNMENT.
"THEY ALL SEEMED NERVOUS. NO ONE SPOKE OR MET OUR EYES UNTIL I LAUNCHED INTO A BRIEF DESCRIPTION OF OUR PLANS:
...AFTER THAT, THE WORLD ECONOMY MUST BE RESTRUCTURED, BROKEN DOWN INTO MORE MANAGEABLE UNITS.
NO, NO, NO! THIS IS ALL QUITE PREPOSTEROUS. WE CAN NEVER ALLOW THIS KIND OF INTERFERENCE WITH THE MARKET.
ALLOW?
AS I WAS SAYING, THIS DE-STRUCTURING OF THE ECONOMY MUST ONLY BE SEEN AS AN INTERIM MEASURE.
MOVING ON FROM THAT...
"AFTERWARDS, I WAS SURPRISED BY AVRIL'S ANGER."
MICHAEL, THAT WAS CHILDISH AND SPITEFUL. THERE WAS NO NEED TO HUMILIATE HER.
WE'RE SUPPOSED TO BE ABOVE THAT.
PRIME MINISTER?
I KNOW THIS MUST HAVE BEEN A DREADFUL SHOCK. IF YOU NEED SOMEONE TO TALK TO, PLEASE GET IN TOUCH.
YES. YES, THANK YOU. THANK YOU, I WILL...
CECIL? C-CAN WE GO NOW, PLEASE?
"THE WAY SHE HUNG ON TO THE MINISTER BESIDE HER, VOICE TOO CHOKED TO SPEAK, HER EYES SO DAZED. WALKING AWAY, SHE LOOKED SO OLD, SO SUDDENLY...
"...I COULD NOT HATE HER.

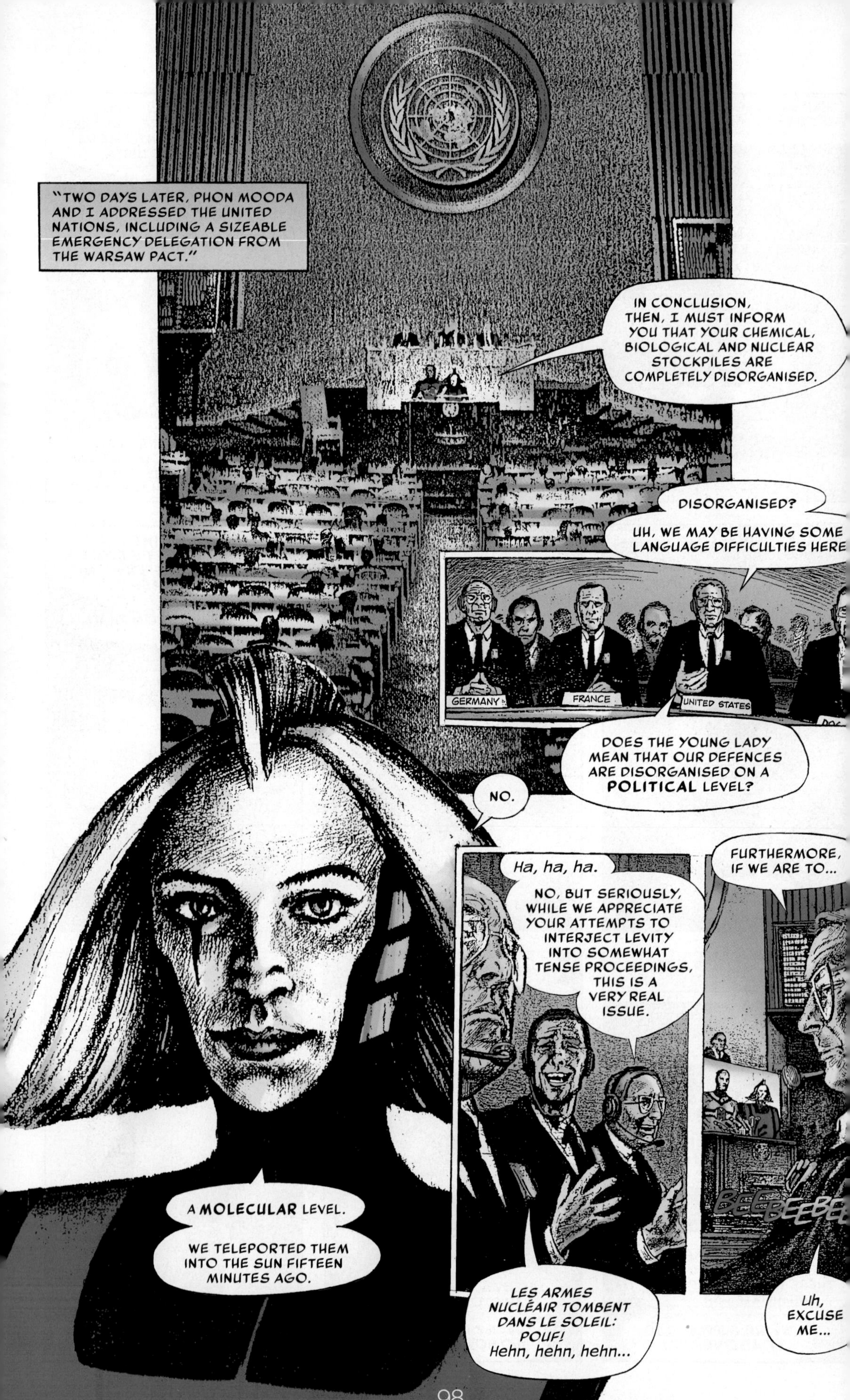
"TWO DAYS LATER, PHON MOODA AND I ADDRESSED THE UNITED NATIONS, INCLUDING A SIZEABLE EMERGENCY DELEGATION FROM THE WARSAW PACT."
IN CONCLUSION, THEN, I MUST INFORM YOU THAT YOUR CHEMICAL, BIOLOGICAL AND NUCLEAR STOCKPILES ARE COMPLETELY DISORGANISED.
DISORGANISED?
UH, WE MAY BE HAVING SOME LANGUAGE DIFFICULTIES HERE
GERMANY
FRANCE
UNITED STATES
DOES THE YOUNG LADY MEAN THAT OUR DEFENCES ARE DISORGANISED ON A POLITICAL LEVEL?
NO.
A MOLECULAR LEVEL.
WE TELEPORTED THEM INTO THE SUN FIFTEEN MINUTES AGO.
Ha, ha, ha.
NO, BUT SERIOUSLY, WHILE WE APPRECIATE YOUR ATTEMPTS TO INTERJECT LEVITY INTO SOMEWHAT TENSE PROCEEDINGS, THIS IS A VERY REAL ISSUE.
LES ARMES NUCLÉAIR TOMBENT DANS LE SOLEIL: POUF! Hehn, hehn, hehn...
FURTHERMORE, IF WE ARE TO...
BEEBEEBEE
Uh, EXCUSE ME...

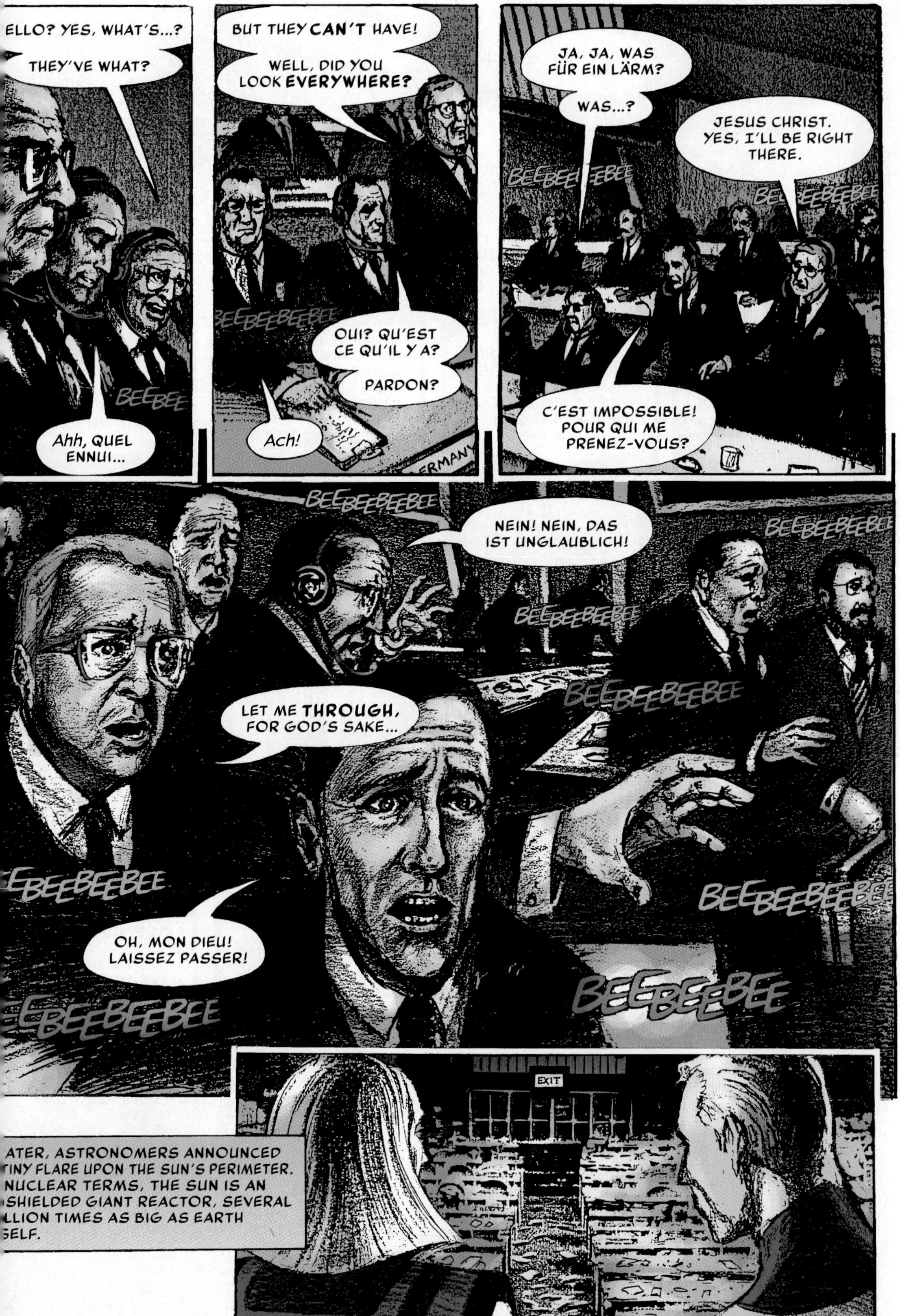
ELLO? YES, WHAT'S...?
THEY'VE WHAT?
Ahh, QUEL ENNUI...
BEEBEE
BUT THEY CAN'T HAVE!
WELL, DID YOU LOOK EVERYWHERE?
BEEBEEBEEBEE
OUI? QU'EST CE QU'IL Y A?
PARDON?
Ach!
JA, JA, WAS FÜR EIN LÄRM?
WAS...?
JESUS CHRIST. YES, I'LL BE RIGHT THERE.
C'EST IMPOSSIBLE! POUR QUI ME PRENEZ-VOUS?
BEEBEEBEEBEE
NEIN! NEIN, DAS IST UNGLAUBLICH!
LET ME THROUGH, FOR GOD'S SAKE...
OH, MON DIEU! LAISSEZ PASSER!
BEEBEEBEEBEE
ATER, ASTRONOMERS ANNOUNCED TINY FLARE UPON THE SUN'S PERIMETER. NUCLEAR TERMS, THE SUN IS AN SHIELDED GIANT REACTOR, SEVERAL LLION TIMES AS BIG AS EARTH SELF.
EXIT

"I DON'T SUPPOSE IT EVEN NOTICED.

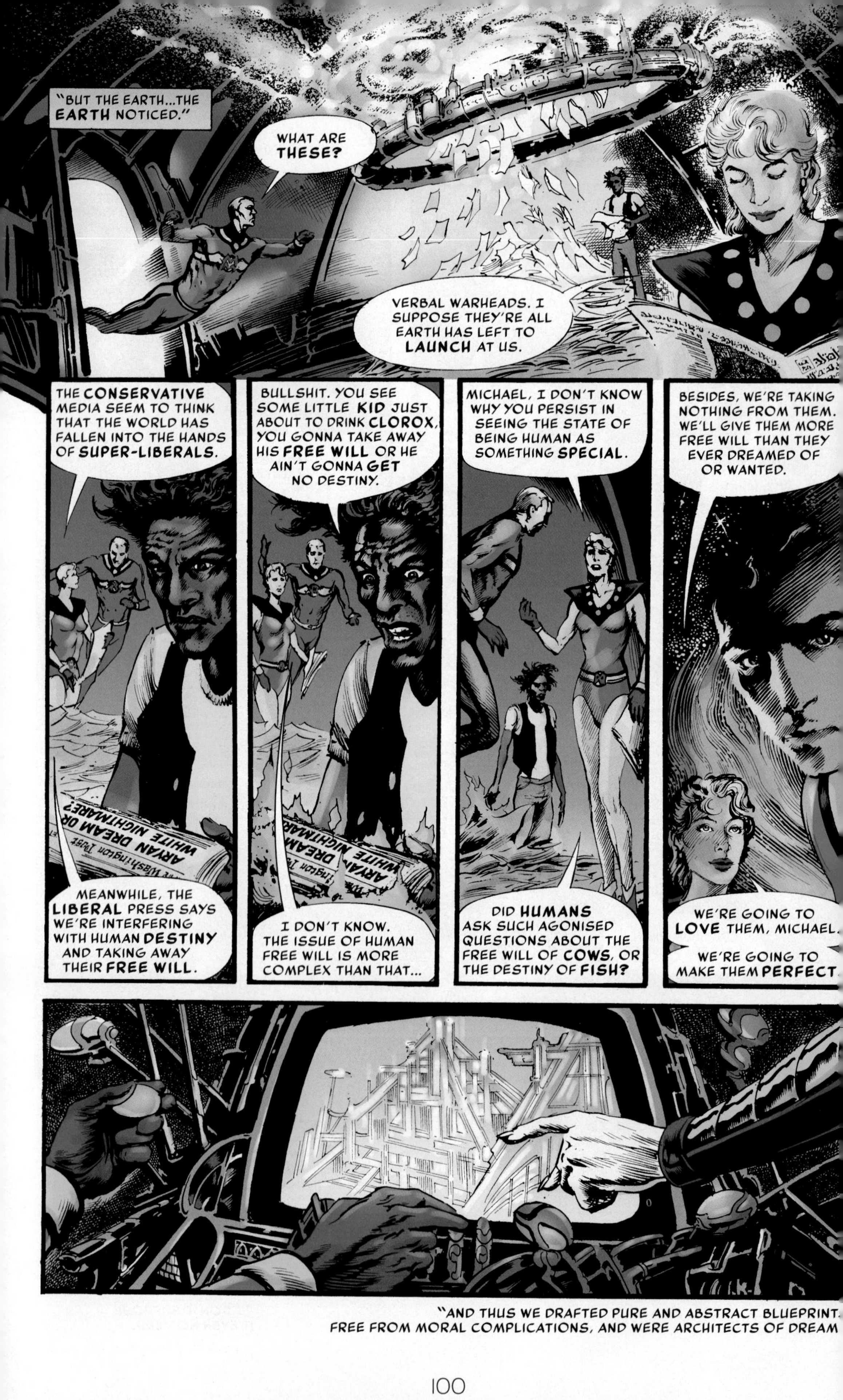
"BUT THE EARTH...THE EARTH NOTICED."
WHAT ARE THESE?
VERBAL WARHEADS. I SUPPOSE THEY'RE ALL EARTH HAS LEFT TO LAUNCH AT US.
THE CONSERVATIVE MEDIA SEEM TO THINK THAT THE WORLD HAS FALLEN INTO THE HANDS OF SUPER-LIBERALS.
The Washington Post
ARYAN DREAM OR WHITE NIGHTMARE?
MEANWHILE, THE LIBERAL PRESS SAYS WE'RE INTERFERING WITH HUMAN DESTINY AND TAKING AWAY THEIR FREE WILL.
BULLSHIT. YOU SEE SOME LITTLE KID JUST ABOUT TO DRINK CLOROX, YOU GONNA TAKE AWAY HIS FREE WILL OR HE AIN'T GONNA GET NO DESTINY.
I DON'T KNOW. THE ISSUE OF HUMAN FREE WILL IS MORE COMPLEX THAN THAT...
MICHAEL, I DON'T KNOW WHY YOU PERSIST IN SEEING THE STATE OF BEING HUMAN AS SOMETHING SPECIAL.
DID HUMANS ASK SUCH AGONISED QUESTIONS ABOUT THE FREE WILL OF COWS, OR THE DESTINY OF FISH?
BESIDES, WE'RE TAKING NOTHING FROM THEM. WE'LL GIVE THEM MORE FREE WILL THAN THEY EVER DREAMED OF OR WANTED.
WE'RE GOING TO LOVE THEM, MICHAEL.
WE'RE GOING TO MAKE THEM PERFECT.

"AND THUS WE DRAFTED PURE AND ABSTRACT BLUEPRINT
FREE FROM MORAL COMPLICATIONS, AND WERE ARCHITECTS OF DREAM

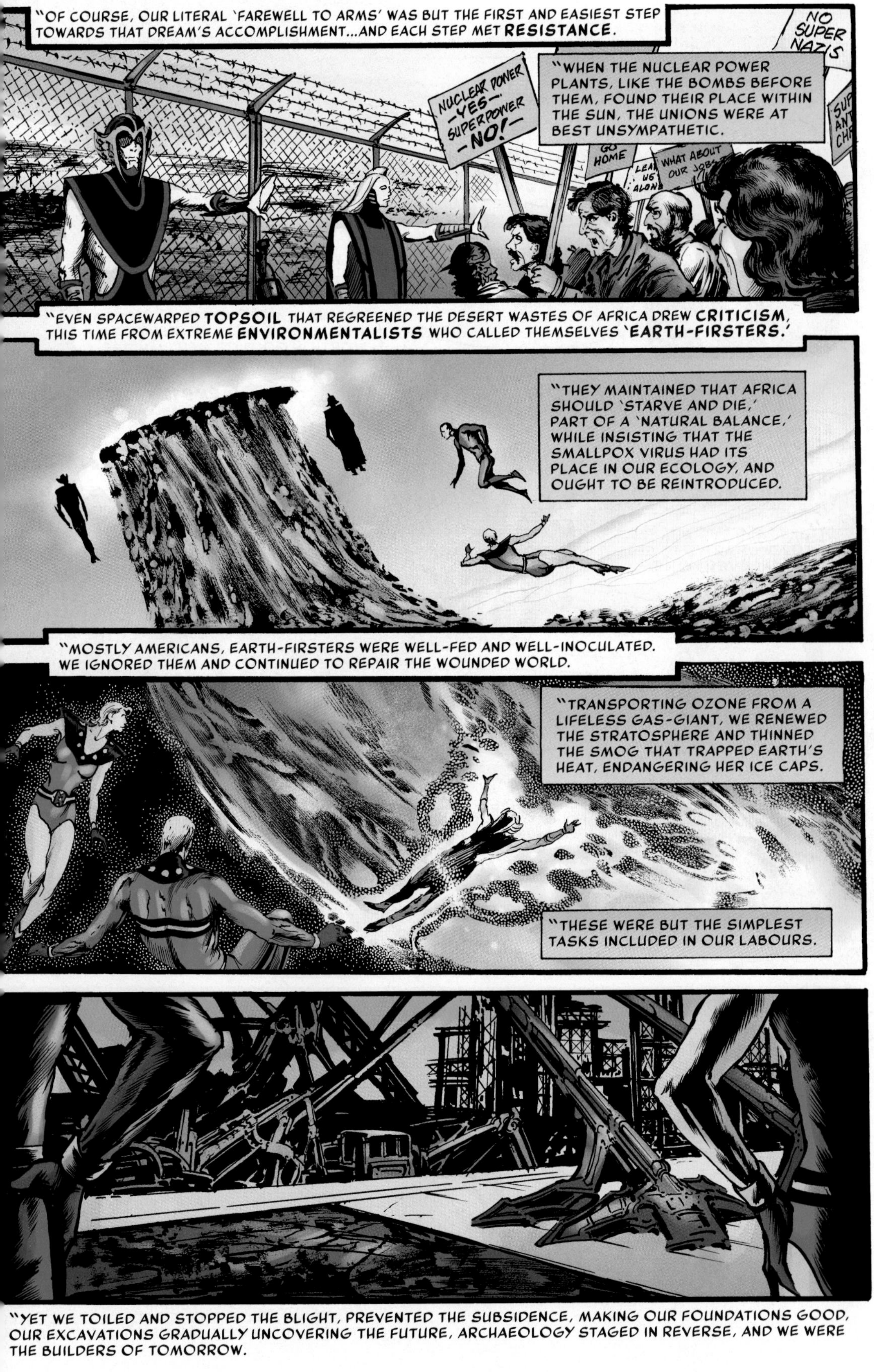
"OF COURSE, OUR LITERAL 'FAREWELL TO ARMS' WAS BUT THE FIRST AND EASIEST STEP TOWARDS THAT DREAM'S ACCOMPLISHMENT...AND EACH STEP MET **RESISTANCE**.
NO SUPER NAZIS
NUCLEAR POWER -YES- SUPERPOWER -NO!-
"WHEN THE NUCLEAR POWER PLANTS, LIKE THE BOMBS BEFORE THEM, FOUND THEIR PLACE WITHIN THE SUN, THE UNIONS WERE AT BEST UNSYMPATHETIC.
GO HOME
WHAT ABOUT OUR JOBS
"EVEN SPACEWARPED **TOPSOIL** THAT REGREENED THE DESERT WASTES OF AFRICA DREW **CRITICISM**, THIS TIME FROM EXTREME **ENVIRONMENTALISTS** WHO CALLED THEMSELVES '**EARTH-FIRSTERS.**'
"THEY MAINTAINED THAT AFRICA SHOULD 'STARVE AND DIE,' PART OF A 'NATURAL BALANCE,' WHILE INSISTING THAT THE SMALLPOX VIRUS HAD ITS PLACE IN OUR ECOLOGY, AND OUGHT TO BE REINTRODUCED.
"MOSTLY AMERICANS, EARTH-FIRSTERS WERE WELL-FED AND WELL-INOCULATED. WE IGNORED THEM AND CONTINUED TO REPAIR THE WOUNDED WORLD.
"TRANSPORTING OZONE FROM A LIFELESS GAS-GIANT, WE RENEWED THE STRATOSPHERE AND THINNED THE SMOG THAT TRAPPED EARTH'S HEAT, ENDANGERING HER ICE CAPS.
"THESE WERE BUT THE SIMPLEST TASKS INCLUDED IN OUR LABOURS.
"YET WE TOILED AND STOPPED THE BLIGHT, PREVENTED THE SUBSIDENCE, MAKING OUR FOUNDATIONS GOOD, OUR EXCAVATIONS GRADUALLY UNCOVERING THE FUTURE, ARCHAEOLOGY STAGED IN REVERSE, AND WE WERE THE BUILDERS OF TOMORROW.

"STILL, TOMORROW WAS NOT SOLELY BUILT WITH EARTH, AIR, ENERGY AND WATER. THERE EXIST **FIVE** ELEMENTS: THE FIFTH IS **MONEY**."

HELLO.

LET'S TALK ABOUT MONEY.

FOR LACK OF IT, BRAZIL MUST LEVEL PRECIOUS **FORESTS**, WITH OTHER NATIONS HUNTING PRECIOUS **WHALE MEAT** TO SURVIVE.

POOR PEOPLE CANNOT PUT THE ENVIRONMENT BEFORE THEIR CHILDREN'S BELLIES.

AND YET, WHAT IS MONEY?

MONEY IS A **PROMISE**, TO REDEEM THE CASH OF EVERY BEARER FOR ITS WORTH IN GOLD OR MERCHANDISE.

RICH NATIONS, HONOURING EACH OTHER'S EMPTY PROMISES, ASSURE THEIR MUTUAL **CREDIBILITY**...

...AND **ALWAYS** WITH THE FORCE OF **ARMS** TO SEE THAT **EVERYONE** BELIEVES!

AN **EMPTY** PROMISE. SHOULD W ALL DEMAND AT ONCE REDEMPTI OF OUR COINS, WE'D LEARN SU WEALTH DOES NOT EXIST.

MONEY'S IMAGINAR REAL IF WE BELIEV IN IT.

NO MORE.

FROM AUGUST, EVERYTHING IS **FREE**; NATIONAL SURPLUS TELEPORTED TO THOSE NATIONS MOST IN NEED UNTIL THEY MASTER SELF-SUFFICIENCY.

EACH SOUL SHALL HAVE FREE CLOTHING, FOOD AND SHELTER, ENTERTAINMENT, EDUCATION, ALL REQUIREMENTS FOR A WORTHWHILE LIFE...

...WITH GREATER LUXURIES FOR THOSE WHO **WISH** TO WORK PROVIDING THE ABOVE.

COME SUMMER, MONEY WON'T EXIST...

...BUT THEN, IT NEVER **DID**.

GOOD NIGHT.

SPECIAL BROADCAST

"...AND THUS WE CALCULATED COSTS AND ALLOCATE PROFITS, AND WE WERE ACCOUNTANTS OF UTOPIA

ONCE THINGS WERE FREE, THE CRIME RATE
PLUMMETED. ENCOURAGING THIS TREND, WE
LEGALISED ALL DRUGS, WHILE SATURATING
EARTH WITH HONEST INFORMATION ON
THEIR TOXIC OR BENIGN EFFECTS.

DRUG SMUGGLING PERISHED, ALMOST OVERNIGHT.
THE CRIME CARTELS INVOLVED, THEIR FISCAL
BASE DESTROYED, WAGED ALL-OUT WAR
THAT WE SHOULD PERISH ALSO.

SOMETIMES I ALMOST
MISS THOSE DARK-EYED
MAFIA PRINCES;
GUATEMALAN PHARMA-
RATS IN THEIR EXQUISITE
COLOURED SHIRTS.
THE PLANET SEEMS SO
QUIET WITHOUT THEM.

"OBVIOUSLY, CRIMINALS STILL
EXISTED, BUT THE WARPSMITHS
HAD SOME FASCINATING NOTIONS
THAT ASSISTED US WITH THESE:

"THEY HAD IDENTIFIED A LARGE
PROPORTION OF COMPULSIVE CRIMINAL
ACTIVITY AS BASED ON PHYSICAL
ADDICTION TO THE BODY'S
OWN ADRENALINE.

"PROVIDING AN ORGANIC
SUBSTITUTE...A LEAF THAT'S
JUICES WERE A NATURAL
ADRENOCHROME...
WE FOUND THAT
CRIME AGAIN
DECREASED.

THAT LEFT THE
PSYCHOPATHS AND BRUTES,
THE RED-FACED MEN AND
ICE-FACED WOMEN. THESE
WERE DEALT WITH INDIVIDUALLY.
SOME ARE PERHAPS INCURABLE,
BUT MANY HAVE RESPONDED WELL.

CHARLES MANSON RUNS A CARE GROUP
NOW FOR INFANTS THAT HAVE BEEN ABUSED.
THOUGH HE STILL FINDS BLACK CHILDREN
HARDER TO RELATE TO, HE PERCEIVES HIS
PROBLEM, WORKING HARD TO COUNTER IT.

"BY 1986, WE HAD
DEMOLISHED EARTH'S
LAST PENITENTIARY.

"THUS WE HEWED STONES, SMOOTHING AWAY
THEIR ROUGHEST EDGES, AND WERE MASONS OF UTOPIA.

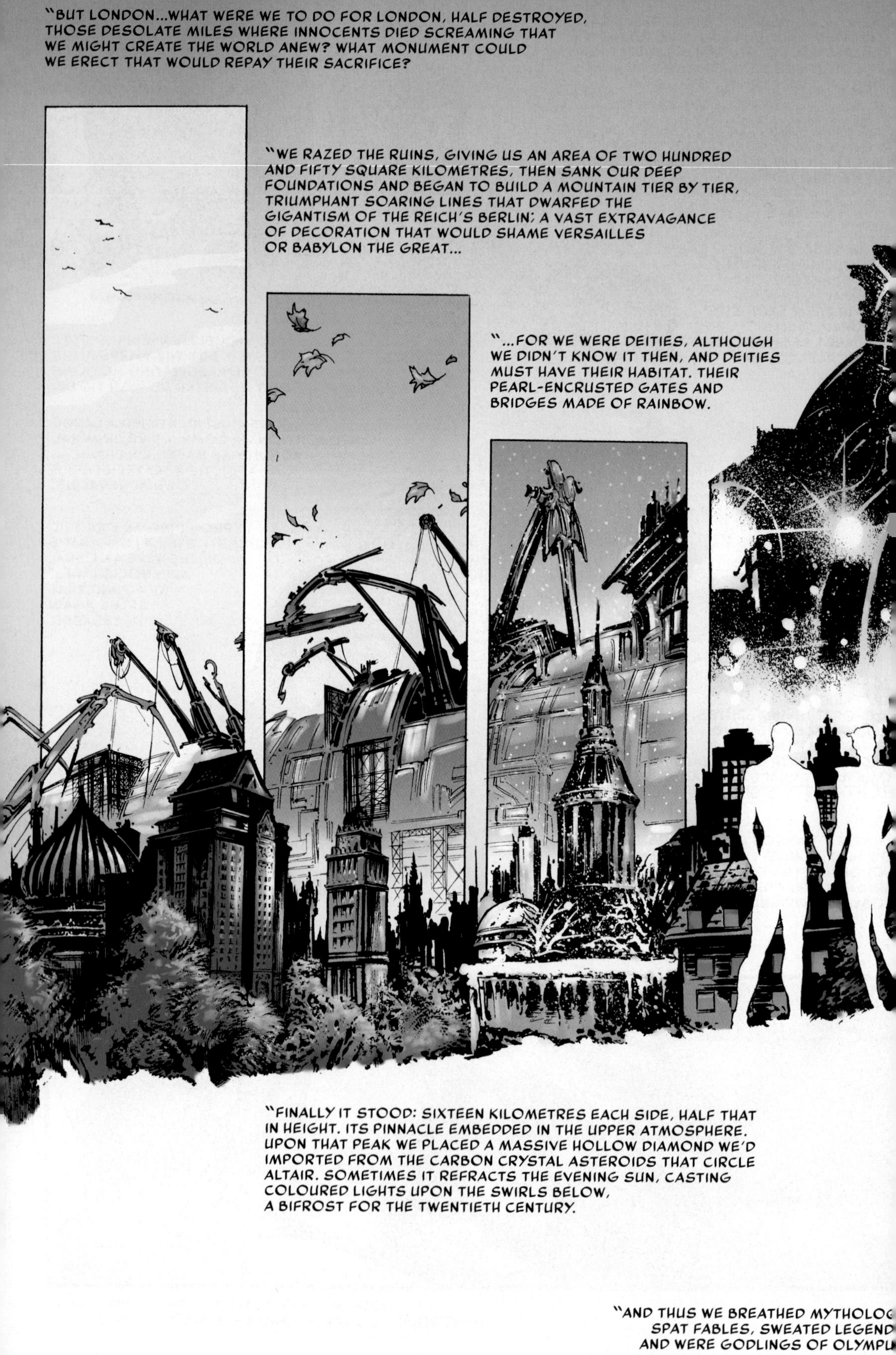
"BUT LONDON...WHAT WERE WE TO DO FOR LONDON, HALF DESTROYED, THOSE DESOLATE MILES WHERE INNOCENTS DIED SCREAMING THAT WE MIGHT CREATE THE WORLD ANEW? WHAT MONUMENT COULD WE ERECT THAT WOULD REPAY THEIR SACRIFICE?
"WE RAZED THE RUINS, GIVING US AN AREA OF TWO HUNDRED AND FIFTY SQUARE KILOMETRES, THEN SANK OUR DEEP FOUNDATIONS AND BEGAN TO BUILD A MOUNTAIN TIER BY TIER, TRIUMPHANT SOARING LINES THAT DWARFED THE GIGANTISM OF THE REICH'S BERLIN; A VAST EXTRAVAGANCE OF DECORATION THAT WOULD SHAME VERSAILLES OR BABYLON THE GREAT...
"...FOR WE WERE DEITIES, ALTHOUGH WE DIDN'T KNOW IT THEN, AND DEITIES MUST HAVE THEIR HABITAT. THEIR PEARL-ENCRUSTED GATES AND BRIDGES MADE OF RAINBOW.
"FINALLY IT STOOD: SIXTEEN KILOMETRES EACH SIDE, HALF THAT IN HEIGHT. ITS PINNACLE EMBEDDED IN THE UPPER ATMOSPHERE. UPON THAT PEAK WE PLACED A MASSIVE HOLLOW DIAMOND WE'D IMPORTED FROM THE CARBON CRYSTAL ASTEROIDS THAT CIRCLE ALTAIR. SOMETIMES IT REFRACTS THE EVENING SUN, CASTING COLOURED LIGHTS UPON THE SWIRLS BELOW, A BIFROST FOR THE TWENTIETH CENTURY.
"AND THUS WE BREATHED MYTHOLOG
SPAT FABLES, SWEATED LEGEND
AND WERE GODLINGS OF OLYMPU

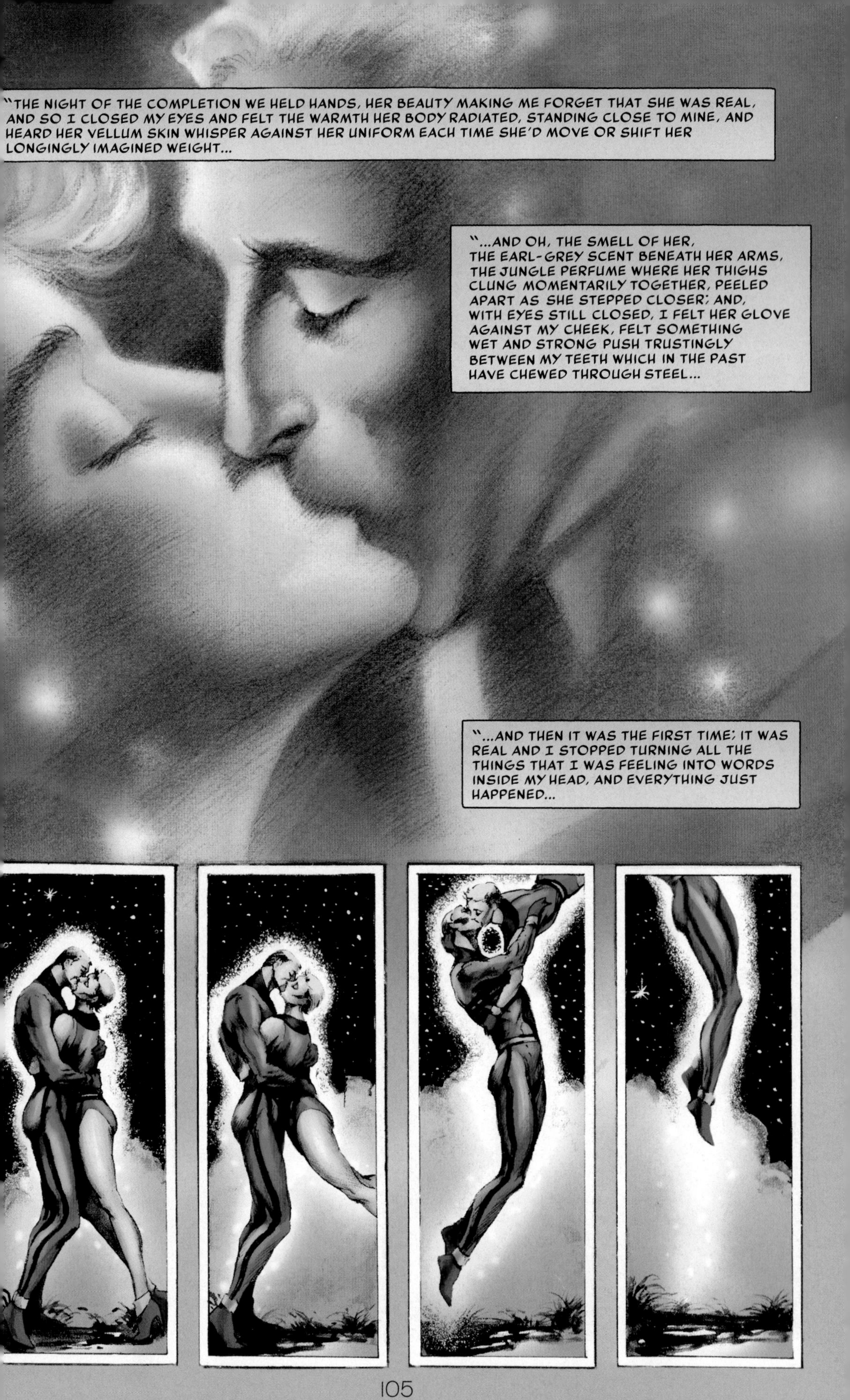
"THE NIGHT OF THE COMPLETION WE HELD HANDS, HER BEAUTY MAKING ME FORGET THAT SHE WAS REAL, AND SO I CLOSED MY EYES AND FELT THE WARMTH HER BODY RADIATED, STANDING CLOSE TO MINE, AND HEARD HER VELLUM SKIN WHISPER AGAINST HER UNIFORM EACH TIME SHE'D MOVE OR SHIFT HER LONGINGLY IMAGINED WEIGHT...
"...AND OH, THE SMELL OF HER, THE EARL-GREY SCENT BENEATH HER ARMS, THE JUNGLE PERFUME WHERE HER THIGHS CLUNG MOMENTARILY TOGETHER, PEELED APART AS SHE STEPPED CLOSER; AND, WITH EYES STILL CLOSED, I FELT HER GLOVE AGAINST MY CHEEK, FELT SOMETHING WET AND STRONG PUSH TRUSTINGLY BETWEEN MY TEETH WHICH IN THE PAST HAVE CHEWED THROUGH STEEL...
"...AND THEN IT WAS THE FIRST TIME; IT WAS REAL AND I STOPPED TURNING ALL THE THINGS THAT I WAS FEELING INTO WORDS INSIDE MY HEAD, AND EVERYTHING JUST HAPPENED...

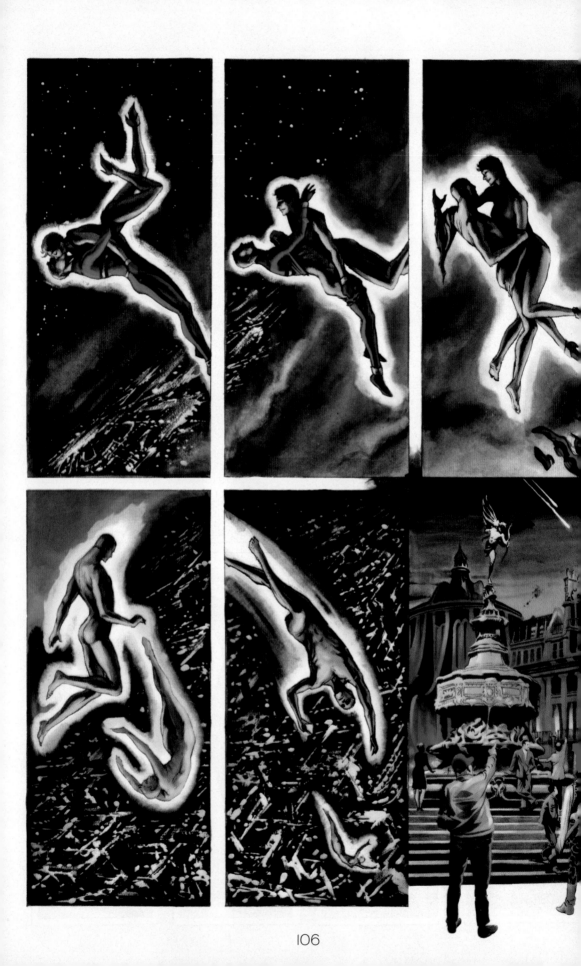

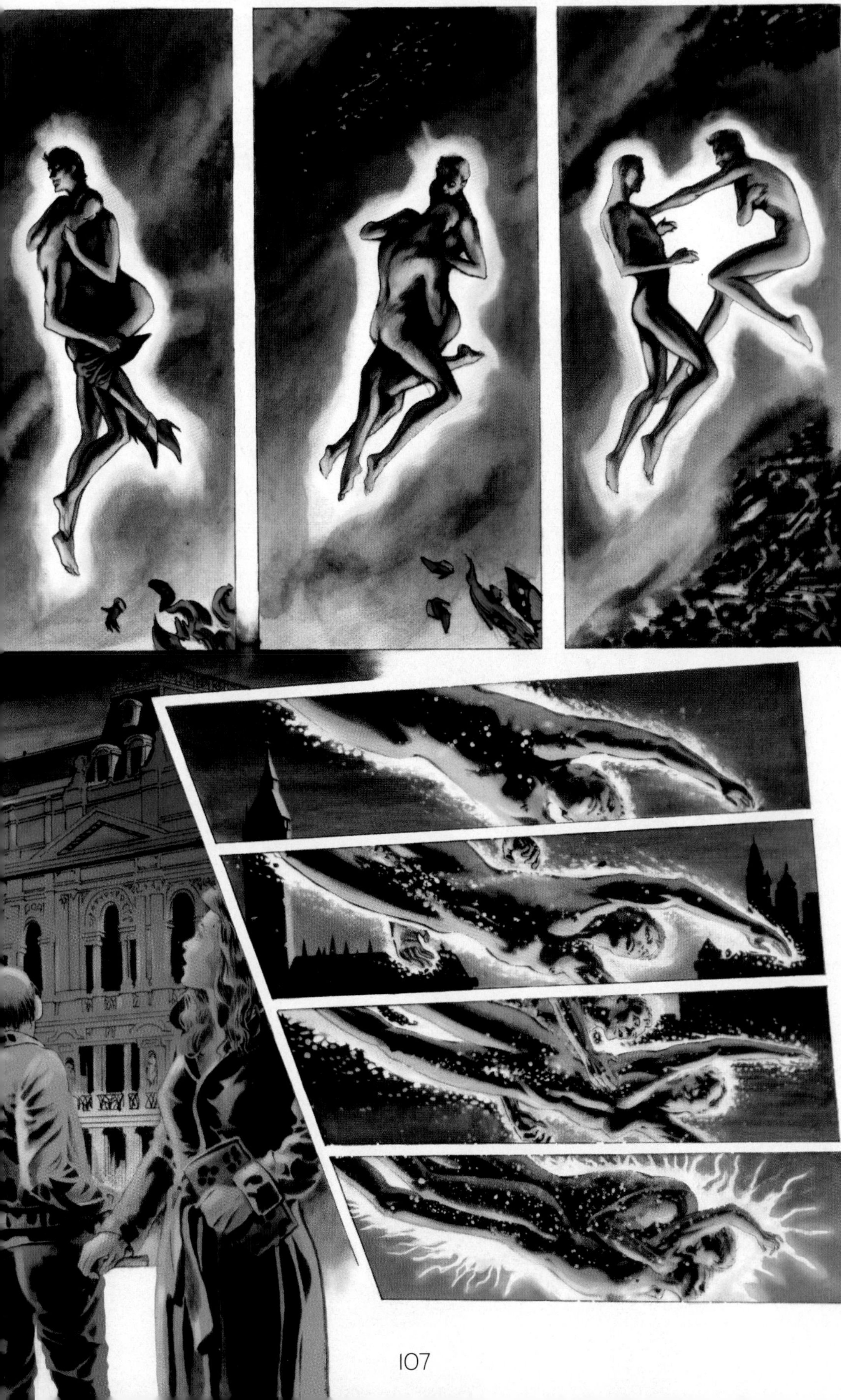

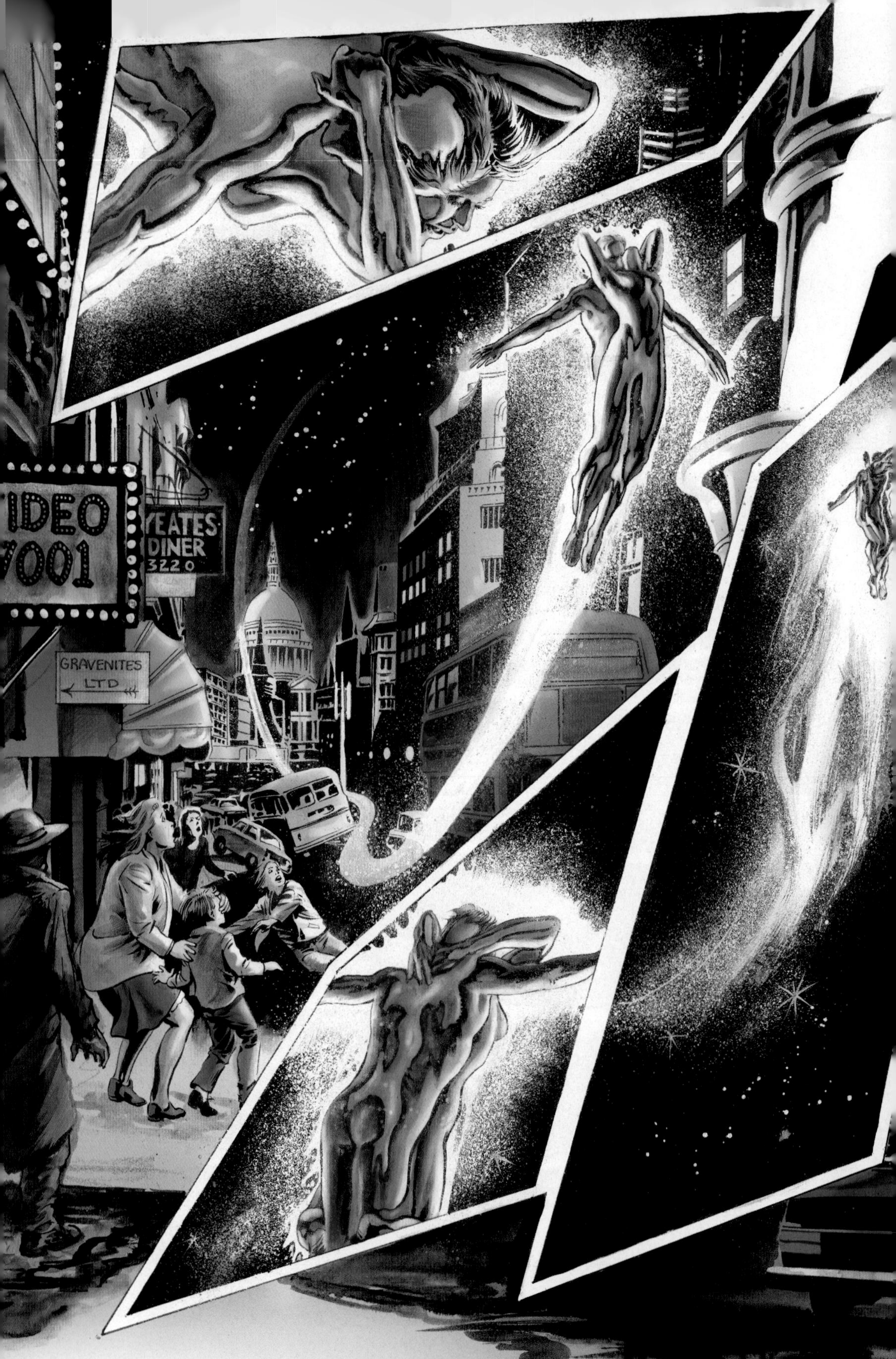
IDEO
7001
YEATES
DINER
3220
GRAVENITES
LTD

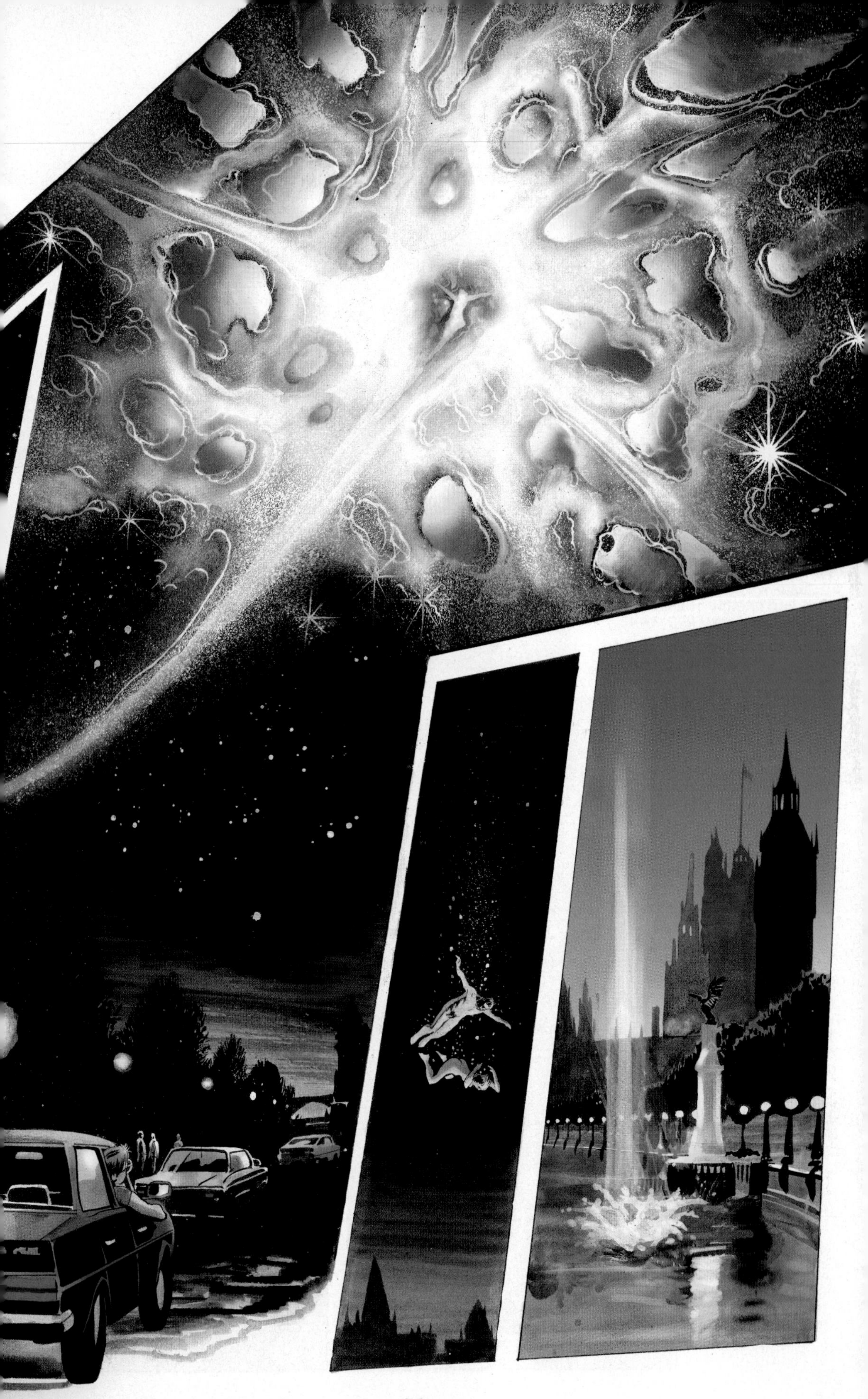

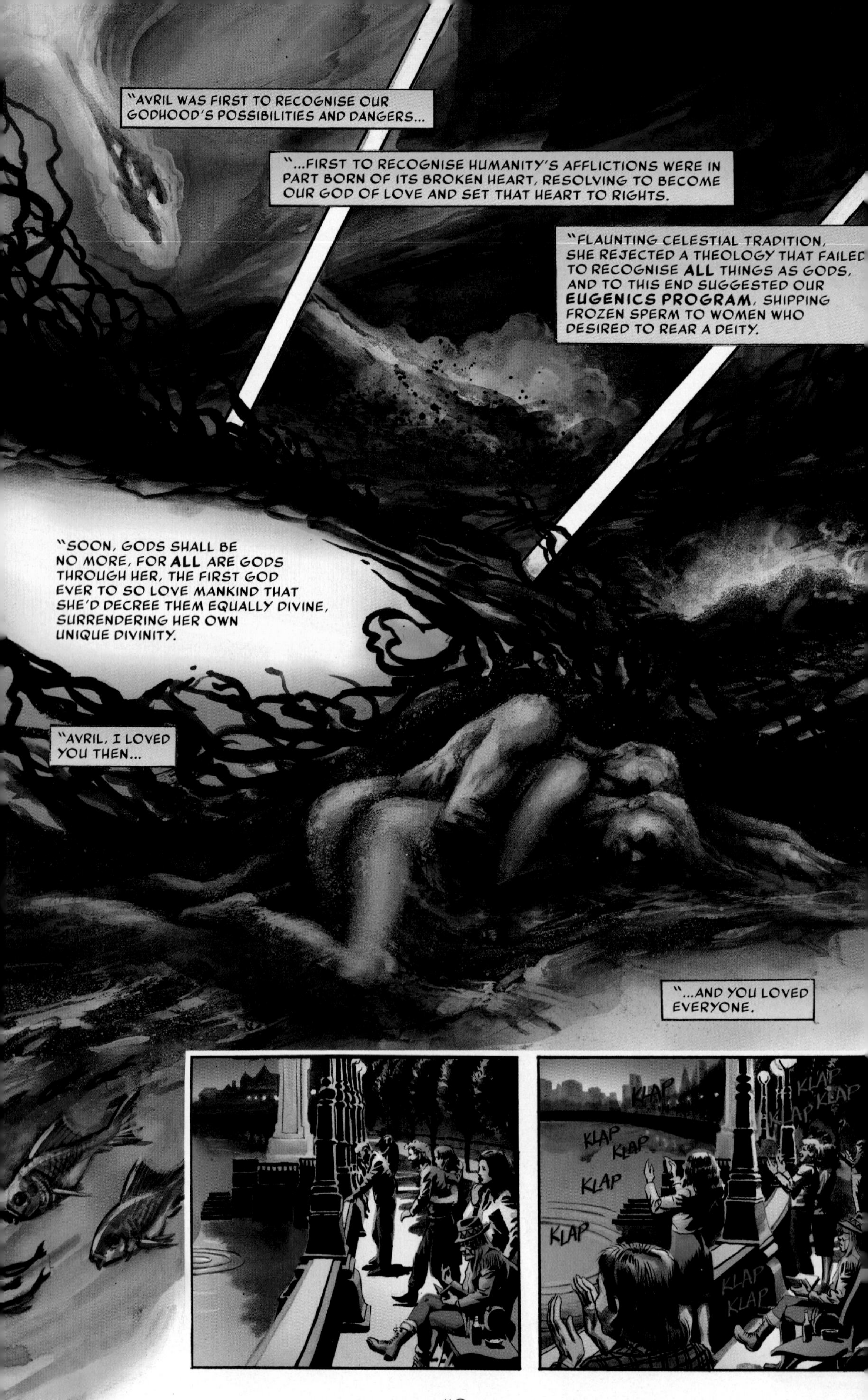
"AVRIL WAS FIRST TO RECOGNISE OUR GODHOOD'S POSSIBILITIES AND DANGERS...
"...FIRST TO RECOGNISE HUMANITY'S AFFLICTIONS WERE IN PART BORN OF ITS BROKEN HEART, RESOLVING TO BECOME OUR GOD OF LOVE AND SET THAT HEART TO RIGHTS.
"FLAUNTING CELESTIAL TRADITION, SHE REJECTED A THEOLOGY THAT FAILED TO RECOGNISE ALL THINGS AS GODS, AND TO THIS END SUGGESTED OUR EUGENICS PROGRAM, SHIPPING FROZEN SPERM TO WOMEN WHO DESIRED TO REAR A DEITY.
"SOON, GODS SHALL BE NO MORE, FOR ALL ARE GODS THROUGH HER, THE FIRST GOD EVER TO SO LOVE MANKIND THAT SHE'D DECREE THEM EQUALLY DIVINE, SURRENDERING HER OWN UNIQUE DIVINITY.
"AVRIL, I LOVED YOU THEN...
"...AND YOU LOVED EVERYONE.
KLAP
KLAP KLAP
KLAP KLAP
KLAP KLAP
KLAP
KLAP
KLAP KLAP

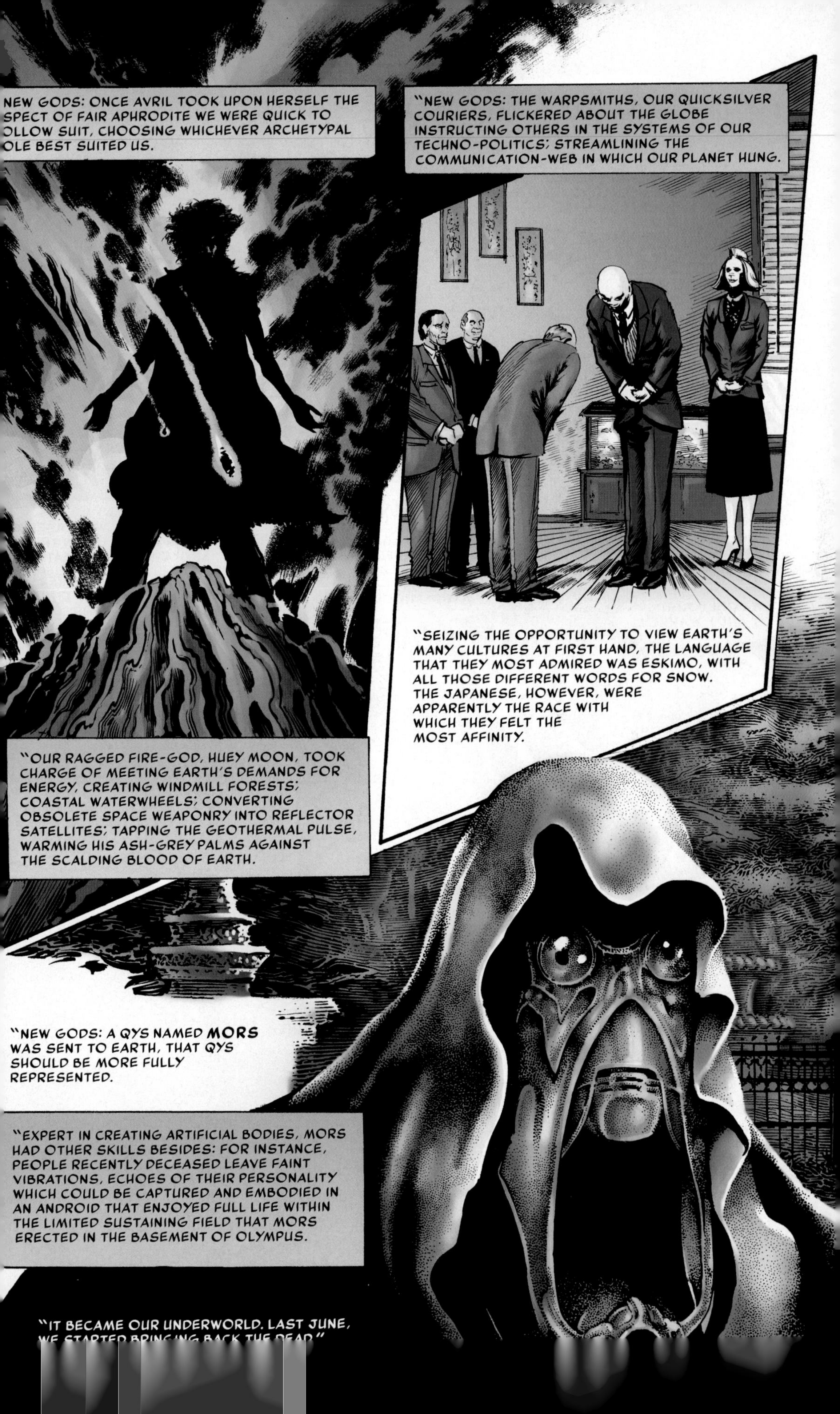
NEW GODS: ONCE AVRIL TOOK UPON HERSELF THE SPECT OF FAIR APHRODITE WE WERE QUICK TO OLLOW SUIT, CHOOSING WHICHEVER ARCHETYPAL OLE BEST SUITED US.
"NEW GODS: THE WARPSMITHS, OUR QUICKSILVER COURIERS, FLICKERED ABOUT THE GLOBE INSTRUCTING OTHERS IN THE SYSTEMS OF OUR TECHNO-POLITICS; STREAMLINING THE COMMUNICATION-WEB IN WHICH OUR PLANET HUNG.
"SEIZING THE OPPORTUNITY TO VIEW EARTH'S MANY CULTURES AT FIRST HAND, THE LANGUAGE THAT THEY MOST ADMIRED WAS ESKIMO, WITH ALL THOSE DIFFERENT WORDS FOR SNOW. THE JAPANESE, HOWEVER, WERE APPARENTLY THE RACE WITH WHICH THEY FELT THE MOST AFFINITY.
"OUR RAGGED FIRE-GOD, HUEY MOON, TOOK CHARGE OF MEETING EARTH'S DEMANDS FOR ENERGY, CREATING WINDMILL FORESTS; COASTAL WATERWHEELS; CONVERTING OBSOLETE SPACE WEAPONRY INTO REFLECTOR SATELLITES; TAPPING THE GEOTHERMAL PULSE, WARMING HIS ASH-GREY PALMS AGAINST THE SCALDING BLOOD OF EARTH.
"NEW GODS: A QYS NAMED MORS WAS SENT TO EARTH, THAT QYS SHOULD BE MORE FULLY REPRESENTED.
"EXPERT IN CREATING ARTIFICIAL BODIES, MORS HAD OTHER SKILLS BESIDES: FOR INSTANCE, PEOPLE RECENTLY DECEASED LEAVE FAINT VIBRATIONS, ECHOES OF THEIR PERSONALITY WHICH COULD BE CAPTURED AND EMBODIED IN AN ANDROID THAT ENJOYED FULL LIFE WITHIN THE LIMITED SUSTAINING FIELD THAT MORS ERECTED IN THE BASEMENT OF OLYMPUS.
"IT BECAME OUR UNDERWORLD. LAST JUNE,

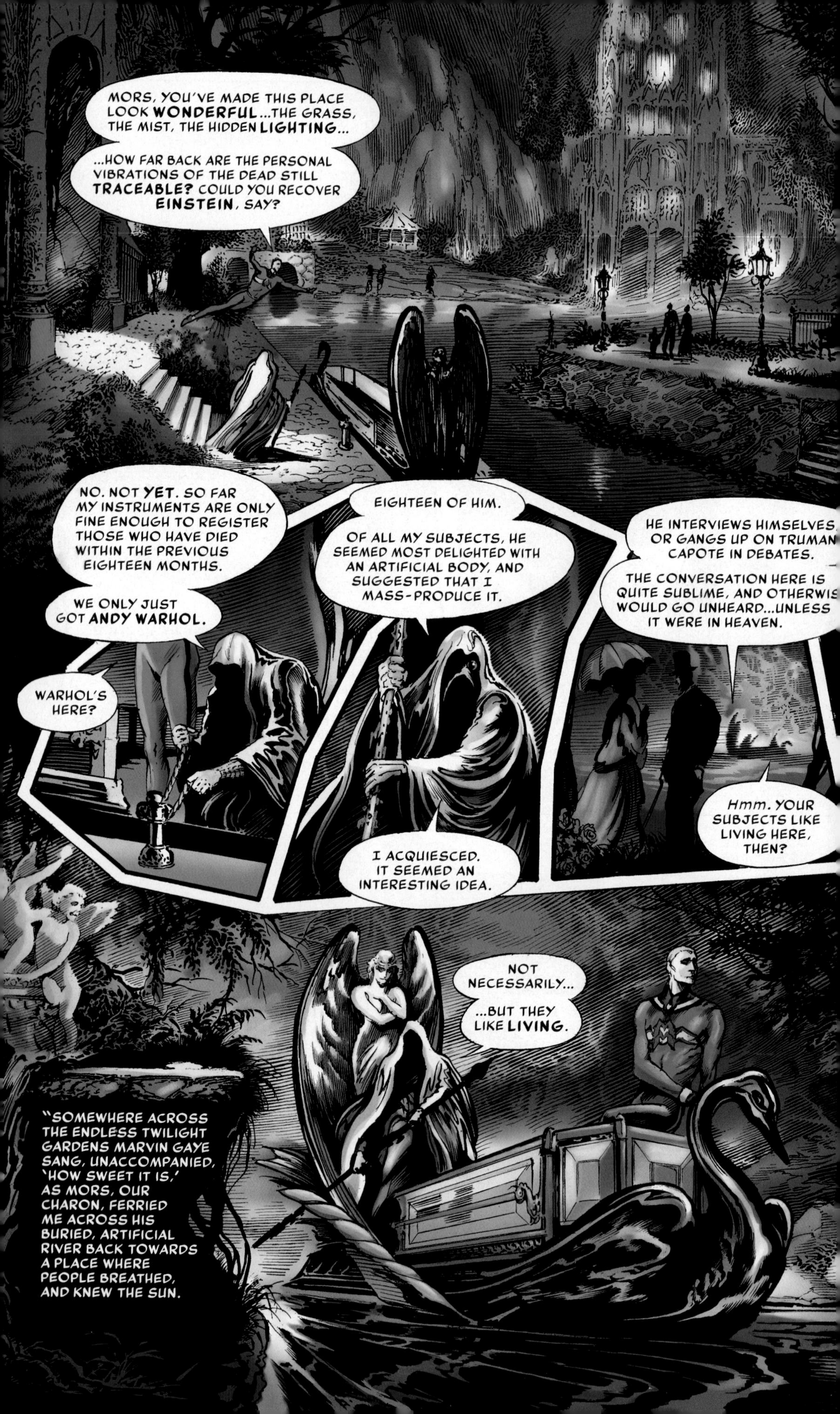
MORS, YOU'VE MADE THIS PLACE LOOK WONDERFUL...THE GRASS, THE MIST, THE HIDDEN LIGHTING...
...HOW FAR BACK ARE THE PERSONAL VIBRATIONS OF THE DEAD STILL TRACEABLE? COULD YOU RECOVER EINSTEIN, SAY?
NO. NOT YET. SO FAR MY INSTRUMENTS ARE ONLY FINE ENOUGH TO REGISTER THOSE WHO HAVE DIED WITHIN THE PREVIOUS EIGHTEEN MONTHS.
WE ONLY JUST GOT ANDY WARHOL.
WARHOL'S HERE?
EIGHTEEN OF HIM.
OF ALL MY SUBJECTS, HE SEEMED MOST DELIGHTED WITH AN ARTIFICIAL BODY, AND SUGGESTED THAT I MASS-PRODUCE IT.
I ACQUIESCED. IT SEEMED AN INTERESTING IDEA.
HE INTERVIEWS HIMSELVES, OR GANGS UP ON TRUMAN CAPOTE IN DEBATES.
THE CONVERSATION HERE IS QUITE SUBLIME, AND OTHERWIS WOULD GO UNHEARD...UNLESS IT WERE IN HEAVEN.
Hmm. YOUR SUBJECTS LIKE LIVING HERE, THEN?
NOT NECESSARILY...
...BUT THEY LIKE LIVING.
"SOMEWHERE ACROSS THE ENDLESS TWILIGHT GARDENS MARVIN GAYE SANG, UNACCOMPANIED, 'HOW SWEET IT IS,' AS MORS, OUR CHARON, FERRIED ME ACROSS HIS BURIED, ARTIFICIAL RIVER BACK TOWARDS A PLACE WHERE PEOPLE BREATHED, AND KNEW THE SUN.

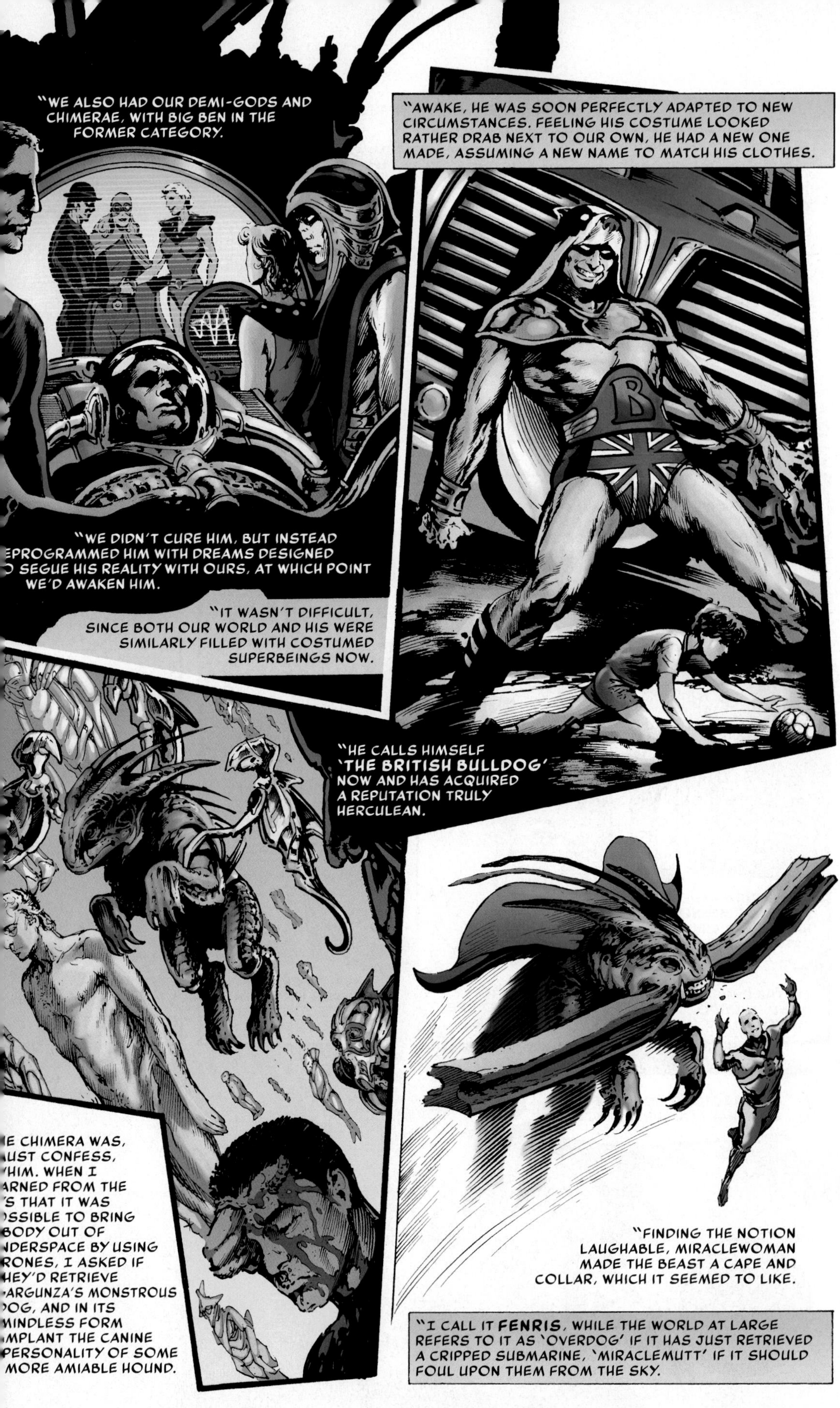
"WE ALSO HAD OUR DEMI-GODS AND CHIMERAE, WITH BIG BEN IN THE FORMER CATEGORY.
"WE DIDN'T CURE HIM, BUT INSTEAD EPROGRAMMED HIM WITH DREAMS DESIGNED O SEGUE HIS REALITY WITH OURS, AT WHICH POINT WE'D AWAKEN HIM.
"IT WASN'T DIFFICULT, SINCE BOTH OUR WORLD AND HIS WERE SIMILARLY FILLED WITH COSTUMED SUPERBEINGS NOW.
"AWAKE, HE WAS SOON PERFECTLY ADAPTED TO NEW CIRCUMSTANCES. FEELING HIS COSTUME LOOKED RATHER DRAB NEXT TO OUR OWN, HE HAD A NEW ONE MADE, ASSUMING A NEW NAME TO MATCH HIS CLOTHES.
"HE CALLS HIMSELF 'THE BRITISH BULLDOG' NOW AND HAS ACQUIRED A REPUTATION TRULY HERCULEAN.
E CHIMERA WAS, UST CONFESS, HIM. WHEN I ARNED FROM THE 'S THAT IT WAS SSIBLE TO BRING BODY OUT OF NDERSPACE BY USING RONES, I ASKED IF HEY'D RETRIEVE ARGUNZA'S MONSTROUS OG, AND IN ITS MINDLESS FORM MPLANT THE CANINE PERSONALITY OF SOME MORE AMIABLE HOUND.
"FINDING THE NOTION LAUGHABLE, MIRACLEWOMAN MADE THE BEAST A CAPE AND COLLAR, WHICH IT SEEMED TO LIKE.
"I CALL IT FENRIS, WHILE THE WORLD AT LARGE REFERS TO IT AS 'OVERDOG' IF IT HAS JUST RETRIEVED A CRIPPED SUBMARINE, 'MIRACLEMUTT' IF IT SHOULD FOUL UPON THEM FROM THE SKY.

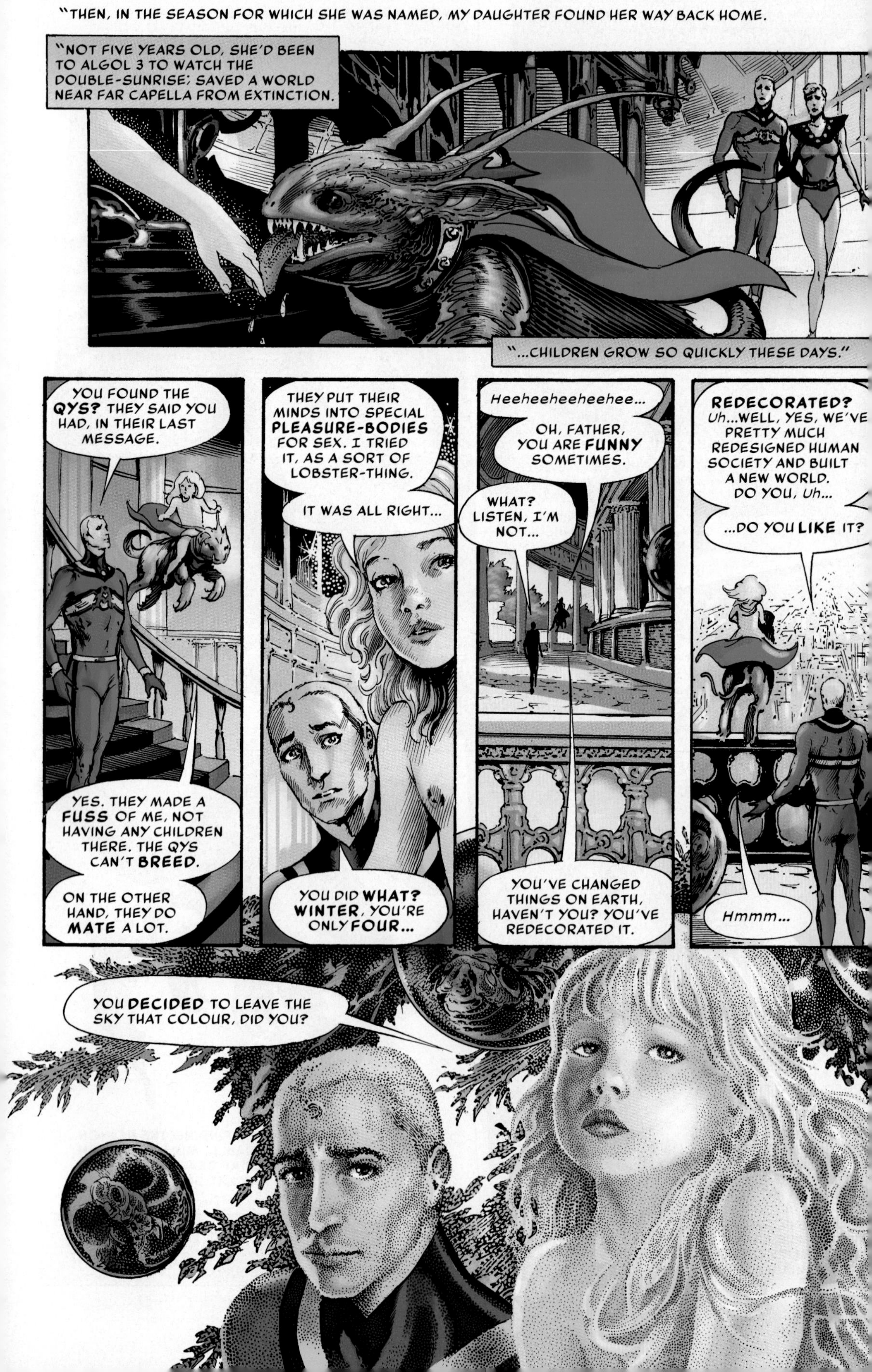

"THEN, IN THE SEASON FOR WHICH SHE WAS NAMED, MY DAUGHTER FOUND HER WAY BACK HOME.
"NOT FIVE YEARS OLD, SHE'D BEEN TO ALGOL 3 TO WATCH THE DOUBLE-SUNRISE; SAVED A WORLD NEAR FAR CAPELLA FROM EXTINCTION.
"...CHILDREN GROW SO QUICKLY THESE DAYS."
YOU FOUND THE QYS? THEY SAID YOU HAD, IN THEIR LAST MESSAGE.
YES. THEY MADE A FUSS OF ME, NOT HAVING ANY CHILDREN THERE. THE QYS CAN'T BREED.
ON THE OTHER HAND, THEY DO MATE A LOT.
THEY PUT THEIR MINDS INTO SPECIAL PLEASURE-BODIES FOR SEX. I TRIED IT, AS A SORT OF LOBSTER-THING.
IT WAS ALL RIGHT...
YOU DID WHAT? WINTER, YOU'RE ONLY FOUR...
Heeheeheeheehee...
OH, FATHER, YOU ARE FUNNY SOMETIMES.
WHAT? LISTEN, I'M NOT...
YOU'VE CHANGED THINGS ON EARTH, HAVEN'T YOU? YOU'VE REDECORATED IT.
REDECORATED? Uh...WELL, YES, WE'VE PRETTY MUCH REDESIGNED HUMAN SOCIETY AND BUILT A NEW WORLD. DO YOU, Uh...
...DO YOU LIKE IT?
Hmmm...
YOU DECIDED TO LEAVE THE SKY THAT COLOUR, DID YOU?

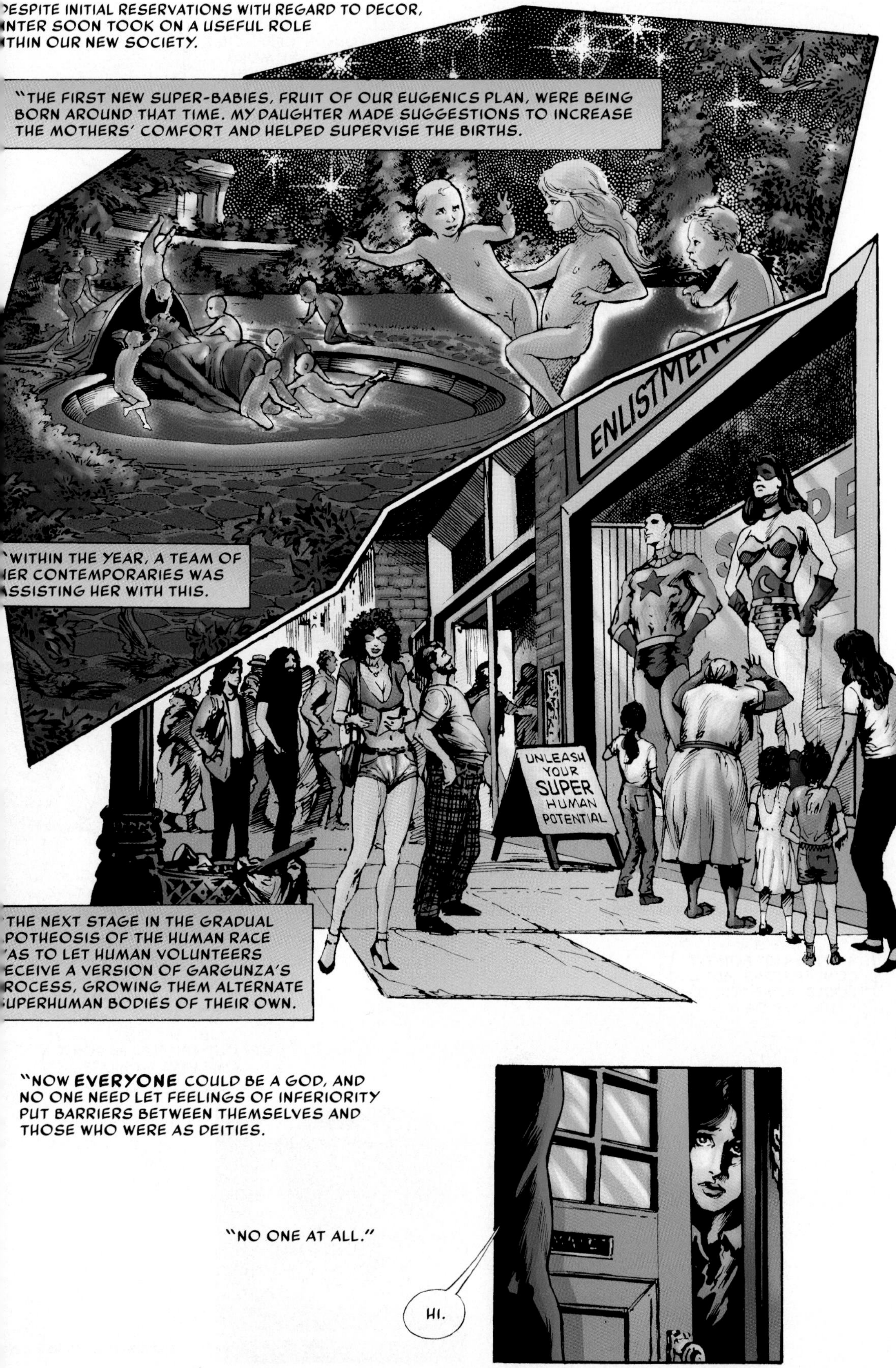

ESPITE INITIAL RESERVATIONS WITH REGARD TO DECOR, NTER SOON TOOK ON A USEFUL ROLE THIN OUR NEW SOCIETY.
"THE FIRST NEW SUPER-BABIES, FRUIT OF OUR EUGENICS PLAN, WERE BEING BORN AROUND THAT TIME. MY DAUGHTER MADE SUGGESTIONS TO INCREASE THE MOTHERS' COMFORT AND HELPED SUPERVISE THE BIRTHS.
"WITHIN THE YEAR, A TEAM OF IER CONTEMPORARIES WAS SSISTING HER WITH THIS.
ENLISTMEN
UNLEASH YOUR SUPER HUMAN POTENTIAL
THE NEXT STAGE IN THE GRADUAL POTHEOSIS OF THE HUMAN RACE 'AS TO LET HUMAN VOLUNTEERS ECEIVE A VERSION OF GARGUNZA'S ROCESS, GROWING THEM ALTERNATE UPERHUMAN BODIES OF THEIR OWN.
"NOW EVERYONE COULD BE A GOD, AND NO ONE NEED LET FEELINGS OF INFERIORITY PUT BARRIERS BETWEEN THEMSELVES AND THOSE WHO WERE AS DEITIES.
"NO ONE AT ALL."
HI.

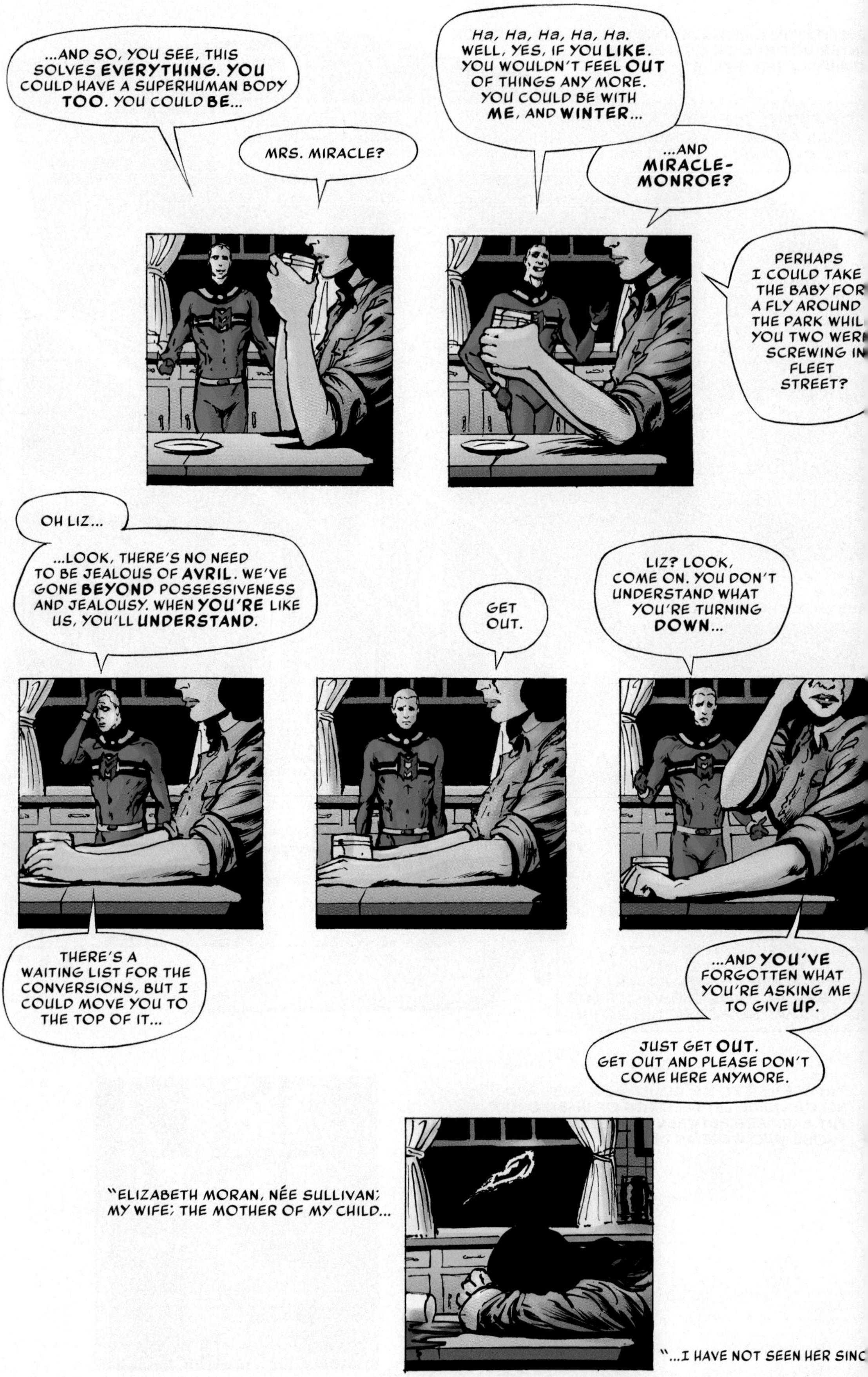

...AND SO, YOU SEE, THIS SOLVES EVERYTHING. YOU COULD HAVE A SUPERHUMAN BODY TOO. YOU COULD BE...
MRS. MIRACLE?
Ha, Ha, Ha, Ha, Ha. WELL, YES, IF YOU LIKE. YOU WOULDN'T FEEL OUT OF THINGS ANY MORE. YOU COULD BE WITH ME, AND WINTER...
...AND MIRACLE-MONROE?
PERHAPS I COULD TAKE THE BABY FOR A FLY AROUND THE PARK WHIL YOU TWO WER SCREWING IN FLEET STREET?
OH LIZ...
...LOOK, THERE'S NO NEED TO BE JEALOUS OF AVRIL. WE'VE GONE BEYOND POSSESSIVENESS AND JEALOUSY. WHEN YOU'RE LIKE US, YOU'LL UNDERSTAND.
THERE'S A WAITING LIST FOR THE CONVERSIONS, BUT I COULD MOVE YOU TO THE TOP OF IT...
GET OUT.
LIZ? LOOK, COME ON. YOU DON'T UNDERSTAND WHAT YOU'RE TURNING DOWN...
...AND YOU'VE FORGOTTEN WHAT YOU'RE ASKING ME TO GIVE UP.
JUST GET OUT. GET OUT AND PLEASE DON'T COME HERE ANYMORE.
"ELIZABETH MORAN, NÉE SULLIVAN; MY WIFE; THE MOTHER OF MY CHILD...
"...I HAVE NOT SEEN HER SINC

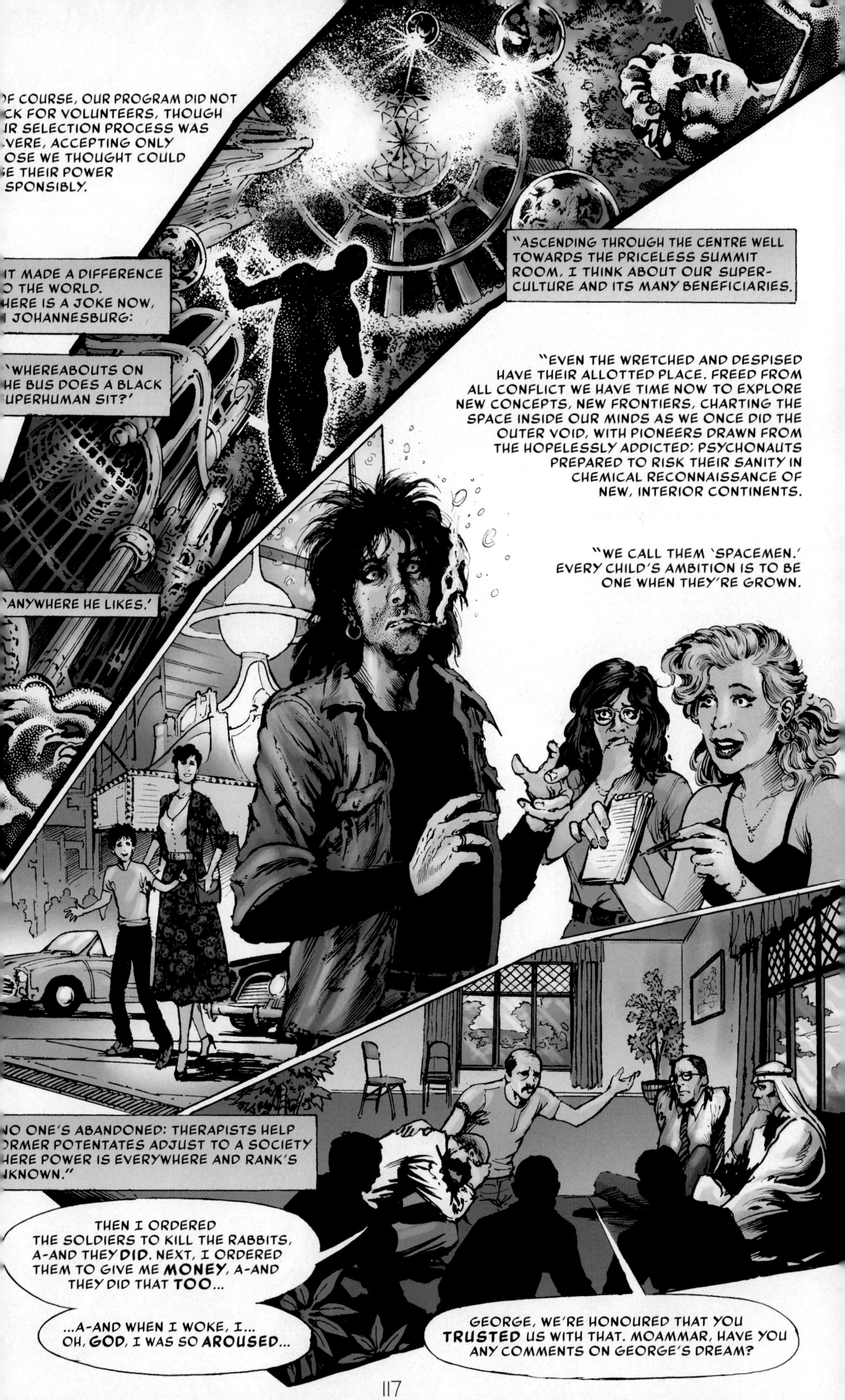

OF COURSE, OUR PROGRAM DID NOT ASK FOR VOLUNTEERS, THOUGH OUR SELECTION PROCESS WAS SEVERE, ACCEPTING ONLY THOSE WE THOUGHT COULD USE THEIR POWER RESPONSIBLY.
"ASCENDING THROUGH THE CENTRE WELL TOWARDS THE PRICELESS SUMMIT ROOM, I THINK ABOUT OUR SUPER-CULTURE AND ITS MANY BENEFICIARIES.
IT MADE A DIFFERENCE TO THE WORLD. THERE IS A JOKE NOW, IN JOHANNESBURG:
'WHEREABOUTS ON THE BUS DOES A BLACK SUPERHUMAN SIT?'
'ANYWHERE HE LIKES.'
"EVEN THE WRETCHED AND DESPISED HAVE THEIR ALLOTTED PLACE. FREED FROM ALL CONFLICT WE HAVE TIME NOW TO EXPLORE NEW CONCEPTS, NEW FRONTIERS, CHARTING THE SPACE INSIDE OUR MINDS AS WE ONCE DID THE OUTER VOID, WITH PIONEERS DRAWN FROM THE HOPELESSLY ADDICTED; PSYCHONAUTS PREPARED TO RISK THEIR SANITY IN CHEMICAL RECONNAISSANCE OF NEW, INTERIOR CONTINENTS.
"WE CALL THEM 'SPACEMEN.' EVERY CHILD'S AMBITION IS TO BE ONE WHEN THEY'RE GROWN.
NO ONE'S ABANDONED: THERAPISTS HELP FORMER POTENTATES ADJUST TO A SOCIETY WHERE POWER IS EVERYWHERE AND RANK'S UNKNOWN."
THEN I ORDERED THE SOLDIERS TO KILL THE RABBITS, A-AND THEY **DID**. NEXT, I ORDERED THEM TO GIVE ME **MONEY**, A-AND THEY DID THAT **TOO**...
...A-AND WHEN I WOKE, I... OH, **GOD**, I WAS SO **AROUSED**...
GEORGE, WE'RE HONOURED THAT YOU **TRUSTED** US WITH THAT. MOAMMAR, HAVE YOU ANY COMMENTS ON GEORGE'S DREAM?

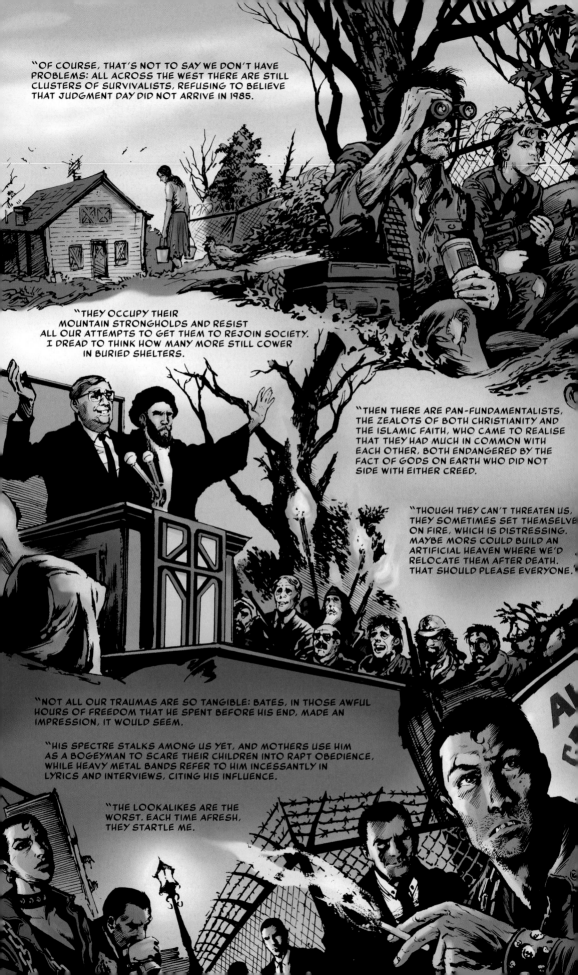

"OF COURSE, THAT'S NOT TO SAY WE DON'T HAVE PROBLEMS: ALL ACROSS THE WEST THERE ARE STILL CLUSTERS OF SURVIVALISTS, REFUSING TO BELIEVE THAT JUDGMENT DAY DID NOT ARRIVE IN 1985.

"THEY OCCUPY THEIR MOUNTAIN STRONGHOLDS AND RESIST ALL OUR ATTEMPTS TO GET THEM TO REJOIN SOCIETY. I DREAD TO THINK HOW MANY MORE STILL COWER IN BURIED SHELTERS.

"THEN THERE ARE PAN-FUNDAMENTALISTS, THE ZEALOTS OF BOTH CHRISTIANITY AND THE ISLAMIC FAITH, WHO CAME TO REALISE THAT THEY HAD MUCH IN COMMON WITH EACH OTHER, BOTH ENDANGERED BY THE FACT OF GODS ON EARTH WHO DID NOT SIDE WITH EITHER CREED.

"THOUGH THEY CAN'T THREATEN US, THEY SOMETIMES SET THEMSELVES ON FIRE, WHICH IS DISTRESSING. MAYBE MORS COULD BUILD AN ARTIFICIAL HEAVEN WHERE WE'D RELOCATE THEM AFTER DEATH. THAT SHOULD PLEASE EVERYONE."

"NOT ALL OUR TRAUMAS ARE SO TANGIBLE: BATES, IN THOSE AWFUL HOURS OF FREEDOM THAT HE SPENT BEFORE HIS END, MADE AN IMPRESSION, IT WOULD SEEM.

"HIS SPECTRE STALKS AMONG US YET, AND MOTHERS USE HIM AS A BOGEYMAN TO SCARE THEIR CHILDREN INTO RAPT OBEDIENCE, WHILE HEAVY METAL BANDS REFER TO HIM INCESSANTLY IN LYRICS AND INTERVIEWS, CITING HIS INFLUENCE.

"THE LOOKALIKES ARE THE WORST. EACH TIME AFRESH, THEY STARTLE ME.

AND YET, THESE FAULTS DO NOT DIMINISH OUR ACHIEVEMENT: ALL HUMANITY PREPARES TO FLY, DRESSED IN THEIR CAPES AND GAUDY PLUMAGE; A MIGRATION OF EXOTIC BIRDS; A FLUTTERING, GORGEOUS CLOUD RESTLESS TO RISE INTO THE UNIVERSE.

"IS THIS PERFECTION, THEN?

"I THINK SO.

"IN THE ANTECHAMBER OF THE CRYSTAL ROOM, MY CEREMONIAL UNIFORM AWAITS, HUNG ON A PEG OF GOLD.

"PERFECTION.

"NOT WITHOUT ITS PROBLEMS, I'LL CONFESS; BUT THEN, WITHOUT THEM, COULD PERFECTION BE?

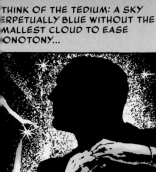

THINK OF THE TEDIUM: A SKY PERPETUALLY BLUE WITHOUT THE SMALLEST CLOUD TO EASE MONOTONY...

"...A POEM WITH NO WORD MISJUDGED...

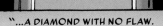

"...A DIAMOND WITH NO FLAW.

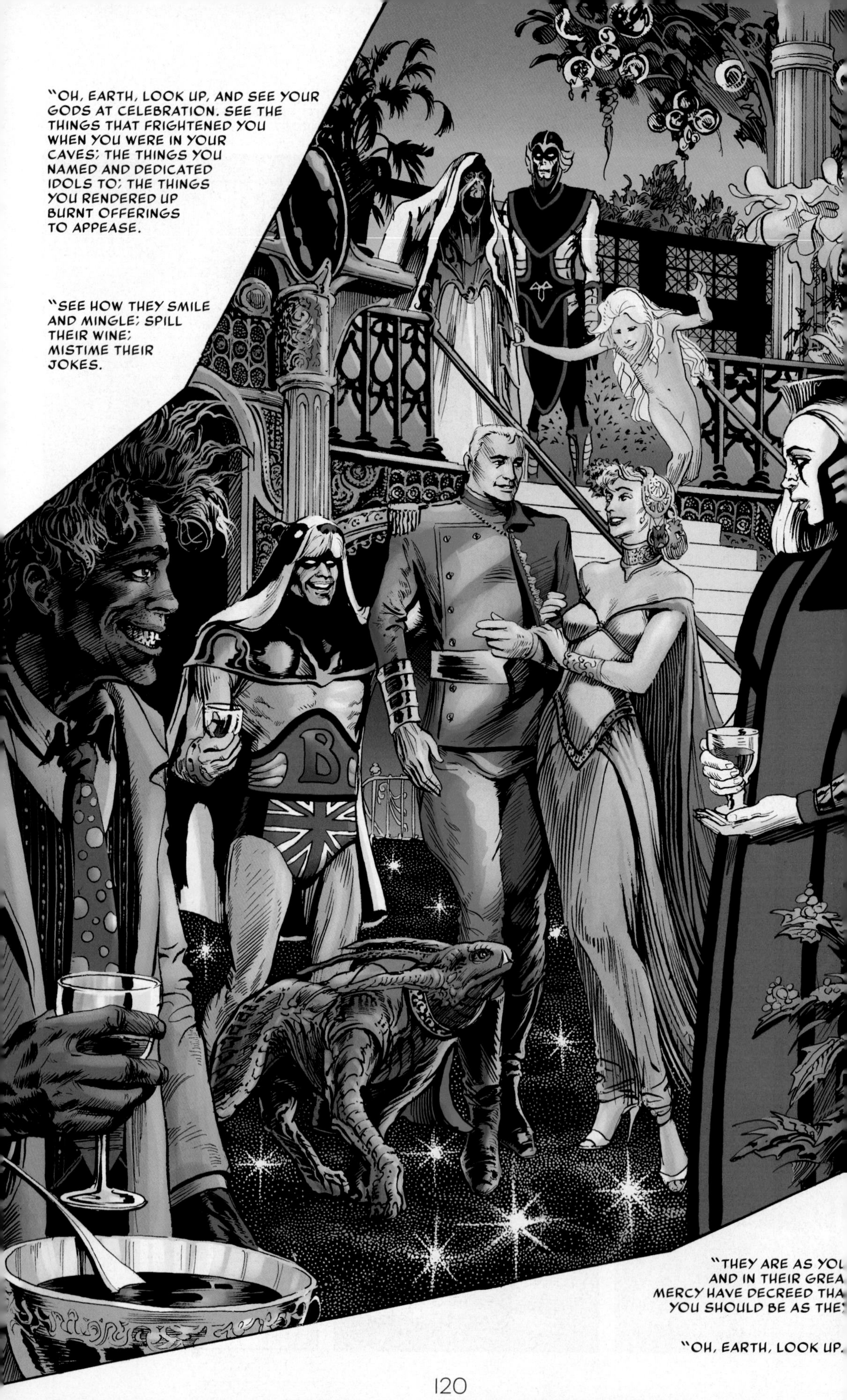
"OH, EARTH, LOOK UP, AND SEE YOUR GODS AT CELEBRATION. SEE THE THINGS THAT FRIGHTENED YOU WHEN YOU WERE IN YOUR CAVES; THE THINGS YOU NAMED AND DEDICATED IDOLS TO; THE THINGS YOU RENDERED UP BURNT OFFERINGS TO APPEASE.
"SEE HOW THEY SMILE AND MINGLE; SPILL THEIR WINE; MISTIME THEIR JOKES.
"THEY ARE AS YOL AND IN THEIR GREA MERCY HAVE DECREED THA YOU SHOULD BE AS THE
"OH, EARTH, LOOK UP.

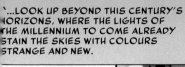

`...LOOK UP BEYOND THIS CENTURY'S HORIZONS, WHERE THE LIGHTS OF THE MILLENNIUM TO COME ALREADY STAIN THE SKIES WITH COLOURS STRANGE AND NEW.

"LOOK UP: WE HAVE REPEALED THE LAWS OF GRAVITY, TORN OFF THE CEILING OF THE WORLD THAT WAS SO VERY LOW.

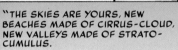

"THE SKIES ARE YOURS, NEW BEACHES MADE OF CIRRUS-CLOUD, NEW VALLEYS MADE OF STRATO-CUMULUS.

"LIFT UP YOUR HEADS! YOU WERE NOT MADE TO GAZE AT GUTTERS, MUD, AND PUDDLES ALL YOUR LIVES, BUT HAVE NOT DARED TO RAISE YOUR SIGHTS IN CASE THE THING YOU LONGED FOR WAS NOT THERE.

"LOOK UP AND SEE IT NOW, THE SHAPE THAT'S HAUNTED HUMAN DREAMS AND LEGENDS SINCE WE FIRST PEERED FROM THE JUNGLES LONG AGO AND WONDERED WHAT MIGHT DWELL UPON THOSE BLUE AND DISTANT HILLS, UPON THOSE MOUNTAINS THERE...

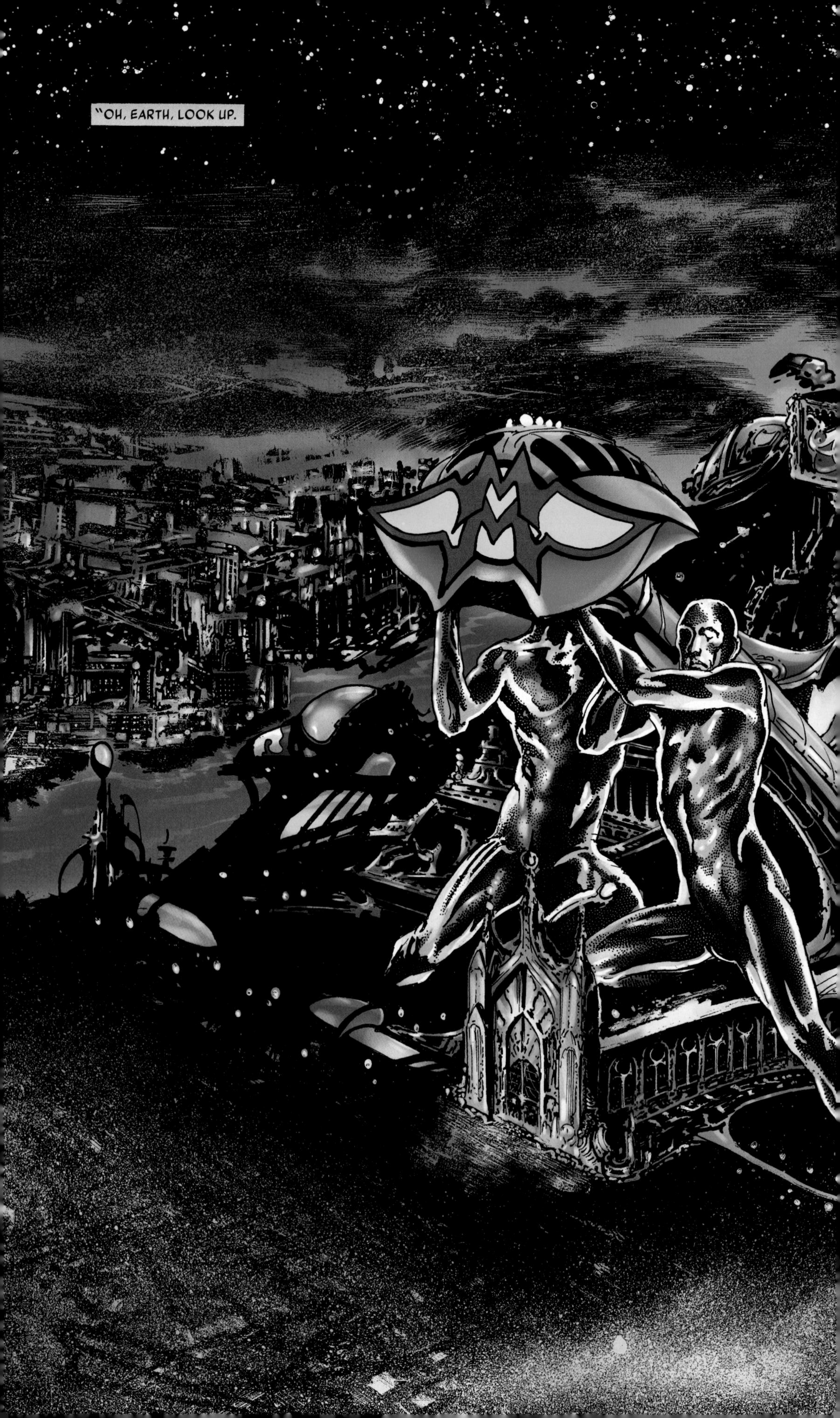
"OH, EARTH, LOOK UP.

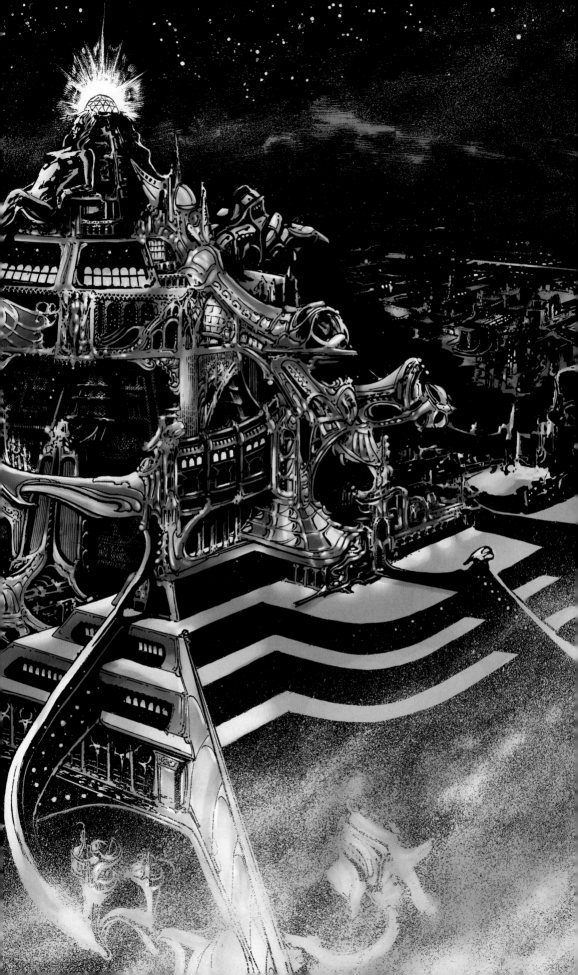

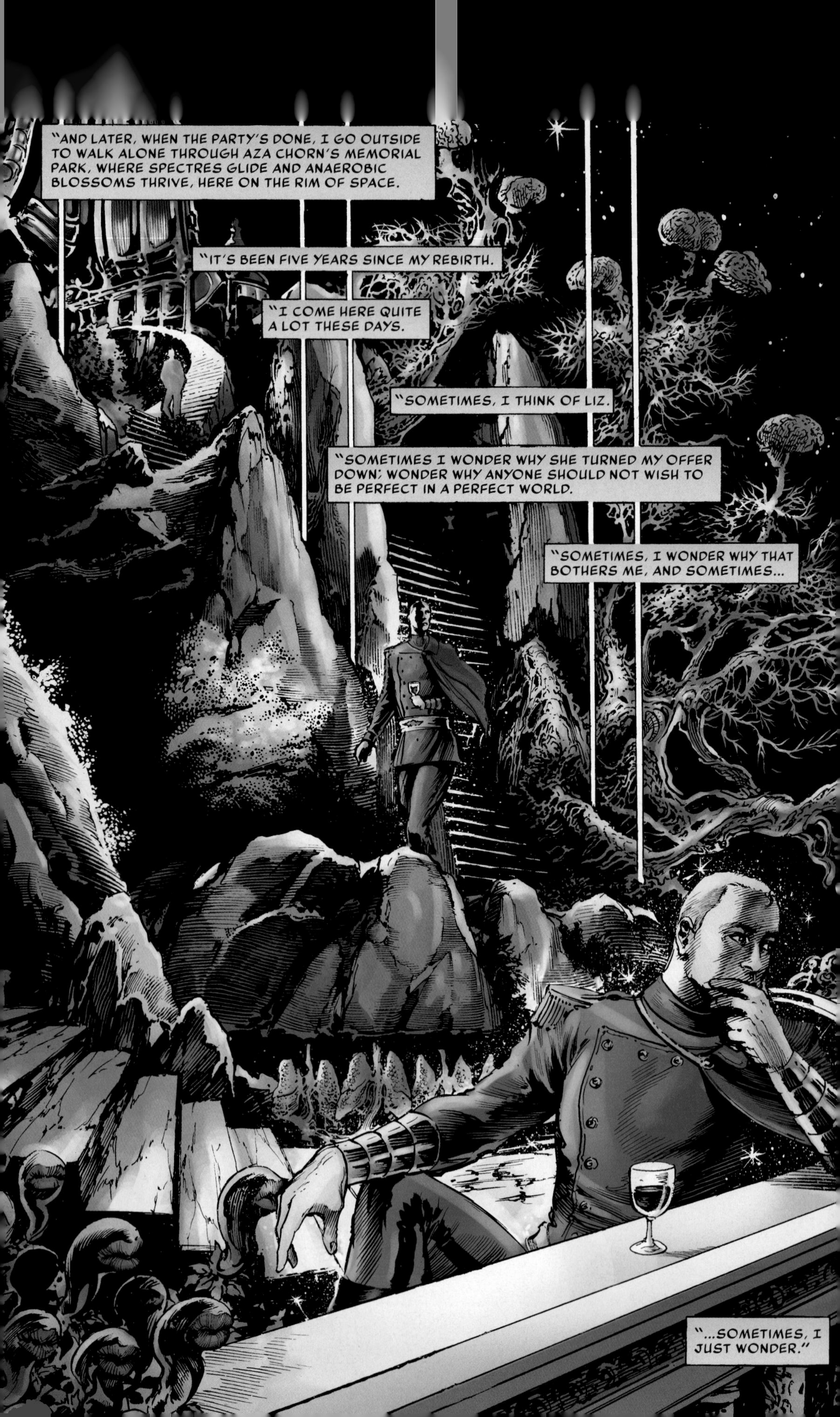
"AND LATER, WHEN THE PARTY'S DONE, I GO OUTSIDE TO WALK ALONE THROUGH AZA CHORN'S MEMORIAL PARK, WHERE SPECTRES GLIDE AND ANAEROBIC BLOSSOMS THRIVE, HERE ON THE RIM OF SPACE.
"IT'S BEEN FIVE YEARS SINCE MY REBIRTH.
"I COME HERE QUITE A LOT THESE DAYS.
"SOMETIMES, I THINK OF LIZ.
"SOMETIMES I WONDER WHY SHE TURNED MY OFFER DOWN; WONDER WHY ANYONE SHOULD NOT WISH TO BE PERFECT IN A PERFECT WORLD.
"SOMETIMES, I WONDER WHY THAT BOTHERS ME, AND SOMETIMES...
"...SOMETIMES, I JUST WONDER."

# LEGENDS & APOCRYPHA

### THE PRIEST & THE DRAGON:
#### "OCTOBER INCIDENT: 1966"

STORY – **GRANT MORRISON**
ART – **JOE QUESADA**
COLOR ART – **RICHARD ISANOVE**
LETTERING – **CHRIS ELIOPOULOS**

One wintry night on the shores of Scotlan
a man of faith and a creature of deat
encountered each other. Three years late
they meet again and the young drago
shares his views on the world he ha
inherited from the old priest.

### THE MIRACLEMAN FAMILY:
#### "SERIOUSLY MIRACULOUS"

STORY – **PETER MILLIGAN**
ART – **MIKE ALLRED**
COLOR ART – **LAURA ALLRED**
LETTERING – **TRAVIS LANHAM**

Featuring the entire Miracleman Famil
this joyous romp pays its respects
both the whimsy and imagination
Miracleman creator Mick Anglo ar
the groundbreaking work of those wh
returned the character to prominence.

EDITORS – **NICK LOWE & CORY SEDLMEIE**
ASSISTANT EDITOR – **CHARLES BEACHA**

**LEFT:** Gabriel Dell-Otto's cover to
*All-New Miracleman Annual #1 (2014).*

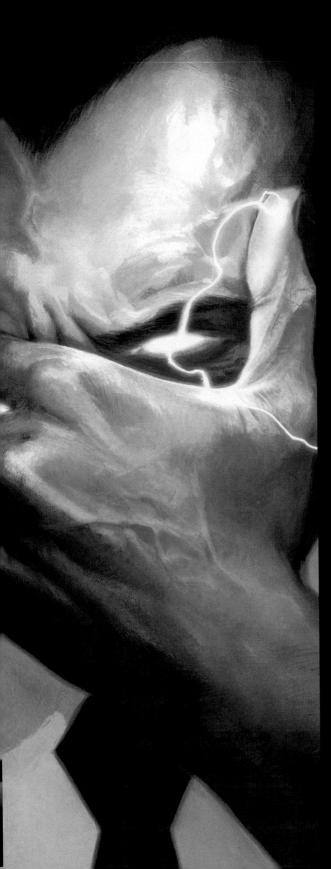

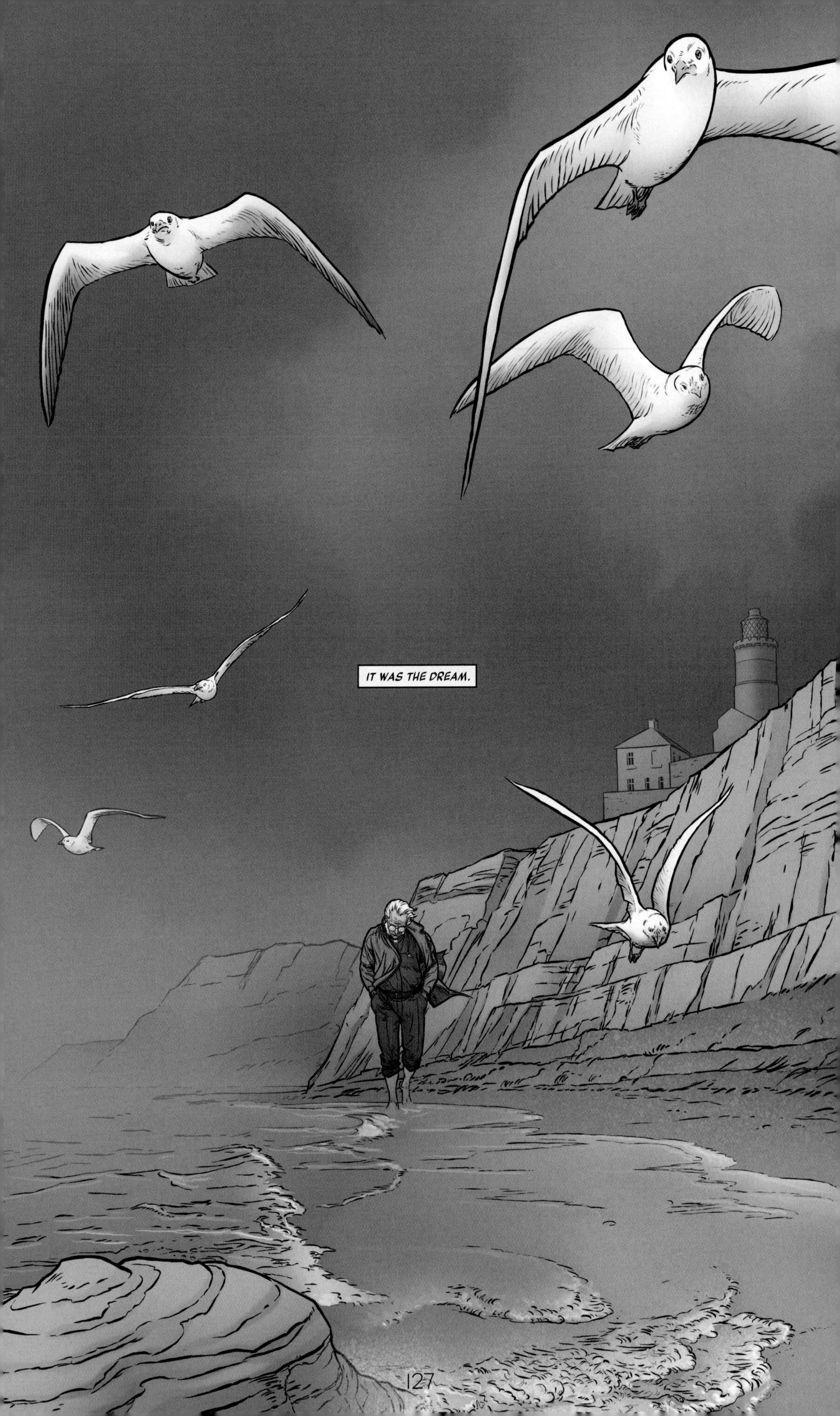
IT WAS THE DREAM.

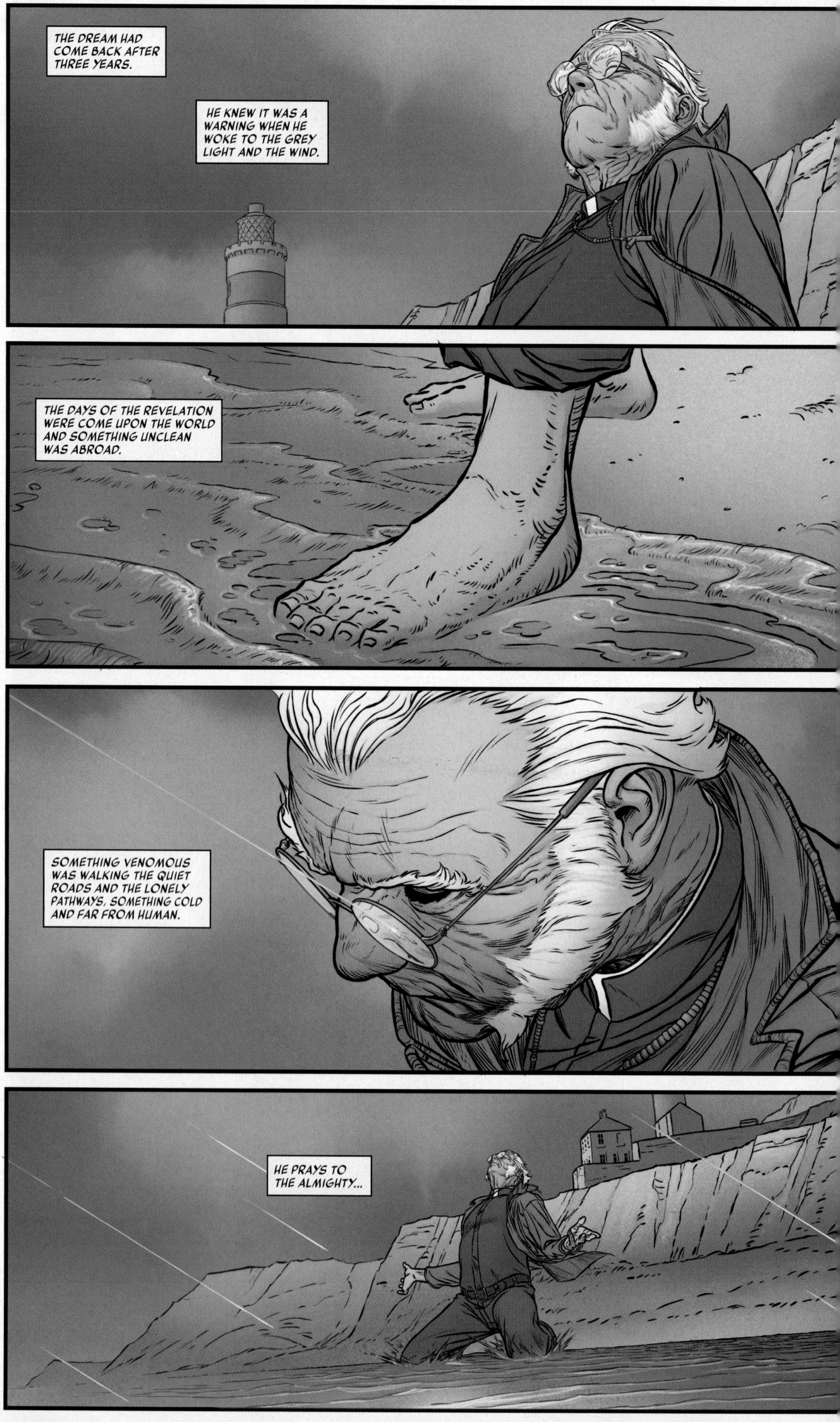
THE DREAM HAD COME BACK AFTER THREE YEARS.
HE KNEW IT WAS A WARNING WHEN HE WOKE TO THE GREY LIGHT AND THE WIND.
THE DAYS OF THE REVELATION WERE COME UPON THE WORLD AND SOMETHING UNCLEAN WAS ABROAD.
SOMETHING VENOMOUS WAS WALKING THE QUIET ROADS AND THE LONELY PATHWAYS, SOMETHING COLD AND FAR FROM HUMAN.
HE PRAYS TO THE ALMIGHTY...

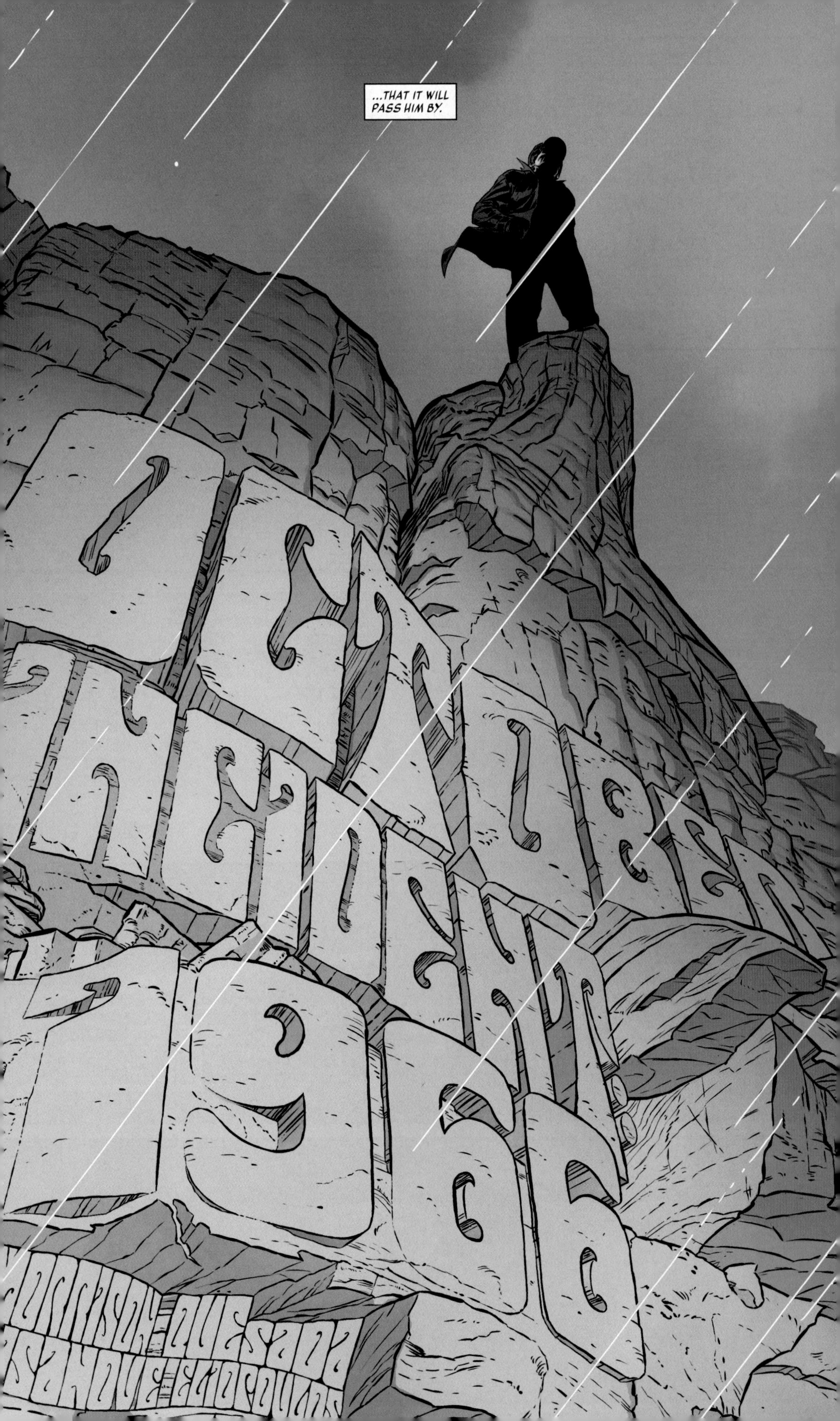
...THAT IT WILL PASS HIM BY.

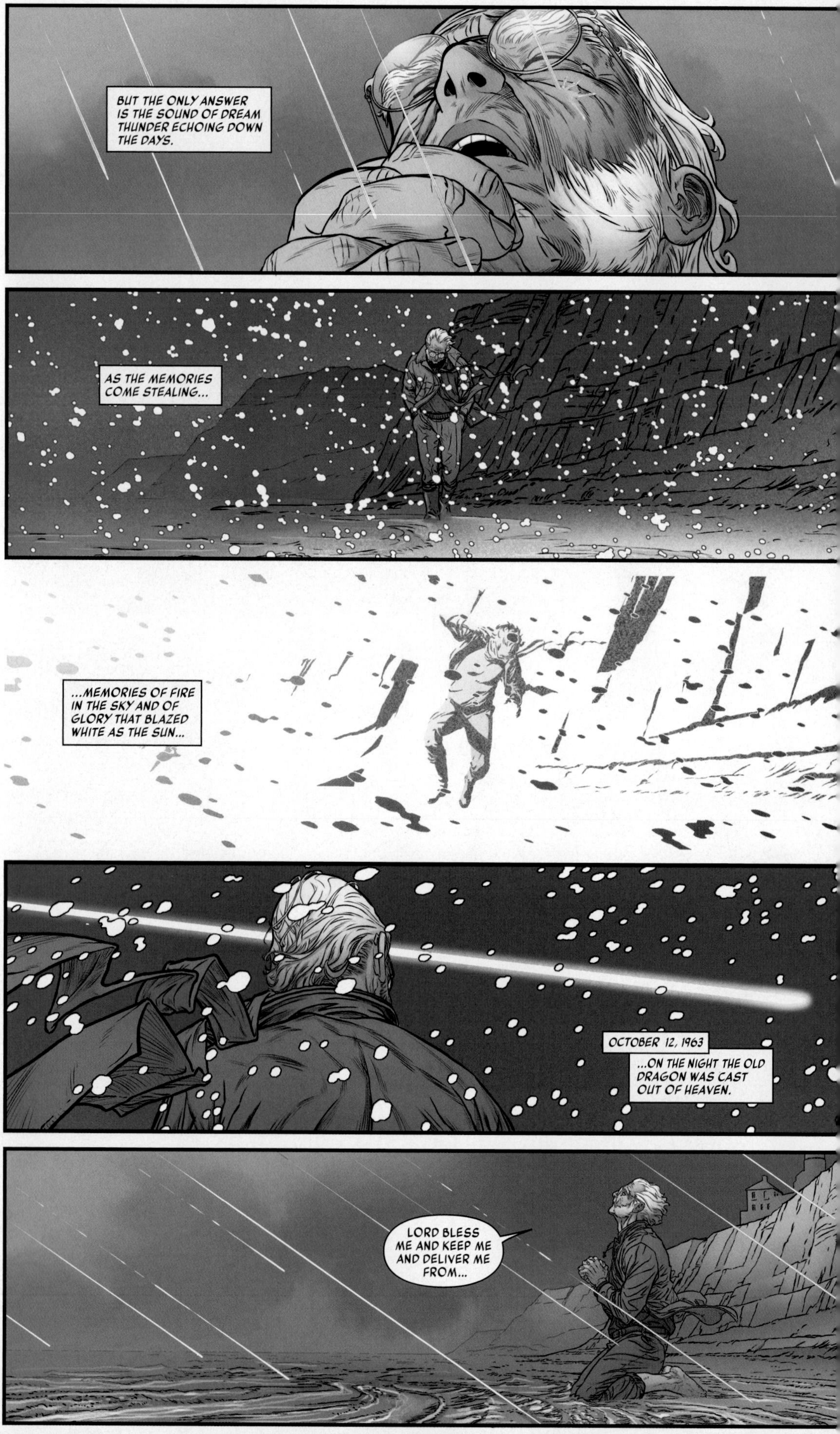
BUT THE ONLY ANSWER IS THE SOUND OF DREAM THUNDER ECHOING DOWN THE DAYS.
AS THE MEMORIES COME STEALING...
...MEMORIES OF FIRE IN THE SKY AND OF GLORY THAT BLAZED WHITE AS THE SUN...
OCTOBER 12, 1963
...ON THE NIGHT THE OLD DRAGON WAS CAST OUT OF HEAVEN.
LORD BLESS ME AND KEEP ME AND DELIVER ME FROM...

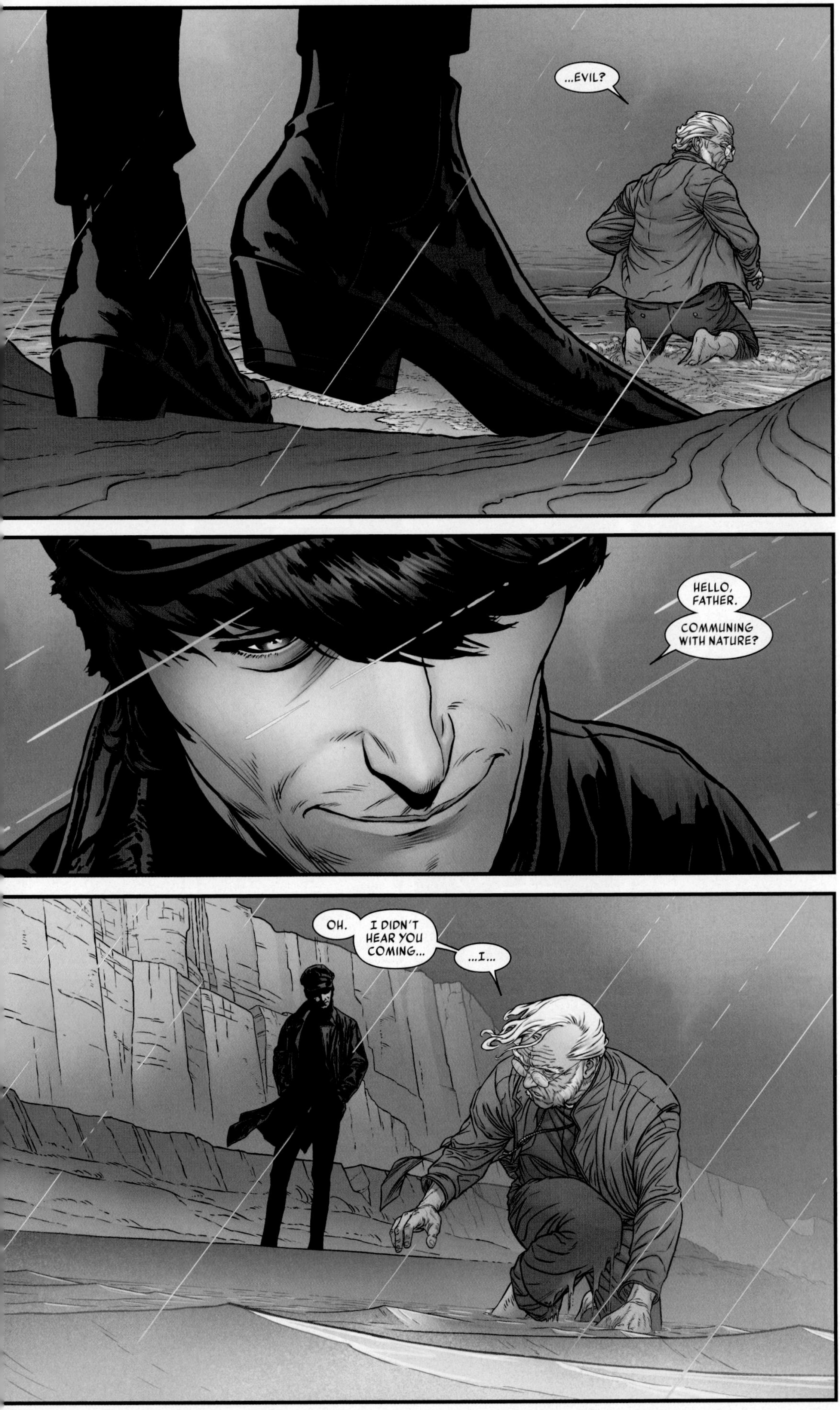
...EVIL?
HELLO, FATHER.
COMMUNING WITH NATURE?
OH.
I DIDN'T HEAR YOU COMING...
...I...

...HAVE...HAVE WE MET BEFORE SOMEWHERE?

A SMELL OF BURNING.

COULD BE. I'VE BEEN HERE BEFORE... ...COUPLE OF YEARS BACK.

A SMELL OF BRIMSTONE.

OH, GOD.

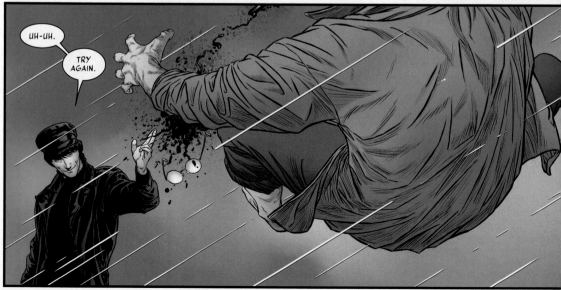

UH-UH.

TRY AGAIN.

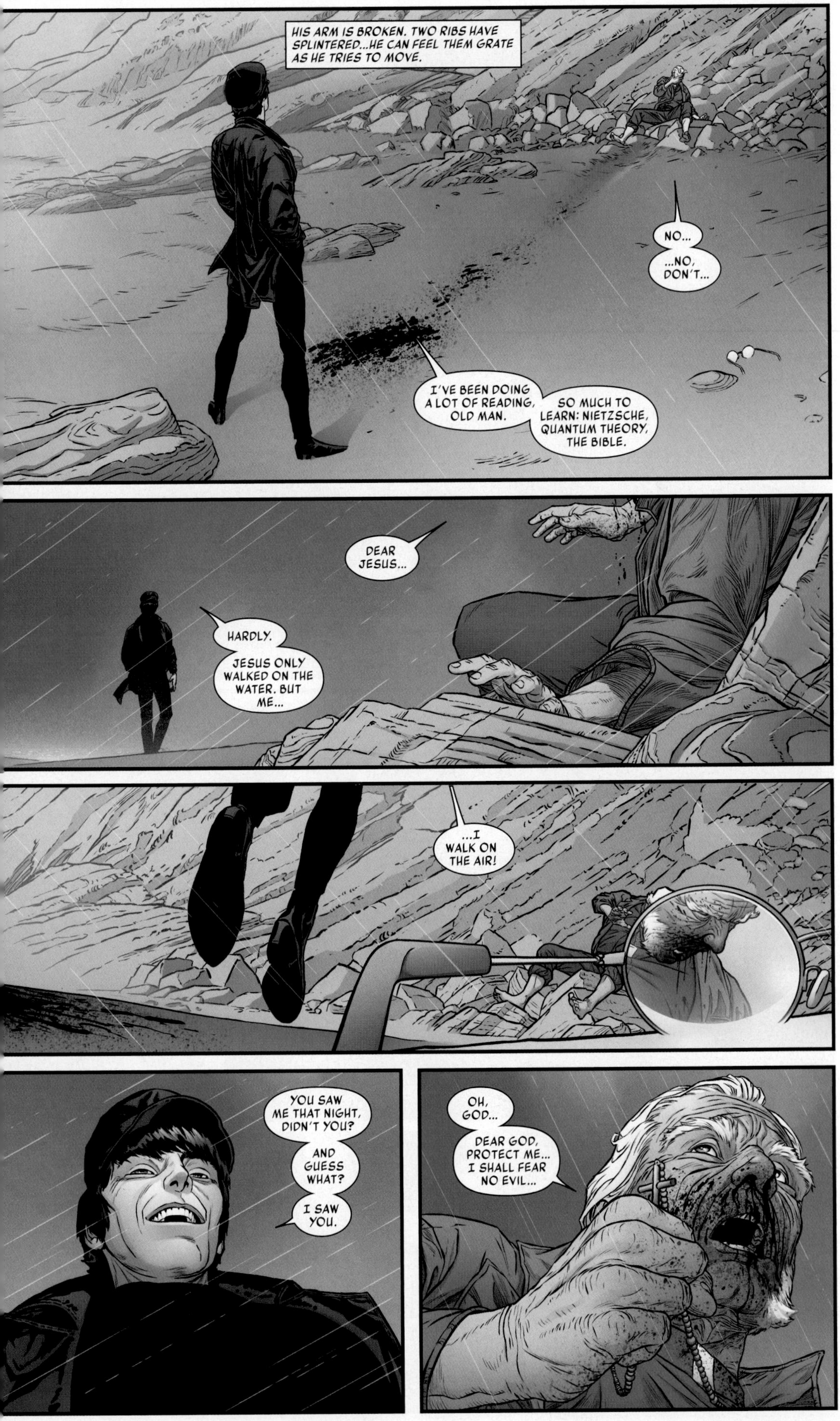

HIS ARM IS BROKEN. TWO RIBS HAVE SPLINTERED...HE CAN FEEL THEM GRATE AS HE TRIES TO MOVE.
NO...
...NO, DON'T...
I'VE BEEN DOING A LOT OF READING, OLD MAN.
SO MUCH TO LEARN: NIETZSCHE, QUANTUM THEORY, THE BIBLE.
DEAR JESUS...
HARDLY.
JESUS ONLY WALKED ON THE WATER. BUT ME...
...I WALK ON THE AIR!
YOU SAW ME THAT NIGHT, DIDN'T YOU?
AND GUESS WHAT?
I SAW YOU.
OH, GOD...
DEAR GOD, PROTECT ME... I SHALL FEAR NO EVIL...

YOU CAN TAKE YOUR CROSS AND STUFF IT! THE APOCALYPSE HAS ARRIVED!

I CAN DO ANY BLOODY THING I WANT AND YOU CAN'T STOP ME, YOU PATHETIC OLD WITCH DOCTOR!

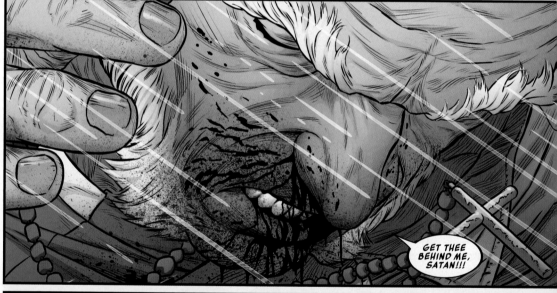

GET THEE BEHIND ME, SATAN!!!

THERE IS A BRIEF STINK OF OZONE...

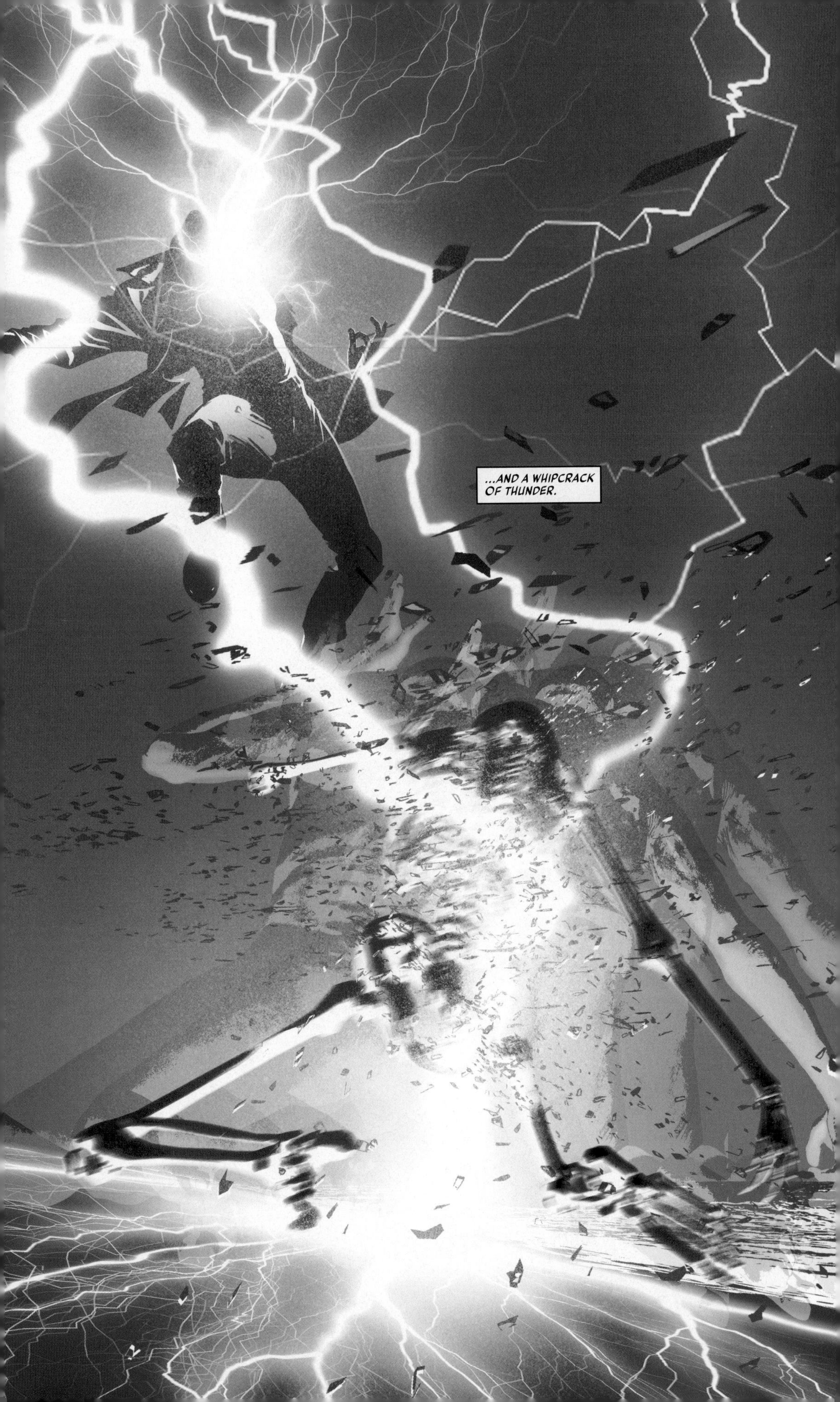
...AND A WHIPCRACK
OF THUNDER.

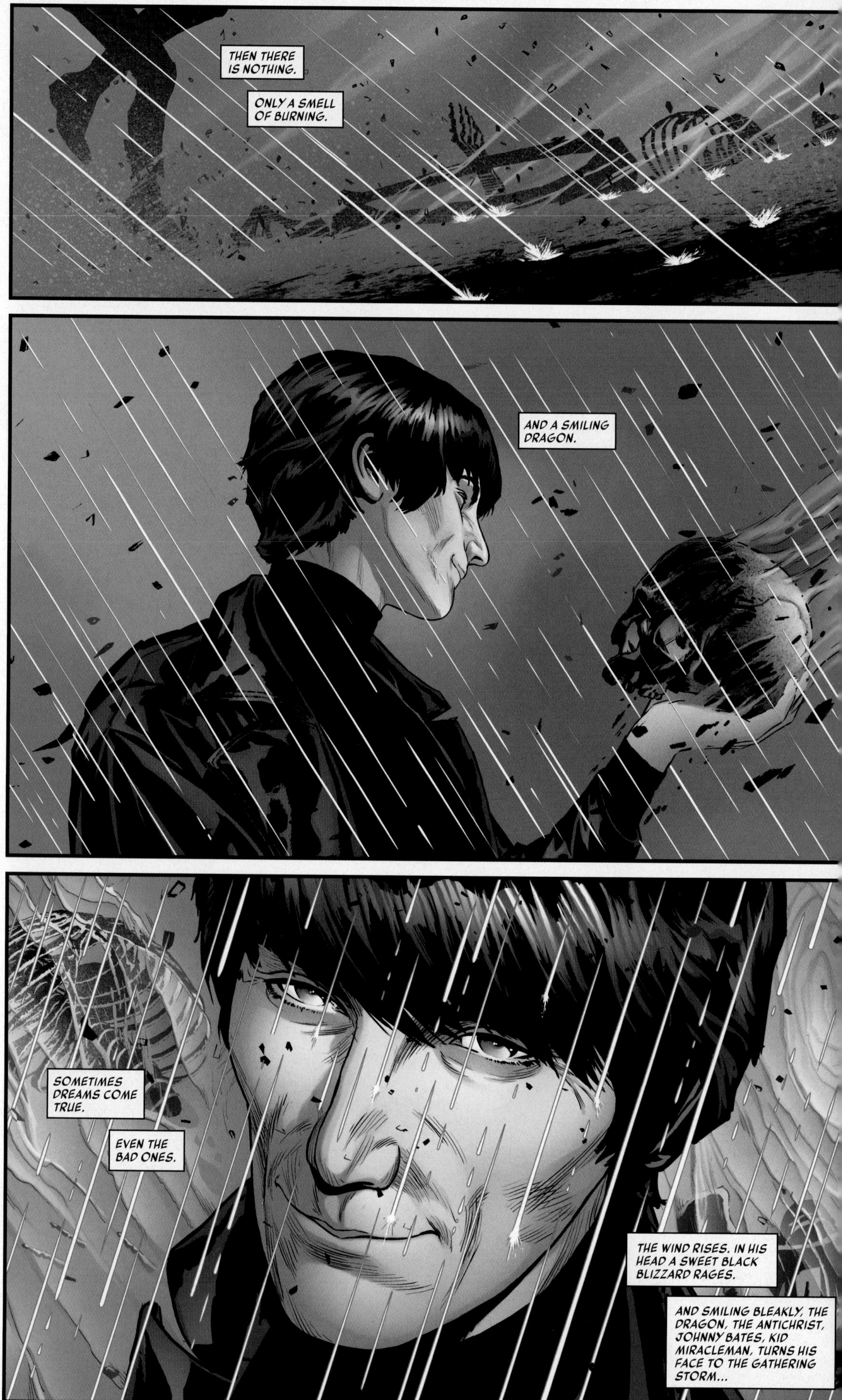
THEN THERE IS NOTHING.
ONLY A SMELL OF BURNING.
AND A SMILING DRAGON.
SOMETIMES DREAMS COME TRUE.
EVEN THE BAD ONES.
THE WIND RISES. IN HIS HEAD A SWEET BLACK BLIZZARD RAGES.
AND SMILING BLEAKLY, THE DRAGON, THE ANTICHRIST, JOHNNY BATES, KID MIRACLEMAN, TURNS HIS FACE TO THE GATHERING STORM...

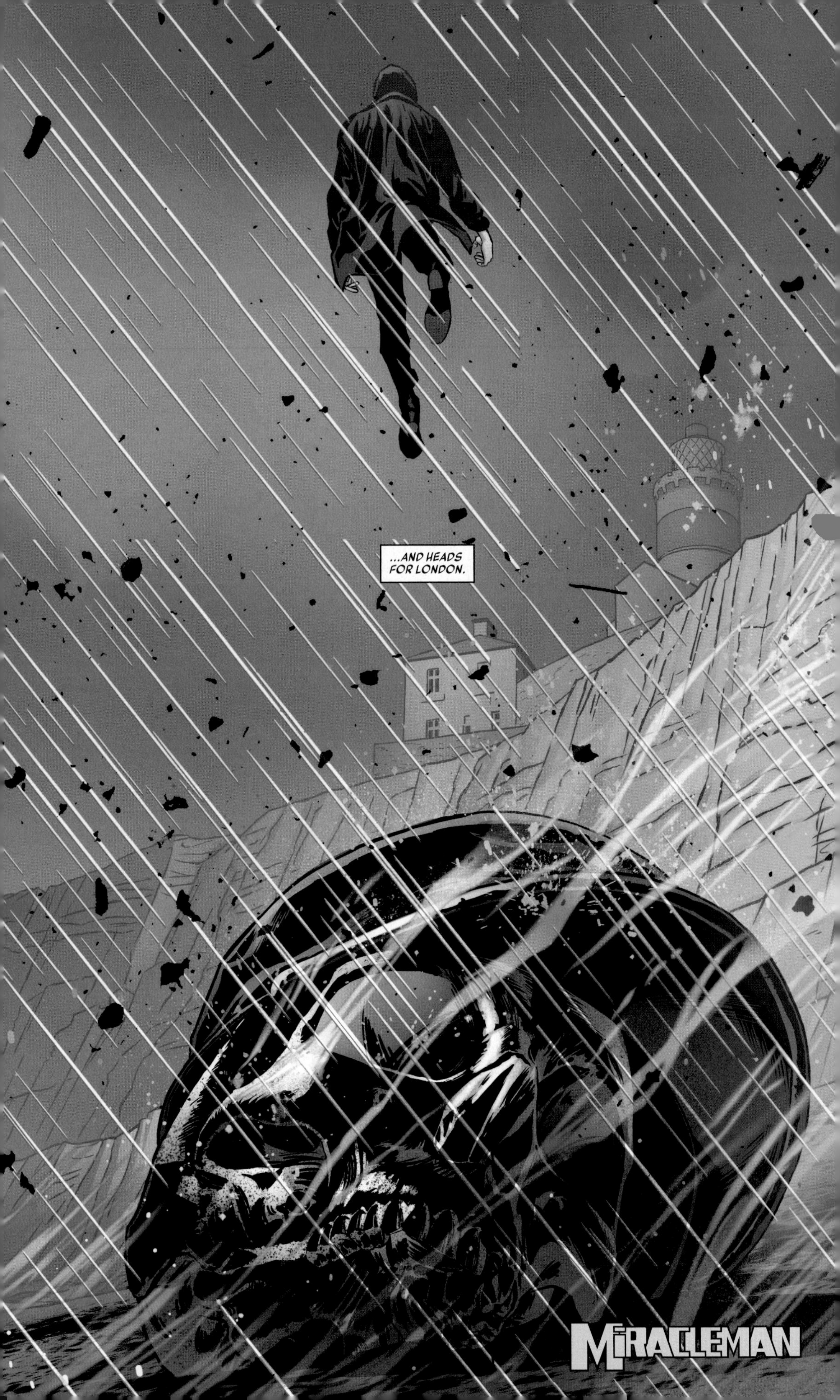
...AND HEADS FOR LONDON.
MIRACLEMAN

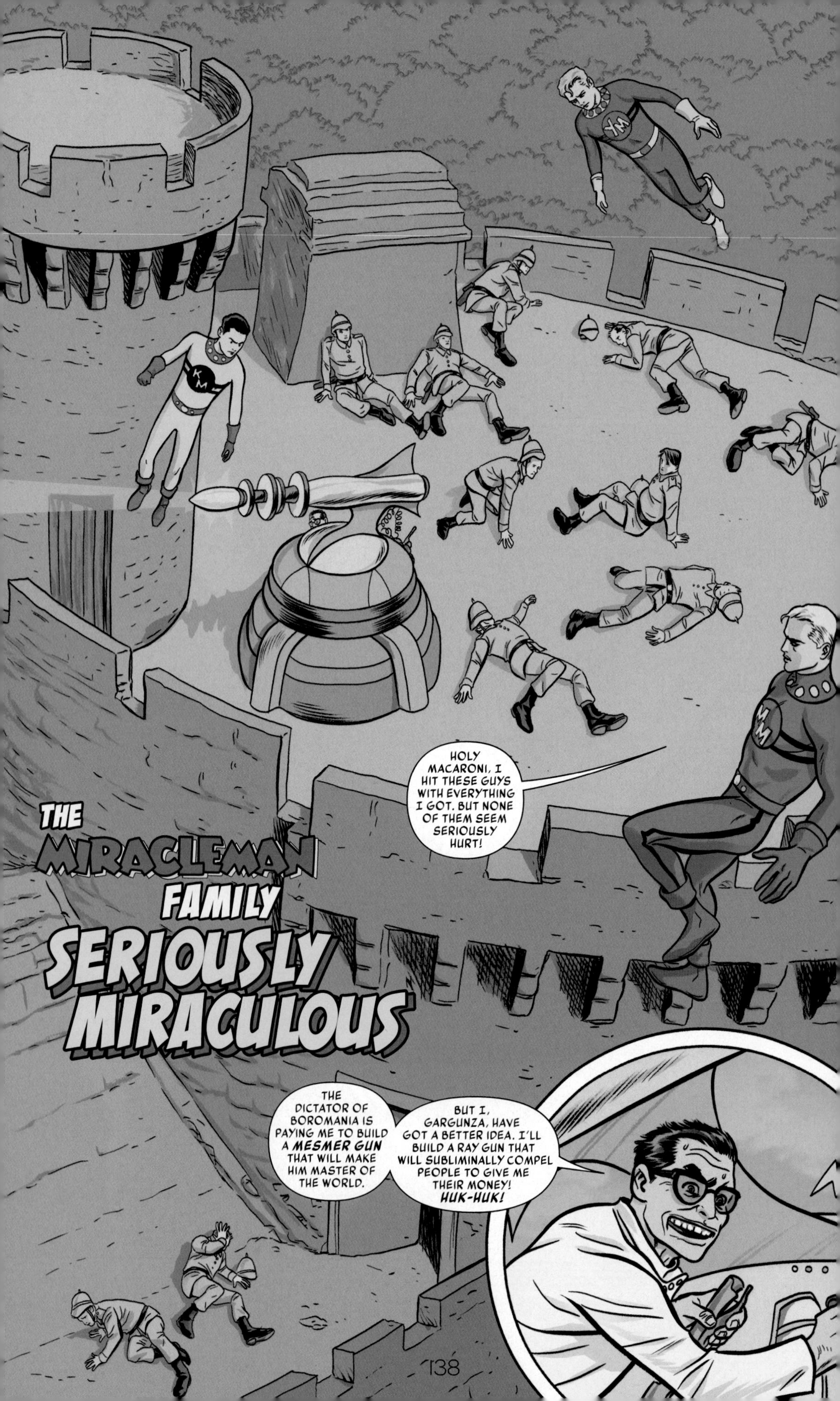
THE MIRACLEMAN FAMILY
SERIOUSLY MIRACULOUS
HOLY MACARONI, I HIT THESE GUYS WITH EVERYTHING I GOT. BUT NONE OF THEM SEEM SERIOUSLY HURT!
THE DICTATOR OF BOROMANIA IS PAYING ME TO BUILD A MESMER GUN THAT WILL MAKE HIM MASTER OF THE WORLD.
BUT I, GARGUNZA, HAVE GOT A BETTER IDEA. I'LL BUILD A RAY GUN THAT WILL SUBLIMINALLY COMPEL PEOPLE TO GIVE ME THEIR MONEY! HUK-HUK!

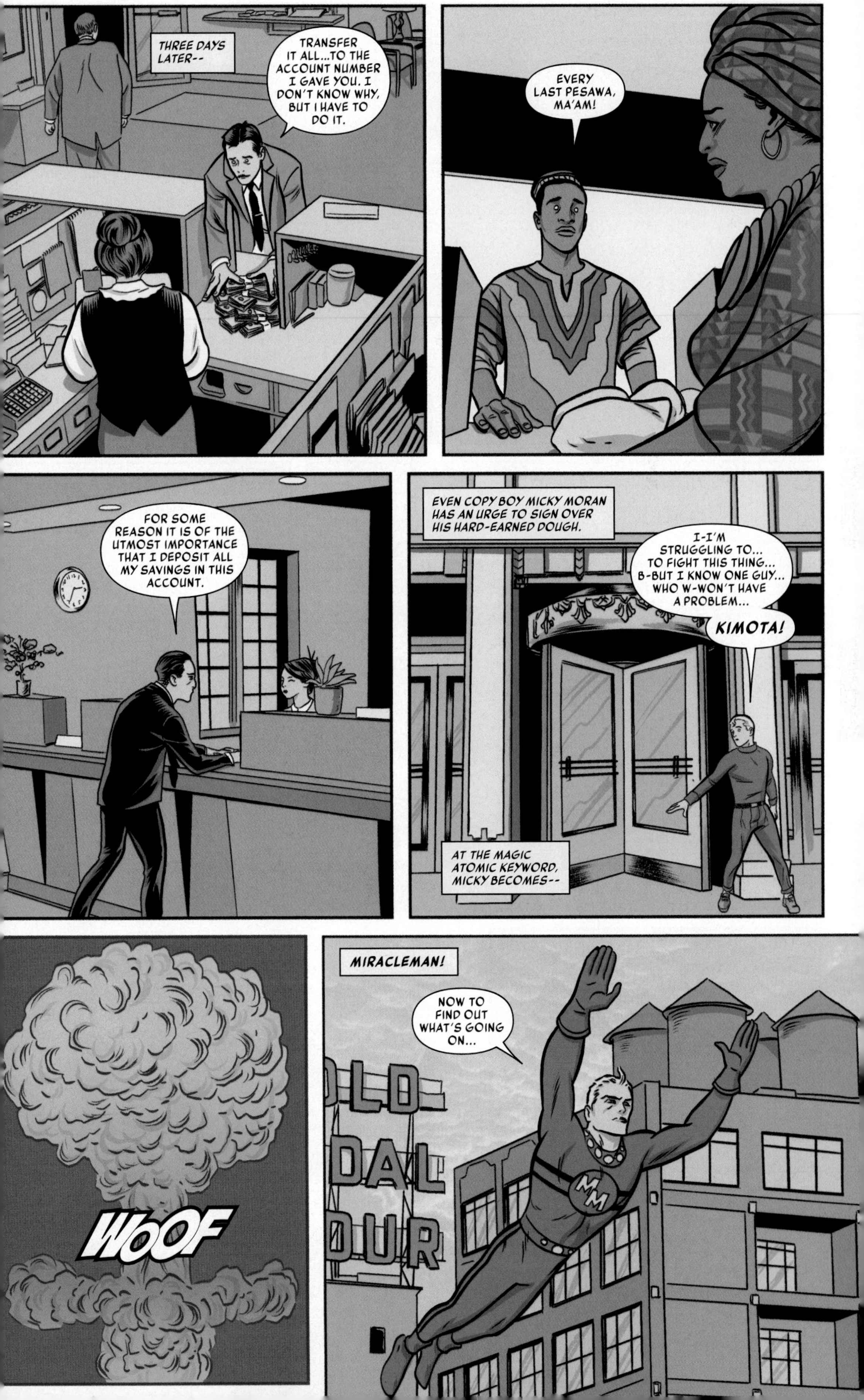
THREE DAYS LATER--
TRANSFER IT ALL...TO THE ACCOUNT NUMBER I GAVE YOU. I DON'T KNOW WHY, BUT I HAVE TO DO IT.
EVERY LAST PESAWA, MA'AM!
FOR SOME REASON IT IS OF THE UTMOST IMPORTANCE THAT I DEPOSIT ALL MY SAVINGS IN THIS ACCOUNT.
EVEN COPY BOY MICKY MORAN HAS AN URGE TO SIGN OVER HIS HARD-EARNED DOUGH.
I-I'M STRUGGLING TO... TO FIGHT THIS THING... B-BUT I KNOW ONE GUY... WHO W-WON'T HAVE A PROBLEM...
KIMOTA!
AT THE MAGIC ATOMIC KEYWORD, MICKY BECOMES--
WOOF
MIRACLEMAN!
NOW TO FIND OUT WHAT'S GOING ON...

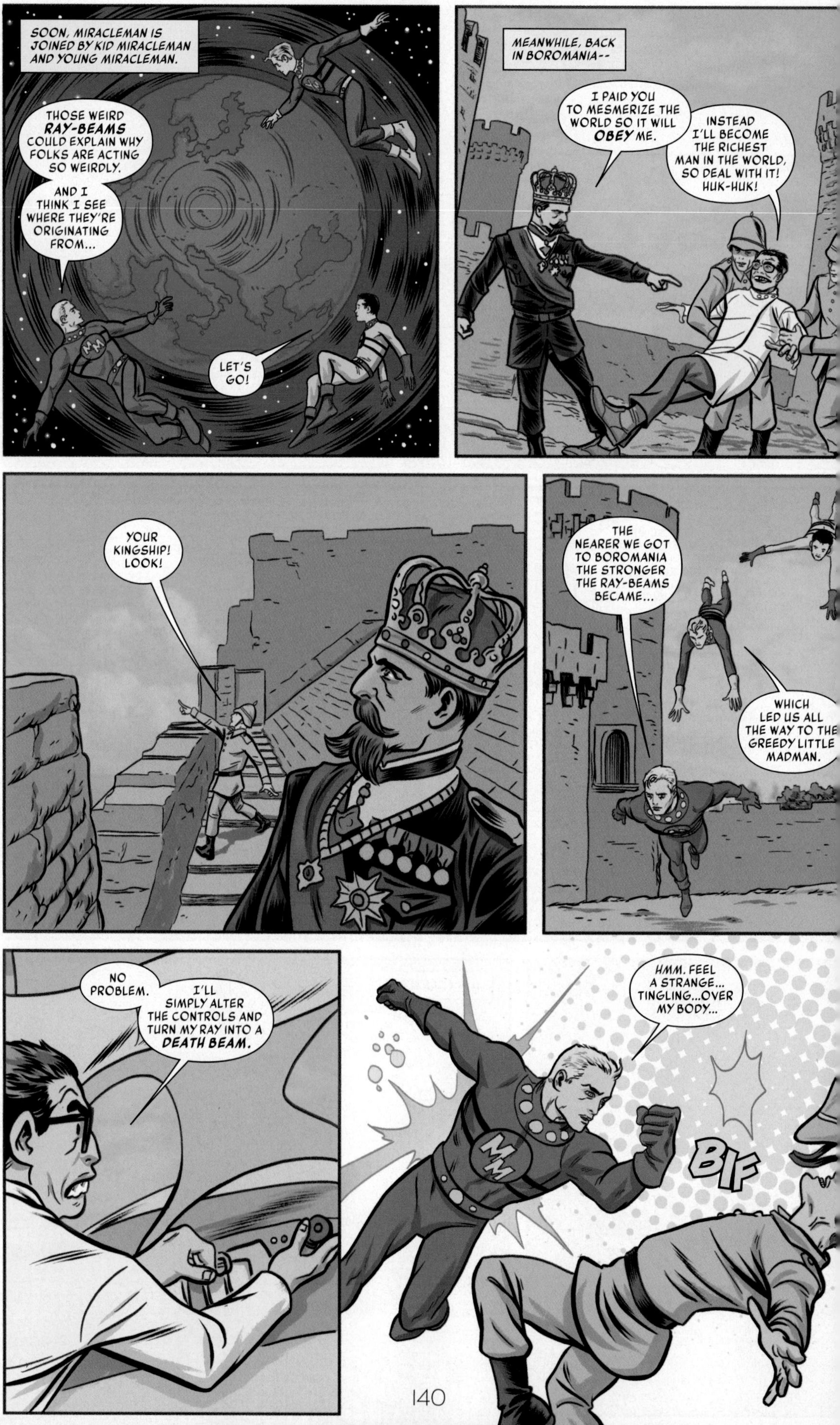

SOON, MIRACLEMAN IS JOINED BY KID MIRACLEMAN AND YOUNG MIRACLEMAN.
THOSE WEIRD RAY-BEAMS COULD EXPLAIN WHY FOLKS ARE ACTING SO WEIRDLY.
AND I THINK I SEE WHERE THEY'RE ORIGINATING FROM...
LET'S GO!
MEANWHILE, BACK IN BOROMANIA--
I PAID YOU TO MESMERIZE THE WORLD SO IT WILL OBEY ME.
INSTEAD I'LL BECOME THE RICHEST MAN IN THE WORLD, SO DEAL WITH IT! HUK-HUK!
YOUR KINGSHIP! LOOK!
THE NEARER WE GOT TO BOROMANIA THE STRONGER THE RAY-BEAMS BECAME...
WHICH LED US ALL THE WAY TO THE GREEDY LITTLE MADMAN.
NO PROBLEM.
I'LL SIMPLY ALTER THE CONTROLS AND TURN MY RAY INTO A DEATH BEAM.
HMM. FEEL A STRANGE... TINGLING...OVER MY BODY...
BIF

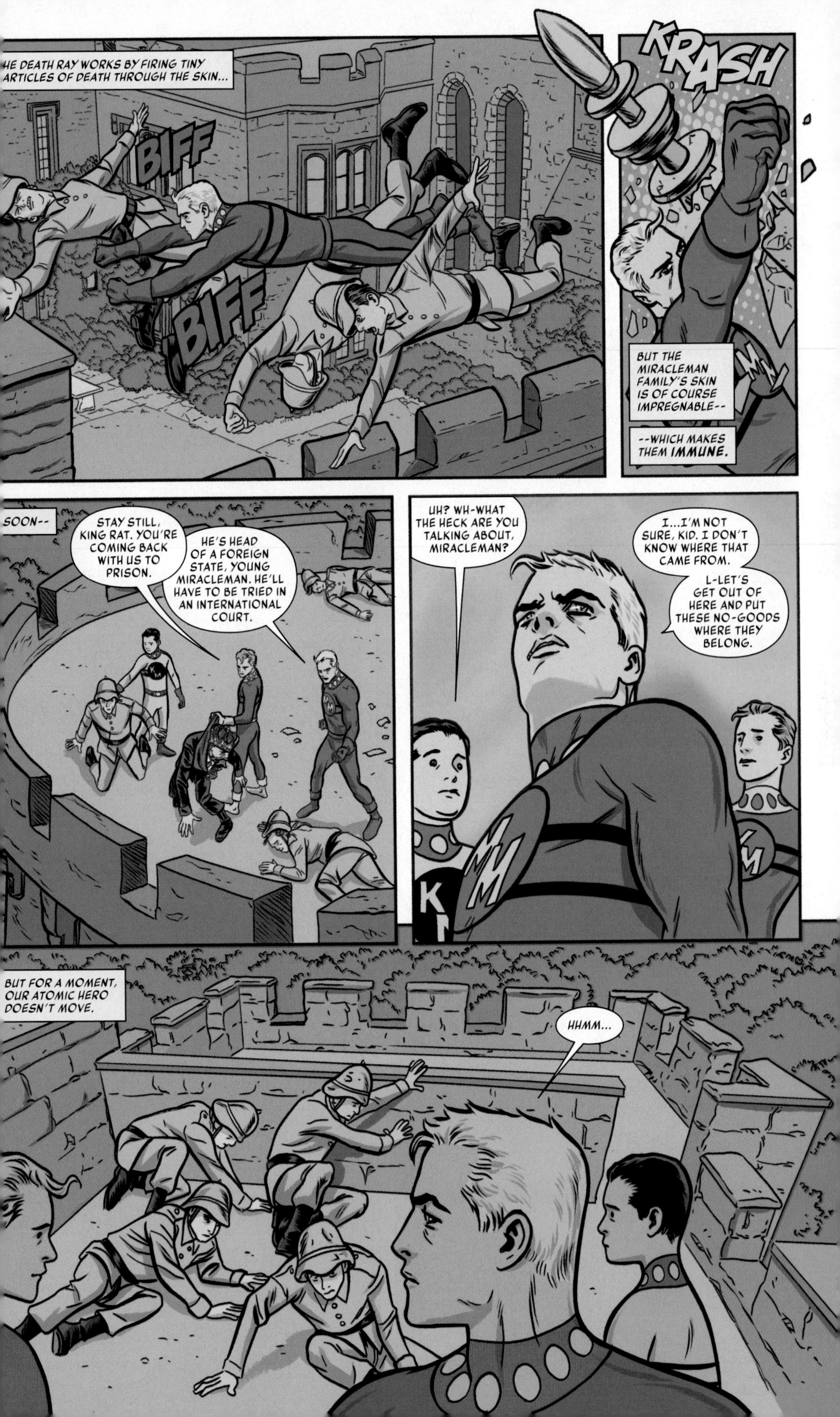

HE DEATH RAY WORKS BY FIRING TINY ARTICLES OF DEATH THROUGH THE SKIN...
BIFF
BIFF
KRASH
BUT THE MIRACLEMAN FAMILY'S SKIN IS OF COURSE IMPREGNABLE--
--WHICH MAKES THEM IMMUNE.
SOON--
STAY STILL, KING RAT. YOU'RE COMING BACK WITH US TO PRISON.
HE'S HEAD OF A FOREIGN STATE, YOUNG MIRACLEMAN. HE'LL HAVE TO BE TRIED IN AN INTERNATIONAL COURT.
UH? WH-WHAT THE HECK ARE YOU TALKING ABOUT, MIRACLEMAN?
I...I'M NOT SURE, KID. I DON'T KNOW WHERE THAT CAME FROM.
L-LET'S GET OUT OF HERE AND PUT THESE NO-GOODS WHERE THEY BELONG.
BUT FOR A MOMENT, OUR ATOMIC HERO DOESN'T MOVE.
HHMM...

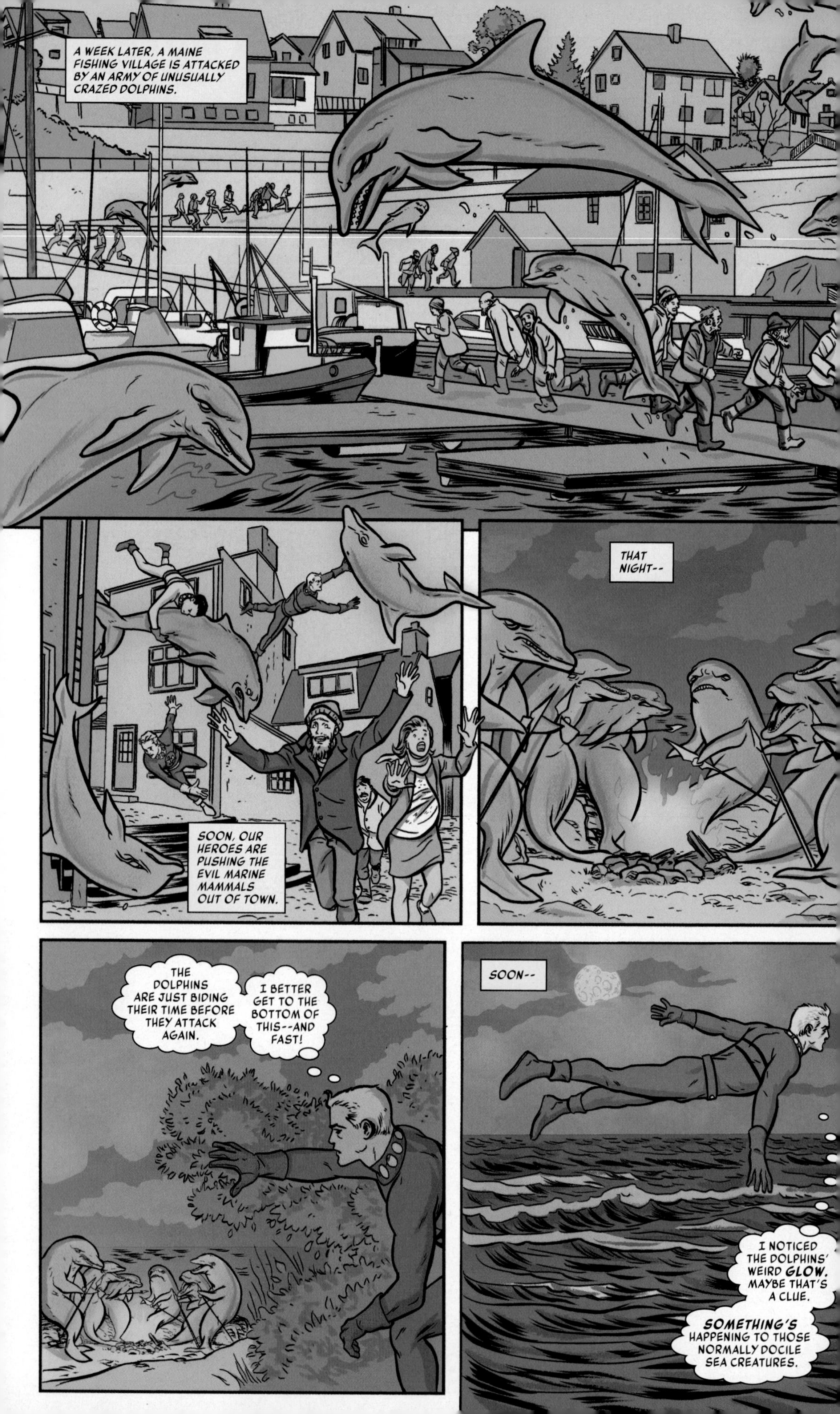
A WEEK LATER, A MAINE FISHING VILLAGE IS ATTACKED BY AN ARMY OF UNUSUALLY CRAZED DOLPHINS.
SOON, OUR HEROES ARE PUSHING THE EVIL MARINE MAMMALS OUT OF TOWN.
THAT NIGHT--
THE DOLPHINS ARE JUST BIDING THEIR TIME BEFORE THEY ATTACK AGAIN.
I BETTER GET TO THE BOTTOM OF THIS--AND FAST!
SOON--
I NOTICED THE DOLPHINS' WEIRD GLOW. MAYBE THAT'S A CLUE.
SOMETHING'S HAPPENING TO THOSE NORMALLY DOCILE SEA CREATURES.

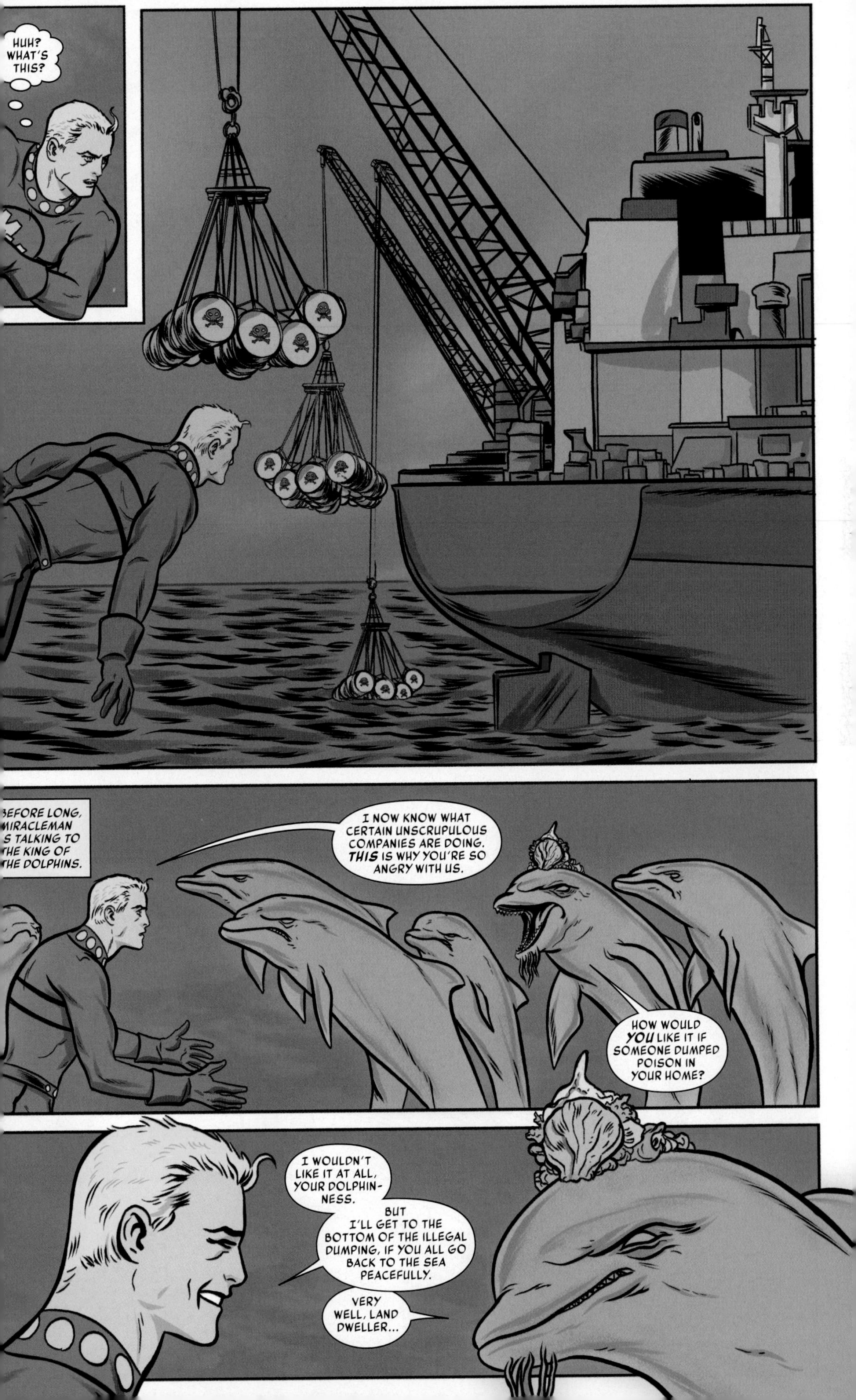
HUH? WHAT'S THIS?
BEFORE LONG, MIRACLEMAN IS TALKING TO THE KING OF THE DOLPHINS.
I NOW KNOW WHAT CERTAIN UNSCRUPULOUS COMPANIES ARE DOING. THIS IS WHY YOU'RE SO ANGRY WITH US.
HOW WOULD YOU LIKE IT IF SOMEONE DUMPED POISON IN YOUR HOME?
I WOULDN'T LIKE IT AT ALL, YOUR DOLPHIN-NESS.
BUT I'LL GET TO THE BOTTOM OF THE ILLEGAL DUMPING, IF YOU ALL GO BACK TO THE SEA PEACEFULLY.
VERY WELL, LAND DWELLER...

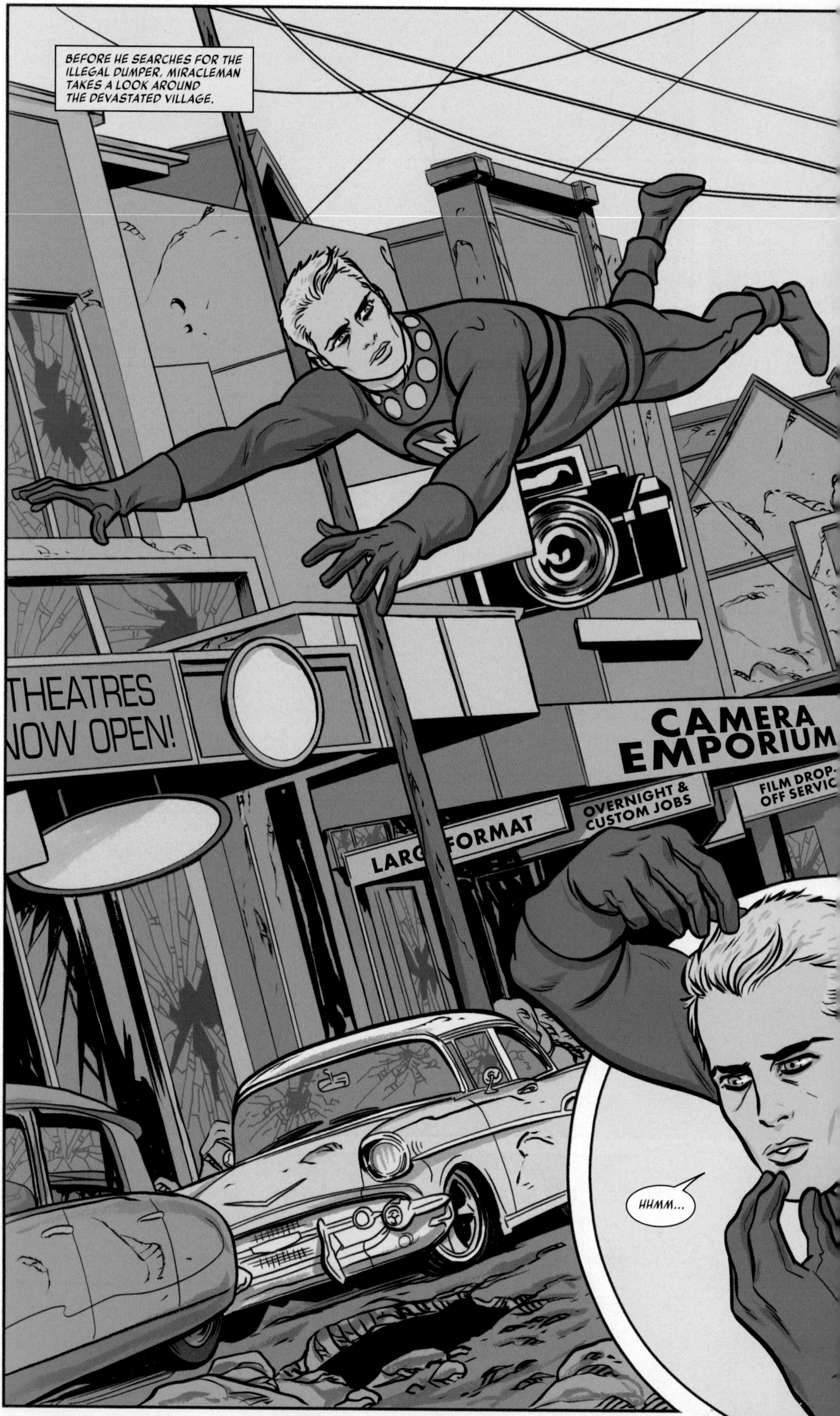
BEFORE HE SEARCHES FOR THE ILLEGAL DUMPER, MIRACLEMAN TAKES A LOOK AROUND THE DEVASTATED VILLAGE.
THEATRES NOW OPEN!
CAMERA EMPORIUM
LARG FORMAT
OVERNIGHT & CUSTOM JOBS
FILM DROP-OFF SERVIC
HHMM...

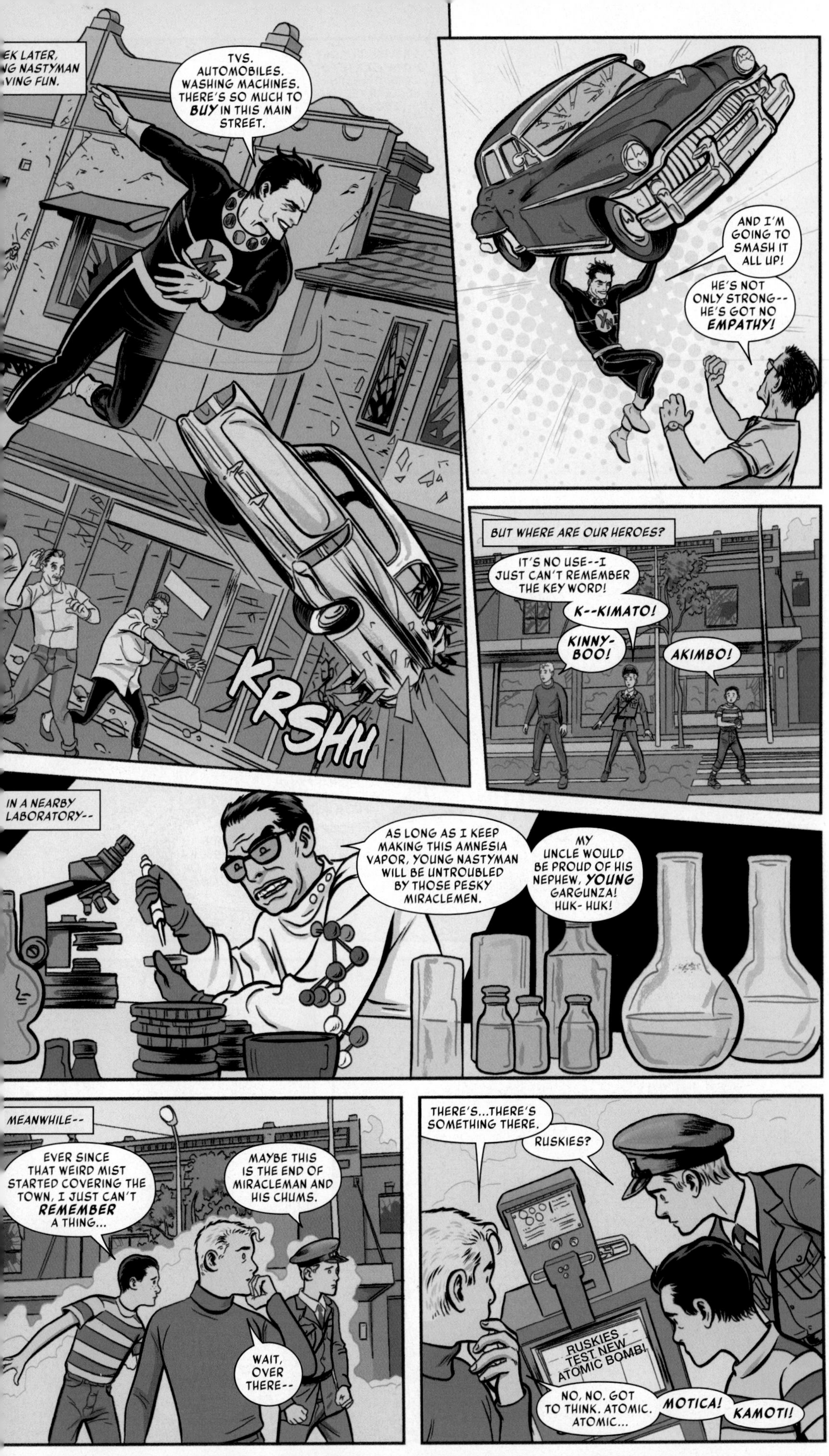
EK LATER,
NG NASTYMAN
VING FUN.
TVS. AUTOMOBILES. WASHING MACHINES. THERE'S SO MUCH TO BUY IN THIS MAIN STREET.
KRSHH
AND I'M GOING TO SMASH IT ALL UP!
HE'S NOT ONLY STRONG-- HE'S GOT NO EMPATHY!
BUT WHERE ARE OUR HEROES?
IT'S NO USE--I JUST CAN'T REMEMBER THE KEY WORD!
K--KIMATO!
KINNY-BOO!
AKIMBO!
IN A NEARBY LABORATORY--
AS LONG AS I KEEP MAKING THIS AMNESIA VAPOR, YOUNG NASTYMAN WILL BE UNTROUBLED BY THOSE PESKY MIRACLEMEN.
MY UNCLE WOULD BE PROUD OF HIS NEPHEW, YOUNG GARGUNZA! HUK- HUK!
MEANWHILE--
EVER SINCE THAT WEIRD MIST STARTED COVERING THE TOWN, I JUST CAN'T REMEMBER A THING...
MAYBE THIS IS THE END OF MIRACLEMAN AND HIS CHUMS.
WAIT, OVER THERE--
THERE'S...THERE'S SOMETHING THERE.
RUSKIES?
RUSKIES TEST NEW ATOMIC BOMB!
NO, NO. GOT TO THINK. ATOMIC. ATOMIC...
MOTICA!
KAMOTI!

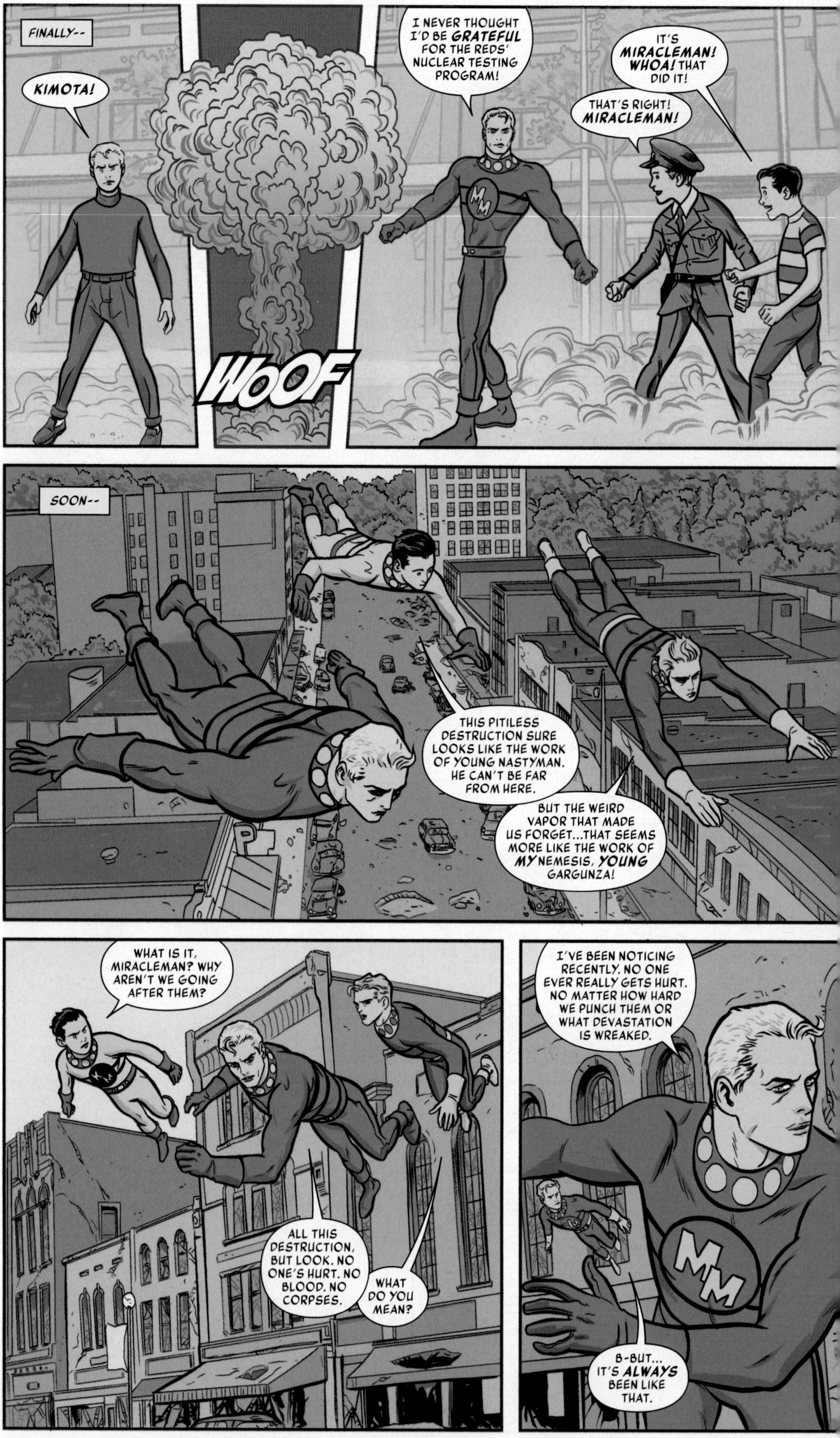
FINALLY--
KIMOTA!
WOOF
I NEVER THOUGHT I'D BE GRATEFUL FOR THE REDS' NUCLEAR TESTING PROGRAM!
IT'S MIRACLEMAN! WHOA! THAT DID IT!
THAT'S RIGHT! MIRACLEMAN!
SOON--
THIS PITILESS DESTRUCTION SURE LOOKS LIKE THE WORK OF YOUNG NASTYMAN. HE CAN'T BE FAR FROM HERE.
BUT THE WEIRD VAPOR THAT MADE US FORGET...THAT SEEMS MORE LIKE THE WORK OF MY NEMESIS, YOUNG GARGUNZA!
WHAT IS IT, MIRACLEMAN? WHY AREN'T WE GOING AFTER THEM?
ALL THIS DESTRUCTION, BUT LOOK. NO ONE'S HURT. NO BLOOD. NO CORPSES.
WHAT DO YOU MEAN?
I'VE BEEN NOTICING RECENTLY. NO ONE EVER REALLY GETS HURT. NO MATTER HOW HARD WE PUNCH THEM OR WHAT DEVASTATION IS WREAKED.
B-BUT... IT'S ALWAYS BEEN LIKE THAT.

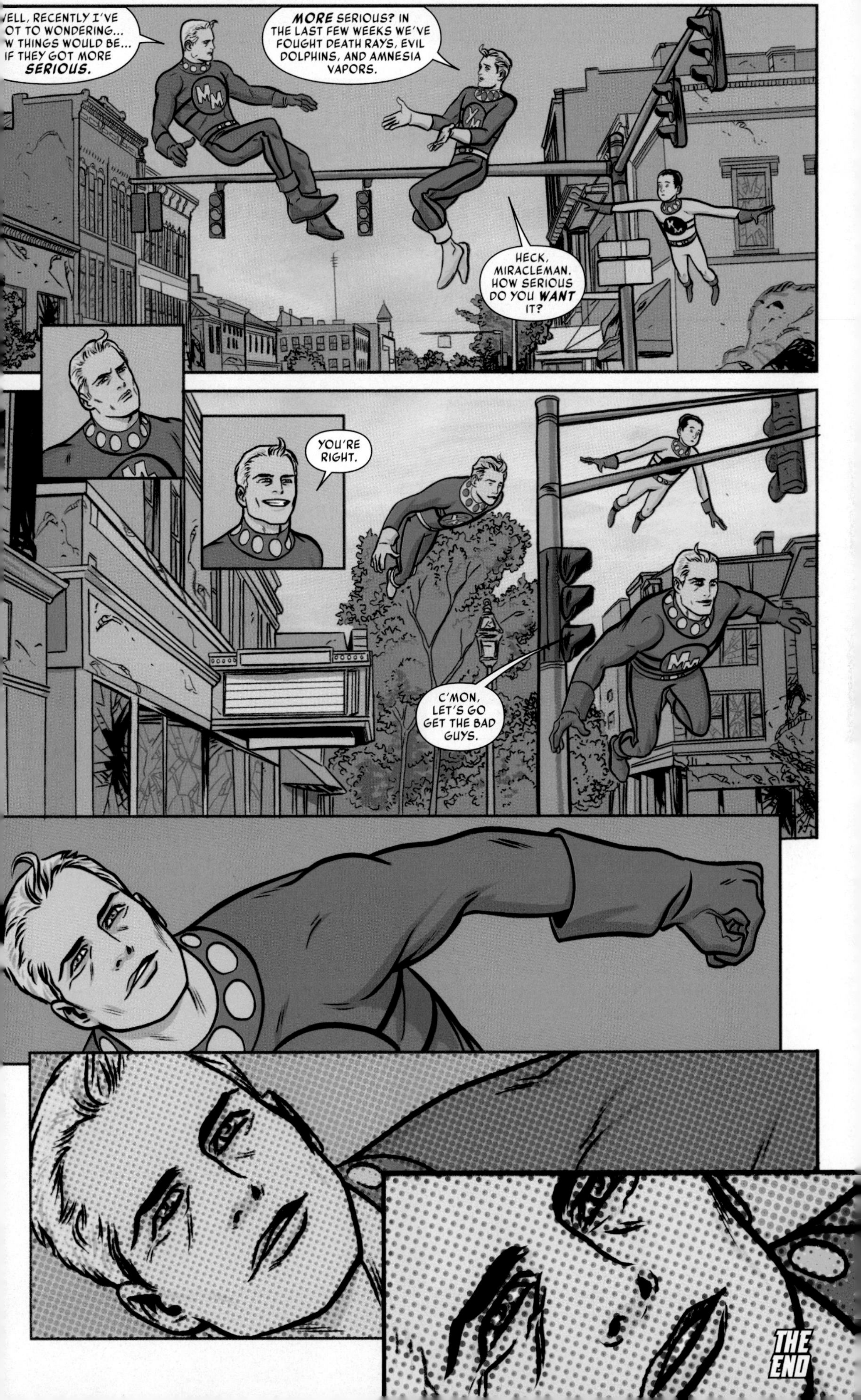

WELL, RECENTLY I'VE GOT TO WONDERING... HOW THINGS WOULD BE... IF THEY GOT MORE SERIOUS.
MORE SERIOUS? IN THE LAST FEW WEEKS WE'VE FOUGHT DEATH RAYS, EVIL DOLPHINS, AND AMNESIA VAPORS.
HECK, MIRACLEMAN. HOW SERIOUS DO YOU WANT IT?
YOU'RE RIGHT.
C'MON, LET'S GO GET THE BAD GUYS.
THE END

# MIRACLEMAN

## BEHIND THE SCENES

Grant Morrison wrote **"October Incident: 1966"** for the British comic magazine *Warrior*, the first home of the revitalized Marvelman/Miracleman. The story was put on hiatus, however, and appeared destined never to see print when *Warrior* ceased publication in 1984. In 2014, Joe Quesada contacted Morrison hoping that the script survived and they agreed to bring the story to readers at last.

1

OCTOBER INCIDENT:1966

FRAME 1 — Long shot. A grey day with drifting,drizzly rain. An old priest is trudging along an empty shore. Waves are surging,seagulls are flying around - all that Ryan's Daughter/French Lieutenant's Woman stuff basically. The priest is wearing a long coat but has no other protection against the elements .

CAP.: IT WAS THE DREAM.

CAP.: THE DREAM HAD COME BACK AFTER THREE YEARS.

MARVEL
Notice: This text and/or artwork may not be reproduced without the permission of the copyright owner.
ALL BLEED ART MUST EXTEND TO SOLID LINE
Book
Issue
Story Page #
Line Up Page #
INSTRUCTIONS FOR DOUBLE PAGE SPREAD: CUT AS SHOWN, ABUT PAGE EDGES, TAPE ON BACK. DO NOT OVERLAP.

MARVEL
Notice: This text and/or artwork may not be reproduced without the permission of the copyright owner.
ALL BLEED ART MUST EXTEND TO SOLID LINE
Book
Issue
Story Page #
Artist(s)
INSTRUCTIONS FOR DOUBLE PAGE SPREAD: CUT AS SHOWN, ABUT PAGE EDGES, TAPE ON BACK. DO NOT OVERLAP.

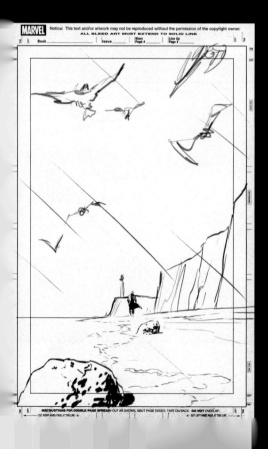

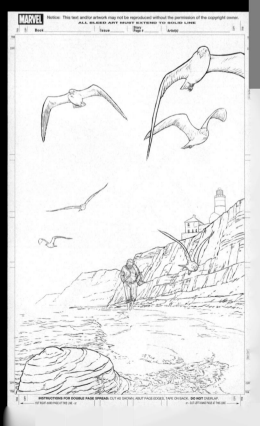

Morrison's script is written in a format that may be unfamiliar to some readers. Rather than specifying the number of panels (or "frames") per page and where page breaks occur, the script is open for the artist to visually pace as suits their storytelling style. The only limitation is the number of pages allocated by the publisher, typically six in *Warrior*.

FRAME 2 The priest staring out to sea, looking rather disturbed.

CAP.: HE KNEW IT WAS A WARNING WHEN HE WOKE TO THE GREY LIGHT AND THE WIND.

CAP.: THE DAYS OF THE REVELATION WERE COME UPON THE WORLD AND SOMETHING UNCLEAN WAS ABROAD.

FRAME 3 The priest has dropped to his knees on the sand and clasped his hands in desperate prayer.

CAP.: SOMETHING VENOMOUS WAS WALKING THE QUIET ROADS AND THE LONELY PATHWAYS, SOMETHING COLD AND FAR FROM HUMAN.

CAP.: HE PRAYS TO THE ALMIGHTY...

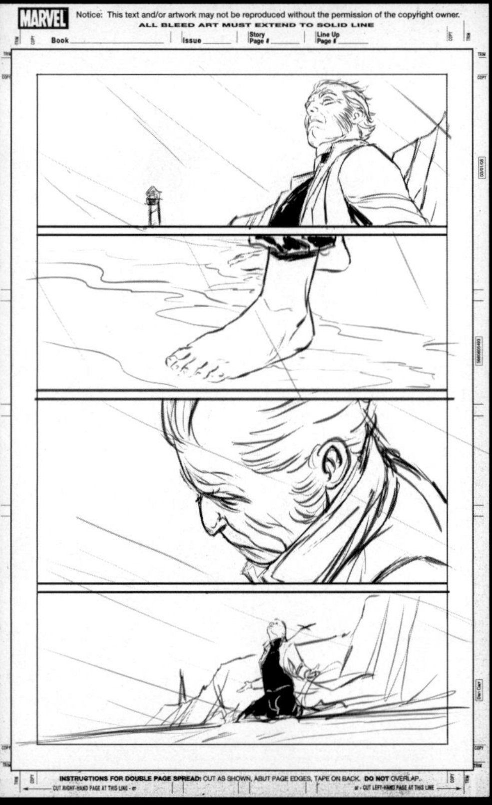
MARVEL
Notice: This text and/or artwork may not be reproduced without the permission of the copyright owner.
ALL BLEED ART MUST EXTEND TO SOLID LINE
INSTRUCTIONS FOR DOUBLE PAGE SPREAD: CUT AS SHOWN, ABUT PAGE EDGES, TAPE ON BACK. DO NOT OVERLAP.

Page 2 (Frames 2-3) layout by Joe Quesada

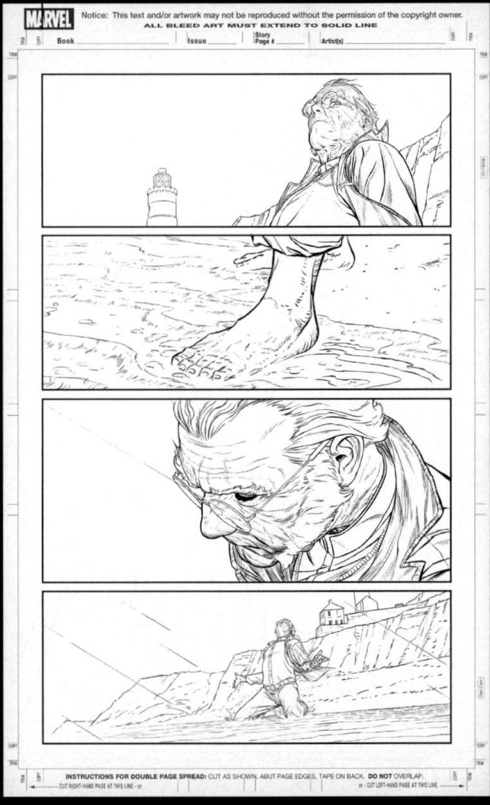
MARVEL
Notice: This text and/or artwork may not be reproduced without the permission of the copyright owner.
ALL BLEED ART MUST EXTEND TO SOLID LINE
INSTRUCTIONS FOR DOUBLE PAGE SPREAD: CUT AS SHOWN, ABUT PAGE EDGES, TAPE ON BACK. DO NOT OVERLAP.

Page 2 (Frames 2-3) art by Joe Quesada

As a lifelong Beatles fan, Quesada likely couldn't resist the opportunity to illustrate Johnny Bates as a "mod angel of death." That, paired with the chance to reveal an early step in Johnny's path to corruption, brought him to the drawing board.

| | |
|---|---|
| FRAME 4 | Large title frame. A path along the sea cliffs. Seen in full figure is a young man whose hair blows in the wind. (It is black and cut in the Beatles style of the time - not too long but covering his ears and reaching just past his collar, with a straight fringe. And would you like a shave too, sir ? ) He is wearing a black vinyl short raincoat, black poloneck jumper, black drainpipe trousers and black chelsea boots. His face is strong and cruel with high cheekbones and slanting eyebrows. He is smiling in a slight, wicked way. His body is slim. He looks like a mod angel of death. |
| CAP.: | THAT IT WILL PASS HIM BY |
| TITLE: | OCTOBER INCIDENT: 1966 |

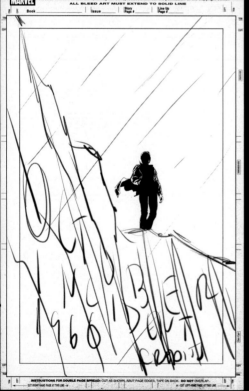

MARVEL
Notice: This text and/or artwork may not be reproduced without the permission of the copyright owner.
ALL BLEED ART MUST EXTEND TO SOLID LINE
INSTRUCTIONS FOR DOUBLE PAGE SPREAD: CUT AS SHOWN, ABUT PAGE EDGES, TAPE ON BACK. DO NOT OVERLAP.
Page 3 (Frame 4) layout by Joe Quesada

MARVEL
Notice: This text and/or artwork may not be reproduced without the permission of the copyright owner.
ALL BLEED ART MUST EXTEND TO SOLID LINE
1966
INSTRUCTIONS FOR DOUBLE PAGE SPREAD: CUT AS SHOWN, ABUT PAGE EDGES, TAPE ON BACK. DO NOT OVERLAP.
Page 3 (Frame 4) art by Joe Quesada

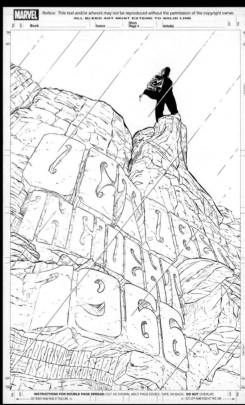

FRAME 5 The priest close up. He is staring heavenward. His hands are clenched at his chin. Rain runs on his face.

CAP.: BUT THE ONLY ANSWER IS THE SOUND OF DREAM THUNDER ECHOING DOWN THE DAYS.

FRAME 6 Flashback. Long shot. The priest walking on the sea cliffs three years earlier. It is night and snow is falling.

2

CAP.: AS THE MEMORIES COME STEALING.

FRAME 7 Flashback. Same view as Frame 6 but lit white as though by a flash of lightning. The priest is turned towards the sea.

CAP.: MEMORIES OF FIRE IN THE SKY AND OF GLORY THAT BLAZED WHITE AS THE SUN...

FRAME 8 Flashback. The priest looking up as what appears to be a small comet hurtles overhead.

CAP.: ON THE NIGHT THE OLD DRAGON WAS CAST OUT OF HEAVEN.

FRAME 9 The priest still kneeling on the sand. The sea has almost reached his knees. His head is bent in fervent prayer. In the background we can see the small dark figure of the young man approaching.

PRIEST: LORD BLESS ME AND KEEP ME AND DELIVER ME FROM...

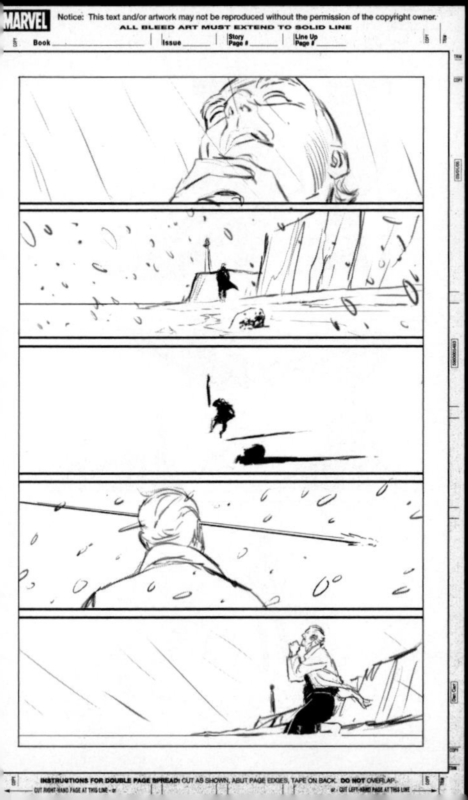
MARVEL
Notice: This text and/or artwork may not be reproduced without the permission of the copyright owner.
ALL BLEED ART MUST EXTEND TO SOLID LINE
Book
Issue
Story Page #
Line Up Page #
INSTRUCTIONS FOR DOUBLE PAGE SPREAD: CUT AS SHOWN, ABUT PAGE EDGES, TAPE ON BACK. DO NOT OVERLAP.

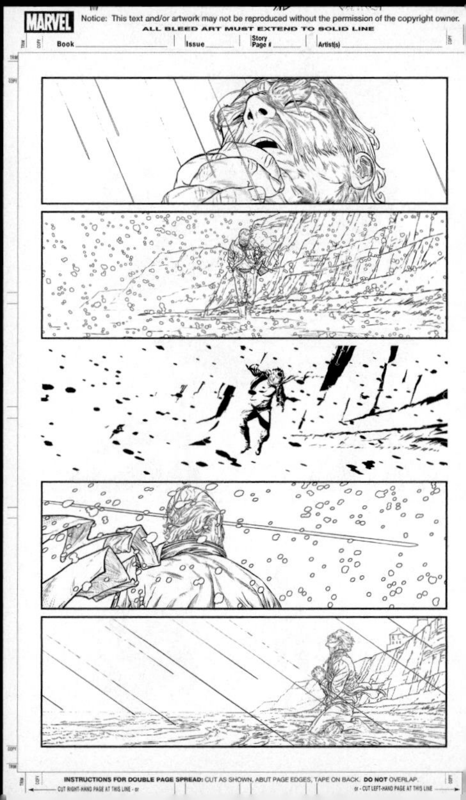
MARVEL
Notice: This text and/or artwork may not be reproduced without the permission of the copyright owner.
ALL BLEED ART MUST EXTEND TO SOLID LINE
Book
Issue
Story Page #
Artist(s)
INSTRUCTIONS FOR DOUBLE PAGE SPREAD: CUT AS SHOWN, ABUT PAGE EDGES, TAPE ON BACK. DO NOT OVERLAP.

ito the scene dressed like another famous John, John Lennon, who wore a similar fisherman's
at during the Beatles' first American tour. Setting the story in 1966 echoes Lennon's controversia
uote from that year: "Christianity will go. It will vanish and shrink. I needn't argue about that; I'm
ght and I'll be proved right. We're more popular than Jesus now; I don't know which will go first—
ock 'n' roll or Christianity. Jesus was all right but his disciples were thick and ordinary. It's them
wisting it that ruins it for me."

---

FRAME 10 — Ground level view. In the foreground is the black-trousered leg of the young man,his boot sunk into the wet sand. Behind that,the priest is turning startled from his devotions.

PRIEST: ...EVIL ?

FRAME 11 — The young man smiling in a mocking,condescending way.

YOUNG MAN: HELLO FATHER.

YOUNG MAN: COMMUNING WITH NATURE ?

FRAME 12 — The priest and the young man. The priest is getting up,with a trapped frightened look on his face.

PRIEST: OH.

PRIEST: I DIDN'T HEAR YOU COMING...

PRIEST: ...I...

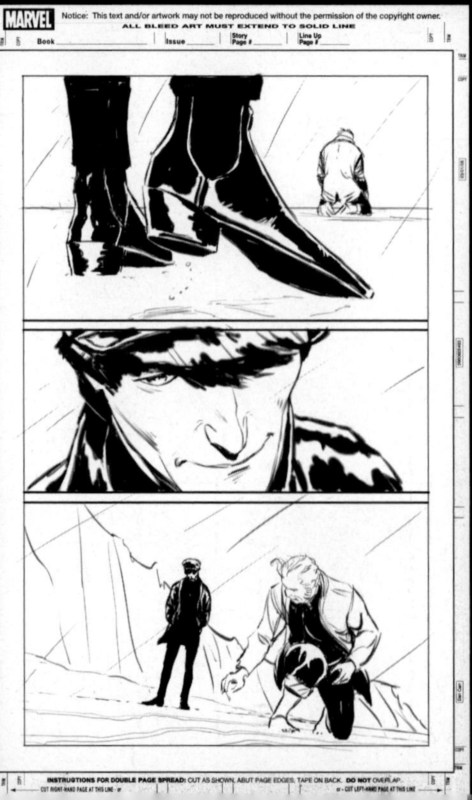

MARVEL
Notice: This text and/or artwork may not be reproduced without the permission of the copyright owner.
ALL BLEED ART MUST EXTEND TO SOLID LINE
Book
Issue
Story Page #
Line Up Page #
INSTRUCTIONS FOR DOUBLE PAGE SPREAD: CUT AS SHOWN, ABUT PAGE EDGES, TAPE ON BACK. DO NOT OVERLAP.


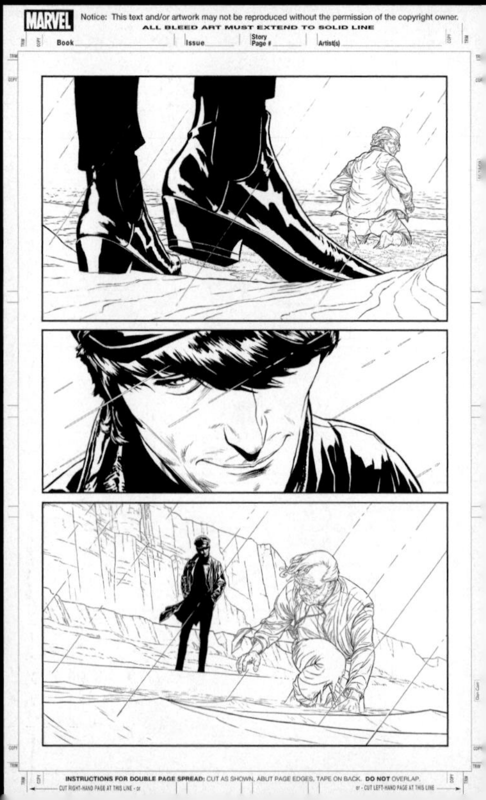

MARVEL
Notice: This text and/or artwork may not be reproduced without the permission of the copyright owner.
ALL BLEED ART MUST EXTEND TO SOLID LINE
Book
Issue
Story Page #
Artist(s)
INSTRUCTIONS FOR DOUBLE PAGE SPREAD: CUT AS SHOWN, ABUT PAGE EDGES, TAPE ON BACK. DO NOT OVERLAP.

FRAME 13 — Close in on the pair. The priest staring into the young man's face.

PRIEST: ...HAVE WE MET BEFORE...

FRAME 14 — First of four slim vertical frames. Flashback. A boy's naked figure stumbling through swirling snow. Smoke drifts off his burnt and strangely glowing form. He has short black hair.

CAP.: '...SOMEWHERE.?'

CAP.: A SMELL OF BURNING.

FRAME 15 — The young man, hands in pockets, standing against the wind and rain. Almost exulting in the storm.

(3)

YOUNG MAN: COULD BE. I'VE BEEN HERE BEFORE...

FRAME 16 — Flashback. Long shot. The smouldering boy stumbling down a quiet road. It is still dark, still snowing. The boy looks like a ghost.

CAP.: 'A COUPLE OF YEARS BACK.'

CAP.: A SMELL OF BRIMSTONE.

FRAME 17 — The priest's stance has crumbled. He looks old and frail, cowering before the storm.

PRIEST: OH GOD.

FRAME 18 — The young man has very lightly slapped the priest who flies backwards across the sand under the force of the blow.

YOUNG MAN: UH-UH.

YOUNG MAN: TRY AGAIN.

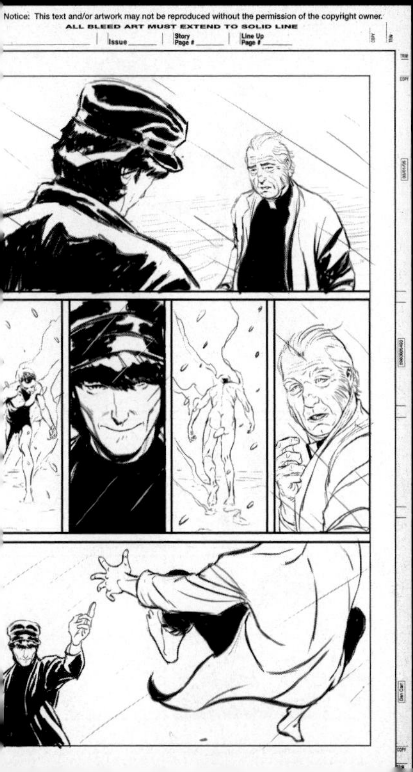
Notice: This text and/or artwork may not be reproduced without the permission of the copyright owner.
ALL BLEED ART MUST EXTEND TO SOLID LINE

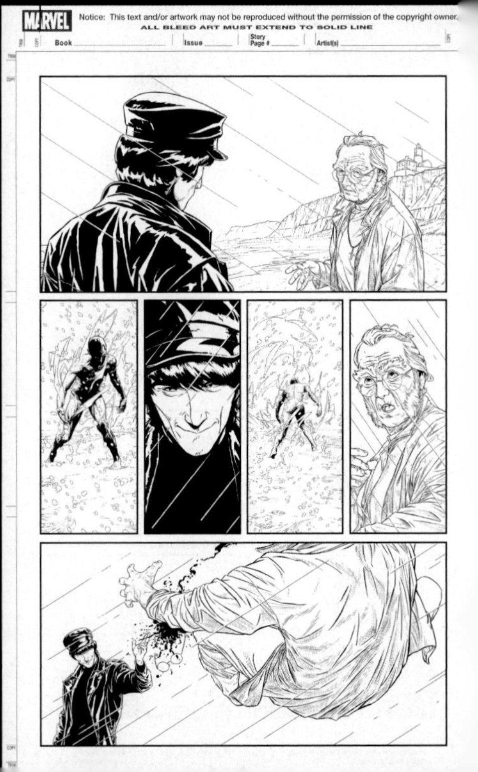
MARVEL
Notice: This text and/or artwork may not be reproduced without the permission of the copyright owner.
ALL BLEED ART MUST EXTEND TO SOLID LINE

FRAME 19 From above. The priest is lying twisted on the tideline at the end of a long skid mark he has left in the sand. The sea is coming in around his body. The young man is walking towards him,implacable.

CAP.: HIS ARM IS BROKEN. TWO RIBS HAVE SPLINTERED...HE CAN FEEL THEM GRATE AS HE TRIES TO MOVE.

PRIEST: NO..

PRIEST: ...NO,DON'T...

FRAME 20 The young man walking across the sand. The priest lies in the foreground.

YOUNG MAN: I'VE BEEN DOING A LOT OF READING,OLD MAN. SO MUCH TO LEARN ; NIETZCHE,QUANTUM THEORY,THE BIBLE.

PRIEST: DEAR JESUS...

FRAME 21 Track in towards the young man,whose feet are seen to be leaving the ground ever so slightly.

YOUNG MAN: HARDLY.

YOUNG MAN: JESUS ONLY WALKED ON THE WATER. BUT ME...

FRAME 22 The young man is stepping up into the air over the priest's head. He is grinning madly,his hair flying in the storm.

YOUNG MAN: I WALK ON THE AIR !

FRAME 23 The priest staring up in terror,grasping at the cross around his neck while the young man hovers above him.

PRIEST: OH GOD...



PRIEST: DEAR GOD PROTECT ME...I SHALL FEAR NO EVIL...

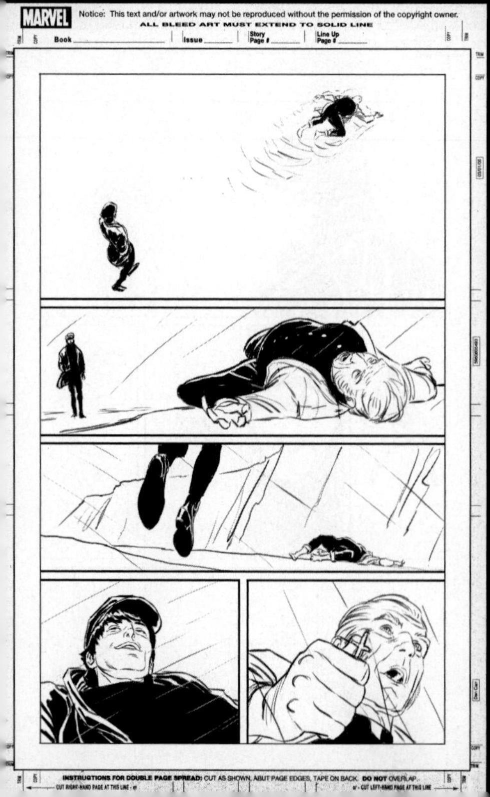
MARVEL
Notice: This text and/or artwork may not be reproduced without the permission of the copyright owner.
ALL BLEED ART MUST EXTEND TO SOLID LINE
Book
Issue
Story Page #
Line Up Page #
INSTRUCTIONS FOR DOUBLE PAGE SPREAD: CUT AS SHOWN, ABUT PAGE EDGES, TAPE ON BACK. DO NOT OVERLAP.

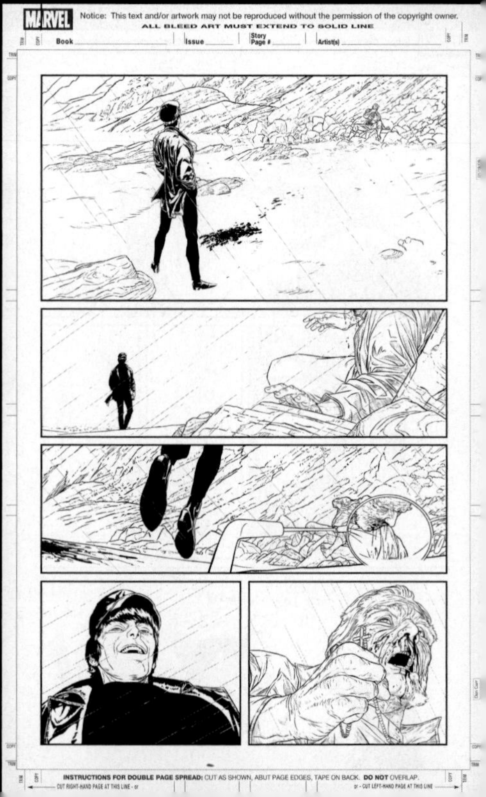
MARVEL
Notice: This text and/or artwork may not be reproduced without the permission of the copyright owner.
ALL BLEED ART MUST EXTEND TO SOLID LINE
Book
Issue
Story Page #
Artist(s)
INSTRUCTIONS FOR DOUBLE PAGE SPREAD: CUT AS SHOWN, ABUT PAGE EDGES, TAPE ON BACK. DO NOT OVERLAP.

That the work of German philosopher Friedrich Wilhelm Nietzsche is amongst Bates' reading material is no accident. In 1882, Nietzsche famously wrote, "God is dead." To Nietzsche, the loss of faith/God meant that the absolute morality imposed by religion was also lost. If one does not believe in the source from which the moral order springs, its morality becomes unenforceable. The result is a struggle to maintain a system of moral values in the face of nihilism (the rejection of morality).

| | |
|---|---|
| FRAME 24 | The young man laughing, hanging in the air as though in parody of the crucifixion. Lightning is crackling around his outstretched hands. |
| YOUNG MAN: | YOU CAN TAKE YOUR CROSS AND STUFF IT! THE APOCALYPSE HAS ARRIVED! |
| YOUNG MAN: | I CAN DO ANY BLOODY THING I WANT AND YOU CAN'T STOP ME YOU PATHETIC OLD WITCH DOCTOR! |
| FRAME 25 | The priest screaming. Wielding his cross like a gun without bullets. |
| PRIEST: | GET THEE BEHIND ME SATAN!!! |

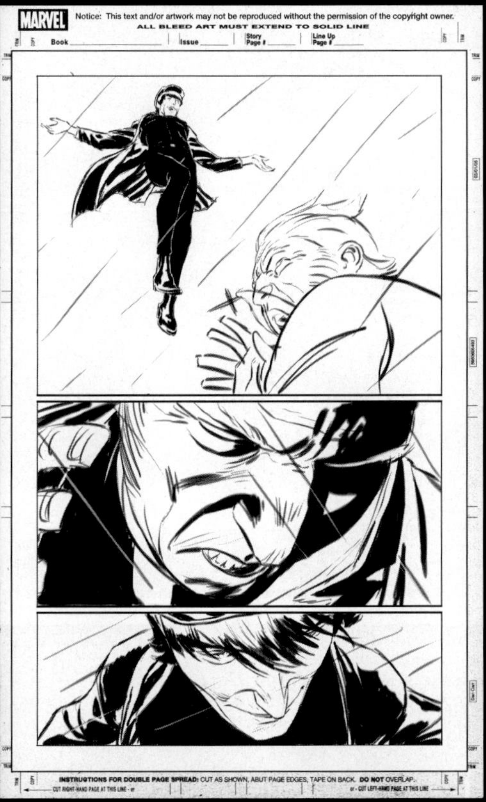
MARVEL
Notice: This text and/or artwork may not be reproduced without the permission of the copyright owner.
ALL BLEED ART MUST EXTEND TO SOLID LINE
INSTRUCTIONS FOR DOUBLE PAGE SPREAD: CUT AS SHOWN, ABUT PAGE EDGES, TAPE ON BACK. DO NOT OVERLAP.

Page 8 (Frames 24-25) layout by Joe Quesada

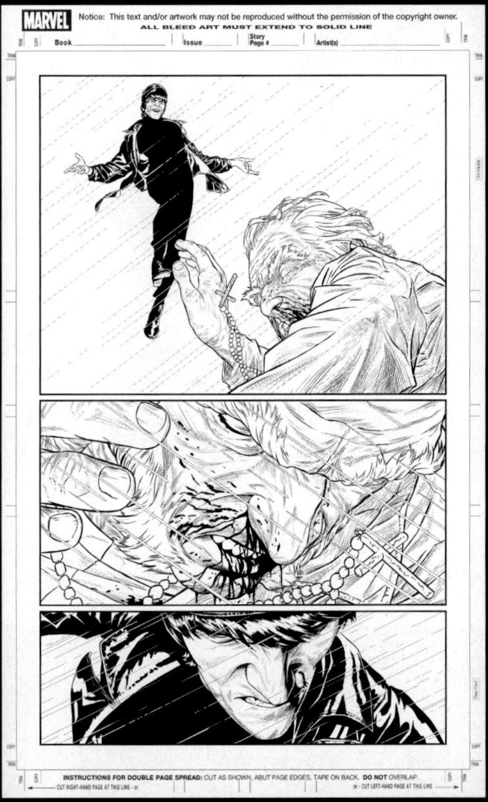
MARVEL
Notice: This text and/or artwork may not be reproduced without the permission of the copyright owner.
ALL BLEED ART MUST EXTEND TO SOLID LINE
INSTRUCTIONS FOR DOUBLE PAGE SPREAD: CUT AS SHOWN, ABUT PAGE EDGES, TAPE ON BACK. DO NOT OVERLAP.

Page 8 (Frames 24-25) art by Joe Quesada

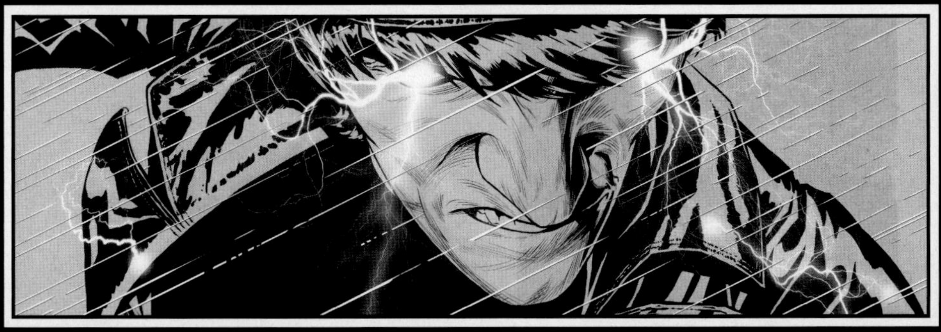

Page 8 with darkened overlay for Bates' lightning effects.

In the three years since the Spookshow attempted to kill the Miracleman Family, Johnny Bates, loose in a world unencumbered by Gargunza's dreams, has transformed from a playful child into a violent murderer. Quesada punctuates Bates' corruption with a full-page splash.

| | |
|---|---|
| FRAME 26 | Long shot. Lightning blasting down to incinerate the priest. The young man's head is thrown back in wild glee. |
| CAP.: | THERE IS A BRIEF STINK OF OZONE AND A WHIPCRACK OF THUNDER. |

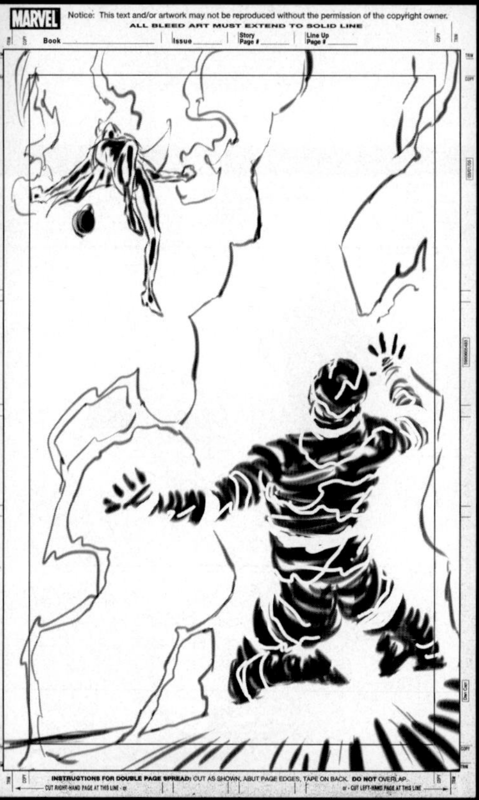
MARVEL
Notice: This text and/or artwork may not be reproduced without the permission of the copyright owner.
ALL BLEED ART MUST EXTEND TO SOLID LINE
Book
Issue
Story Page #
Line Up Page #
INSTRUCTIONS FOR DOUBLE PAGE SPREAD: CUT AS SHOWN, ABUT PAGE EDGES, TAPE ON BACK. DO NOT OVERLAP.

Page 9 (Frame 26) layout by Joe Quesada

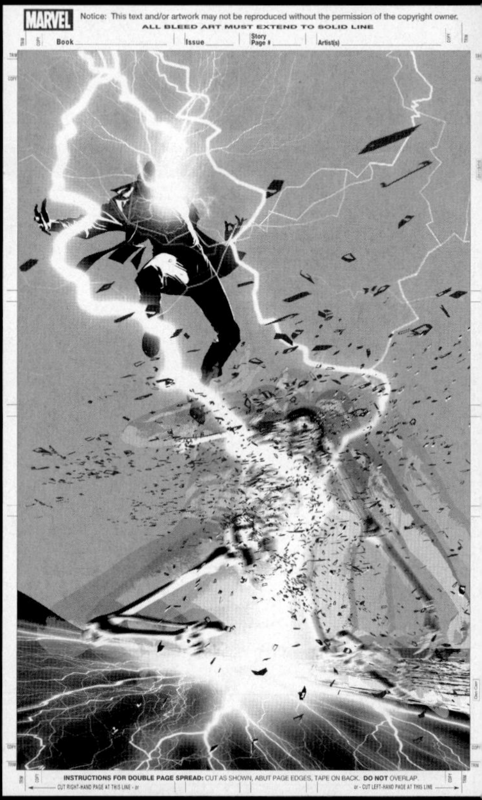
MARVEL
Notice: This text and/or artwork may not be reproduced without the permission of the copyright owner.
ALL BLEED ART MUST EXTEND TO SOLID LINE
Book
Issue
Story Page #
Artist(s)
INSTRUCTIONS FOR DOUBLE PAGE SPREAD: CUT AS SHOWN, ABUT PAGE EDGES, TAPE ON BACK. DO NOT OVERLAP.

Page 9 (Frame 26) art with effects overlay by Joe Quesada

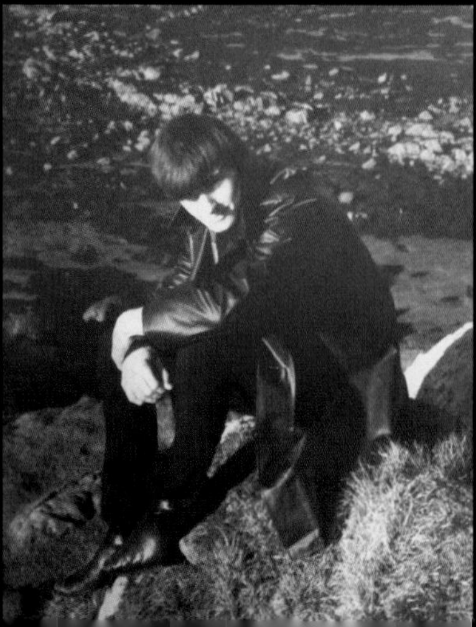

Quesada used this photograph of Morrison, taken the year the story was written, as reference for Bates' Beatles-inspired fashions.

Grant Morrison, Culzean Castle, Scotland, 1984
Photo by Judy Cartwright

Heightening the moment's drama, Quesada extends Bates' inspection of his work, adding a reference to *Hamlet*'s gravedigger scene. Bates takes the place of mad Prince Hamlet, while the priest's skull stands in for that of Yorick, the beloved court jester who entertained the prince in his youth. The moment also foreshadows Miracleman crushing Johnny's skull 20 years later.

| | |
|---|---|
| FRAME 27 | The young man standing over a smoking,charred pile. He is looking down with an inhuman grin,as though inspecting the results of a successful experiment. |
| CAP.: | THEN THERE IS NOTHING. |
| CAP.: | ONLY A SMELL OF BURNING. |
| CAP.: | AND A SMILING DRAGON. |
| FRAME 28 | View from the cliffs down to the beach. The young man is walking in mid air up towards 'camera'. |
| CAP.: | SOMETIMES DREAMS CAN COME TRUE. |
| CAP.: | EVEN THE BAD ONES. |

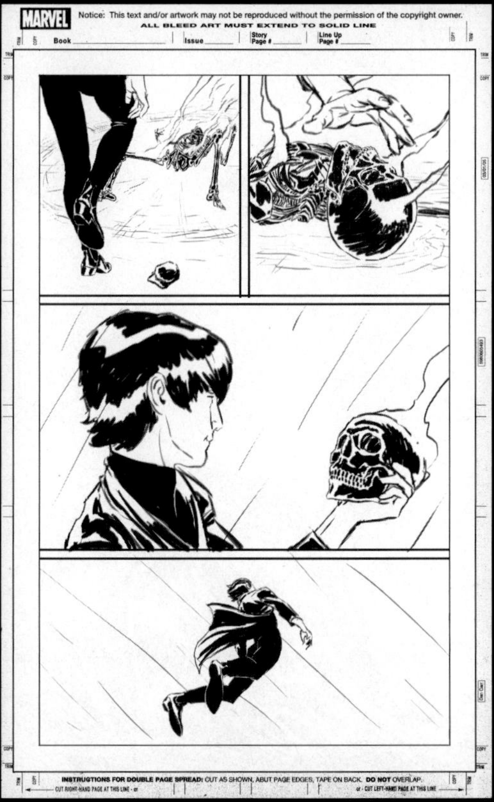
MARVEL
Notice: This text and/or artwork may not be reproduced without the permission of the copyright owner.
ALL BLEED ART MUST EXTEND TO SOLID LINE
Book
Issue
Story Page #
Line Up Page #
INSTRUCTIONS FOR DOUBLE PAGE SPREAD: CUT AS SHOWN, ABUT PAGE EDGES, TAPE ON BACK. DO NOT OVERLAP.
Page 10 (Frames 27-28) layout by Joe Quesada

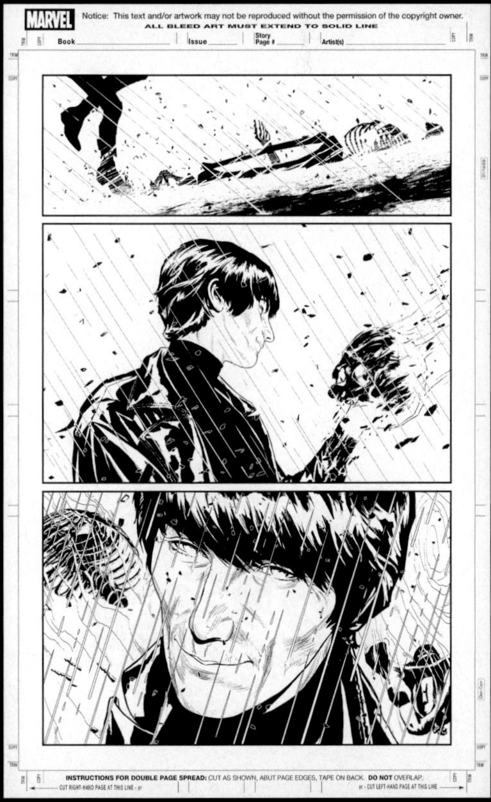
MARVEL
Notice: This text and/or artwork may not be reproduced without the permission of the copyright owner.
ALL BLEED ART MUST EXTEND TO SOLID LINE
Book
Issue
Story Page #
Artist(s)
INSTRUCTIONS FOR DOUBLE PAGE SPREAD: CUT AS SHOWN, ABUT PAGE EDGES, TAPE ON BACK. DO NOT OVERLAP.
Page 10 (Frames 27-28) art by Joe Quesada

In *Also Sprach Zarathustra*, Nietzsche presented his concept of the *Übermensch* (originally translated as "Beyond-Man," but since interpreted as "superman" or "overman"). The *Übermensch* will rise above nihilism to create mankind's new system of moral values. In *Miracleman*, Bates becomes a horrifying embodiment of nihilism, while Miracleman follows the path of the potential *Übermensch*.

FRAME 29 Long shot down a road as the young man walks off into empty country. The rain falls and leaves whirl in the wind.

CAP.: THE WIND RISES. IN HIS HEAD A SWEET BLACK BLIZZARD RAGES.

CAP.: AND SMILING BLEAKLY, THE DRAGON, THE ANTICHRIST, JOHNNY BATES, KID MIRACLEMAN, TURNS HIS FACE TO THE GATHERING STORM AND HEADS FOR LONDON.

****************************************

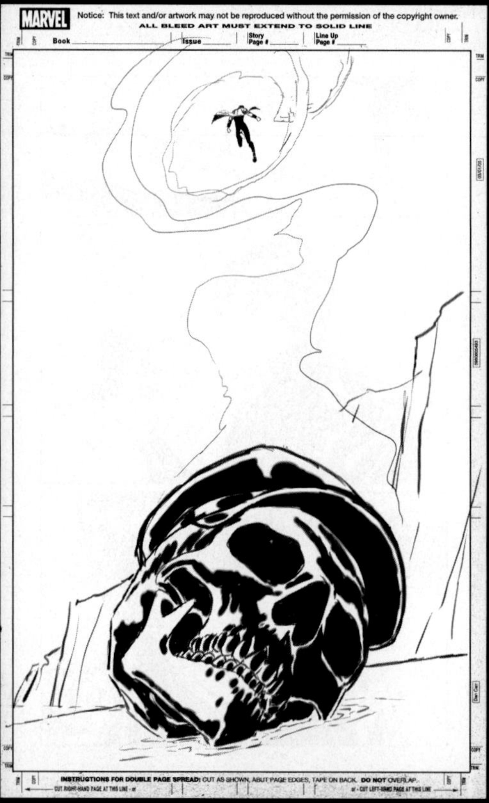

MARVEL
Notice: This text and/or artwork may not be reproduced without the permission of the copyright owner.
ALL BLEED ART MUST EXTEND TO SOLID LINE
INSTRUCTIONS FOR DOUBLE PAGE SPREAD: CUT AS SHOWN, ABUT PAGE EDGES, TAPE ON BACK. DO NOT OVERLAP.


Page 11 (Frame 29) layout by Joe Quesada

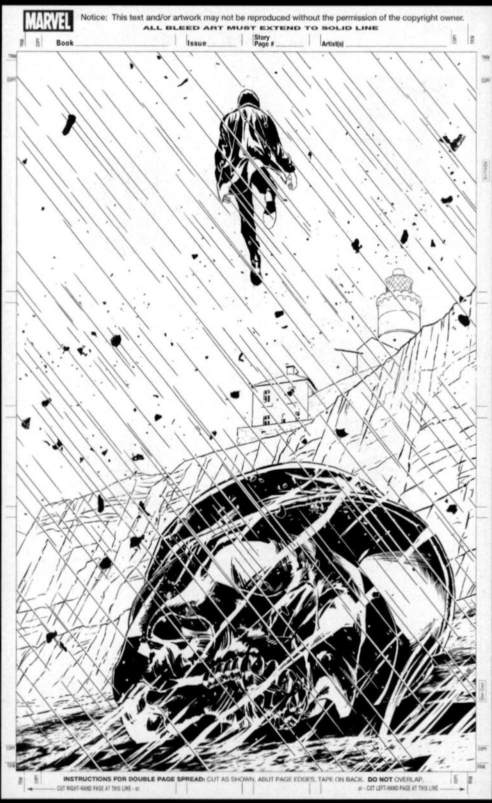

MARVEL
Notice: This text and/or artwork may not be reproduced without the permission of the copyright owner.
ALL BLEED ART MUST EXTEND TO SOLID LINE
INSTRUCTIONS FOR DOUBLE PAGE SPREAD: CUT AS SHOWN, ABUT PAGE EDGES, TAPE ON BACK. DO NOT OVERLAP.


Page 11 (Frame 29) art by Joe Quesada

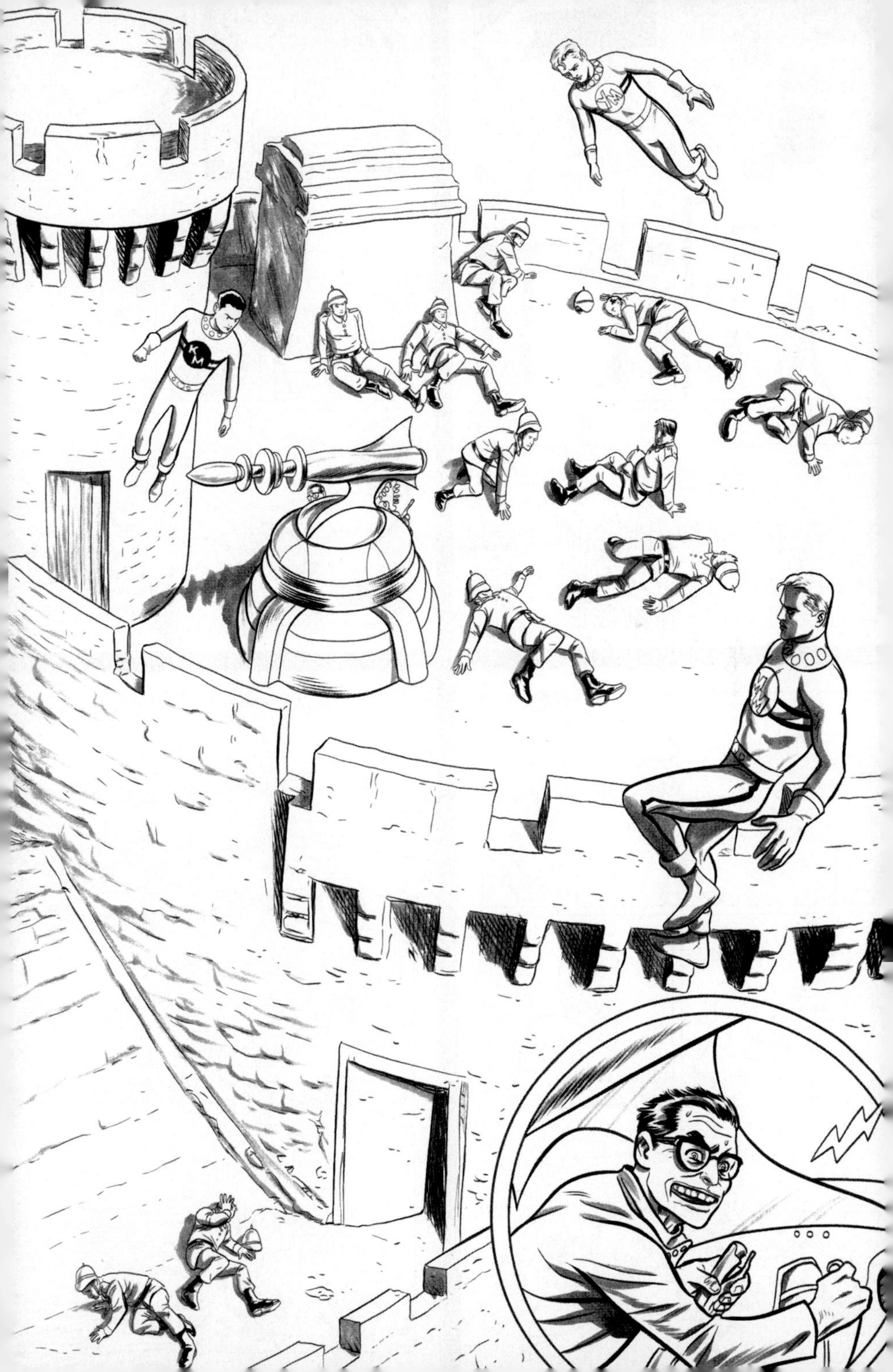

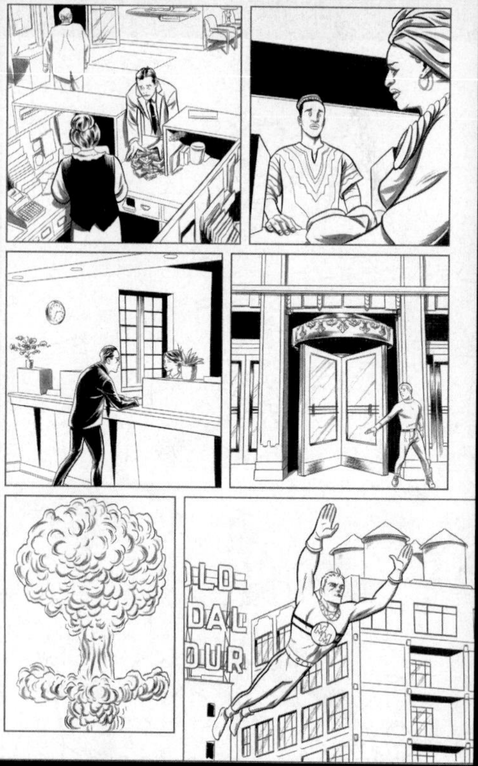

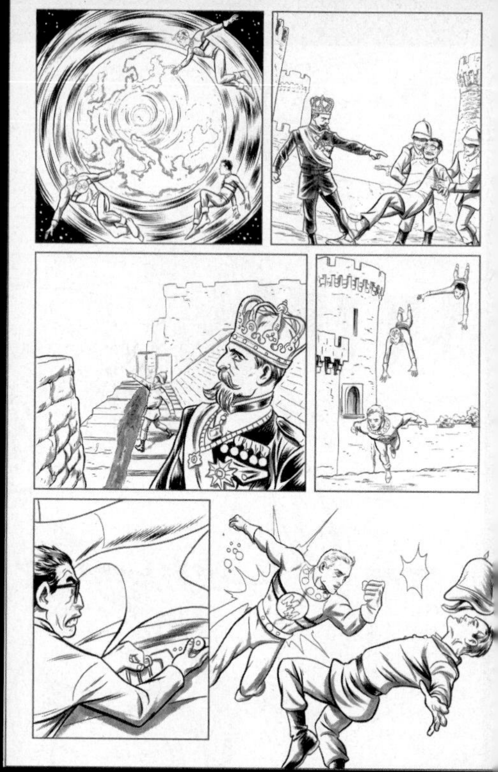

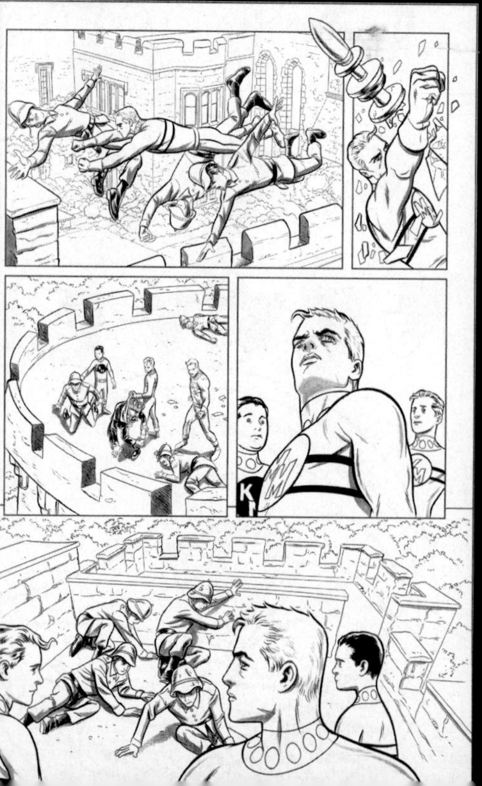

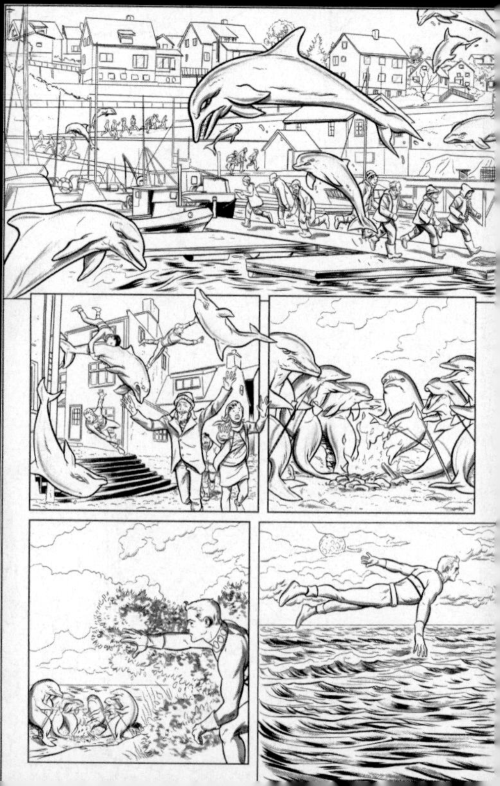

*All New Miracleman Annual* #1, "Seriously Miraculous," pages 2-5 original artwork, pencil, India ink and ink washes on illustration board by Mike Allred.

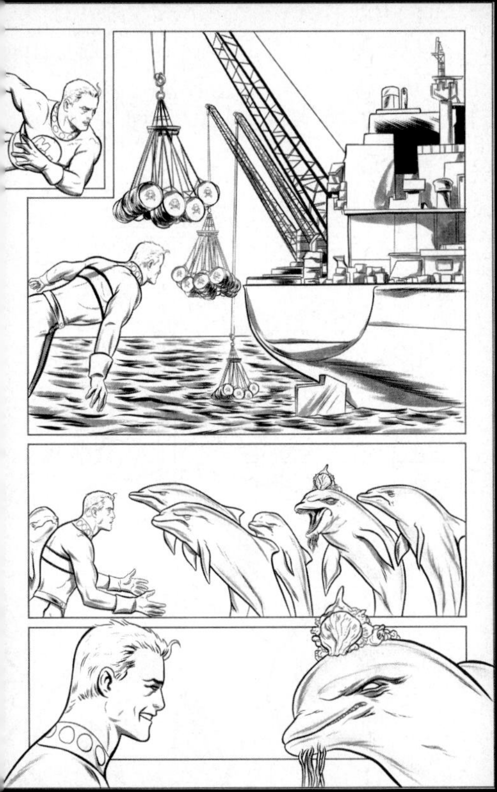

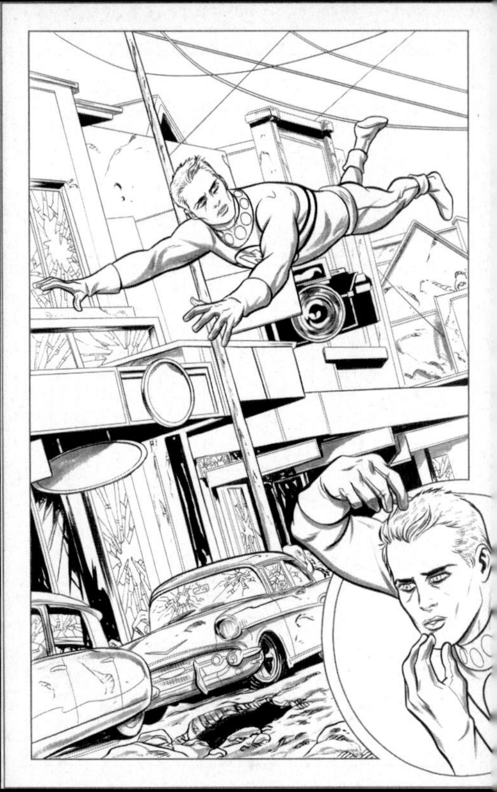

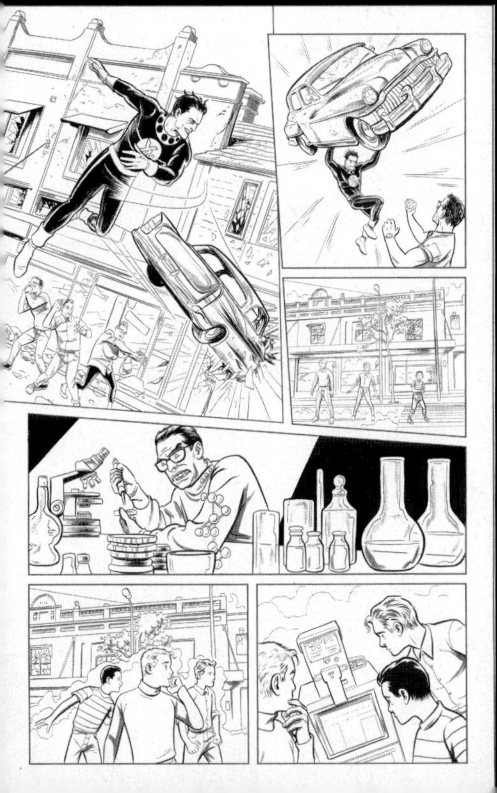

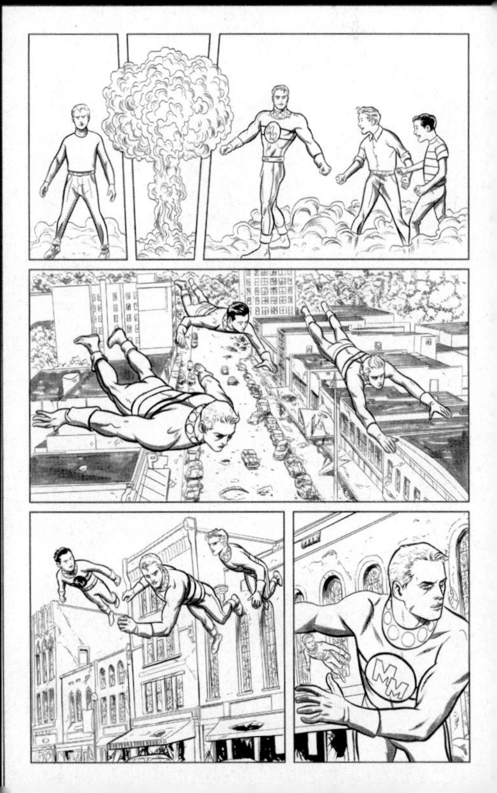

"Seriously Miraculous" ends with an homage to the Original Writer and Garry Leach's *Thus Spake Zarathustra* zoom-in page from *Miracleman* #1. **CLOCKWISE FROM TOP-LEFT:** Mike Allred's pencils; inks; colors by Laura Allred; Garry Leach's page from *Miracleman* #1, colors by Steve Oliff.

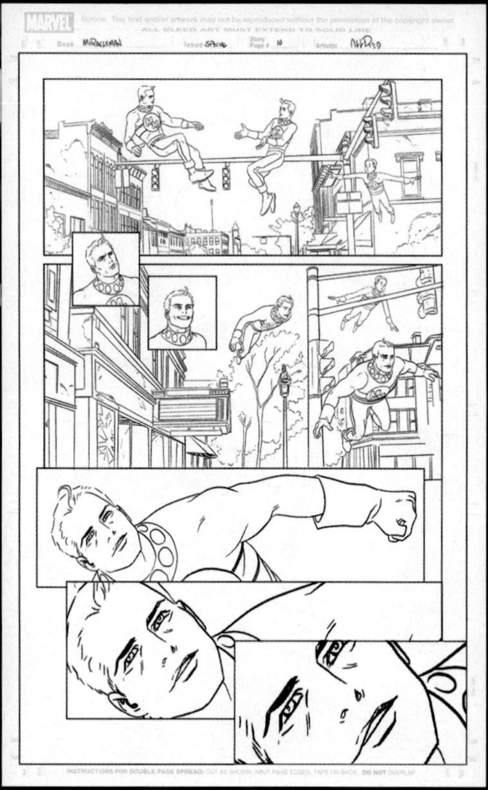

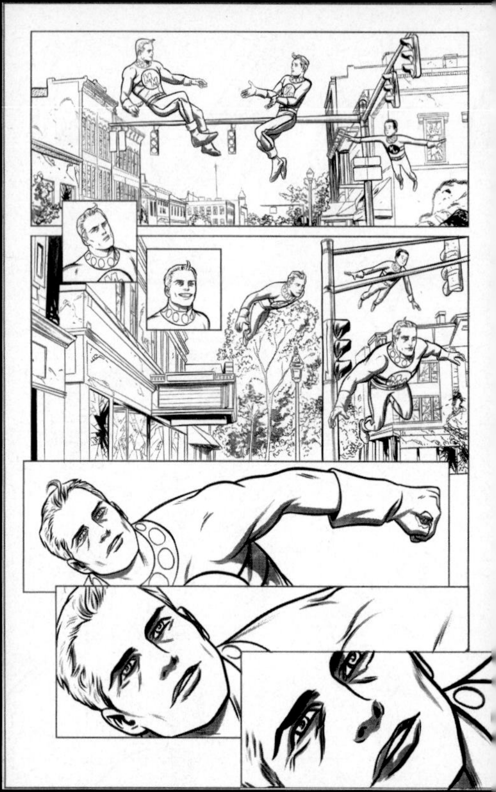

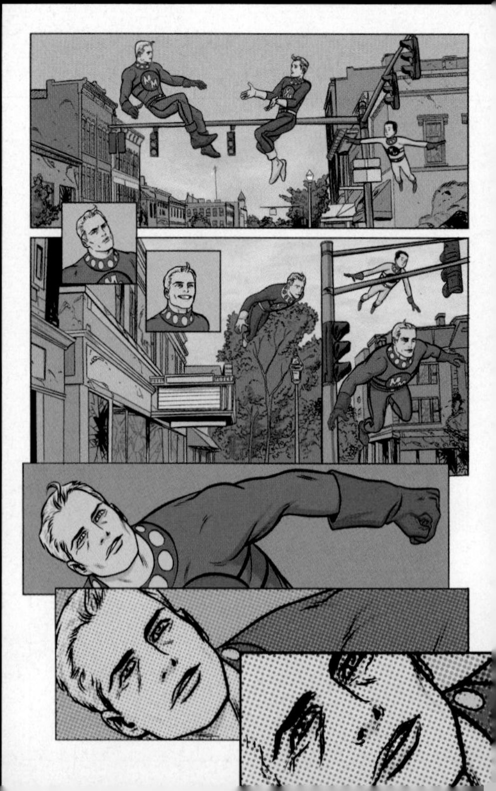

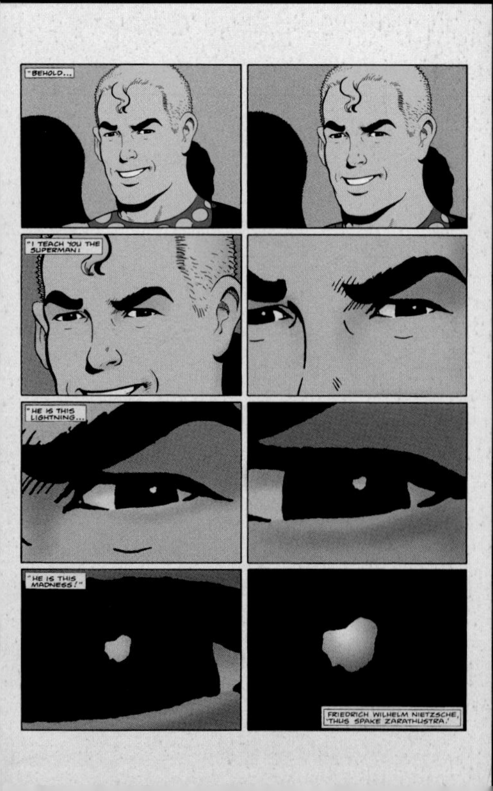
"BEHOLD...
"I TEACH YOU THE SUPERMAN!
"HE IS THIS LIGHTNING...
"HE IS THIS MADNESS!"
FRIEDRICH WILHELM NIETZSCHE, 'THUS SPAKE ZARATHUSTRA.'

*Miracleman* #11, page 1 pencils by John Totleben. For Book Three's 1987 scenes, inspiration was found in the work of Winsor McCay. McCay's newspaper comic strips *Little Nemo in Slumberland* and *In the Land of Wondeful Dreams* were famous for their giant, broadsheet depictions of Slumberland's fantastic dreamscapes. Totleben renders Olympus using an open line style evoking McCay's work and capturing the pyramid's endless wonders and godlike scale.

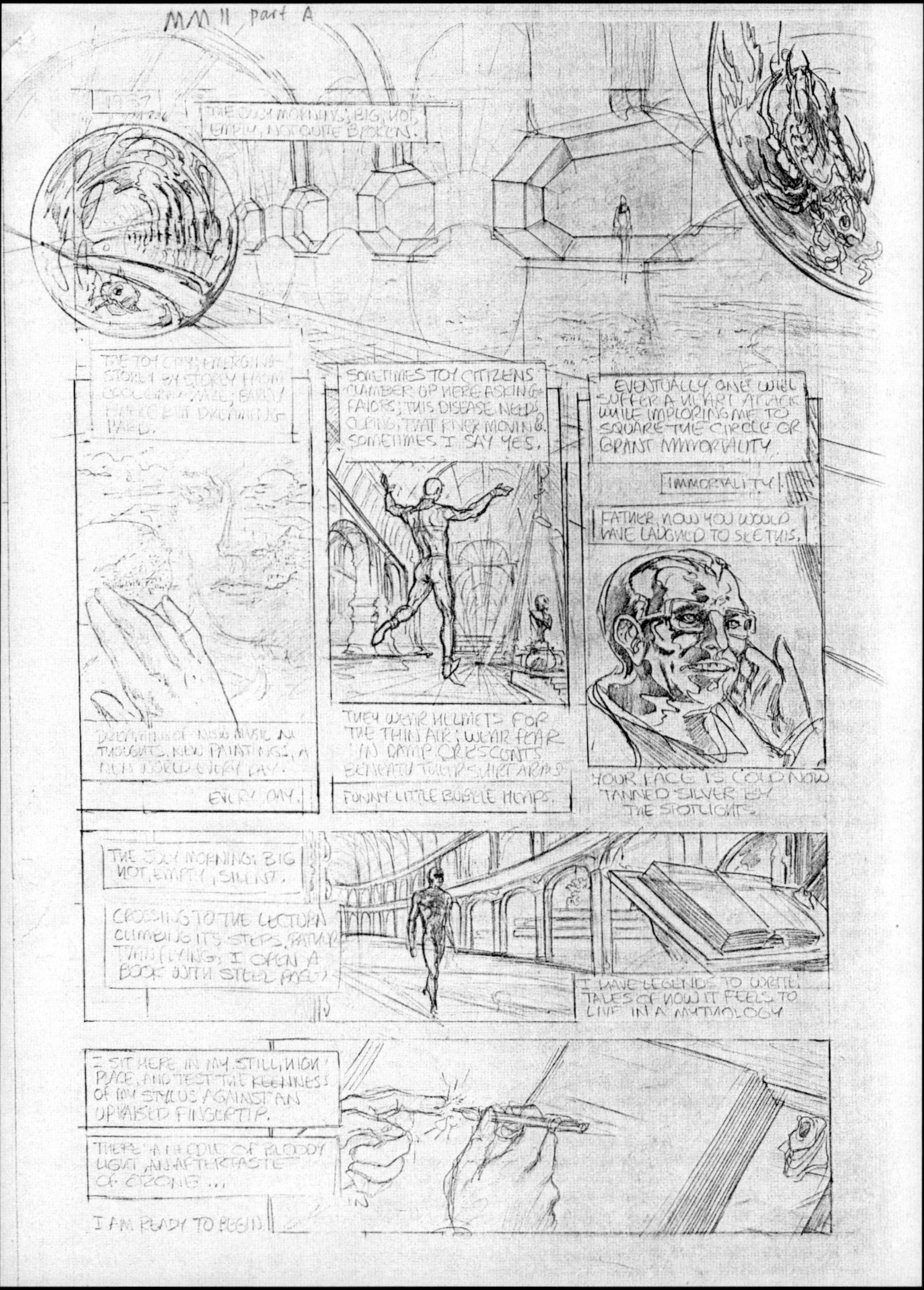
MM 11 part A
SOMETIMES TOY CITIZENS CLAMBER UP HERE ASKING FAVORS; THIS DISEASE NEEDS CURING, THAT RIVER MOVING. SOMETIMES I SAY YES.
EVENTUALLY ONE WILL SUFFER A HEART ATTACK WHILE IMPLORING ME TO SQUARE THE CIRCLE OR GRANT IMMORTALITY.
IMMORTALITY.
FATHER, HOW YOU WOULD HAVE LAUGHED TO SEE THIS.
EVERY DAY.
THEY WEAR HELMETS FOR THE THIN AIR; WEAR FEAR IN DAMP CRESCENTS BENEATH THEIR SHIRT ARMS.
FUNNY LITTLE BUBBLE HEADS.
YOUR FACE IS COLD NOW TANNED SILVER BY THE SPOTLIGHTS.
NOT, EMPTY, SILENT.
CROSSING TO THE LECTURN CLIMBING ITS STEPS, I OPEN A BOOK WITH STEEL PAGES
I HAVE LEGENDS TO WRITE; TALES OF HOW IT FEELS TO LIVE IN A MYTHOLOGY
I SIT HERE IN MY STILL, HIGH PLACE, AND TEST THE KEENNESS OF MY STYLUS AGAINST AN UPRAISED FINGERTIP.
OF OZONE ...
I AM READY TO BEGIN.

*Miracleman* #11, page 2 pencils by John Totleben. In Greek mythology Cronos was a Titan, an early generation of gods, and the father of Zeus and the Olympians. He is destined to be overthrown by his children and battles them in a war to decide which gods will rule the universe.

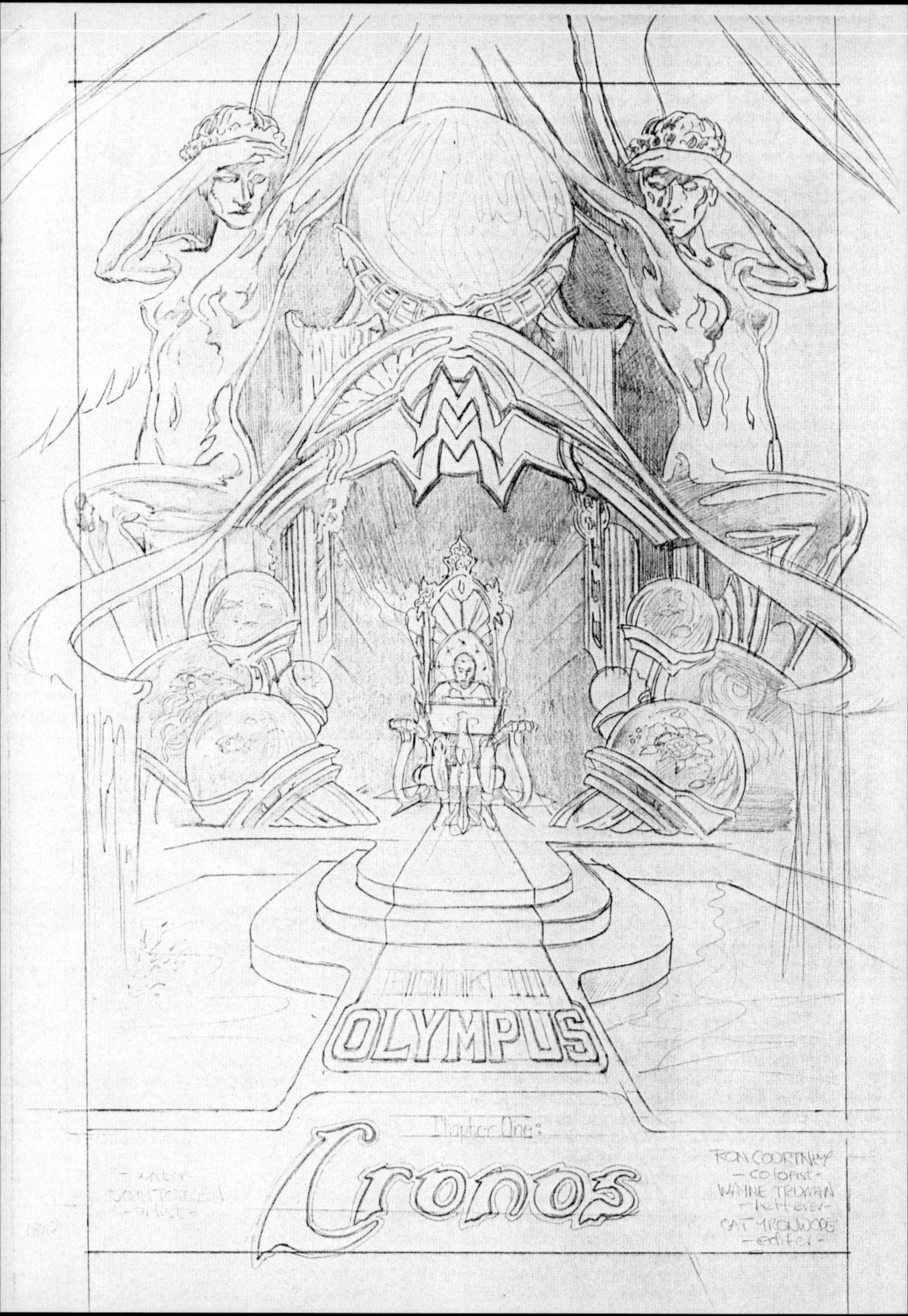
OLYMPUS
Chapter One:
Cronos
RON COURTNEY
- colorist -
WAYNE TRUMAN
- letterer -
CAT YRONWODE
- editor -

*Miracleman* #11, page 5 pencils by John Totleben. In contrast to the 1987 Olympus setting, for the 1982 scenes Totleben employs more frequent spotted blacks and heavy crosshatching. Set in enclosed rooms, tight spaces and dead ends, the techniques amplify the tension and emphasize the human scale.

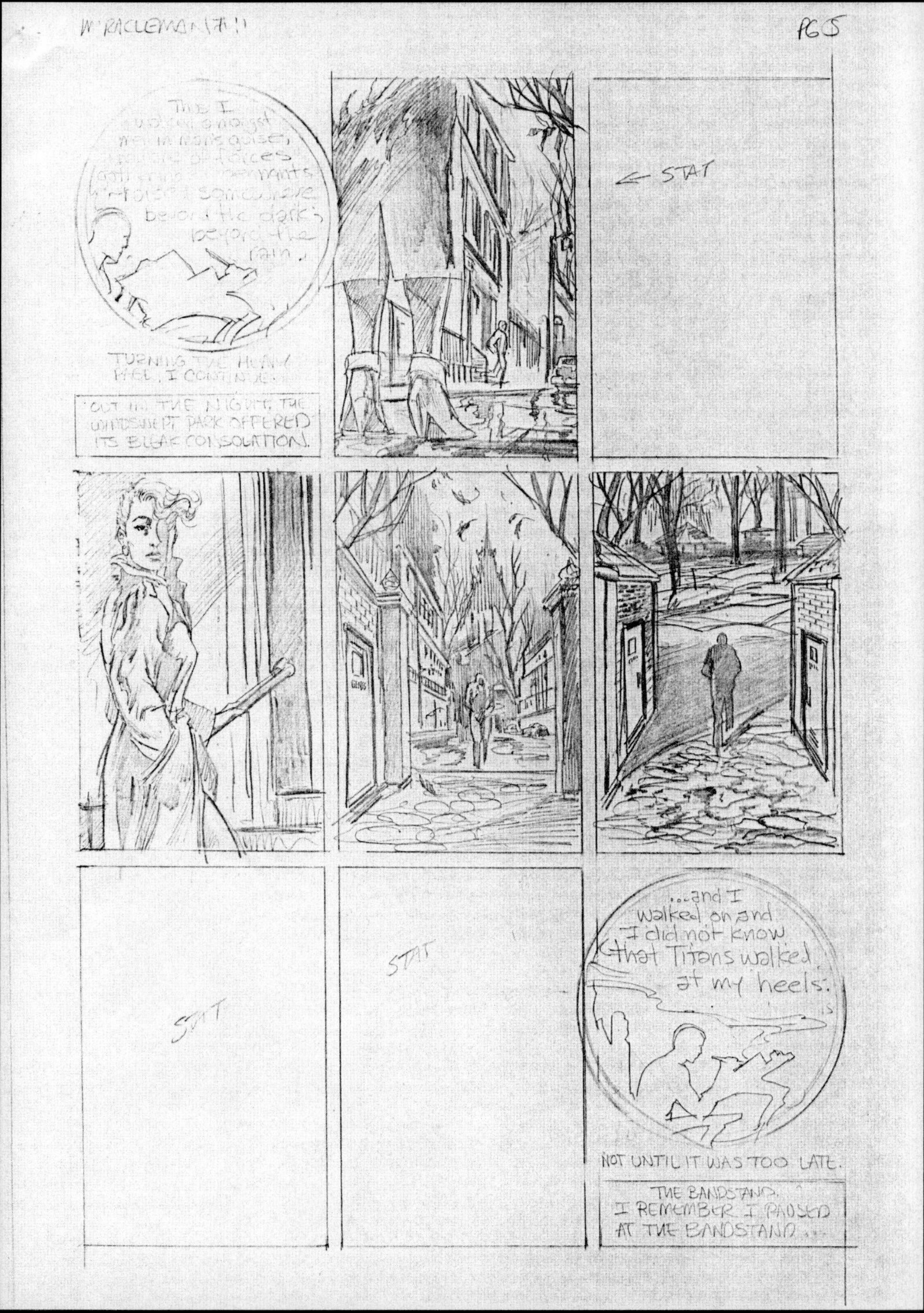
PG 5
TURNING THE HEAVY PAGE, I CONTINUE.
OUT IN THE NIGHT, THE WINDSWEPT PARK OFFERED ITS BLEAK CONSOLATION.
STAT
...and I walked on and I did not know that Titans walked at my heels:
NOT UNTIL IT WAS TOO LATE.
THE BANDSTAND. I REMEMBER I PAUSED AT THE BANDSTAND...
STAT

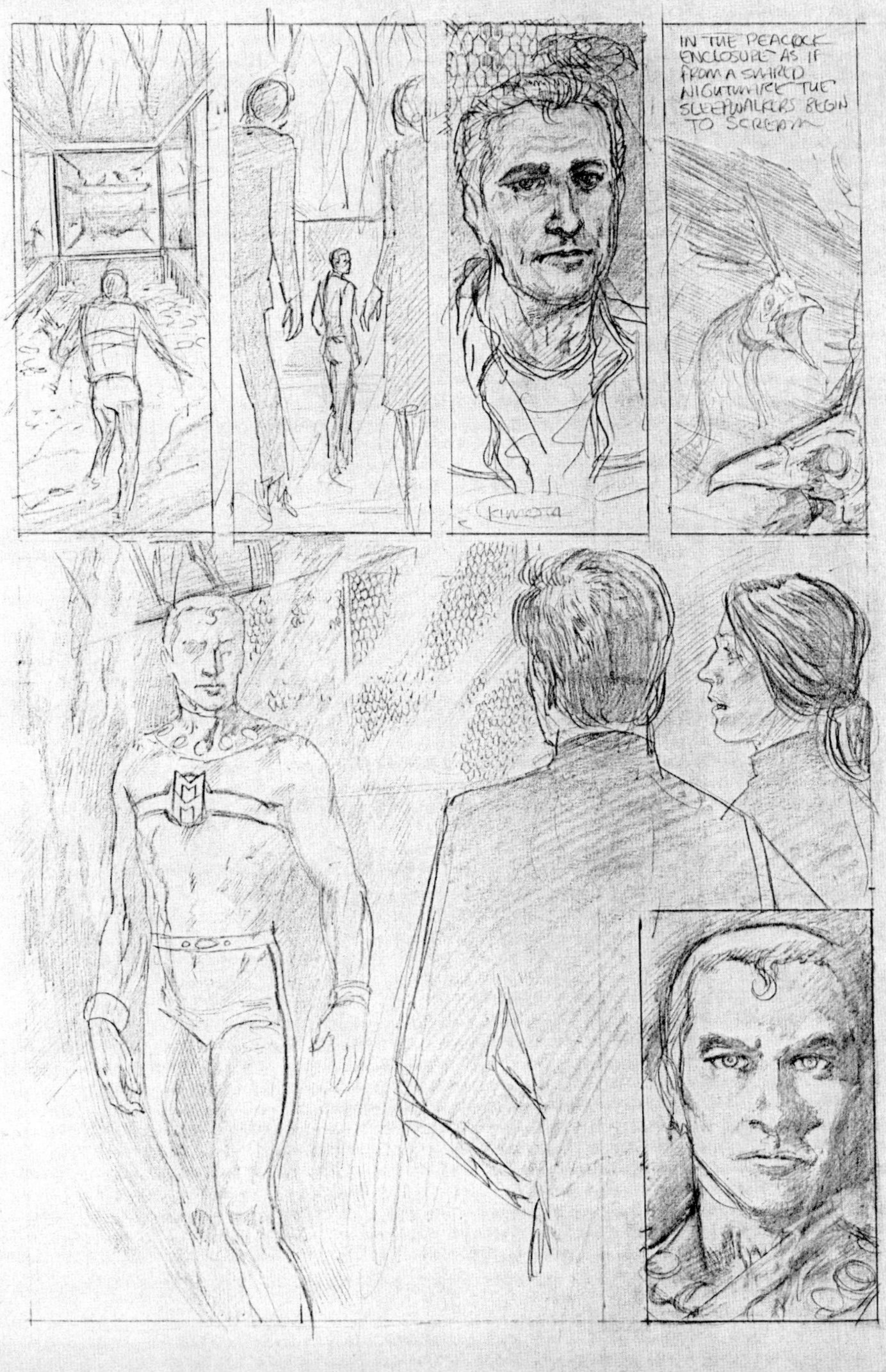
IN THE PEACOCK ENCLOSURE AS IF FROM A SHARED NIGHTMARE THE SLEEPWALKERS BEGIN TO SCREAM
KIMOTA

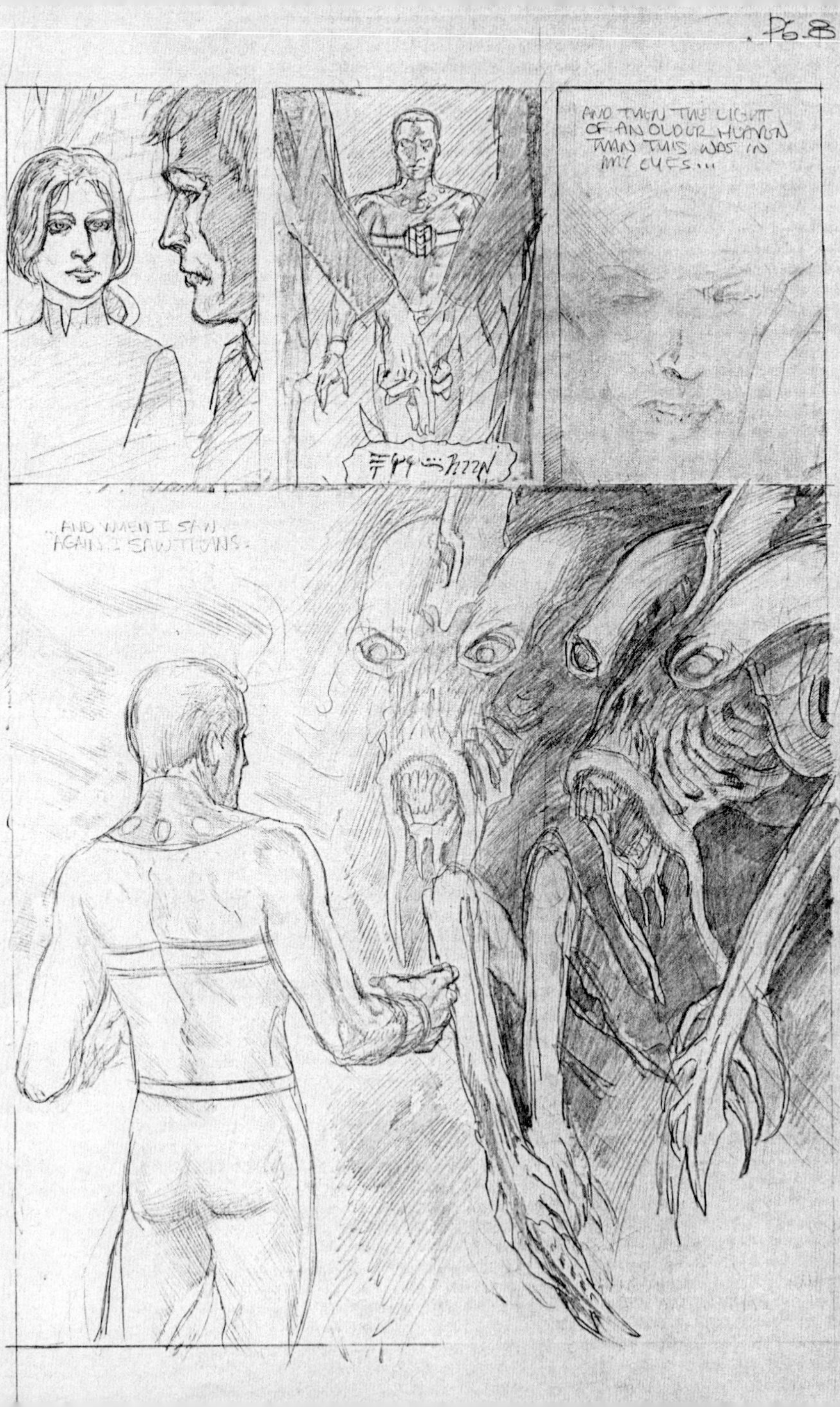
Pg 8
AND THEN THE LIGHT OF AN OLDER HEAVEN THAN THIS WAS IN MY EYES...
...AND WHEN I SAW AGAIN I SAW TITANS.

*Miracleman* #11, page 9 pencils by John Totleben. During action scenes, Totleben drops the traditional panel-grid layout for angular freestyle compositions that emphasize motion, speed and power. The change also visually underscores Miracleman's loss of control.

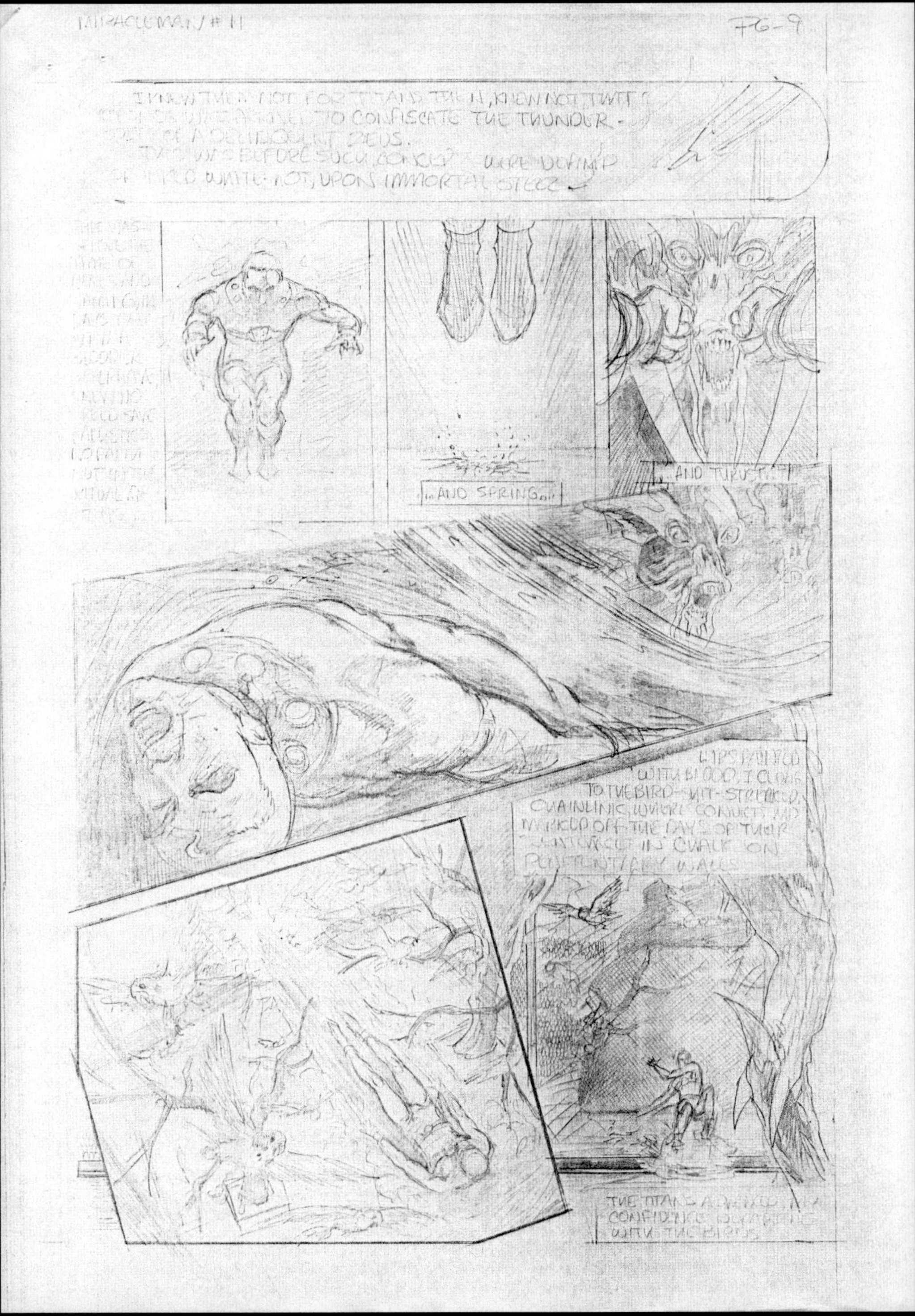

...AND SPRING...
AND THRUST...

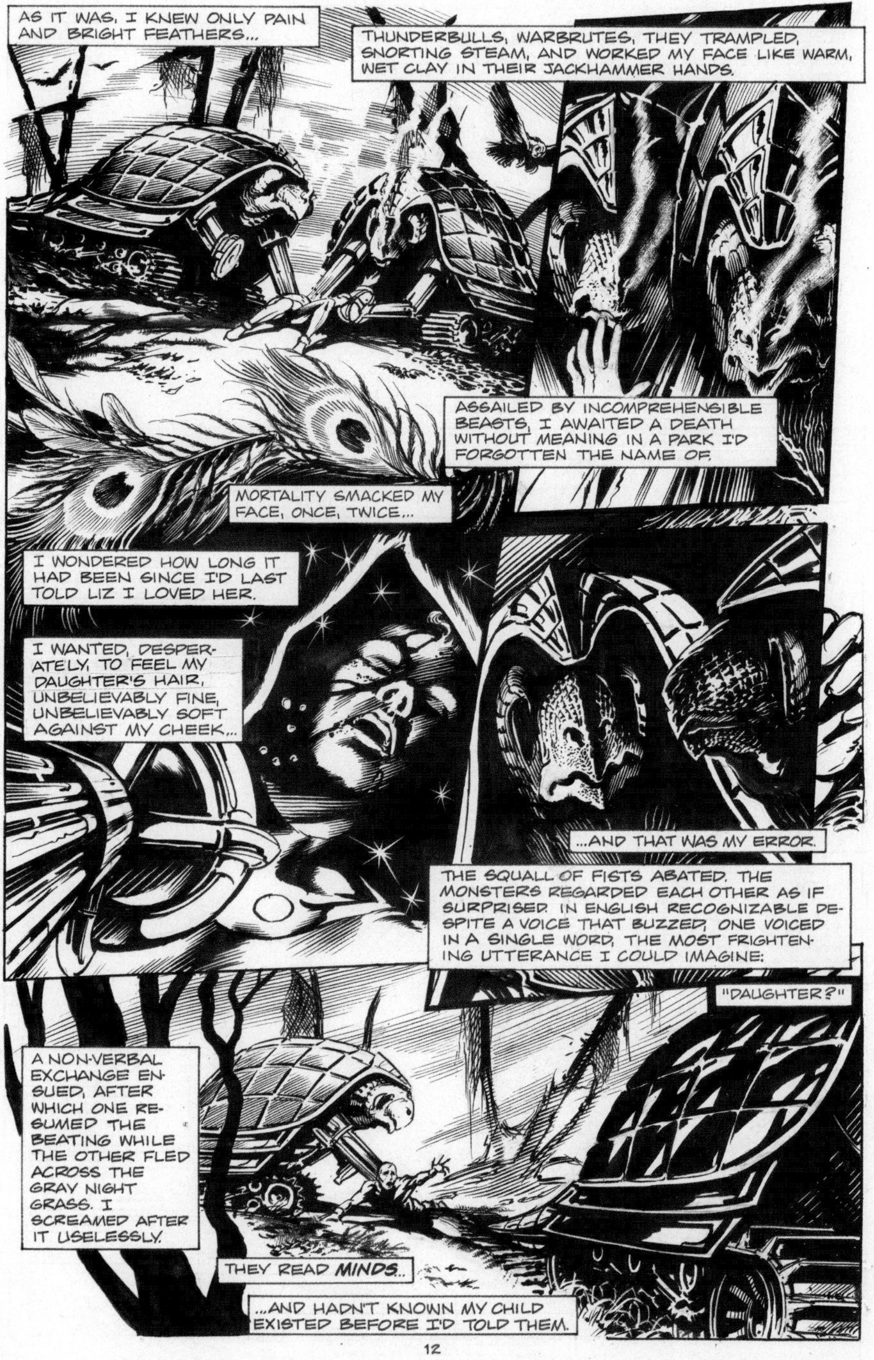
AS IT WAS, I KNEW ONLY PAIN AND BRIGHT FEATHERS...
THUNDERBULLS, WARBRUTES, THEY TRAMPLED, SNORTING STEAM, AND WORKED MY FACE LIKE WARM, WET CLAY IN THEIR JACKHAMMER HANDS.
ASSAILED BY INCOMPREHENSIBLE BEASTS, I AWAITED A DEATH WITHOUT MEANING IN A PARK I'D FORGOTTEN THE NAME OF.
MORTALITY SMACKED MY FACE, ONCE, TWICE...
I WONDERED HOW LONG IT HAD BEEN SINCE I'D LAST TOLD LIZ I LOVED HER.
I WANTED, DESPERATELY, TO FEEL MY DAUGHTER'S HAIR, UNBELIEVABLY FINE, UNBELIEVABLY SOFT AGAINST MY CHEEK...
...AND THAT WAS MY ERROR.
THE SQUALL OF FISTS ABATED. THE MONSTERS REGARDED EACH OTHER AS IF SURPRISED. IN ENGLISH RECOGNIZABLE DESPITE A VOICE THAT BUZZED, ONE VOICED IN A SINGLE WORD, THE MOST FRIGHTENING UTTERANCE I COULD IMAGINE:
"DAUGHTER?"
A NON-VERBAL EXCHANGE ENSUED, AFTER WHICH ONE RESUMED THE BEATING WHILE THE OTHER FLED ACROSS THE GRAY NIGHT GRASS. I SCREAMED AFTER IT USELESSLY.
THEY READ MINDS...
...AND HADN'T KNOWN MY CHILD EXISTED BEFORE I'D TOLD THEM.

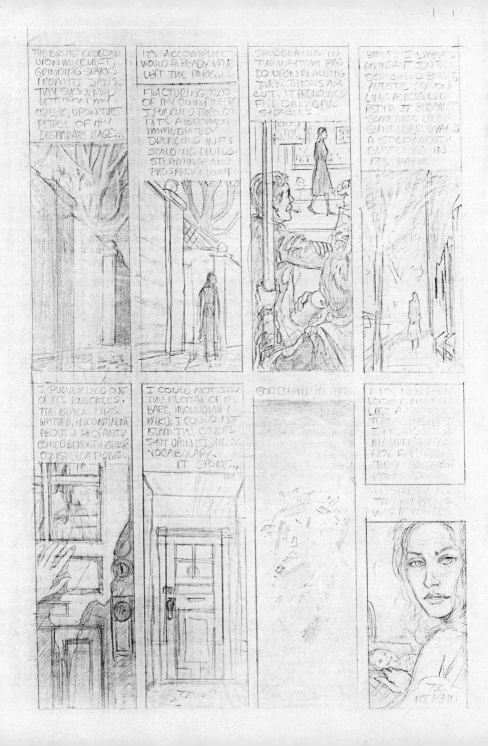

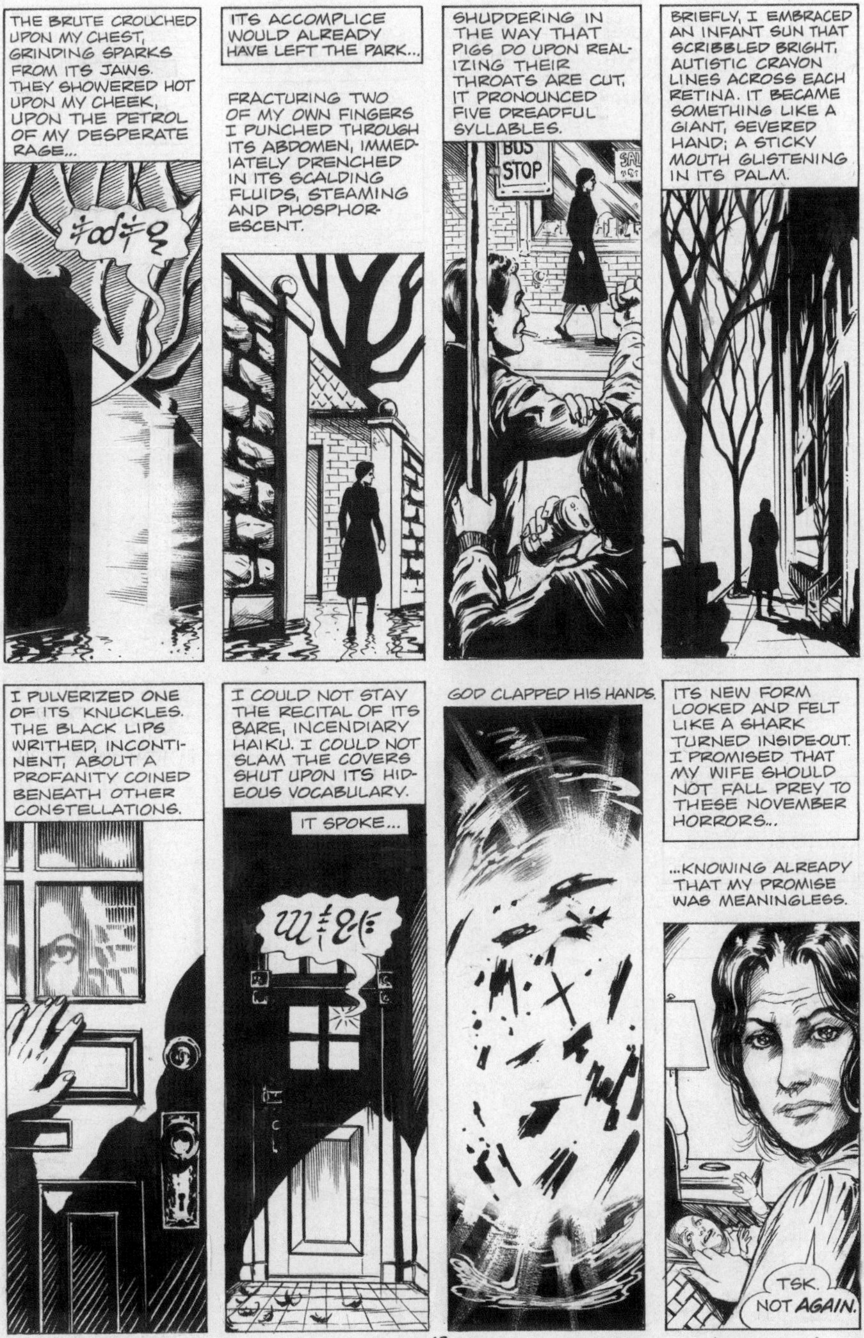
THE BRUTE CROUCHED UPON MY CHEST, GRINDING SPARKS FROM ITS JAWS. THEY SHOWERED HOT UPON MY CHEEK, UPON THE PETROL OF MY DESPERATE RAGE...
ITS ACCOMPLICE WOULD ALREADY HAVE LEFT THE PARK...
FRACTURING TWO OF MY OWN FINGERS I PUNCHED THROUGH ITS ABDOMEN, IMMEDIATELY DRENCHED IN ITS SCALDING FLUIDS, STEAMING AND PHOSPHORESCENT.
SHUDDERING IN THE WAY THAT PIGS DO UPON REALIZING THEIR THROATS ARE CUT, IT PRONOUNCED FIVE DREADFUL SYLLABLES.
BUS STOP
BRIEFLY, I EMBRACED AN INFANT SUN THAT SCRIBBLED BRIGHT, AUTISTIC CRAYON LINES ACROSS EACH RETINA. IT BECAME SOMETHING LIKE A GIANT, SEVERED HAND; A STICKY MOUTH GLISTENING IN ITS PALM.
I PULVERIZED ONE OF ITS KNUCKLES. THE BLACK LIPS WRITHED, INCONTINENT, ABOUT A PROFANITY COINED BENEATH OTHER CONSTELLATIONS.
I COULD NOT STAY THE RECITAL OF ITS BARE, INCENDIARY HAIKU. I COULD NOT SLAM THE COVERS SHUT UPON ITS HIDEOUS VOCABULARY.
IT SPOKE...
GOD CLAPPED HIS HANDS.
ITS NEW FORM LOOKED AND FELT LIKE A SHARK TURNED INSIDE-OUT. I PROMISED THAT MY WIFE SHOULD NOT FALL PREY TO THESE NOVEMBER HORRORS...
...KNOWING ALREADY THAT MY PROMISE WAS MEANINGLESS.
TSK. NOT AGAIN.
TOTLEBEN

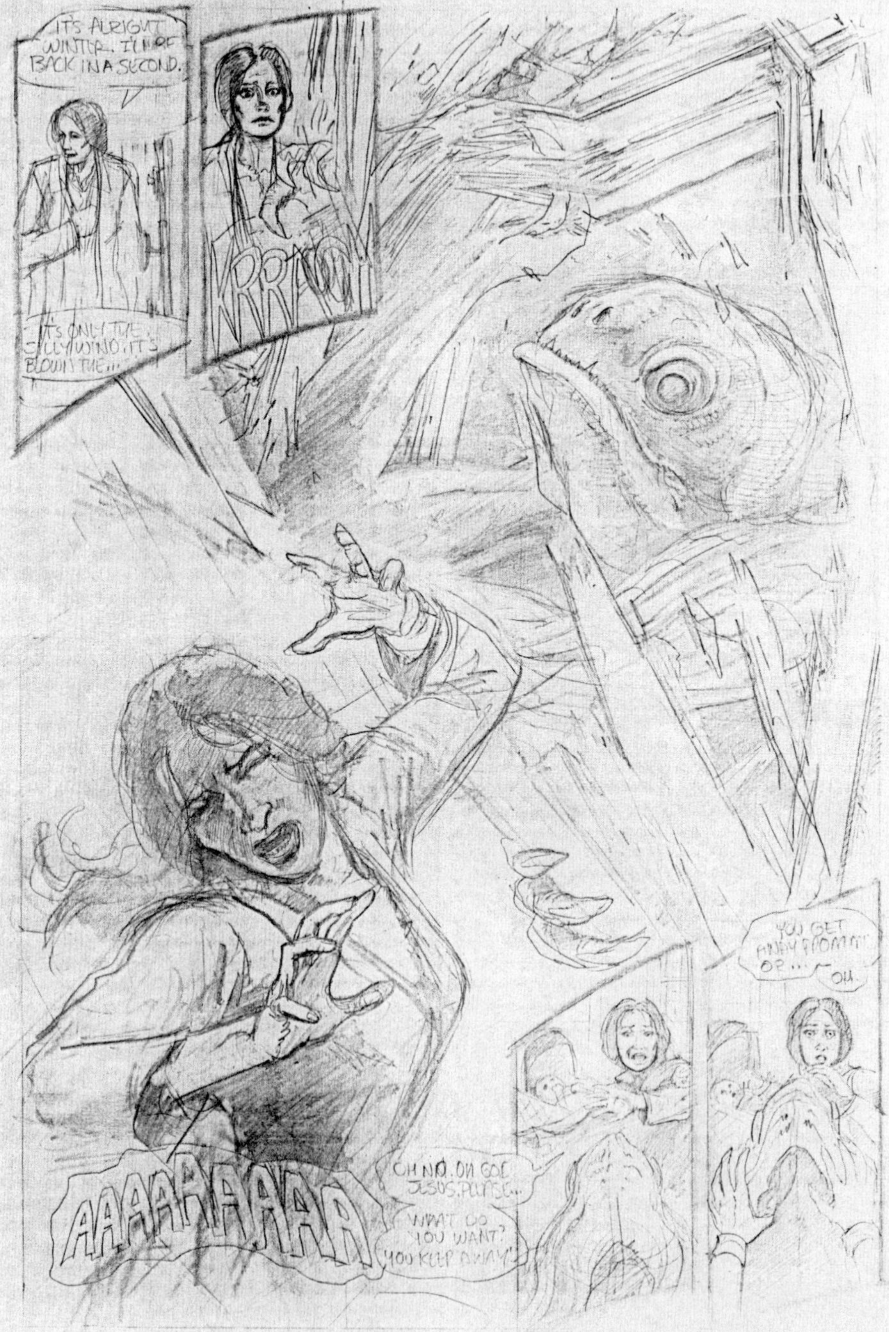
IT'S ALRIGHT WINTER. I'LL BE BACK IN A SECOND.
IT'S ONLY THE SILLY WIND. IT'S BLOWIN THE...
AAAAAAAAR
OH NO. OH GOD JESUS, PLEASE...
WHAT DO YOU WANT? YOU KEEP AWAY!
YOU GET AWAY FROM M OR...
OH.

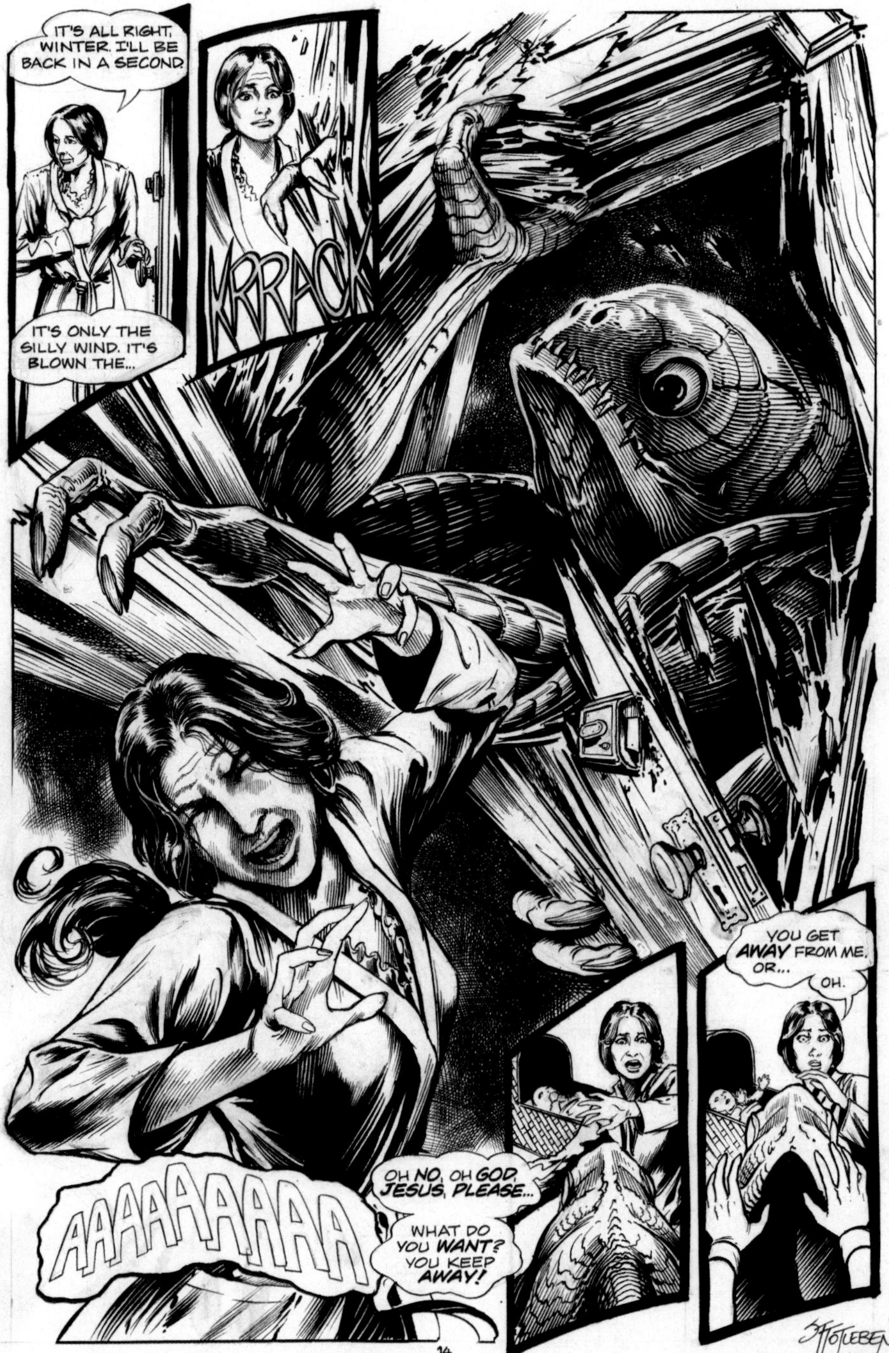
IT'S ALL RIGHT, WINTER. I'LL BE BACK IN A SECOND.
IT'S ONLY THE SILLY WIND. IT'S BLOWN THE...
KRRACK
AAAAAAAAAA
OH NO, OH GOD. JESUS, PLEASE...
WHAT DO YOU WANT? YOU KEEP AWAY!
YOU GET AWAY FROM ME, OR...
OH.
TOTLEBEN

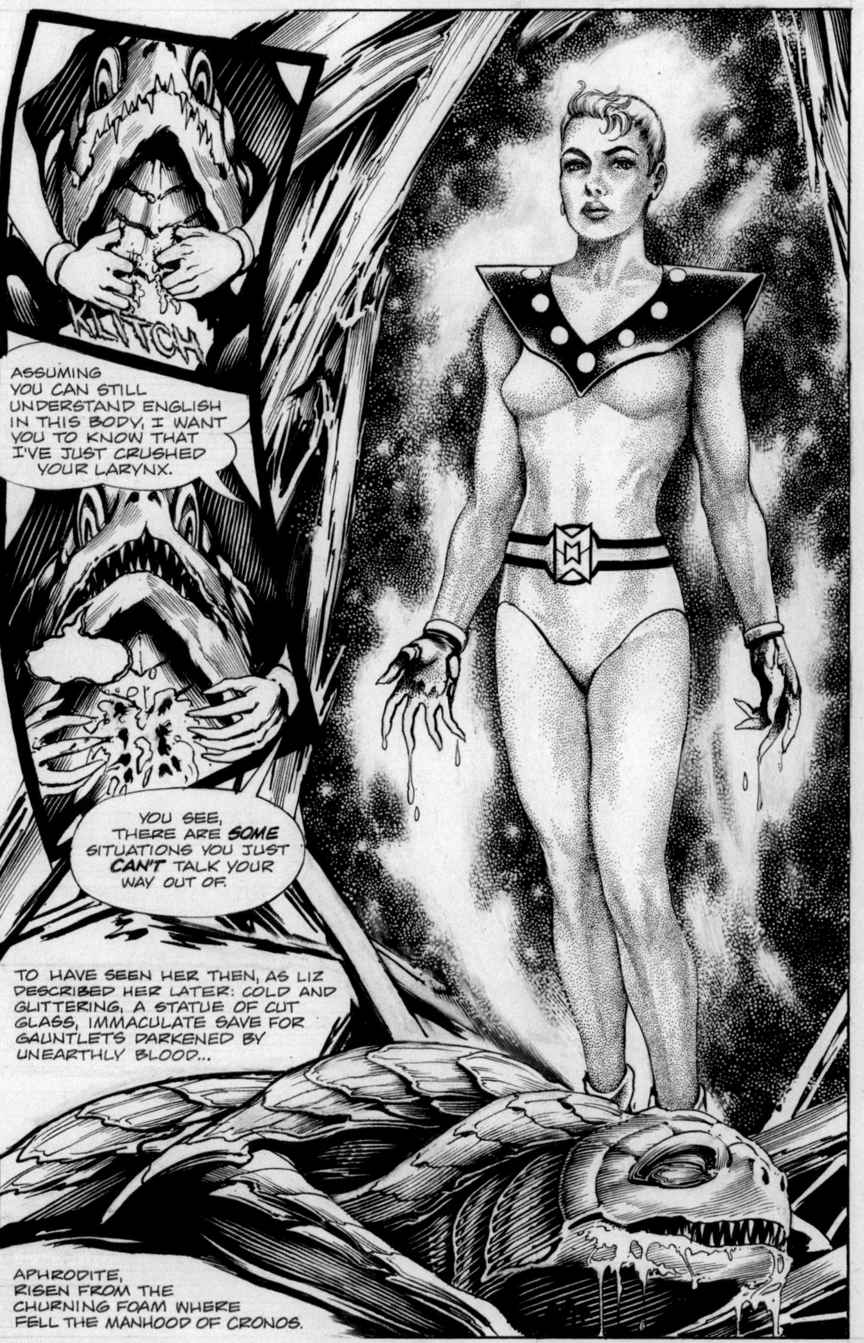
KLITCH
ASSUMING YOU CAN STILL UNDERSTAND ENGLISH IN THIS BODY, I WANT YOU TO KNOW THAT I'VE JUST CRUSHED YOUR LARYNX.
YOU SEE, THERE ARE SOME SITUATIONS YOU JUST CAN'T TALK YOUR WAY OUT OF.
TO HAVE SEEN HER THEN, AS LIZ DESCRIBED HER LATER: COLD AND GLITTERING, A STATUE OF CUT GLASS, IMMACULATE SAVE FOR GAUNTLETS DARKENED BY UNEARTHLY BLOOD...
APHRODITE, RISEN FROM THE CHURNING FOAM WHERE FELL THE MANHOOD OF CRONOS.

MY WORDS SMOULDER, COOLING UPON THE OPEN PAGE. I CROSS TO THE WINDOWS, HEELS DUSTED WITH SHARD...

TO THE NORTH THE DIMMER HAZE DRIFT... PAINTED SAILS COLD AND WIN... ELECTRICITY FROM NOW...

THE GREAT TIDES DRIFT, UPON A... KITES, GORGEOUS AND HYPNOTIC AS THE FANS OF OPTHISMS...

MORE THAN A THOUSAND... CLOCKS, PHOSON... WIND-DRIVEN CLOUDS LIKE... OBSIDIAN OBSCURELY... AND SHADOW AMONG THE WAKING CITY...

LOOKING DOWN, LONDON BECOMES A COMPOSITION OF TRAFFIC BLUE AND FORTIES... TUM-GRAY VIEWED BY AN ABSTRACT PAINTER, OR ONE SUFFERING FROM APHA...

THE MIRROR SIDEWALK BOTTOM IN THE SKY'S OLYMPIUMS, IMAGINARY CLOUDS... ISOLATED... UNDER GLASS...

FROM... WANT... WORLD AS... THOUSAND BOY... OR... PAUSE... OF...

EACH MORNING I WATCH THEM, MY MARVELLOUS EYES PIERCING CLOTHING AND SKIN, ABLE TO SEE AT DIFFERENT SPEEDS, SLOW MOTION ILLUSOS TO THE COLOUR ONES, A BOVINE ANIMAL DIGNI...

AND SCATTER TO THE MIGHTY COLD VISTORS THE ASHES OF THEIR ORDAINED MARKLES...

EVERY EVENING I WAKE THE ALL... AND...

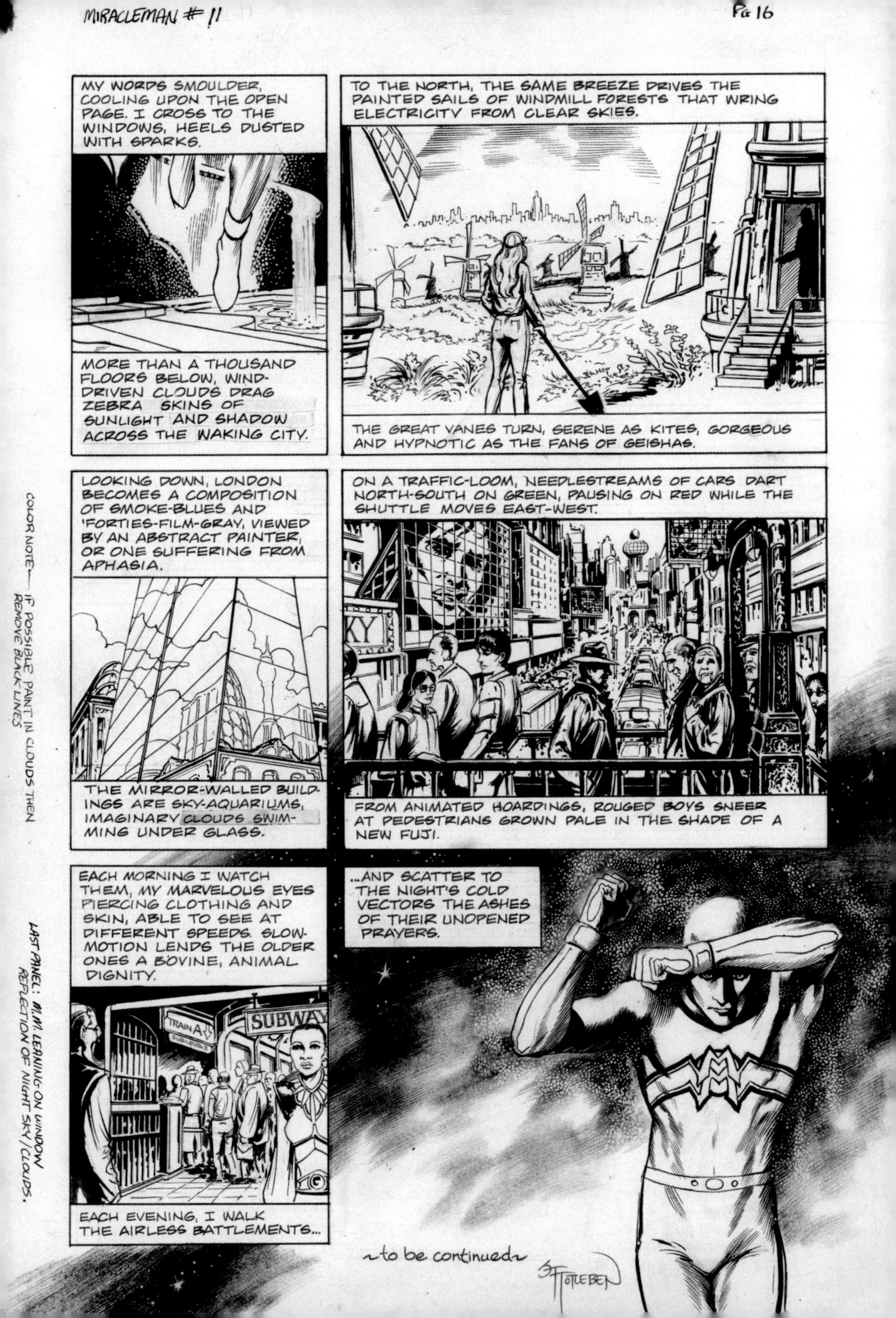
MIRACLEMAN #11
PG 16
MY WORDS SMOULDER, COOLING UPON THE OPEN PAGE. I CROSS TO THE WINDOWS, HEELS DUSTED WITH SPARKS.
MORE THAN A THOUSAND FLOORS BELOW, WIND-DRIVEN CLOUDS DRAG ZEBRA SKINS OF SUNLIGHT AND SHADOW ACROSS THE WAKING CITY.
TO THE NORTH, THE SAME BREEZE DRIVES THE PAINTED SAILS OF WINDMILL FORESTS THAT WRING ELECTRICITY FROM CLEAR SKIES.
THE GREAT VANES TURN, SERENE AS KITES, GORGEOUS AND HYPNOTIC AS THE FANS OF GEISHAS.
LOOKING DOWN, LONDON BECOMES A COMPOSITION OF SMOKE-BLUES AND 'FORTIES-FILM-GRAY, VIEWED BY AN ABSTRACT PAINTER, OR ONE SUFFERING FROM APHASIA.
THE MIRROR-WALLED BUILDINGS ARE SKY-AQUARIUMS, IMAGINARY CLOUDS SWIMMING UNDER GLASS.
ON A TRAFFIC-LOOM, NEEDLESTREAMS OF CARS DART NORTH-SOUTH ON GREEN, PAUSING ON RED WHILE THE SHUTTLE MOVES EAST-WEST.
KY
FROM ANIMATED HOARDINGS, ROUGED BOYS SNEER AT PEDESTRIANS GROWN PALE IN THE SHADE OF A NEW FUJI.
EACH MORNING I WATCH THEM, MY MARVELOUS EYES PIERCING CLOTHING AND SKIN, ABLE TO SEE AT DIFFERENT SPEEDS. SLOW-MOTION LENDS THE OLDER ONES A BOVINE, ANIMAL DIGNITY.
TRAIN A
SUBWAY
EACH EVENING, I WALK THE AIRLESS BATTLEMENTS...
...AND SCATTER TO THE NIGHT'S COLD VECTORS THE ASHES OF THEIR UNOPENED PRAYERS.
~to be continued~
S. TOTLEBEN
COLOR NOTE — IF POSSIBLE PAINT IN CLOUDS THEN REMOVE BLACK LINES
LAST PANEL: M.M. LEANING ON WINDOW REFLECTION OF NIGHT SKY/CLOUDS.

Miracleman #12, page 1 pencils by John Totleben. In Olympus, Miracleman has gathered every wonder and piece of human history and mythology imaginable: Babylonian hanging gardens, a zoo akin to Noah's ark, classic cars — even thundering storm clouds traverse its halls.

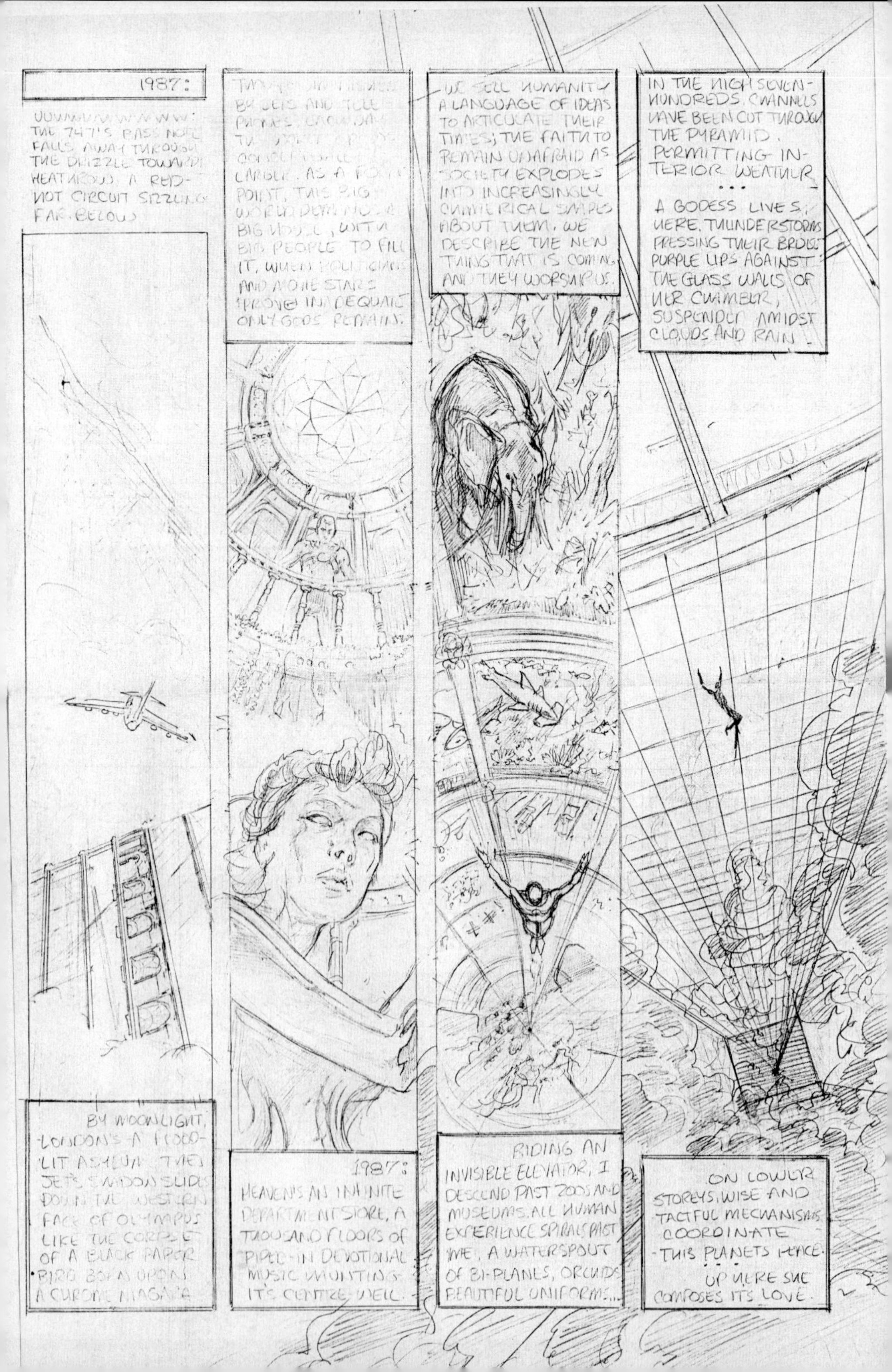

1987:
UUWWWWWWWWW: THE 747'S BASS NOTE FALLS AWAY THROUGH THE DRIZZLE TOWARDS HEATHROW. A RED-HOT CIRCUIT SIZZLING FAR BELOW
LARGER. AS A FOCAL POINT, THIS BIG WORLD DEMANDS A BIG HOUSE, WITH BIG PEOPLE TO FILL IT. WHEN POLITICIANS AND MOVIE STARS PROVED INADEQUATE ONLY GODS REMAIN.
WE SELL HUMANITY A LANGUAGE OF IDEAS TO ARTICULATE THEIR TIMES; THE FAITH TO REMAIN UNAFRAID AS SOCIETY EXPLODES INTO INCREASINGLY CHIMERICAL SHAPES ABOUT THEM. WE DESCRIBE THE NEW THING THAT IS COMING AND THEY WORSHIP US.
IN THE HIGH SEVEN-HUNDREDS, CHANNELS HAVE BEEN CUT THROUGH THE PYRAMID, PERMITTING INTERIOR WEATHER...
A GODESS LIVES HERE. THUNDERSTORMS PRESSING THEIR BRUISE PURPLE LIPS AGAINST THE GLASS WALLS OF HER CHAMBER, SUSPENDED AMIDST CLOUDS AND RAIN.
BY MOONLIGHT, LONDON'S A FLOOD-LIT ASYLUM. THE JET'S SHADOW SLIDES DOWN THE WESTERN FACE OF OLYMPUS LIKE THE CORPSE OF A BLACK PAPER BIRD BORN UPON A CHROME NIAGARA
1987:
HEAVEN'S AN INFINITE DEPARTMENT STORE, A THOUSAND FLOORS OF PIPED-IN DEVOTIONAL MUSIC HAUNTING IT'S CENTRE WELL.
RIDING AN INVISIBLE ELEVATOR, I DESCEND PAST ZOOS AND MUSEUMS. ALL HUMAN EXPERIENCE SPIRALS PAST ME. A WATERSPOUT OF BI-PLANES, ORCHIDS BEAUTIFUL UNIFORMS...
ON LOWER STOREYS, WISE AND TACTFUL MECHANISMS COORDINATE THIS PLANETS PEACE...
UP HERE SHE COMPOSES ITS LOVE.

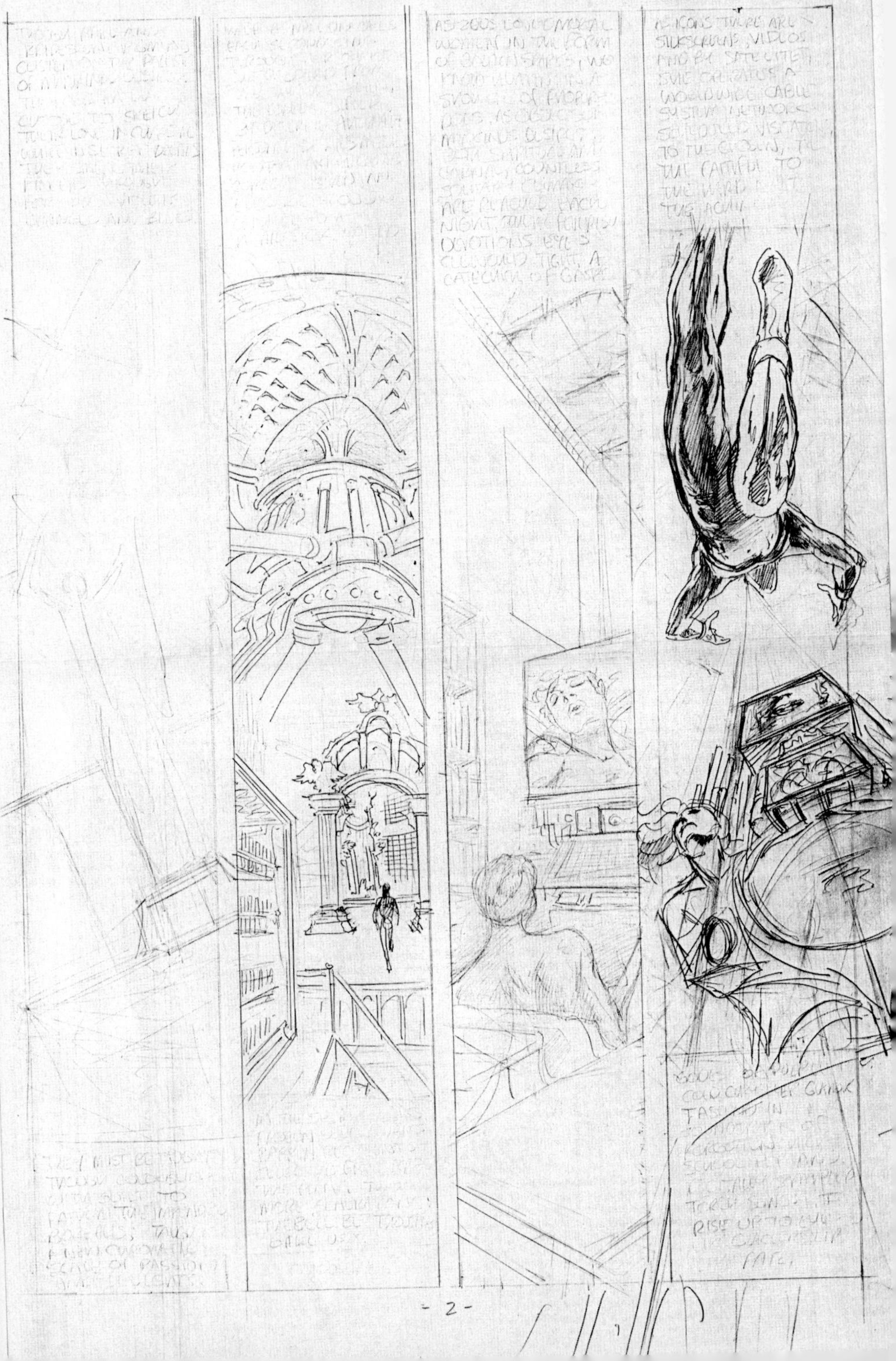

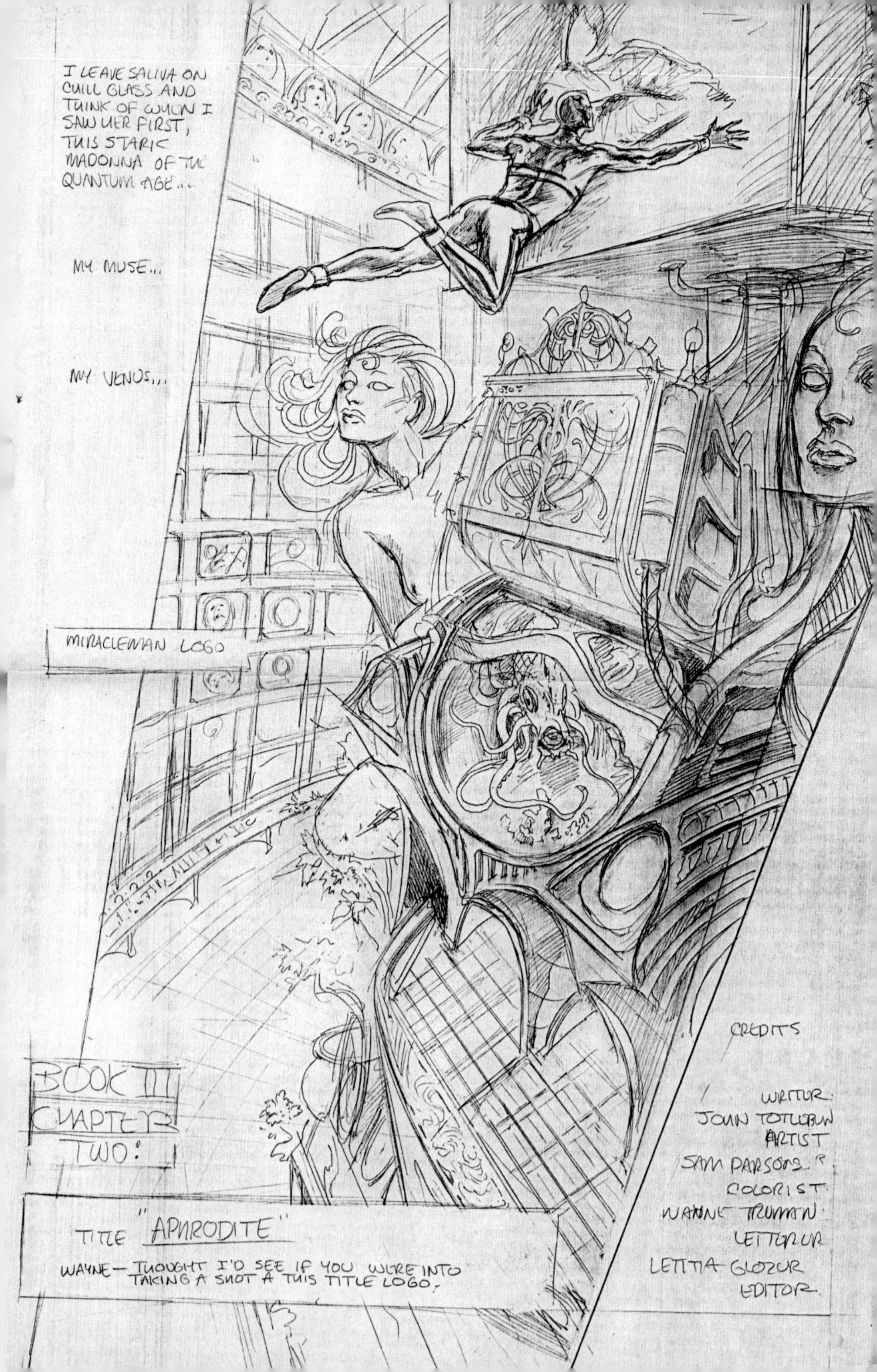
I LEAVE SALIVA ON CHILL GLASS AND THINK OF WHEN I SAW HER FIRST, THIS STARK MADONNA OF THE QUANTUM AGE...
MY MUSE...
MY VENUS...
MIRACLEMAN LOGO
BOOK III CHAPTER TWO:
TITLE "APHRODITE"
WAYNE— THOUGHT I'D SEE IF YOU WERE INTO TAKING A SHOT A THIS TITLE LOGO.
CREDITS
WRITER:
JOHN TOTLEBEN
ARTIST
SAM PARSONS
COLORIST
WAYNE TRUMAN
LETTERER
LETITIA GLOZER
EDITOR

NOVEMBER, 1982

THE MILL OF PUNISHMENT THAT GROUND MY BODY PAUSED AS TO WHAT IT SEEMED TO BE ITS HAND AS IT HOVED A MURDER IN THE GLOOM WHILE I HEARD ONLY RAIN UPON DEAD LEAVES

THERE CAME A WORD WITH SYLLABLES THAT RATTLED LIKE A NIGHT TRAIN STORMING NEARER THROUGH THE BLACKNESS WITH ITS CYCLOPS LANTERN GLARING TIL IT HIT AND ALL THE WORLD WAS BURNED AWAY IN ONE WHITE MOMENT

VANING EXCHANGED A FORM THAT PULVERIZED FOR ONE THAT FLEW IT LIFTED EERILY INTO THE RAINY LO ANCHOR, SAVE ITS SHADOW DRAGGED ACROSS THE GRASS DEFLATING AS IT WENT

GUESSING ITS PURPOSE I GAVE CHASE

TOO FAST TO BE SEEN EXCEPT BY EACH OTHER WE WERE DANGEROUS BLURS IN A WORLD WITHOUT MOTION DODGING BETWEEN THE FREEZE-FRAME BIRDS THAT HUNG TRAPPED IN A SOLID GLASS SKY

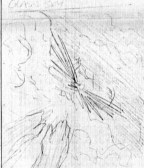

WE DROPPED AS ONE, A NANO-SECONDS BREATH BETWEEN US, WHILE BELOW THE STREET WHERE I LIVED AS A MAN GREW LARGER, CLOSER, RAPIDLY EMBROIDERING ITSELF WITH DETAIL ON APPROACH

THROUGH THE SPLINTERED DOOR THE DISTANT CARS AND INCIDENTAL NIGHT NOISE ALTERED BY VELOCITY, BECAME A VIOLIN CRESCENDO SHRIEKING, RISING AS I HURTLED UP THE STAIRS ONLY TO BE CONFRONTED BY BEWILDERMENT...

...THOUGH NOT MINE...

—4—

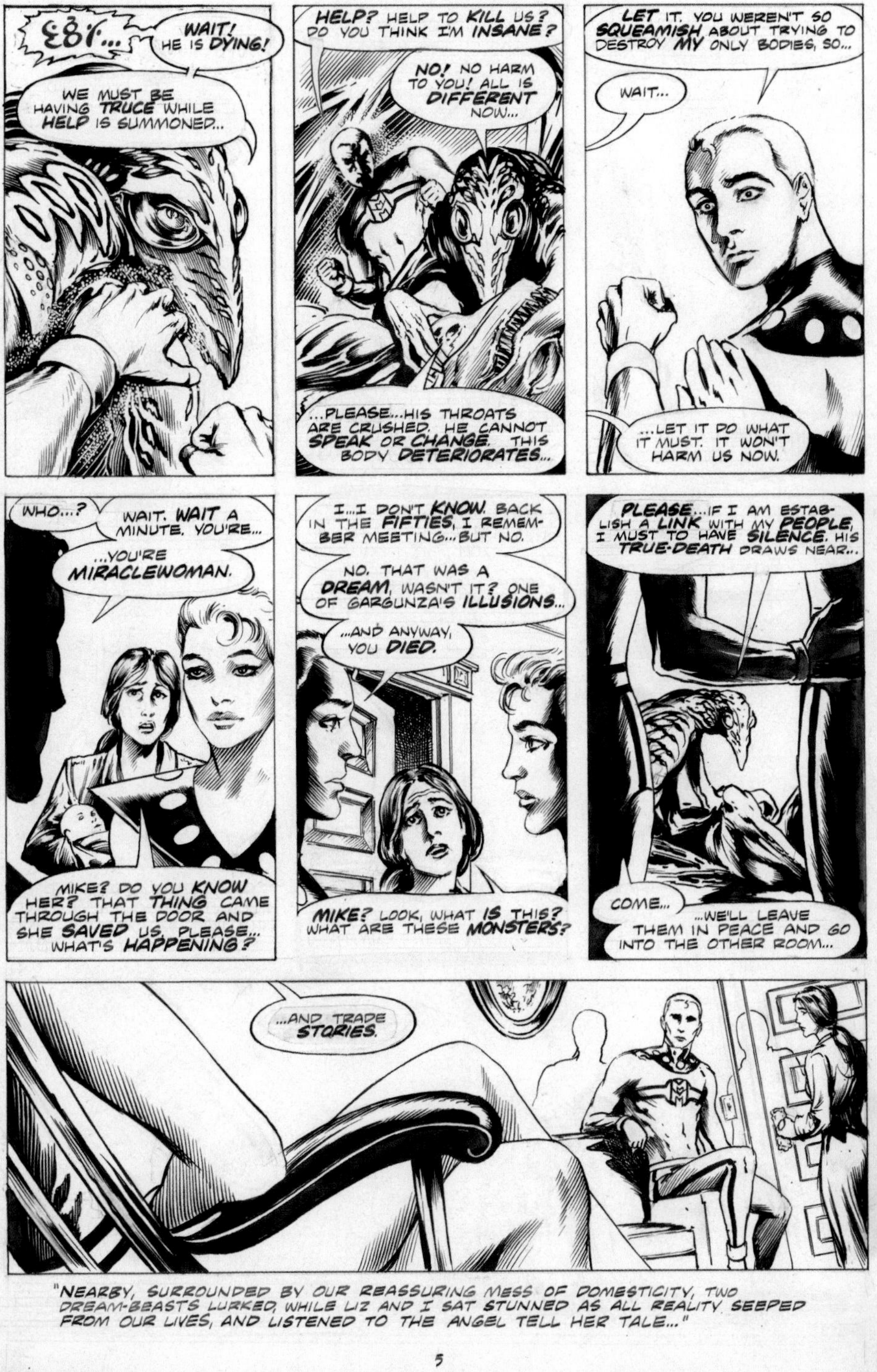
WAIT! HE IS DYING!
WE MUST BE HAVING TRUCE WHILE HELP IS SUMMONED...
HELP? HELP TO KILL US? DO YOU THINK I'M INSANE?
NO! NO HARM TO YOU! ALL IS DIFFERENT NOW...
...PLEASE...HIS THROATS ARE CRUSHED. HE CANNOT SPEAK OR CHANGE. THIS BODY DETERIORATES...
LET IT. YOU WEREN'T SO SQUEAMISH ABOUT TRYING TO DESTROY MY ONLY BODIES, SO...
WAIT...
...LET IT DO WHAT IT MUST. IT WON'T HARM US NOW.
WHO...?
WAIT. WAIT A MINUTE. YOU'RE...
...YOU'RE MIRACLEWOMAN.
MIKE? DO YOU KNOW HER? THAT THING CAME THROUGH THE DOOR AND SHE SAVED US. PLEASE... WHAT'S HAPPENING?
I...I DON'T KNOW. BACK IN THE FIFTIES, I REMEMBER MEETING...BUT NO.
NO. THAT WAS A DREAM, WASN'T IT? ONE OF GARGUNZA'S ILLUSIONS...
...AND ANYWAY, YOU DIED.
MIKE? LOOK, WHAT IS THIS? WHAT ARE THESE MONSTERS?
PLEASE...IF I AM ESTABLISH A LINK WITH MY PEOPLE, I MUST TO HAVE SILENCE. HIS TRUE-DEATH DRAWS NEAR...
COME...
...WE'LL LEAVE THEM IN PEACE AND GO INTO THE OTHER ROOM...
...AND TRADE STORIES.
"NEARBY, SURROUNDED BY OUR REASSURING MESS OF DOMESTICITY, TWO DREAM-BEASTS LURKED, WHILE LIZ AND I SAT STUNNED AS ALL REALITY SEEPED FROM OUR LIVES, AND LISTENED TO THE ANGEL TELL HER TALE..."

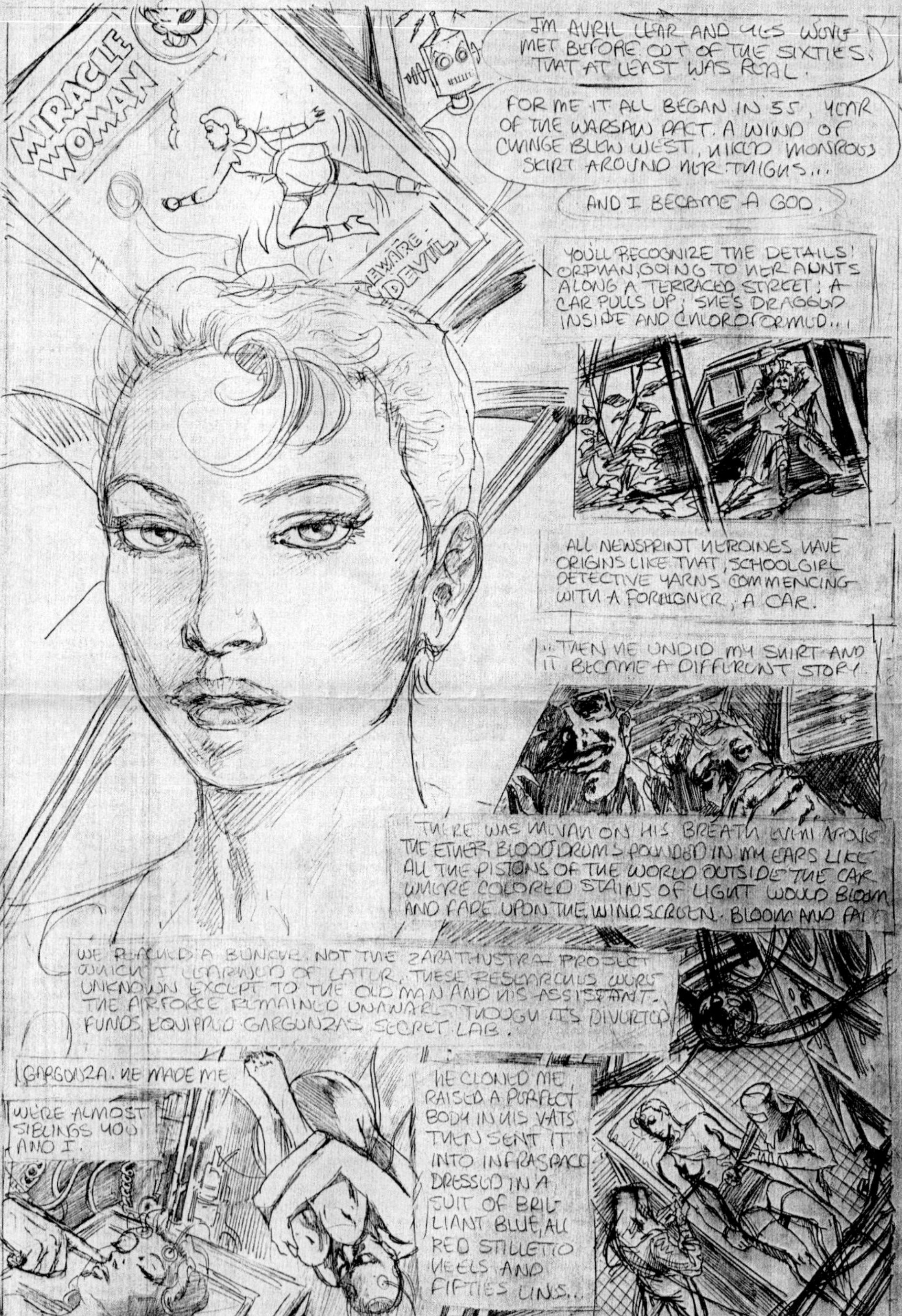
MIRACLE WOMAN
BEWARE DEVIL
I'M AVRIL LEAR AND YES WE'VE MET BEFORE OUT OF THE SIXTIES. THAT AT LEAST WAS REAL.
FOR ME IT ALL BEGAN IN 55, YEAR OF THE WARSAW PACT. A WIND OF CHANGE BLEW WEST, HIKED MONROE'S SKIRT AROUND HER THIGHS...
AND I BECAME A GOD.
YOU'LL RECOGNIZE THE DETAILS! ORPHAN, GOING TO HER AUNTS ALONG A TERRACED STREET; A CAR PULLS UP; SHE'S DRAGGED INSIDE AND CHLOROFORMED...
ALL NEWSPRINT HEROINES HAVE ORIGINS LIKE THAT, SCHOOLGIRL DETECTIVE YARNS COMMENCING WITH A FOREIGNER, A CAR.
...THEN HE UNDID MY SHIRT AND IT BECAME A DIFFERENT STORY.
THERE WAS ON HIS BREATH EVEN ABOVE THE ETHER. BLOODDRUMS POUNDED IN MY EARS LIKE ALL THE PISTONS OF THE WORLD OUTSIDE THE CAR WHERE COLORED STAINS OF LIGHT WOULD BLOOM AND FADE UPON THE WINDSCREEN. BLOOM AND FA
WE REACHED A BUNKER. NOT THE ZARATHUSTRA PROJECT WHICH I LEARNED OF LATER. THESE RESEARCHES WERE UNKNOWN EXCEPT TO THE OLD MAN AND HIS ASSISTANT. THE AIRFORCE REMAINED UNAWARE THOUGH ITS DIVERTED FUNDS EQUIPPED GARGUNZA'S SECRET LAB.
GARGUNZA. HE MADE ME.
WE'RE ALMOST SIBLINGS YOU AND I.
HE CLONED ME, RAISED A PERFECT BODY IN HIS VATS THEN SENT IT INTO INFRASPACE DRESSED IN A SUIT OF BRILLIANT BLUE, ALL RED STILETTO HEELS AND FIFTIES LINES...
GIVEN THE TASTES OF MY COUTURIER, UPON REFLECTION, I COULD HAVE DONE WORSE.

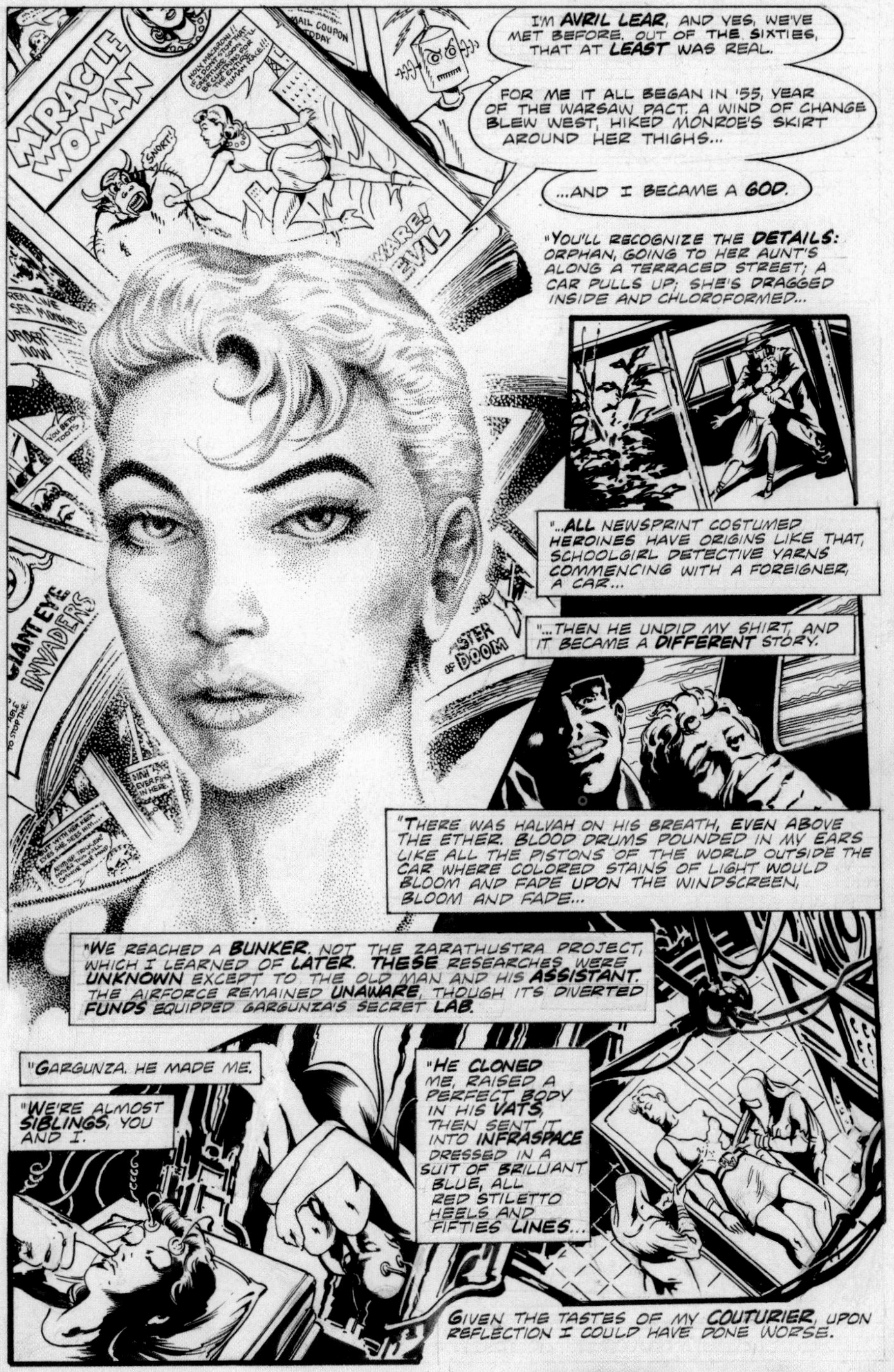
I'M AVRIL LEAR, AND YES, WE'VE MET BEFORE. OUT OF THE SIXTIES, THAT AT LEAST WAS REAL.
FOR ME IT ALL BEGAN IN '55, YEAR OF THE WARSAW PACT. A WIND OF CHANGE BLEW WEST, HIKED MONROE'S SKIRT AROUND HER THIGHS...
...AND I BECAME A GOD.
"YOU'LL RECOGNIZE THE DETAILS: ORPHAN, GOING TO HER AUNT'S ALONG A TERRACED STREET; A CAR PULLS UP; SHE'S DRAGGED INSIDE AND CHLOROFORMED...
"...ALL NEWSPRINT COSTUMED HEROINES HAVE ORIGINS LIKE THAT, SCHOOLGIRL DETECTIVE YARNS COMMENCING WITH A FOREIGNER, A CAR...
"...THEN HE UNDID MY SHIRT, AND IT BECAME A DIFFERENT STORY.
"THERE WAS HALVAH ON HIS BREATH, EVEN ABOVE THE ETHER. BLOOD DRUMS POUNDED IN MY EARS LIKE ALL THE PISTONS OF THE WORLD OUTSIDE THE CAR WHERE COLORED STAINS OF LIGHT WOULD BLOOM AND FADE UPON THE WINDSCREEN, BLOOM AND FADE...
"WE REACHED A BUNKER. NOT THE ZARATHUSTRA PROJECT, WHICH I LEARNED OF LATER. THESE RESEARCHES WERE UNKNOWN EXCEPT TO THE OLD MAN AND HIS ASSISTANT. THE AIRFORCE REMAINED UNAWARE, THOUGH ITS DIVERTED FUNDS EQUIPPED GARGUNZA'S SECRET LAB.
"GARGUNZA. HE MADE ME.
"WE'RE ALMOST SIBLINGS, YOU AND I.
"HE CLONED ME, RAISED A PERFECT BODY IN HIS VATS, THEN SENT IT INTO INFRASPACE DRESSED IN A SUIT OF BRILLIANT BLUE, ALL RED STILETTO HEELS AND FIFTIES LINES...
GIVEN THE TASTES OF MY COUTURIER, UPON REFLECTION I COULD HAVE DONE WORSE.
MIRACLE WOMAN
SNORT!
GIANT EYE INVADERS
MASTER OF DOOM

FOR REASONS WHOLLY UNCONNECTED WITH THE MILITARY USE HIS SUPERIORS HAD INTENDED WHEN THEY FUNDED YOU, HE KEPT THREE OF US THERE...

MYSELF, A HIDEOUS ALTERED DOG, AND TERRENCE REBBECK WHO BECAME YOUNG NASTYMAN.

THERE. I SEE YOU'RE STARTING TO REMEMBER.

POOR TERRY, AIRFORCE ORPHAN, JUST LIKE US. THEY PUT AN IMPLANT IN HIS HEAD, GAVE HIM A SKIN-TIGHT SUIT OF BLACK AND DROPPED HIM DOWN THEIR WARP WELL INTO INFRASPACE TO JOIN THE REST OF DR. G'S MENAGERIE...

...EXCEPT THAT HE AND I WERE SPECIAL CASES. GRANTED, YOU AND YOUR TWO PARTNERS WERE ABUSED, BUT YOU WERE KNOWN ABOUT AND THUS GARGUNZA DARED NOT GO TOO FAR.

NOT SO WITH US.

WITH US, HE COULD DO ANYTHING HE LIKED.

HE FIRST BECAME A RAPIST AGED FOURTEEN. DID YOU KNOW THAT?

WITH US, HE'D FIRST DISMISS HIS AIDE, THEN BY THE DREAMSCREEN'S LIGHT, UN-DRESS. SAVE FOR HIS SPECTACLES.

I WATCHED THE VID... APL'S. HE'D MADE YEARS LATER. NAKED, HE WAS PITIFUL; A TROLL MOUNTING A GODDESS WHILE SHE SLEPT.

WATCHING MYSELF VIOLATED I JUST LAUGHED, HE'D HAD NO PART OF ME.

I WAS ELSEWHERE. A COSMOS FULL OF COLORS AND EMOTIONS THAT WERE SIMPLE, BRIGHT AND WONDERFULLY GARISH. FREE FROM HINDERING LOGIC I EXPLORED A REALM OF INCANDE-SCENT COMIC BOOK IDEAS.

HE GAVE ME FREEDOM, IN A PERFECT WORLD, RECEIVING IN RETURN MY CROTCH. I LAUGHED AND LAUGHED.

Miracleman #12, page 8 pencils by John Totleben. The artist employs a simpler art style inspired by pulp illustration and 1950s teen "good girl" comic books for Miraclewoman's dream adventures.

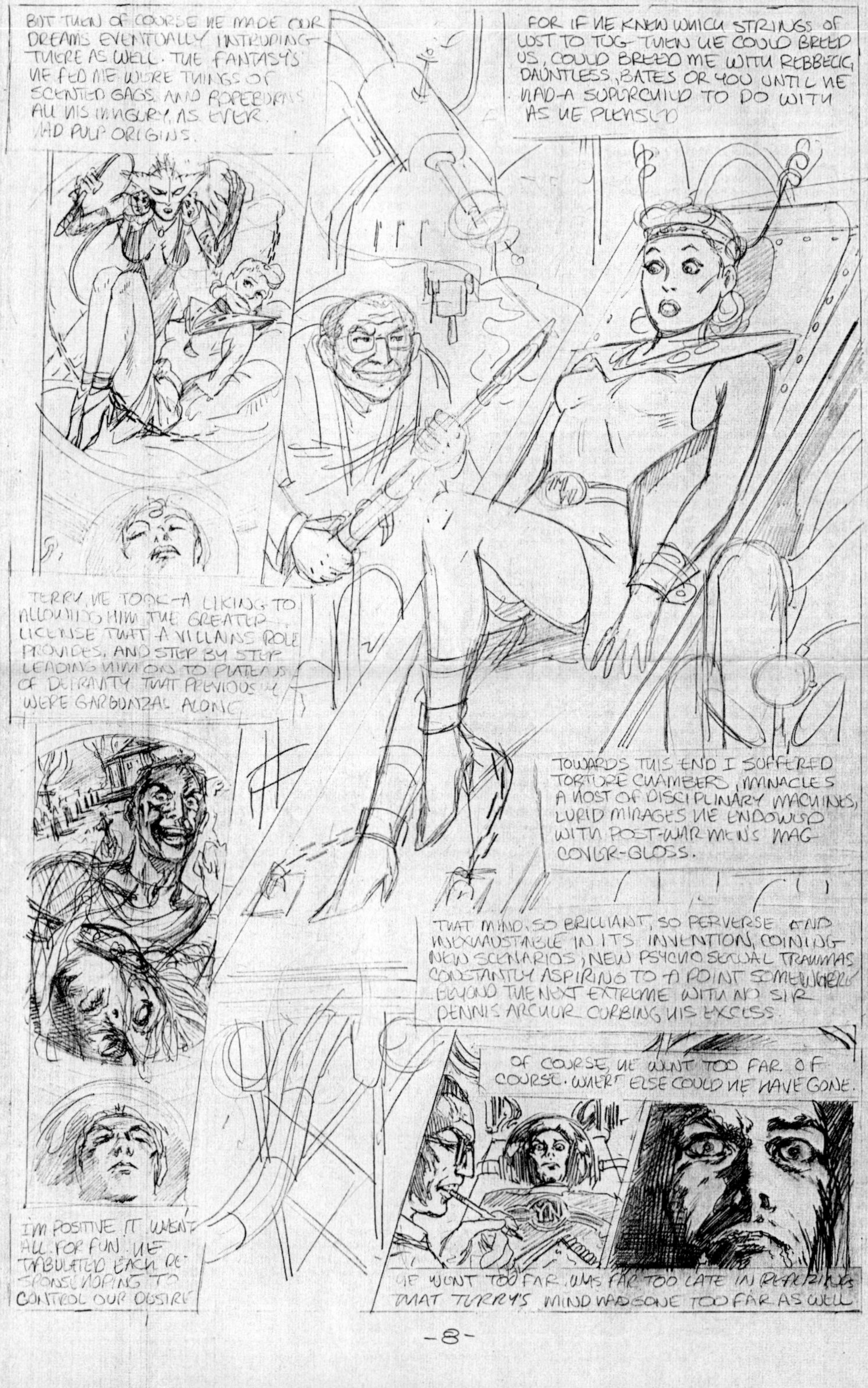
BUT THEN OF COURSE HE MADE OUR DREAMS EVENTUALLY INTRUDING THERE AS WELL. THE FANTASY'S HE FED ME WERE THINGS OF SCENTED GAGS AND ROPEBURNS ALL HIS IMAGERY, AS EVER, HAD PULP ORIGINS.
FOR IF HE KNEW WHICH STRINGS OF LUST TO TUG THEN HE COULD BREED US, COULD BREED ME WITH REBBECK, DAUNTLESS, BATES OR YOU UNTIL HE HAD A SUPERCHILD TO DO WITH AS HE PLEASED
TERRY, HE TOOK A LIKING TO ALLOWING HIM THE GREATER LICENSE THAT A VILLAINS ROLE PROVIDES, AND STEP BY STEP LEADING HIM ON TO PLATEAUS OF DEPRAVITY THAT PREVIOUSLY WERE GARGANTUAL ALONE
TOWARDS THIS END I SUFFERED TORTURE CHAMBERS, MANACLES A HOST OF DISCIPLINARY MACHINES, LURID MIRAGES HE ENDOWED WITH POST-WAR MEN'S MAG COVER-GLOSS.
THAT MIND, SO BRILLIANT, SO PERVERSE AND INEXHAUSTABLE IN ITS INVENTION, COINING NEW SCENARIOS, NEW PSYCHOSEXUAL TRAUMAS CONSTANTLY ASPIRING TO A POINT SOMEWHERE BEYOND THE NEXT EXTREME WITH NO SIR DENNIS ARCHER CURBING HIS EXCESS.
OF COURSE, HE WENT TOO FAR. OF COURSE. WHERE ELSE COULD HE HAVE GONE.
I'M POSITIVE IT WASN'T ALL FOR FUN. HE TABULATED EACH RESPONSE HOPING TO CONTROL OUR DESIRE
HE WENT TOO FAR. WAS FAR TOO LATE IN REALIZING THAT TERRY'S MIND HAD GONE TOO FAR AS WELL
-8-

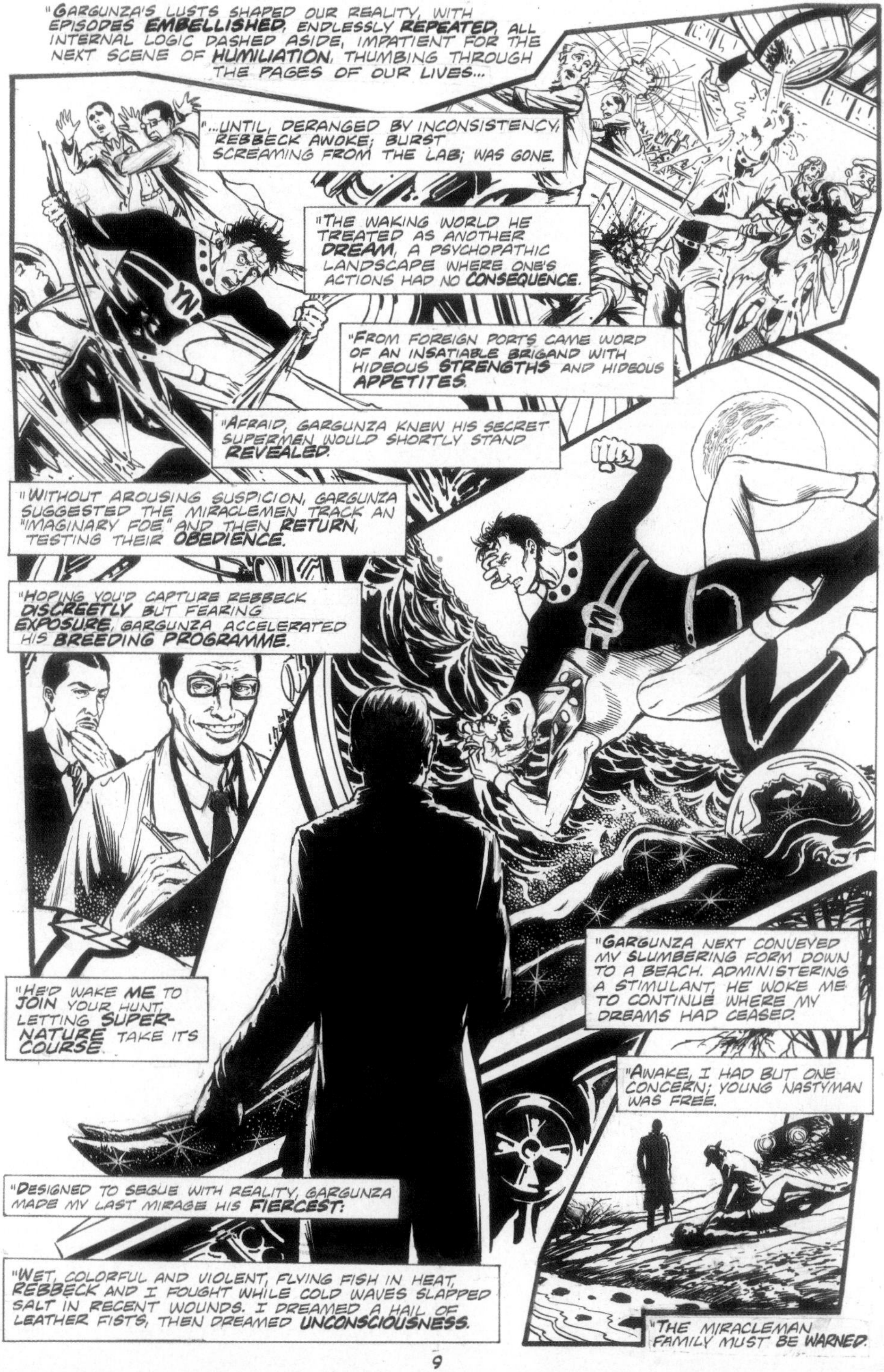
"GARGUNZA'S LUSTS SHAPED OUR REALITY, WITH EPISODES EMBELLISHED, ENDLESSLY REPEATED, ALL INTERNAL LOGIC DASHED ASIDE, IMPATIENT FOR THE NEXT SCENE OF HUMILIATION, THUMBING THROUGH THE PAGES OF OUR LIVES...
"...UNTIL, DERANGED BY INCONSISTENCY, REBBECK AWOKE; BURST SCREAMING FROM THE LAB; WAS GONE.
"THE WAKING WORLD HE TREATED AS ANOTHER DREAM, A PSYCHOPATHIC LANDSCAPE WHERE ONE'S ACTIONS HAD NO CONSEQUENCE.
"FROM FOREIGN PORTS CAME WORD OF AN INSATIABLE BRIGAND WITH HIDEOUS STRENGTHS AND HIDEOUS APPETITES.
"AFRAID, GARGUNZA KNEW HIS SECRET SUPERMEN WOULD SHORTLY STAND REVEALED.
"WITHOUT AROUSING SUSPICION, GARGUNZA SUGGESTED THE MIRACLEMEN TRACK AN "IMAGINARY FOE" AND THEN RETURN, TESTING THEIR OBEDIENCE.
"HOPING YOU'D CAPTURE REBBECK DISCREETLY BUT FEARING EXPOSURE, GARGUNZA ACCELERATED HIS BREEDING PROGRAMME.
"HE'D WAKE ME TO JOIN YOUR HUNT, LETTING SUPER-NATURE TAKE IT'S COURSE.
"GARGUNZA NEXT CONVEYED MY SLUMBERING FORM DOWN TO A BEACH. ADMINISTERING A STIMULANT, HE WOKE ME TO CONTINUE WHERE MY DREAMS HAD CEASED.
"AWAKE, I HAD BUT ONE CONCERN; YOUNG NASTYMAN WAS FREE.
"DESIGNED TO SEGUE WITH REALITY, GARGUNZA MADE MY LAST MIRAGE HIS FIERCEST:
"WET, COLORFUL AND VIOLENT, FLYING FISH IN HEAT, REBBECK AND I FOUGHT WHILE COLD WAVES SLAPPED SALT IN RECENT WOUNDS. I DREAMED A HAIL OF LEATHER FISTS, THEN DREAMED UNCONSCIOUSNESS.
"THE MIRACLEMAN FAMILY MUST BE WARNED.

MIRACLEMAN #12/PG 13

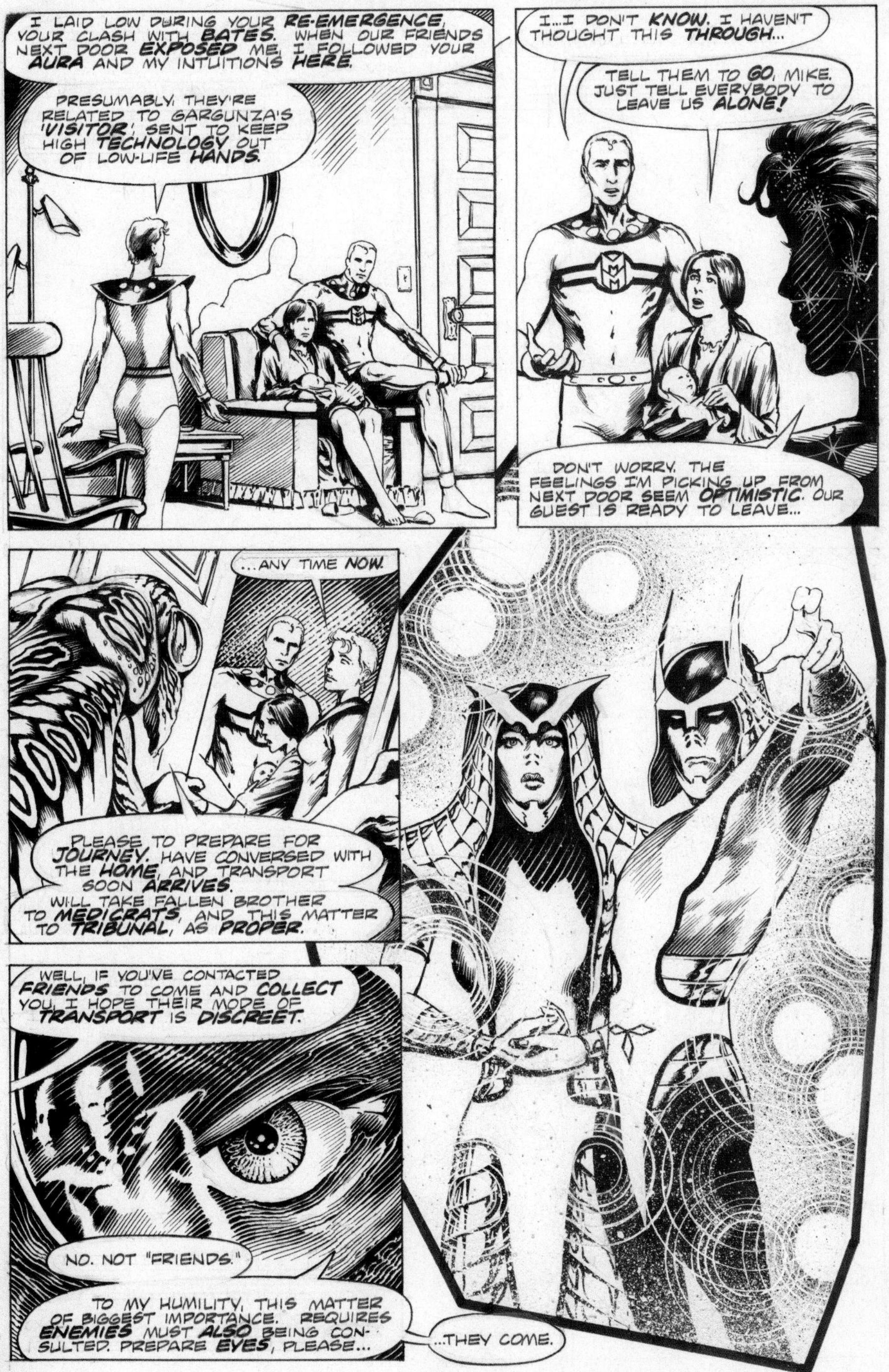
I LAID LOW DURING YOUR RE-EMERGENCE, YOUR CLASH WITH BATES. WHEN OUR FRIENDS NEXT DOOR EXPOSED ME, I FOLLOWED YOUR AURA AND MY INTUITIONS HERE.
PRESUMABLY, THEY'RE RELATED TO GARGUNZA'S 'VISITOR', SENT TO KEEP HIGH TECHNOLOGY OUT OF LOW-LIFE HANDS.
I...I DON'T KNOW. I HAVEN'T THOUGHT THIS THROUGH...
TELL THEM TO GO, MIKE. JUST TELL EVERYBODY TO LEAVE US ALONE!
DON'T WORRY. THE FEELINGS I'M PICKING UP FROM NEXT DOOR SEEM OPTIMISTIC. OUR GUEST IS READY TO LEAVE...
...ANY TIME NOW.
PLEASE TO PREPARE FOR JOURNEY. HAVE CONVERSED WITH THE HOME, AND TRANSPORT SOON ARRIVES.
WILL TAKE FALLEN BROTHER TO MEDICRATS, AND THIS MATTER TO TRIBUNAL, AS PROPER.
WELL, IF YOU'VE CONTACTED FRIENDS TO COME AND COLLECT YOU, I HOPE THEIR MODE OF TRANSPORT IS DISCREET.
NO. NOT "FRIENDS."
TO MY HUMILITY, THIS MATTER OF BIGGEST IMPORTANCE. REQUIRES ENEMIES MUST ALSO BEING CONSULTED. PREPARE EYES, PLEASE...
...THEY COME.



NOTE: SEE COVER OF WARRIOR #10 FOR COLORING OF AZA CHORN'S GARB.

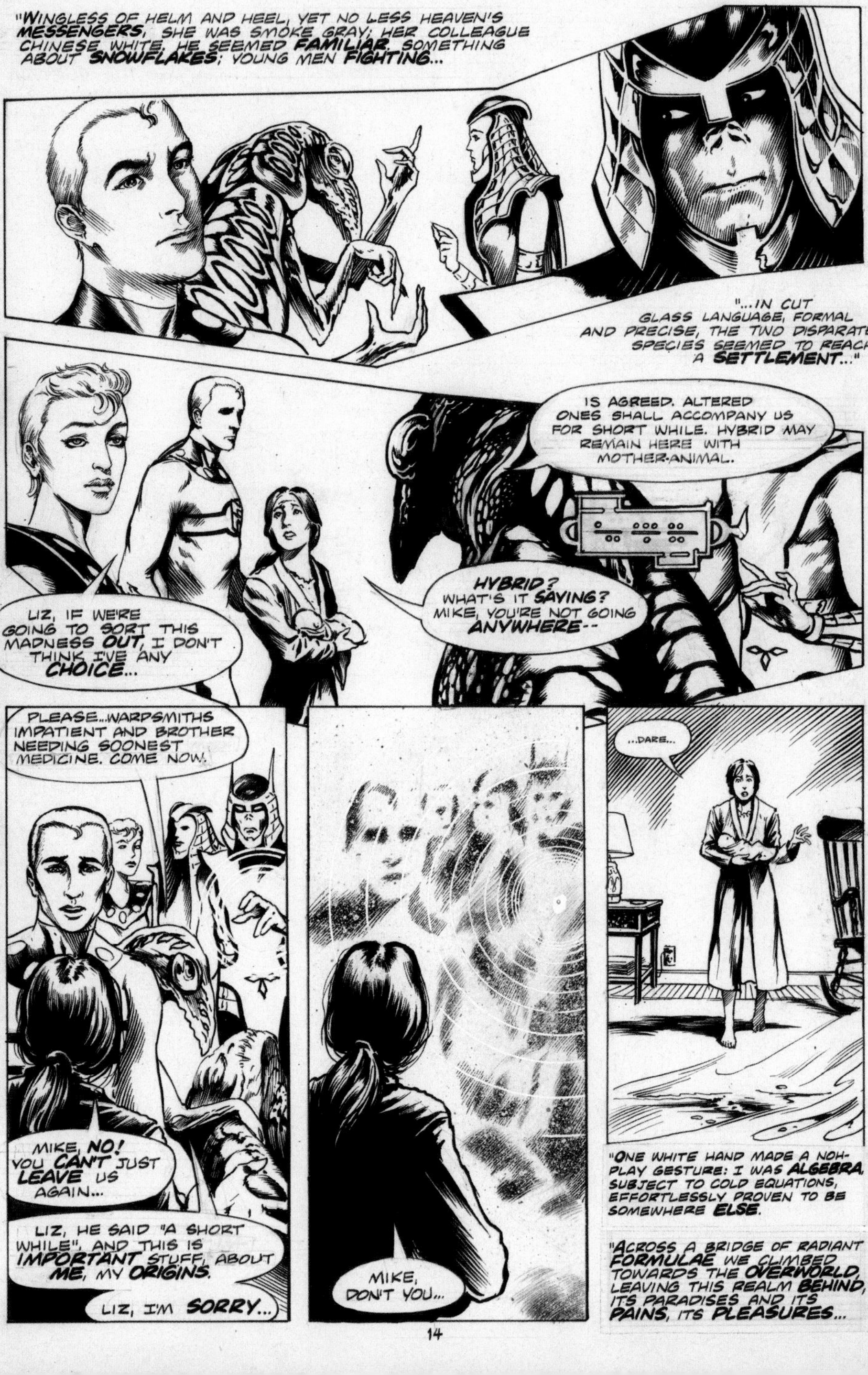
"WINGLESS OF HELM AND HEEL, YET NO LESS HEAVEN'S MESSENGERS, SHE WAS SMOKE GRAY; HER COLLEAGUE CHINESE WHITE. HE SEEMED FAMILIAR, SOMETHING ABOUT SNOWFLAKES; YOUNG MEN FIGHTING...
"...IN CUT GLASS LANGUAGE, FORMAL AND PRECISE, THE TWO DISPARATE SPECIES SEEMED TO REACH A SETTLEMENT..."
IS AGREED. ALTERED ONES SHALL ACCOMPANY US FOR SHORT WHILE. HYBRID MAY REMAIN HERE WITH MOTHER-ANIMAL.
HYBRID? WHAT'S IT SAYING? MIKE, YOU'RE NOT GOING ANYWHERE--
LIZ, IF WE'RE GOING TO SORT THIS MADNESS OUT, I DON'T THINK I'VE ANY CHOICE...
PLEASE...WARPSMITHS IMPATIENT AND BROTHER NEEDING SOONEST MEDICINE. COME NOW.
MIKE, NO! YOU CAN'T JUST LEAVE US AGAIN...
LIZ, HE SAID "A SHORT WHILE", AND THIS IS IMPORTANT STUFF, ABOUT ME, MY ORIGINS.
LIZ, I'M SORRY...
MIKE, DON'T YOU...
...DARE...
"ONE WHITE HAND MADE A NOH-PLAY GESTURE: I WAS ALGEBRA, SUBJECT TO COLD EQUATIONS, EFFORTLESSLY PROVEN TO BE SOMEWHERE ELSE.
"ACROSS A BRIDGE OF RADIANT FORMULAE WE CLIMBED TOWARDS THE OVERWORLD, LEAVING THIS REALM BEHIND, ITS PARADISES AND ITS PAINS, ITS PLEASURES...

Miracleman #12, page 15 original artwork, pencil, India ink and white acrylic on illustration board by John Totleben.

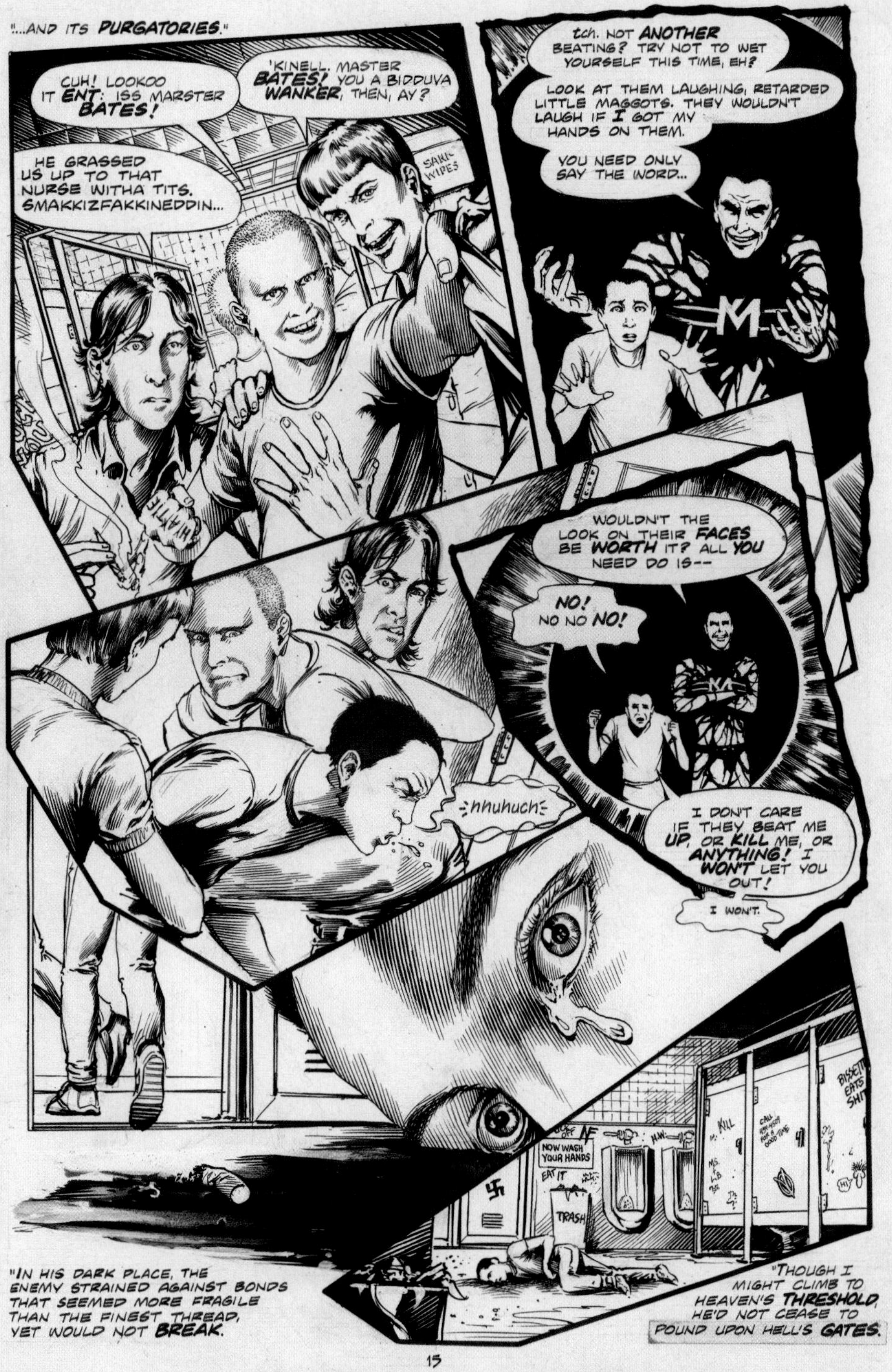

"...AND ITS PURGATORIES."
CUH! LOOKOO IT ENT: ISS MARSTER BATES!
'KINELL. MASTER BATES! YOU A BIDDUVA WANKER, THEN, AY?
HE GRASSED US UP TO THAT NURSE WITHA TITS. SMAKKIZFAKKINEDDIN...
SAKI WIPES
tch. NOT ANOTHER BEATING? TRY NOT TO WET YOURSELF THIS TIME, EH?
LOOK AT THEM LAUGHING, RETARDED LITTLE MAGGOTS. THEY WOULDN'T LAUGH IF I GOT MY HANDS ON THEM.
YOU NEED ONLY SAY THE WORD...
WOULDN'T THE LOOK ON THEIR FACES BE WORTH IT? ALL YOU NEED DO IS--
NO! NO NO NO!
hhuhuch
I DON'T CARE IF THEY BEAT ME UP, OR KILL ME, OR ANYTHING! I WON'T LET YOU OUT!
I WON'T.
NOW WASH YOUR HANDS
EAT IT
TRASH
KILL
BISSETT EATS SHIT
"IN HIS DARK PLACE, THE ENEMY STRAINED AGAINST BONDS THAT SEEMED MORE FRAGILE THAN THE FINEST THREAD, YET WOULD NOT BREAK.
"THOUGH I MIGHT CLIMB TO HEAVEN'S THRESHOLD, HE'D NOT CEASE TO POUND UPON HELL'S GATES.
15

*Miracleman* #12, page 16 pencils by John Totleben. The flight through Miraclewoman's suite in panels 1-3 was inspired by the January 27, 1907, installment of *Little Nemo* from "The Palace of Ice" serial.

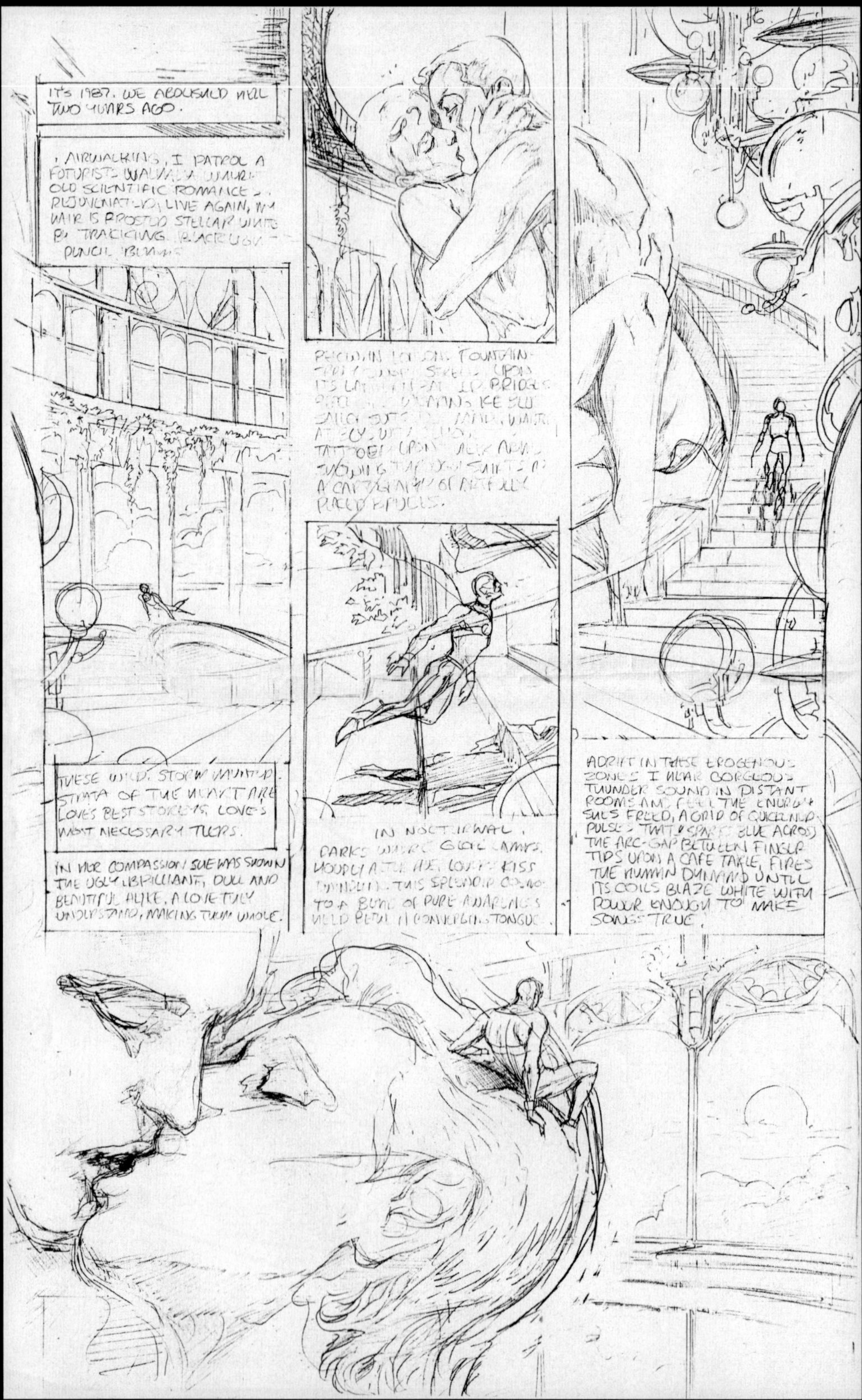
TWO YEARS AGO.
AIRWALKING, I PATROL A
OLD SCIENTIFIC ROMANCE
LIVE AGAIN,
ADRIFT IN THESE EROGENOUS
THUNDER SOUND IN DISTANT
THE ARC-GAP BETWEEN FINGER
TIPS UPON A CAFE TABLE, FIRES
ITS COILS BLAZE WHITE WITH
POWER ENOUGH TO MAKE
SONGS TRUE.
STRATA OF THE HEART ARE
LOVE'S BEST
MOST NECESSARY
IN HER COMPASSION SHE WAS SHOWN
THE UGLY, BRILLIANT, DULL AND
BEAUTIFUL ALIKE,
MAKING THEM WHOLE.
IN NOCTURNAL
TO A BLEND OF PURE

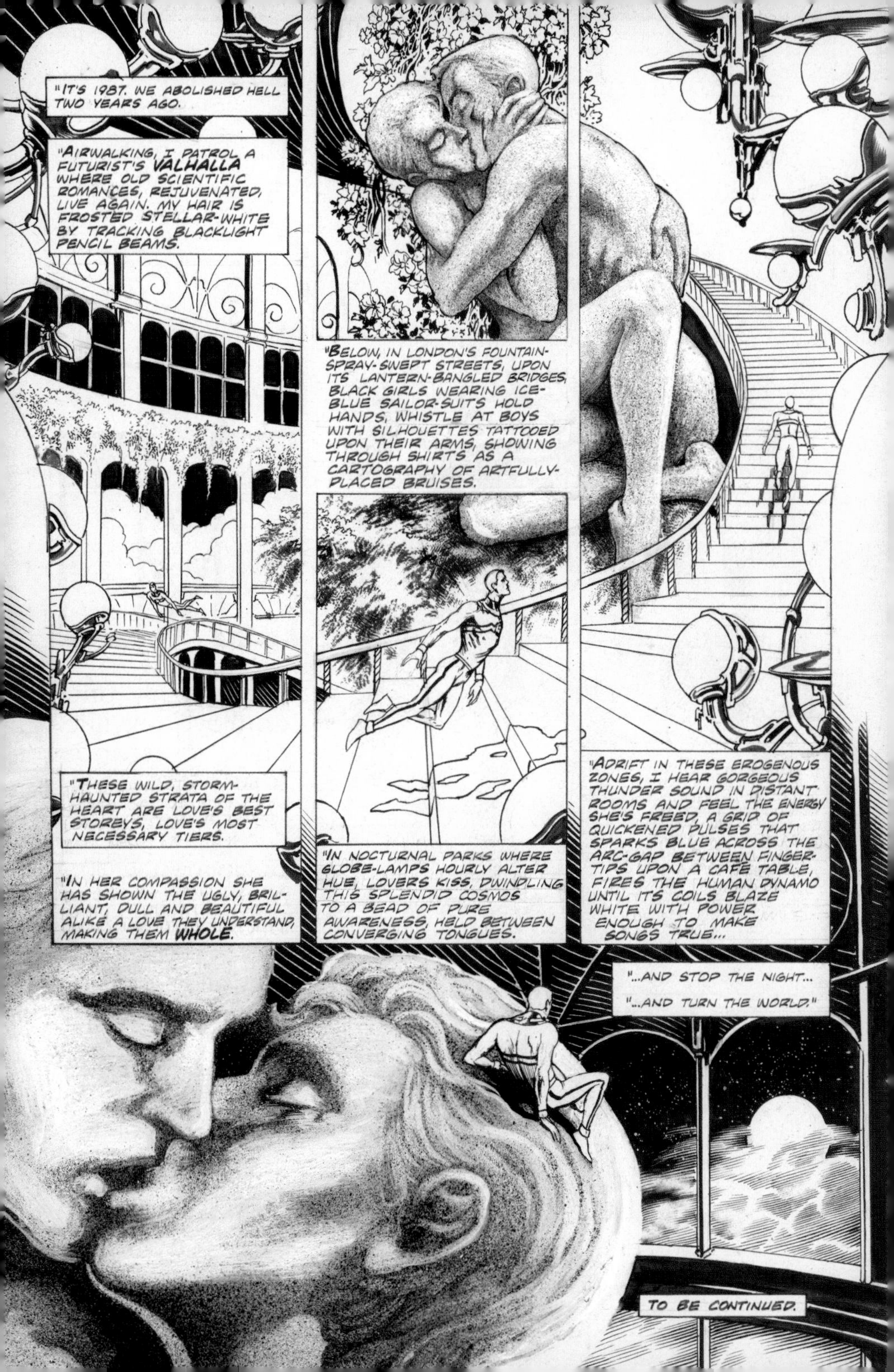
"IT'S 1987. WE ABOLISHED HELL TWO YEARS AGO.
"AIRWALKING, I PATROL A FUTURIST'S VALHALLA WHERE OLD SCIENTIFIC ROMANCES, REJUVENATED, LIVE AGAIN. MY HAIR IS FROSTED STELLAR-WHITE BY TRACKING BLACKLIGHT PENCIL BEAMS.
"BELOW, IN LONDON'S FOUNTAIN-SPRAY-SWEPT STREETS, UPON ITS LANTERN-BANGLED BRIDGES, BLACK GIRLS WEARING ICE-BLUE SAILOR-SUITS HOLD HANDS, WHISTLE AT BOYS WITH SILHOUETTES TATTOOED UPON THEIR ARMS, SHOWING THROUGH SHIRTS AS A CARTOGRAPHY OF ARTFULLY-PLACED BRUISES.
"THESE WILD, STORM-HAUNTED STRATA OF THE HEART ARE LOVE'S BEST STOREYS, LOVE'S MOST NECESSARY TIERS.
"IN HER COMPASSION SHE HAS SHOWN THE UGLY, BRILLIANT, DULL AND BEAUTIFUL ALIKE A LOVE THEY UNDERSTAND, MAKING THEM WHOLE.
"IN NOCTURNAL PARKS WHERE GLOBE-LAMPS HOURLY ALTER HUE, LOVERS KISS, DWINDLING THIS SPLENDID COSMOS TO A BEAD OF PURE AWARENESS, HELD BETWEEN CONVERGING TONGUES.
"ADRIFT IN THESE EROGENOUS ZONES, I HEAR GORGEOUS THUNDER SOUND IN DISTANT ROOMS AND FEEL THE ENERGY SHE'S FREED, A GRID OF QUICKENED PULSES THAT SPARKS BLUE ACROSS THE ARC-GAP BETWEEN FINGERTIPS UPON A CAFE TABLE, FIRES THE HUMAN DYNAMO UNTIL ITS COILS BLAZE WHITE WITH POWER ENOUGH TO MAKE SONGS TRUE...
"...AND STOP THE NIGHT...
"...AND TURN THE WORLD."
TO BE CONTINUED.

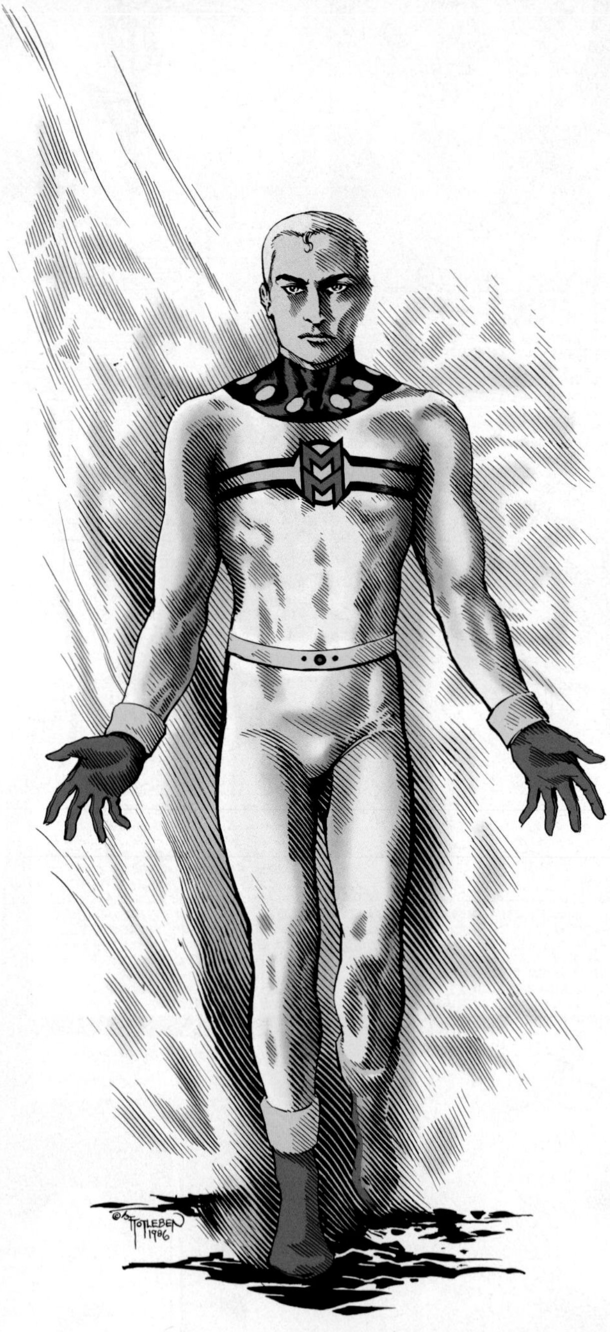

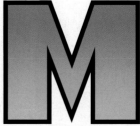

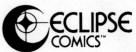

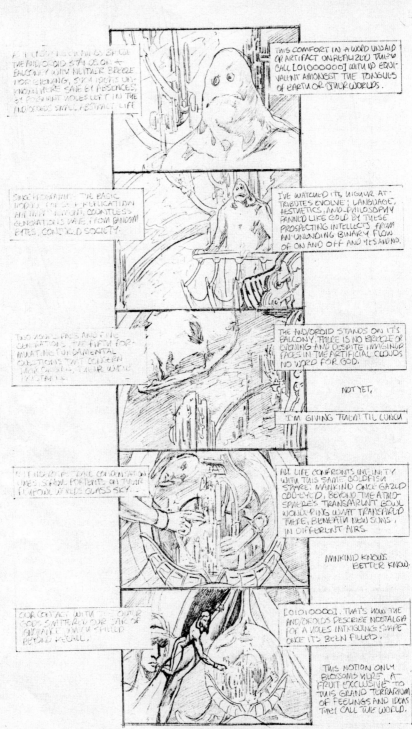

(— THICK BORDERLINES ON PANELS / REGULAR LINE-WIDTH ON CAPTION BORDERS)

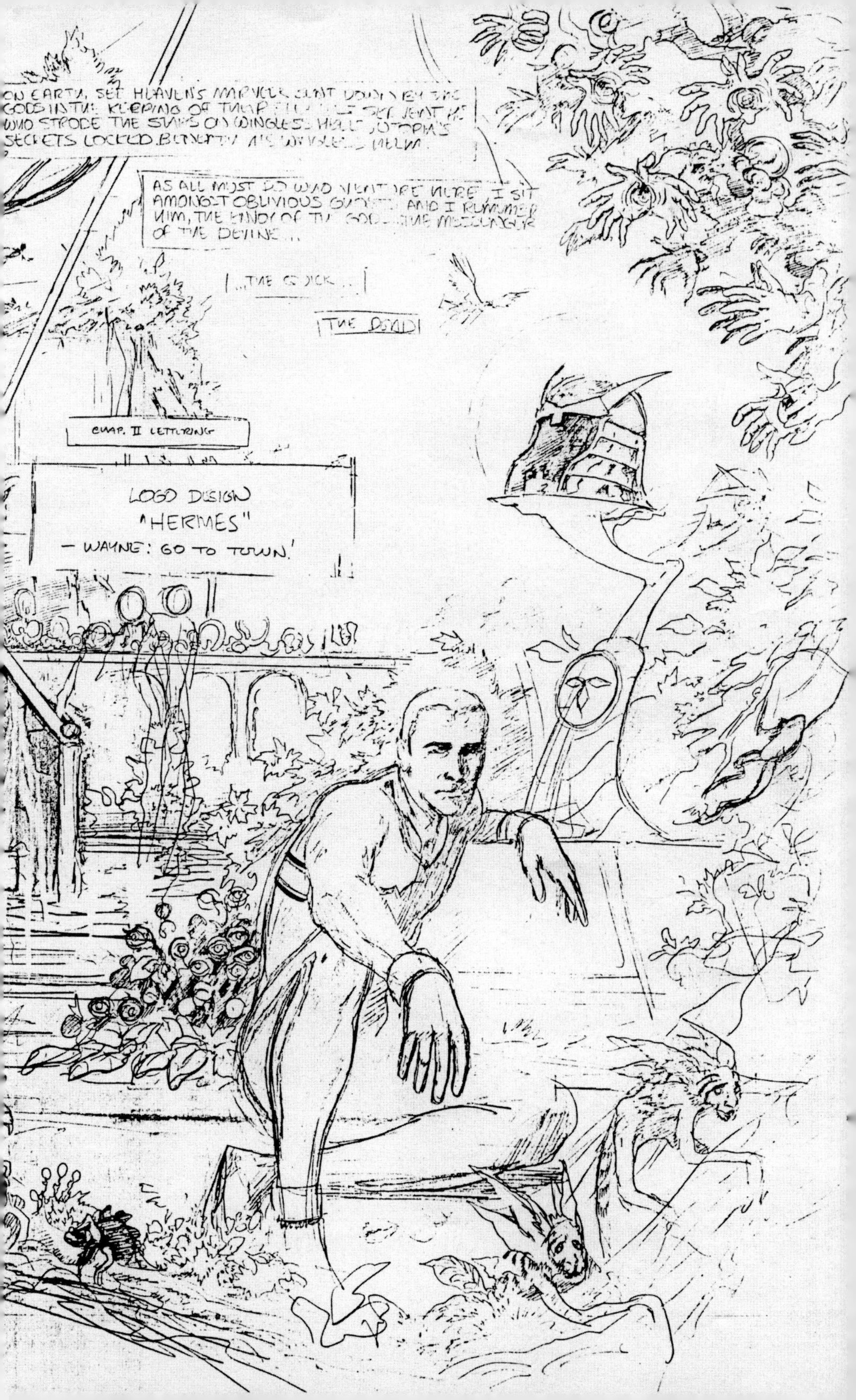
...THE QUICK...
THE DEAD
CHAP. II LETTERING
LOGO DESIGN
"HERMES"
— WAYNE: GO TO TOWN!

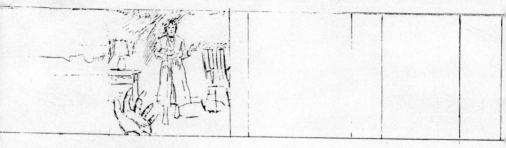

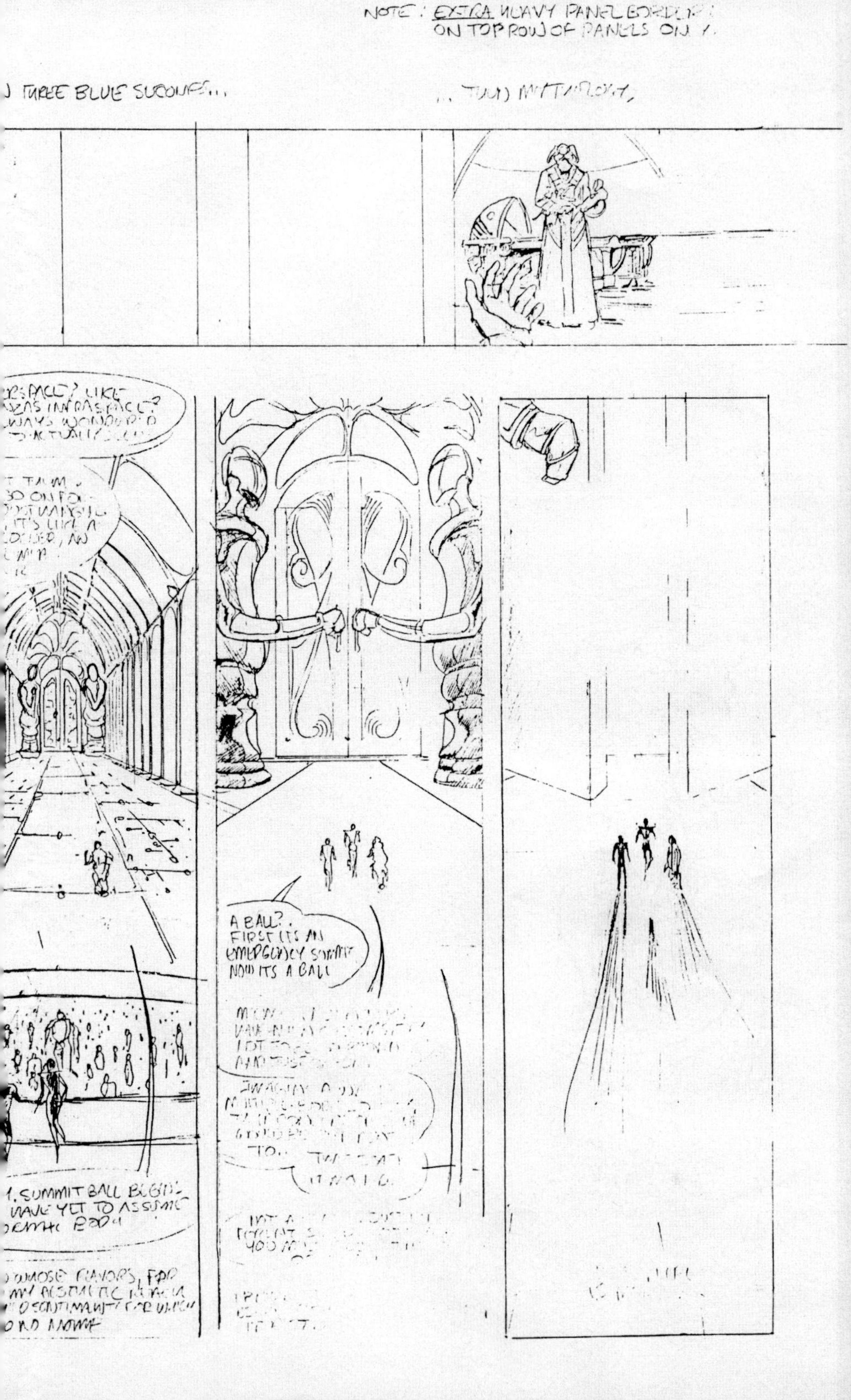

NOTE: EXTRA HEAVY PANEL BORDERS ON TOP ROW OF PANELS ONLY.
A BALL? FIRST ITS AN EMERGENCY SUMMIT NOW ITS A BALL

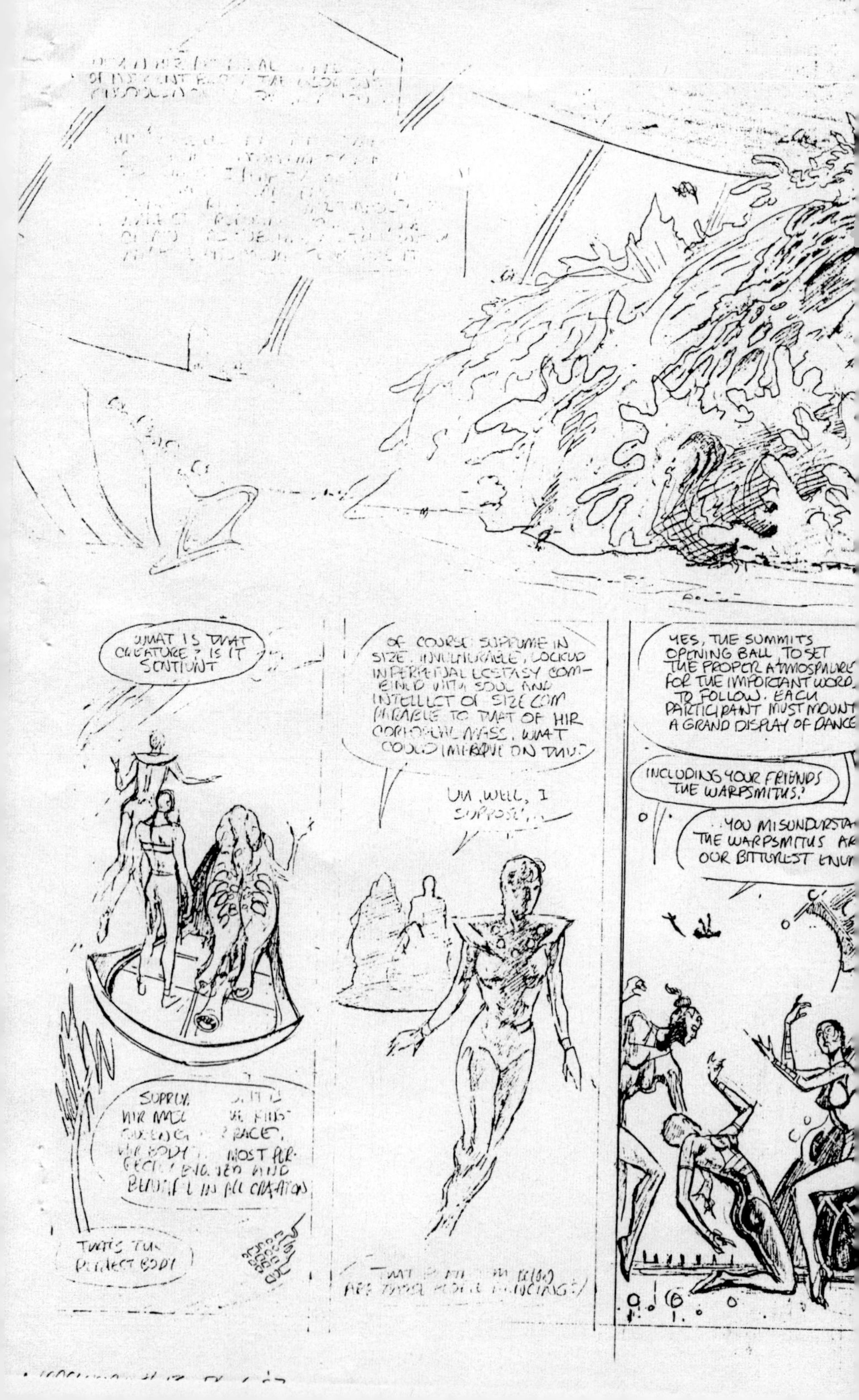
WHAT IS THAT CREATURE? IS IT SENTIENT
OF COURSE: SUPREME IN SIZE. INVULNERABLE, LOCKED IN PERPETUAL ECSTASY COMBINED WITH SOUL AND INTELLECT OF SIZE COMPARABLE TO THAT OF HIR CORPOREAL MASS. WHAT COULD IMPROVE ON THIS?
UH, WELL, I SUPPOSE...
YES, THE SUMMITS OPENING BALL TO SET THE PROPER ATMOSPHERE FOR THE IMPORTANT WORDS TO FOLLOW. EACH PARTICIPANT MUST MOUNT A GRAND DISPLAY OF DANCE
INCLUDING YOUR FRIENDS THE WARPSMITHS?
...YOU MISUNDERSTA THE WARPSMITHS AR OUR BITTEREST ENE
THAT'S THE PERFECT BODY

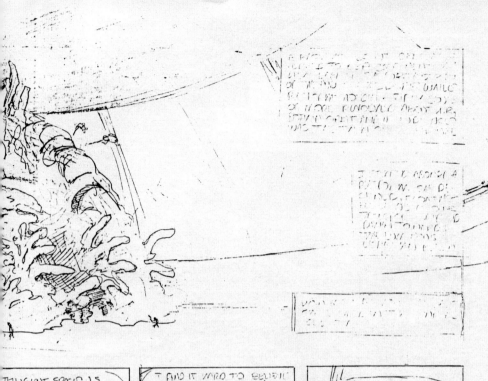

TWILIGHT SPACE IS
VOID BETWEEN THE OVS
PURIUM AND THE GULF
WORLDS CONFEDERACY.
UNTIL WARPSMITH RULE.

PERPETUAL COLD WAR DUAD
OUR VAST EMPIRES CO-
ST HAVE DONE SO FOR
TENS THOUSAND JUMPS

I FIND IT HARD TO BELIEVE
A RACE AS POWERFUL AS
YOUR OWN COULD HAVE TO
BROKER THE WAR OF
ELSEWHERE NEXT.

AHH BUT YOU DO NOT
UNDERSTAND THAT
WARPSMITHS, YOU SEE
THE WARPSMITHS
ARE FEW.

LET'S HOPE WE HAVEN'T
KEPT THEM WAITING LONG

WELL HAVE YOU ASSURED
YET NOT THEY STOOD TO
GREET US FAINT ABOUT THE
UKURKITE THE UNKNOWN COR-
REER CALLING UNTIL THE TITLE
TION CREEDS OF THE MANS
WHITE BAND

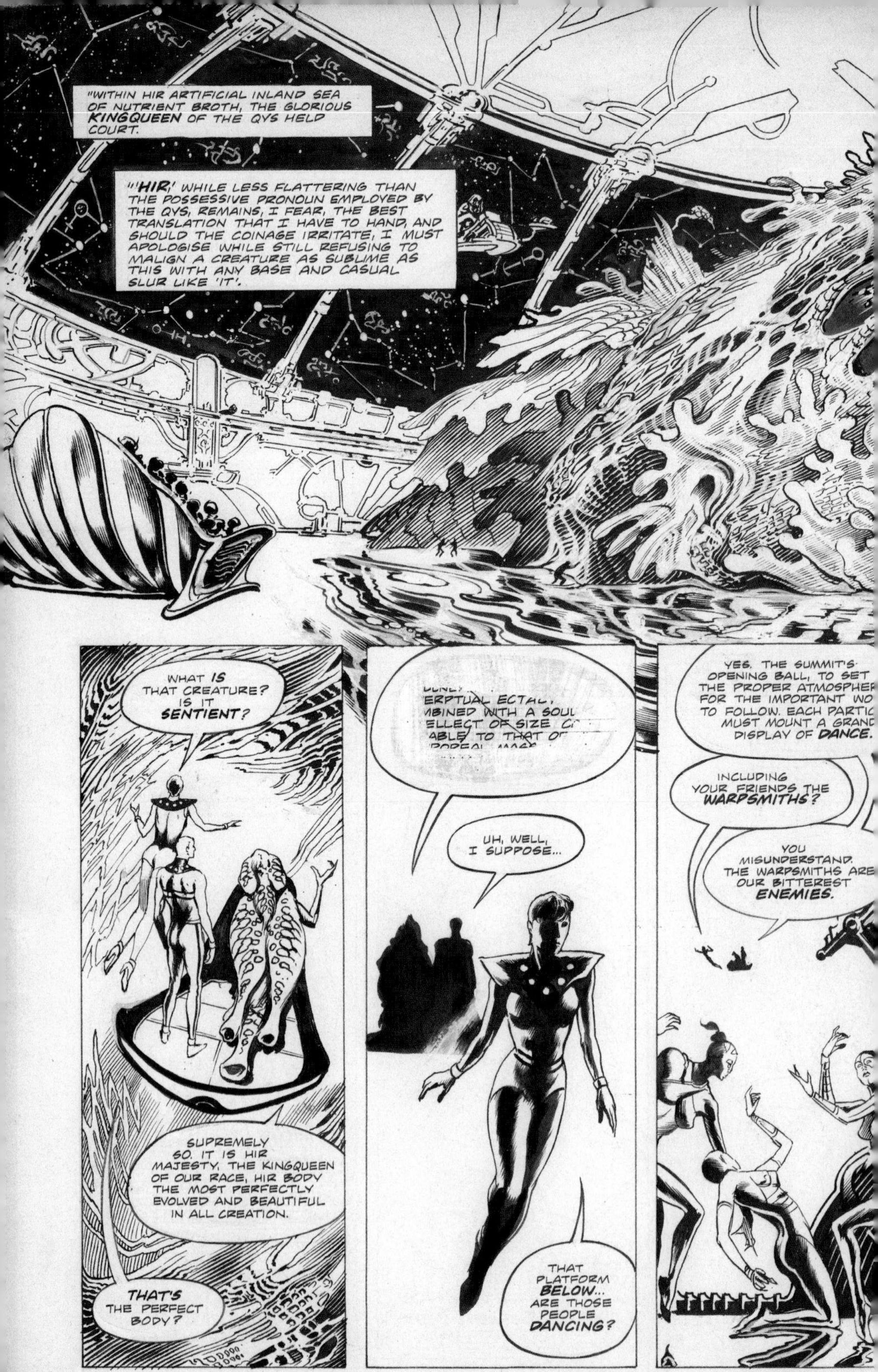

"WITHIN HIR ARTIFICIAL INLAND SEA OF NUTRIENT BROTH, THE GLORIOUS KINGQUEEN OF THE QYS HELD COURT.
"'HIR,' WHILE LESS FLATTERING THAN THE POSSESSIVE PRONOUN EMPLOYED BY THE QYS, REMAINS, I FEAR, THE BEST TRANSLATION THAT I HAVE TO HAND, AND SHOULD THE COINAGE IRRITATE, I MUST APOLOGISE WHILE STILL REFUSING TO MALIGN A CREATURE AS SUBLIME AS THIS WITH ANY BASE AND CASUAL SLUR LIKE 'IT'.
WHAT IS THAT CREATURE? IS IT SENTIENT?
SUPREMELY SO. IT IS HIR MAJESTY, THE KINGQUEEN OF OUR RACE, HIR BODY THE MOST PERFECTLY EVOLVED AND BEAUTIFUL IN ALL CREATION.
THAT'S THE PERFECT BODY?
UH, WELL, I SUPPOSE...
THAT PLATFORM BELOW... ARE THOSE PEOPLE DANCING?
YES. THE SUMMIT'S OPENING BALL, TO SET THE PROPER ATMOSPHER FOR THE IMPORTANT WO TO FOLLOW. EACH PARTIC MUST MOUNT A GRAND DISPLAY OF DANCE.
INCLUDING YOUR FRIENDS THE WARPSMITHS?
YOU MISUNDERSTAND. THE WARPSMITHS ARE OUR BITTEREST ENEMIES.

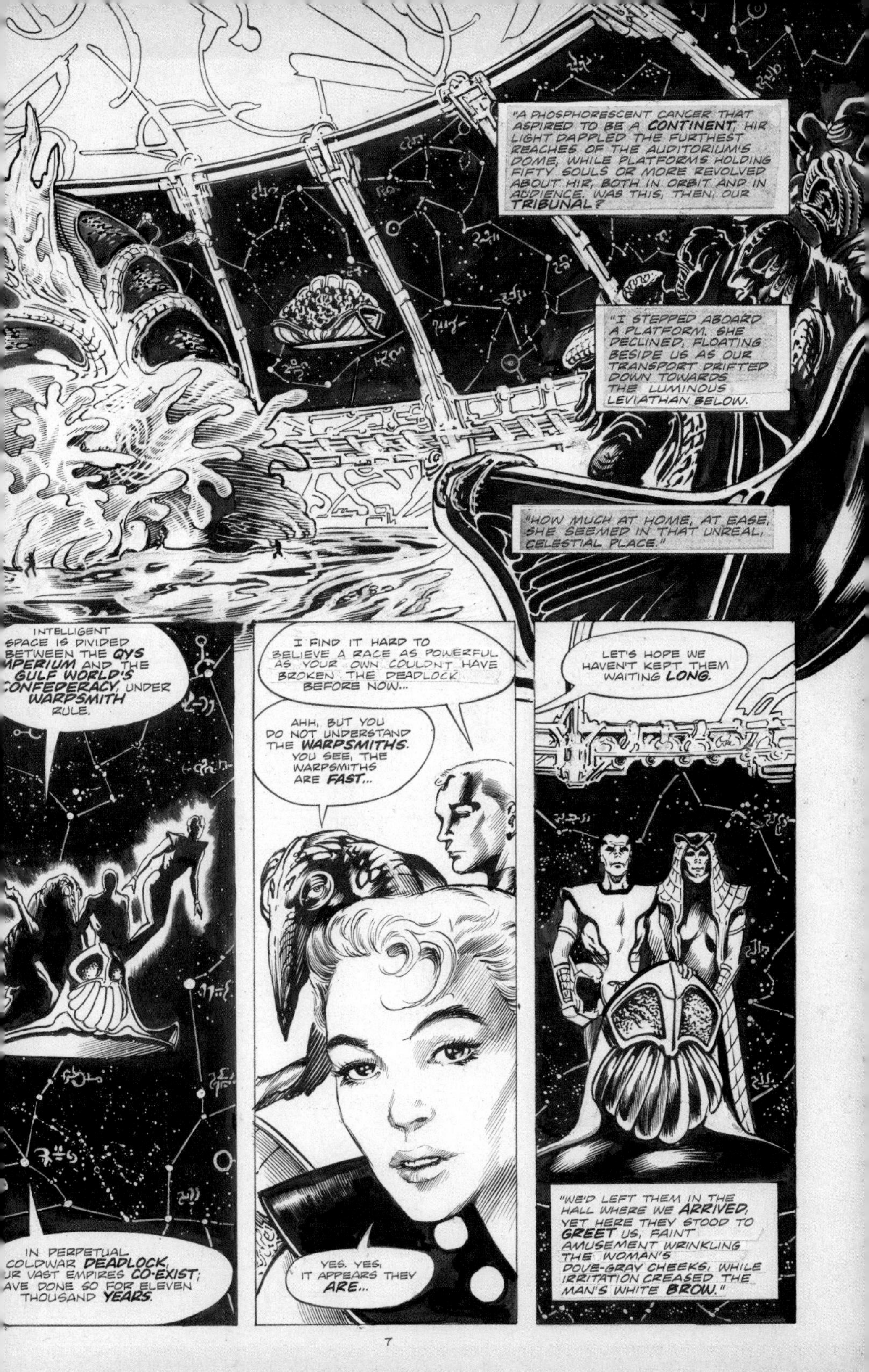
"A PHOSPHORESCENT CANCER THAT ASPIRED TO BE A CONTINENT, HIR LIGHT DAPPLED THE FURTHEST REACHES OF THE AUDITORIUM'S DOME, WHILE PLATFORMS HOLDING FIFTY SOULS OR MORE REVOLVED ABOUT HIR, BOTH IN ORBIT AND IN AUDIENCE. WAS THIS, THEN, OUR TRIBUNAL?
"I STEPPED ABOARD A PLATFORM. SHE DECLINED, FLOATING BESIDE US AS OUR TRANSPORT DRIFTED DOWN TOWARDS THE LUMINOUS LEVIATHAN BELOW.
"HOW MUCH AT HOME, AT EASE, SHE SEEMED IN THAT UNREAL, CELESTIAL PLACE."
INTELLIGENT SPACE IS DIVIDED BETWEEN THE QYS IMPERIUM AND THE GULF WORLD'S CONFEDERACY, UNDER WARPSMITH RULE.
IN PERPETUAL COLDWAR DEADLOCK, OUR VAST EMPIRES CO-EXIST; HAVE DONE SO FOR ELEVEN THOUSAND YEARS.
I FIND IT HARD TO BELIEVE A RACE AS POWERFUL AS YOUR OWN COULDN'T HAVE BROKEN THE DEADLOCK BEFORE NOW...
AHH, BUT YOU DO NOT UNDERSTAND THE WARPSMITHS. YOU SEE, THE WARPSMITHS ARE FAST...
YES. YES, IT APPEARS THEY ARE...
LET'S HOPE WE HAVEN'T KEPT THEM WAITING LONG.
"WE'D LEFT THEM IN THE HALL WHERE WE ARRIVED, YET HERE THEY STOOD TO GREET US, FAINT AMUSEMENT WRINKLING THE WOMAN'S DOVE-GRAY CHEEKS, WHILE IRRITATION CREASED THE MAN'S WHITE BROW."

*Miracleman* #13, page 9 pencils by John Totleben. Johnny Bates stands before his own tribunal — with Kid Miracleman as his only counsel.

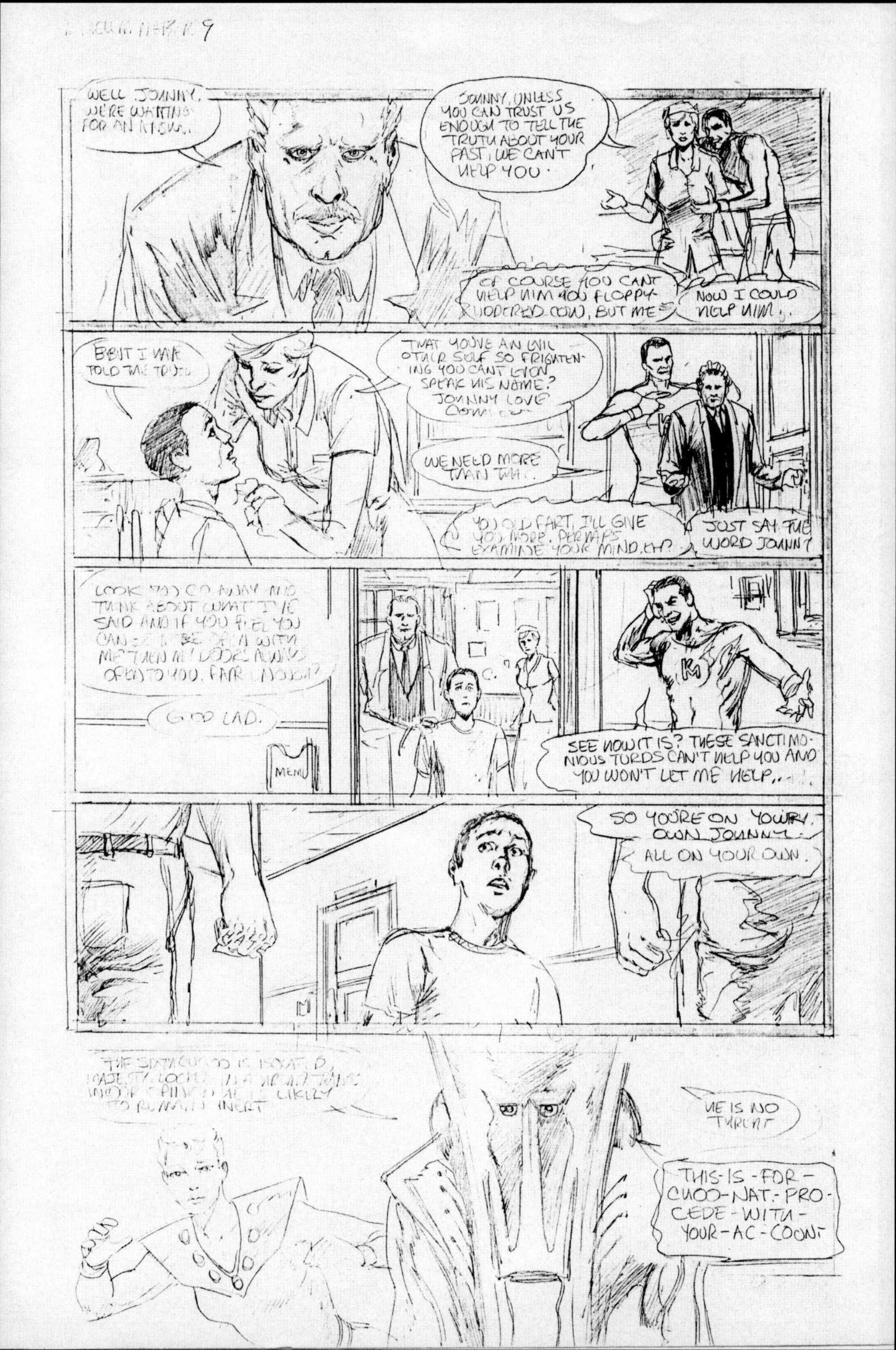
JOHNNY, UNLESS YOU CAN TRUST US ENOUGH TO TELL THE TRUTH ABOUT YOUR PAST, WE CAN'T HELP YOU.
OF COURSE YOU CAN'T HELP HIM YOU FLOPPY-UDDERED COW, BUT ME
NOW I COULD HELP HIM.
BUT I HAVE TOLD THE TRUTH
SPEAK HIS NAME?
WE NEED MORE THAN THAT.
YOU OLD FART, I'LL GIVE YOU MORE. PERHAPS EXAMINE YOUR MIND, EH?
JUST SAY THE WORD JOHNNY
GOOD LAD.
MENU
SEE HOW IT IS? THESE SANCTIMONIOUS TURDS CAN'T HELP YOU AND YOU WON'T LET ME HELP...
SO YOU'RE ON YOUR OWN JOHNNY...
ALL ON YOUR OWN.
HE IS NO THREAT
THIS-IS-FOR-CHOO-NAT.-PRO-CEDE-WITH-YOUR-AC-COUNT

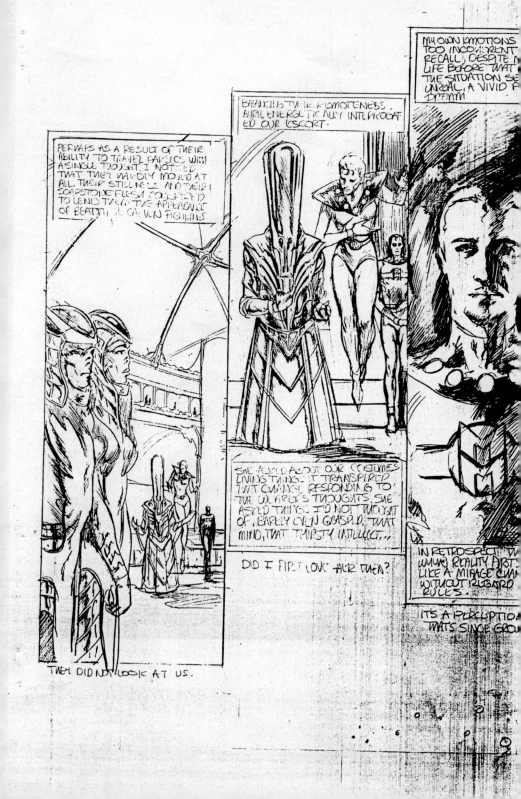

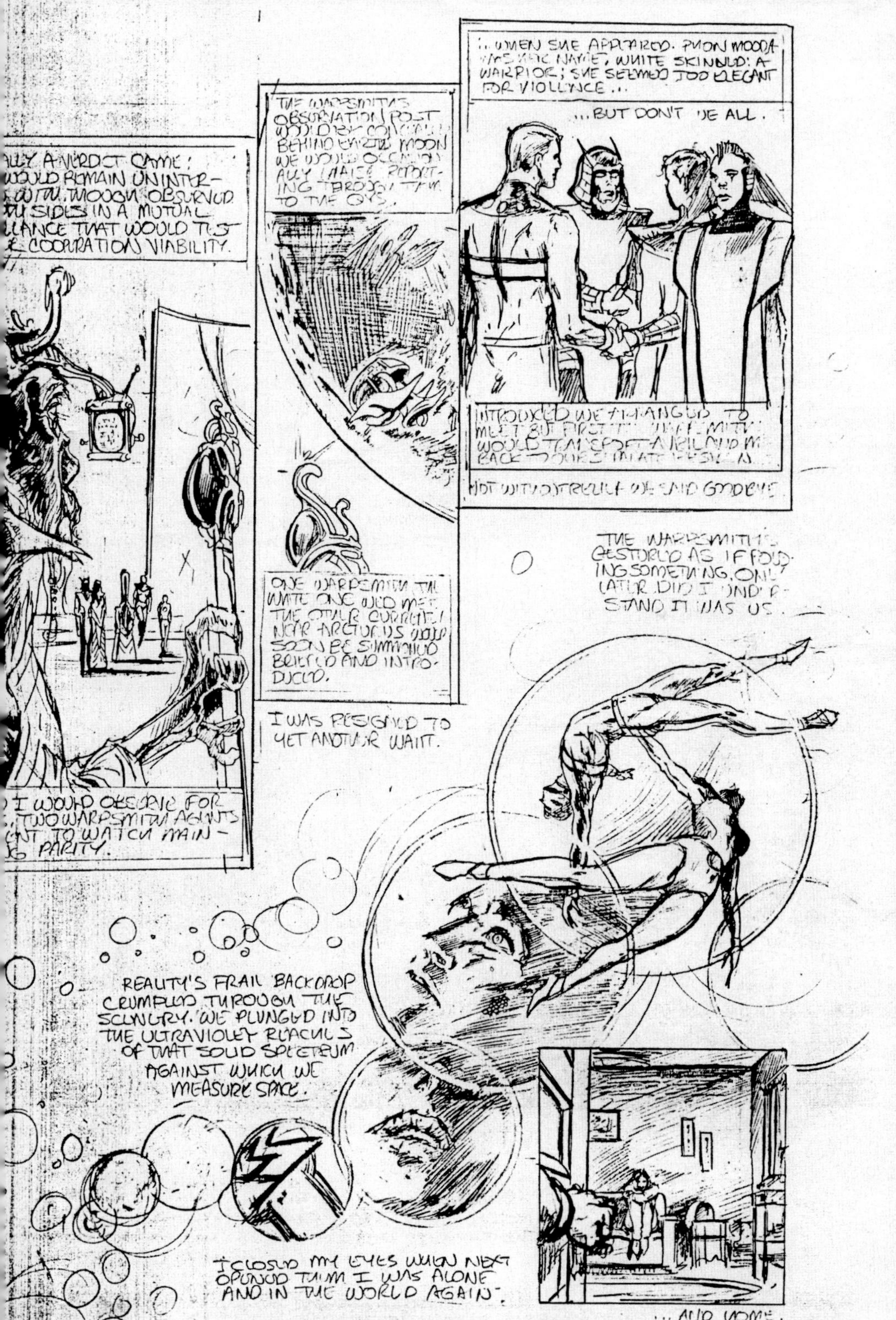
A VERDICT CAME:
WOULD REMAIN UNINTER-
SIDES IN A MUTUAL
ALLIANCE THAT WOULD TEST
COOPERATION VIABILITY.
THE WARPSMITH'S OBSERVATION POST
BEHIND EARTH'S MOON
TO THE OYS.
...WHEN SHE APPEARED.
WHITE SKINNED: A WARRIOR; SHE SEEMED TOO ELEGANT FOR VIOLENCE...
...BUT DON'T WE ALL.
I WOULD OBSERVE FOR
TWO WARPSMITH AGENTS
TO WATCH MAIN-
PARITY.
ONE WARPSMITH THE WHITE ONE WE'D MET.
THE OTHER CURRENTLY NEAR ARCTURUS WOULD SOON BE SUMMONED BRIEFED AND INTRODUCED.
I WAS RESIGNED TO YET ANOTHER WAIT.
THE WARPSMITHS GESTURED AS IF FOLDING SOMETHING. ONLY LATER DID I UNDERSTAND IT WAS US.
REALITY'S FRAIL BACKDROP CRUMPLED THROUGH THE SCENERY. WE PLUNGED INTO THE ULTRAVIOLET REACHES OF THAT SOLID SPECTRUM AGAINST WHICH WE MEASURE SPACE.
I CLOSED MY EYES WHEN NEXT OPENED THEM I WAS ALONE AND IN THE WORLD AGAIN.
...AND HOME.

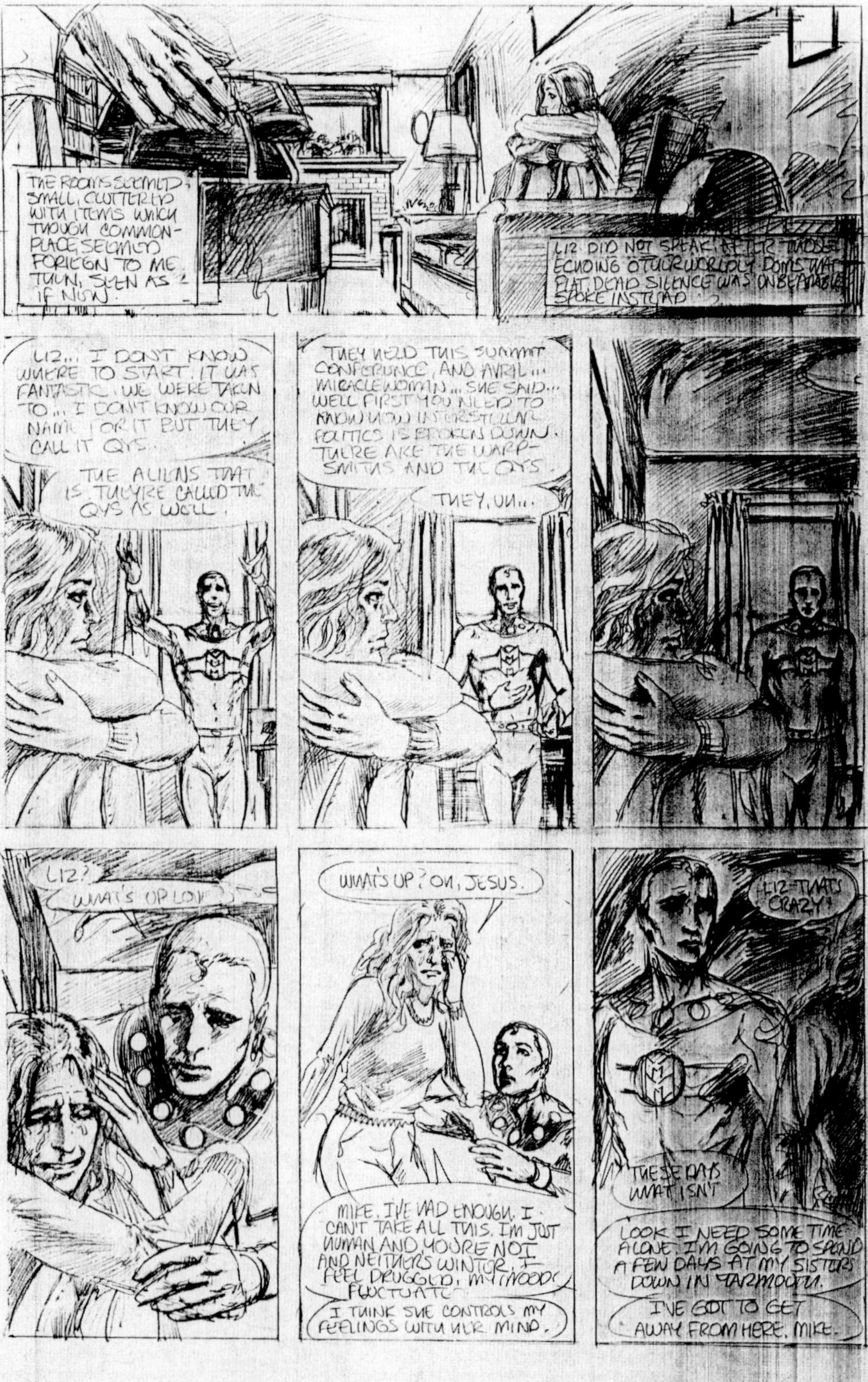
THE ROOMS SEEMED SMALL, CLUTTERED WITH ITEMS WHICH THOUGH COMMONPLACE, SEEMED FOREIGN TO ME. THEN, SEEN AS IF NEW.
LIZ DID NOT SPEAK. AFTER THOSE ECHOING OTHERWORLDLY DOOMS THAT FLAT, DEAD SILENCE WAS UNBEARABLE. SPOKE INSTEAD
LIZ... I DON'T KNOW WHERE TO START. IT WAS FANTASTIC. WE WERE TAKEN TO... I DON'T KNOW OUR NAME FOR IT BUT THEY CALL IT QYS.
THE ALIENS THAT IS. THEY'RE CALLED THE QYS AS WELL.
THEY HELD THIS SUMMIT CONFERENCE, AND AVRIL... MIRACLEWOMAN... SHE SAID... WELL FIRST YOU NEED TO KNOW HOW INTERSTELLAR POLITICS IS BROKEN DOWN. THERE ARE THE WARPSMITHS AND THE QYS.
THEY, UH...
LIZ?
WHAT'S UP LOVE
WHAT'S UP? OH, JESUS.
MIKE. I'VE HAD ENOUGH. I CAN'T TAKE ALL THIS. I'M JUST HUMAN AND YOU'RE NOT. AND NEITHER'S WINTER. I FEEL DRUGGED. MY MOODS FLUCTUATE
I THINK SHE CONTROLS MY FEELINGS WITH HER MIND.
LIZ - THAT'S CRAZY!
THESE DAYS WHAT ISN'T
LOOK I NEED SOME TIME ALONE. I'M GOING TO SPEND A FEW DAYS AT MY SISTER'S DOWN IN YARMOUTH.
I'VE GOT TO GET AWAY FROM HERE, MIKE.

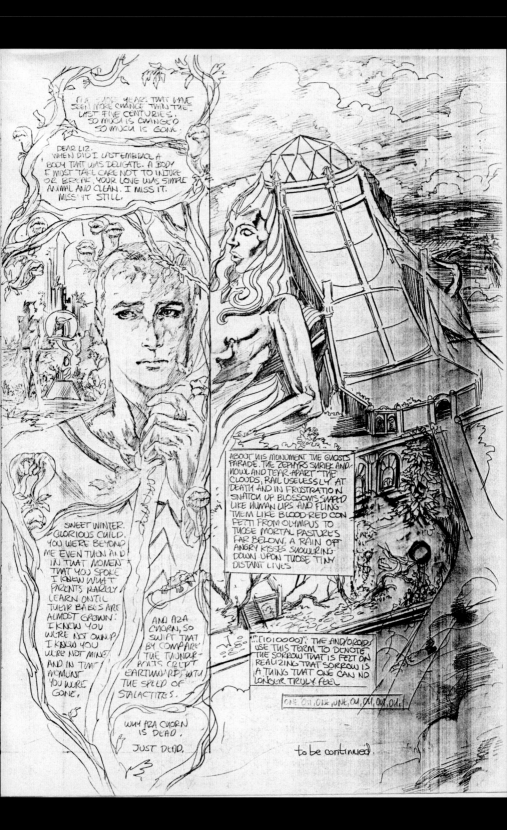

Miracleman #15, page 16 original artwork, pencil, India ink and white acrylic on illustration board by John Totleben.

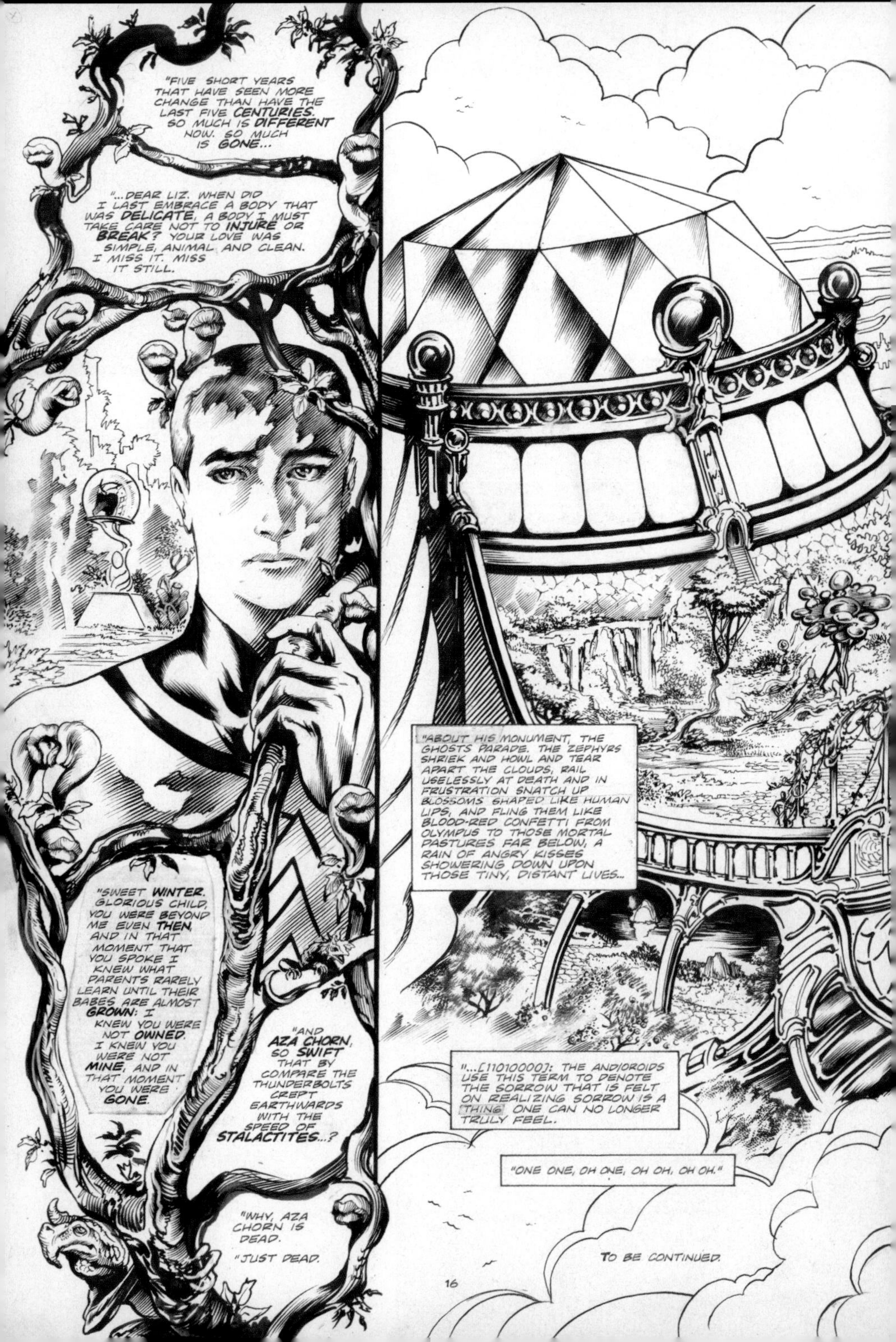

"FIVE SHORT YEARS THAT HAVE SEEN MORE CHANGE THAN HAVE THE LAST FIVE CENTURIES. SO MUCH IS DIFFERENT NOW. SO MUCH IS GONE...
"...DEAR LIZ. WHEN DID I LAST EMBRACE A BODY THAT WAS DELICATE, A BODY I MUST TAKE CARE NOT TO INJURE OR BREAK? YOUR LOVE WAS SIMPLE, ANIMAL AND CLEAN. I MISS IT. MISS IT STILL.
"SWEET WINTER. GLORIOUS CHILD, YOU WERE BEYOND ME EVEN THEN, AND IN THAT MOMENT THAT YOU SPOKE I KNEW WHAT PARENTS RARELY LEARN UNTIL THEIR BABES ARE ALMOST GROWN: I KNEW YOU WERE NOT OWNED. I KNEW YOU WERE NOT MINE, AND IN THAT MOMENT YOU WERE GONE.
"AND AZA CHORN, SO SWIFT THAT BY COMPARE THE THUNDERBOLTS CREPT EARTHWARDS WITH THE SPEED OF STALACTITES...?
"WHY, AZA CHORN IS DEAD.
"JUST DEAD.
"ABOUT HIS MONUMENT, THE GHOSTS PARADE. THE ZEPHYRS SHRIEK AND HOWL AND TEAR APART THE CLOUDS, RAIL USELESSLY AT DEATH AND IN FRUSTRATION SNATCH UP BLOSSOMS SHAPED LIKE HUMAN LIPS, AND FLING THEM LIKE BLOOD-RED CONFETTI FROM OLYMPUS TO THOSE MORTAL PASTURES FAR BELOW, A RAIN OF ANGRY KISSES SHOWERING DOWN UPON THOSE TINY, DISTANT LIVES...
"...[11010000]: THE ANDIOROIDS USE THIS TERM TO DENOTE THE SORROW THAT IS FELT ON REALIZING SORROW IS A THING ONE CAN NO LONGER TRULY FEEL.
"ONE ONE, OH ONE, OH OH, OH OH."
TO BE CONTINUED.
16

*Miracleman* #13, page 16 pencil studies, pencil on drawing paper by John Totleben.

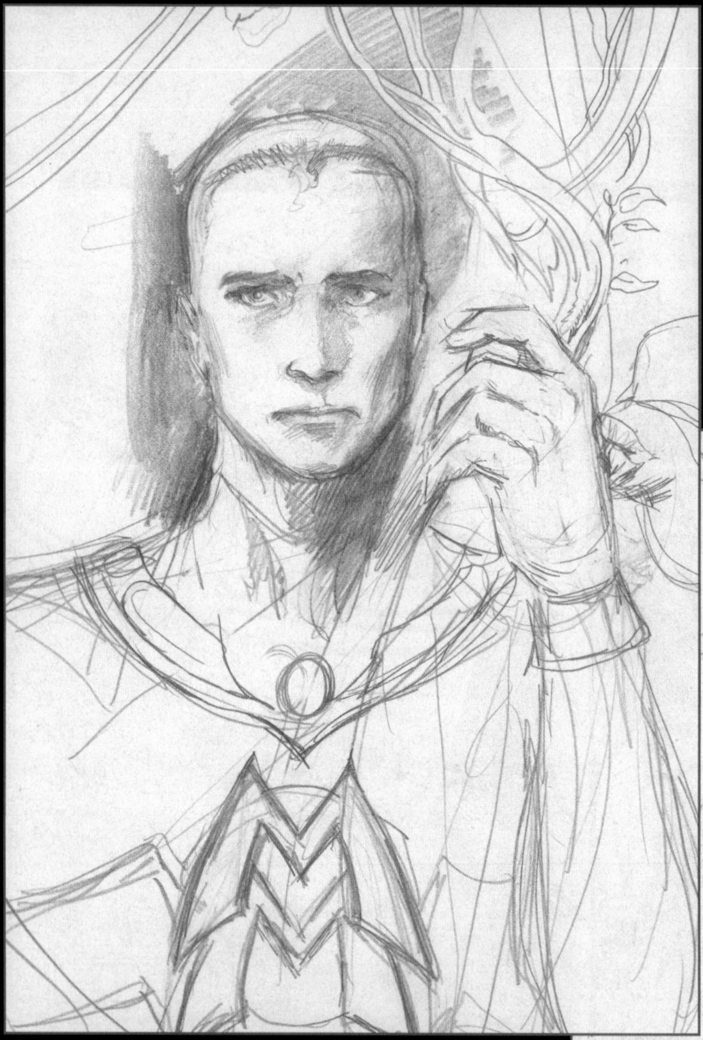

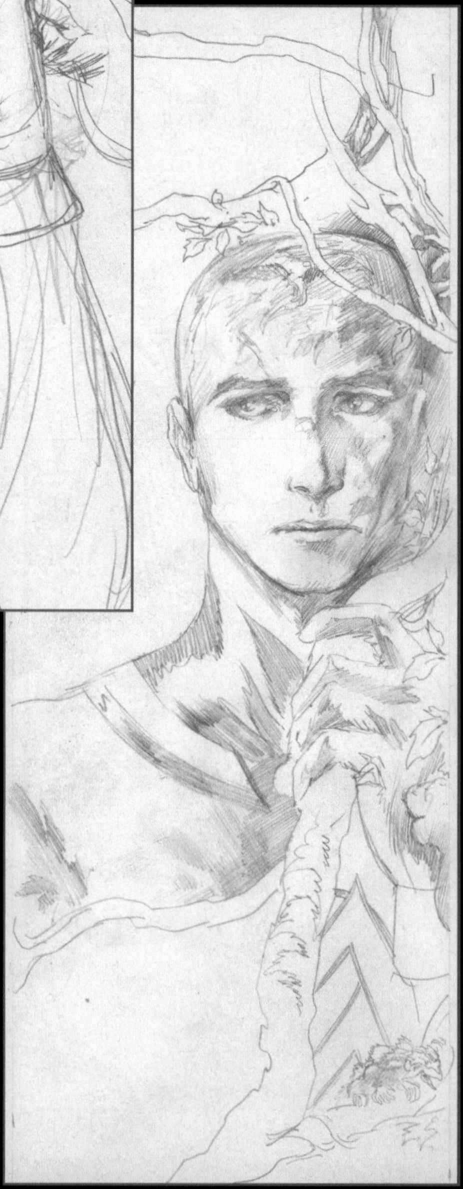

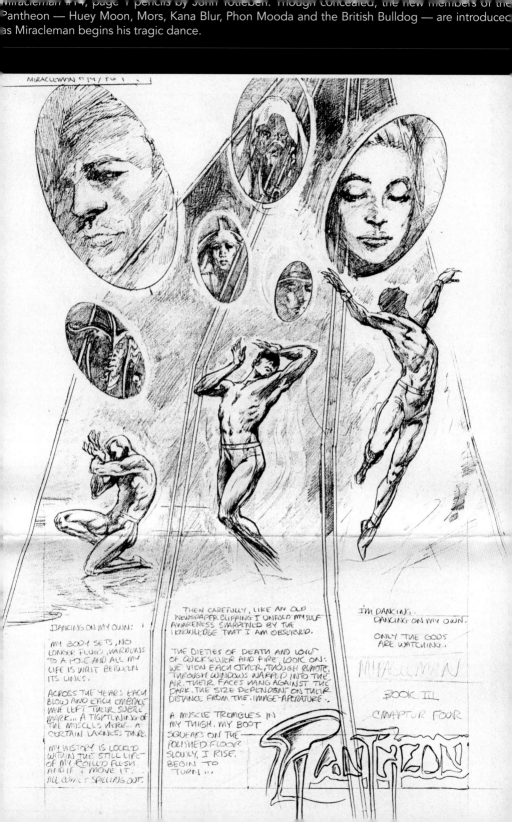

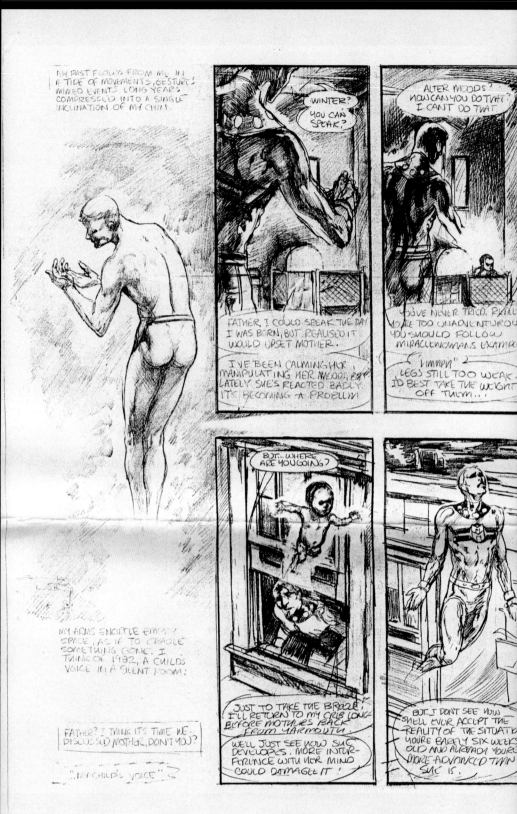

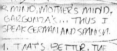

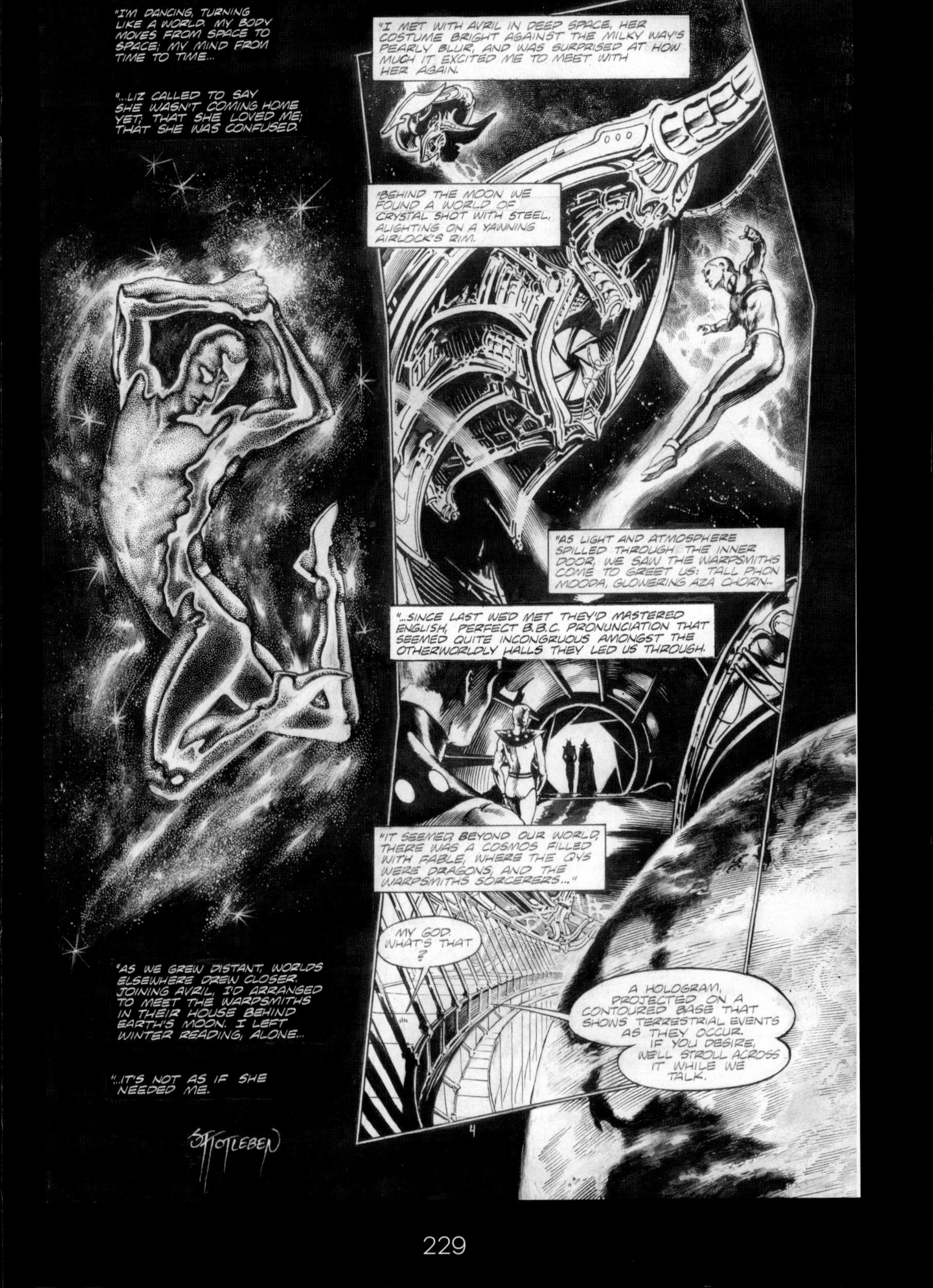
"I'M DANCING, TURNING LIKE A WORLD. MY BODY MOVES FROM SPACE TO SPACE; MY MIND FROM TIME TO TIME...
"...LIZ CALLED TO SAY SHE WASN'T COMING HOME YET; THAT SHE LOVED ME; THAT SHE WAS CONFUSED.
"AS WE GREW DISTANT, WORLDS ELSEWHERE DREW CLOSER. JOINING AVRIL, I'D ARRANGED TO MEET THE WARPSMITHS IN THEIR HOUSE BEHIND EARTH'S MOON. I LEFT WINTER READING, ALONE...
"...IT'S NOT AS IF SHE NEEDED ME.
"I MET WITH AVRIL IN DEEP SPACE, HER COSTUME BRIGHT AGAINST THE MILKY WAY'S PEARLY BLUR, AND WAS SURPRISED AT HOW MUCH IT EXCITED ME TO MEET WITH HER AGAIN.
"BEHIND THE MOON WE FOUND A WORLD OF CRYSTAL SHOT WITH STEEL, ALIGHTING ON A YAWNING AIRLOCK'S RIM.
"AS LIGHT AND ATMOSPHERE SPILLED THROUGH THE INNER DOOR, WE SAW THE WARPSMITHS COME TO GREET US: TALL PHON MOODA, GLOWERING AZA CHORN...
"...SINCE LAST WE'D MET THEY'D MASTERED ENGLISH, PERFECT B.B.C. PRONUNCIATION THAT SEEMED QUITE INCONGRUOUS AMONGST THE OTHERWORLDLY HALLS THEY LED US THROUGH.
"IT SEEMED, BEYOND OUR WORLD, THERE WAS A COSMOS FILLED WITH FABLE, WHERE THE QYS WERE DRAGONS, AND THE WARPSMITHS SORCERERS..."
MY GOD. WHAT'S THAT?
A HOLOGRAM, PROJECTED ON A CONTOURED BASE THAT SHOWS TERRESTRIAL EVENTS AS THEY OCCUR. IF YOU DESIRE, WE'LL STROLL ACROSS IT WHILE WE TALK.

*Miracleman* #14, page 5 pencils by John Totleben. The Pantheon stand as giant figures astride the
the world; their towering forms and whimsical demeanor channel McCay's *Little Nemo*.

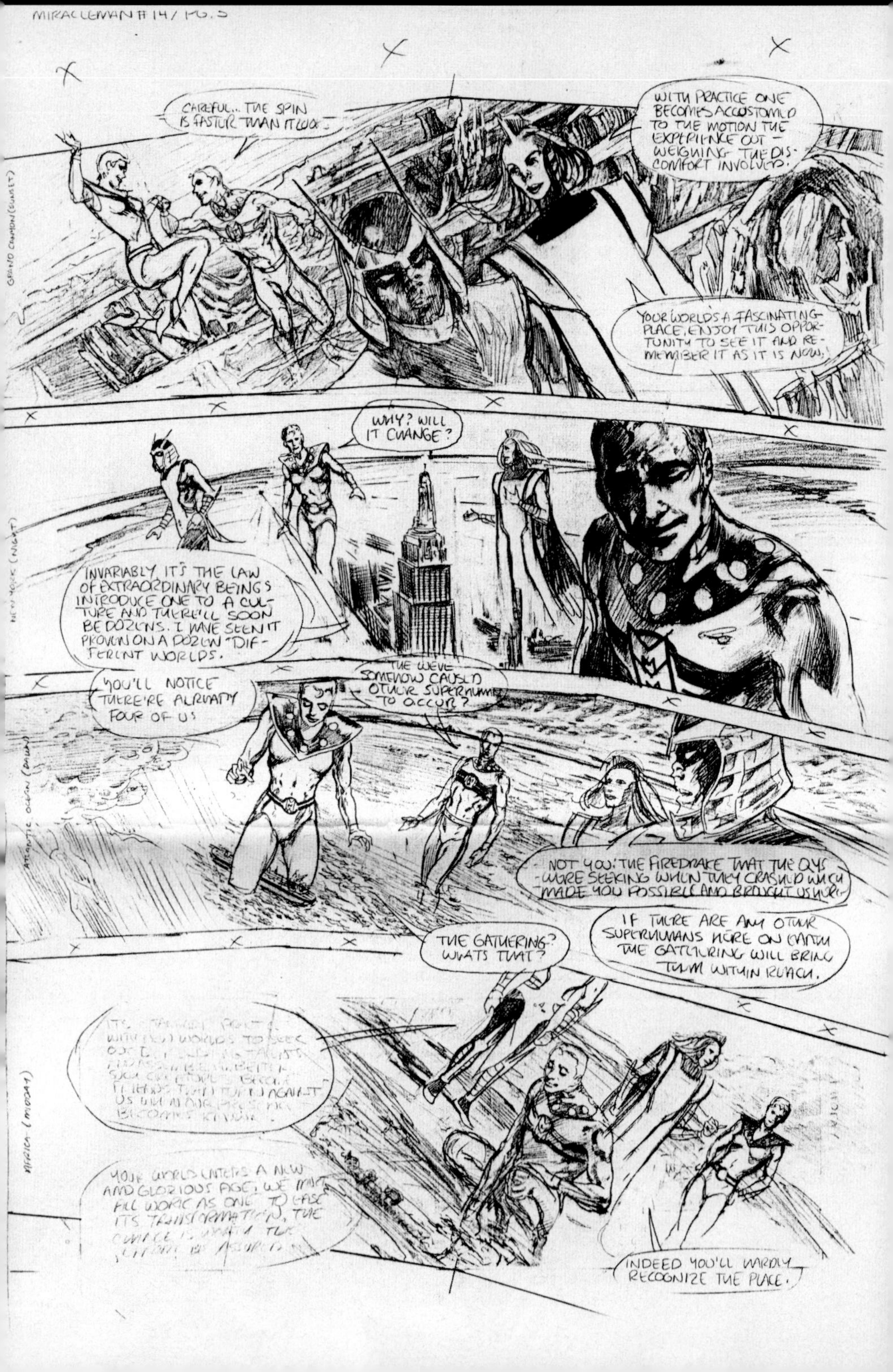

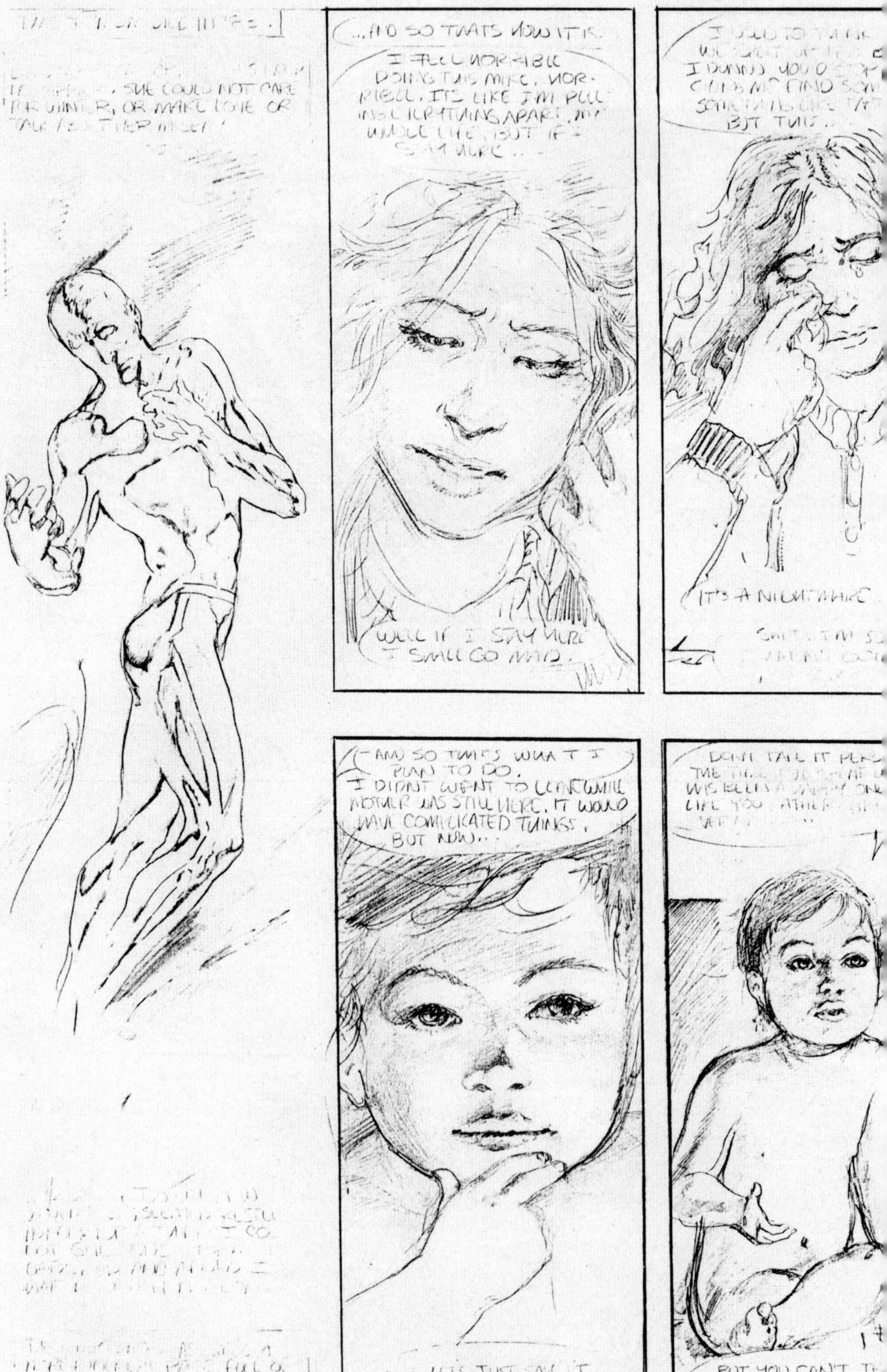

...AND SO THATS HOW IT IS.
WELL IF I STAY HERE I SHALL GO MAD.
IT'S A NIGHTMARE
I DIDN'T WANT TO LEAVE WHILE MOTHER WAS STILL HERE. IT WOULD HAVE COMPLICATED THINGS. BUT NOW...
BUT YOU CAN'T

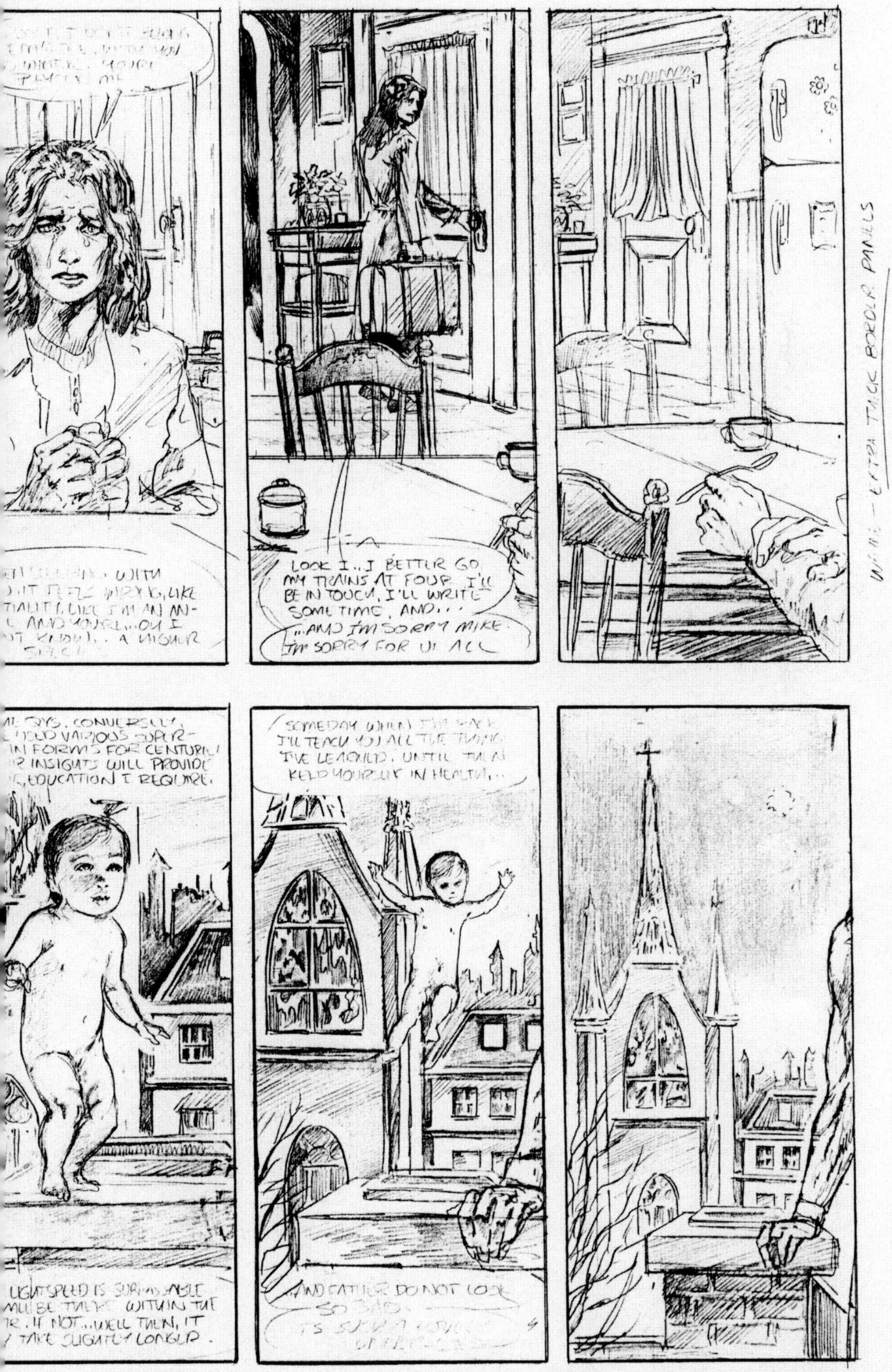

LOOK I.. I BETTER GO. MY TRAIN'S AT FOUR. I'LL BE IN TOUCH, I'LL WRITE SOME TIME, AND...
...AND I'M SORRY MIKE. I'M SORRY FOR US ALL
INSIGHTS WILL PROVIDE EDUCATION I REQUIRE.
SOMEDAY WHEN I'M BACK I'LL TEACH YOU ALL THE THINGS I'VE LEARNED. UNTIL THEN KEEP YOURSELF IN HEALTH...
LIGHTSPEED IS SURPASSABLE WILL BE THERE WITHIN THE IF NOT... WELL THEN, IT TAKE SLIGHTLY LONGER.
...AND FATHER DO NOT LOOK SO SAD.
WHITE — EXTRA THICK BORDER PANELS

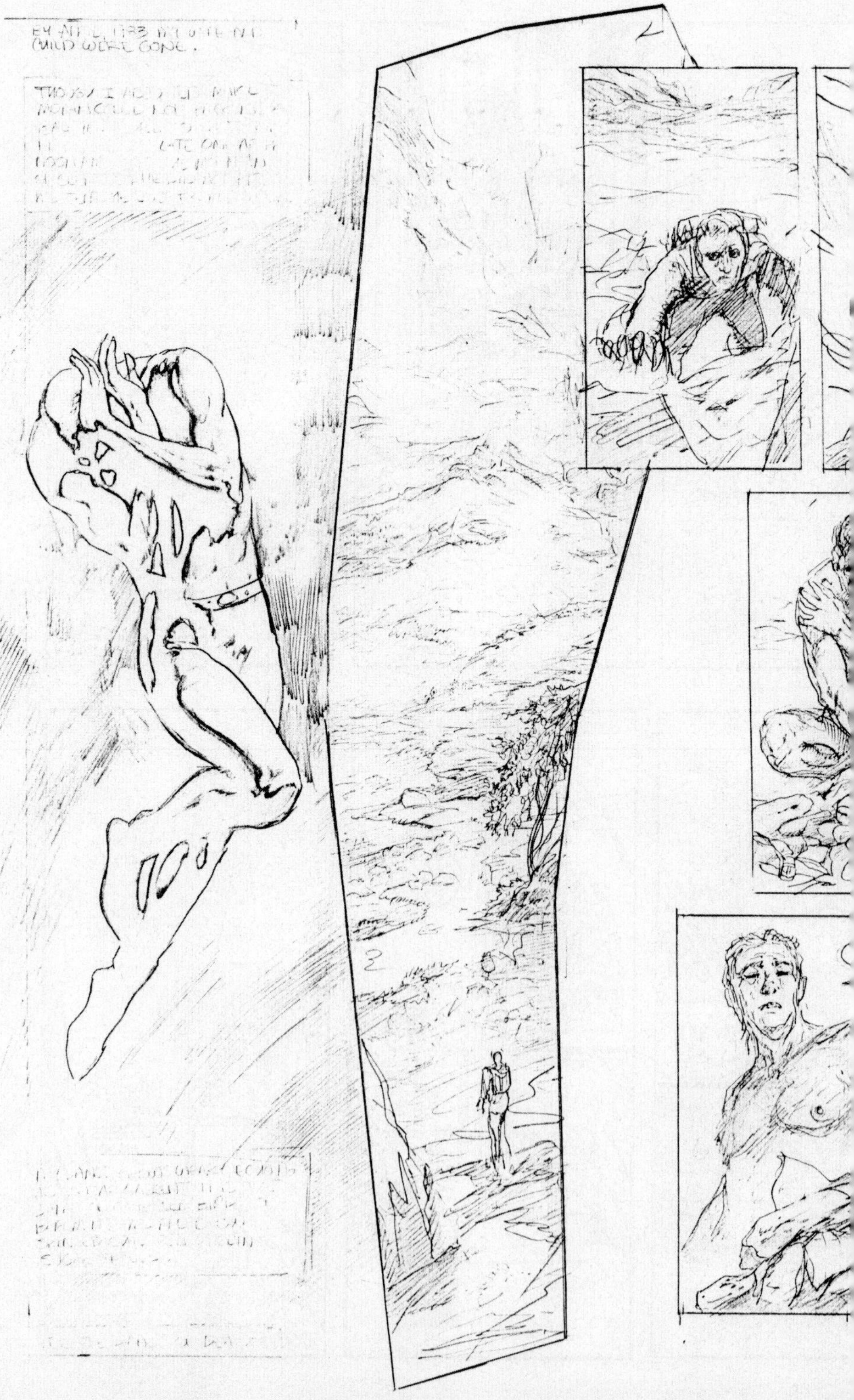
CHILD WERE GONE.

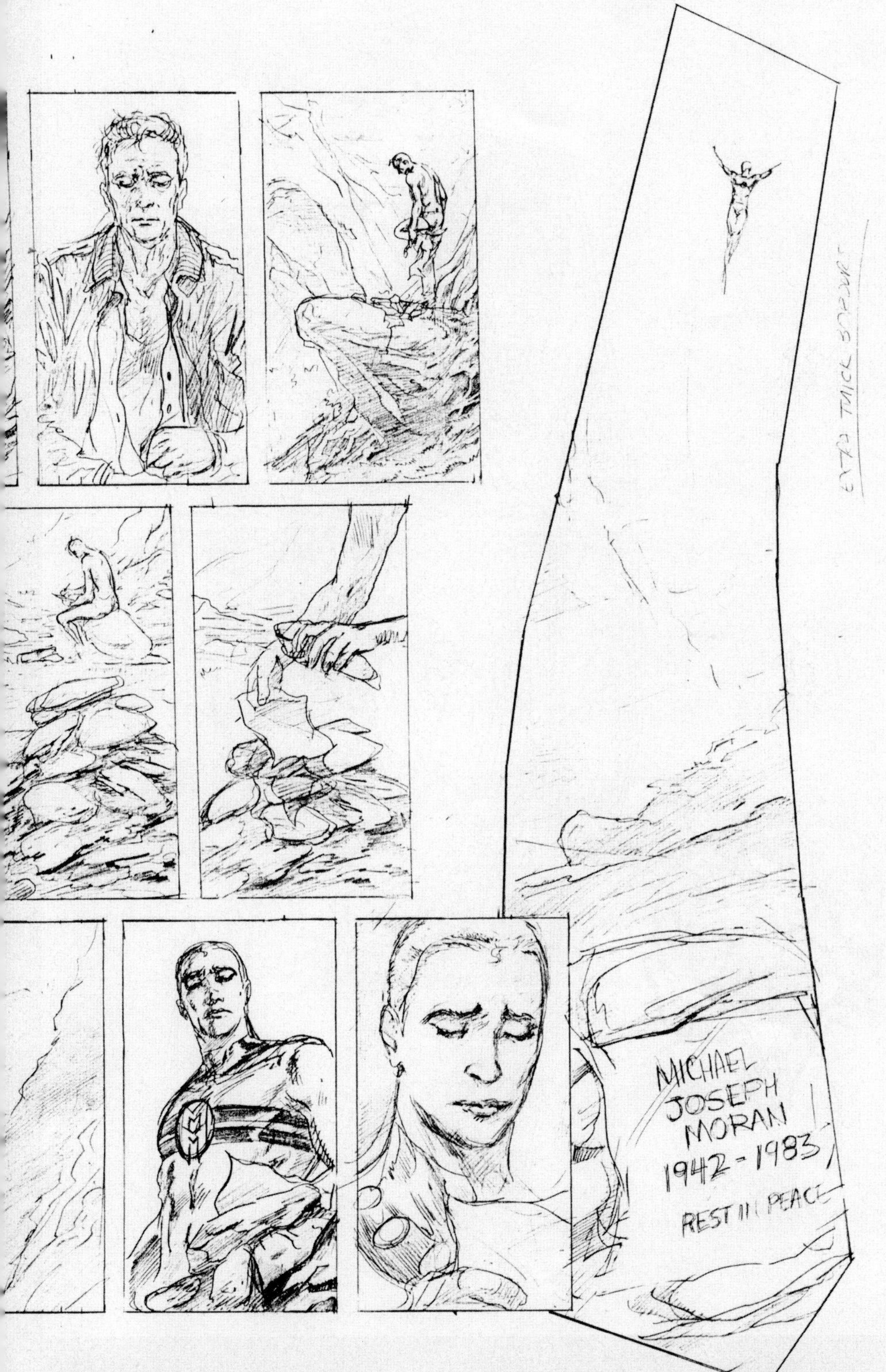
EXTRA THICK BORDER
MICHAEL
JOSEPH
MORAN
1942 - 1983
REST IN PEACE

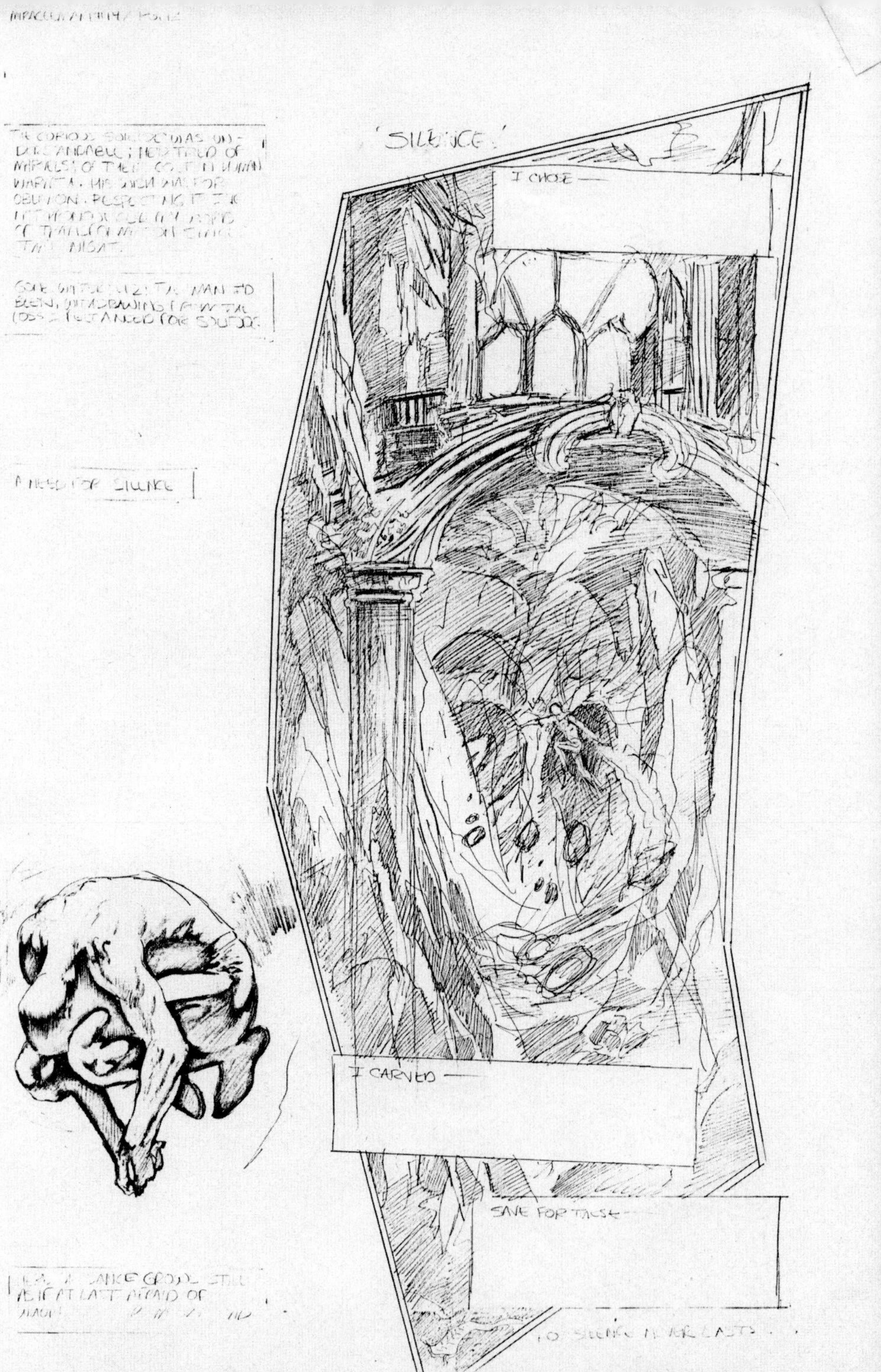
'SILENCE!'
I CHOSE —
A NEED FOR SILENCE
I CARVED —
SAVE FOR THOSE —
SILENCE NEVER LASTS.

*Miracleman* #14, page 12 original artwork, pencil, India ink and white acrylic on illustration board by John Totleben.

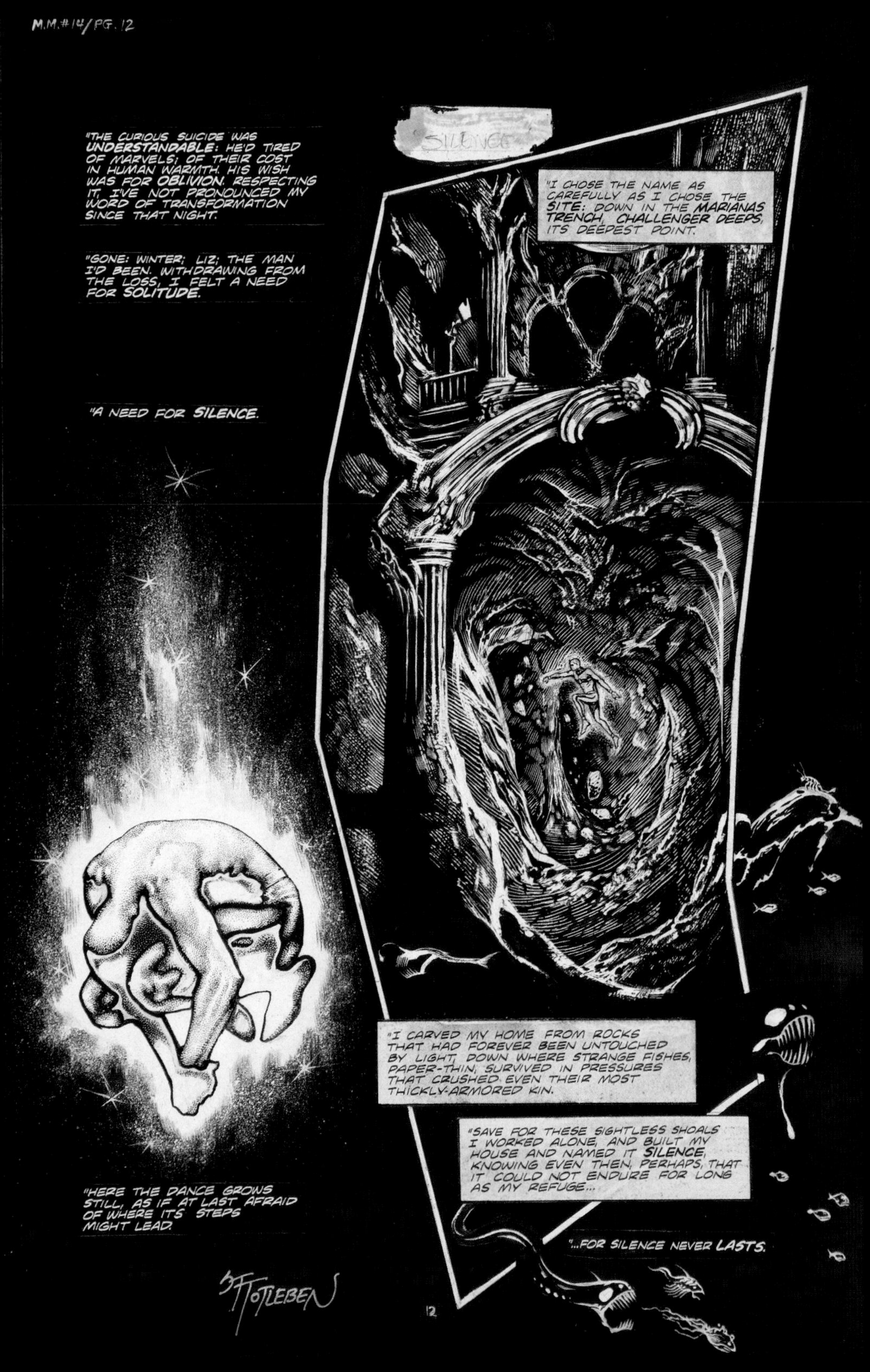
M.M.#14/PG.12
"THE CURIOUS SUICIDE WAS UNDERSTANDABLE: HE'D TIRED OF MARVELS; OF THEIR COST IN HUMAN WARMTH. HIS WISH WAS FOR OBLIVION. RESPECTING IT, I'VE NOT PRONOUNCED MY WORD OF TRANSFORMATION SINCE THAT NIGHT.
"GONE: WINTER; LIZ; THE MAN I'D BEEN. WITHDRAWING FROM THE LOSS, I FELT A NEED FOR SOLITUDE.
"A NEED FOR SILENCE.
"HERE THE DANCE GROWS STILL, AS IF AT LAST AFRAID OF WHERE ITS STEPS MIGHT LEAD.
"I CHOSE THE NAME AS CAREFULLY AS I CHOSE THE SITE: DOWN IN THE MARIANAS TRENCH, CHALLENGER DEEPS, ITS DEEPEST POINT.
"I CARVED MY HOME FROM ROCKS THAT HAD FOREVER BEEN UNTOUCHED BY LIGHT, DOWN WHERE STRANGE FISHES, PAPER-THIN, SURVIVED IN PRESSURES THAT CRUSHED EVEN THEIR MOST THICKLY-ARMORED KIN.
"SAVE FOR THESE SIGHTLESS SHOALS I WORKED ALONE, AND BUILT MY HOUSE AND NAMED IT SILENCE, KNOWING EVEN THEN, PERHAPS, THAT IT COULD NOT ENDURE FOR LONG AS MY REFUGE...
"...FOR SILENCE NEVER LASTS.
J.TOTLEBEN
12

Miracleman #14, page 13 pencils by John Totleben. Miracleman explodes into motion. The agony of what follows is written across his face as he raises his arms and looks up, searching for answers.

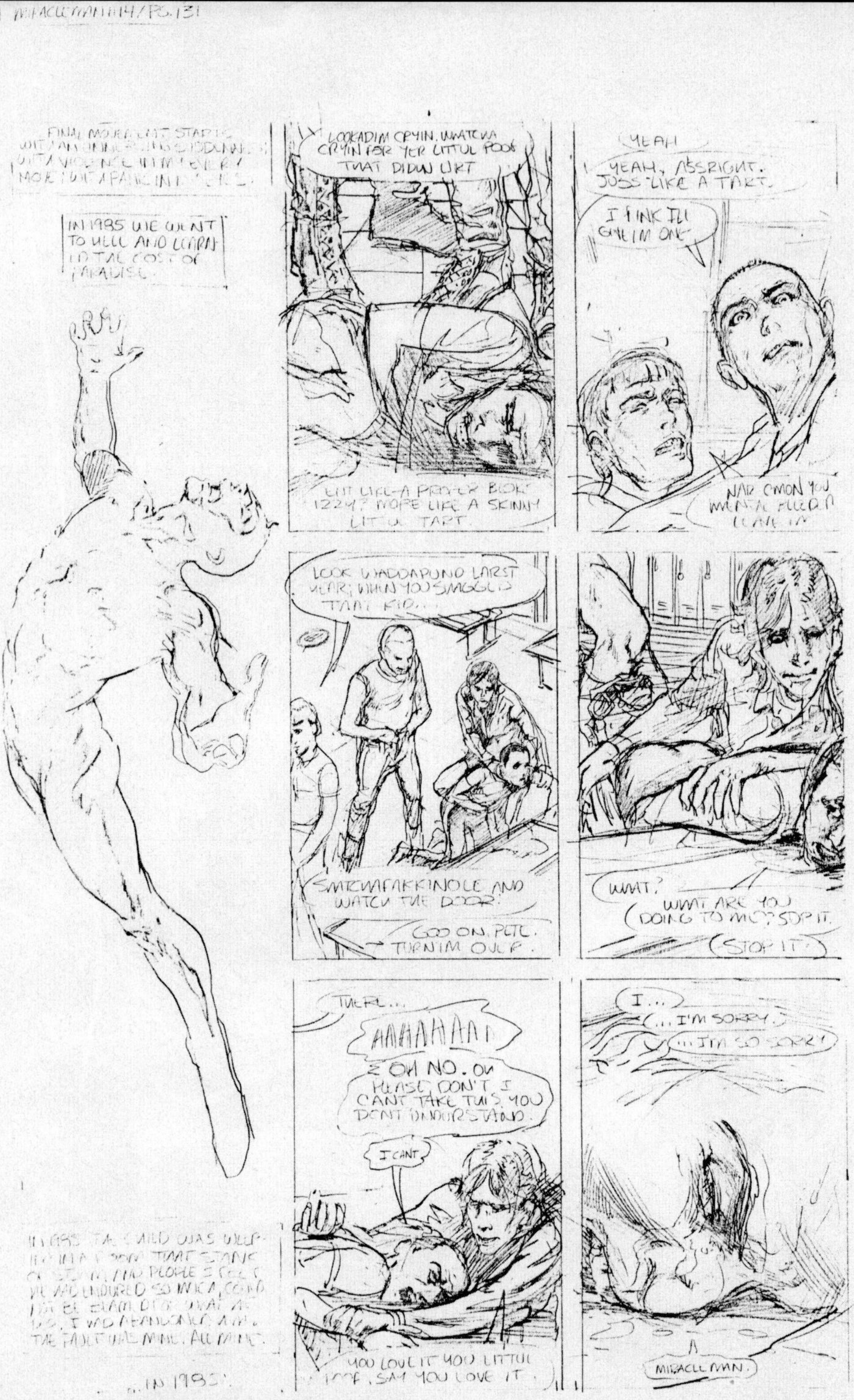
LOOKADIM CRYIN. WHATCHA CRYIN FOR YER LITTUL POOF THAT DIDN URT
YEAH
YEAH, ASSRIGHT. JUSS LIKE A TART.
I FINK I'LL GIVE IM ONE
LOOK WADDAPUND LARST YEAR, WHEN YOU SMAGGED THAT KID...
GOO ON, PETE. TURNIM OVER.
WHAT?
WHAT ARE YOU DOING TO ME? STOP IT.
STOP IT.
THERE...
AAAAAAAA
OH NO. OH PLEASE DON'T. I CAN'T TAKE THIS. YOU DON'T UNDERSTAND.
I CAN'T
YOU LOVE IT YOU LITTUL POOF. SAY YOU LOVE IT.
I...
...I'M SORRY.
...I'M SO SORRY.
MIRACLEMAN.
...IN 1985.

Miracleman #14, page 14 pencils by John Totleben. After three years trapped by Johnny Bates, Kid Miracleman returns in a blinding flash. An open, white panel captures the reader's shock and the limitless horrors to be imagined.

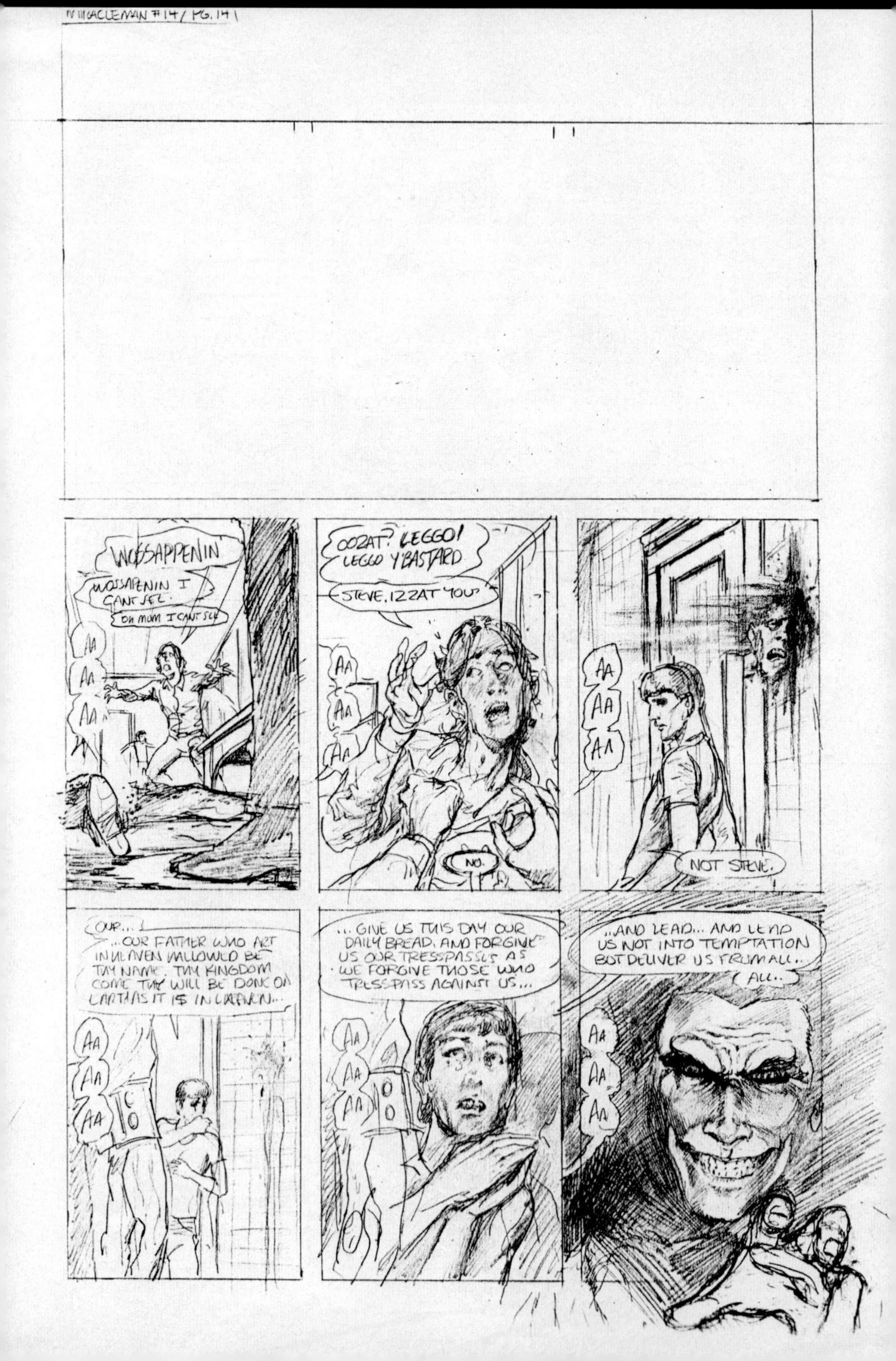

MIRACLEMAN #14/ PG. 14
WOSSAPPENIN'
WOSSAPENIN I CANT SEE.
OH MUM I CANT SEE
AA AA AA
OOZAT? LEGGO! LEGGO Y'BASTARD
STEVE, IZZAT YOU?
AA AA AA
NO.
AA AA AA
NOT STEVE.
OUR...
...OUR FATHER WHO ART IN HEAVEN HALLOWED BE THY NAME. THY KINGDOM COME THY WILL BE DONE ON EARTH AS IT IS IN HEAVEN...
AA AA AA
...GIVE US THIS DAY OUR DAILY BREAD, AND FORGIVE US OUR TRESSPASSES AS WE FORGIVE THOSE WHO TRESSPASS AGAINST US...
AA AA AA
...AND LEAD... AND LEAD US NOT INTO TEMPTATION BUT DELIVER US FROM ALL...
ALL..
AA AA AA

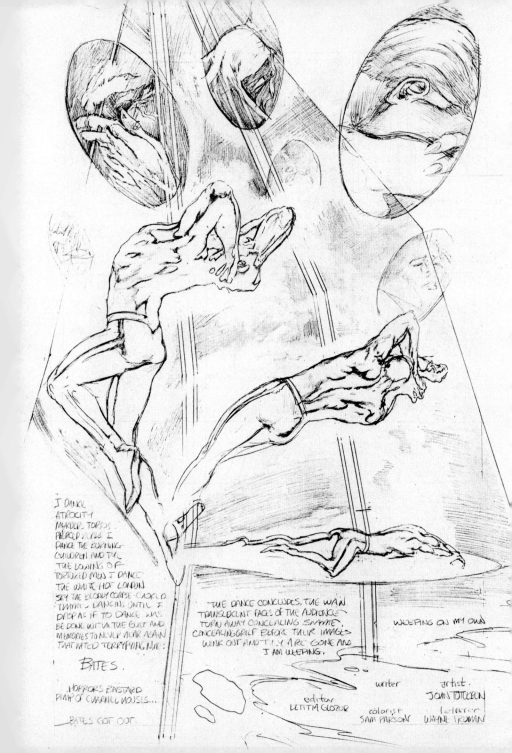

I DANCE
ATROCITY
MURDER, TORSOS
PIERCED, KNIVES I
DANCE THE BURNING
CHILDREN AND THE
THE LOWING OF
TORTURED MEN. I DANCE
THE WHITE HOT LONDON
SKY THE BLOODY CORPSE-COLD
TWINING, DANCING UNTIL I
DROP AS IF TO DANCE WAS
TO BE DONE WITH THE GUILT AND
MEMORIES TO NEVER WEAR AGAIN
THAT HATED TERRIFYING NAME:

BATES.

...HORRORS BASTARD
PIMP OF CHARNEL HOUSES...

...BATES GOT OUT.

THE DANCE CONCLUDES, THE WAN
TRANSLUCENT FACES OF THE AUDIENCE
TURN AWAY CONCEALING SHAME,
CONCEALING GRIEF BEFORE THEIR IMAGES
WINK OUT AND THEY ARE GONE AND
I AM WEEPING.

WEEPING ON MY OWN

writer
JOHN TOTLEBEN

artist
JOHN TOTLEBEN

editor
LETITIA GLOZER

colorist
SAM PARSON

letterer
WAYNE TRUMAN

Among all John Totleben's exceptional art on *Miracleman*, his work on the dance sequence in "Pantheon" is perhaps the most striking. Totleben did numerous figure studies (pencil and India ink on tracing paper) to capture Miracleman's dance. The results are beautiful expressions of figure and motion, anguish and regret — an intimate emotional prelude to the horror to come.

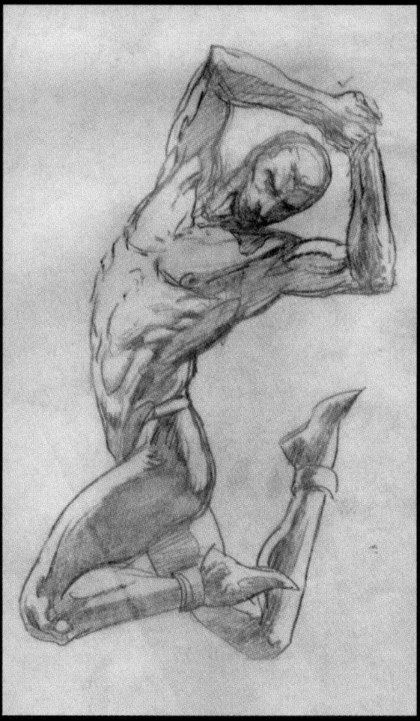
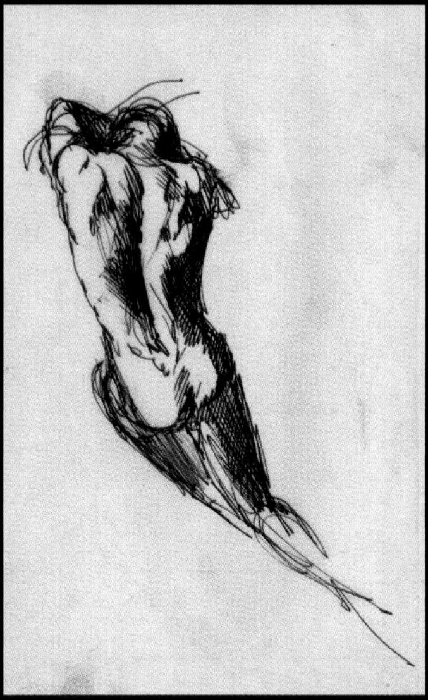
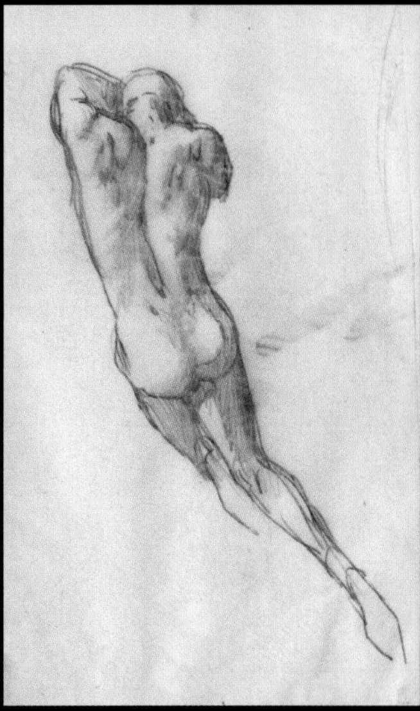
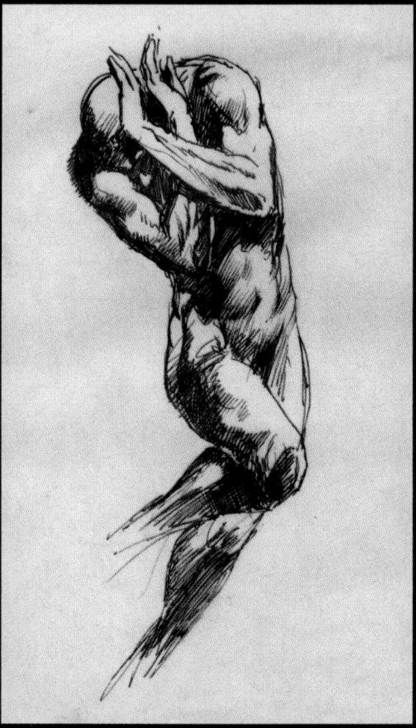
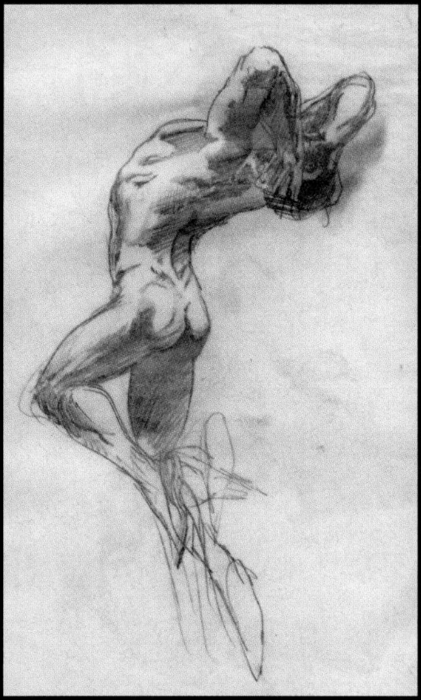
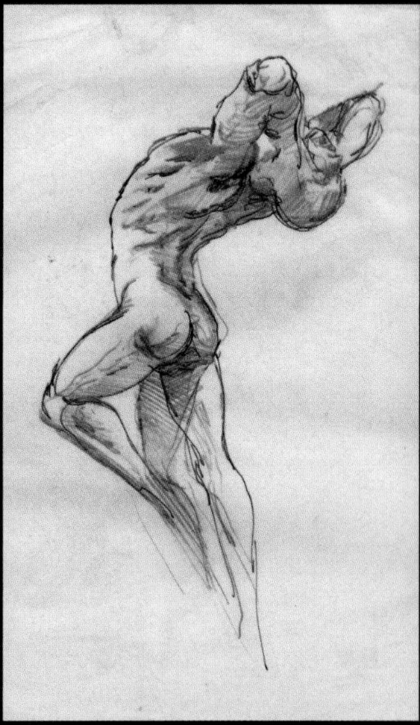
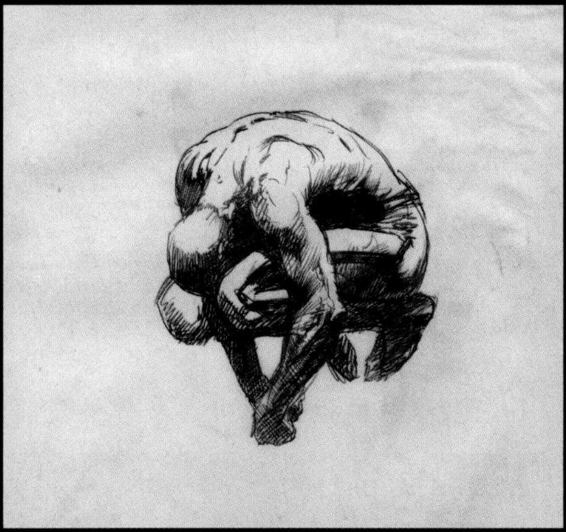

Miracleman #15, page 1 original artwork, pencil, India ink and white acrylic on illustration board by John Totleben. (*N.B. Pencil art photocopies have not survived for issue #15's story pages.*)

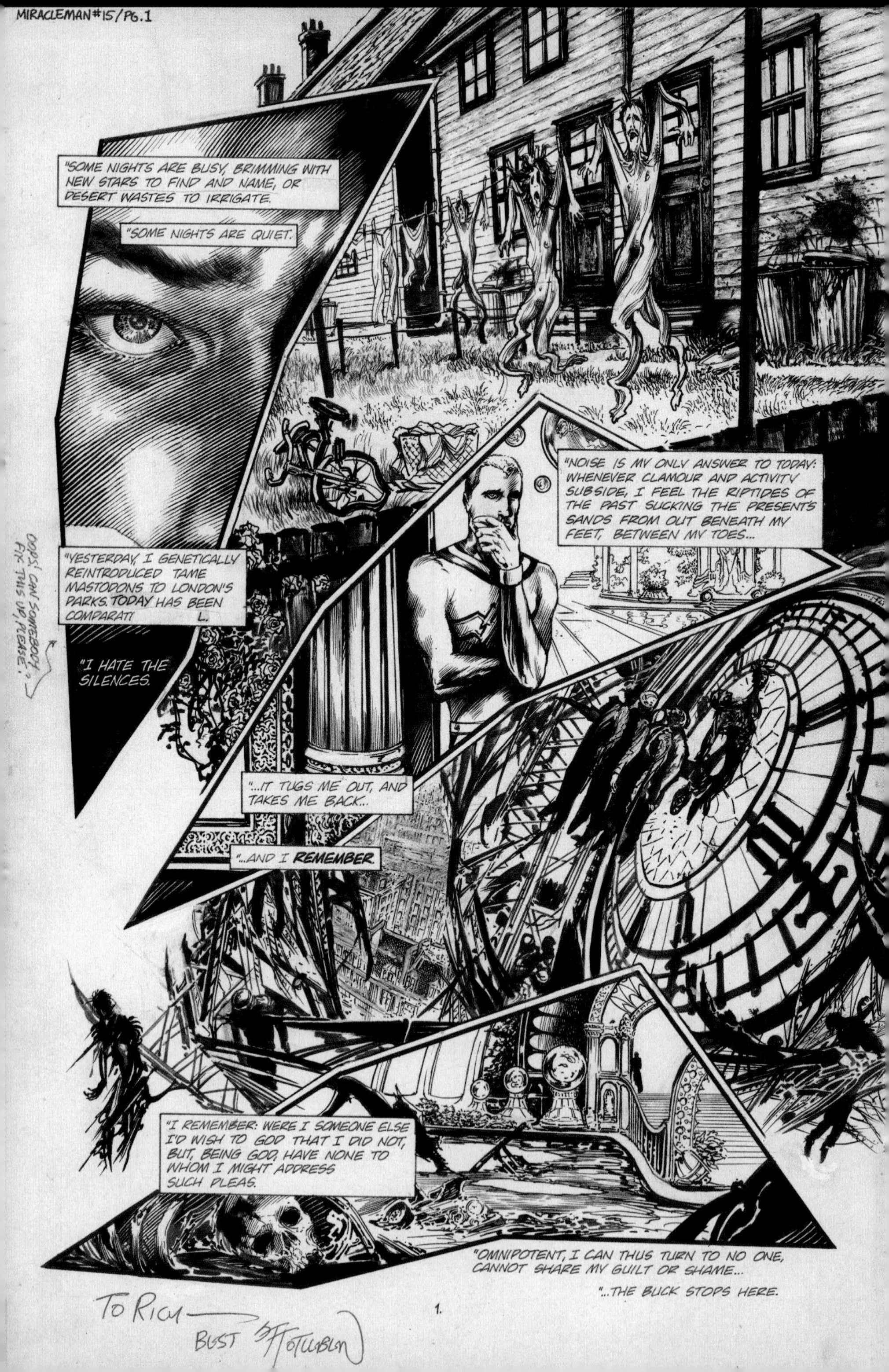

MIRACLEMAN #15/PG. 1
"SOME NIGHTS ARE BUSY, BRIMMING WITH NEW STARS TO FIND AND NAME, OR DESERT WASTES TO IRRIGATE.
"SOME NIGHTS ARE QUIET.
"YESTERDAY, I GENETICALLY REINTRODUCED TAME MASTODONS TO LONDON'S PARKS. TODAY HAS BEEN COMPARATI L.
OOPS! CAN SOMEBODY FIX THIS UP, PLEASE?
"I HATE THE SILENCES.
"NOISE IS MY ONLY ANSWER TO TODAY: WHENEVER CLAMOUR AND ACTIVITY SUBSIDE, I FEEL THE RIPTIDES OF THE PAST SUCKING THE PRESENT'S SANDS FROM OUT BENEATH MY FEET, BETWEEN MY TOES...
"...IT TUGS ME OUT, AND TAKES ME BACK...
"...AND I REMEMBER.
"I REMEMBER: WERE I SOMEONE ELSE I'D WISH TO GOD THAT I DID NOT, BUT, BEING GOD, HAVE NONE TO WHOM I MIGHT ADDRESS SUCH PLEAS.
"OMNIPOTENT, I CAN THUS TURN TO NO ONE, CANNOT SHARE MY GUILT OR SHAME...
"...THE BUCK STOPS HERE.
1.
TO RICH — BEST

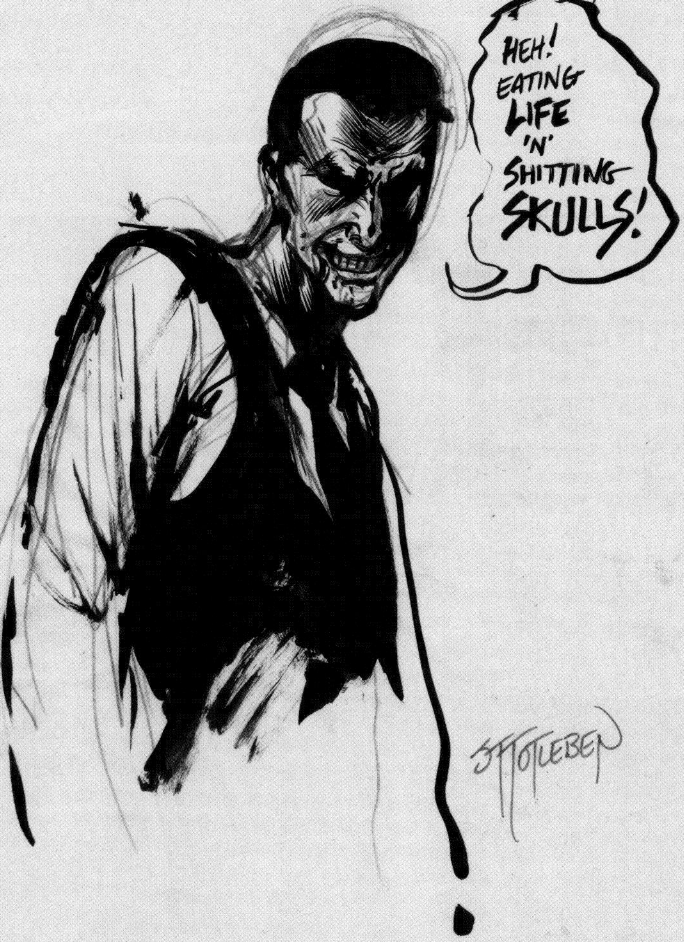
HEH! EATING LIFE 'N' SHITTING SKULLS!
STTOTLEBEN

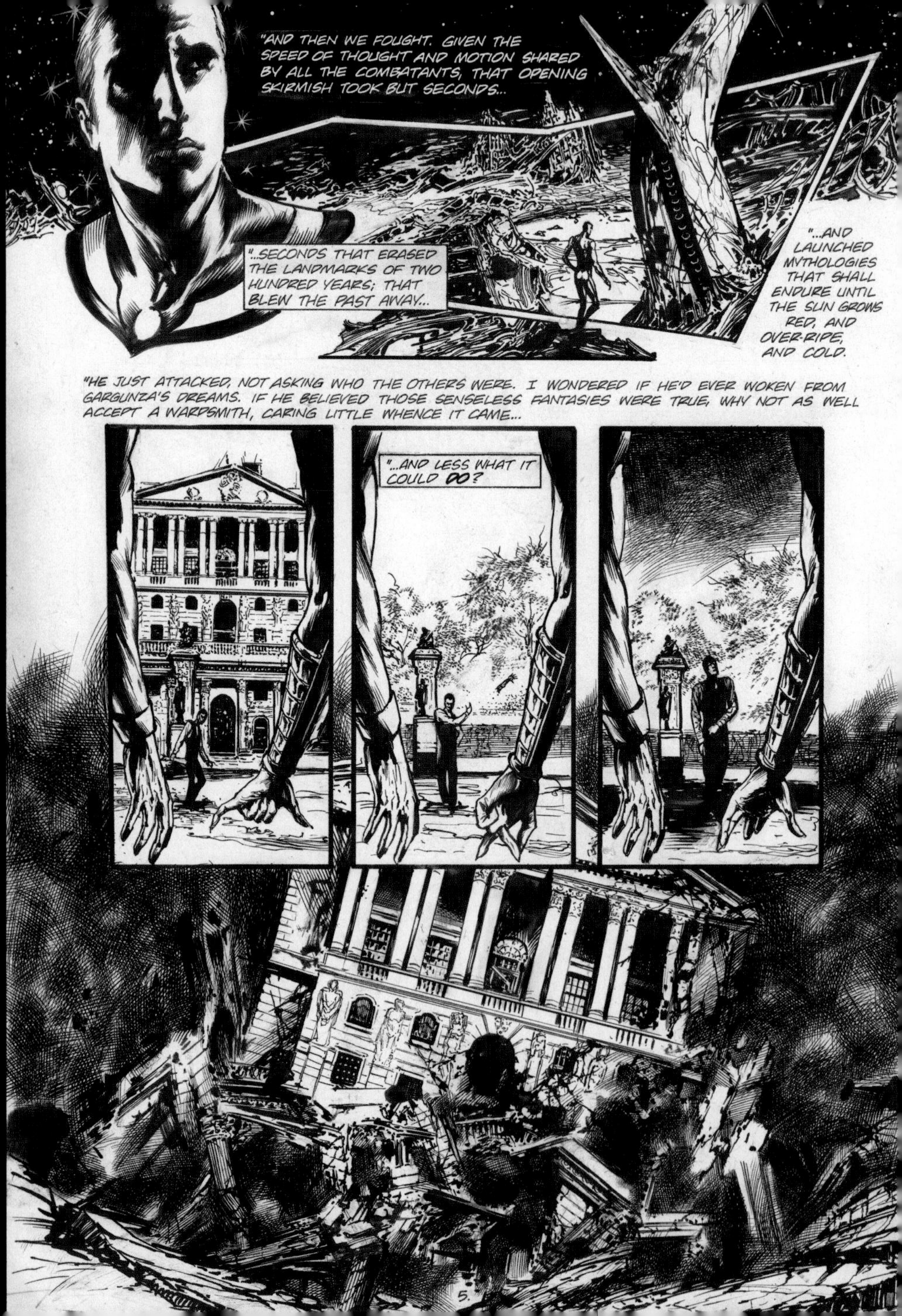

"AND THEN WE FOUGHT. GIVEN THE SPEED OF THOUGHT AND MOTION SHARED BY ALL THE COMBATANTS, THAT OPENING SKIRMISH TOOK BUT SECONDS...
"...SECONDS THAT ERASED THE LANDMARKS OF TWO HUNDRED YEARS; THAT BLEW THE PAST AWAY...
"...AND LAUNCHED MYTHOLOGIES THAT SHALL ENDURE UNTIL THE SUN GROWS RED, AND OVER-RIPE, AND COLD.
"HE JUST ATTACKED, NOT ASKING WHO THE OTHERS WERE. I WONDERED IF HE'D EVER WOKEN FROM GARGUNZA'S DREAMS. IF HE BELIEVED THOSE SENSELESS FANTASIES WERE TRUE, WHY NOT AS WELL ACCEPT A WARDSMITH, CARING LITTLE WHENCE IT CAME...
"...AND LESS WHAT IT COULD DO?

*Miracleman* #15, page 10 original artwork, pencil, India ink and white acrylic on illustration board by John Totleben. This page both recaps and mythologizes the Book One story "The Yesterday Gambit."

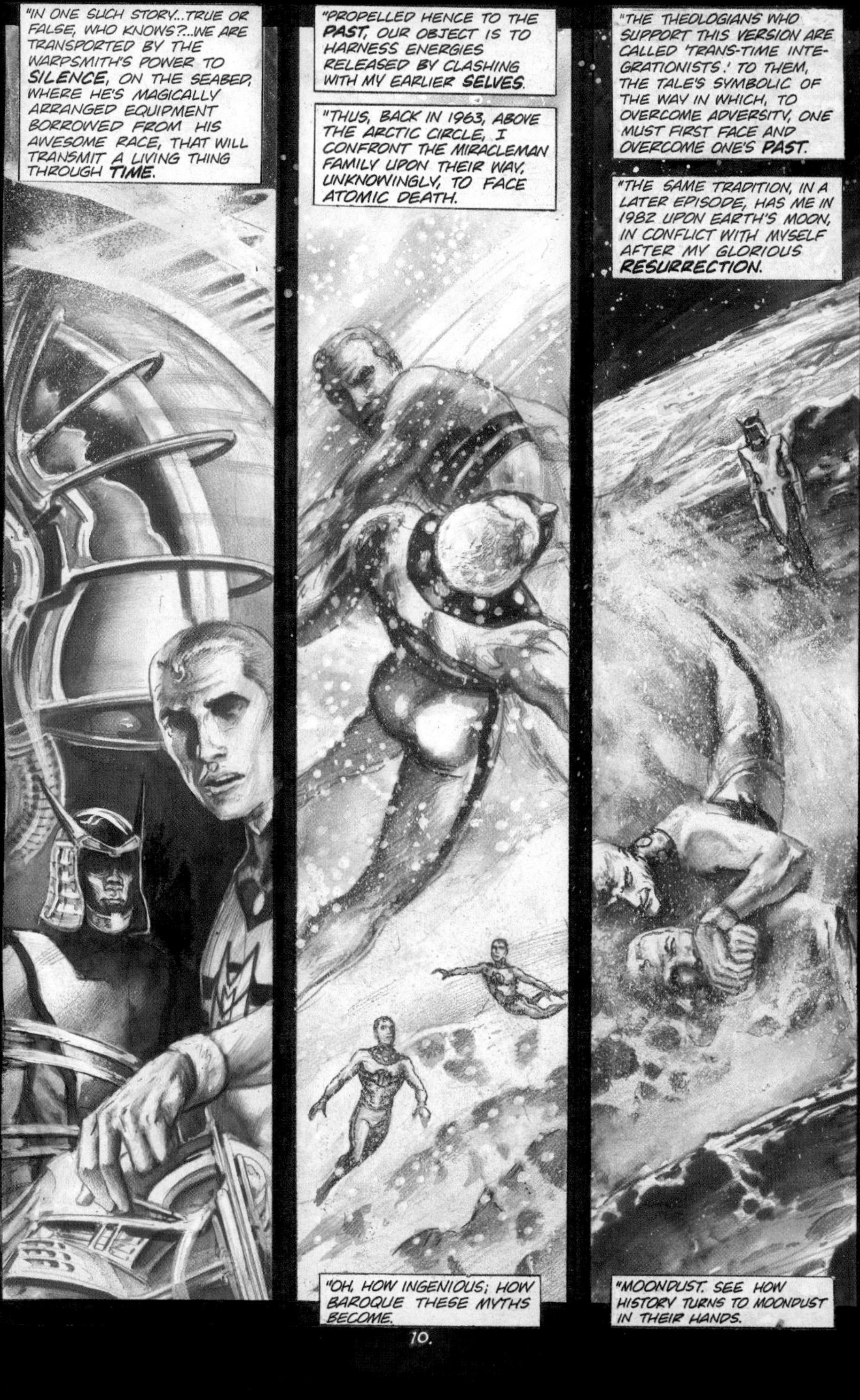

"IN ONE SUCH STORY...TRUE OR FALSE, WHO KNOWS?...WE ARE TRANSPORTED BY THE WARPSMITH'S POWER TO SILENCE, ON THE SEABED, WHERE HE'S MAGICALLY ARRANGED EQUIPMENT BORROWED FROM HIS AWESOME RACE, THAT WILL TRANSMIT A LIVING THING THROUGH TIME.
"PROPELLED HENCE TO THE PAST, OUR OBJECT IS TO HARNESS ENERGIES RELEASED BY CLASHING WITH MY EARLIER SELVES.
"THUS, BACK IN 1963, ABOVE THE ARCTIC CIRCLE, I CONFRONT THE MIRACLEMAN FAMILY UPON THEIR WAY, UNKNOWINGLY, TO FACE ATOMIC DEATH.
"OH, HOW INGENIOUS; HOW BAROQUE THESE MYTHS BECOME.
"THE THEOLOGIANS WHO SUPPORT THIS VERSION ARE CALLED 'TRANS-TIME INTEGRATIONISTS.' TO THEM, THE TALE'S SYMBOLIC OF THE WAY IN WHICH, TO OVERCOME ADVERSITY, ONE MUST FIRST FACE AND OVERCOME ONE'S PAST.
"THE SAME TRADITION, IN A LATER EPISODE, HAS ME IN 1982 UPON EARTH'S MOON, IN CONFLICT WITH MYSELF AFTER MY GLORIOUS RESURRECTION.
"MOONDUST. SEE HOW HISTORY TURNS TO MOONDUST IN THEIR HANDS.
10.

*Miracleman* #15, page 13 original artwork, pencil, India ink and white acrylic on illustration board by John Totleben. Kid Miracleman's nihilistic drive is unequivocally captured in the page's dialogue.

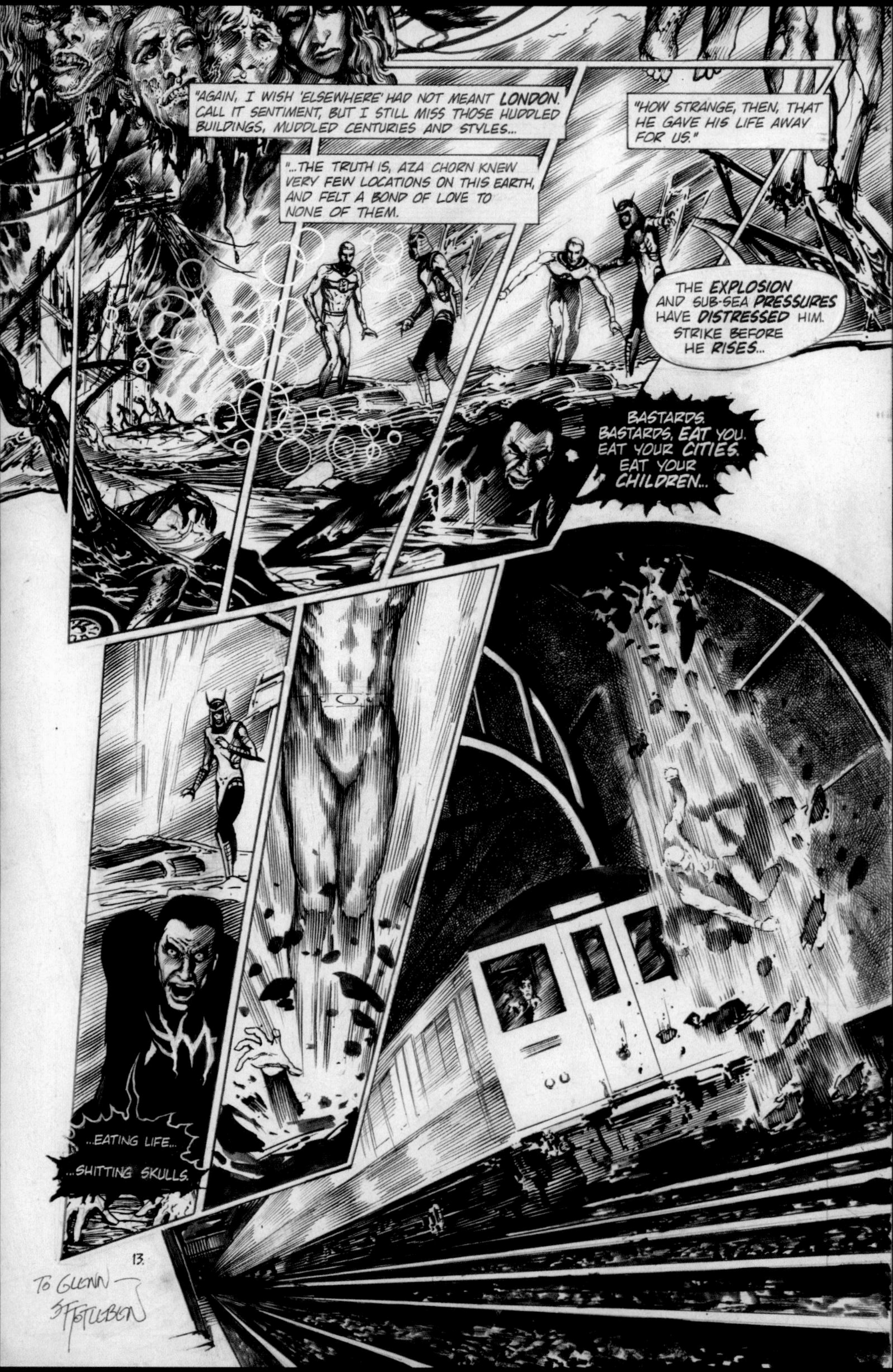
"AGAIN, I WISH 'ELSEWHERE' HAD NOT MEANT LONDON. CALL IT SENTIMENT, BUT I STILL MISS THOSE HUDDLED BUILDINGS, MUDDLED CENTURIES AND STYLES...
"...THE TRUTH IS, AZA CHORN KNEW VERY FEW LOCATIONS ON THIS EARTH, AND FELT A BOND OF LOVE TO NONE OF THEM.
"HOW STRANGE, THEN, THAT HE GAVE HIS LIFE AWAY FOR US."
THE EXPLOSION AND SUB-SEA PRESSURES HAVE DISTRESSED HIM. STRIKE BEFORE HE RISES...
BASTARDS. BASTARDS, EAT YOU. EAT YOUR CITIES. EAT YOUR CHILDREN...
...EATING LIFE...
...SHITTING SKULLS.
13.
TO GLENN

*Miracleman* #15, page 13, panel 6 and page 14, panels 3-4 studies, pencil and India ink on tracing paper by John Totleben.

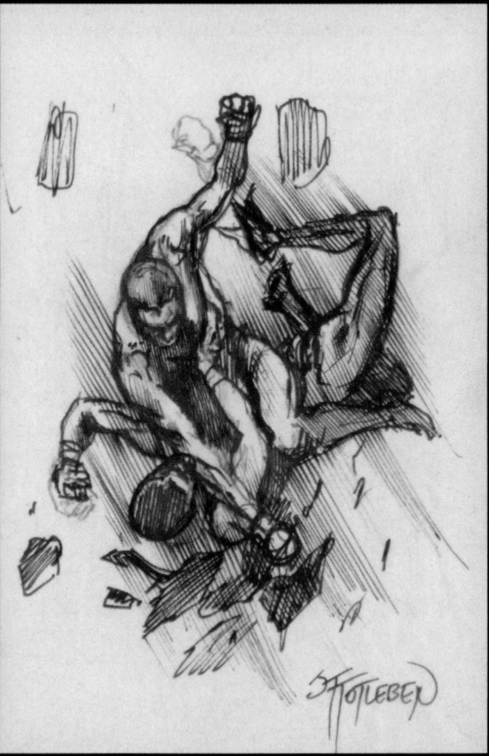

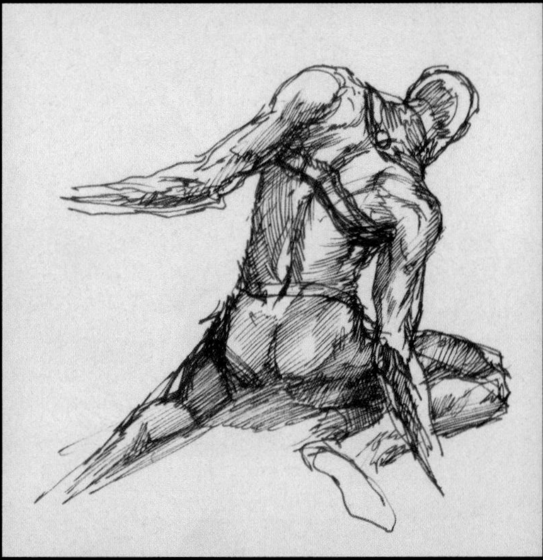

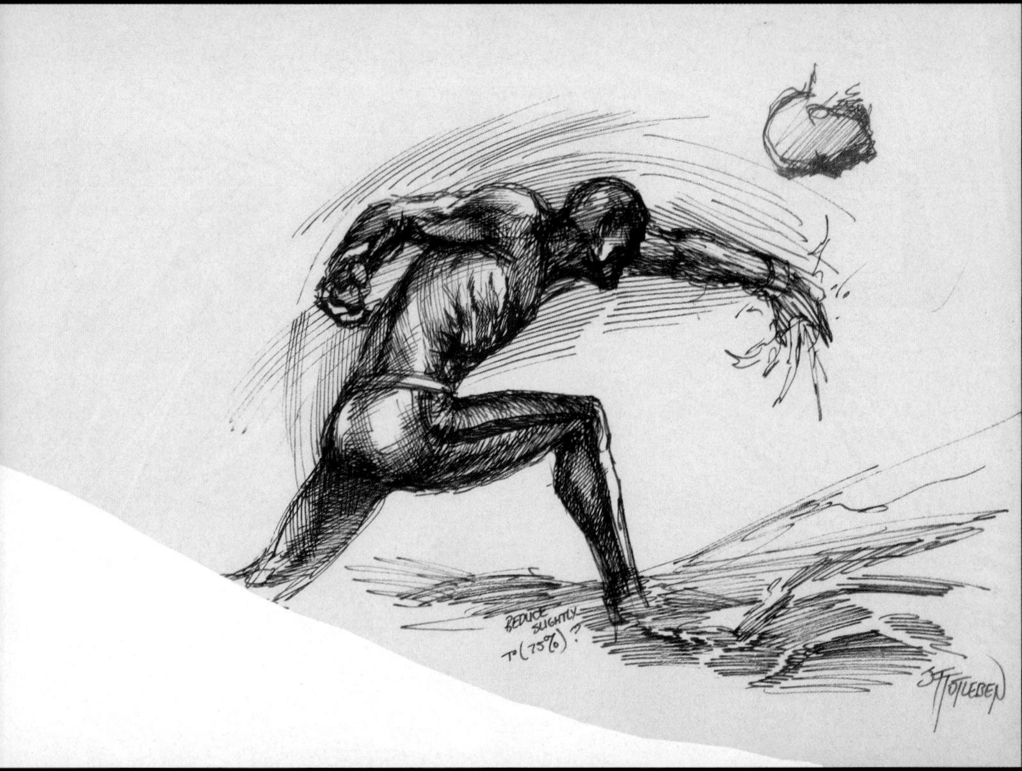
REDUCE SLIGHTLY TO (75%)?

*Miracleman* #15, page 14 original artwork, pencil, India ink and white acrylic on illustration board by John Totleben. The creators' goal for the story was not to be gruesome or extreme, but to depict the plausible damage inflicted by a battle of superhumans — to show the real horror of violence.

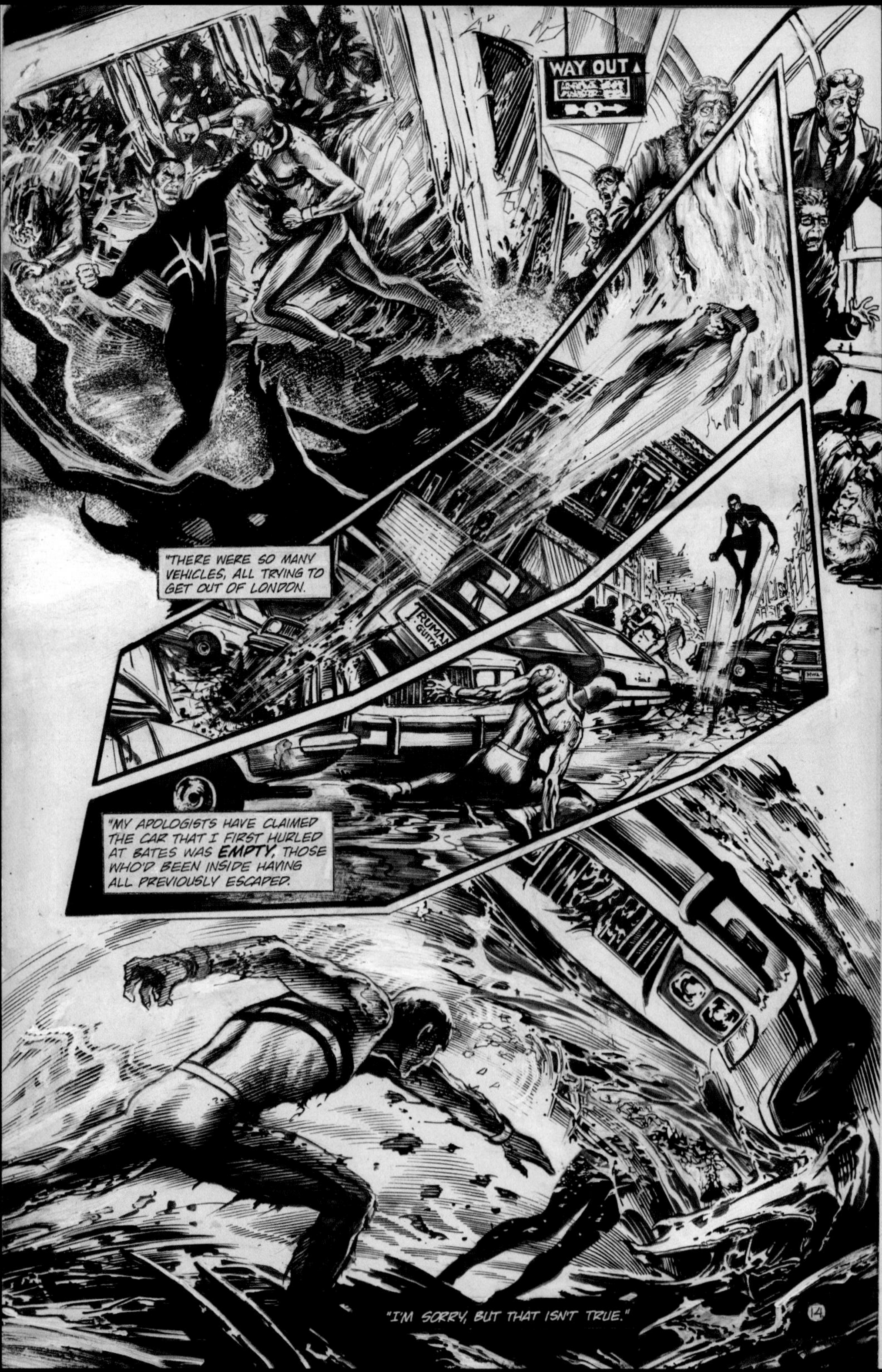
WAY OUT
"THERE WERE SO MANY VEHICLES, ALL TRYING TO GET OUT OF LONDON.
TRUMAN
"MY APOLOGISTS HAVE CLAIMED THE CAR THAT I FIRST HURLED AT BATES WAS **EMPTY**, THOSE WHO'D BEEN INSIDE HAVING ALL PREVIOUSLY ESCAPED.
"I'M SORRY, BUT THAT ISN'T TRUE."
14

*Miracleman* #15, page 15 original artwork, pencil, India ink and white acrylic on illustration board by John Totleben. Action in fantasy-adventure entertainment often has no meaningful impact — everything is back to normal in the end, which can be seen as a glorification. Here the results are awful and true.

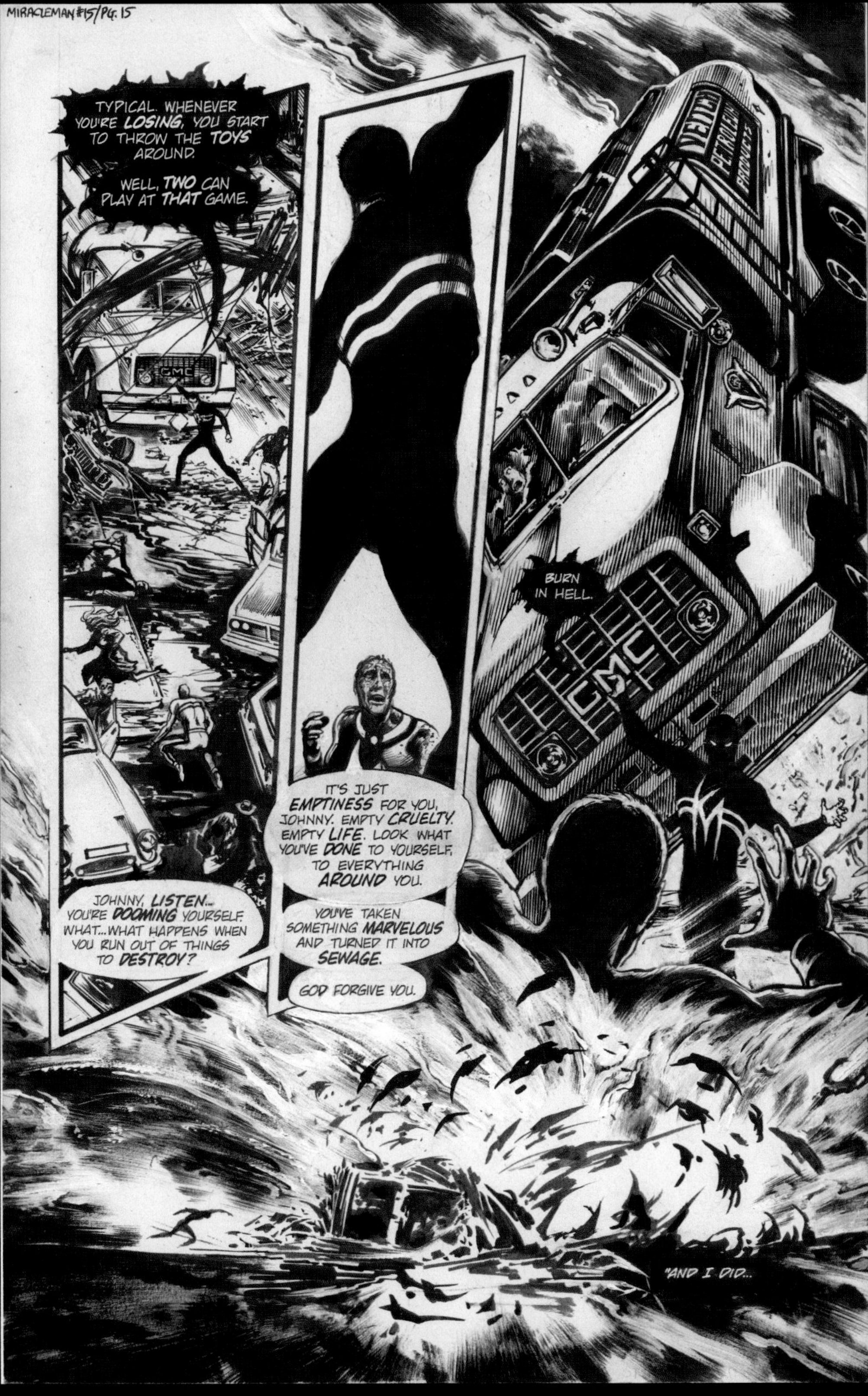

MIRACLEMAN #15/PG. 15
TYPICAL. WHENEVER YOU'RE LOSING, YOU START TO THROW THE TOYS AROUND.
WELL, TWO CAN PLAY AT THAT GAME.
NEWTECH PETROLEUM PRODUCTS
GMC
BURN IN HELL.
IT'S JUST EMPTINESS FOR YOU, JOHNNY. EMPTY CRUELTY. EMPTY LIFE. LOOK WHAT YOU'VE DONE TO YOURSELF, TO EVERYTHING AROUND YOU.
JOHNNY, LISTEN... YOU'RE DOOMING YOURSELF. WHAT...WHAT HAPPENS WHEN YOU RUN OUT OF THINGS TO DESTROY?
YOU'VE TAKEN SOMETHING MARVELOUS AND TURNED IT INTO SEWAGE.
GOD FORGIVE YOU.
"AND I DID...

*Miracleman* #15, page 16 study, pencil on sketchbook paper by John Totleben. Totleben did numerous sketches to capture Kid Miracleman's demise.

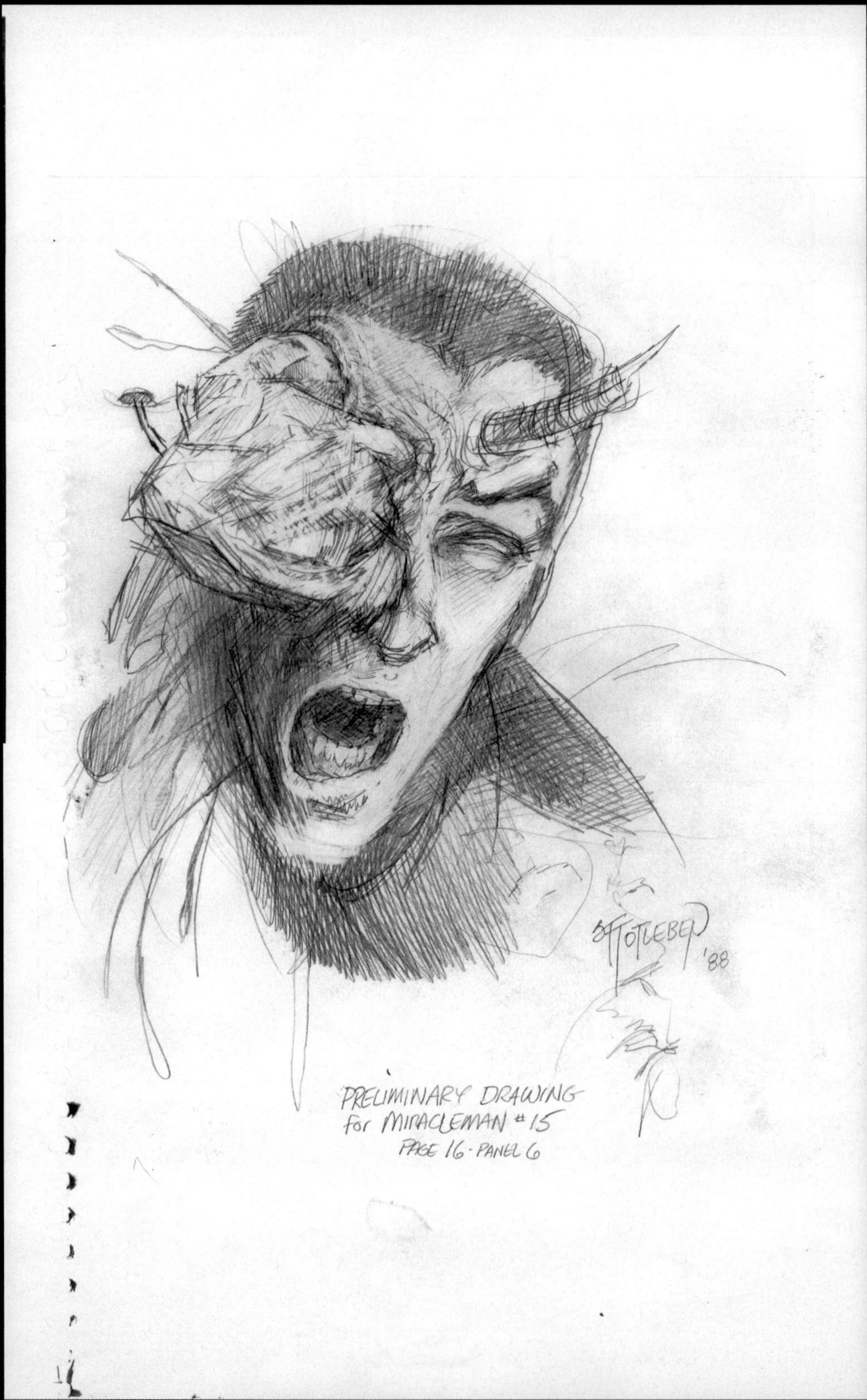

TOTLEBEN '88
PRELIMINARY DRAWING
for MIRACLEMAN #15
PAGE 16 - PANEL 6

*Miracleman* #15, page 17 study, India ink, marker and ballpoint pen on sketchbook paper by John Totleben. In complete agony, Bates escapes the pain the only way he can: "Miracleman."

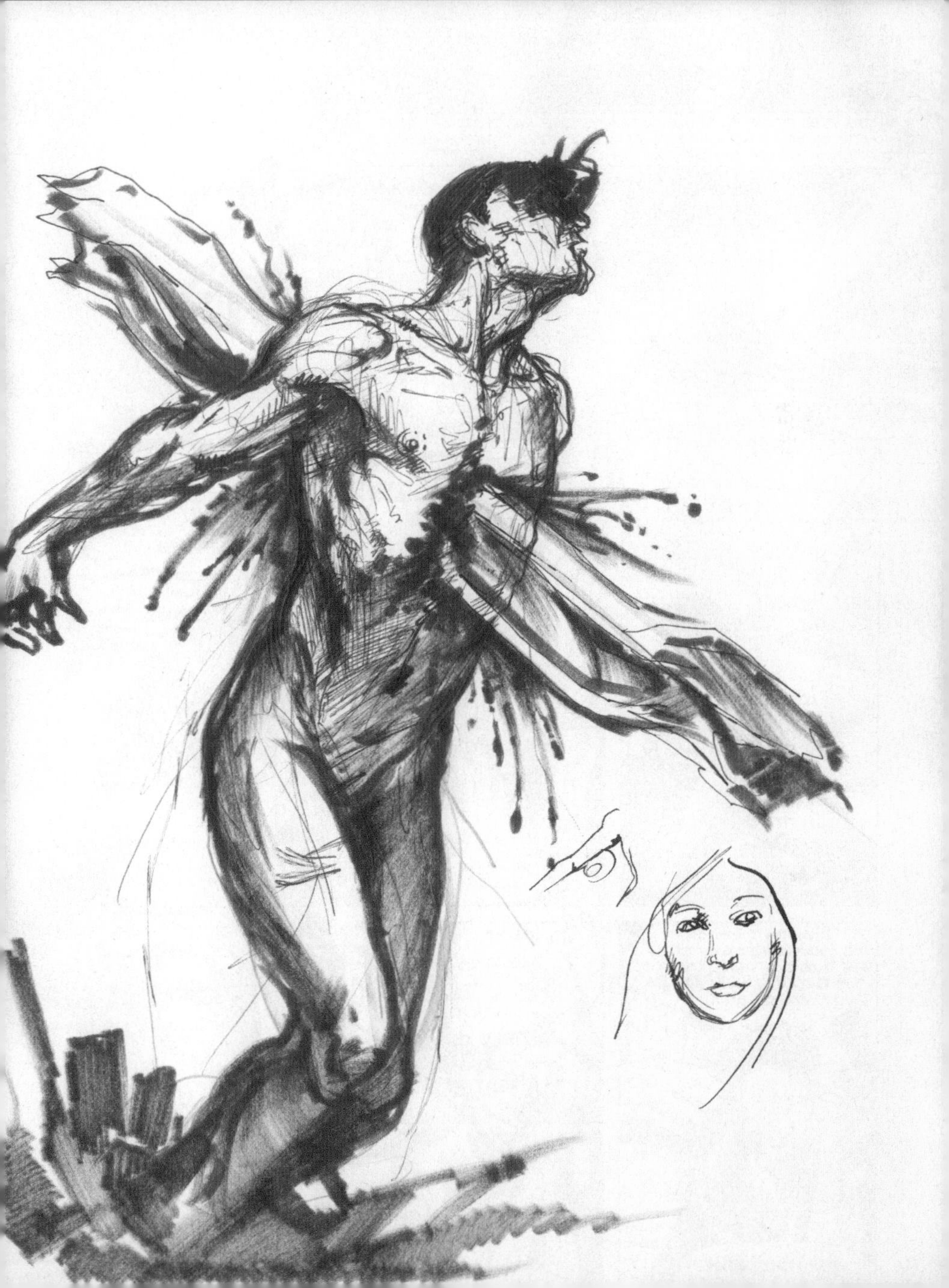

Miracleman #15, page 18 original artwork, pencil, India ink and white acrylic on illustration board by John Totleben. As delicate as it is shocking, Totleben masterfully captures Johnny's desperation and Miracleman's awful resignation. Their relationship comes to its tragic end.

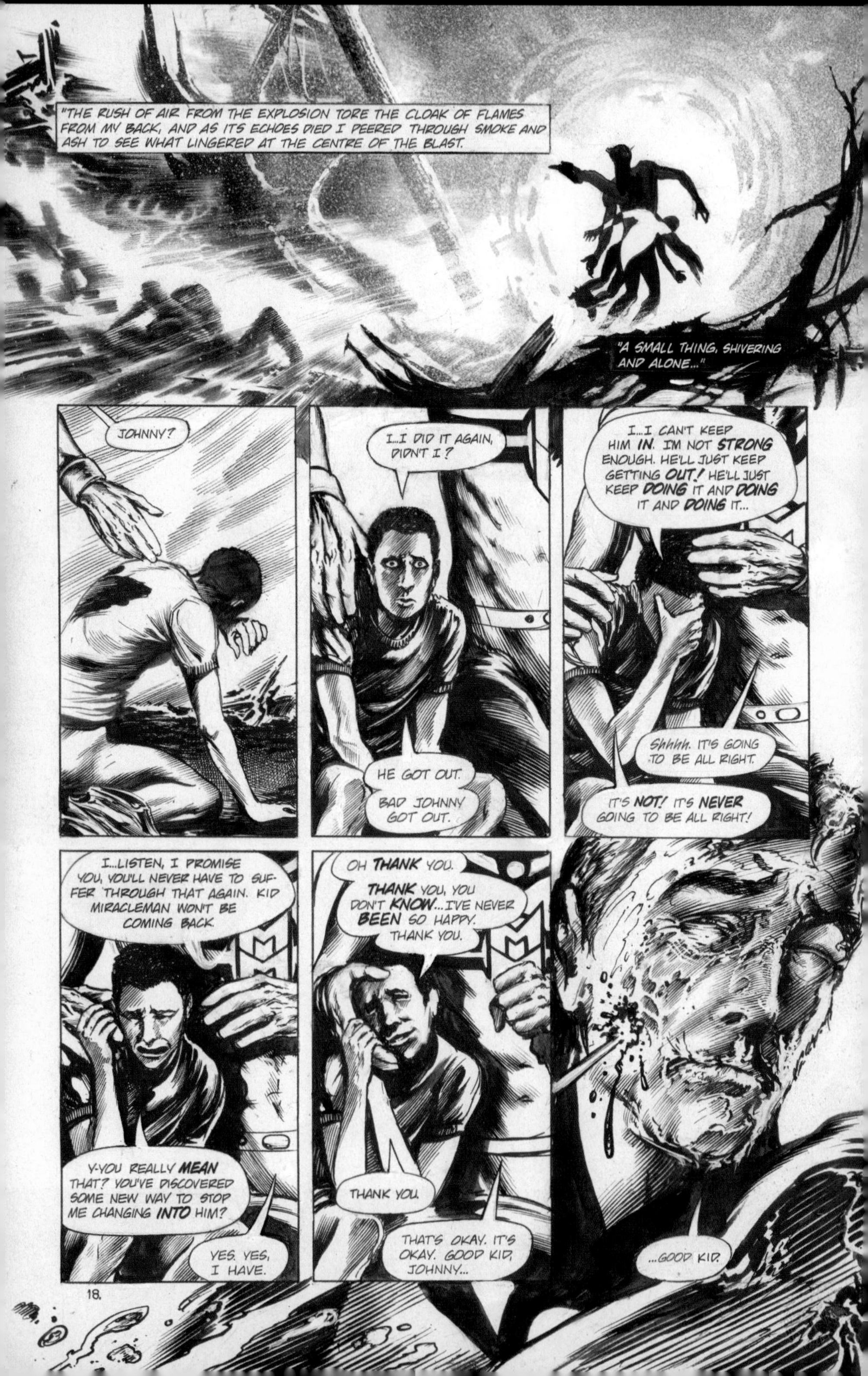

"THE RUSH OF AIR FROM THE EXPLOSION TORE THE CLOAK OF FLAMES FROM MY BACK, AND AS ITS ECHOES DIED I PEERED THROUGH SMOKE AND ASH TO SEE WHAT LINGERED AT THE CENTRE OF THE BLAST.
"A SMALL THING, SHIVERING AND ALONE..."
JOHNNY?
I...I DID IT AGAIN, DIDN'T I?
HE GOT OUT.
BAD JOHNNY GOT OUT.
I...I CAN'T KEEP HIM IN. I'M NOT STRONG ENOUGH. HE'LL JUST KEEP GETTING OUT! HE'LL JUST KEEP DOING IT AND DOING IT AND DOING IT...
Shhhh. IT'S GOING TO BE ALL RIGHT.
IT'S NOT! IT'S NEVER GOING TO BE ALL RIGHT!
I...LISTEN, I PROMISE YOU, YOU'LL NEVER HAVE TO SUFFER THROUGH THAT AGAIN. KID MIRACLEMAN WON'T BE COMING BACK.
Y-YOU REALLY MEAN THAT? YOU'VE DISCOVERED SOME NEW WAY TO STOP ME CHANGING INTO HIM?
YES. YES, I HAVE.
OH THANK YOU.
THANK YOU, YOU DON'T KNOW...I'VE NEVER BEEN SO HAPPY. THANK YOU.
THANK YOU.
THAT'S OKAY. IT'S OKAY. GOOD KID, JOHNNY...
...GOOD KID.
18.

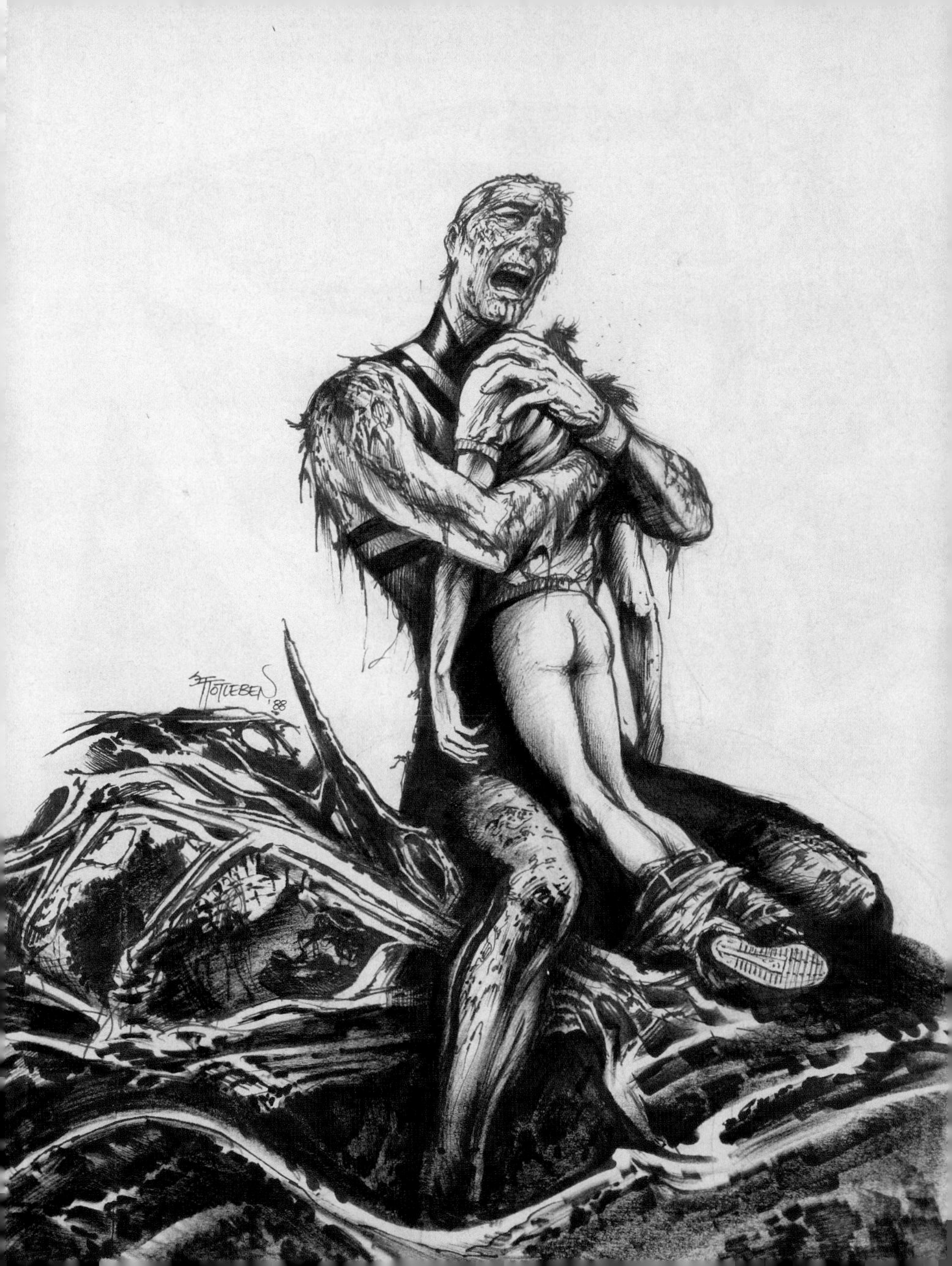

TOTLEBEN
'88

*Miracleman* #15, page 19 production photostat. Totleben composed page 19 by duplicating and modifying the backgrounds to the same illustration of Miracleman and Johnny Bates.

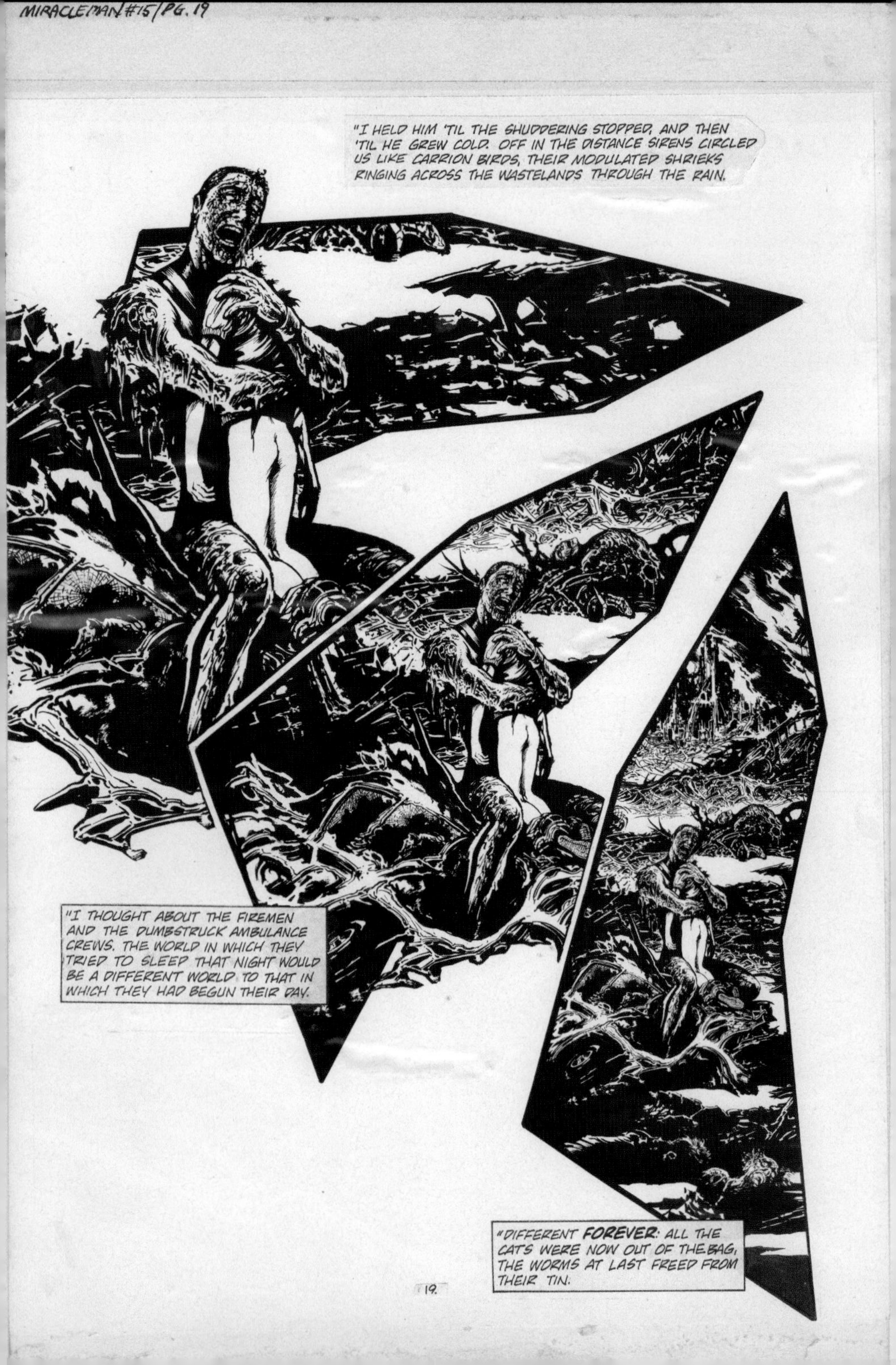

MIRACLEMAN #15/PG. 19
"I HELD HIM 'TIL THE SHUDDERING STOPPED, AND THEN 'TIL HE GREW COLD. OFF IN THE DISTANCE SIRENS CIRCLED US LIKE CARRION BIRDS, THEIR MODULATED SHRIEKS RINGING ACROSS THE WASTELANDS THROUGH THE RAIN.
"I THOUGHT ABOUT THE FIREMEN AND THE DUMBSTRUCK AMBULANCE CREWS. THE WORLD IN WHICH THEY TRIED TO SLEEP THAT NIGHT WOULD BE A DIFFERENT WORLD TO THAT IN WHICH THEY HAD BEGUN THEIR DAY.
"DIFFERENT FOREVER: ALL THE CATS WERE NOW OUT OF THE BAG, THE WORMS AT LAST FREED FROM THEIR TIN.
19.

...acleman #15, page 17 unused layout by John Totleben. Pages 17-21 were scripted as a ...e, but feeling this key moment needed more space, Totleben expanded it to convey the Miracleman's anguish and the extent of London's destruction.

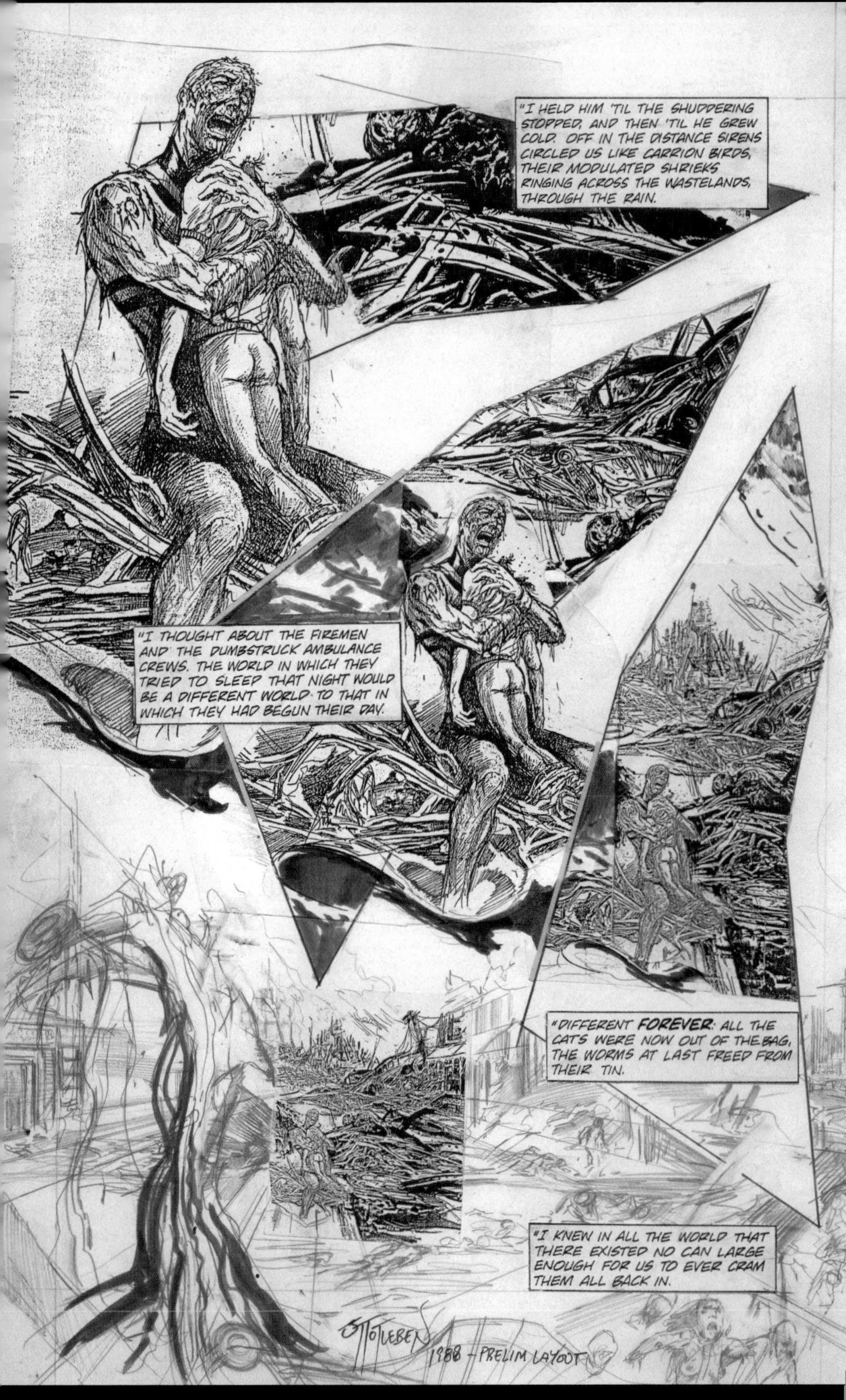
"I HELD HIM 'TIL THE SHUDDERING STOPPED, AND THEN 'TIL HE GREW COLD. OFF IN THE DISTANCE SIRENS CIRCLED US LIKE CARRION BIRDS, THEIR MODULATED SHRIEKS RINGING ACROSS THE WASTELANDS, THROUGH THE RAIN.
"I THOUGHT ABOUT THE FIREMEN AND THE DUMBSTRUCK AMBULANCE CREWS. THE WORLD IN WHICH THEY TRIED TO SLEEP THAT NIGHT WOULD BE A DIFFERENT WORLD TO THAT IN WHICH THEY HAD BEGUN THEIR DAY.
"DIFFERENT FOREVER: ALL THE CATS WERE NOW OUT OF THE BAG, THE WORMS AT LAST FREED FROM THEIR TIN.
"I KNEW IN ALL THE WORLD THAT THERE EXISTED NO CAN LARGE ENOUGH FOR US TO EVER CRAM THEM ALL BACK IN.
TOTLEBEN
1988 - PRELIM LAYOUT

...LLOWING PAGES: *Miracleman* #15, pages 20-21 original artwork, pencil, India ink and

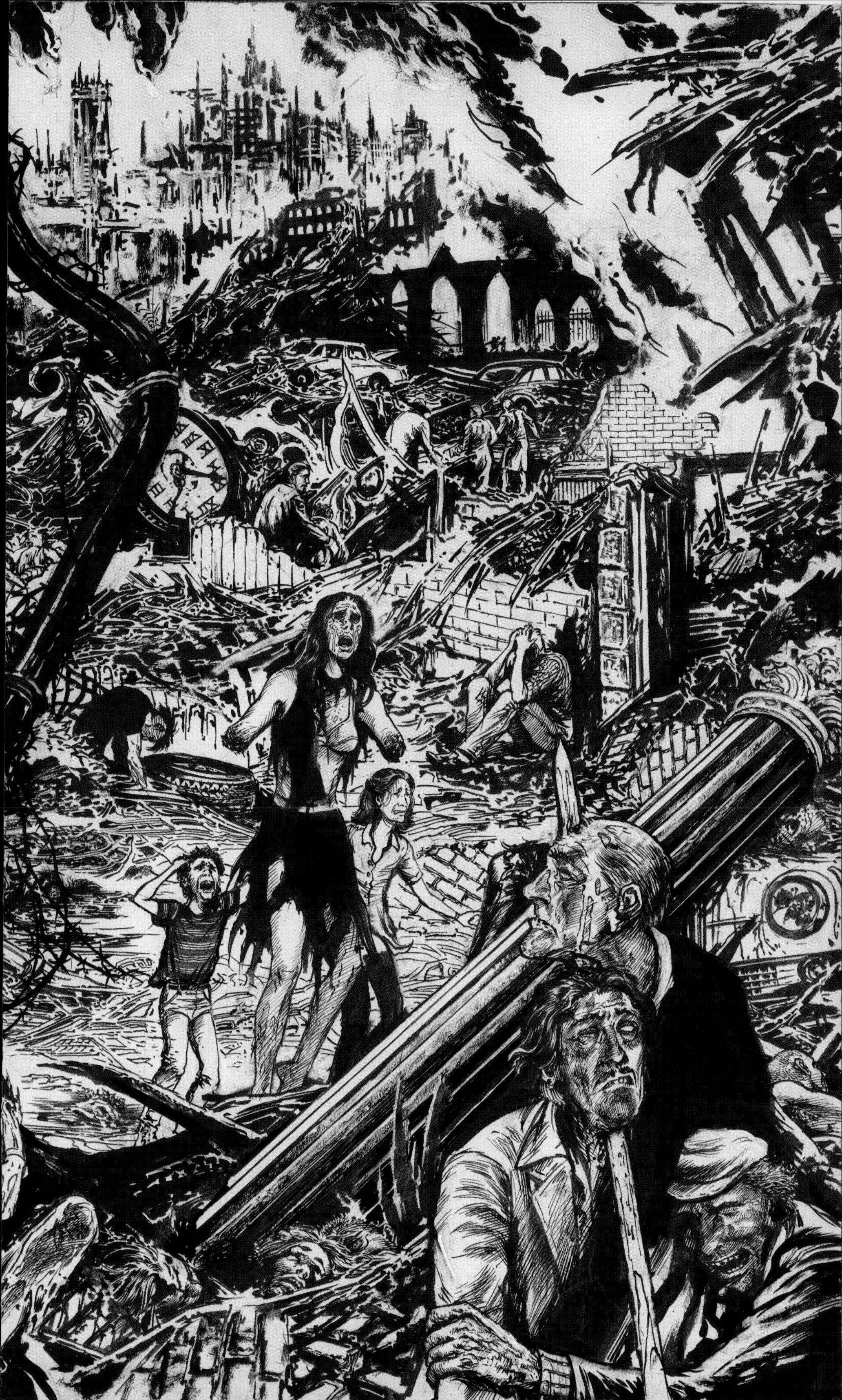

**TOP:** Kid Miracleman pencil sketches from the back of the *Miracleman* #15, page 15 art board.
**BOTTOM:** *Miracleman* #14, page 15 and *Miracleman* #15 pencil studies, pencil on sketchbook paper by John Totleben.

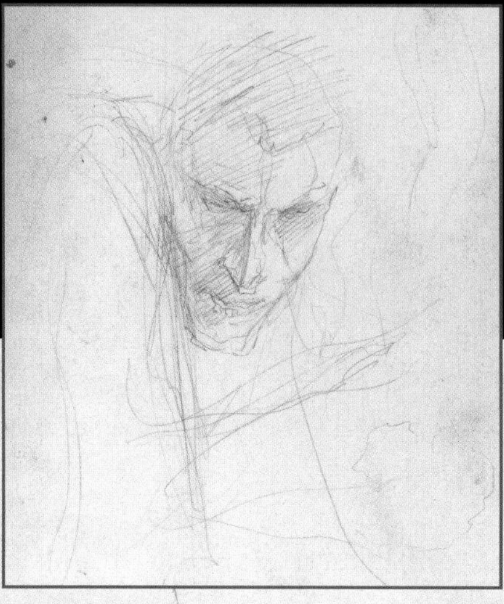

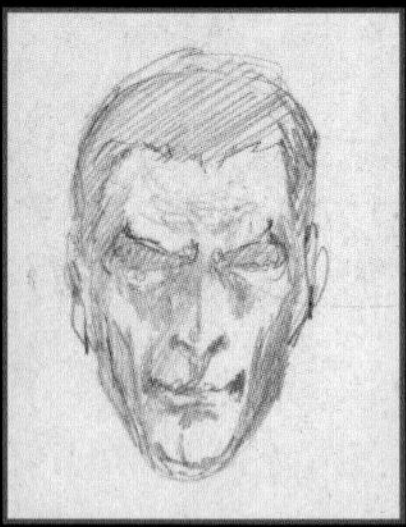

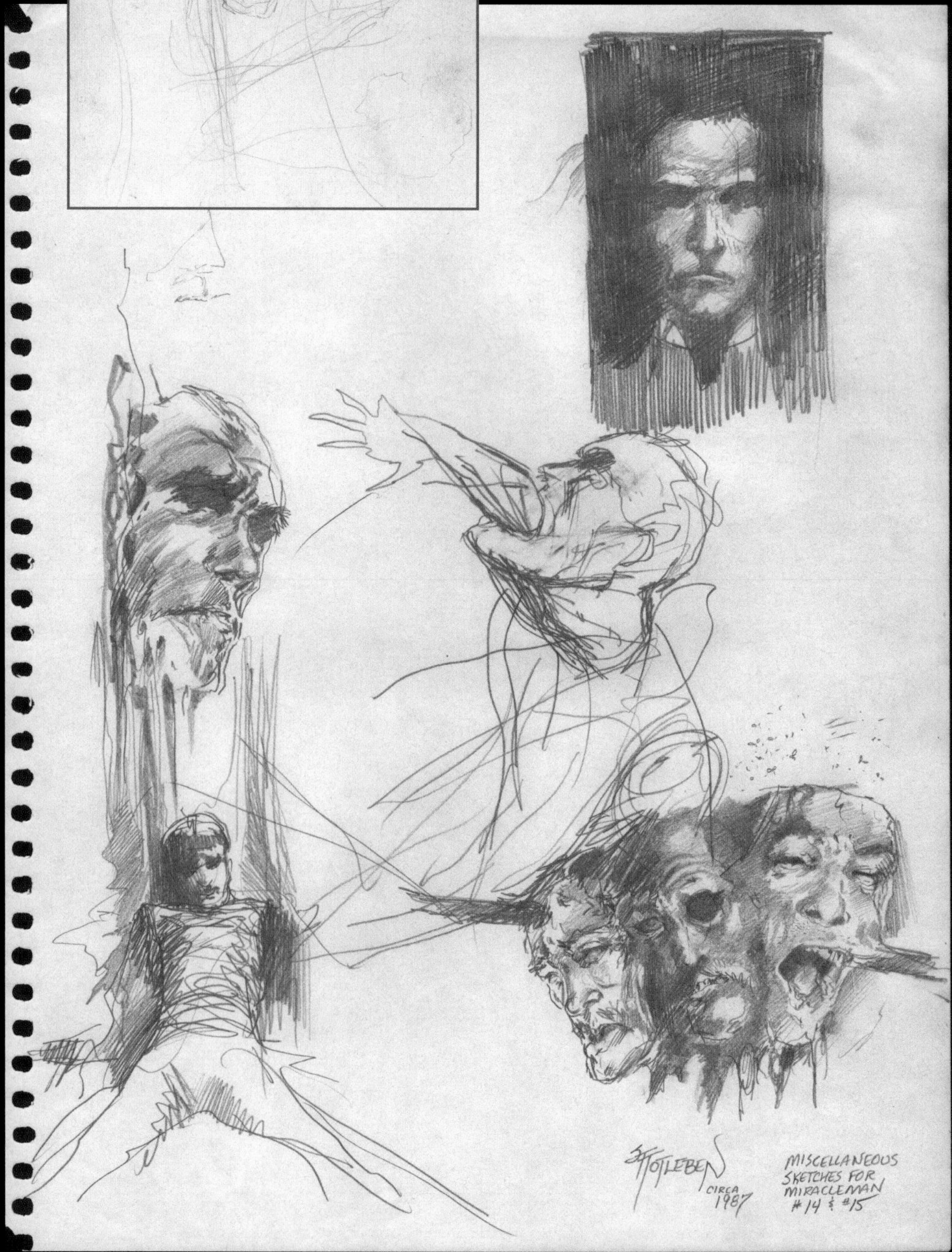
TOTLEBEN
CIRCA 1987
MISCELLANEOUS SKETCHES FOR MIRACLEMAN #14 & #15

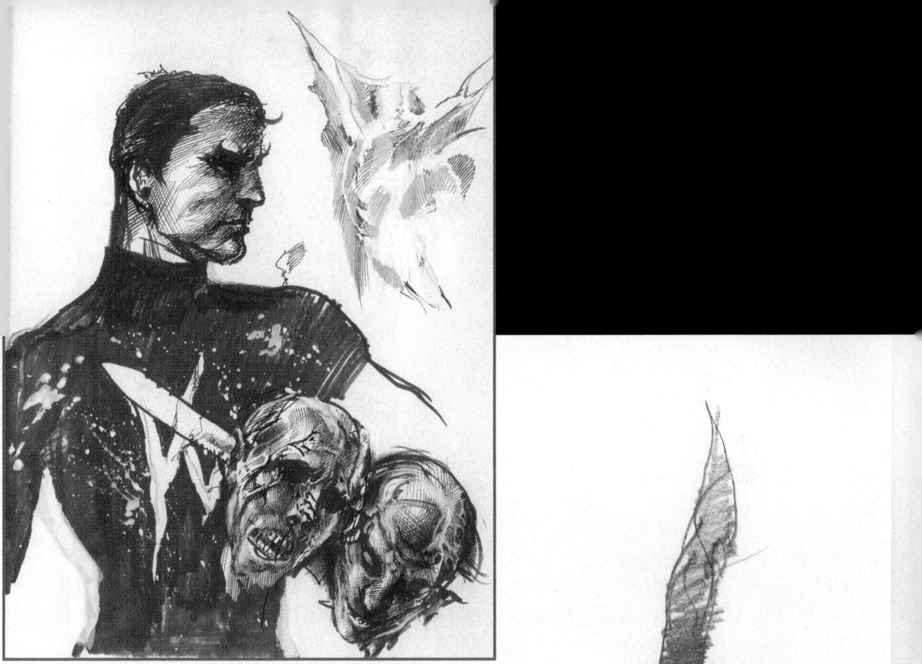

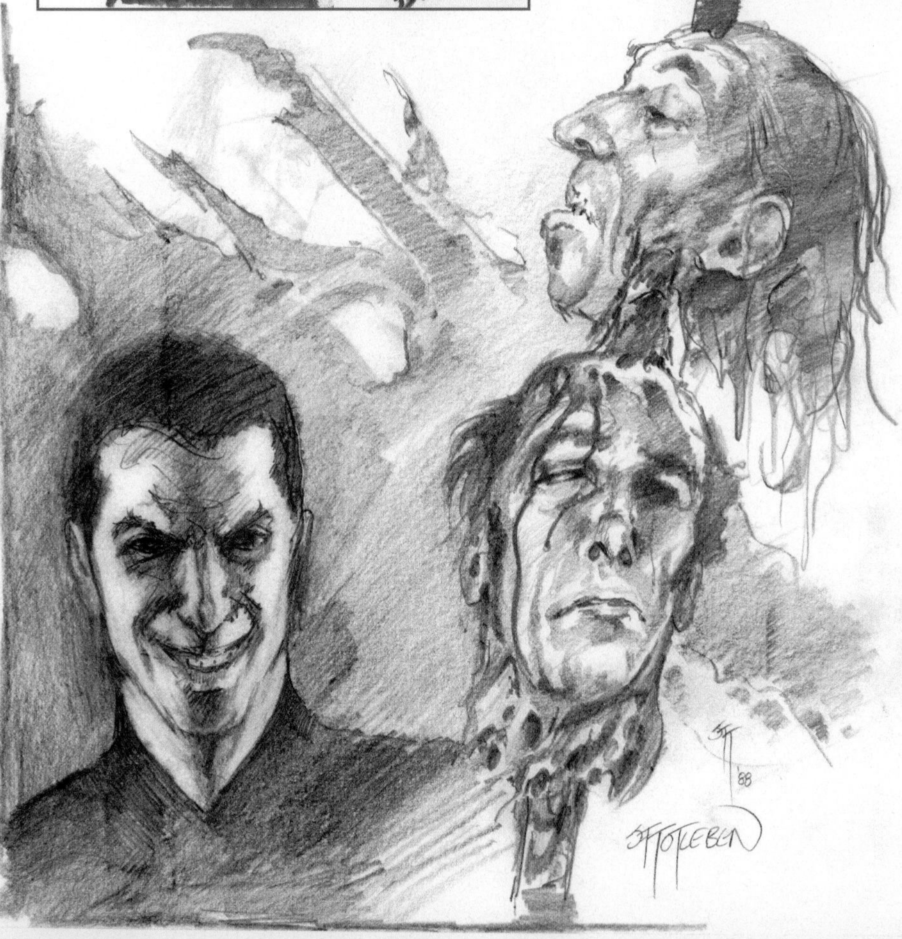

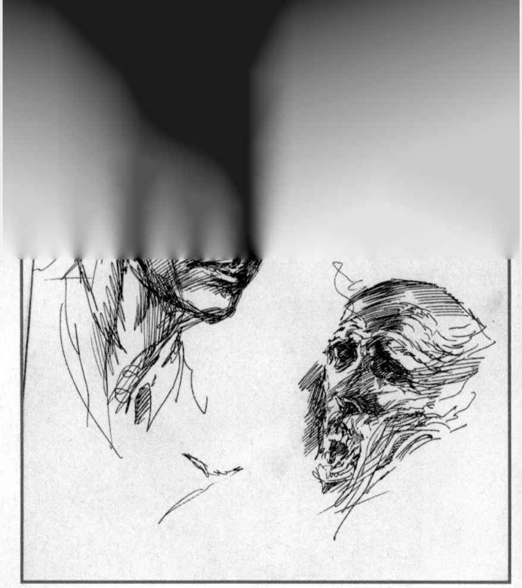

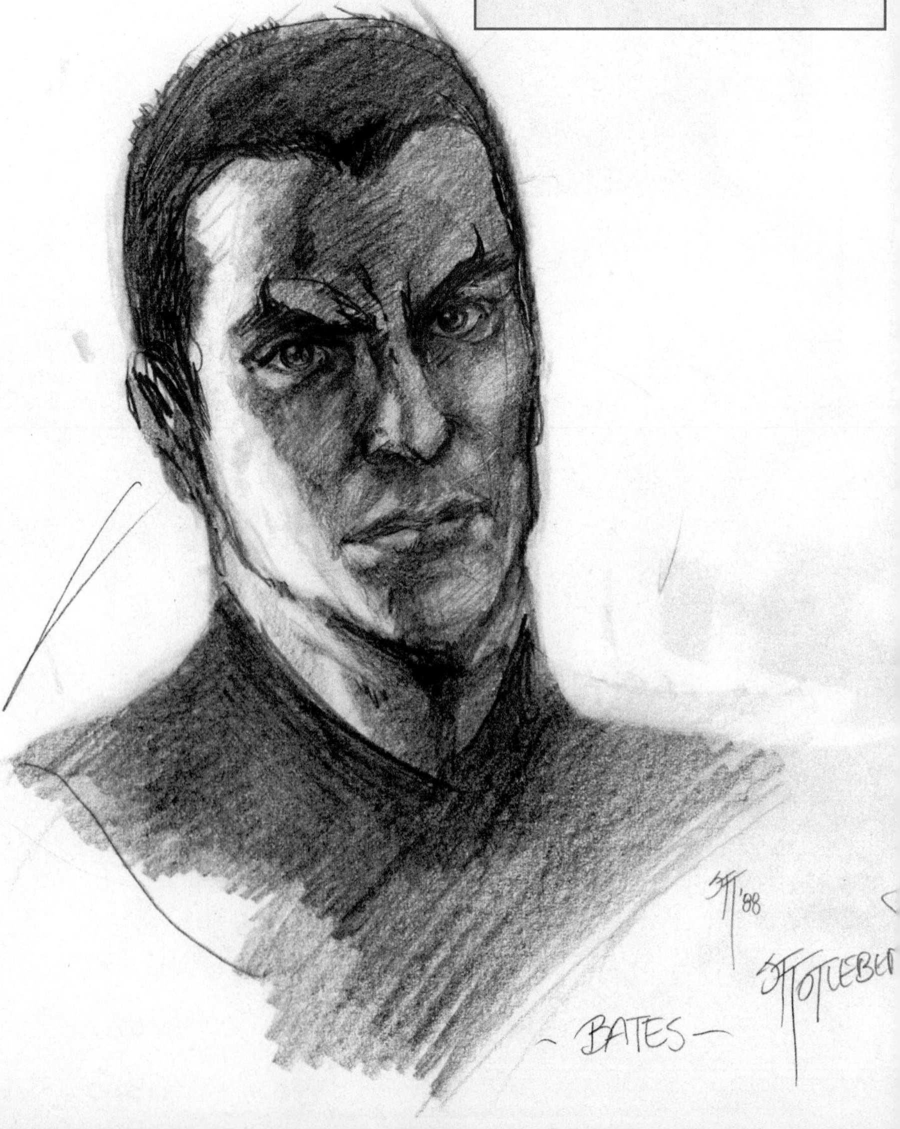
– BATES –

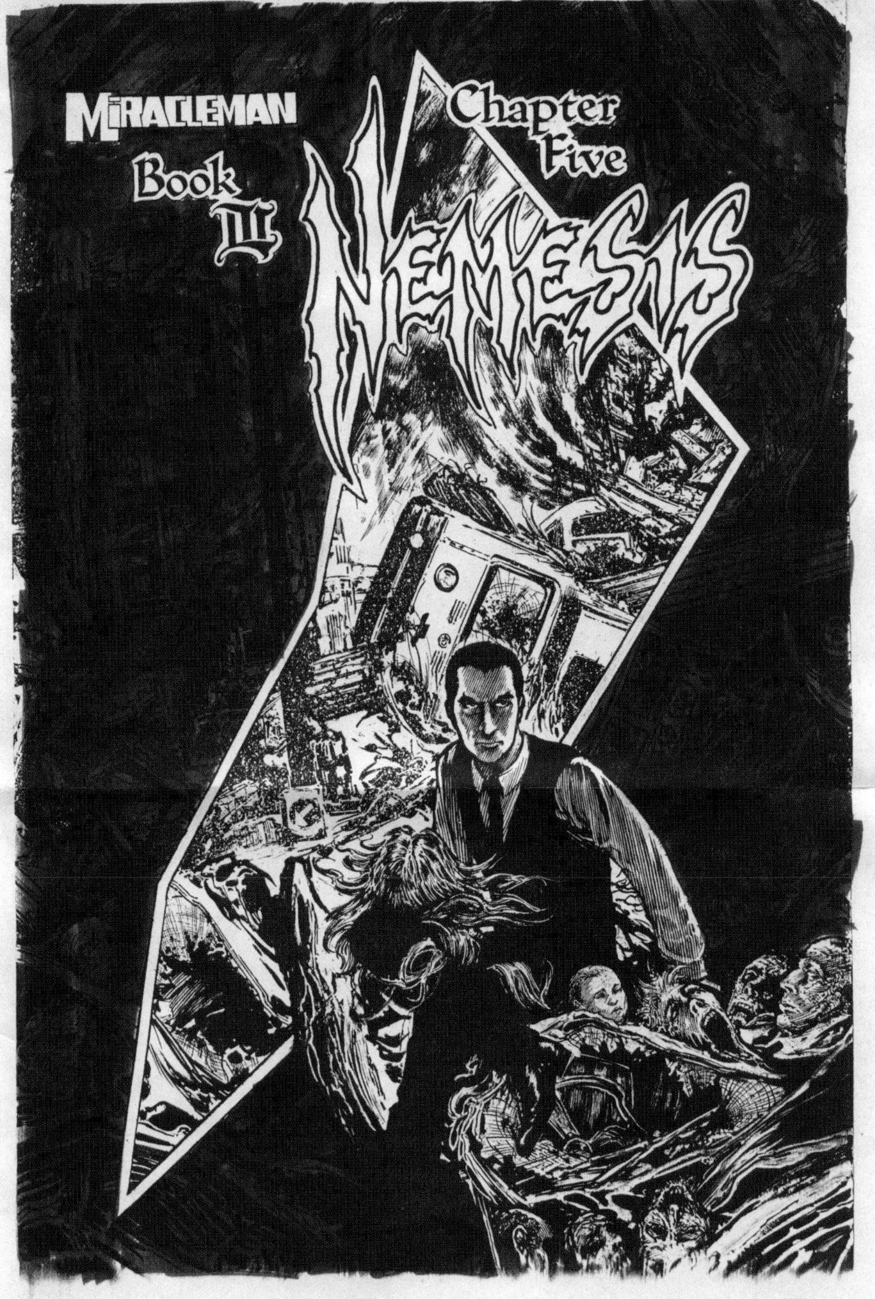
MIRACLEMAN
Book III
Chapter Five
NEMESIS

HI LETITIA —
THIS SPLASH PG. DESIGN MIGHT WORK WELL AS AN AD. WITH THE BACKGROUND BLACKED-OUT IT DOESN'T GIVE THE FULL IMPACT AWAY AND SERVES AS A BIT OF A TEASER. ANYWAY, JUST THOUGHT I'D SUGGEST.
— JOHN

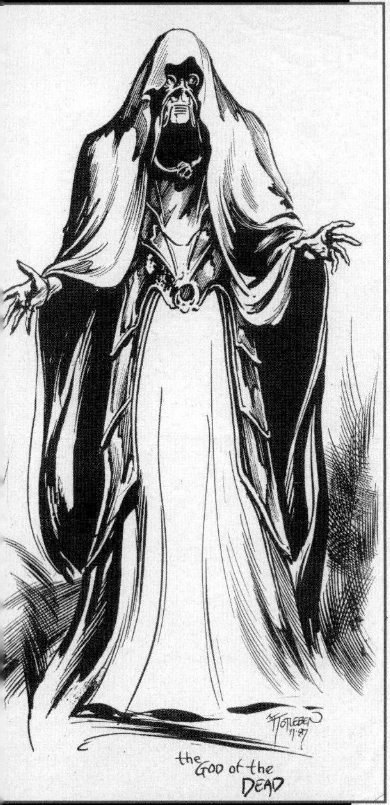
the GOD of the DEAD

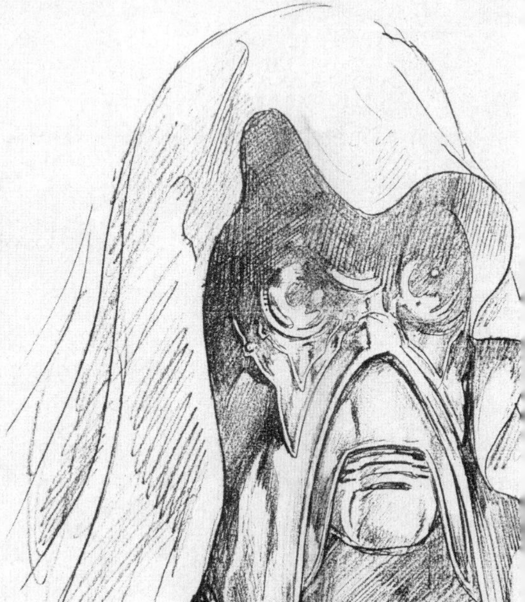
the God of the Dead

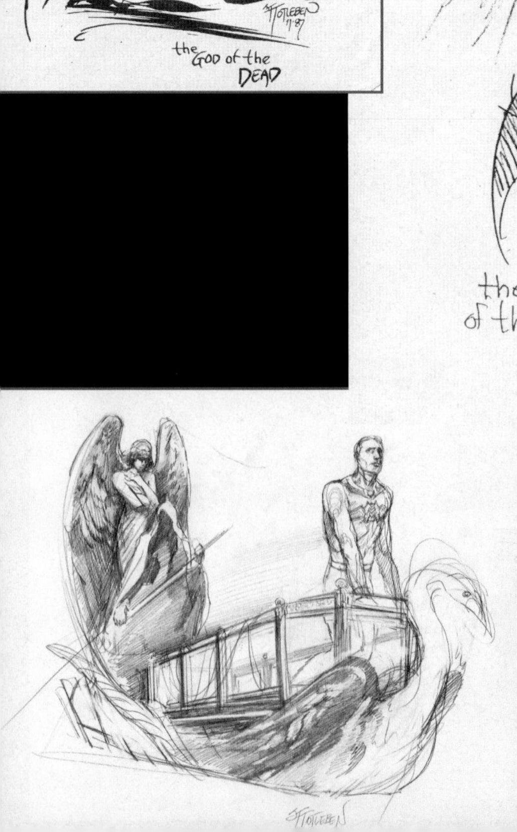

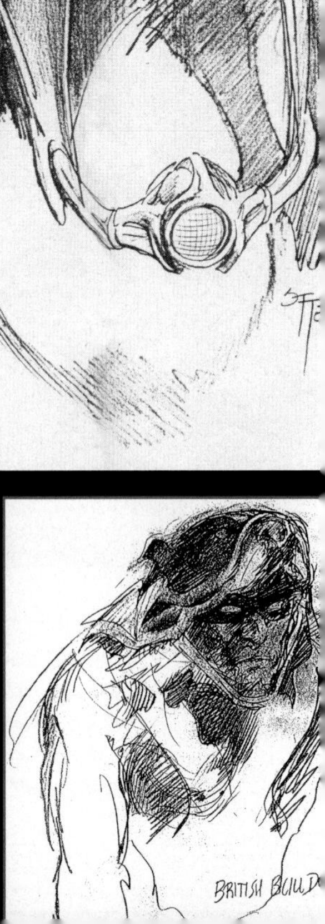
BRITISH BUILD

Three's final chapter, Totleben produced the designs earlier in the series for their issue #14 can

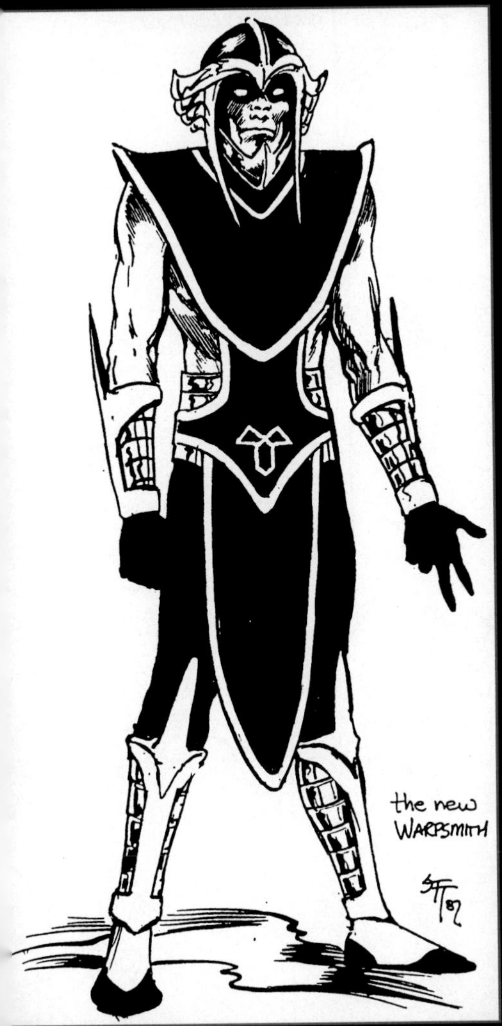
the new
WARPSMITH

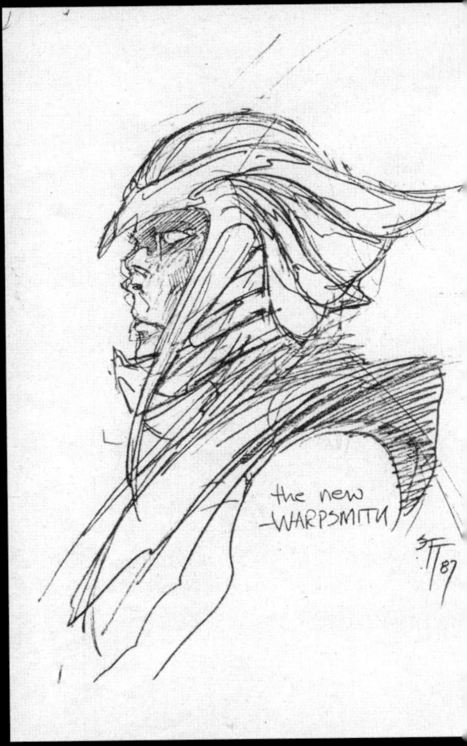
the new
WARPSMITH

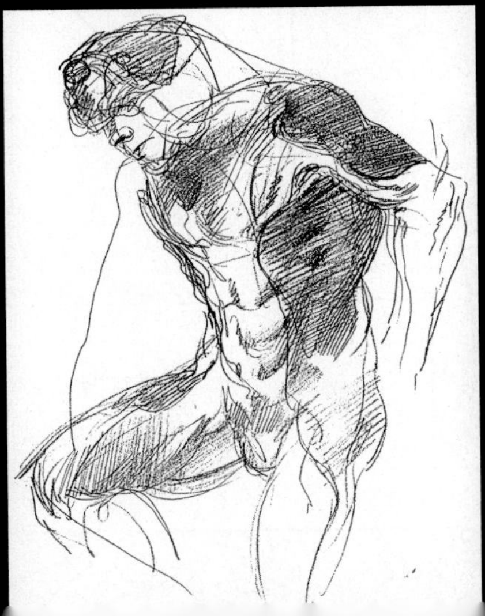

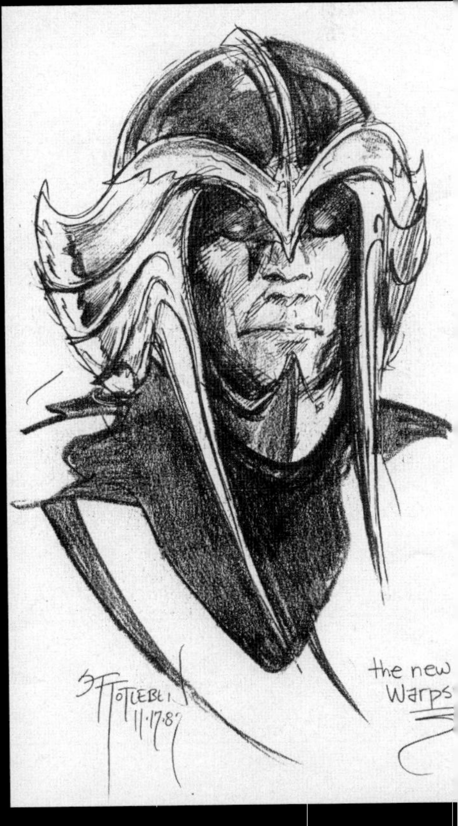
11·17·87
the new
Warps

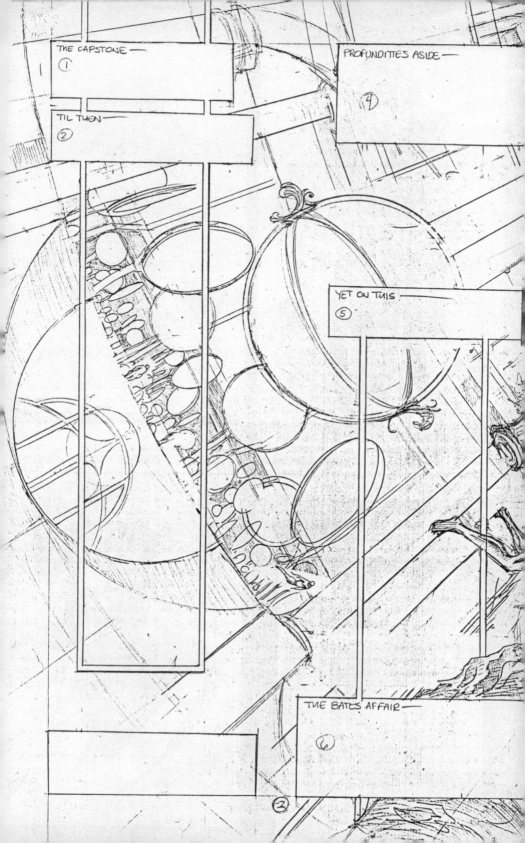

THE CAPSTONE — ①

TIL THEN — ②

PROFUNDITIES ASIDE — ④

YET ON THIS — ⑤

THE BATES AFFAIR — ⑥

③

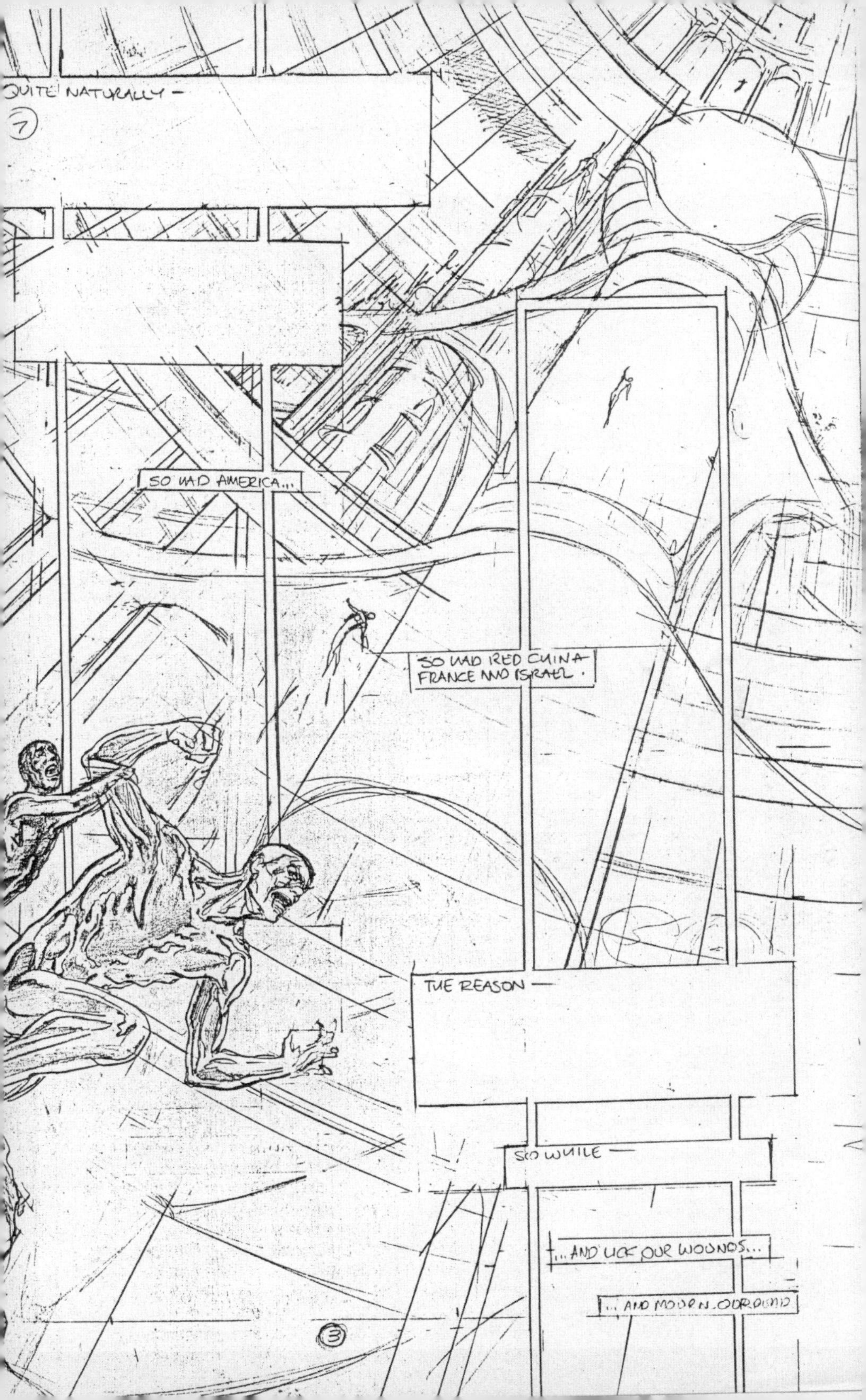
QUITE NATURALLY —
SO HAD AMERICA...
SO HAD RED CHINA
FRANCE AND ISRAEL.
THE REASON —
SO WHILE —
...AND LICK OUR WOUNDS...

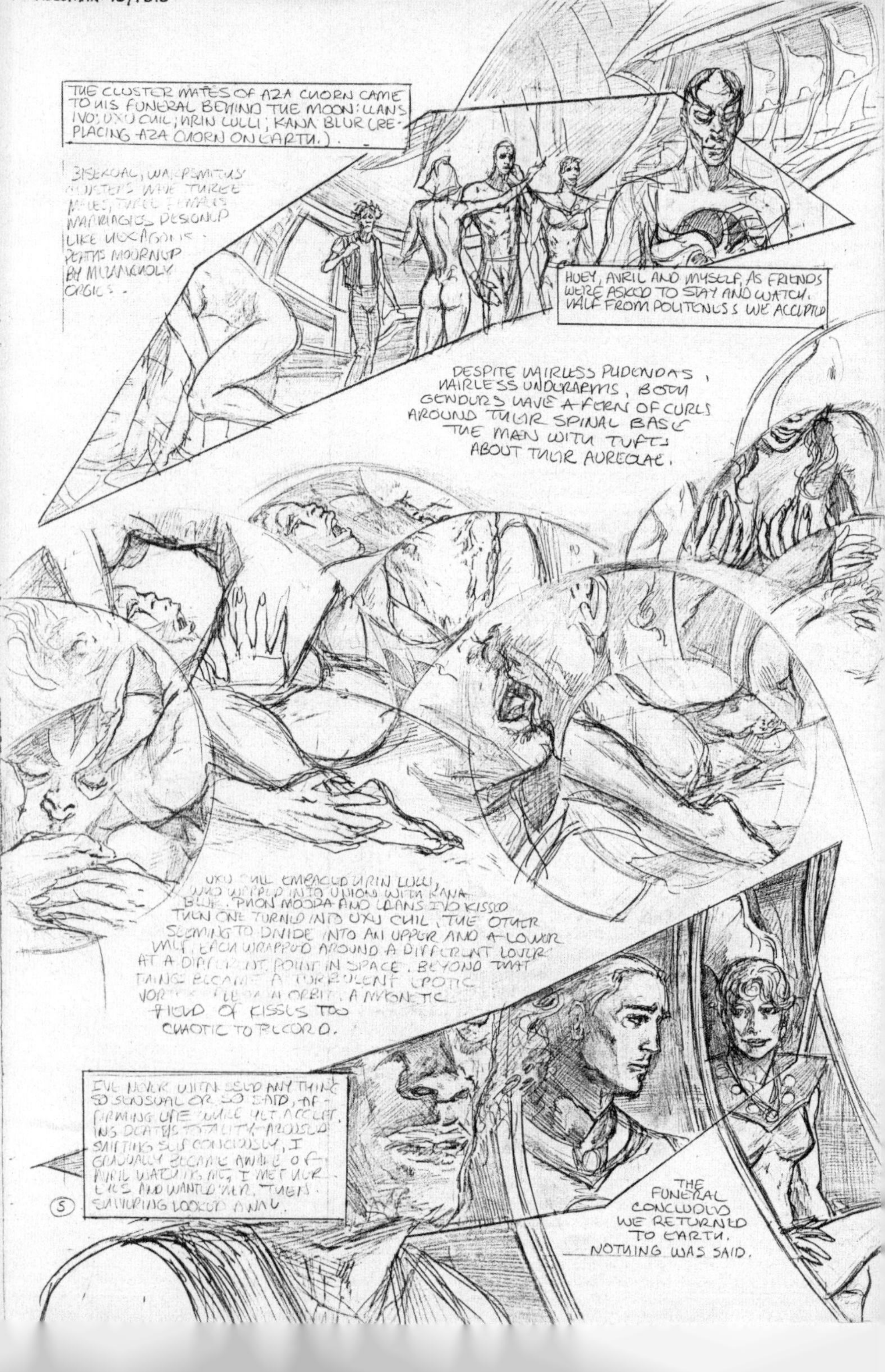
THE CLUSTER MATES OF AZA CHORN CAME TO HIS FUNERAL BEHIND THE MOON: LLANS IVO; UXU CHIL; VRIN LULLI; KANA BLUR (REPLACING AZA CHORN ON EARTH.).
BISEXUAL, HERMAPHRODITES. CLUSTERS HAVE THREE MALES, THREE FEMALES. MARRIAGES DESIGNED LIKE HEXAGONS. DEATHS MOURNED BY MELANCHOLY ORGIES.
HUEY, AVRIL AND MYSELF, AS FRIENDS WERE ASKED TO STAY AND WATCH. HALF FROM POLITENESS WE ACCEPTED.
DESPITE HAIRLESS PUDENDAS, HAIRLESS UNDERARMS, BOTH GENDERS HAVE A FERN OF CURLS AROUND THEIR SPINAL BASE THE MEN WITH TUFTS ABOUT THEIR AUREOLAE.
UXU CHIL EMBRACED VRIN LULLI, WHO WHIPPED INTO UNION WITH KANA BLUR. PHON MOORA AND LLANS IVO KISSED THEN ONE TURNED INTO UXU CHIL, THE OTHER SEEMING TO DIVIDE INTO AN UPPER AND A LOWER HALF, EACH WRAPPED AROUND A DIFFERENT LOVER AT A DIFFERENT POINT IN SPACE. BEYOND THAT THINGS BECAME A TURBULENT EROTIC VORTEX ORBIT. A MAGNETIC FIELD OF KISSES TOO CHAOTIC TO RECORD.
I'VE NEVER WITNESSED ANYTHING SO SENSUAL OR SO SAD, AFFIRMING LIFE WHILE YET ACCEPTING DEATH'S TOTALITY. AROUSED SHIFTING SELF CONSCIOUSLY, I GRADUALLY BECAME AWARE OF AVRIL WATCHING ME. I MET HER EYES AND WANTED HER. THEN SHIVERING LOOKED AWAY.
5
THE FUNERAL CONCLUDED WE RETURNED TO EARTH. NOTHING WAS SAID.

**TOP:** *Miracleman* #16, page 7, panel 3-5 pencils by John Totleben. For pages 7-8 and 11-12, Totleben penciled individual panels and photocopied them to create the pages' final look.
**BOTTOM:** Olympus design sketches, pencil on sketchbook paper by John Totleben.

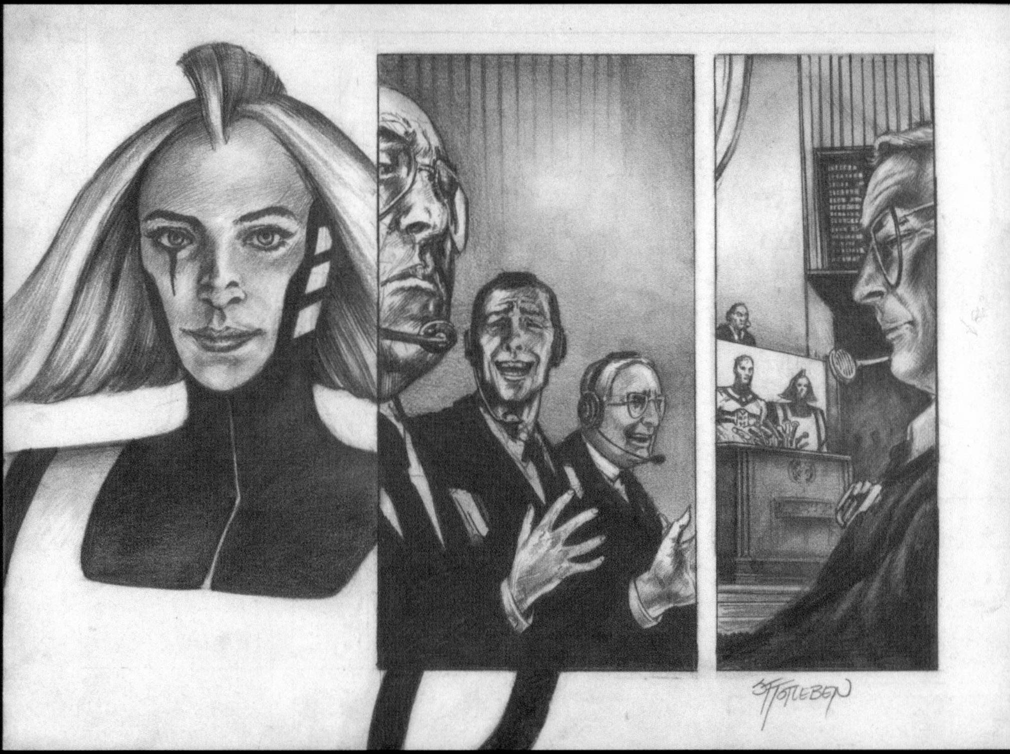

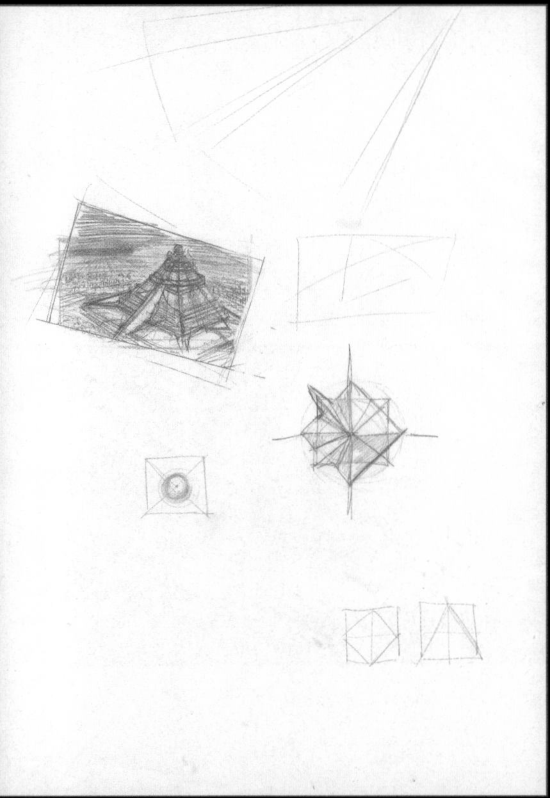

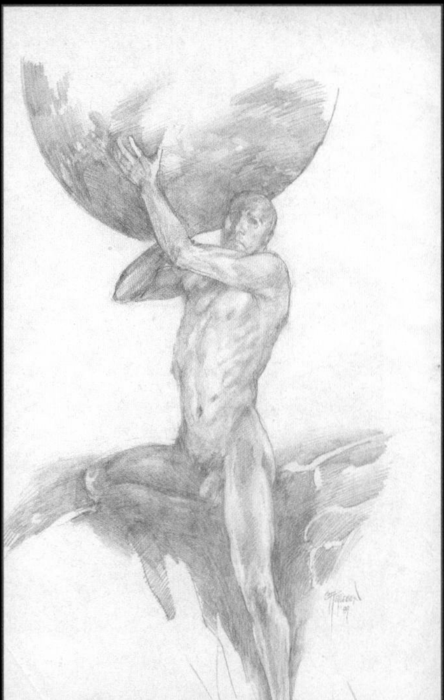

Miracleman #16, page 7 pencils by John Totleben. The headline "Aryan Dream or White Nightmare?" references Nazi Germany's appropriation of Nietzsche's philosophy and questions whether Miracleman is the world's savior or its most successful dictator.

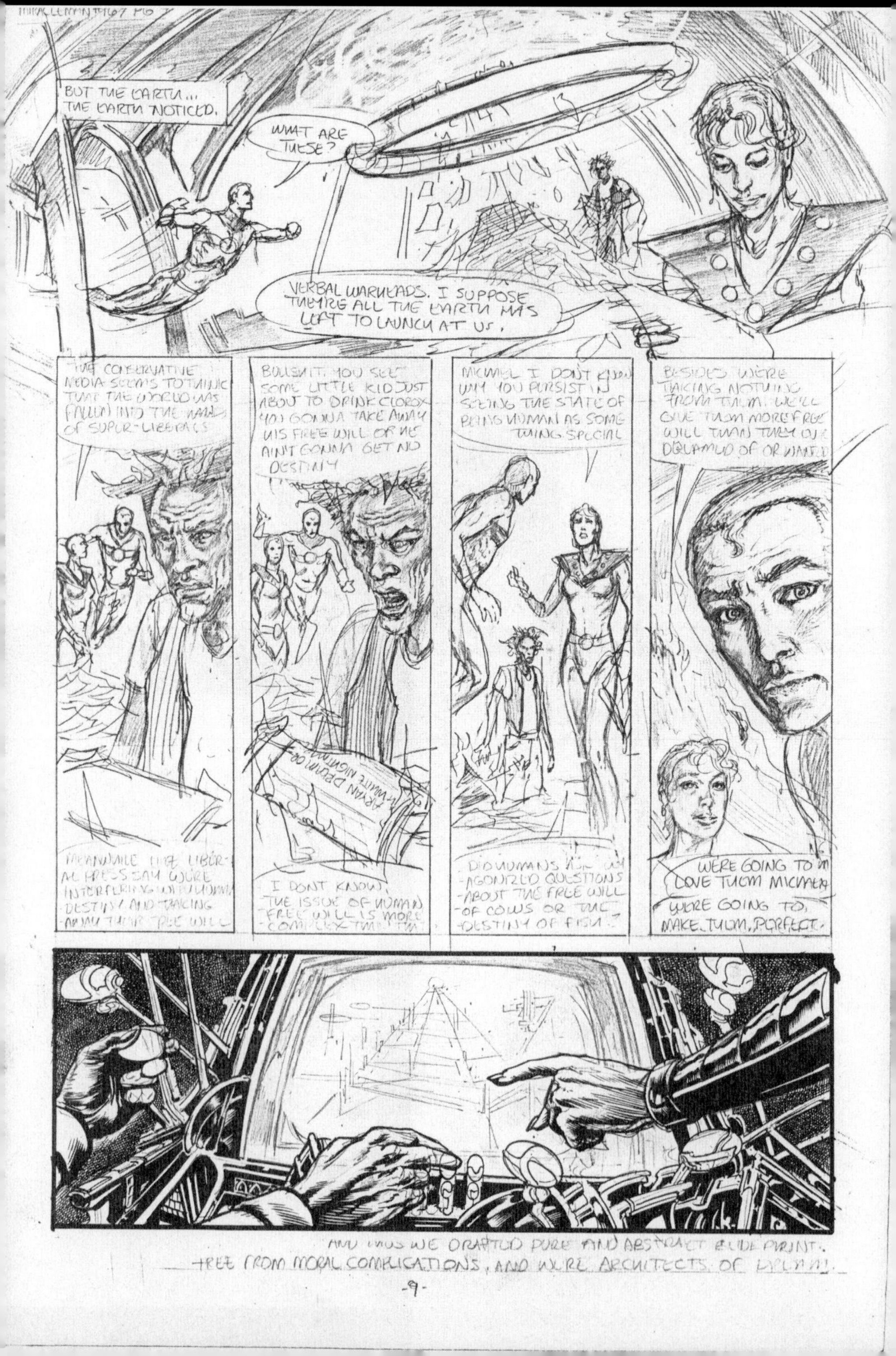
BUT THE EARTH... THE EARTH NOTICED.
WHAT ARE THESE?
VERBAL WARHEADS. I SUPPOSE THEY'RE ALL THE EARTH HAS LEFT TO LAUNCH AT US.
THE CONSERVATIVE MEDIA SEEMS TO THINK THAT THE WORLD HAS FALLEN INTO THE HANDS OF SUPER-LIBERALS
BULLSHIT. YOU SEE SOME LITTLE KID JUST ABOUT TO DRINK CLOROX YOU GONNA TAKE AWAY HIS FREE WILL OR HE AIN'T GONNA GET NO DESTINY
MICHAEL I DON'T KNOW WHY YOU PERSIST IN SEEING THE STATE OF BEING HUMAN AS SOMETHING SPECIAL
BESIDES WE'RE TAKING NOTHING FROM THEM. WE'LL GIVE THEM MORE FREE WILL THAN THEY EVER DREAMED OF OR WANTED
MEANWHILE THE LIBERAL PRESS SAY WE'RE INTERFERING WITH HUMAN DESTINY AND TAKING AWAY THEIR FREE WILL
I DON'T KNOW. THE ISSUE OF HUMAN FREE WILL IS MORE COMPLEX
DO HUMANS ASK AGONIZED QUESTIONS ABOUT THE FREE WILL OF COWS OR THE DESTINY OF FISH?
WE'RE GOING TO LOVE THEM MICHAEL. WE'RE GOING TO MAKE THEM PERFECT.
AND THUS WE CRAFTED PURE AND ABSTRACT BLUEPRINT. FREE FROM MORAL COMPLICATIONS, AND WE'RE ARCHITECTS OF
-9-

*Miracleman* #16, page 10 pencils by John Totleben. There is opposition at every stage as Miracleman's new society is built. Despite mankind's protests, the unremitting march forward is measured by Olympus' rise at the bottom, the foundation, of pages 9-12. Finally, it ascends into the sky on page 13.

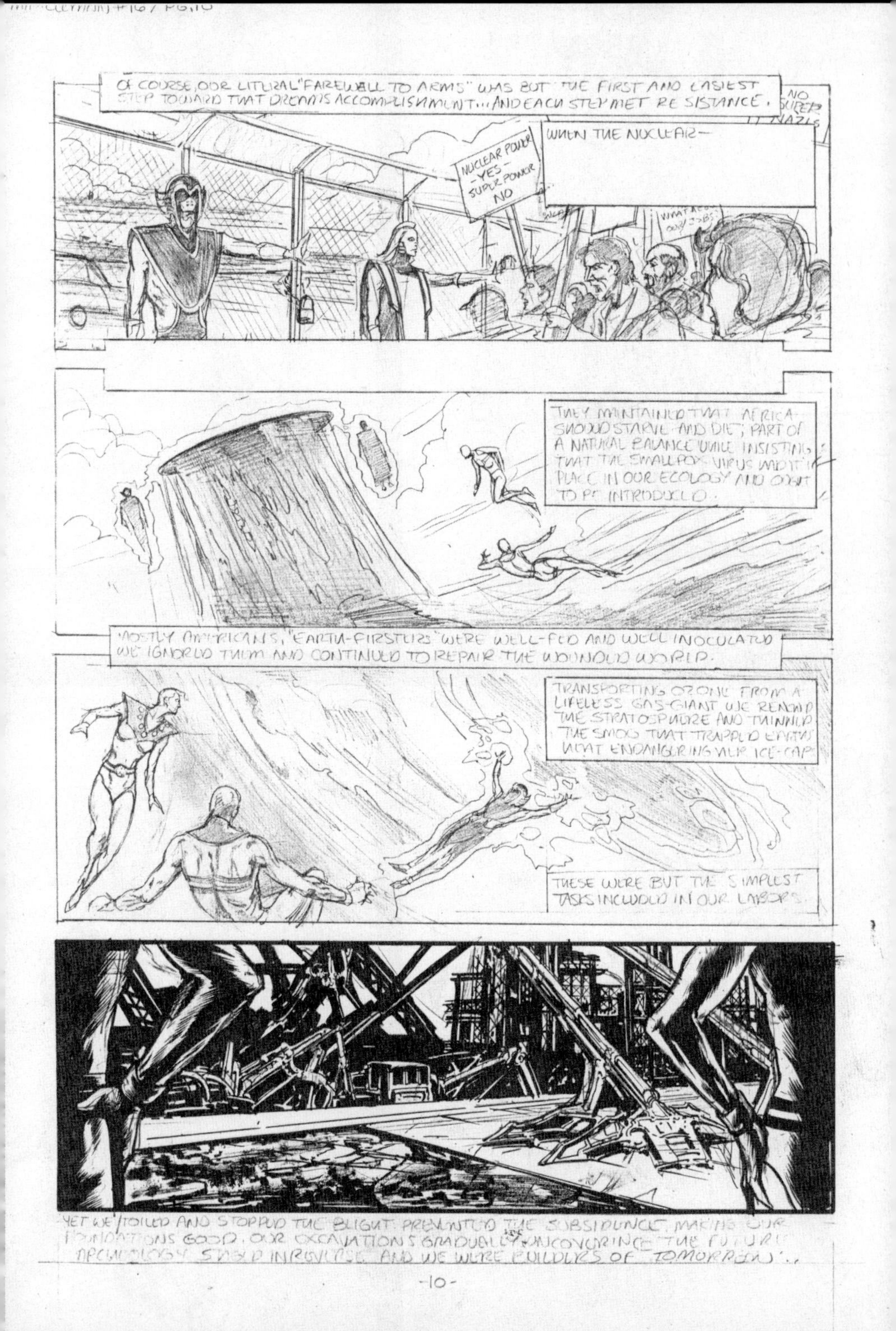

OF COURSE, OUR LITERAL "FAREWELL TO ARMS" WAS BUT THE FIRST AND EASIEST STEP TOWARD THAT DREAM'S ACCOMPLISHMENT... AND EACH STEP MET RESISTANCE.
NO SUPER NAZIS
WHEN THE NUCLEAR—
NUCLEAR POWER -YES- SUPER POWER NO
THEY MAINTAINED THAT AFRICA SHOULD STARVE AND DIE; PART OF A NATURAL BALANCE WHILE INSISTING THAT THE SMALLPOX VIRUS HAD IT'S PLACE IN OUR ECOLOGY AND OUGHT TO BE INTRODUCED.
MOSTLY AMERICANS, "EARTH-FIRSTERS" WERE WELL-FED AND WELL INOCULATED. WE IGNORED THEM AND CONTINUED TO REPAIR THE WOUNDED WORLD.
TRANSPORTING OZONE FROM A LIFELESS GAS-GIANT WE RENEWED THE STRATOSPHERE AND THINNED THE SMOG THAT TRAPPED EARTH'S HEAT ENDANGERING THE ICE-CAP.
THESE WERE BUT THE SIMPLEST TASKS INCLUDED IN OUR LABORS.
YET WE TOILED AND STOPPED THE BLIGHT, PREVENTED THE SUBSIDENCE, MAKING OUR FOUNDATIONS GOOD. OUR EXCAVATIONS GRADUALLY UNCOVERING THE FUTURE ... AND WE WERE BUILDERS OF TOMORROW...
-10-

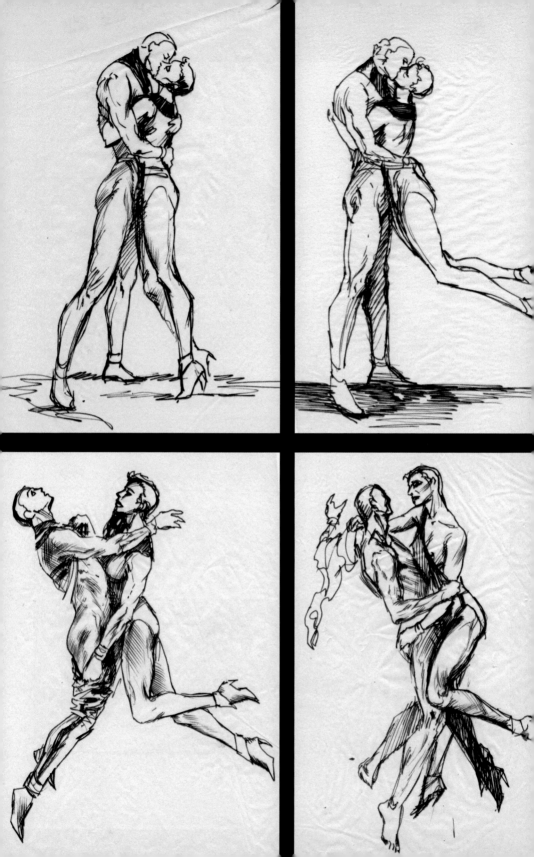

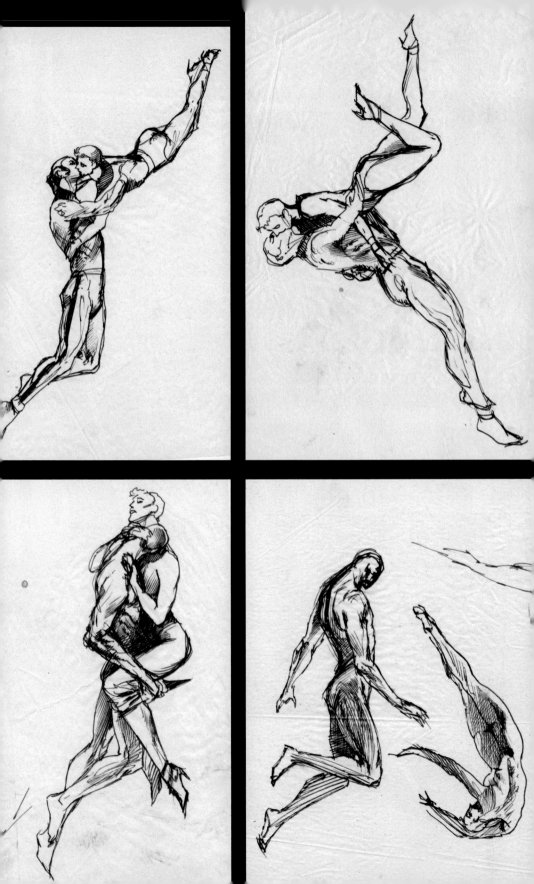

*Miracleman* #16, pages 17-18 original artwork, pencil, India ink, ink washes and white acrylic on illustration board by Thomas Yeates with additional effects by John Totleben.

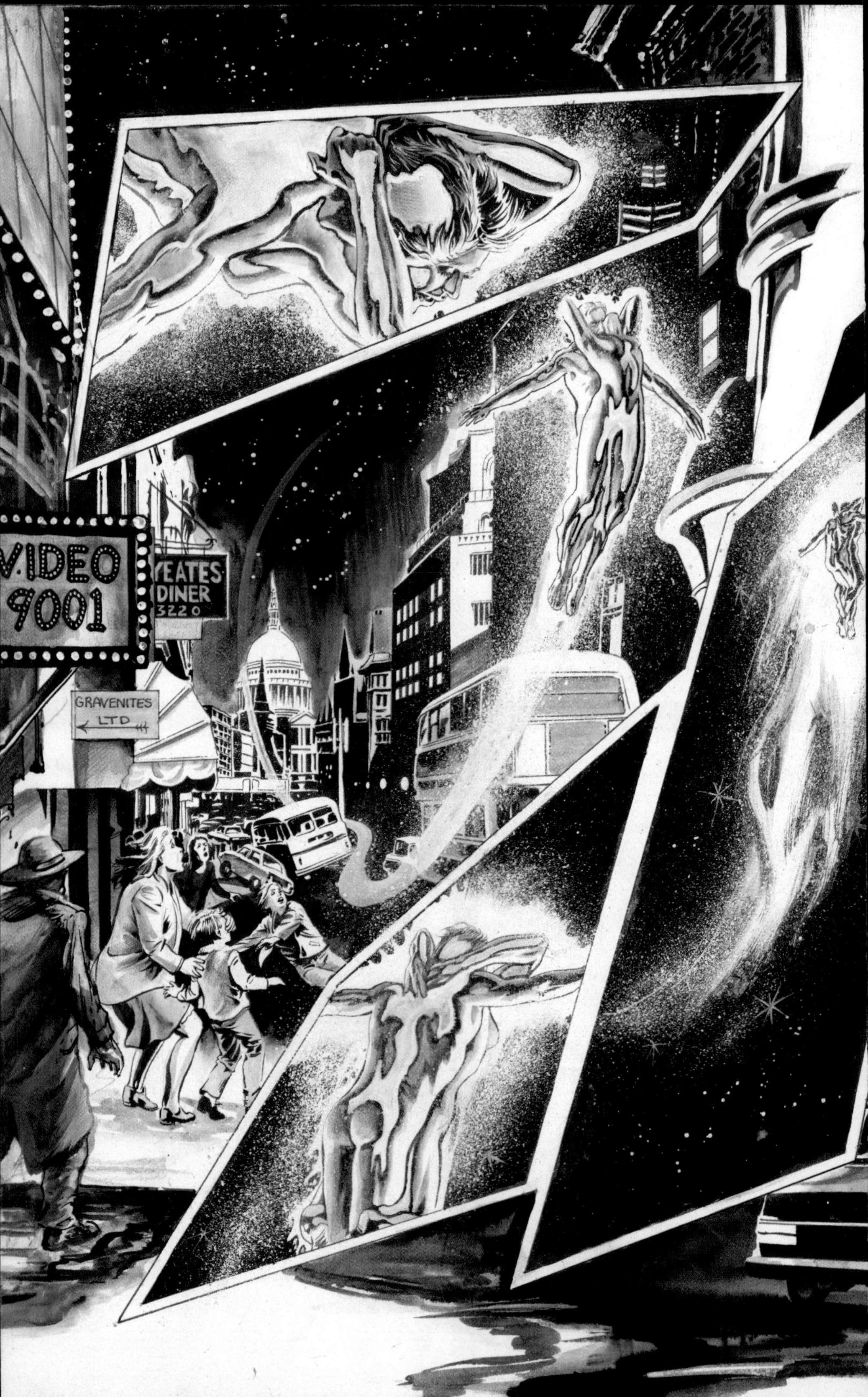
VIDEO 9001
YEATES DINER 3220
GRAVENITES LTD

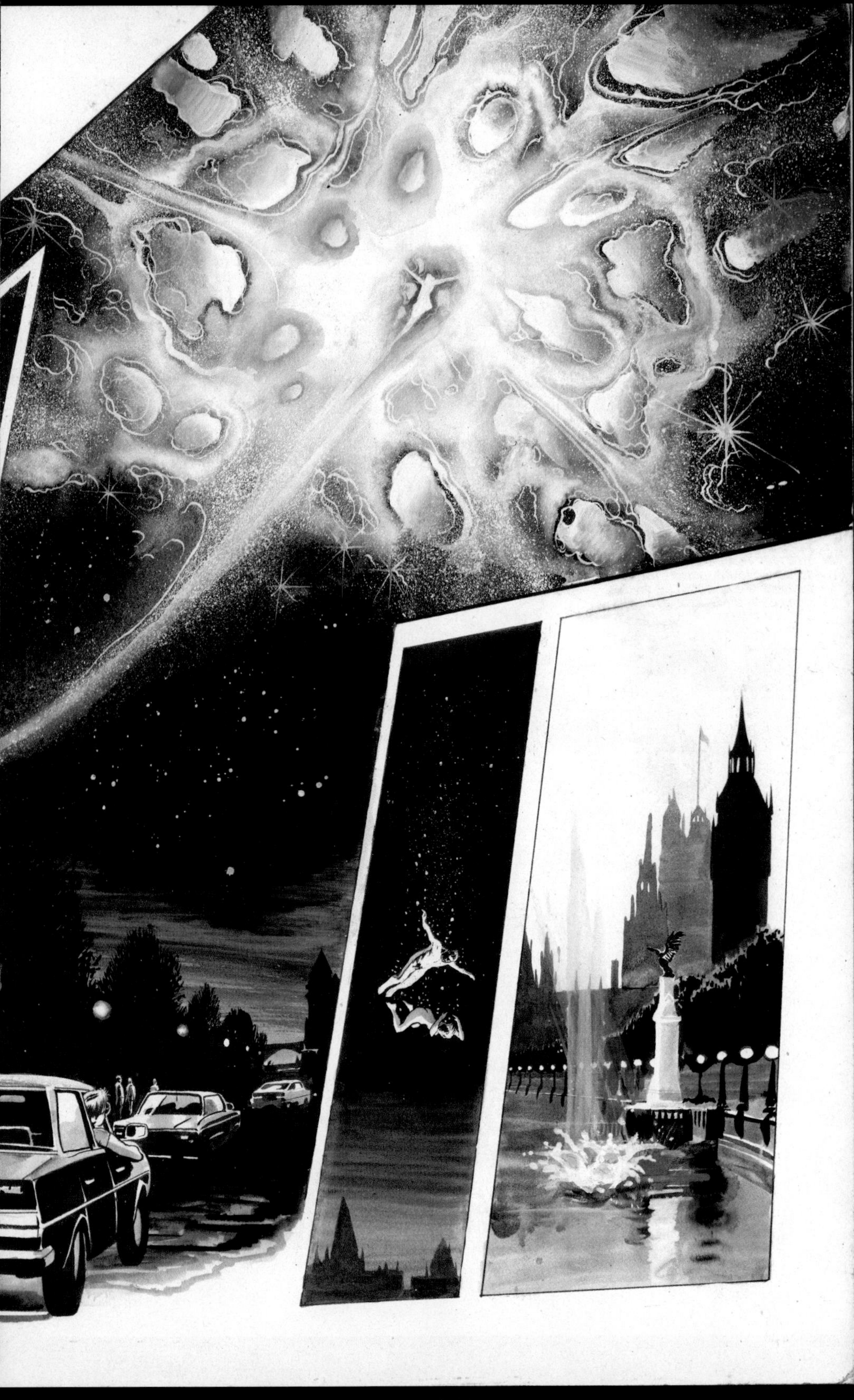

Miracleman #16, page 19 original artwork, pencil, India ink, ink washes and white acrylic on illustration board. Panels 1-3 by John Totleben; panels 4-5 by Thomas Yeates.

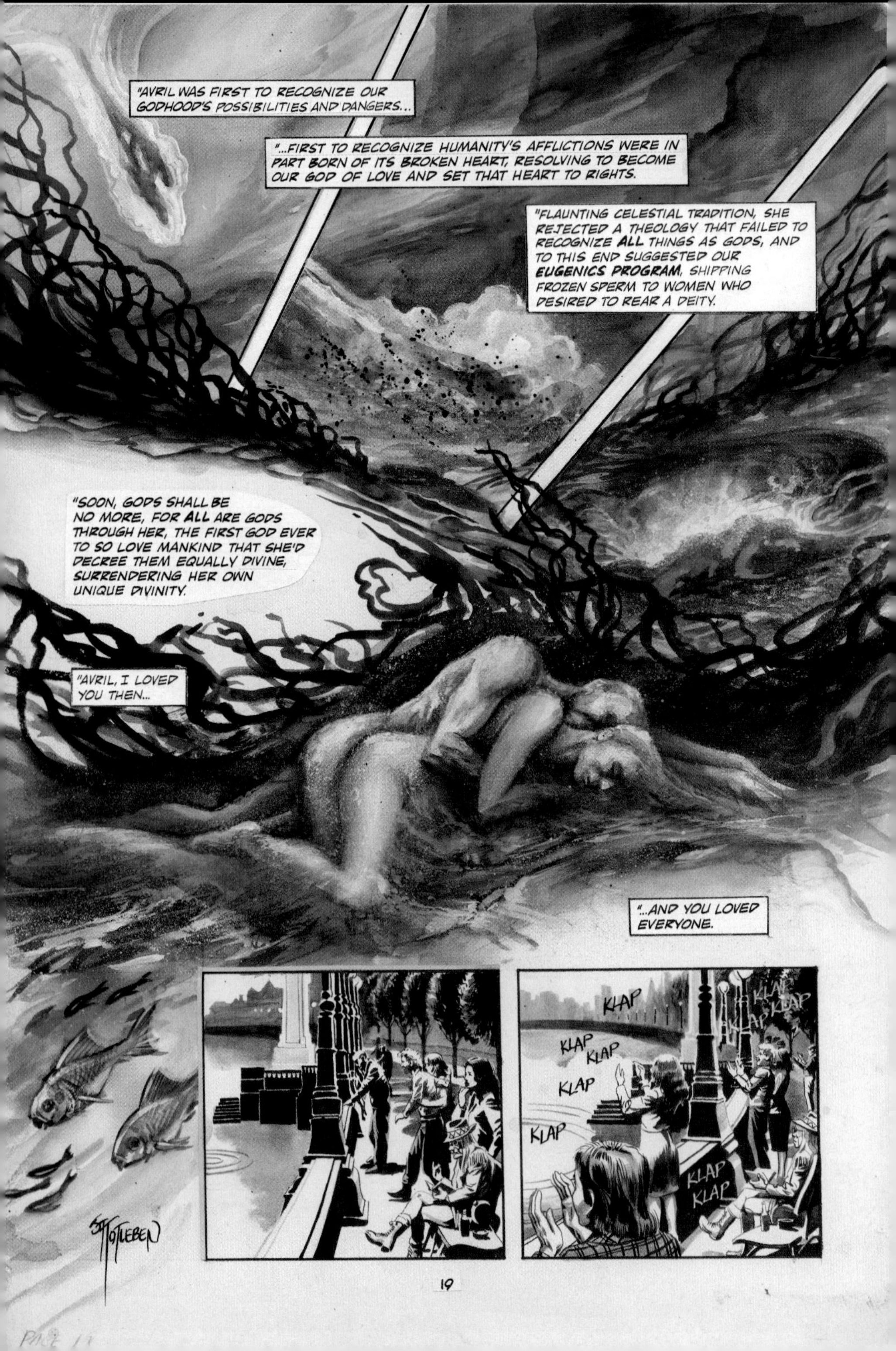
"AVRIL WAS FIRST TO RECOGNIZE OUR GODHOOD'S POSSIBILITIES AND DANGERS...
"...FIRST TO RECOGNIZE HUMANITY'S AFFLICTIONS WERE IN PART BORN OF ITS BROKEN HEART, RESOLVING TO BECOME OUR GOD OF LOVE AND SET THAT HEART TO RIGHTS.
"FLAUNTING CELESTIAL TRADITION, SHE REJECTED A THEOLOGY THAT FAILED TO RECOGNIZE ALL THINGS AS GODS, AND TO THIS END SUGGESTED OUR EUGENICS PROGRAM, SHIPPING FROZEN SPERM TO WOMEN WHO DESIRED TO REAR A DEITY.
"SOON, GODS SHALL BE NO MORE, FOR ALL ARE GODS THROUGH HER, THE FIRST GOD EVER TO SO LOVE MANKIND THAT SHE'D DECREE THEM EQUALLY DIVINE, SURRENDERING HER OWN UNIQUE DIVINITY.
"AVRIL, I LOVED YOU THEN...
"...AND YOU LOVED EVERYONE.
KLAP
KLAP KLAP
KLAP
KLAP
KLAP
KLAP KLAP
TOTLEBEN
19

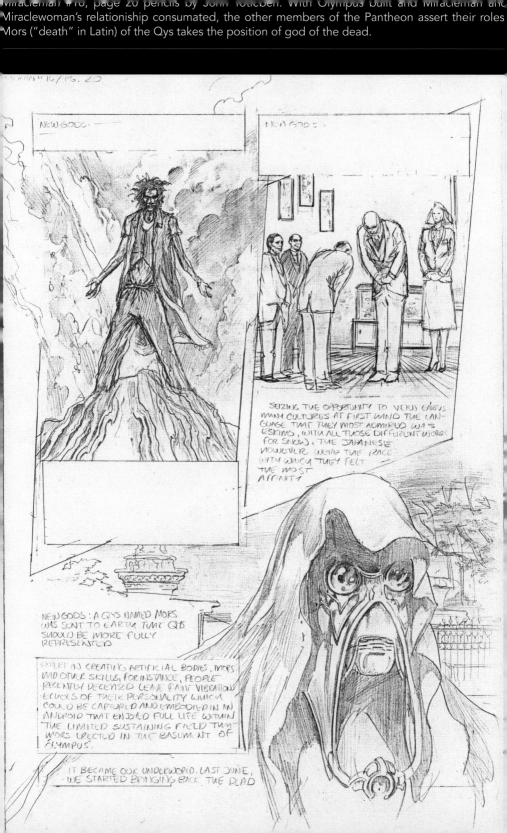

*Miracleman* #16, page 22 pencils by John Totleben. Big Ben is reborn as the new Hercules with a British bulldog's pelt in the place of a lion's. Miracledog becomes the Pantheon's Fenris. In Norse mythology, Fenris the wolf is Loki's son and swallows Odin during Ragnarök.

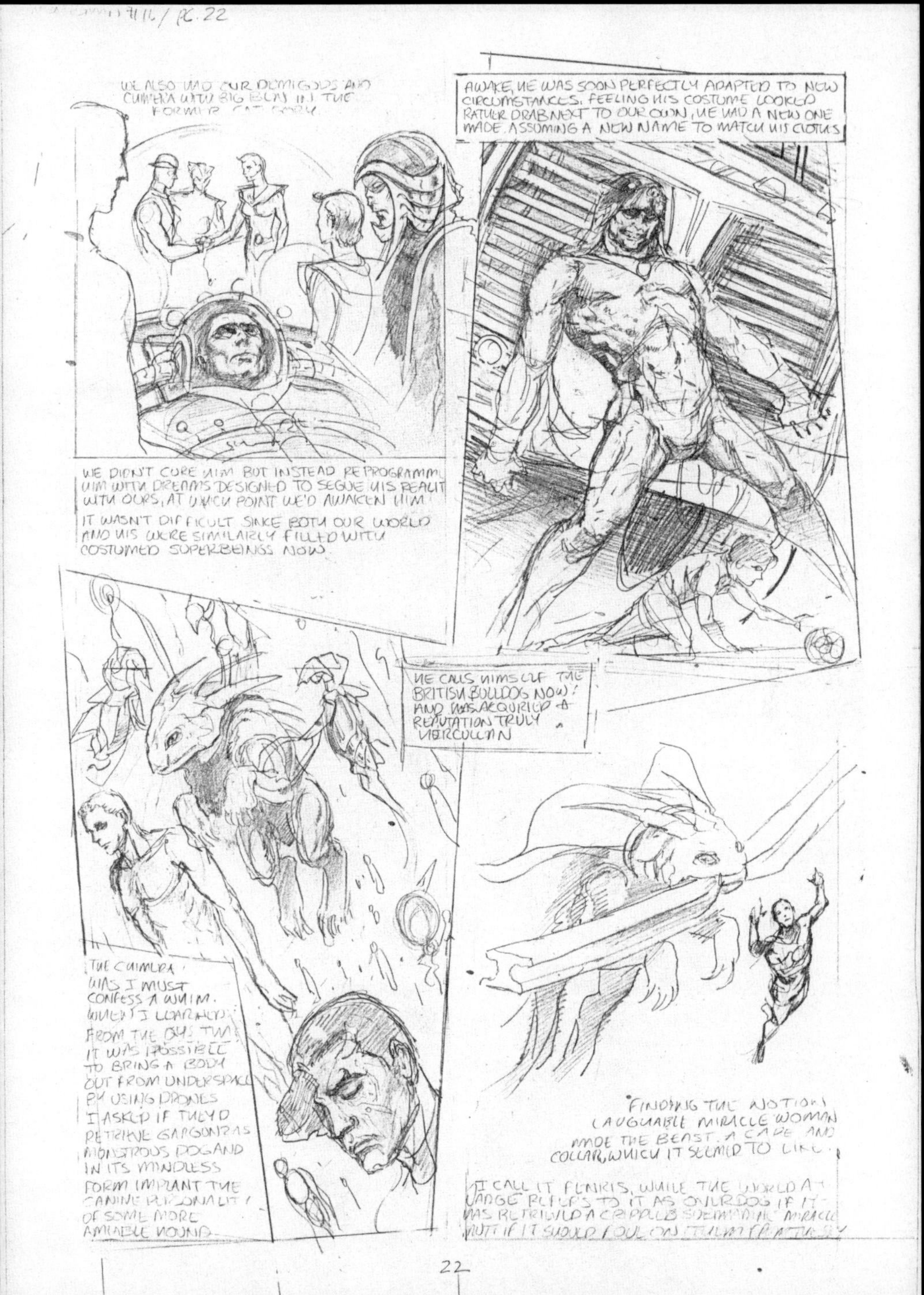
AWAKE, HE WAS SOON PERFECTLY ADAPTED TO NEW CIRCUMSTANCES. FEELING HIS COSTUME LOOKED RATHER DRAB NEXT TO OUR OWN, HE HAD A NEW ONE MADE, ASSUMING A NEW NAME TO MATCH HIS CLOTHES
WE DIDN'T CURE HIM BUT INSTEAD REPROGRAMMED HIM WITH DREAMS DESIGNED TO SEGUE HIS REALITY WITH OURS, AT WHICH POINT WE'D AWAKEN HIM
IT WASN'T DIFFICULT SINCE BOTH OUR WORLD AND HIS WERE SIMILARLY FILLED WITH COSTUMED SUPERBEINGS NOW
HE CALLS HIMSELF THE BRITISH BULLDOG NOW! AND HAS ACQUIRED A REPUTATION TRULY HERCULEAN
THE CHIMERA WAS I MUST CONFESS A WHIM. FROM THE QYS TIM IT WAS POSSIBLE TO BRING A BODY OUT FROM UNDERSPACE BY USING DRONES. I ASKED IF THEY'D RETRIEVE MONSTROUS DOG AND IN ITS MINDLESS FORM IMPLANT THE CANINE PERSONALITY OF SOME MORE AMIABLE HOUND
FINDING THE NOTION LAUGHABLE MIRACLE WOMAN MADE THE BEAST A CAPE AND COLLAR, WHICH IT SEEMED TO LIKE.
22

Miracleman #16, page 24 pencils by John Totleben. Winter welcomes miracle babies into the world in her role in the Pantheon, while those that weren't born gods must decide whether to leave humanity behind and receive superhuman enchancements.

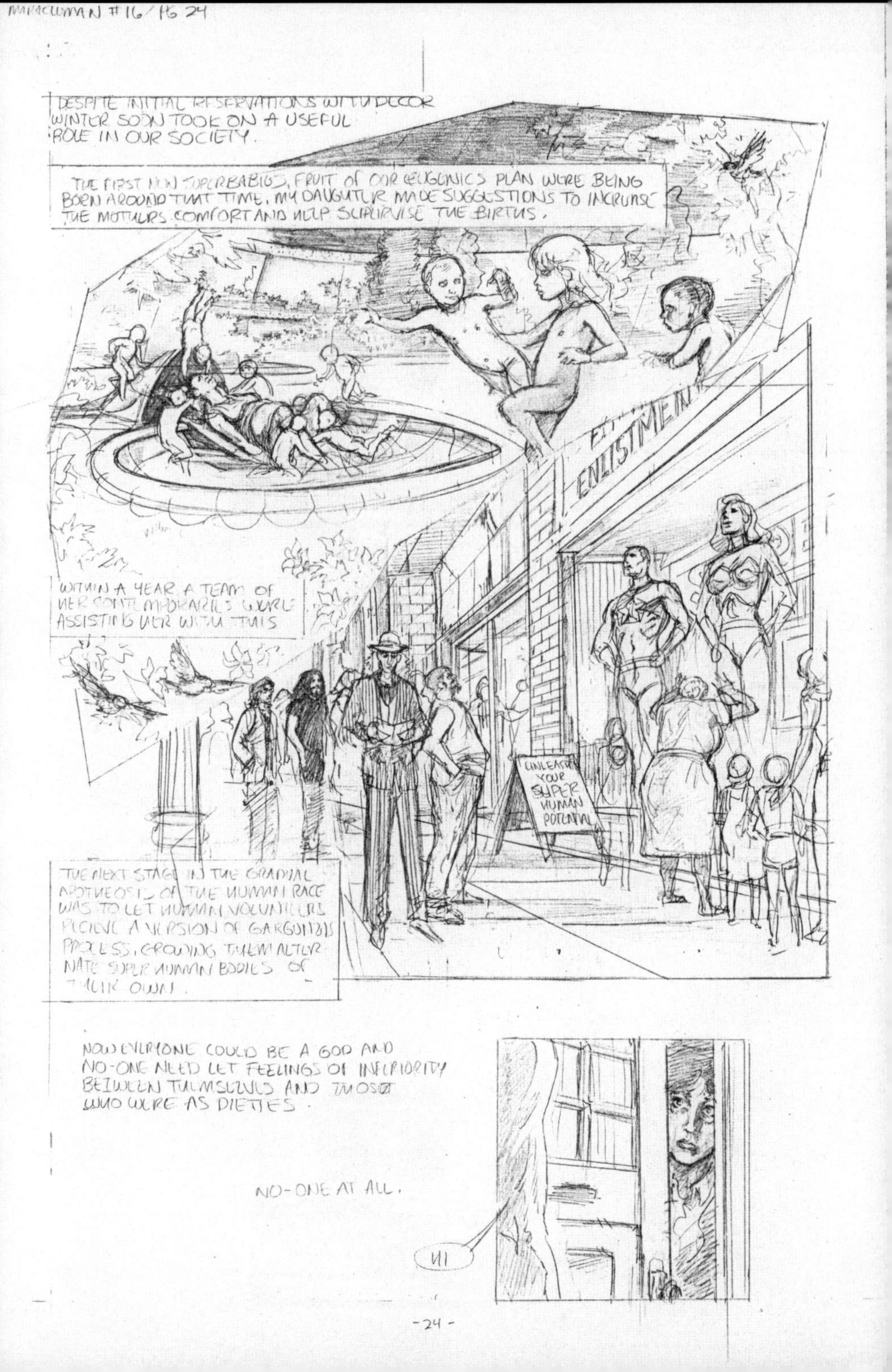
MIRACLEMAN #16 / PG 24
DESPITE INITIAL RESERVATIONS WITH DECOR WINTER SOON TOOK ON A USEFUL ROLE IN OUR SOCIETY.
THE FIRST NEW SUPERBABIES, FRUIT OF OUR EUGENICS PLAN WERE BEING BORN AROUND THAT TIME. MY DAUGHTER MADE SUGGESTIONS TO INCREASE THE MOTHERS COMFORT AND HELP SUPERVISE THE BIRTHS.
ENLISTMENT
WITHIN A YEAR A TEAM OF HER CONTEMPORARIES WERE ASSISTING HER WITH THIS
UNLEASH YOUR SUPER HUMAN POTENTIAL
THE NEXT STAGE IN THE GRADUAL APOTHEOSIS OF THE HUMAN RACE WAS TO LET HUMAN VOLUNTEERS RECEIVE A VERSION OF GARGUNZA'S PROCESS, GROWING THEM ALTERNATE SUPERHUMAN BODIES OF THEIR OWN.
NOW EVERYONE COULD BE A GOD AND NO-ONE NEED LET FEELINGS OF INFERIORITY BETWEEN THEMSELVES AND THOSE WHO WERE AS DIETIES.
NO-ONE AT ALL.
-24-

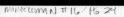

*Miracleman* #16, page 25 pencils and partial inks by John Totleben. For Miracleman/Michael Moran's wife, Liz, there's no decision to be made. Their final parting of ways is a study in posture and contrast. Miracleman gesticulates widely; Liz, cropped just below the eyes to emphasize her small contained movements, struggles with a loss he cannot comprehend.

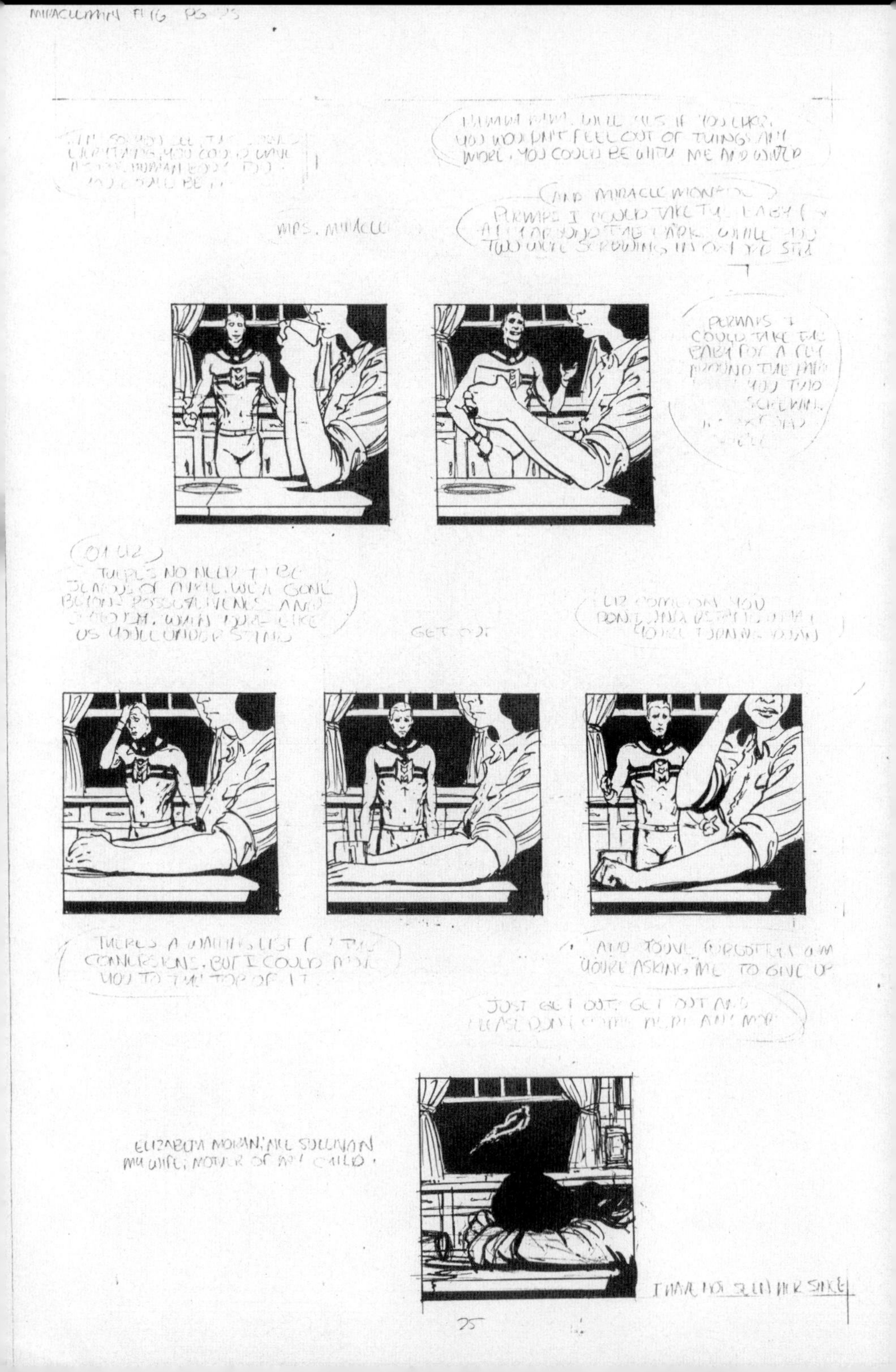

MRS. MIRACLE
ELIZABETH MORAN; NEE SULLIVAN
MY WIFE; MOTHER OF MY CHILD.

*Miracleman* #16, page 26 pencils by John Totleben. The wonders of other worlds have come to Earth, so inner space — with drug use as its launch pad — has become the new frontier. Meanwhile, men formerly of political and military power confess their insecurities in group therapy. Totleben's opening panel tilts the reader back, forcing them to reassess their balance.

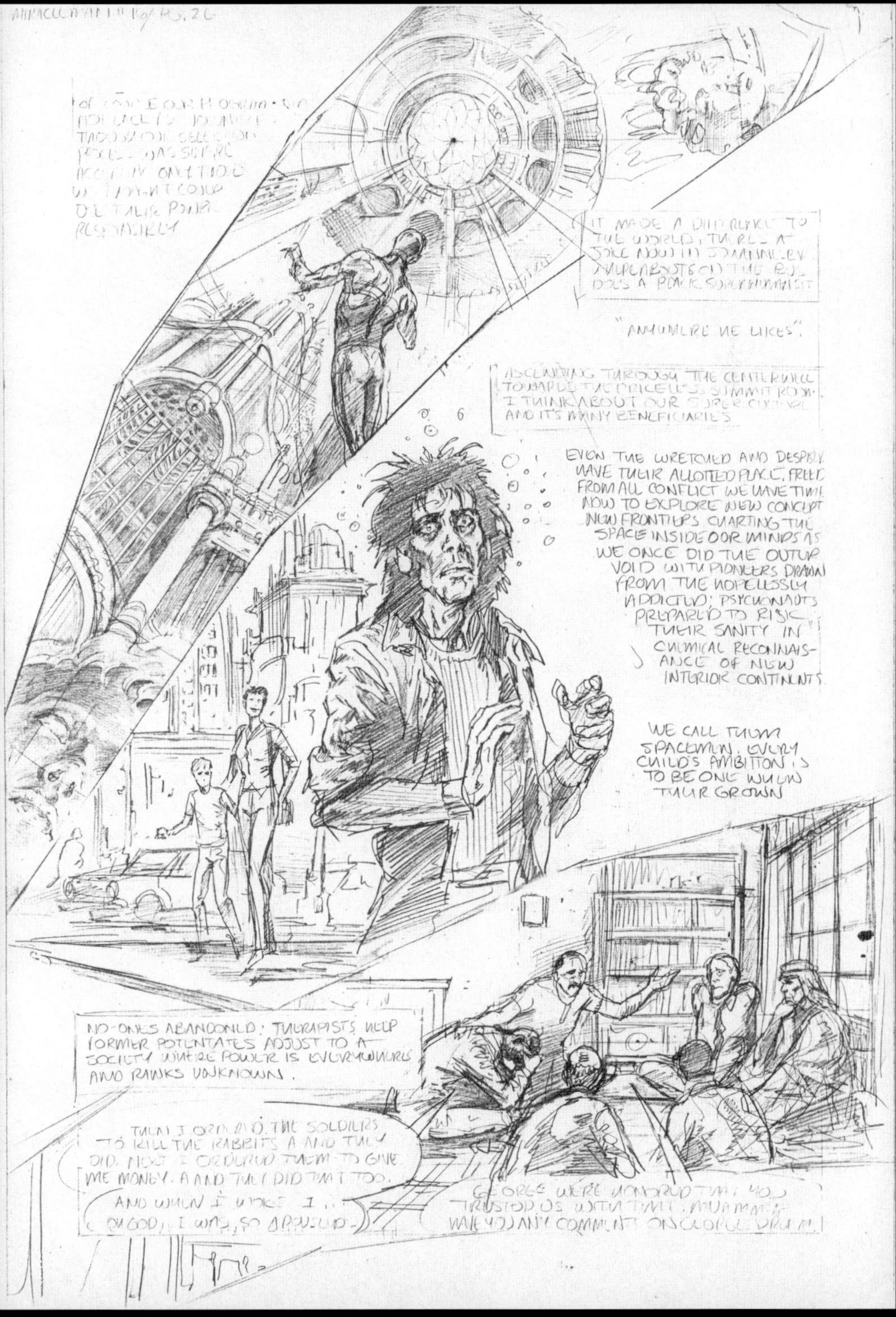
"ANYWHERE HE LIKES".
ASCENDING THROUGH THE CENTERWELL TOWARD THE PRICELESS SUMMIT ROOM, I THINK ABOUT OUR SUPERCULTURE AND IT'S MANY BENEFICIARIES
EVEN THE WRETCHED AND DESPERATE HAVE THEIR ALLOTTED PLACE. FREED FROM ALL CONFLICT WE HAVE TIME NOW TO EXPLORE NEW CONCEPTS NEW FRONTIERS CHARTING THE SPACE INSIDE OUR MINDS AS WE ONCE DID THE OUTER VOID WITH PIONEERS DRAWN FROM THE HOPELESSLY ADDICTED; PSYCHONAUTS PREPARED TO RISK THEIR SANITY IN CHEMICAL RECONNAISSANCE OF NEW INTERIOR CONTINENTS.
WE CALL THEM SPACEMEN. EVERY CHILD'S AMBITION IS TO BE ONE WHEN THEY'RE GROWN
NO-ONES ABANDONED: THERAPISTS HELP FORMER POTENTATES ADJUST TO A SOCIETY WHERE POWER IS EVERYWHERE AND RANKS UNKNOWN.
THEN I ORDERED THE SOLDIERS TO KILL THE RABBITS AND THEY DID. NEXT I ORDERED THEM TO GIVE ME MONEY. AND THEY DID THAT TOO.
AND WHEN I WOKE I... OH GOD, I WAS SO AROUSED-
GEORGE, WE'RE HONORED THAT YOU TRUSTED US WITH THAT. MUAMMAR, HAVE YOU ANY COMMENTS ON GEORGE'S DREAM?

*Miracleman* #16, page 28 pencils by John Totleben. Finally, we arrive at the present, February 1987. Miracleman dresses for a celebration of his rebirth. His ceremonial uniform is undoubtedly formal, possibly authoritarian.

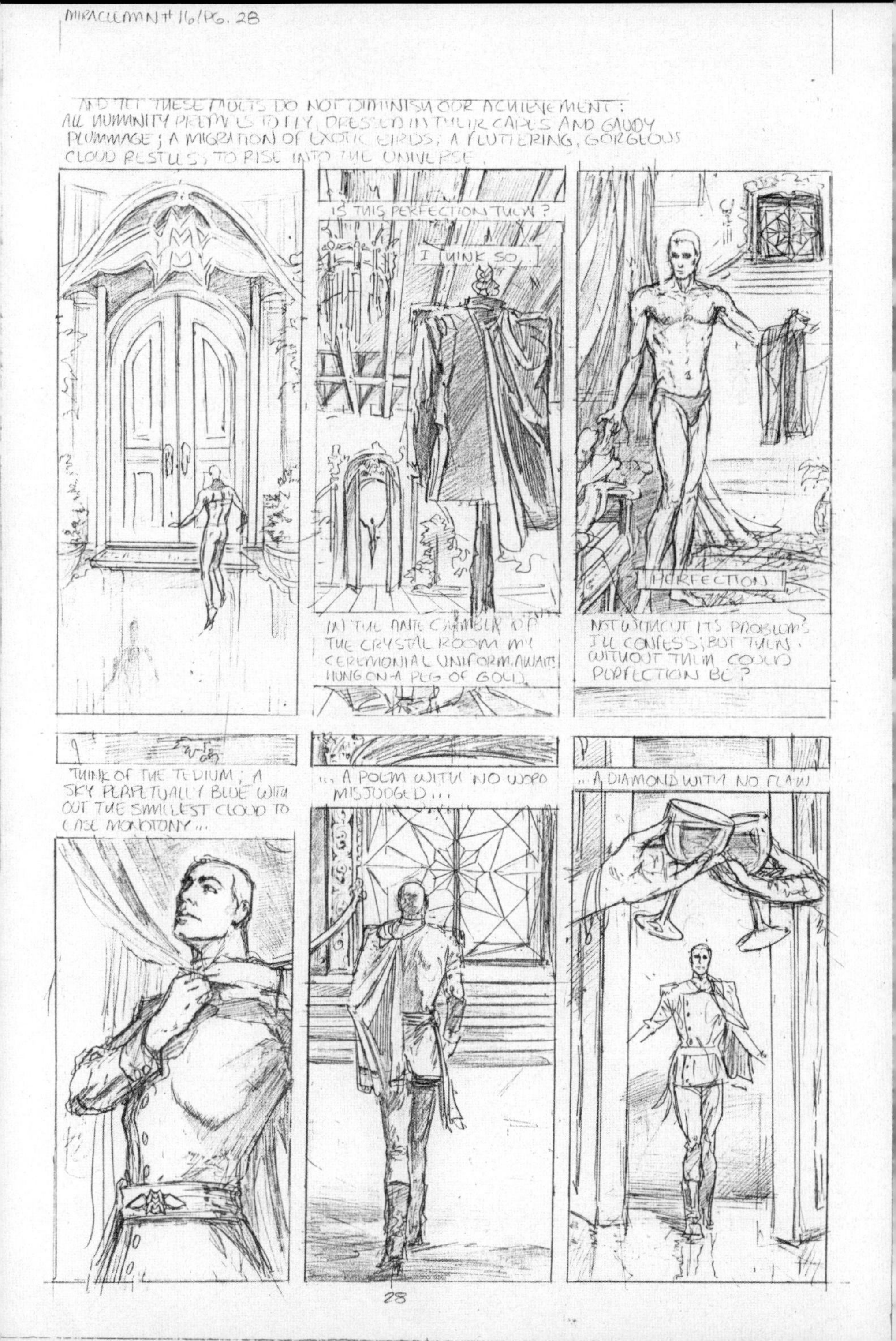
MIRACLEMAN #16/PG. 28
AND YET THESE FAULTS DO NOT DIMINISH OUR ACHIEVEMENT: ALL HUMANITY PREPARES TO FLY, DRESSED IN THEIR CAPES AND GAUDY PLUMMAGE; A MIGRATION OF EXOTIC BIRDS; A FLUTTERING, GORGEOUS CLOUD RESTLESS TO RISE INTO THE UNIVERSE.
IS THIS PERFECTION THEN?
I THINK SO.
IN THE ANTE CHAMBER OF THE CRYSTAL ROOM MY CEREMONIAL UNIFORM AWAITS HUNG ON A PEG OF GOLD.
PERFECTION.
NOT WITHOUT ITS PROBLEMS I'LL CONFESS; BUT THEN, WITHOUT THEM COULD PERFECTION BE?
THINK OF THE TEDIUM; A SKY PERPETUALLY BLUE WITHOUT THE SMALLEST CLOUD TO EASE MONOTONY...
...A POEM WITH NO WORD MISJUDGED...
...A DIAMOND WITH NO FLAW
28

Miracleman #16, page 29 pencils by John Totleben. With his story of how the world was remade complete, Miracleman gathers together with the new Miracleman Family atop Olympus' peak.

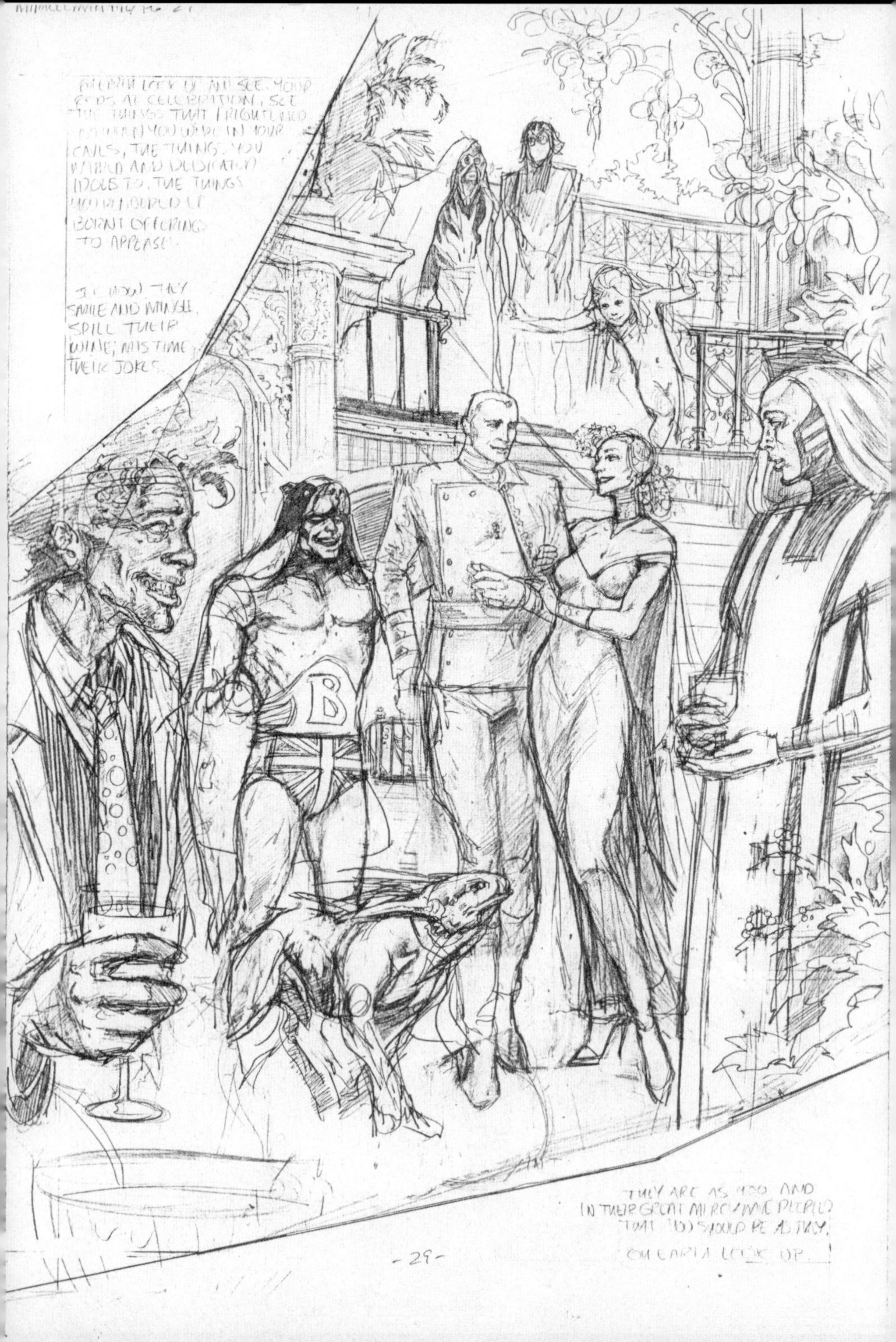
GODS AT CELEBRATION. SEE
IDOLS TO. THE THINGS
BURNT OFFERINGS
TO APPEASE.
SMILE AND MINGLE,
SPILL THEIR
WINE; MISTIME
THEIR JOKES.
THEY ARE AS GODS AND
ON EARTH LOOK UP.
-29-

*Miracleman* #16, page 30 pencils by John Totleben. The camera moves outside, and the Pantheon are seen through Olympus' diamond capstone. As each panel pulls farther away, the figures become more and more diffused, fading, like a dream.

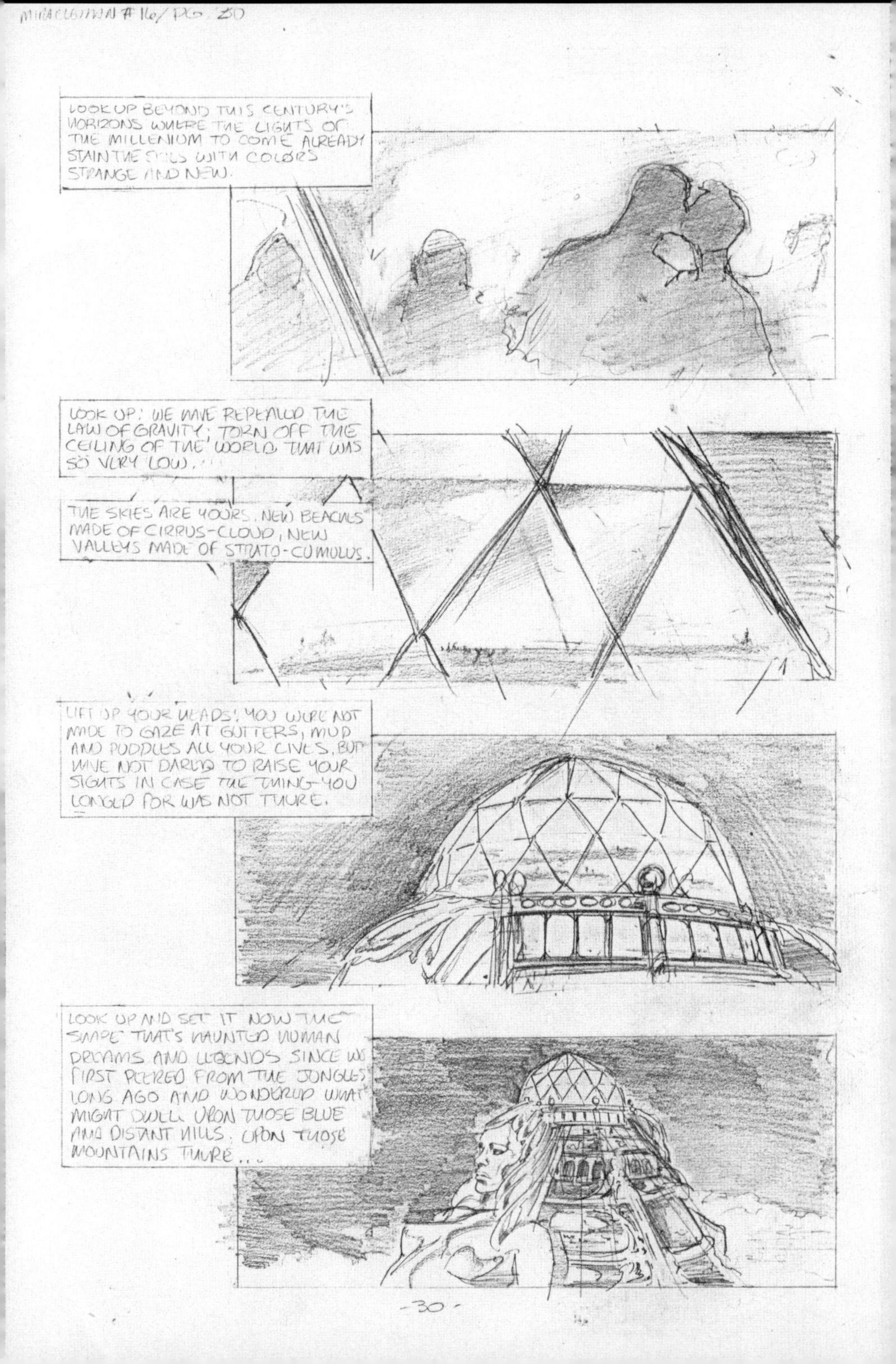

MIRACLEMAN #16/PG 30
LOOK UP BEYOND THIS CENTURY'S HORIZONS WHERE THE LIGHTS OF THE MILLENIUM TO COME ALREADY STAIN THE SKIES WITH COLORS STRANGE AND NEW.
LOOK UP: WE HAVE REPEALED THE LAW OF GRAVITY; TORN OFF THE CEILING OF THE WORLD THAT WAS SO VERY LOW...
THE SKIES ARE YOURS. NEW BEACHES MADE OF CIRRUS-CLOUD, NEW VALLEYS MADE OF STRATO-CUMULUS.
LIFT UP YOUR HEADS! YOU WERE NOT MADE TO GAZE AT GUTTERS, MUD AND PUDDLES ALL YOUR LIVES, BUT HAVE NOT DARED TO RAISE YOUR SIGHTS IN CASE THE THING YOU LONGED FOR WAS NOT THERE.
LOOK UP AND SEE IT NOW THE SHAPE THAT'S HAUNTED HUMAN DREAMS AND LEGENDS SINCE WE FIRST PEERED FROM THE JUNGLES LONG AGO AND WONDERED WHAT MIGHT DWELL UPON THOSE BLUE AND DISTANT HILLS. UPON THOSE MOUNTAINS THERE...
-30-

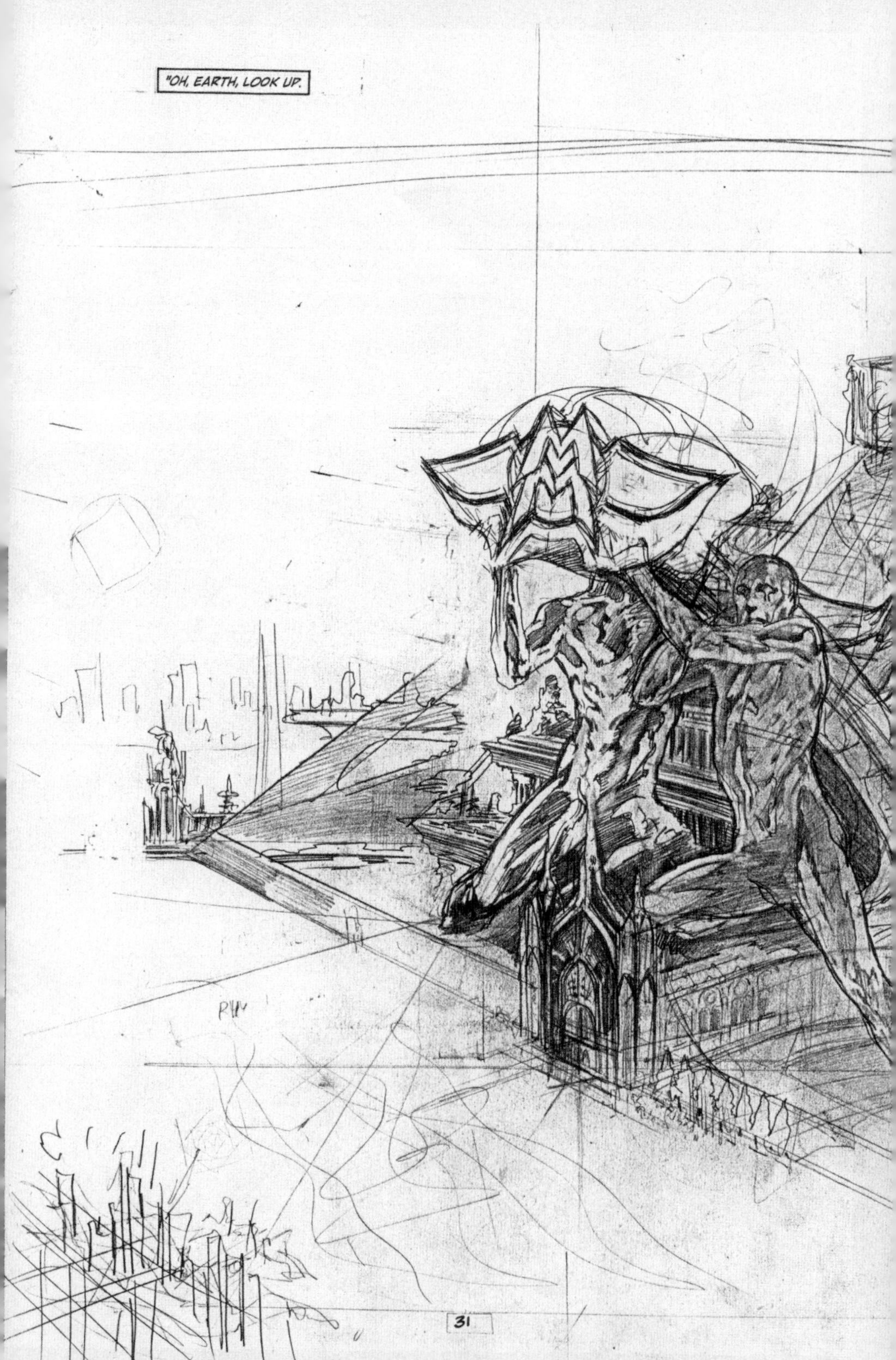
"OH, EARTH, LOOK UP.

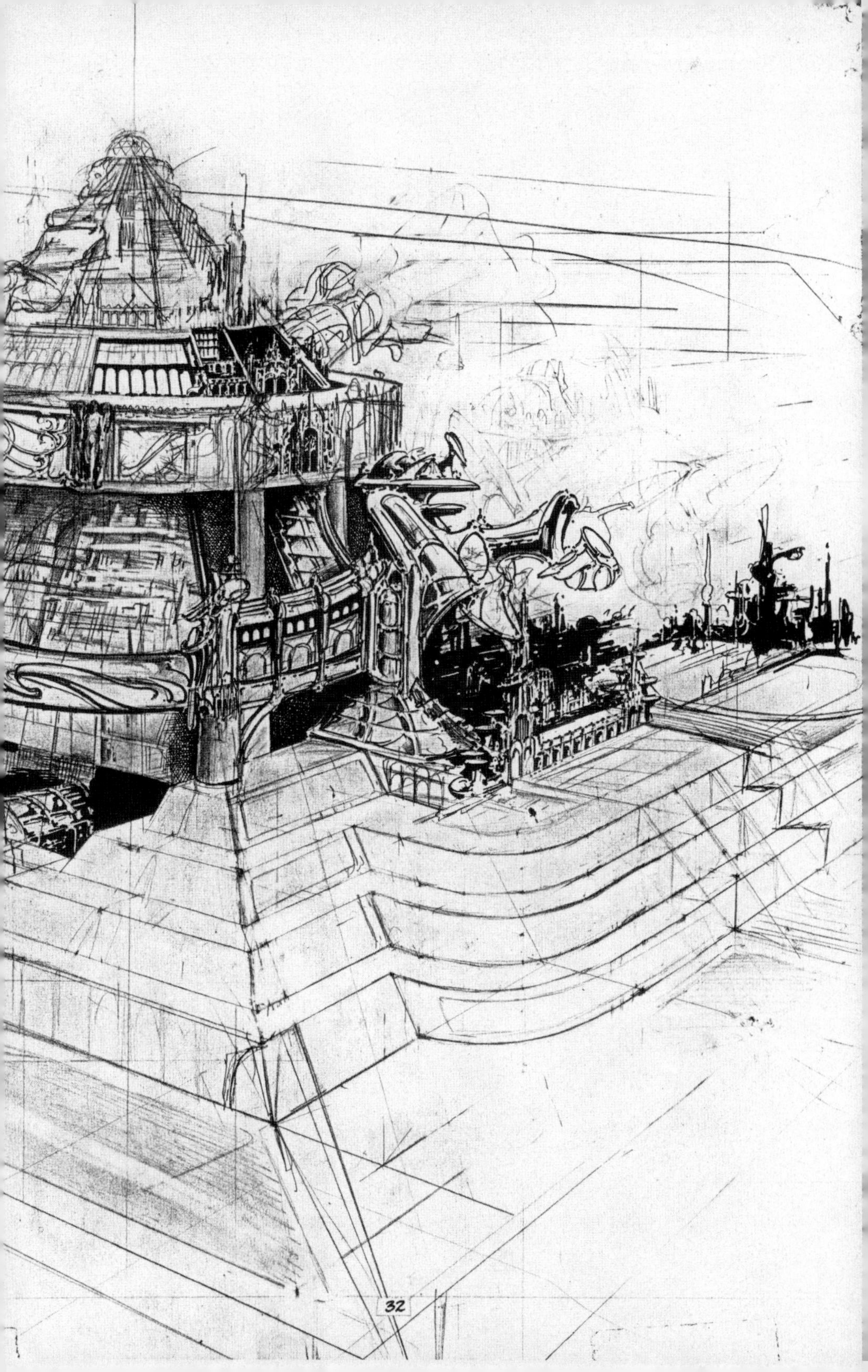

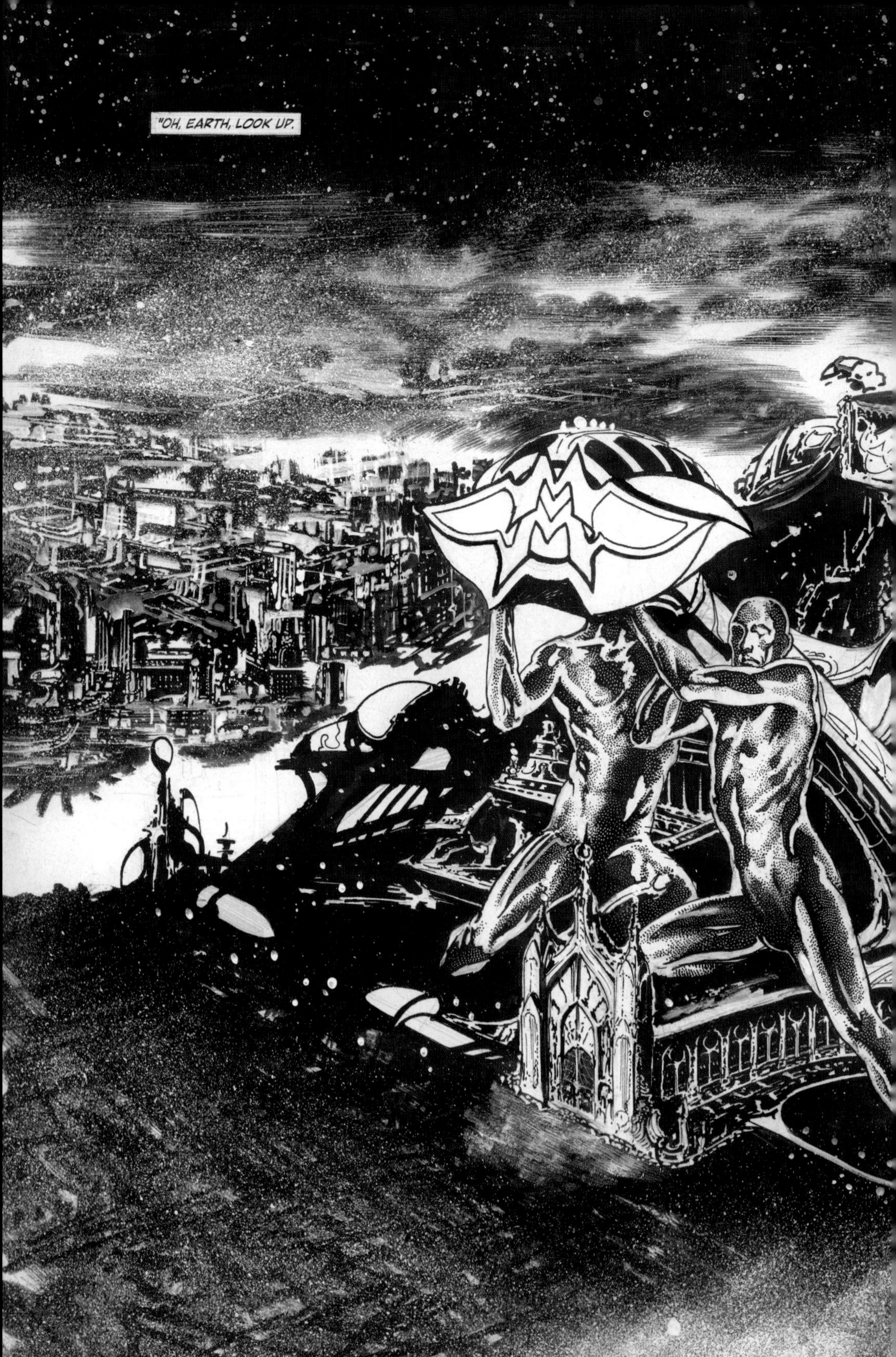
"OH, EARTH, LOOK UP.

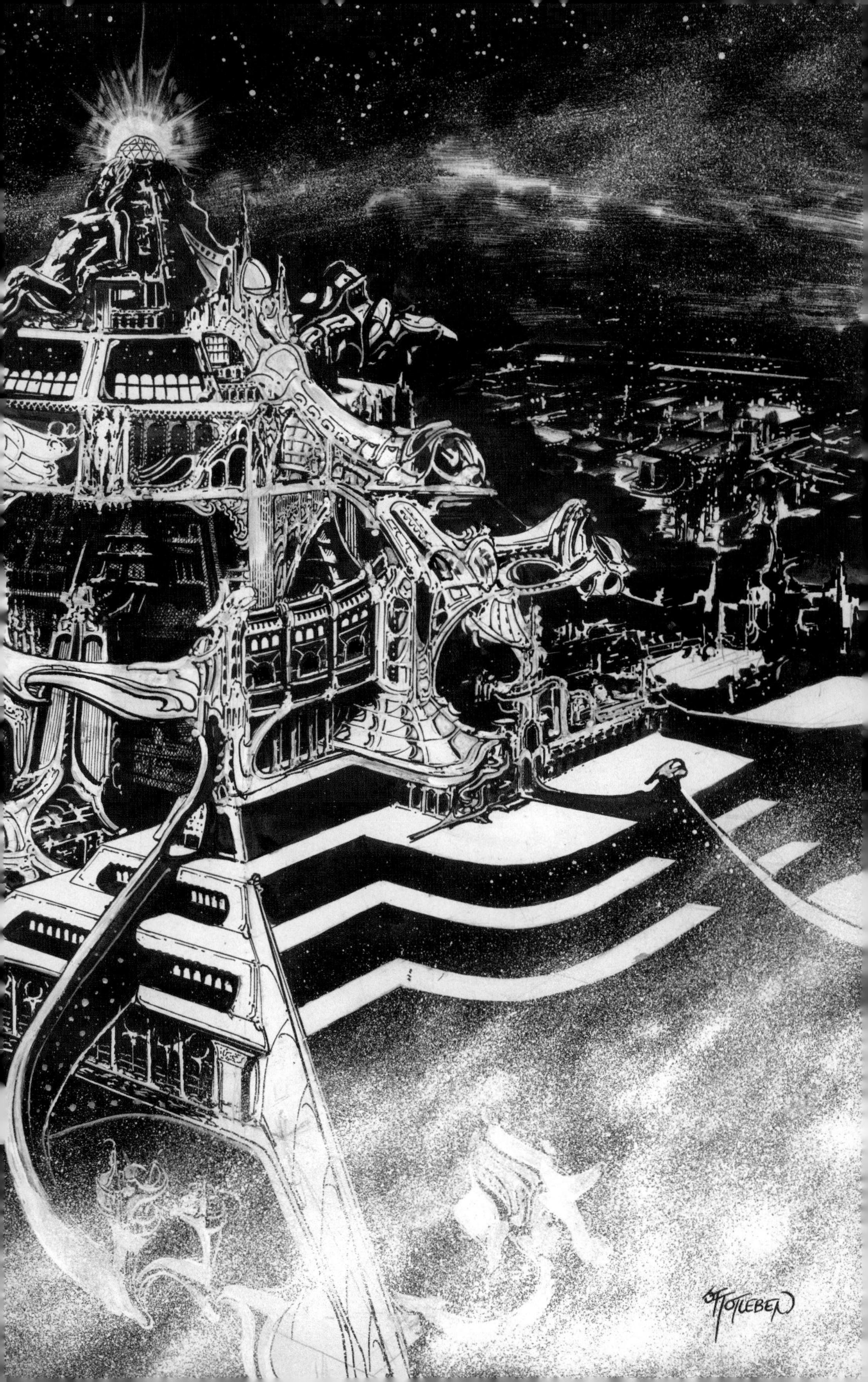

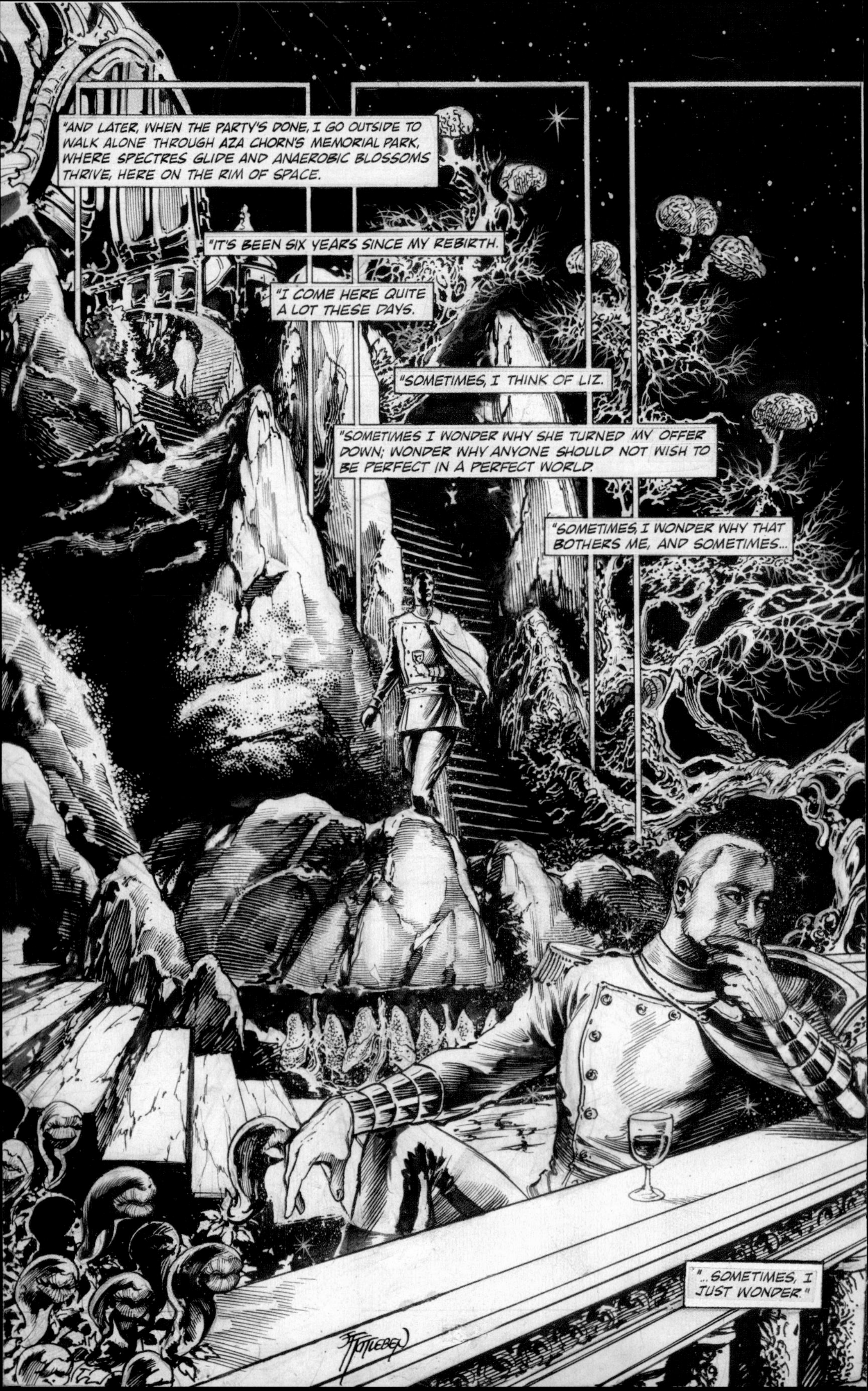
"AND LATER, WHEN THE PARTY'S DONE, I GO OUTSIDE TO WALK ALONE THROUGH AZA CHORN'S MEMORIAL PARK, WHERE SPECTRES GLIDE AND ANAEROBIC BLOSSOMS THRIVE, HERE ON THE RIM OF SPACE.
"IT'S BEEN SIX YEARS SINCE MY REBIRTH.
"I COME HERE QUITE A LOT THESE DAYS.
"SOMETIMES, I THINK OF LIZ.
"SOMETIMES I WONDER WHY SHE TURNED MY OFFER DOWN; WONDER WHY ANYONE SHOULD NOT WISH TO BE PERFECT IN A PERFECT WORLD.
"SOMETIMES, I WONDER WHY THAT BOTHERS ME, AND SOMETIMES...
"...SOMETIMES, I JUST WONDER."
TOTLEBEN

the published version of the cover, Totleben revised it after publication, bringing out the detail in Miracleman's face and removing his "tinkerbell effect." He also brightened the background, added leaves to the trees and changed the Qys' eyes from yellow to red.

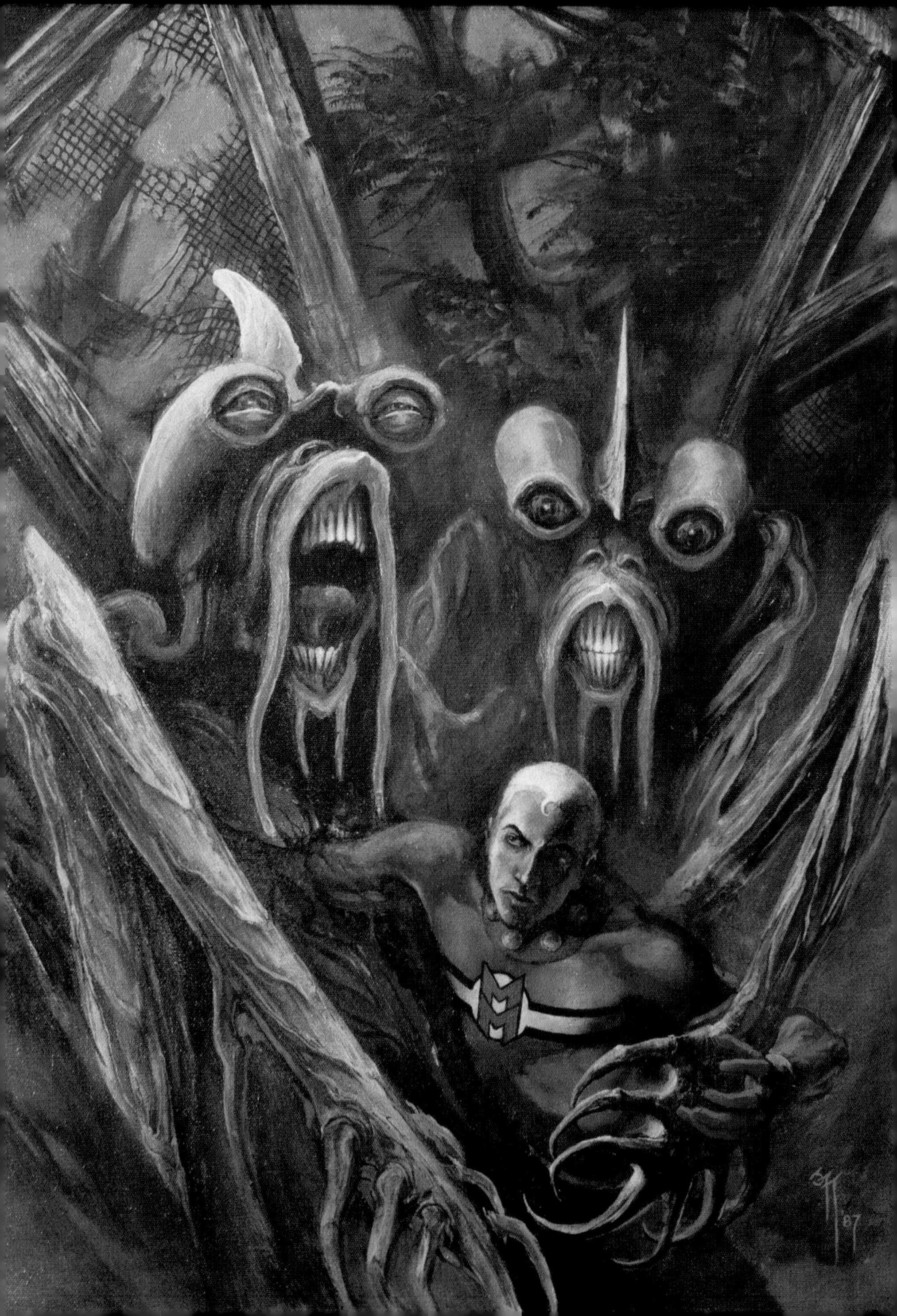

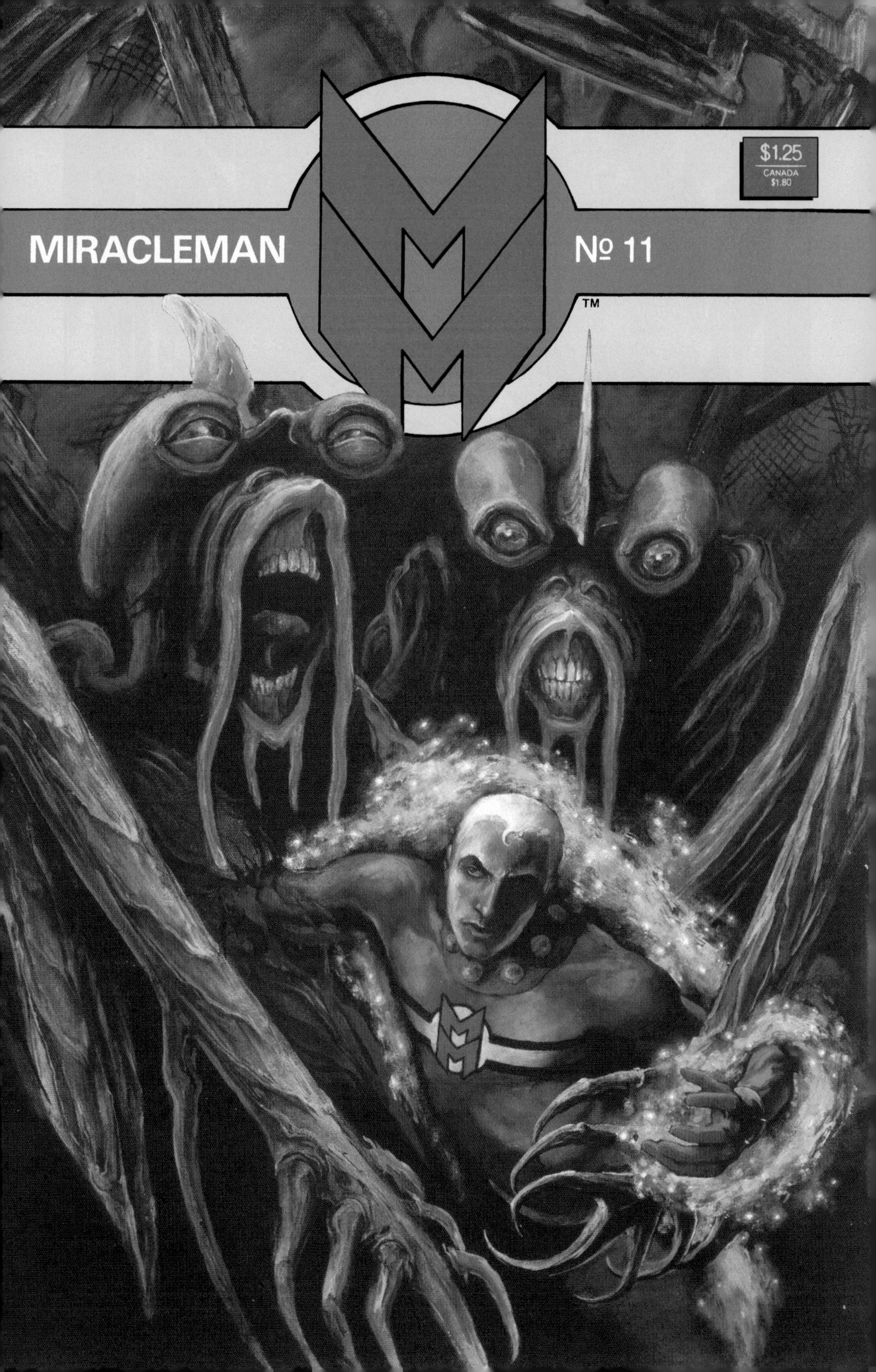

$1.25
CANADA
$1.80
MIRACLEMAN
№ 11
TM

*Miracleman* #12 cover original artwork, pencil, India ink and white acrylic on illustration board by John Totleben.

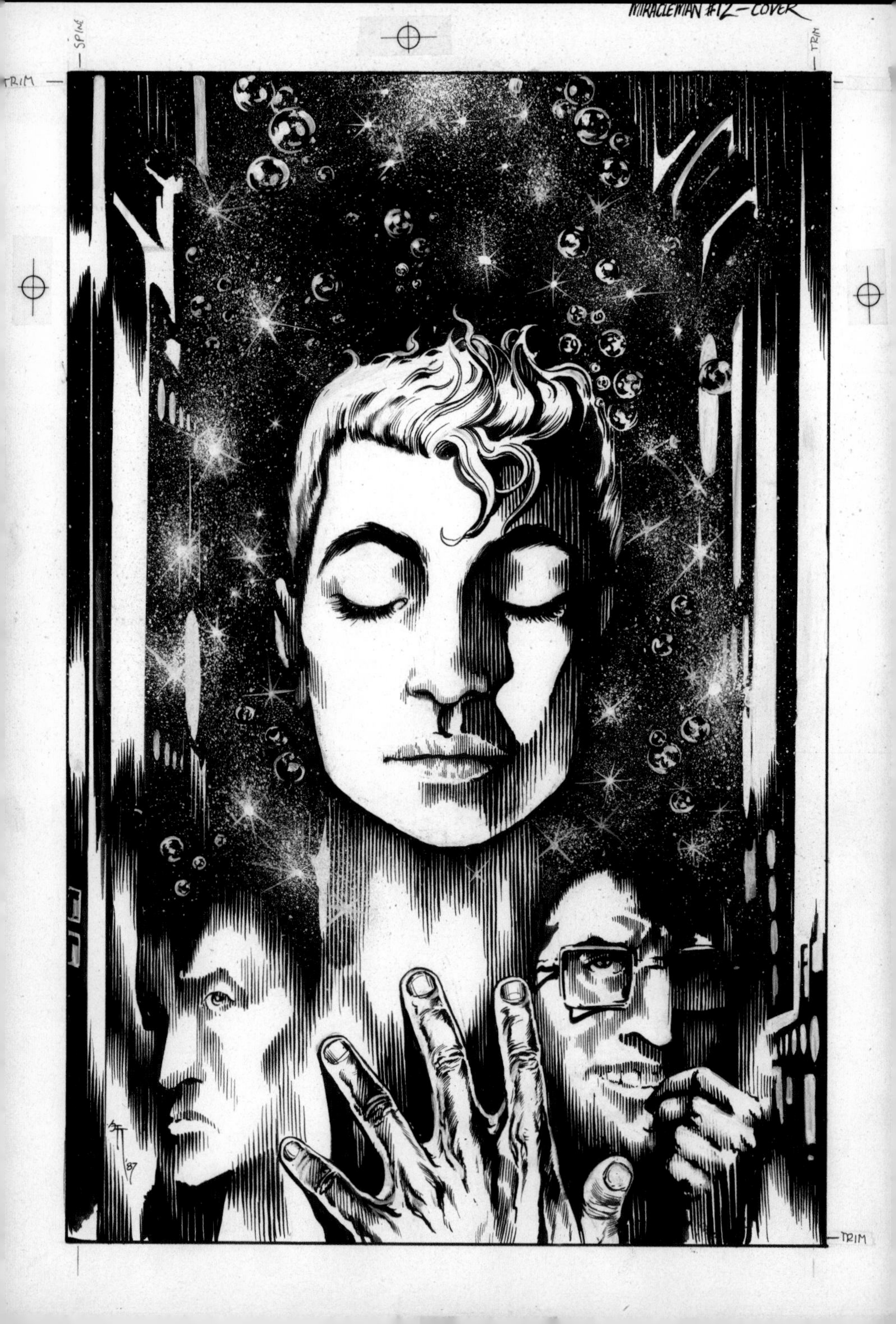
MIRACLEMAN #12—COVER
SPINE
TRIM
TRIM
TRIM

*Miracleman* #12 (September 1987) cover by John Totleben.

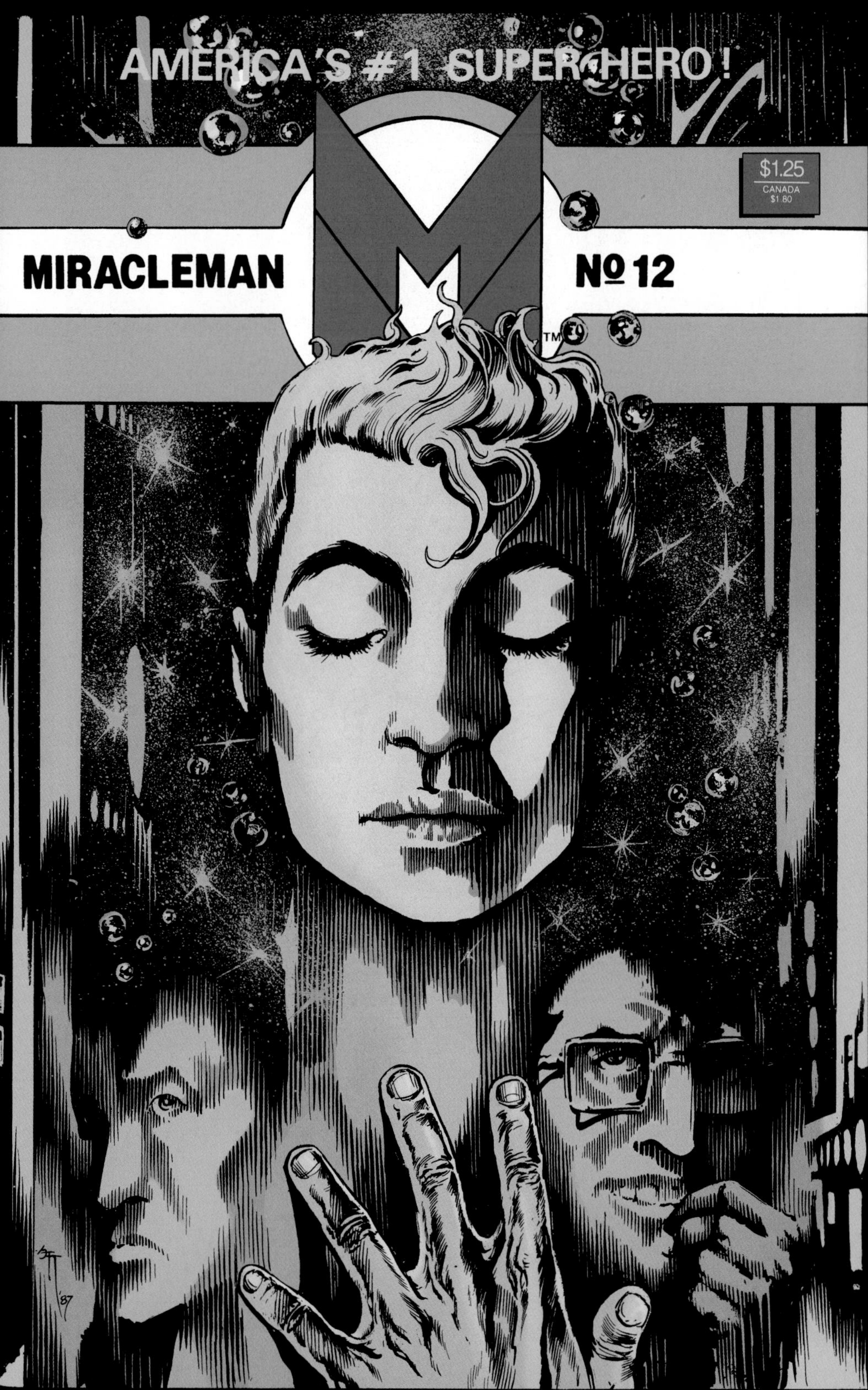
AMERICA'S #1 SUPER-HERO!
$1.25
CANADA
$1.80
MIRACLEMAN
№ 12

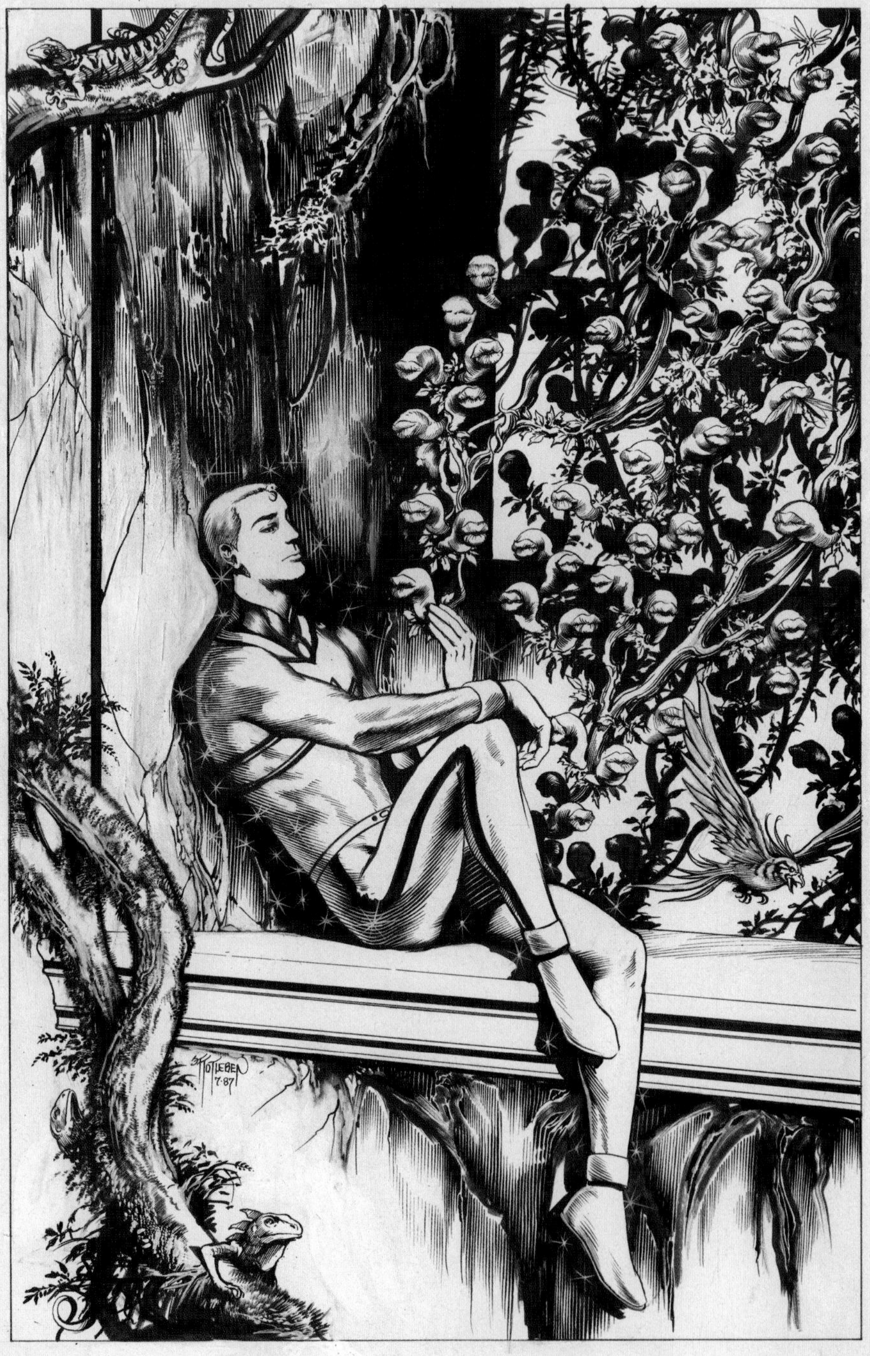

COLOR NOTES:— THESE LITTLE "LIP-PLANTS" SHOULD BE FLESH COLOR WITH THE "LIPS" COLORED PINK
LEAVES & VINES GREENISH, AS NORMAL.

COLOR NOTE — THE LIZARDS & BIRD CAN BE COLORED
HOWEVER YOU LIKE SINCE I MADE 'EM UP.

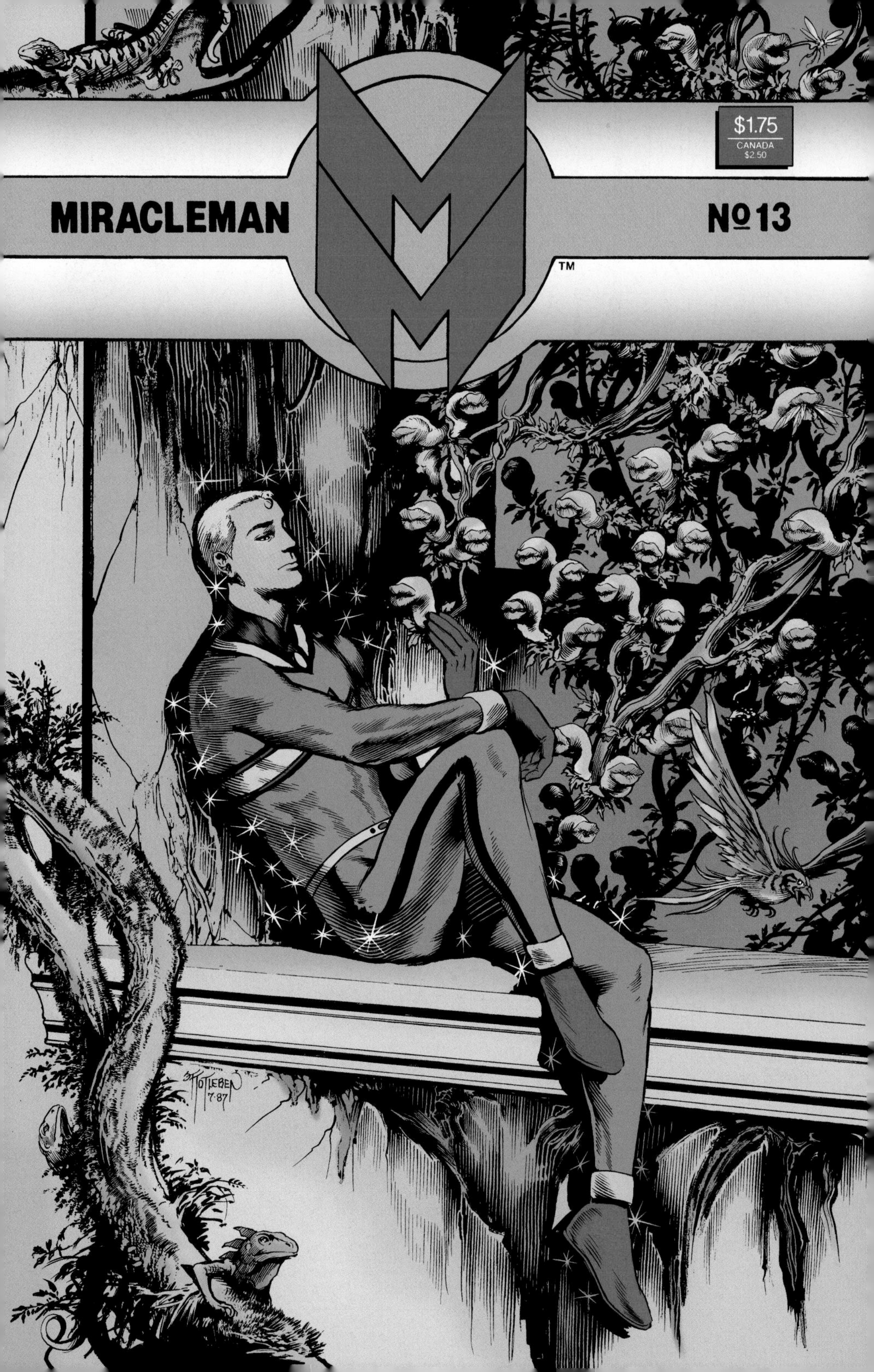
$1.75
CANADA
$2.50
MIRACLEMAN
№13
TM
BISSETTE TOTLEBEN 7·87

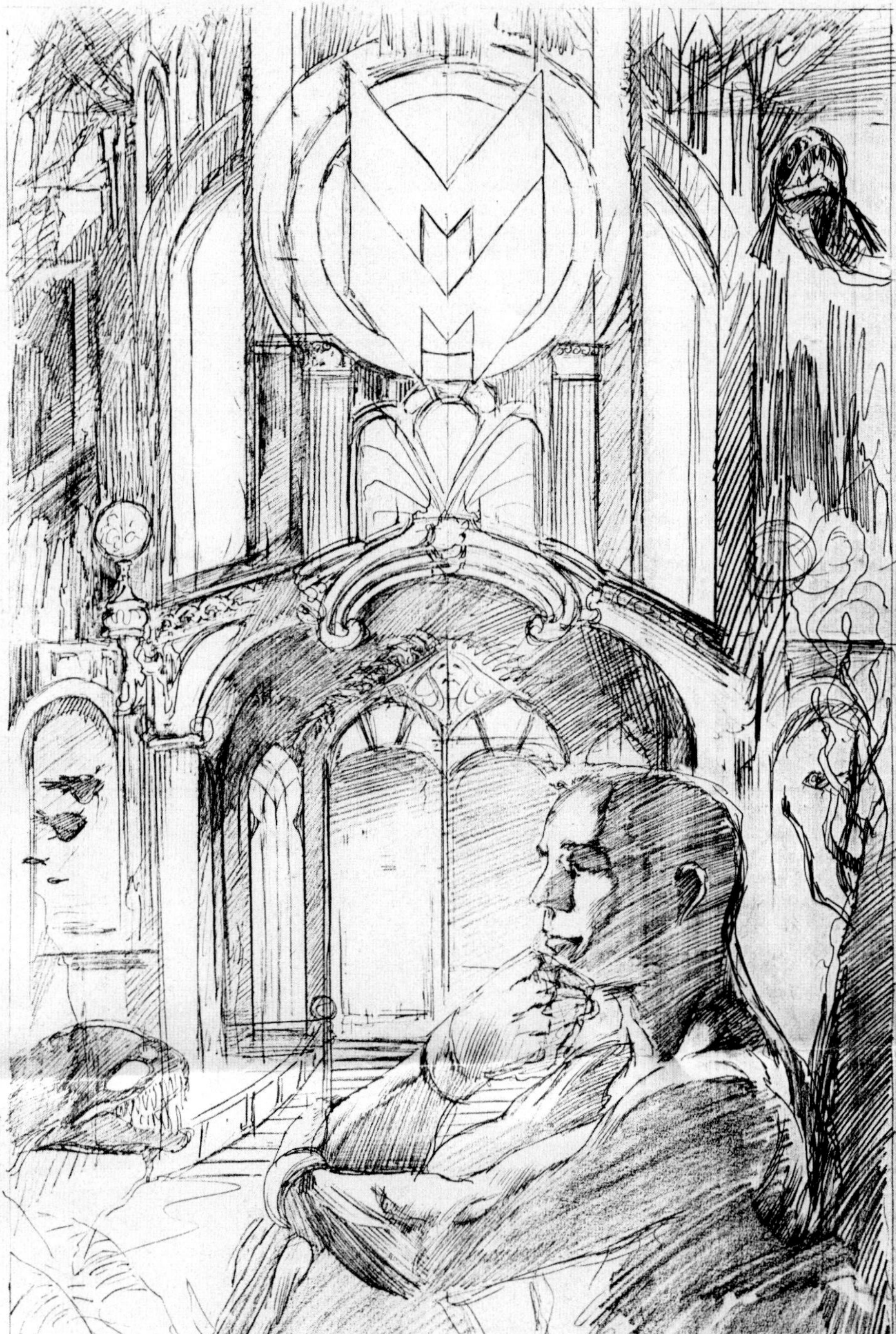

LOTS OF SPARKLES & GLITTER
AROUND M.M.

FOLD LINE AT EDGE

Sam- this is underwater!

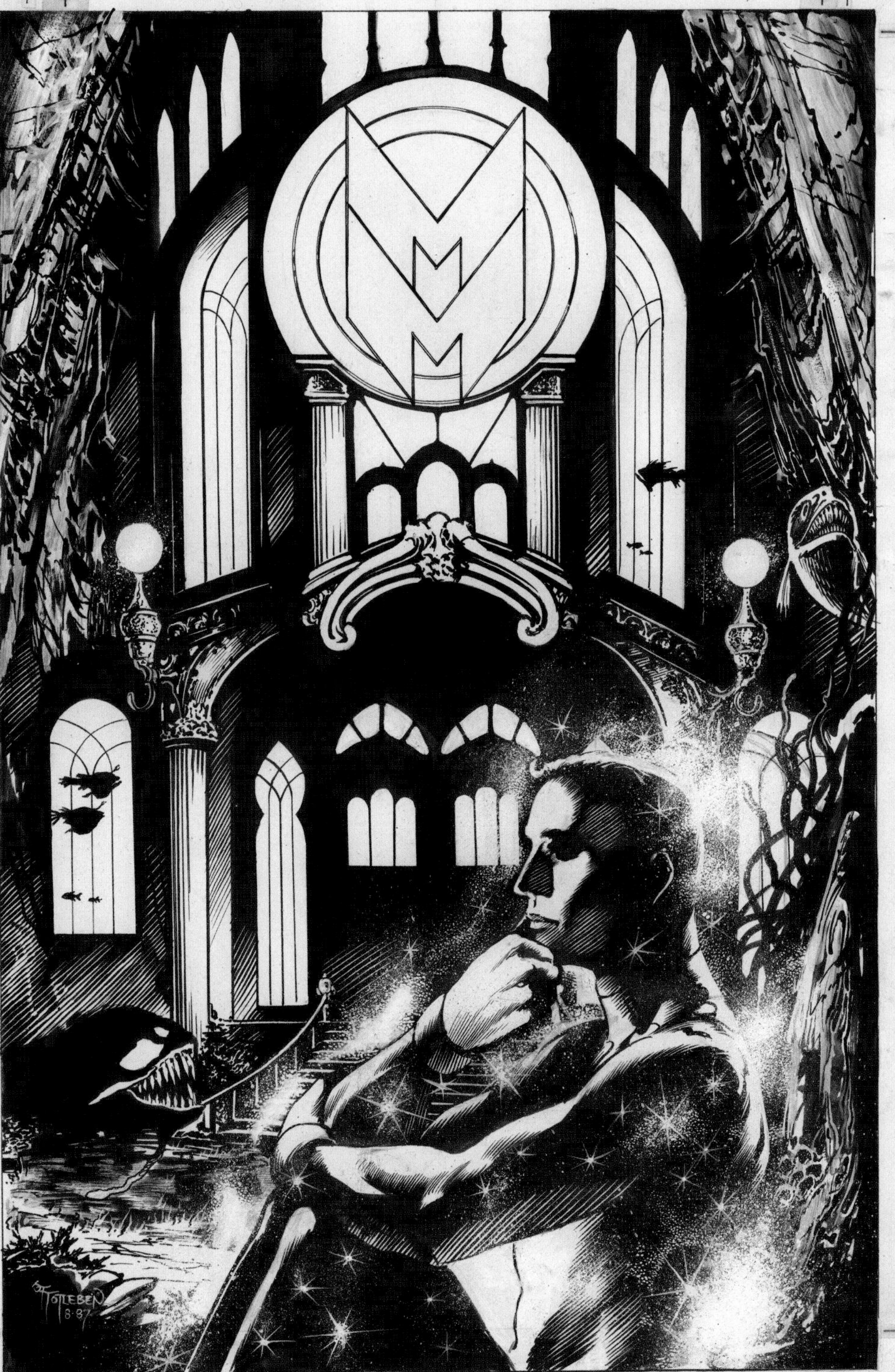
TOTLEBEN
8·87

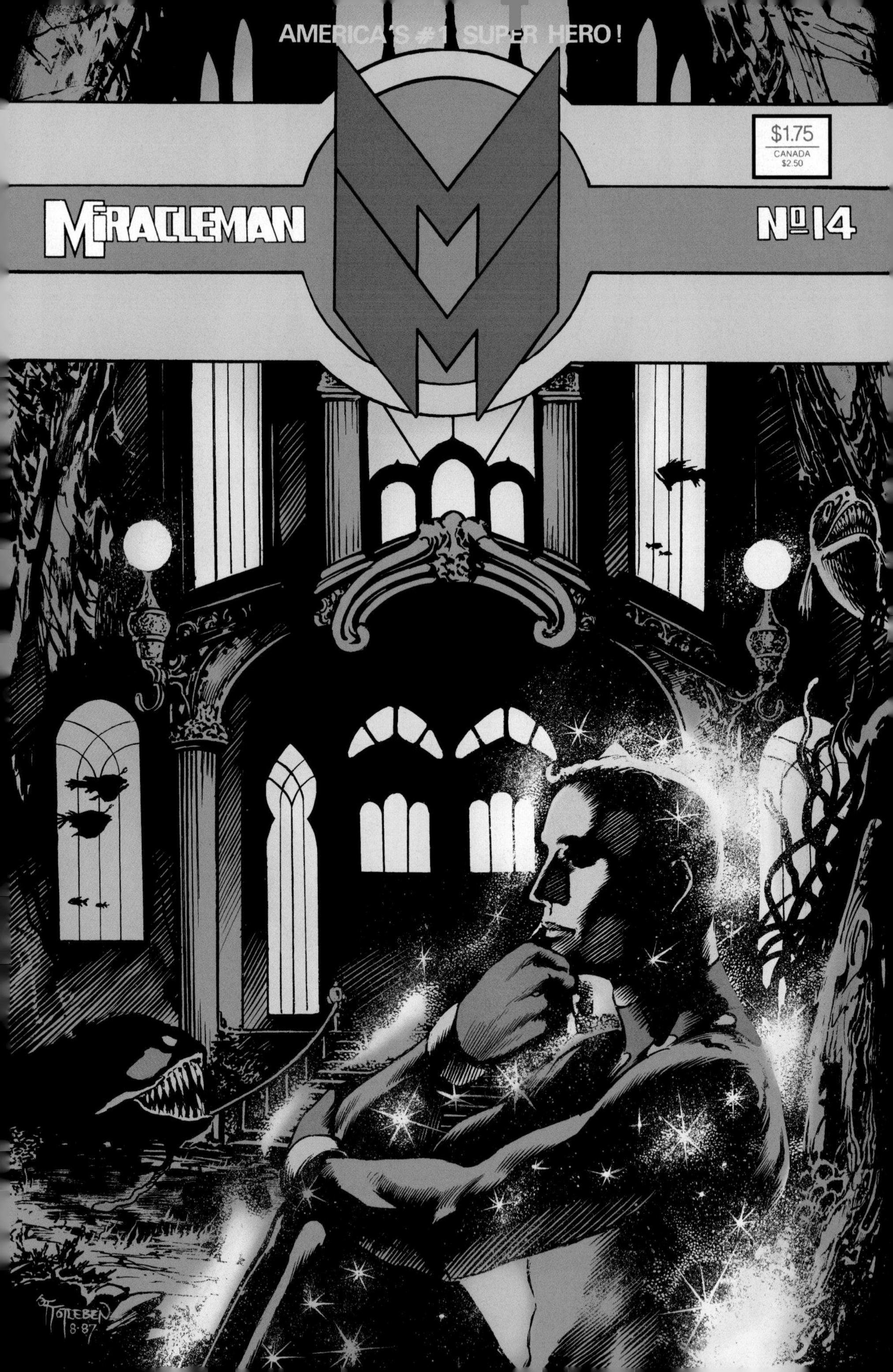
AMERICA'S #1 SUPER HERO!
$1.75
CANADA
$2.50
MIRACLEMAN
Nº 14
TOTLEBEN
8·87

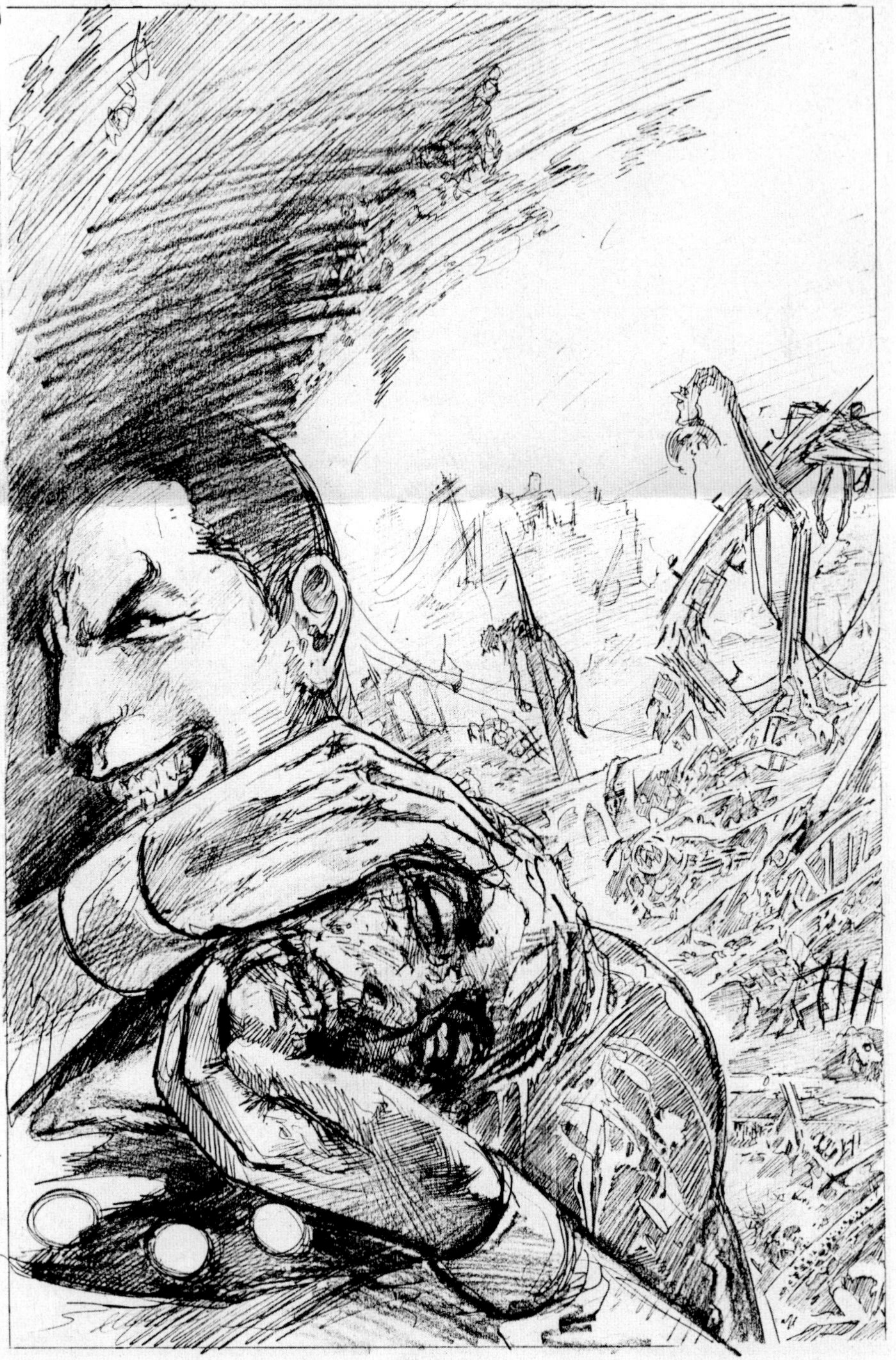

MIRACLEMAN #15

TRIM

TRIM

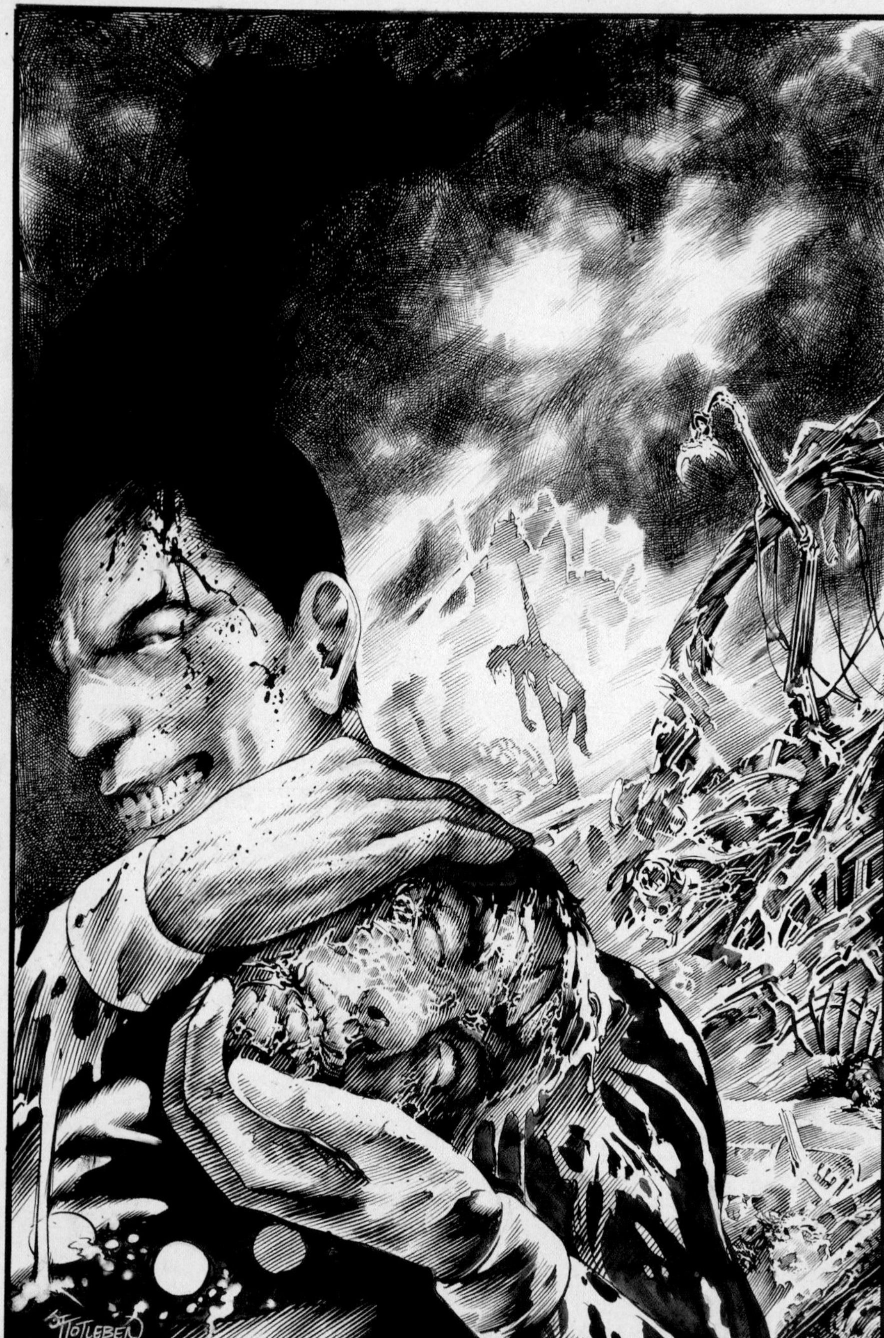

TRIM

TRIM

69% TRIM

NOTE— COLORING SHOULD REFLECT THE APOCALYPTIC FLAVOR OF THIS COVER
ALSO—BATES & M.M. SHOULD BE COVERED WITH BLOOD. SAM— LET LOOSE & PULL NO PUNCHES.

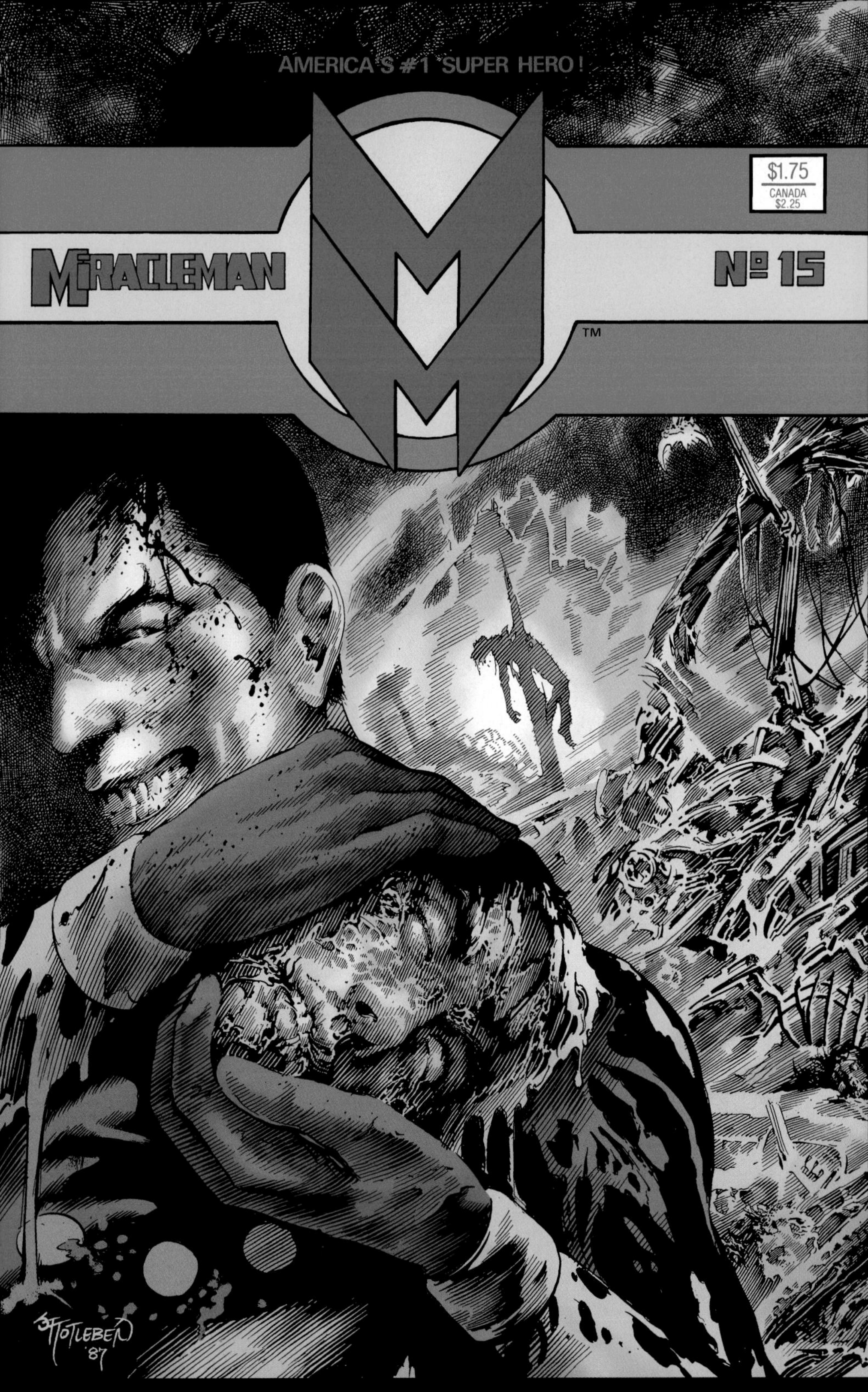
AMERICA'S #1 SUPER HERO!
$1.75
CANADA $2.25
MIRACLEMAN
№ 15
TM
STOTLEBEN '87

*Miracleman* #16 cover original artwork, pencil, India ink and white acrylic on illustration board by John Totleben.

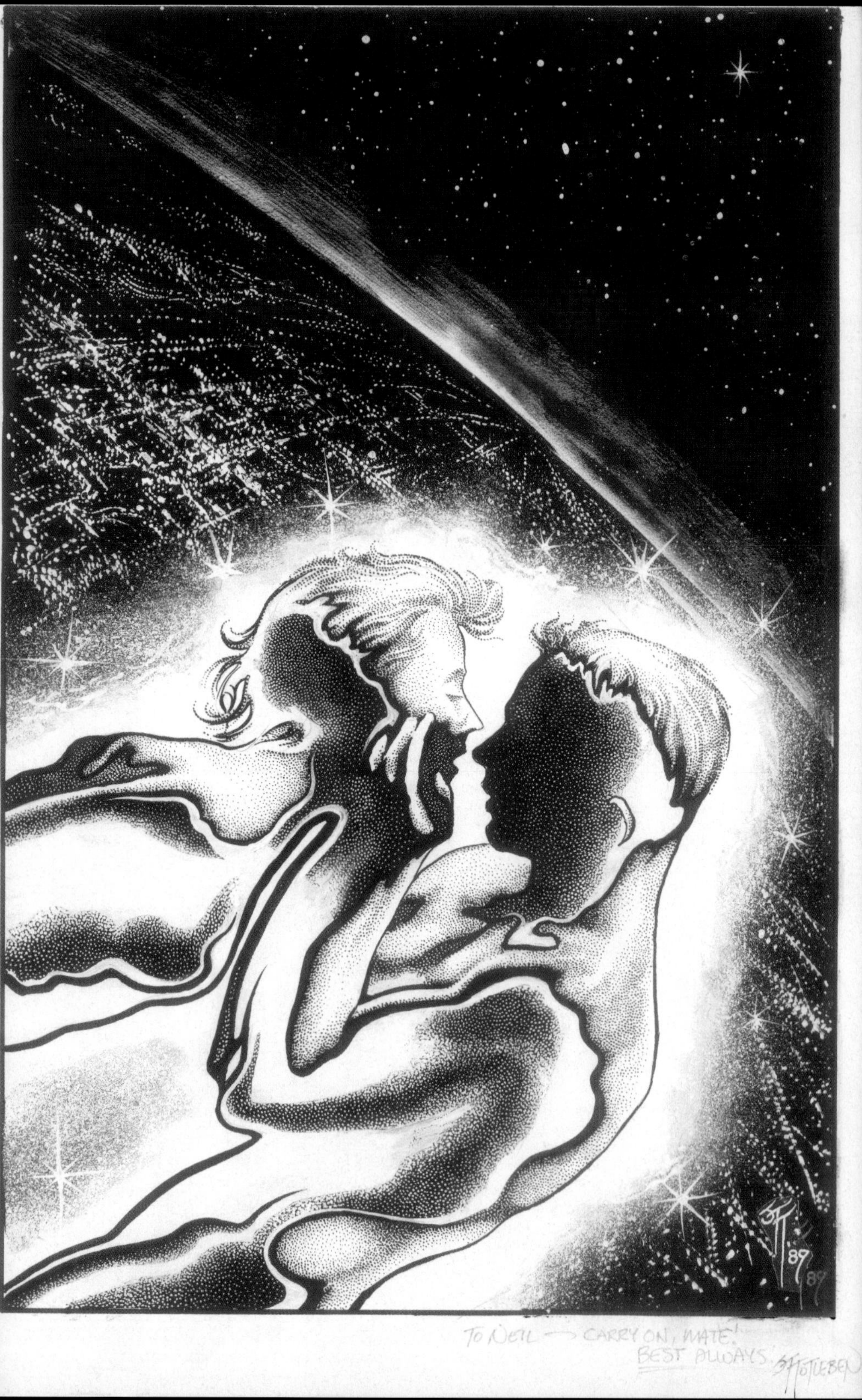

'89
TO NEIL — CARRY ON, MATE!
BEST ALWAYS, S.J. TOTLEBEN

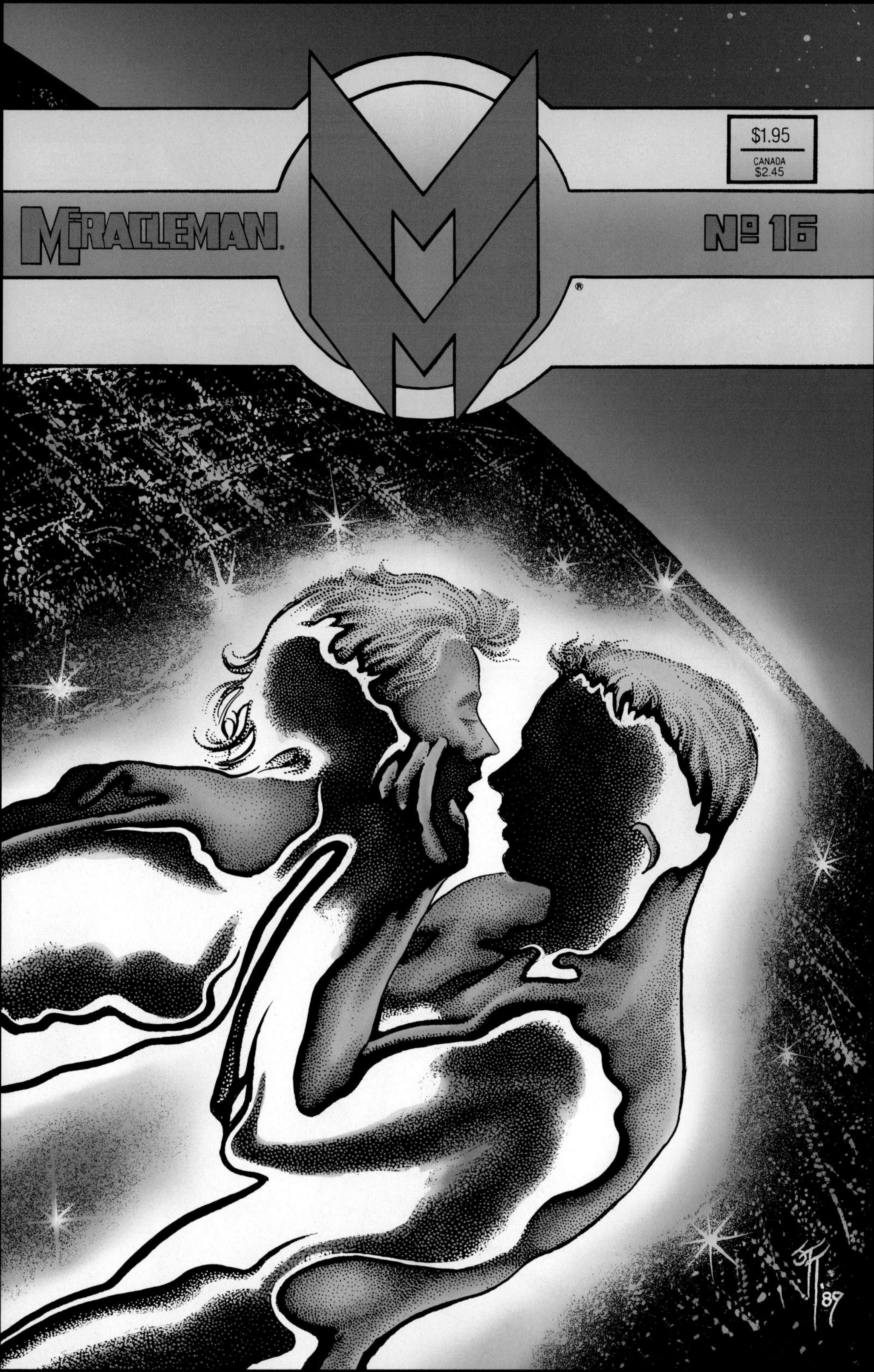
$1.95
CANADA
$2.45
MIRACLEMAN
№ 16

**TOP:** *Miracleman* #16 cover sketches, pencil on notebook paper by John Totleben.

**BOTTOM:** *Miracleman* #16 unused cover sketches, pencil and tempera on drawing paper by John Totleben.

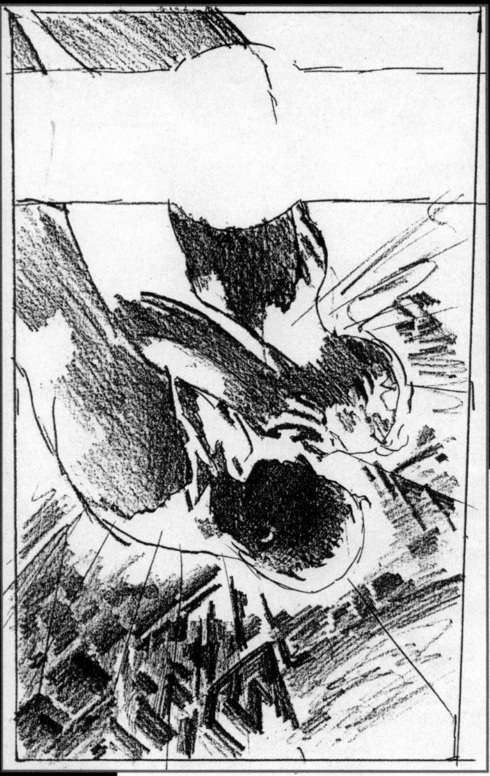

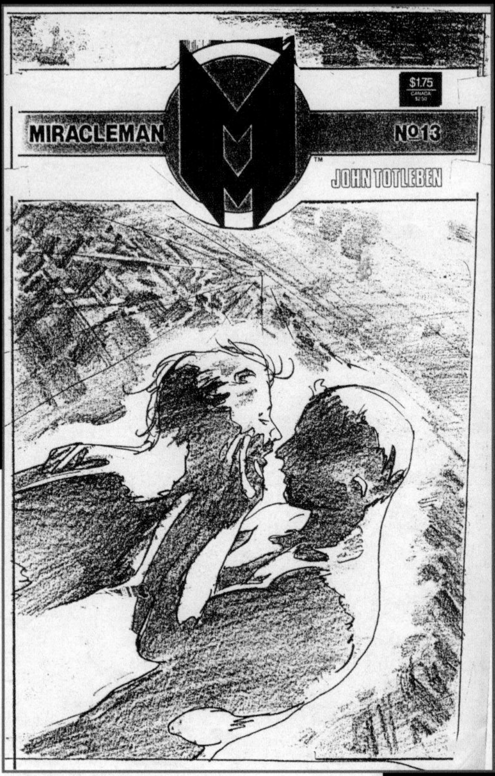
$1.75
MIRACLEMAN
Nº13
JOHN TOTLEBEN

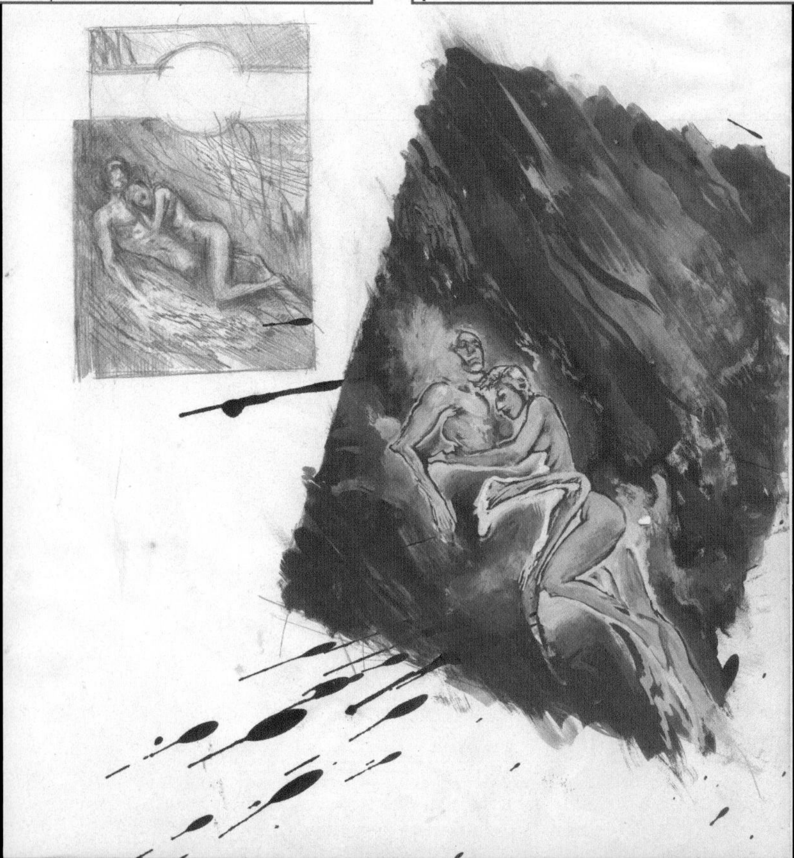

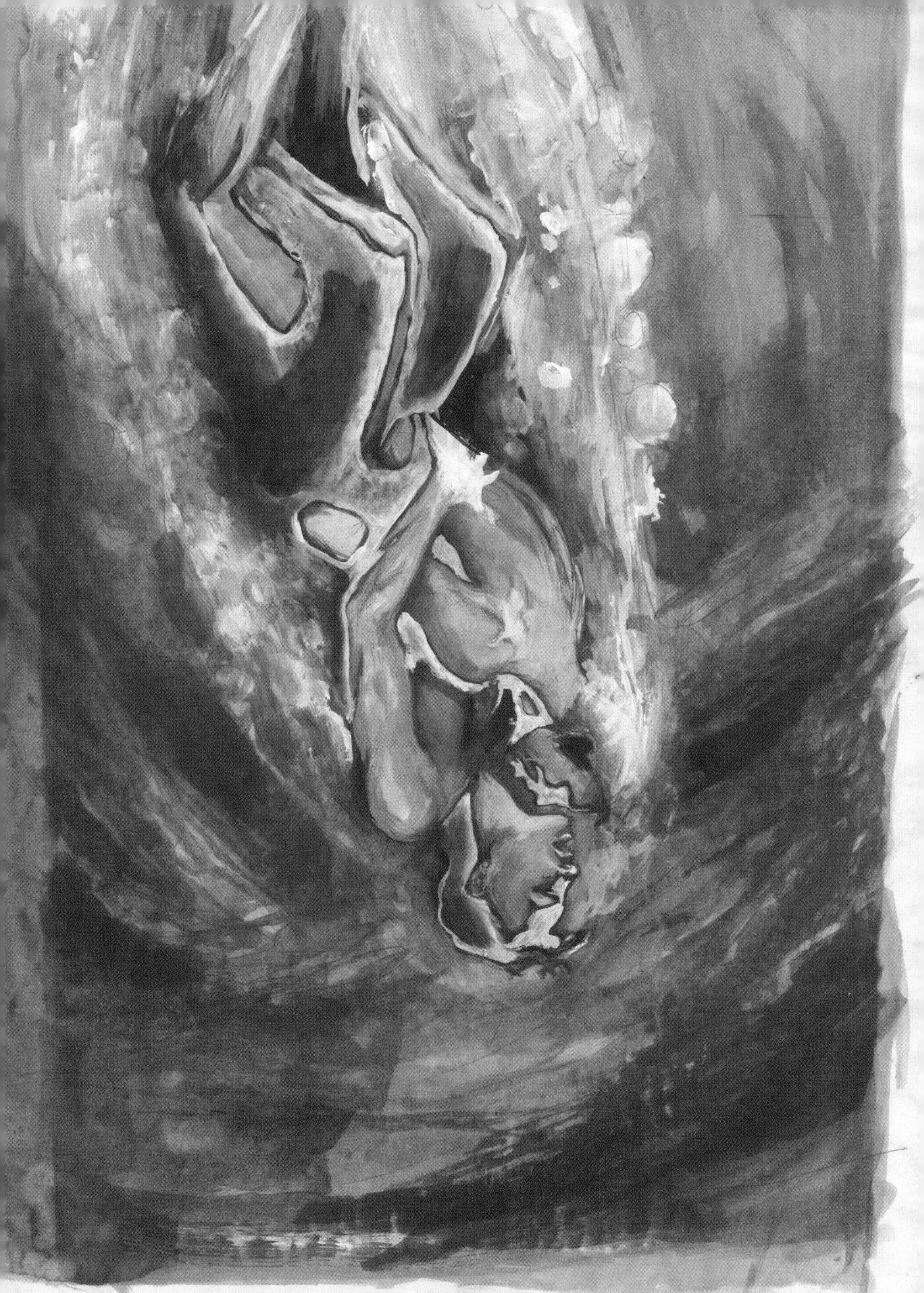

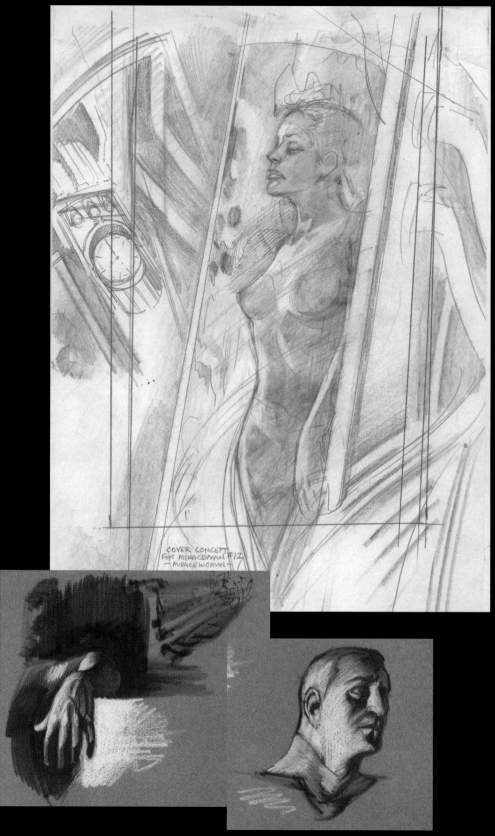

COVER CONCEPT
FOR MIRACLEMAN #12
—MIRACLEWOMAN—

*Miracleman Book Three: Olympus* (1990) cover painting, oil on canvas by John Totleben.

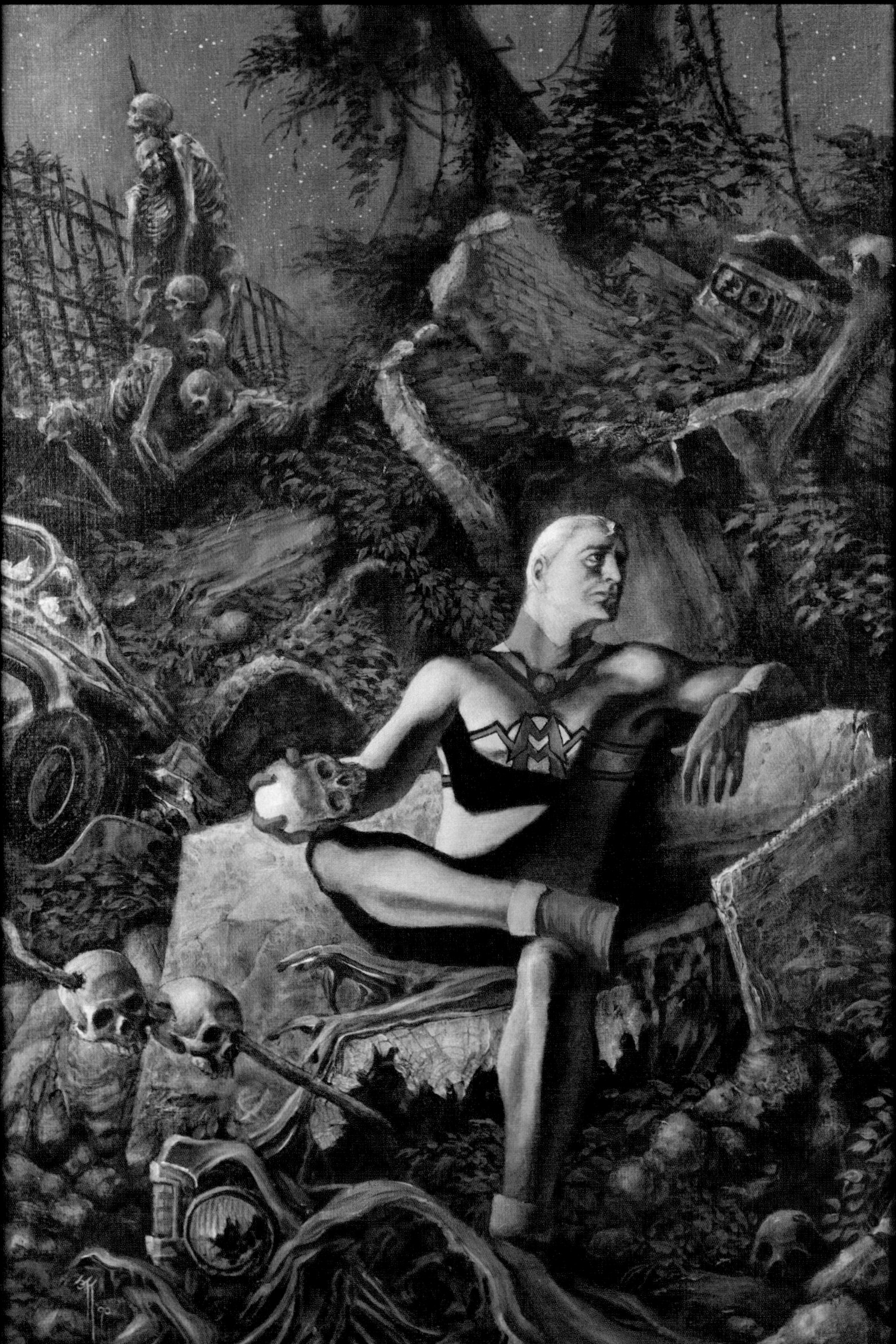

*Miracleman* #11 (2014) cover art by John Totleben & Ralf Beredo.

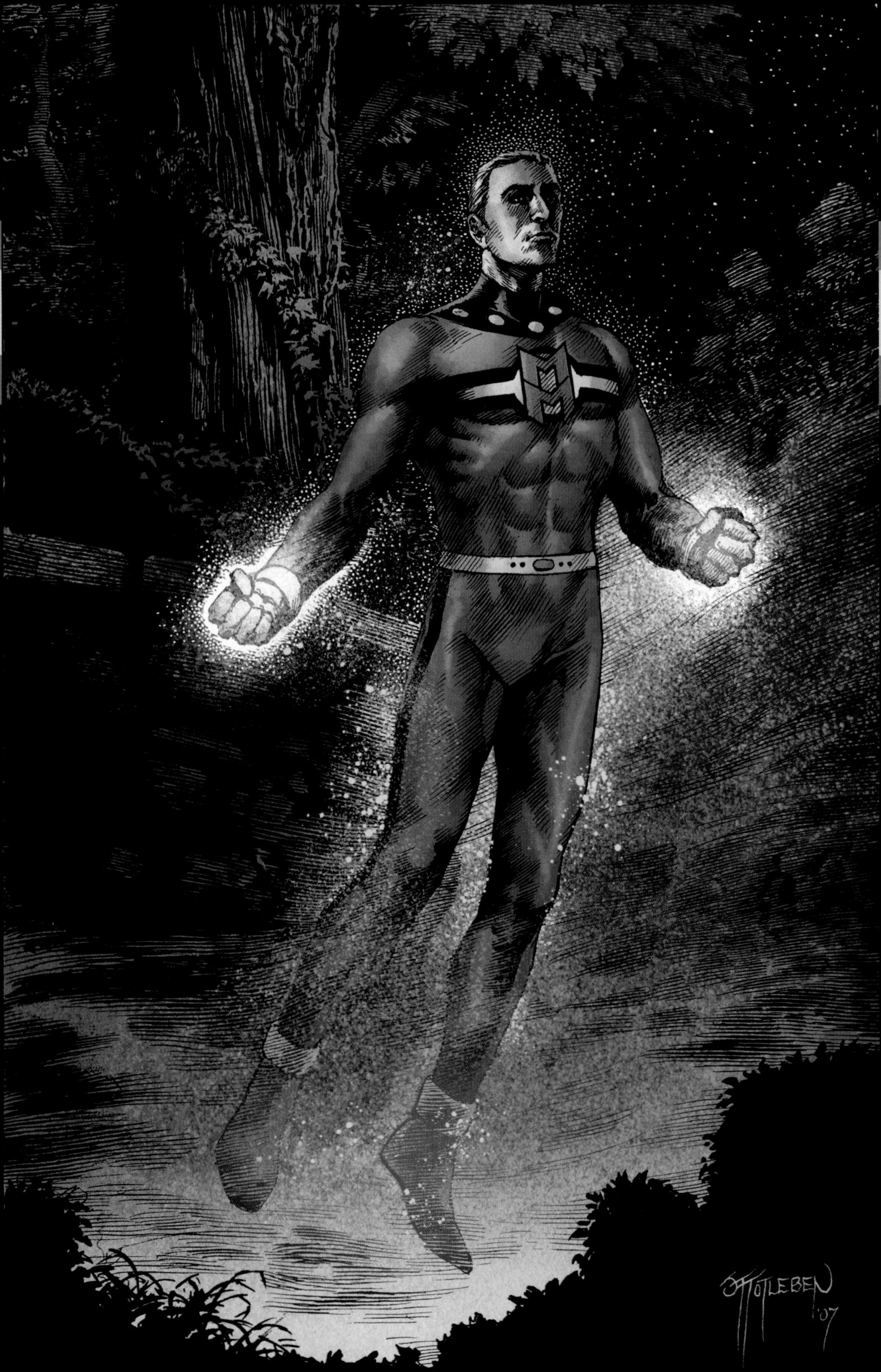
JH TOTLEBEN
'07

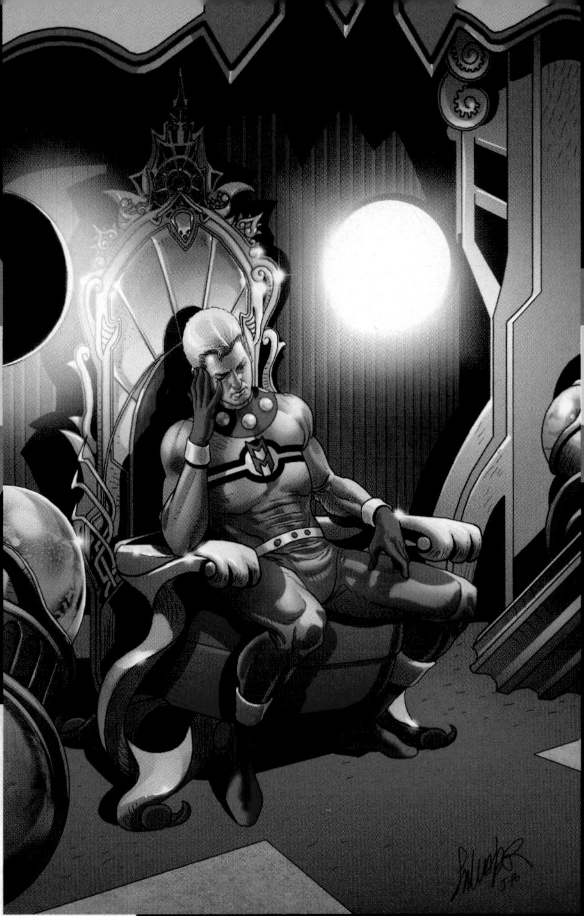

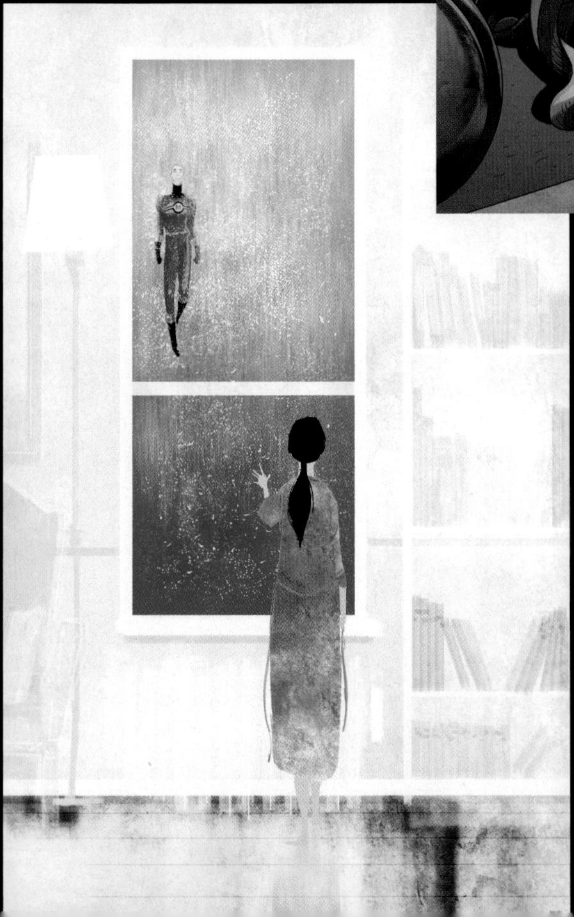

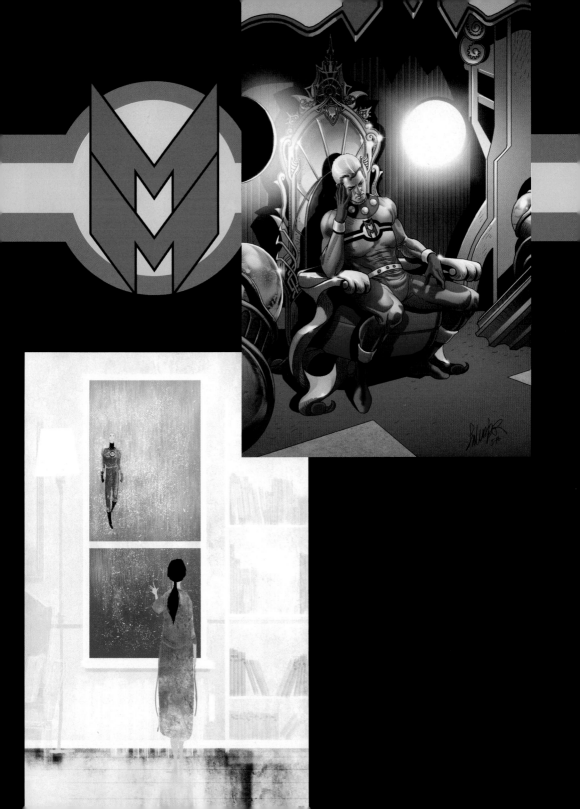

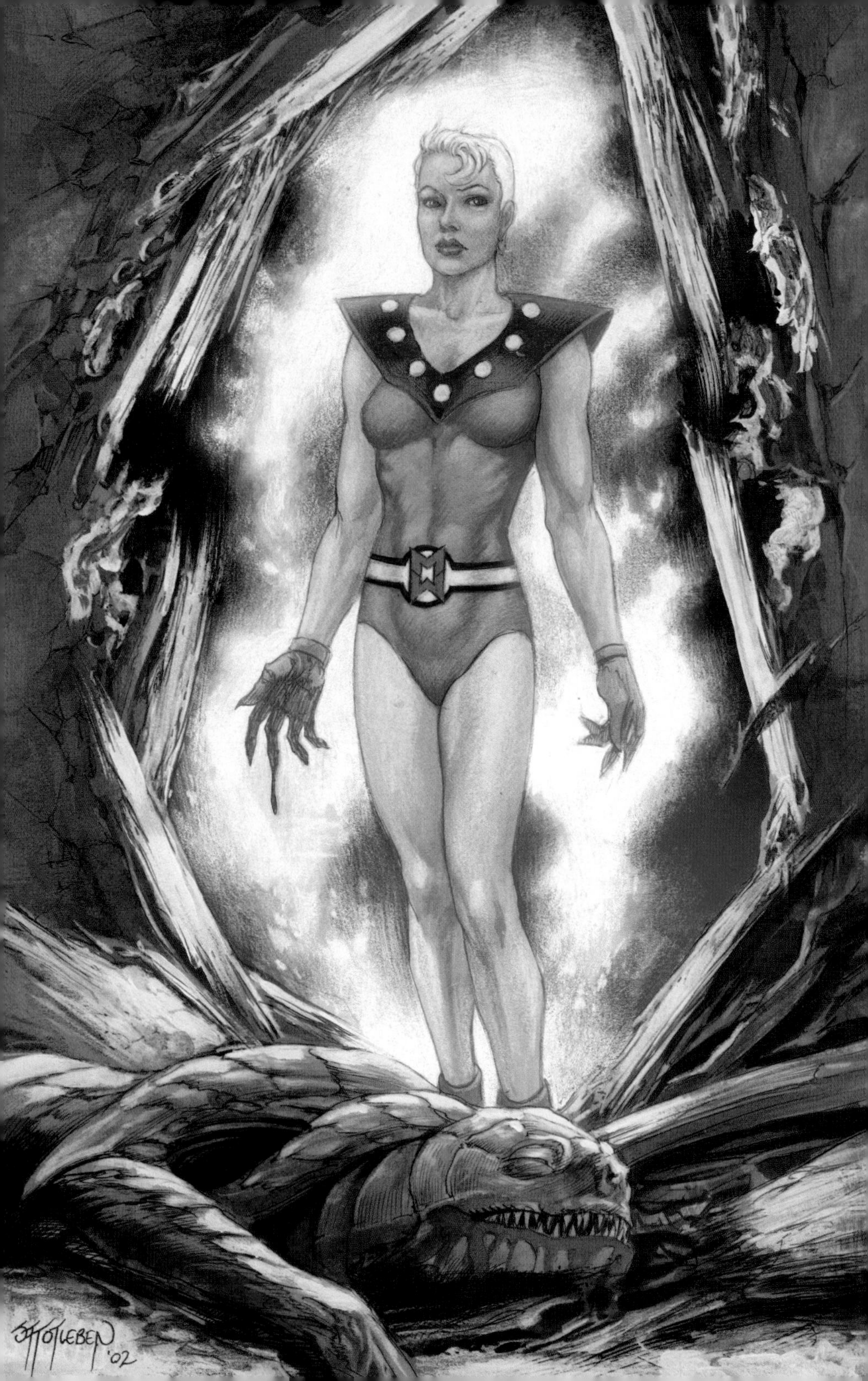

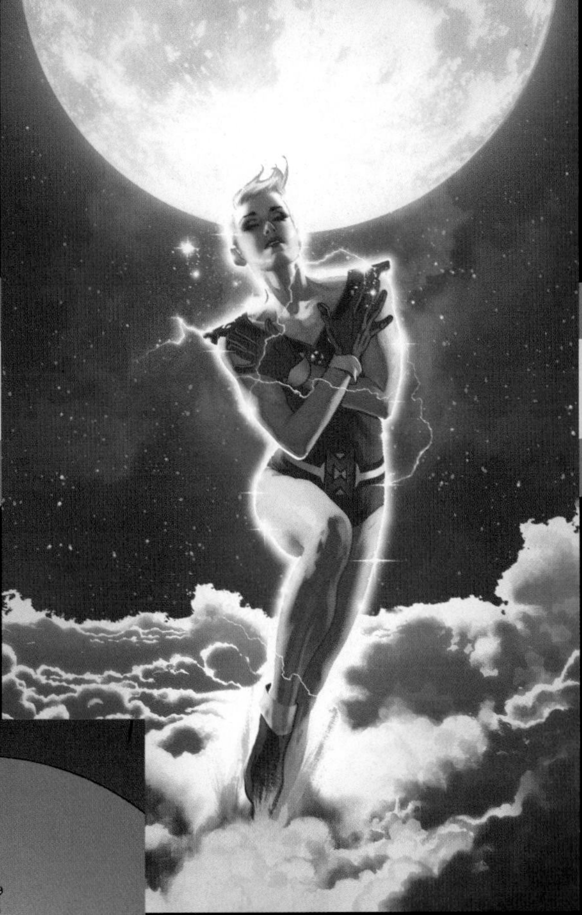

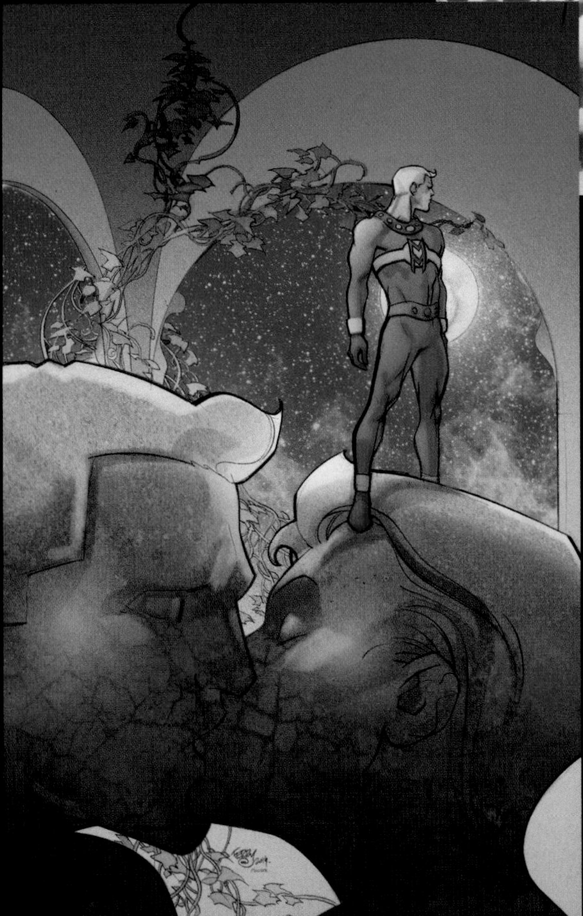

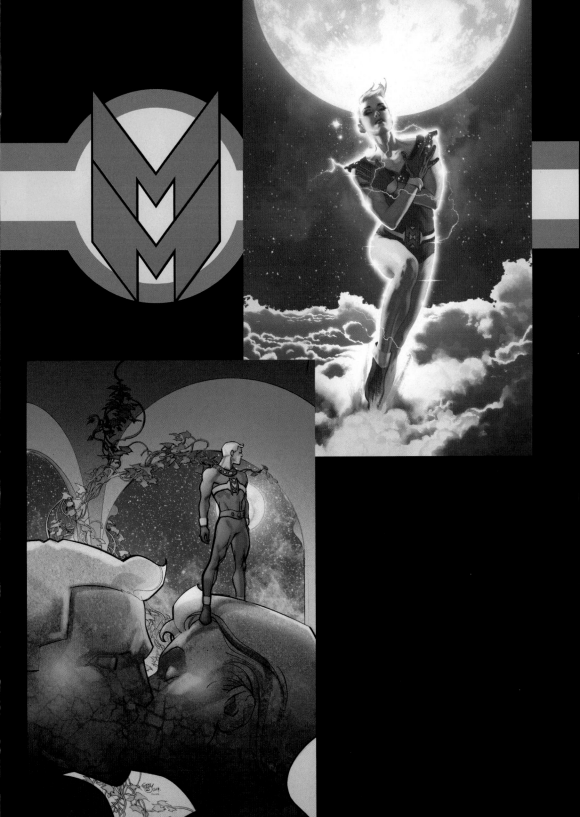

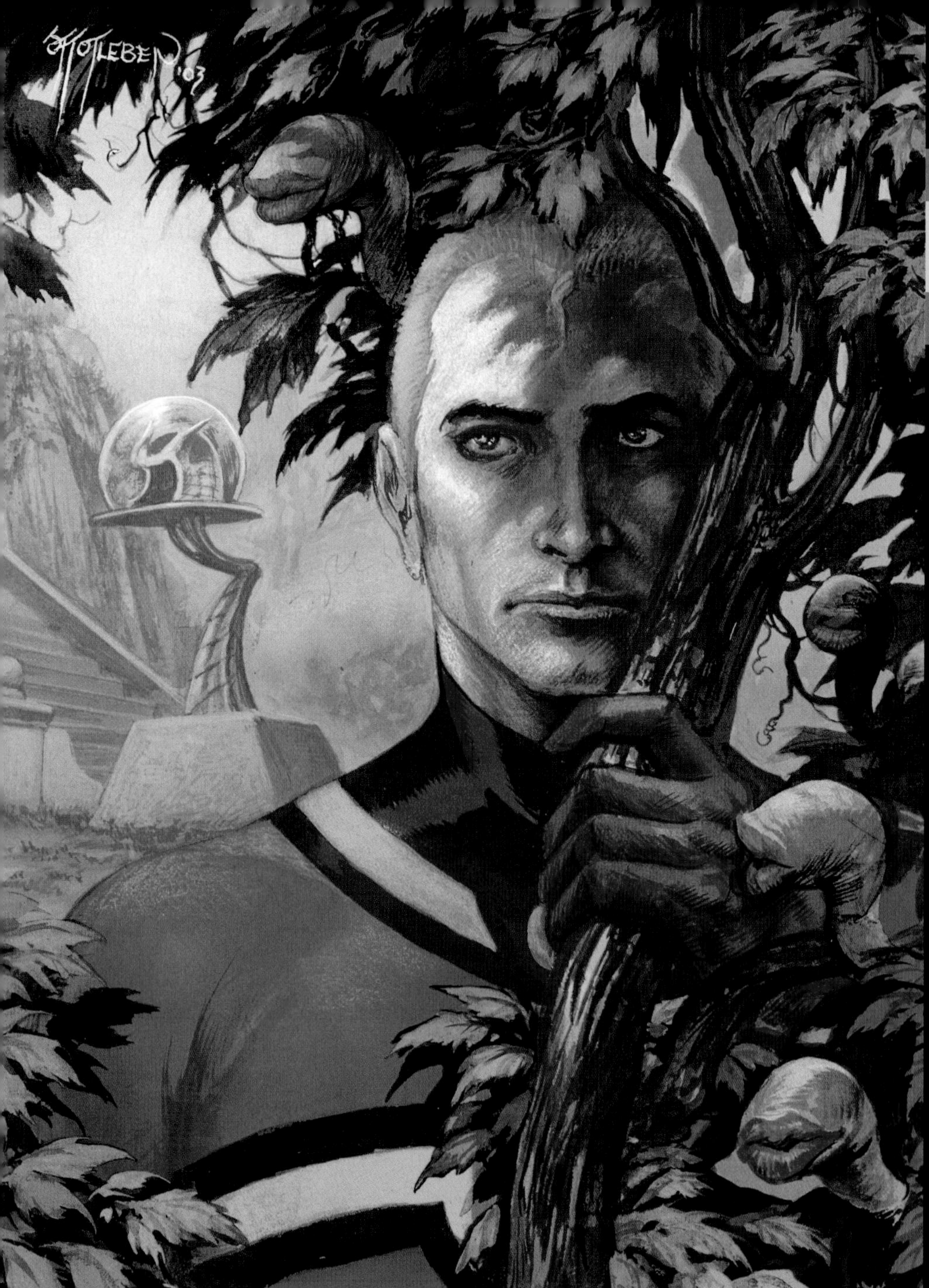
KOTLEBEN '03

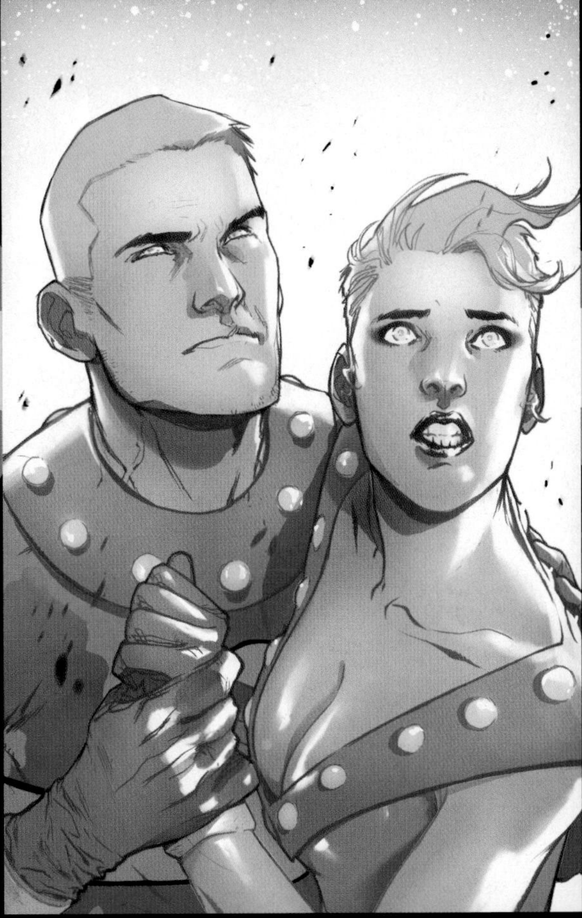
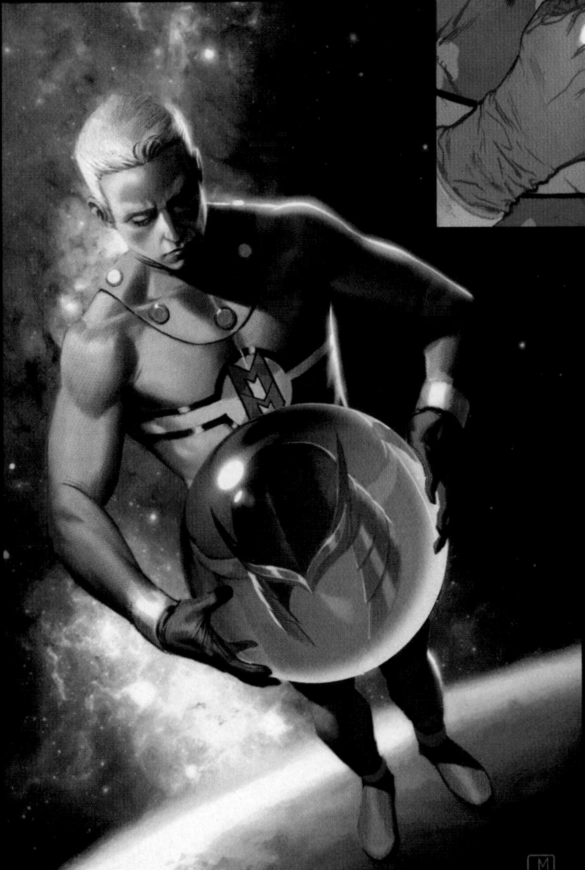

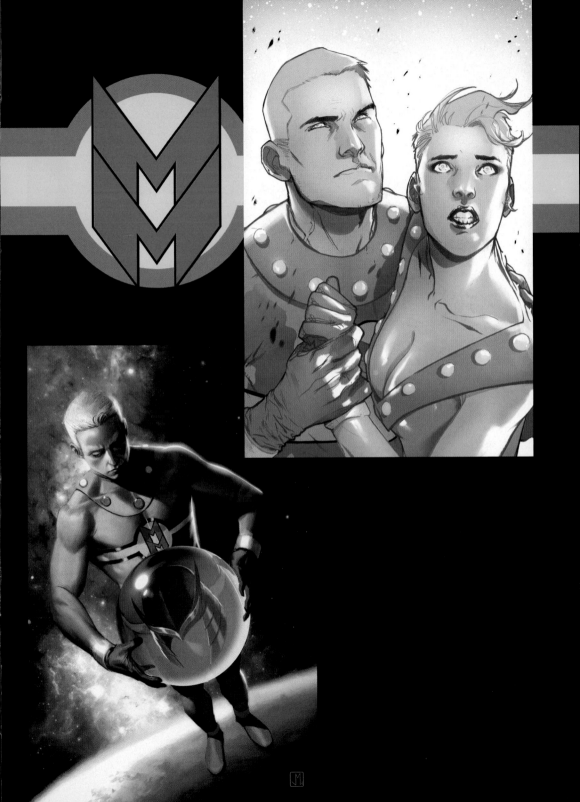

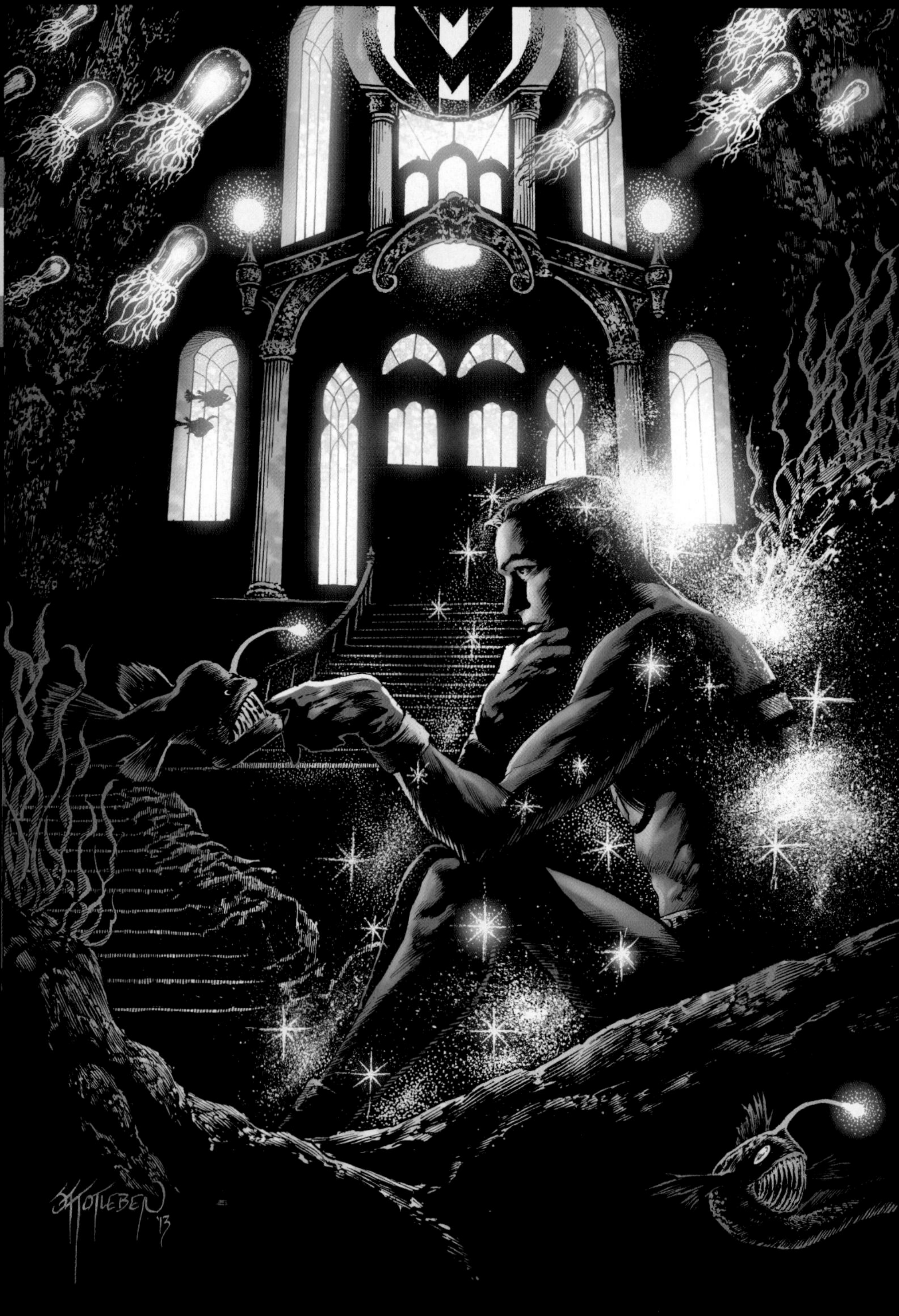
KOTLEBEN '13

*Miracleman* #14 (2014) variant cover art by Brandon Peterson (top) and Lee Weeks & Laura Martin (bottom).

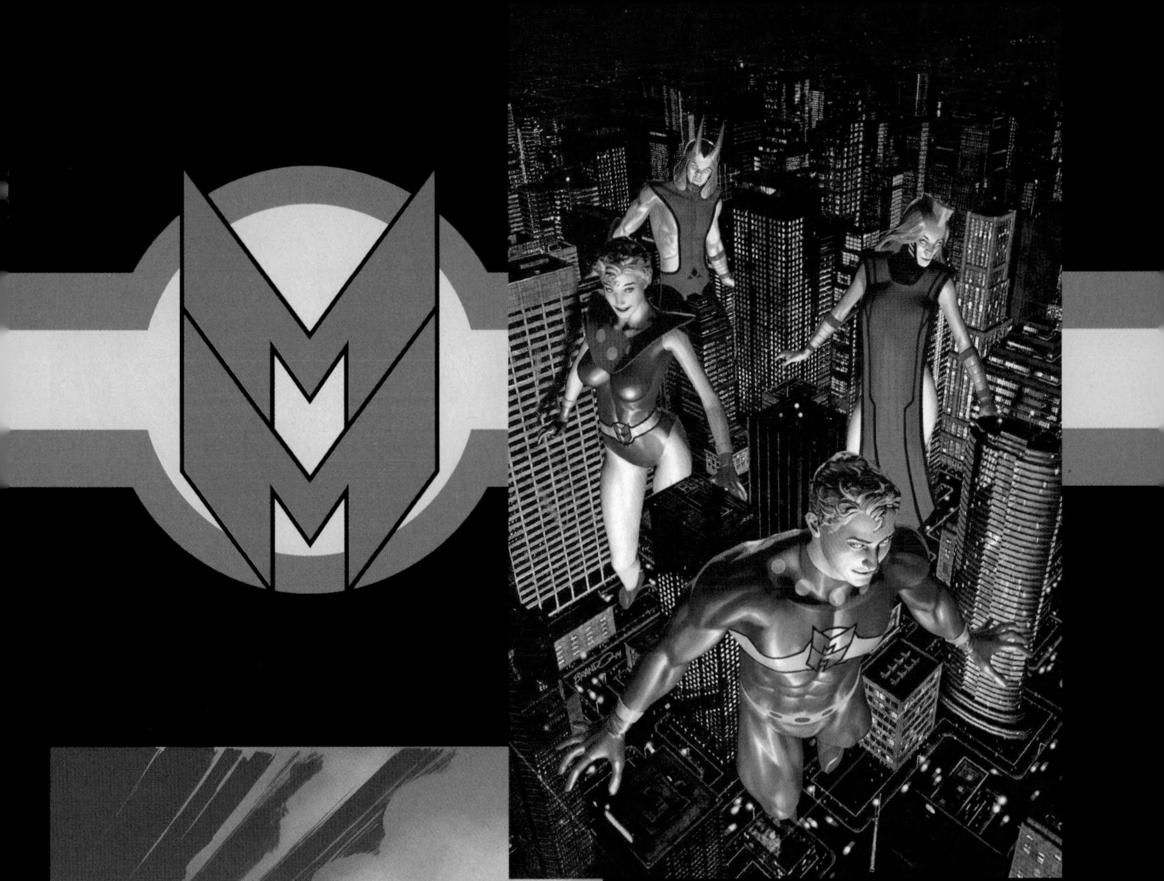

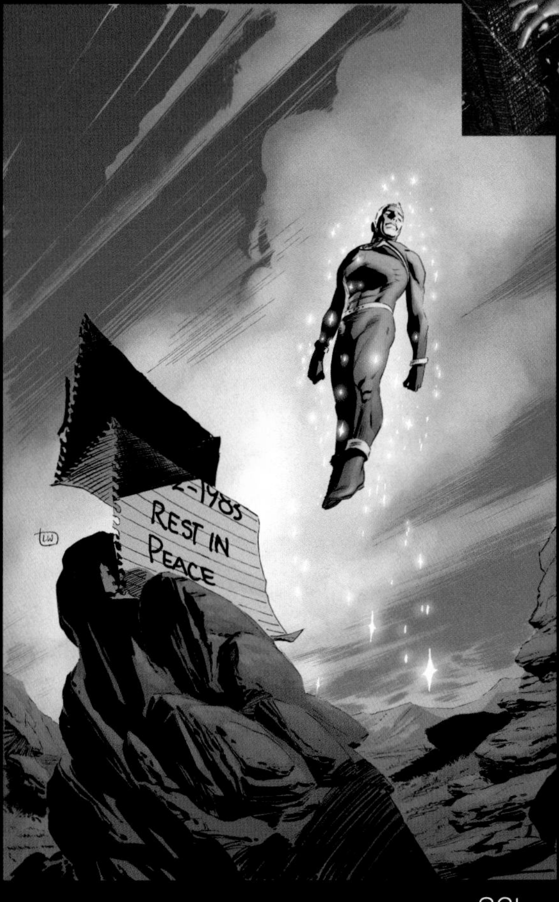
REST IN PEACE

*Miracleman* #13 (2014) cover art by John Totleben & Rain Beredo.

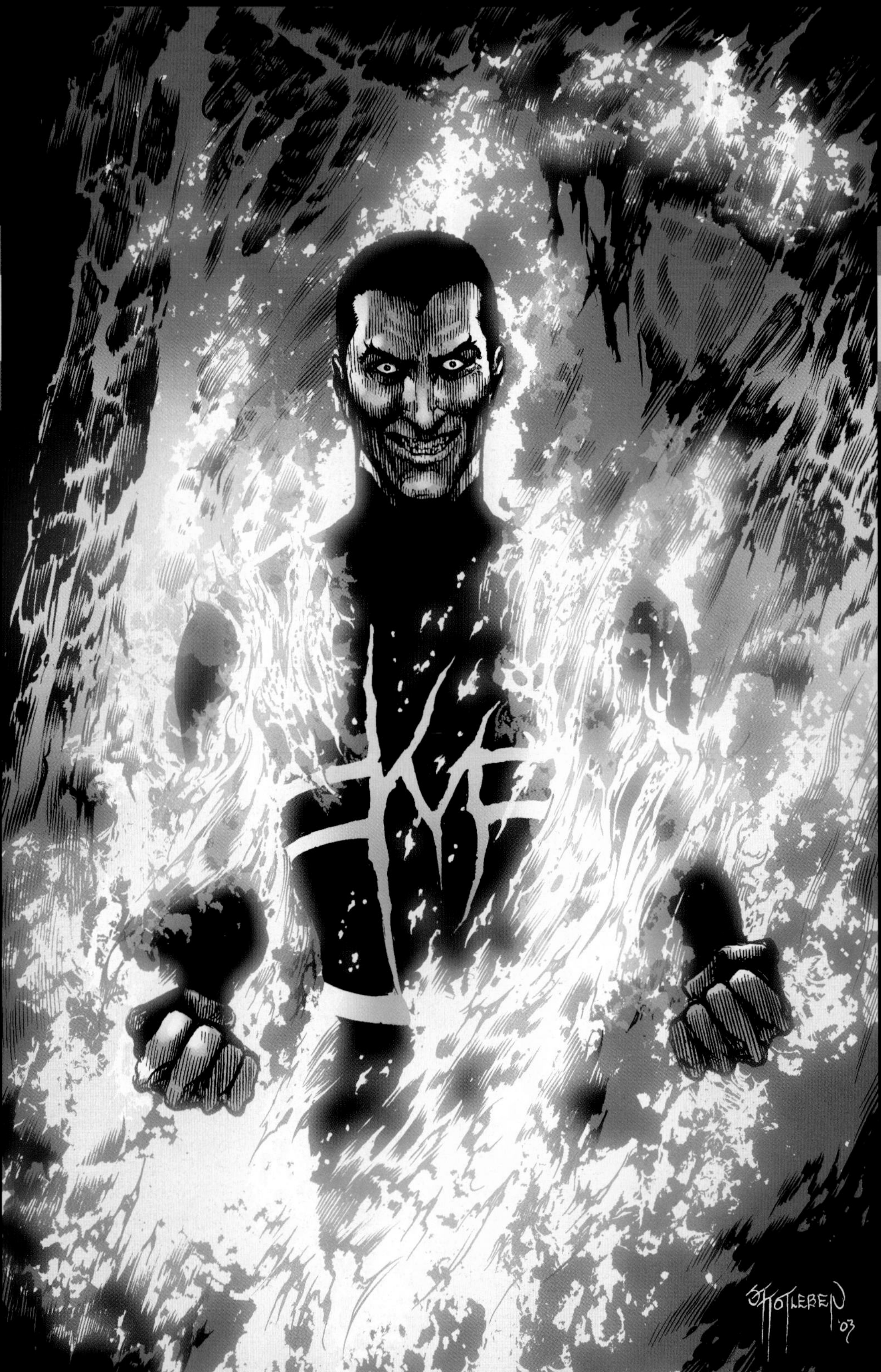

*Miracleman* #15 (2014) variant cover art Bill Sienkiewicz (top) and Tim Sale & Dave Stewart (bottom).

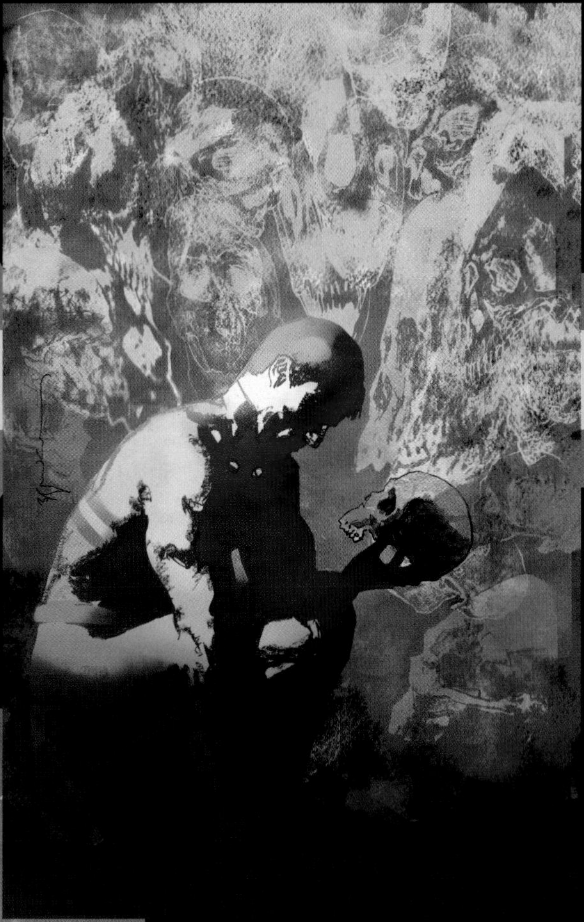

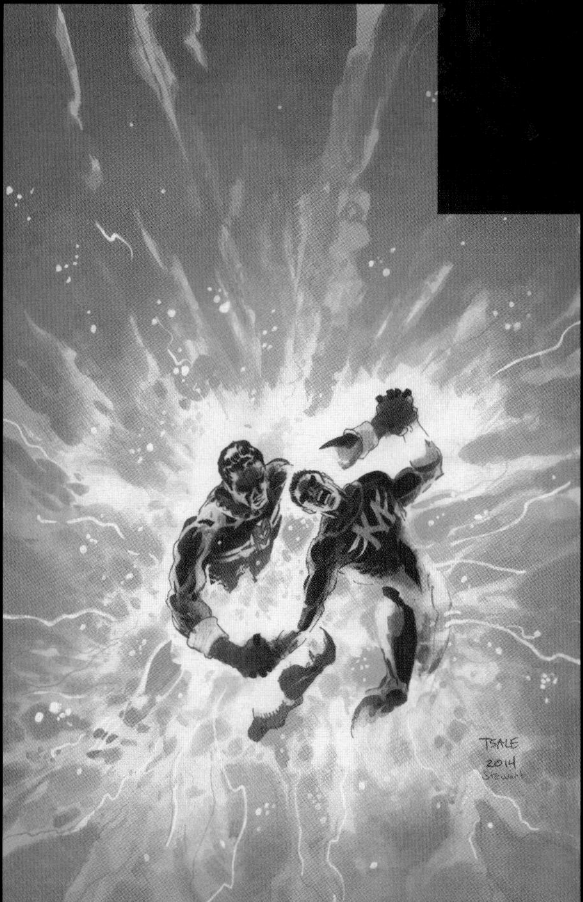
TSALE
2014
Stewart

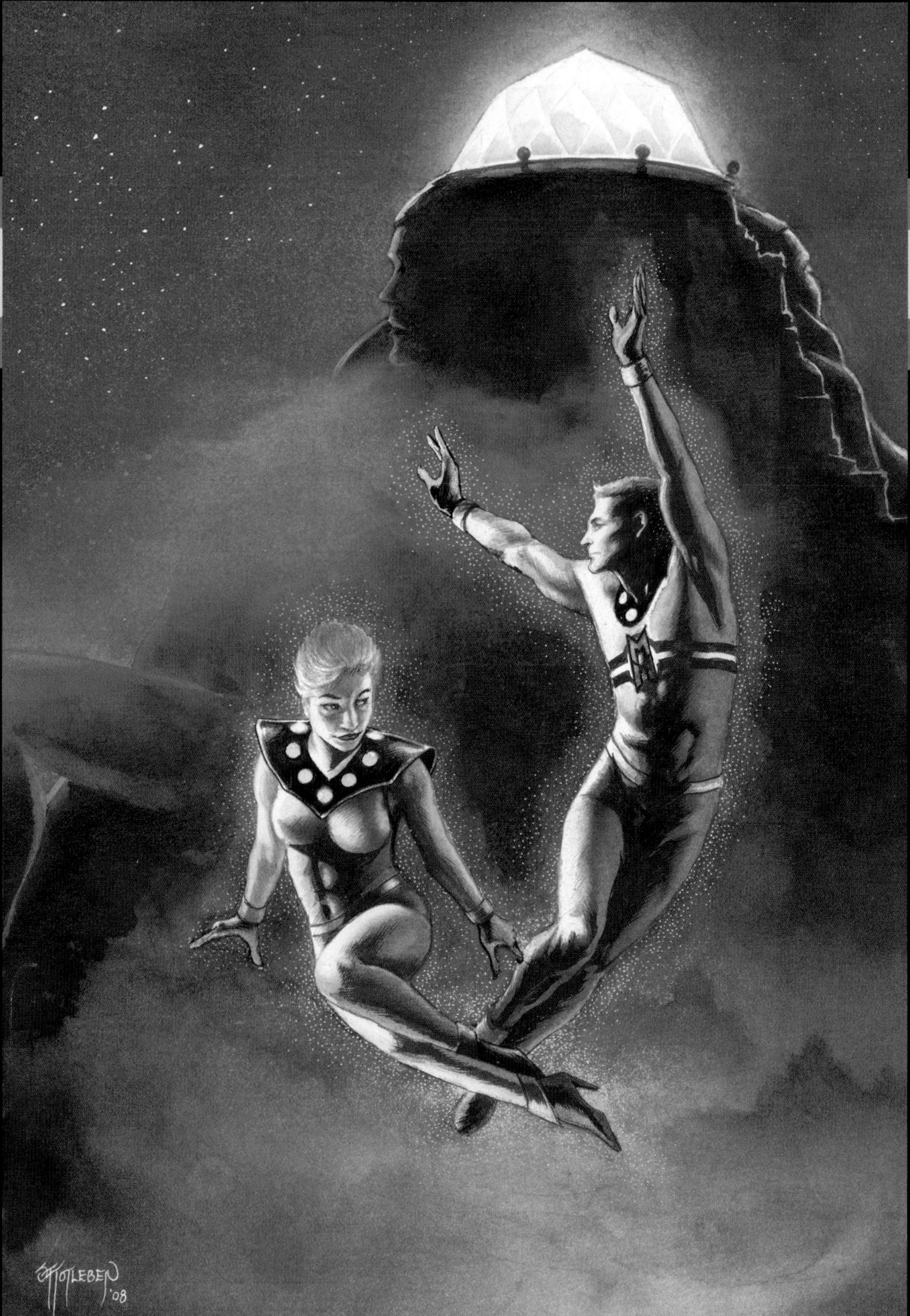
KOTLEBEN
'08

*Miracleman* #16 (2014) variant cover art by Garry Leach (top) and Esteban Maroto & Rain Beredo (bottom).

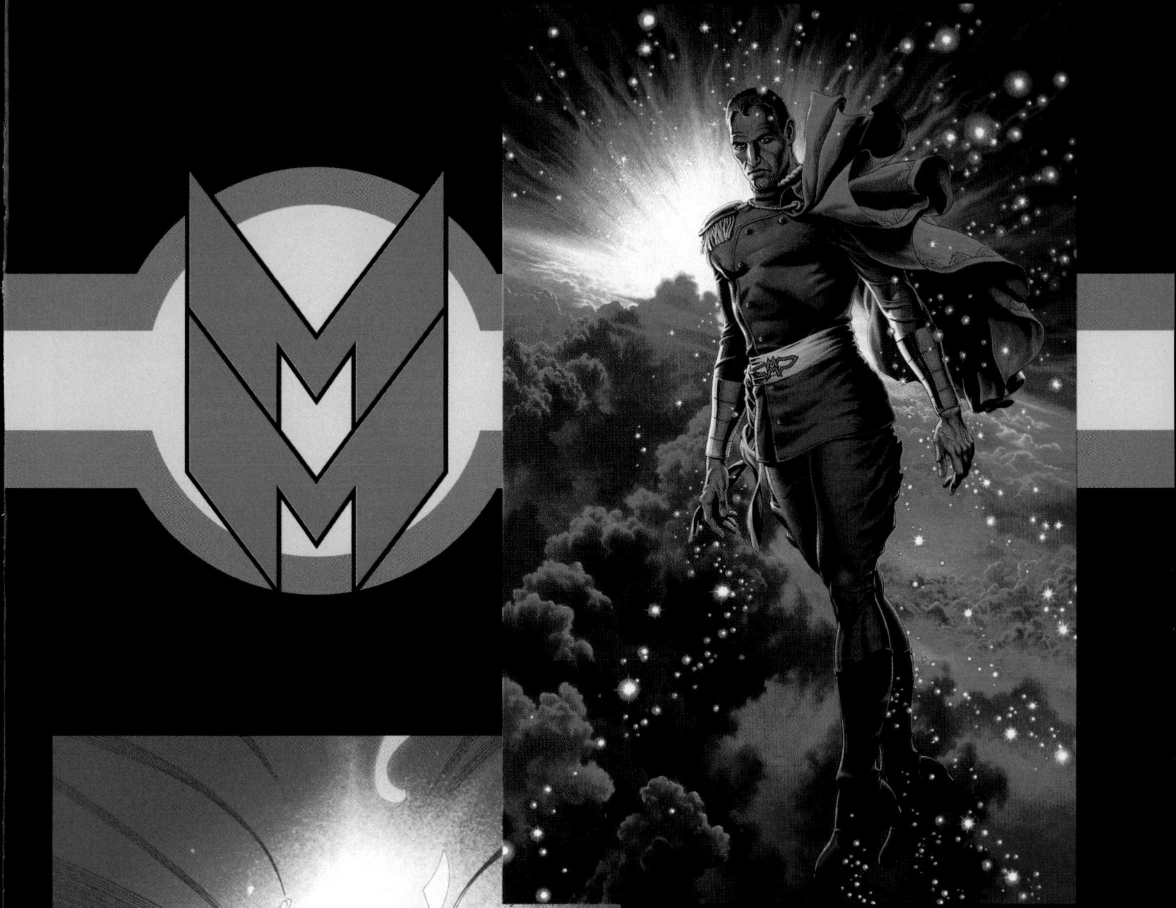

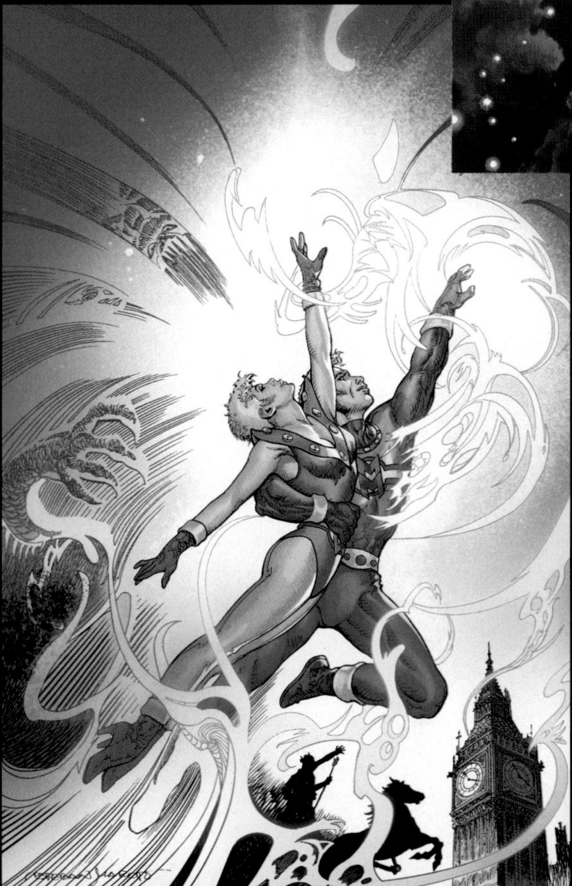

*All-New Miracleman Annual* #1 (2014) cover art by Gabriele Dell'Otto.

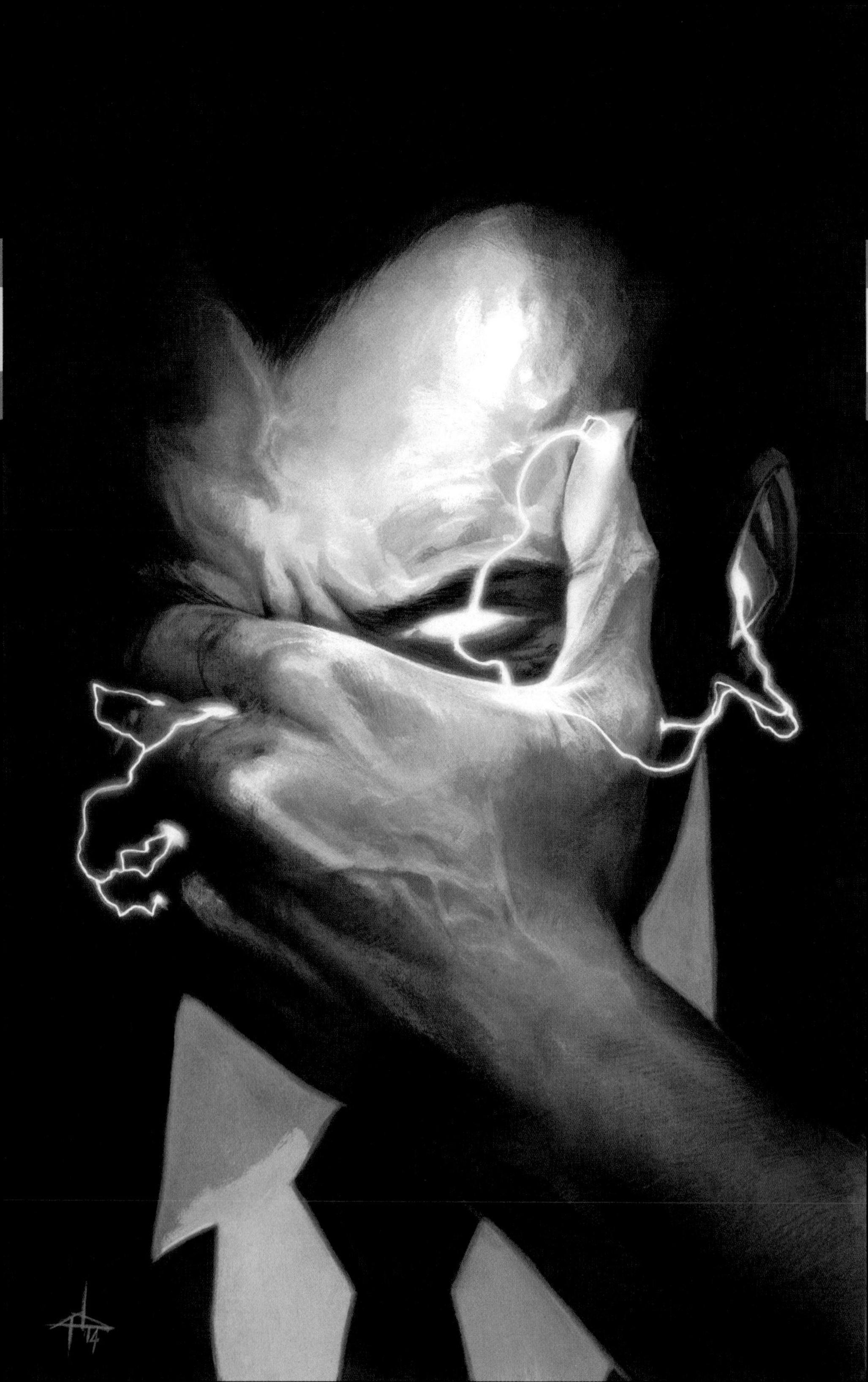

*All-New Miracleman Annual* #1 (2014) variant cover art by Jeff Smith & Thomas James Gaadt (top) and Joe Quesada (bottom).

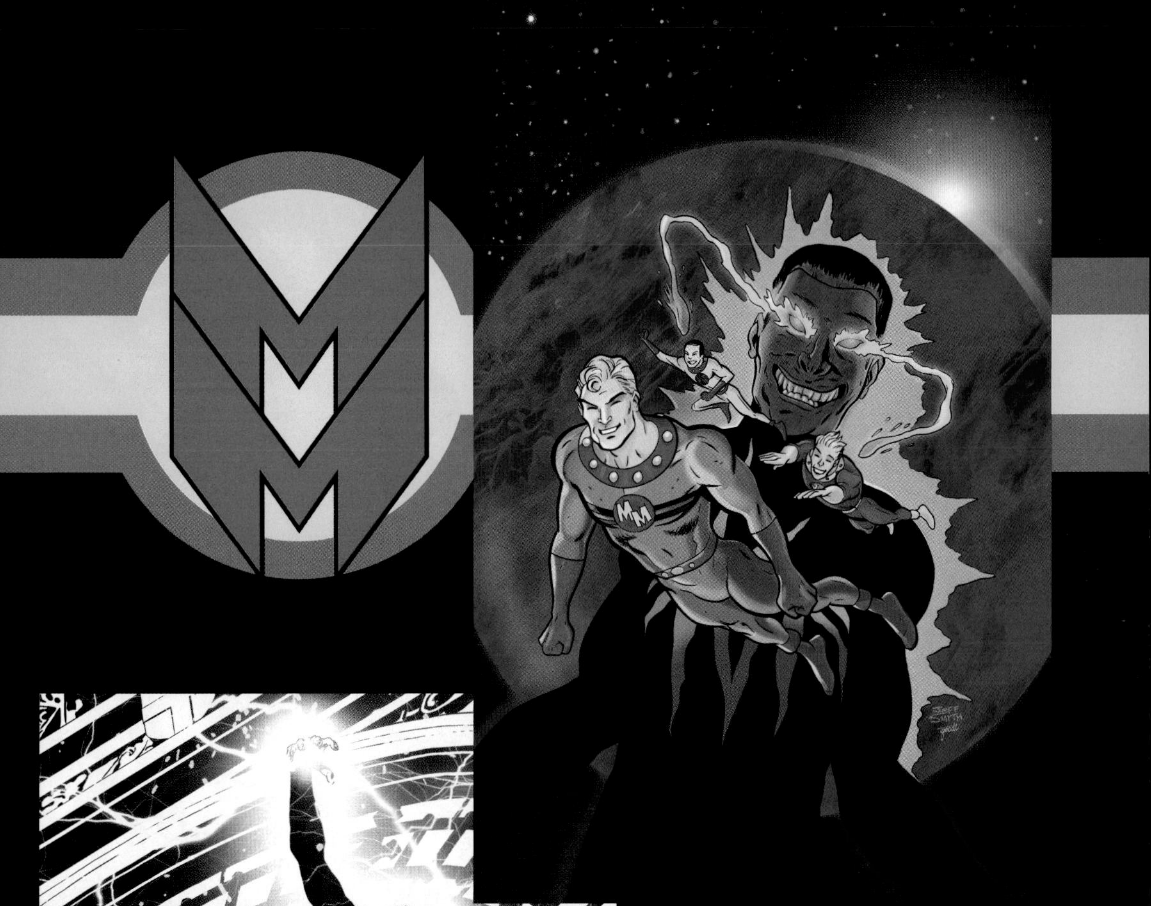

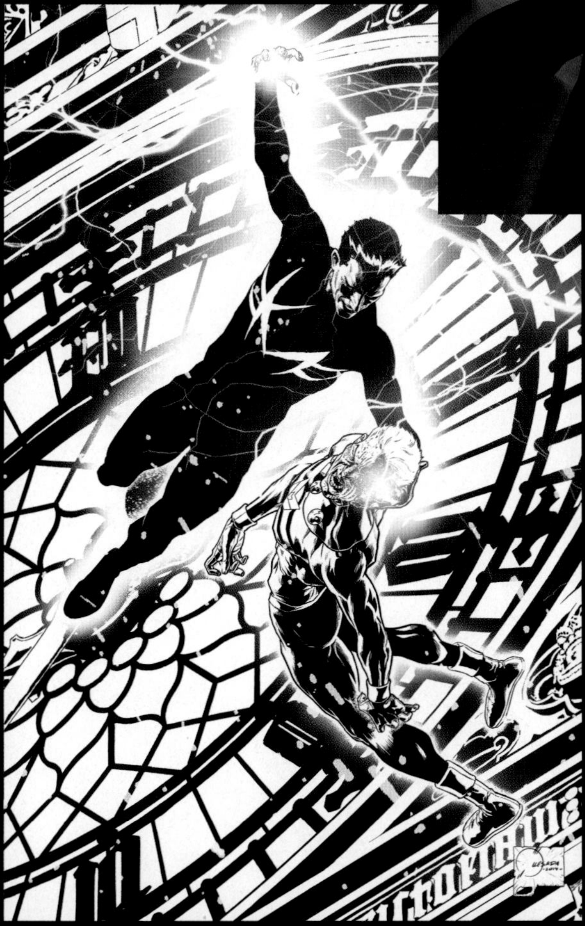

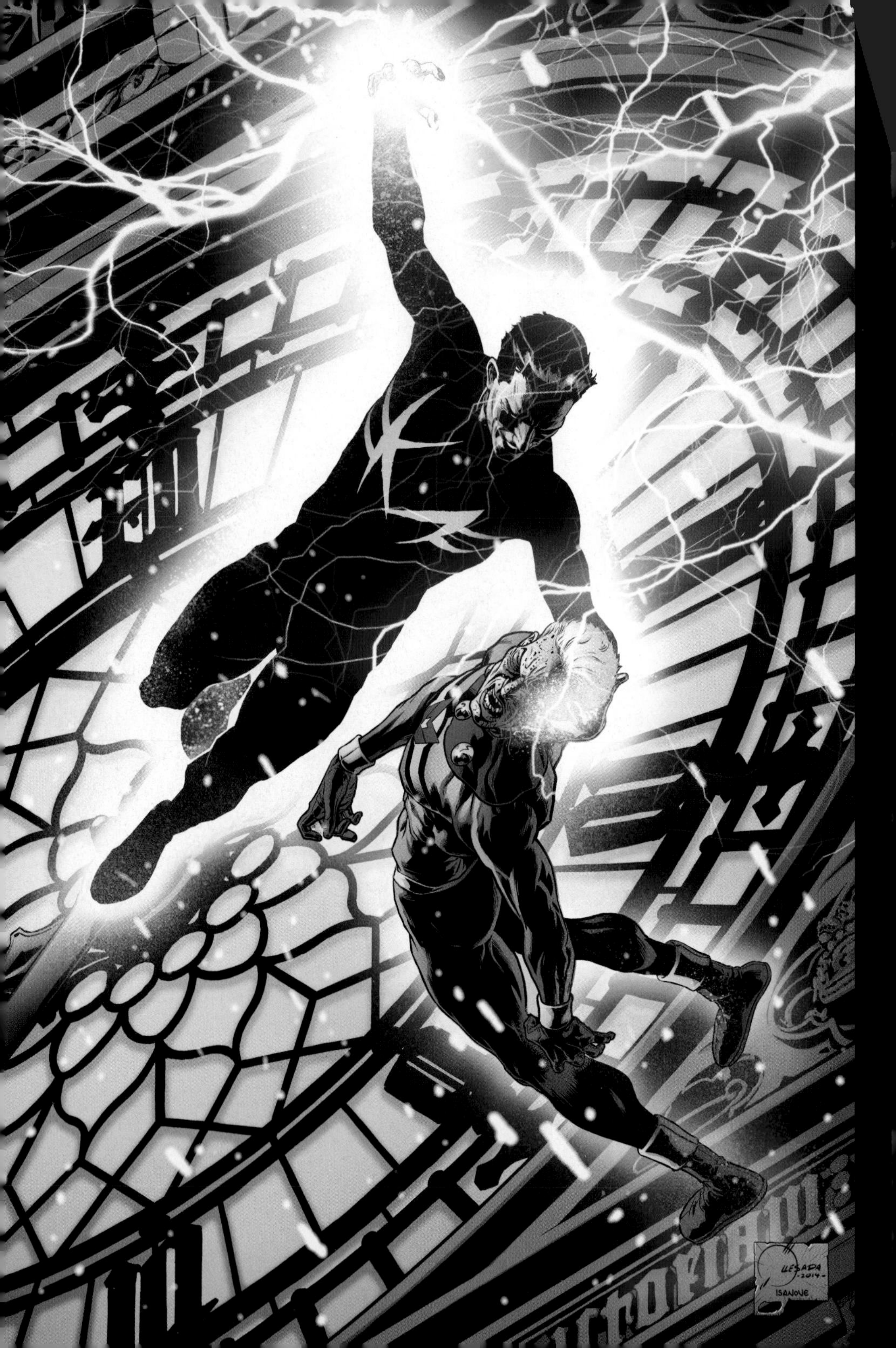
QUESADA
-2014-
ISANOVE